Black Ball and
the Boardwalk

Black Ball and the Boardwalk

The Bacharach Giants of Atlantic City, 1916–1929

James E. Overmyer

McFarland & Company, Inc., Publishers
Jefferson, North Carolina

ISBN 978-0-7864-7237-6 (softcover : acid free paper) ∞
ISBN 978-1-4766-1708-4 (ebook)

LIBRARY OF CONGRESS CATALOGUING DATA ARE AVAILABLE

British Library cataloguing data are available

© 2014 James E. Overmyer. All rights reserved

No part of this book may be reproduced or transmitted in any form or by any means, electronic or mechanical, including photocopying or recording, or by any information storage and retrieval system, without permission in writing from the publisher.

On the cover: *foreground* the 1921 Bacharach Giants, gathered around co-owner and business manager John W. Connor (National Baseball Hall of Fame and Library, Cooperstown, New York); *background* the boardwalk in Atlantic City, New Jersey (Library of Congress)

Printed in the United States of America

*McFarland & Company, Inc., Publishers
Box 611, Jefferson, North Carolina 28640
www.mcfarlandpub.com*

To Ellen

Table of Contents

Preface 1

1 ❖ A Long Train Ride to Fame 7
2 ❖ Surviving the Great War 29
3 ❖ Under New Management 51
4 ❖ Back Home in Atlantic City 85
5 ❖ In the Big Leagues 111
6 ❖ The Championship Seasons 141
7 ❖ Down in the Standings, and Out of the City ... 170

Epilogue 193
Appendix A: Game Log 199
Appendix B: Rosters 224
Appendix C: Batting and Pitching Statistics by Year ... 232
Chapter Notes 259
Bibliography 268
Index 271

Preface

A few years ago I wrote a chapter on black baseball at Ebbets Field, home of the Brooklyn Dodgers, for the book *Ebbets Field: Essays and Memories of Brooklyn's Historic Ballpark*. Two-thirds of the assignment was easy—I had written in the past about the black teams that used Ebbets as a home park in the 1930s and 1940s. But the team that played there in the 1920s, the Bacharach Giants, was relatively unknown to me and required some digging. One of the first things one finds out about the Giants, often with no elaboration, is that the team was named after Harry Bacharach, the mayor of Atlantic City, New Jersey. Which made no sense. Sports teams, at least on the professional level, are not often named after individuals. If they are, the namesake usually owns the team, which Mayor Harry did not.

This was a tantalizing peculiarity. It turned out that two men from Atlantic City's black community, veteran baseball man Henry Tucker and Thomas Jackson, a political supporter of the mayor, recruited the core of the best African American semi-pro team in Jacksonville, Florida, in the spring of 1916. They brought the players to Atlantic City to represent Bacharach in a local league, probably to hype the mayor's chances in an approaching election and thus Jackson's own chances of advancement in municipal employment. The team Tucker and Jackson put together was far too good for the local league, and soon found itself playing fast competition in Philadelphia, then New York, emerging as one of the best black teams in the East.

I found the fact of the mayor as the Giants' namesake to be like an odd-looking something sticking out of the ground that, once one started to dig around it, turned out to be the tip of something much bigger. The digging led to a tale of Atlantic City in the early twentieth century, when it was a resort town known for giving its fun-loving visitors what they wanted, the law (particularly Prohibition) be damned. The story included the intensely personal nature of the city's machine politics, where sports teams could be extensions of public figures. The tale's trail also led to New York City, as stories about East Coast black baseball often do. There team owners, their efforts sometimes fueled by the profits of illegal enterprises, struggled mightily to escape the iron grip of the white semi-pro baseball establishment. Then there was the striving on their part to establish what became known as the Negro Leagues, which legitimized their side of the segregated sport as had the founding of white leagues in previous decades.

And, by the way, there was terrific baseball involved. Some of the best black players of the day, including shortstops John Henry Lloyd and Dick Lundy and pitcher Dick

Redding, played for the Giants, who won two pennants and came close to winning two Negro World Series.

While the story of the Bacharach Giants is primarily one of their exploits against Negro League opponents, the complete account includes play against many white semi-pro teams. In the first half of the twentieth century, good players could live comfortably on the combination of non-baseball employment and weekend and evening semi-pro ball. The careers of two regular Bacharach opponents, Adam "Ad" Swigler, who abandoned big league ball to become a Philadelphia dentist and semi-pro, and Raymond "Ike" Nelson, an Atlantic City–area plumber who played baseball part-time for many years in Southern New Jersey and Philadelphia, show how well this could work.

Cities had dozens of teams, and the best part-time squads could mount a serious challenge to all but white major league teams. Often, their rosters included former big leaguers and minor leaguers, and youngsters just out of high school who were bound for professional ball. The Bacharachs played, and often defeated, the recognized Northeast cream of these teams—the Bushwicks from Brooklyn, the Paterson, New Jersey, Silk Sox, and teams from the Delaware County League near Philadelphia, for example. The Giants also were regular opponents of a short-lived but important category of teams, the highly skilled squads recruited by World War I defense industries that were able to put major and minor leaguers on their payrolls when the players chose defense work over the military draft.

They played teams that featured players with some sort of exotic appearance, such as the bearded House of David squad from a Christian cult community in Michigan. (Of course, when the Bacharachs came to some small, mostly white, communities when on tour, they rather fit this description themselves.) Then there were the local teams sponsored by athletic clubs or religious or social organizations. Philadelphia, an easy 60-mile trip from Atlantic City, was full of these squads, and the Bacharachs played many of them. In other words, the Giants' history is a nearly complete slice of the history of professional and semi-pro baseball in the early part of their century. They even played at least one game against a "Bloomer Girls" women's aggregation. The research for this book has attempted to find as many of these games as possible against all varieties of teams at the different levels of competition to tell the Giants' whole story.

Collecting the raw data on black baseball games is more difficult than it might sound to the reader not immersed in blackball history. The black teams, primarily supported by the African American minority of the nation's population, often were not covered thoroughly (and sometimes were covered not at all) by white-owned urban daily newspapers. To compound this lack of regular game accounts and box scores, the black leagues only infrequently invested in statistical services that compiled regular, reliable individual statistics. When they did, the focus was on players' accomplishments only in league games.

The numbers for this book, however, were compiled by a team of Negro Leagues researchers who have been collecting blackball statistics for 15 years. Larry Lester and Dick Clark, co-chairs of the Society for American Baseball Research's Negro Leagues Committee, launched the effort in 2000 as one major portion of a project to thoroughly research the history of African American baseball in America. The entire project, funded by Major League Baseball, supervised by the National Baseball Hall of Fame and called the Negro League Researchers and Authors Group (NLRAG), produced as its major accomplishments a comprehensive historical manuscript and a statistical database with deep and broad game coverage.

Lester and Clark, along with a third Negro Leagues Committee member, Wayne Stivers, have maintained the database and have continued to compile game accounts and box scores. They did me the invaluable service of combining the data I had gathered with theirs to produce the year-by-year batting and pitching numbers for Bacharach players.

Black baseball game accounts and box scores are found in old newspapers. These are usually the weeklies put out by black publishers for the African American community. Happily for this project, though, the white Atlantic City and Philadelphia daily newspapers covered all baseball in their circulation areas zealously in the early twentieth century, as did the *Brooklyn Daily Eagle*, which blanketed sports in that New York City borough, regardless of the color of the players.

Mining not only these mainstream white and African American newspapers but many local papers published in the smaller towns the Bacharachs visited, where the arrival of an out-of-town team for a game was always big news, we have come up with an average of 110 games per season. While the Giants undoubtedly played more often than that, what we've found represents a majority of their contests and is sufficient for the calculation of statistics that reliably reflect how the team and its individual players performed each year, even though their precise numbers cannot be determined.

Game accounts gathered for the Bacharach project included detailed stories with box scores (included in 85 percent of our finds) and sometimes even play-by-play information. To a lesser extent there are short game stories without boxes but perhaps with a line score that identified the pitchers and catchers and, on occasion, nothing more than a very short item indicating an opponent and a score. All of this data was useful to determine the team's won-lost record in what are referred to as the "discovered" or "found" games. Games for which there are box scores or game stories with pitching information, even without a box, are used for the pitching statistics. Games with boxes provide the data for the batting stats. So, in each season, there are a certain number of "discovered" games, a slightly smaller number of games in the pitching stats and a still slightly smaller number in batting.

The old box scores, even when available, sometimes have shortcomings, at least as compared to our modern conception of a box. A minimalist box score makes some offensive details such as extra-base hits, bases on balls and stolen bases unrecoverable, although they can often, but not always, be gleaned from the game story. Consequently those numbers for individual players are likely to be lower than what was actually achieved. But given the assumption that the lost data affects all players more or less equally, the fastest runners, most powerful sluggers and players with the most judicious batting eyes can still be identified.

As to pitching, a close examination of the game story and box score can often turn up information missing from the box such as strikeouts and walks and when a pitcher was replaced by a reliever (although the majority of starters for black teams threw complete games, as did their white semi-pro mound opponents). Again, strikeouts and walks may sometimes be lacking, but the hardest throwers and hurlers with the best control still stand out.

Two other notes on the data we compiled:

- Black teams often had to use ballparks at the sufferance of other teams who owned or controlled them (although the Bacharachs were fortunate in this respect, often having dibs on a home field). This made it very difficult to reschedule rain or darkness-shortened contests and ties so the games could be played to completion. In the white major and minor leagues the ties usually stood for the record, but the games that didn't go the regulation five innings were replayed and the player statistics from the first attempt wiped out. We have included all the information on every game, however foreshortened, to give a fuller picture of the Bacharachs' accomplishments.
- Each season includes player records in all the discovered games, but also a separate subset against "league-level opponents." These are teams that played with the Giants in the Negro Leagues beginning in 1920 and those same squads prior to that year. It also includes black teams that didn't join the Negro Leagues, such as the Pennsylvania Red Caps and Richmond Giants, which nonetheless were substantial opponents, and the very best white semi-pro outfits such as the Bushwicks, regarded as certainly the equal of many Negro League teams. In the case of the Bacharachs, there is the occasional end-of-season game against an actual white major league team, or at least a representative group from its roster.

That the statistics we present here are certainly not complete for any season, or for most players, is a given in the world of Negro League stats because of the limitations on finding primary sources of game accounts. This undoubtedly will be the case forever, no matter how diligent future searches are. It's actually a bit painful to think of a professional baseball game's results as have been lost to history because the newspaper edition that reported it was not preserved, or possibly because the game never got into print in the first place. But this is the case for some black baseball games.

However, the number of Bacharach games collected provides a sufficient sample size to determine the comparative abilities of the players. Superstars such as Lundy, Lloyd and Redding, along with other outstanding players like Chaney White, Oliver Marcell and Arthur "Rats" Henderson stand out, as might be expected. But the steady production of longtime regulars such as Nap Cummings, Ambrose Reid, Willie Jones, Roy Roberts and Hubert Lockhart is also revealed, as are the prospects who failed to live up to expectations when acquired by the Giants. To state it more simply, these statistics give a picture of a whole team, with its strongest and weakest players and most regular contributors.

This less than complete outcome may be disappointing to someone who wants the numbers for any league to be as precisely available as those for the current major leagues. Black baseball stats work in a different way, though. Their validity can be compared to that of the national unemployment rate or the Gross Domestic Product. Everyone knows those periodically calculated numbers don't precisely represent the economic factors they measure, but they include sufficient data and are figured in an accepted way so that they are taken as valid indicators of how the U.S. economy is doing. Lots of politicians and economists certainly get excited when they change in either direction.

In addition to the year by year player statistics, the book also contains annual team rosters and a listing of all the discovered games, including when and where they were played and the outcome. The point of all this is to treat this particular Negro League team like one of its white major league counterparts would be treated. The anecdotal history of baseball is always fascinating, but no white big league team history would be considered complete without the additional information we have assembled for the Bacharach Giants, at least to the best of our ability. The stats fellows and I believe that, although long gone from the baseball scene, the black teams of the late nineteenth century and the first half of the twentieth were an integral part of not only the history of American sports, but of African American social history of the time. Here, we try to treat them in that way.

It has been one of the enjoyable experiences of researching and writing this book to have teamed up again with some of the other Negro League Researchers and Authors Group members in addition to Larry Lester, Dick Clark and Wayne Stivers. Chief among them are Dr. Lawrence Hogan and Dr. Neil Lanctot. Larry Hogan, professor emeritus at Union County College in Cranford, New Jersey, is my oldest friend and associate in black baseball research, and provided me with his files on the history of the Bacharachs and Atlantic City, in addition to many insights on those topics. Neil, in the history department at the University of Delaware, is in my opinion the leading authority on the business side of the Negro Leagues. His willingness to give me guidance at any time on that topic and many others was important in my goal of giving depth to the Bacharachs as an organization, as opposed to writing just an account of their wins and losses.

There are many people in Atlantic City who have a deep consideration for their city's history. I was fortunate to renew acquaintances with some and meet others for the first time as they provided their help. Michael Everett, a director of the John Henry "Pop" Lloyd Committee that keeps alive the memory of not only that outstanding Negro Leaguer but the Bacharach Giants and black baseball in general, shared much time and access to his files. The help of the staff of the Atlantic City Free Public Library, in particular Heather Halpin Pérez, archivist of the Atlantic City Heritage Collections, and Pam Richter, archivist and information services librarian, was crucial to the project. The library staff at Richard Stockton College near Atlantic City, which holds the Pop Lloyd Committee archives, were also of great assistance. Atlantic County Superior Court Judge Nelson Johnson, author of two city histories, "Boardwalk Empire" and "The Northside," gave me direction on researching the city's history. Former New Jersey Supreme Court Justice John E. Wallace, whose grandfather Reginald Weekes and two great-uncles were part-owners of the Bacharachs, filled me in on that family's history.

The depth of research that went into this work could not have been possible without the decisions made decades ago by Atlantic City newspapermen to devote extensive coverage to the Bacharach Giants' games, even though in many cities the Negro League teams didn't get anything approaching thorough coverage from the white-owned and operated dailies. So a very belated thanks to *Atlantic City Daily Press* Sports Editor Louis

Greenberg and Stewart R. Thorbahn, who covered the Giants during their pennant-winning years, and to the other reporters dispatched to the ballpark.

And, closer to home in the current day, I have often been asked to critique my wife Ellen Weiden's professional writing, advising her to lead with attention-getting introductions and keep her sentences brisk and to the point. She read the drafts of important parts of this manuscript, and reminded me to follow my own advice.

Chapter 1

A Long Train Ride to Fame

1916

There they were in early May, a group of good young black ballplayers working out in a city park in the resort city of Atlantic City, New Jersey. Most of them were 900 miles north of the place they had called home. They had been enticed away from a thoroughly segregated city by probably the only person they knew at the New Jersey Shore. This new location, with its own informal, but obvious, discrimination, still provided great possibilities, greater than maybe any of them knew. They were about to go into action wearing the colors of a Jewish politician who was almost certainly a complete stranger to them.

There may have been worse places than Jacksonville, Florida, for an African American in 1916. But many of its black residents, particularly its young men, thought of it as a good place to get away from. Overall Jacksonville was a prosperous and growing community, the largest city in Florida, with half of its 58,000 population black. Bouncing back immediately from a disastrous fire in 1901 that had leveled nearly 2,400 buildings over 140 city blocks, the city reached upward (a ten-story downtown skyscraper) and outward (several new suburbs), with new schools and a Carnegie library replacing fire-ravaged predecessors.[1]

But the African American half of the city did not share equally in the recovery. Jacksonville lay in the northern section of Florida that considered itself a true part of the South. In these first years of the twentieth century, American blacks still did not have full access to the civil rights supposedly assured by the Fourteenth Amendment to the U.S. Constitution. At Jacksonville's Carnegie library, which had 8,000 books for white members to borrow, a mere two rooms, holding only 609 books, were set aside for blacks in a segregated second-floor section. The head librarian recommended a branch library in the black section of town (85 percent of the black adults in the city were literate), but it was never built. In the schools, although there were only slightly more buildings for white students than blacks, per-pupil expenditures for white children were more than double that for the African Americans, and white teacher salaries were about 40 percent greater than those for their black counterparts.[2]

None of this inequality was unique to the city—this was pretty much a national theme. But in terms of race relations Jacksonville was changing, and not for the better. There had long been African American elected and appointed representatives in the city government, but in 1907 the city's wards were gerrymandered to guarantee white majorities in all of them and snuff out the careers of the last black councilmen. Then the all-white government began the process of expelling blacks from all supervisory positions and "except for menial jobs, city employment became all-white." The rise of all-white government set a tone that encouraged vigilante actions against blacks. In 1909 a black who had allegedly assaulted a white woman in rural Duval County outside the city was shot and killed by a mob before the sheriff could arrive. Black boxer Jack Johnson's July 4, 1910, victory over white opponent Jim Jeffries set off white mob actions against celebrating blacks in many U.S. cities. In Jacksonville 40 white men were arrested after a night of assaulting African Americans and destroying their property.[3]

The Negro writer and educator James Weldon Johnson, a native of Jacksonville who had lived there in the 1870s and 1880s, lamented the change, which he laid to the transfer of white power from old aristocratic families "who were sensitive to the code, noblesse oblige," to poor whites, who held a grudge against blacks that went back to slavery, when many slaves were seen to have lived better than they did. "The aristocratic families have lost control and the old conditions have been changed," he explained; "Jacksonville is today a one hundred per cent Cracker town."[4]

The growing inhospitable attitude toward blacks was exacerbated in 1915 by two otherwise unrelated dire events, the attack of the boll weevil on the South's cotton crop following on the heels of the German invasion of neighboring countries that ignited World War I. The boll weevil, a beetle about a quarter of an inch long, feeds on young cotton plants in the spring. Coming from Mexico, the weevil reached the southern United States that spring and rapidly spread. The infestation, combined with severe flooding, reduced the year's crop by about 30 percent. The crop failure also disrupted the financial rhythm of cotton farmers, who ordinarily borrowed in the spring against the crop that would be harvested later that year. The indebtedness resulting from the widespread crop failure led to a great reduction in the numbers of field workers, mostly tenant farming blacks.

At the same time the outbreak of war in Europe cut the continent's immigration to America by more than 70 percent in 1915. That number, 326,700, would fall again in 1916 to under 300,000. Most of this immigration had been to the industrialized North, and companies whose labor forces were being undermined actively began to recruit unemployed Southerners to fill the gap, focusing on blacks. Railroads, in particular need of workers, went so far as to offer free train rides north to prospective employees. The Pennsylvania and Erie railroads in the summer of 1916 began dispatching whole trainloads of African Americans out of its Jacksonville depots. As James Weldon Johnson summed up, "if the white people of the South dream that the Negro, because he is silent, does not resent ... the bitter injustice to which he is so often subjected, they are mistaken.... Whenever economic conditions open for him elsewhere, he will leave."[5]

Jacksonville's Board of Health reported that the city's black population declined by 5,000, including 2,500 laborers, between the summers of 1915 and 1916. That estimate may have been exaggerated, but African Americans certainly left the city. It is true that, after a wartime industrial boom reversed the population decline, the 1920 U.S. Census showed whites in the majority (54 percent) for the first time since the Reconstruction era.[6]

Eight particular black men left Jacksonville for the North in the spring of 1916, recruited by a northern business. But they weren't fated to lay track anonymously for a Pennsylvania railroad, or make steel in a Pittsburgh foundry, or constantly bend over in a Connecticut tobacco field. They would find themselves welcomed and feted upon their arrival in their new home, given paying work that many people considered play, and read about themselves in the newspapers on almost a daily basis. Some of them are talked about even today when the history of their profession is recounted.

The eight, Dick Lundy, Napoleon Cummings, Leroy Roberts, Dan Johnson, Arthur Dilworth, Willis Crump, Michael Tucker and Frank Crockett, became the nucleus of a baseball team in Atlantic City. The new team, the Bacharach Giants, quickly became one of the dominant squads in the hotbed of semi-pro and amateur baseball around the city. While some of these players wouldn't have long careers in professional baseball, the organization they helped found would last for 14 years, growing in renown and winning two championships in one of the first black major leagues.

In Jacksonville these players had been members of the locally esteemed Duval Giants, named after the county in which the city was located. They were homed in on by Henry Tucker, a Jacksonville native who had once played for and managed the Roman Cities team there. Tucker had migrated to Atlantic City to work in its resort hotels, but he was dispatched in something of an emergency that March not just to scout his old turf for some likely talent, but to bring back a whole baseball team. Tucker essentially transported the Duval Giants, even the nickname, back to the ocean resort. The circumstances were typical Atlantic City, which is to say, they were unique to this place that had an existence all its own. At the turn of the twentieth century there was no community like Atlantic City anywhere in the country. "It has always had a singular purpose for its existence— to provide leisure-time activities for tourists," according to Nelson Johnson, one of its leading historians.[7]

In the first part of the nineteenth century Absecon Island, the low, sandy, barrier island that became the site of Atlantic City, was ridden by mosquitoes and greenhead flies that could drive both man and beast half-crazy in the summer. Jonathan Pitney, a local doctor, prized Absecon for its unspoiled serenity, the bugs notwithstanding. Pitney's idea was to develop a beachside colony that would cater to the well-off seeking relaxation and sea air. But the existing resort towns on the South Jersey coast at Cape May and Long Beach were already growing and unlikely to be overtaken by sandy Absecon.

The trick, then, was to cater to another set of customers. There were more than 400,000 people in Philadelphia and its environs, only 60 miles distant across the New Jersey Pine Barrens, a terrain that more or less resembles a pool table. This made the Barrens a prime route for a railroad, and the Camden-Atlantic line opened in 1854 to take vacationers from the city to the ocean. Originally the road began at Camden, New Jersey, across the river from Philadelphia, and ended on the mainland across the marshes behind Absecon (ferries finished the job on both ends until bridges could be built). Both ends of the tracks were barely above sea level, and the highest elevation anywhere along the line probably never exceeded 100 feet. The tracks ran straight as a string northwest from Atlantic City for about half of the total distance, and didn't curve much more as they got closer to Philadelphia. The one-way trip only took about an hour.

The railroad company built a 600-room hotel, the first in Atlantic City, establishing the community's identity as a resort destination. The pace of growth was pedestrian, however, until 1877, when Samuel Richards, a wealthy regional entrepreneur who had been involved in building the first railroad, quit that company and spearheaded a rival line, the Philadelphia-Atlantic City Railway. This road followed the same general path of the first line, but was even straighter. Its opening not only doubled the passenger capacity for Atlantic City, it set off a fare war that made it affordable for middle- and working-class Philadelphians to vacation at the Jersey shore. Atlantic City's permanent population increased from about 2,000 to 30,000 between 1875 and 1900, but the summertime population was estimated as high as 200,000, up to 300,000 on weekends.[8]

Atlantic City has never had an industrial base, nor anything as lucrative as, say, agriculture or mining (the salty water table is so close to the island's surface that, to this day, drinking water has to be piped from the mainland, passing deceased residents being transported back to inland cemeteries). Its reason for being was well understood by its business and community leaders: "The city's very existence was dependent on money spent by out-of-towners, and resort merchants had something for everyone."[9]

This required that the vacationers be offered not merely the obvious attractions such as sunshine, ocean bathing, bracing sea air and a stroll along the famous Boardwalk. Those choices could get old fast. There had to be more. There were holdouts for morality who from time to time got their way, but for the most part the city's economy thrived from providing what was fun, even if it might be illegal. When drinking and entertainment were taboo on Sundays, you could imbibe and have fun on the Lord's Day in Atlantic City. When Prohibition became the law in 1920 and public drinking became illegal, that stricture was barely noticeable in the vicinity of the Boardwalk and the blocks inland. Activities banned on any day of the week in any recent decade up to then, such as gambling and prostitution, also thrived.

To carry on this way required participation by city and county officials, ranging from just looking the other way to providing explicit protection. That protection, at first for the locally-perceived good of the community, eventually came with a price, both financially in the form of payoffs, and politically in the establishment of an administrative machine with tight-fisted control over all municipal activities that made machine politicians elsewhere envious. The machine was Republican, but that was just because that party happened to dominate the area's politics. Ideology had nothing to do with this city's government, unless resistance to reform could be regarded as ideological.

The dominance of a city with a fairly small voting population by a tightly-run political machine led to the development of a cult of personality among the leading politicians. Louis Kuehnle, who ran a popular hotel started by his father, was the first "strongman" to organize both the necessary municipal improvements to the city and the optional political graft that came with them. He was called "The Commodore," a title that he had not earned in anyone's navy—he was the head of the Atlantic City Yacht Club. His successor, Enoch "Nucky" Johnson, began his political career by serving as Atlantic County sheriff. He succeeded his father, Smith Johnson, performing a neat end run around a reformist state law limiting sheriffs to one consecutive term to prohibit dominance of this important law enforcement post by an entrenched official.

The Bacharach Giants were exceptional from the minute they got their team name, since it's virtually unknown for a team to be named for an individual who doesn't own or otherwise play a dominant role in the organization. Black baseball had the Leland Giants in Chicago and Gilkerson's Union Giants in Southern Illinois, but Frank Leland and Bob Gilkerson owned those teams. The Brooklyn Dodgers were popularly known as the Robins for awhile in the early twentieth century, but that was because their field manager was the popular Wilbert Robinson. Harry Bacharach, after whom the Atlantic City team was named, was one of five city commissioners and an aspirant to become mayor when the Giants came to town in 1916. Bacharach, although a member of the local political machine, seems to have been the kind of fellow who could lie down with dogs and get up with very few fleas. He left behind a reputation as an energetic, progressive leader who pushed the sort of street and public utility improvements that were vital to the growth of the resort business.

Since Atlantic City was subject to state and federal laws, many of its prominent leaders and their underlings wound up being indicted by grand juries for their alleged personal disregard for criminal statutes. Kuehnle served a short prison term for letting some of the money spent on municipal improvements line his own pocket. Johnson, who in succeeding Kuehnle both refined and defined corrupt government in the city, served a four-year stretch when Federal authorities finally caught up to him in 1941. Bacharach himself was named in an indictment for election fraud. The election of 1910 featured so many instances of illegal voting that the Republican gubernatorial candidate received more votes in Atlantic City than there were registered voters. The electoral math was so bad that the corruption could not be ignored. Of course, New Jersey's new reform-minded governor, Woodrow Wilson, the winning Democrat against whom the fraud had been perpetrated, had no intention of turning a blind eye. The state legislature did a full-scale investigation and the local authorities fought back. Two grand juries, one run by the state and the other by Atlantic County, indicted principal characters from both sides of the election.[10]

In Bacharach's case the charge languished in the county court and was eventually dismissed in 1914. Was Bacharach, existing as he did in the atmosphere of corruption, also corrupt? It's clear that he played the political rewards game as seriously as anybody in a city government where almost no one's job

Harry Bacharach's official mayoral portrait from 1913, just before the Bacharach Giants were brought to Atlantic City and named after him (Atlantic City Heritage Collections, Atlantic City Free Public Library).

was perfectly safe if a new mayor took office. But except for the election fraud indictment, an occupational hazard in Atlantic City politics, no one ever hung any serious charges on him. Bacharach's father, Jacob, was a very successful clothier. Harry had begun working at Bacharach and Sons, but had gained the Atlantic City postmaster appointment, a Federal political plum, before he was 30. Later he was president or vice president of real estate and banking ventures. His brother Isaac had a political career of his own, first in the New Jersey legislature and then as a congressman for 22 years. They and other family members founded the nearby Betty Bacharach Home for Afflicted Children in memory of their mother. Harry was a leader of the local Jewish community and a serial joiner of social organizations, having been an Elk, Freemason and Moose, as well as the longtime president of the Morris Guards, a prominent quasi-military men's social club.

The Atlantic City political machine depended significantly on the support of the city's black community, proportionately large by the standards of northern cities. In fact, in 1915 the city's 11,000 African American residents made up more than a quarter of the city's permanent population. During the summer, when seasonal hotel and restaurant jobs were open to blacks, the resident black population swelled to 40 percent. Blacks flocked to the island, often from the near South, to get those jobs. The pay was good, the work often more interesting than the manual labor positions usually available to Negroes. Also,

> There was a hierarchy of positions within the hotel-resort industry, giving black workers the opportunity to advance from one type of job to another.... A result of this phenomenon was the development of a black social structure far more complex than that of other northern cities. By virtue of their higher income, property-ownership and greater responsibility attached to their hotel positions, a substantial number of Atlantic City's black residents were, by comparison to blacks nationally, part of the middle and upper class.[11]

The city's African Americans also voted for the Republican machine for two reasons. The historical reason was that before the Great Depression brought about disgrace to Herbert Hoover's GOP administration and the ascendency of Franklin D. Roosevelt's New Deal, most black voters were Republicans, still following the "Party of Lincoln" that had been responsible for the abolishment of slavery and initial movements to end discrimination following the Civil War.

The more immediate local reason was that beginning with Louis Kuehnle, the local administration made sure the black community shared in coal and food relief efforts that kept many families alive through the long, jobless winters until the tourists again flocked to the beach. In the 1912 election for city commissioner a black physician, P. J. Hawkins, polled 2,154 votes in the primary and 2,355 in the general election, likely an accurate count of the African American voting strength. This was not an insignificant number. Total voter registration was estimated as no more than about 9,000.[12]

While in the city's earlier days neighborhoods were racially mixed, the steady growth of the black population brought about the development of a primarily black neighborhood, a ghetto in other words: "in 1880, more than 70 percent of the black households in the resort had white neighbors; by 1915, the percentage shrank to less than 20 percent."[13] In Atlantic City blacks migrated to the northern part of the island, their community becoming known as the Northside, located north of the railroads, away from the Boardwalk. Restricted from equally sharing many of the city's amenities such as restaurants, theaters, beaches and amusement piers, the blacks began to create their own homogeneous community, easy to locate and easy to influence politically.

Harry Bacharach was perfectly aware of the standard ways to use handouts to court the Northside's voters, but his attention to the black population went beyond that. Most significantly, in the waning hours of his first brief term as mayor in 1912, he appointed a black druggist, James F. Bourne, to the city's Board of Education. In his election campaigns he made pitches directly to the Northside's respectable black working and middle-class residents.[14]

Tucker and Thomas H. Jackson, the men who created the Bacharach Giants, were permanent, respectable residents of Northside and in Jackson's case a loyal worker for the Republican machine, particularly when Bacharach was in the driver's seat. They hatched a plan in the spring of 1916 to honor Bacharach by renaming one of the teams in the Atlantic City Colored League after him. Bacharach, who had his first mayoral term cut short in 1912 by the city's changeover to the five-commissioner form of government, had become one of the five leaders but had not succeeded in having his fellow commissioners again name him mayor.

Now he was out for re-election to the commission and wanted the top job, too, which he got by leading the ballot on May 9. This was before Prohibition thoroughly corrupted the city's government. It was still a time when reform sentiments, held primarily by Boardwalk hotel owners who disliked the riffraff encouraged by the city's laissez-faire approach to public behavior, ministers and their flocks and the minority who were just plain fed up with the political situation, could occasionally win the day. They backed Bacharach's ticket while the existing corps of city hall employees, particular the police and firemen, came out strongly for the opposition. The city election, as usual, was hard fought. Bacharach and the members of his ticket may or may not had ever actually tinkered with past elections, but they certainly knew what that sort of skullduggery looked like. They ran a newspaper ad just before the election imploring potential voters that "If you are not legally entitled to vote, do not attempt it on Tuesday next. If you are entitled, do not be intimidated or harassed by anyone. The combined armies of Europe, assisted by the 'Strong Arm Coppers' of Atlantic City, could not interfere with you."[15]

The birth of the Bacharach Giants provided Harry Bacharach with the sort of political advertising he couldn't have bought at any price. There had already been a buildup in the press while the team was assembled and had begun practicing. But here, the Saturday before the election, was baseball opening day with the much-ballyhooed new black team playing on the Northside, Bacharach's name sewn on each and every uniform. It also didn't hurt that, as the commissioner in charge of the city's parks, he presided over the opening day parade to the ball field. He threw out the first pitch on city playground property at New York and Adriatic Avenues, probably made available through his influence. The *Atlantic City Daily Press* said he threw a spitball, which is probably just a bit of humor worked into the upbeat story. But in truth, a celebratory spitball from City Hall would have been so very much the Atlantic City way.[16]

Getting this tribute to become reality took a lot of work, though. Initially Jackson was going to have a strong existing black team, the Atlantic City Giants, name itself after

Bacharach. But in late March came the news that those Giants had declined to join the league and would play independently. That killed that plan. This disappointing news was followed immediately by the dispatch of Tucker to Jacksonville, where he picked up the eight players from the Duval Giants, plus some others on the way back north. They were feted on their arrival by the black community, and more importantly, were looked after by the city administration: as Nap Cummings later recalled, "We were only here a few days until we got registered to vote."[17] The city was so welcoming to this group of ballplayers that Cummings made it his permanent home, and Dilworth and Crockett also lived there for several years after their careers with the Bacharachs were over.

The support network didn't benefit just the new players. The changing of administrations was invariably accompanied by a large-scale turnover at City Hall, where employment was strongly dependent upon political affiliation. In June Tom Jackson was appointed a rubbish inspector as part of an expansion of the Health Department by Mayor Bacharach, who was quoted as saying, presumably with a straight face, that he wanted "a Spotless City." How much rubbish Jackson might have inspected is unknown, although it's true that real cleanliness was on Bacharach's mind. He was praised in 1916 for a vigorous and successful campaign against a widespread epidemic of infantile paralysis (polio) that included a public sanitation drive.[18]

Bacharach never was involved in the day to day operations of the club, but his influence behind the scenes was significant, starting with providing a free place to play. The city owned several blocks of open land in the Northside, which was used as public parks. Bacharach's oversight of the parks proved to be highly advantageous that May, and a portion of the parkland was turned into a ballpark, complete with a 1,600-seat grandstand. The field quickly became known as Bacharach Park, the first of several locations used by the Giants to bear that name. There were other advantages to having the city as an unofficial sponsor. For the first few years of the team's existence, Loraine Melcher, a clerk in the city's finance office, served as the contact for booking games.[19]

This cozy relationship wasn't lost on the press or public. When the headline writer for the *Daily Press* sports pages needed a short descriptive word for the team to fit in a one-column space, he often just called the Giants the "Mayors." Calling the Giants the "Bacharach" Giants was actually part of a tradition in Atlantic City of putting politicians' names on athletic teams, whether or not the name had any particular connection to the namesake. Bacharach seems not to either have been much of an athlete or a keen follower of sports. His successor as mayor, Edward L. Bader, had been a pro football player and had an all-around athletics club named for him—his son Dan was star pitcher for the baseball team. Frank S. "Hap" Farley, the last Atlantic City political boss, was a multi-sport athlete and sponsored a black baseball club, the Farley Stars. Those Stars were the successors to the Johnson Stars, walking billboards for machine boss "Nucky" Johnson.

As to why Jackson and Tucker nicknamed their team the Giants, the easy answer is that most African American teams were called that in those days. The constant use of the term seems to have stemmed from the first fully professional black team, the Cuban Giants, founded in 1886. (If calling a team the Giants might have been a sort of code to identify a black squad in those days when teams often barnstormed from one town to another for games, the use of the word "Cuban" was a reference of another sort entirely—

late nineteenth-century Negro players often tried to pass as Hispanics from the Caribbean to get around segregationist attitudes). At any rate, the Bacharach Giants had originally been the Duval Giants and a great many of their black opponents, from Atlantic City, Philadelphia, Virginia, New York City and other locales had the same nickname.

The Atlantic City Colored League into which the Bacharachs were recruited had been founded in 1915. It might have been established just to allow black players and fans to have some fun, but nothing was that simple in Atlantic City, where nearly everything that happened was judged by its effect on tourism. It was publicly stated that "the primary object of organizing the League was to keep the colored element off the Boardwalk during the afternoon by providing ball games for them."[20]

The league had six teams. The other five all had more solid ties to the city than the Giants, who so far as the league was concerned were sort of reverse carpetbaggers, African Americans from the South come North. One of the teams, the Vandal Athletic Club, had a connection to the black YMCA. The Cyclones were made up of waiters at the tony St. Charles Hotel. The Rudolfs were named after another major hotel but were made up of "rolling chair pushers" who maneuvered the man-powered wicker cabs that cruised tourists up and down the Boardwalk. The team called "Big Six" was probably not named after Christy Mathewson, the standout major league pitcher with that nickname. More likely its name was a reference to the local tourism label for the top six summer weekends when the city was flooded with visitors and many residents made a big chunk of their annual incomes. It's not clear how the Manhattans got their name, but their owner, Prince Baltimore, was a restaurant and entertainment man, and may have been looking for a suitably cosmopolitan handle.

Tucker and Jackson's hard work putting the Bacharachs together resulted in their widely overshooting their mark of just putting a team on the field that would do credit to Harry Bacharach. This was good for the Giants, bad for the league and, temporarily, a big headache for Jackson. The Bacharachs were much too strong for everyone else, and their dominance contributed to jealousy-fueled bad feelings that had Jackson personally under siege by July. The league opener set the trend, when the Giants easily beat the Vandals, 12–2. Dilworth pitched a four-hitter and struck out 16. The Giants defeated the Cyclones, 15–5, on May 12, knocking out 19 hits, including five by Michael Tucker and three by Lundy. Then it was on to the Manhattans, beaten 15–3 on May 18 in another 19-hit onslaught, and the Rudolfs, walloped 13–2 on May 22 by 17 hits (four by Cummings) behind a two-hitter from Roy Roberts.

The imbalance was getting embarrassing, although the Vandals scored a moral victory, and almost a real one, on May 25. The Giants were leading 3–2 in the sixth inning when the umpire called the game on account of darkness. It's impossible to say at this late date just what the field conditions were, but most league games began at 3:30 p.m. and ordinarily there should still been plenty of daylight when the game was called. On the other hand, extreme darkness due to heavily overcast skies had forced the end of a Philadelphia Athletics home game at about that same time. In Atlantic City both teams protested the halt and the crowd surged onto the field, making it impossible to continue anyway. Matters got only more confusing, however, when the umpire awarded the game to the Vandals. Press accounts offered no explanation but quoted Jackson as saying he would appeal to the league directors. He seems to have won his case, because subsequent published standings didn't count the loss against the Giants.

The Cyclones came close on May 28 with a five-run sixth inning that forced Roberts to relieve Dilworth, but the Giants still won, 9–7. The Vandals got walloped 12–5 on May 29 and the Giants had won seven in a row (counting the disputed previous Vandals game) before the Cyclones finally found them vulnerable on the 31st and beat them, 2–1. The setback was only temporary. The Bacharachs reeled off six straight league wins as the season moved into June, scoring ten or more runs four times and never giving up more than three except for a 16–11 slugfest with the Manhattans on June 23. The *Daily Press* headlines described the streak with little mercy for the losers: "Mayors Pummel Manhattans, 10–1," "Bacharachs Scalp Vandals; 8 to 2," "Bacharachs Win in Slugging Bee."[21]

The rolling chair pushers from Rudolf managed to beat the Bacharachs, 4–3, on June 26, but the Giants ended June with a 7–5 win over the Vandals, and regular league play ceased. The Bacharachs had won 14 of 16, including the "forfeit" on May 25, and had zoomed away from all the competition. There was also a game being played off the field toward the end of the season—a strenuous effort among the other five teams to turn on the Bacharachs, but as Tom Jackson told a reporter, "it is a poor trick that does not work both ways."

Jealousy of the Giants' success had sprung up among the other owners. The Bacharachs were the most popular team in the league, and their shares of the gate contributed to the league treasury were more "than all the others put together. They proved [to] be the chief drawing card and thousands attended the game daily at the Bacharach Park to see the Boy Wonders pull the big league stuff." The other teams clamored for their turn at the New York and Adriatic park on Sundays, and Charles D. White, the city commissioner who had succeeded Mayor Bacharach as head of city parks, ruled that all teams should have an equal shot at Sundays in this city-owned ball yard. Having won this opportunity, the other teams then came up with a myriad of excuses as to why they couldn't actually play:

> Prince Baltimore of the Manhattans said he was a deacon in the church and could not countenance Sunday baseball. The Cyclones, composed of St. Charles Hotel waiters, said that patrons eat late on Sunday and they would pass it up. The Vandal players were members of the local colored Y.M.C.A. and they, too, would have to quit the national game on the Sabbath. The Rudolf nine, chair pushers, declared Sunday was a big day for them and agreed with the Big Six team to pass it up.

This didn't mean the teams were exactly ready to give up their newly-won claims on Sundays. They couldn't play for all those various reasons, but the Bacharachs could if Jackson and Tucker bought out their dates. Sunday baseball had been a hot issue in prior years as part of the political debate between the reformers and the "open city" supporters, and Harry Bacharach himself had banned it as mayor in 1912, apparently to appease the reform contingent. But this dance within the Colored League councils was pure opportunism, and so, the *Press* noted sarcastically, "then were the Bacharach Giants picked to be the Sunday sinners."[22]

As Jackson said, a good trick cuts both ways. The Giants immediately abandoned the first Bacharach Park for another field next to the Absecon Inlet that separates the city's island from the next one to the north. Inlet Park wasn't included in the African American Northside neighborhood. It was near the city's yacht basin, the well-known Inlet Hotel, the storage and repair facility for pioneer aviator Glen Curtiss' seaplane outfit and the Pennsylvania Railroad's West Jersey and Seashore line railroad yards. The railroad owned the property, which eliminated the need to deal with the other Colored League clubs.

But even unofficial politics were complicated in Atlantic City, and by July 18 the Giants had been locked out of Inlet Park by the railroad. The reason was the company's fear that the capacity crowds the Bacharachs usually drew might dangerously overload the stands. But city inspectors had already been satisfied by $150 worth of repairs financed by Jackson and had no objection to Inlet's use.[23] The railroad's sudden reluctance was never adequately explained, and may have been just another step in the back and forth flow of Colored League politics. The Bacharachs returned to the city's Bacharach Park, but by then there was no objection from the rest of the league, because the league was dead. Figuratively the Bacharachs had destroyed it by completely outdistancing the competition. Literally, the league committed suicide through the other owners' envy of the Giants, who in the end had the most important votes—those of the fans, who gladly bought tickets to their games.

Not that the other black owners had given up. In mid-July figures from the late Colored League reportedly tried to have Jackson arrested for keeping league-owned uniforms. Later that month the Bacharachs were the intended victims of a bizarre plot to break up the team. Some scouts from Trenton, assisted by the Atlantic City Giants, still playing independently but overshadowed by the new team, reportedly treated several Bacharachs to a "liquid banquet" at a Northside hotel, intending to persuade them to jump to a new club in Northern New Jersey. This particular method of recruitment wasn't unusual in black baseball circles in those days, but in this case, the upstate club didn't exist—the plan was to strand the defecting Bacharachs far from Atlantic City without sufficient funds to get back. The plot didn't work, and the team played on.[24]

Thereafter the Giants played the former Colored League teams only infrequently. They beat the Rudolfs, 8–1, on July 14 and played an "all-star" team representing Big Six five times between July 28 and August 21, winning four games. The Atlantic City Giants showed up on the Bacharachs' schedule, instead of in the hotel bar, three times in mid-September. The Bacharachs won all three games.

Although Jackson and Henry Tucker continued to bolster the team with acquisitions after it arrived in Atlantic City, most of the regulars arrived via Tucker's expedition to Jacksonville and back. The youngest of Tucker's finds, Dick Lundy, turned out to be the best of the group, among the very best ever to put on a Bacharachs uniform. Lundy was only 17 when he took the train north. He immediately became a starter, initially at third base but later at shortstop. He prospered until 1937 when, having played 21 seasons with major black teams, all or part of 13 with the Bacharachs, he finally stopped, at only age 37. He's considered one of the best shortstops ever to play in the black leagues, bridging the gap between two Hall of Famers, John Henry Lloyd and Willie Wells. Lundy, who acquired the nickname "King Richard," came close to the Hall himself. He was nominated for induction in 2006 when the Hall conducted a special election to expand the number of black baseball figures honored with those brass plaques, but he didn't get enough votes to get in.

Due to the lack of coverage of black teams by the white press and the unevenness of the attention played by the black papers, gathering reliable statistics on the Negro Leagues and the independent teams that preceded them is hard work. Statistics for games against high-level black teams capture 2,268 plate appearances by Lundy and credit him with a lifetime .305 batting average. In the field he was "a superb fielder with a wide range and an exceptionally strong arm that allowed him to play a deep shortstop."[25]

Lundy was a Jacksonville native, raised by his mother Millie, a dressmaker who was widowed by 1910. Lundy had an opportunity for a good education, as least so far as the strictly segregated Jacksonville school system provided at the time. He attended the Cookman Institute for Boys, which provided education through high school for African American youths, in 1914 and 1915. He began playing semi-pro baseball for the Duval Giants in 1915, and while he appears to have wintered back in Jacksonville for a few years, he really became a citizen of the world—the world of baseball. In the 1920 U.S. census he simply described his occupation as "ball player." His athletic abilities aside, Lundy built a substantial reputation in black baseball based on his personality. He was said to have been "a natural leader respected by teammates and opponents alike."[26]

When Lundy moved over from third base to shortstop in the spring of 1916, he displaced the men who had been sharing the position. One of them was his uncle. Willis Crump was a younger brother of Millie Lundy, but only eight years older than his nephew. He had been playing semi-pro ball in Jacksonville since 1907 and was most recently with the Duval Giants. Now, at the age of 27, he also headed north. Crump couldn't hit well enough at the higher level the Bacharachs soon entered, and he became a utility outfielder and infielder. By 1920 he was back in Jacksonville, working as a watchman at the local post office, but he must have kept his baseball skills sharp because in 1923, with his nephew managing the Bacharachs, he returned for another season on the bench.[27]

The train that carried the future Bacharachs out of Jacksonville included the three main starting pitchers, Arthur Dilworth, Roy Roberts and Dan Johnson. All right-handers, they could each throw hard, too hard for the average Southern New Jersey or Philadelphia semi-pro batter. They also sometimes played field positions when not pitching, a common practice among black teams with small rosters.

Dilworth was 21 when he became a Bacharach. He was so successful a starter that the papers often called him "The Mighty Dilworth." His career in high-level black baseball was short, lasting only until 1919, possibly due to an injury. He remained in Atlantic City, however, and could often be found playing for lesser black teams both locally and as far away as New York City. In addition to his pitching, he caught and played outfield, and was a powerful hitter, usually batting in the middle of the lineup.

Roberts was also 21 when the 1916 season began. His appearance in Atlantic City marked the beginning of a long black baseball career, most of it spent with the Bacharachs, lasting until 1934. Roberts could throw hard, and sports reporters often called him "Speed Boy." He also was subject to occasional stretches when he found it hard to find the strike zone, and then the writers called him "Wild Boy." Later in his career he was described as having "the reputation of walking more men and yet winning more games than any pitcher in the country," an exaggeration that nevertheless contained more than a grain of truth. He was the Giants' substitute second baseman in the team's early years, and played some outfield, too.[28]

Johnson, whose long-standing nickname was "Shang," was the second-youngest Bacharach, only 19 days older than Lundy. This sometimes got him called "The Boy Wonder" when he threw a good game, which he usually did. Another strikeout artist in his youth, Johnson, like Dilworth, had a relatively short career. He was gone from high-level black ball by 1921. He, too, could catch in a pinch, and often played outfield when not on the mound.

Frank Crockett, 27 in that first season, was the center fielder and usually hit either leadoff or second. Although he sometimes played for other teams in the Northeast, he became for a time a permanent Atlantic City resident. Crockett left the Bacharachs after 1917 but returned in 1922 and 1923 when Lundy became manager. His top-level career ended at that point, and he returned to Jacksonville to work as a "Redcap" porter at the new Union Depot, which had replaced the old station from which he had departed. There's no evidence pointing to a family relationship between Henry Tucker and Michael Tucker, one of Henry's recruits. Michael was an outfielder and sometimes pitcher who stayed with the club through the 1917 season.

Napoleon "Chance" Cummings didn't have Lundy's kind of career, but among the eight Duval Giants his was the longest and most productive next to King Richard's. A slick-fielding first baseman, he played until 1928, mostly with the Bacharachs. Through hard work he acquired a reputation as a smooth-fielding first baseman. His nickname was a reference to the white first base ace of the time, Frank Chance of the Chicago Cubs. Cummings, who was not a shy fellow, claimed he was "the guy that made Dick Lundy" by taming the young shortstop's wild throws to first. A thorough student of the game, Cummings was an adept base stealer, not afraid to swipe home if the opportunity arose.[29]

He was also good at intuiting the habits of other teams to try to predict what opponents would do in certain situations. Adept at clowning on the field, a feature of black baseball added to amuse the fans, Cummings used his antics to hide his keen sense of observation. "They always thought I was dumb," he said, but he was an ace at outright stealing the other team's signs: "I had the other team's signals as soon as a man got on first base."[30] Although not a power hitter, Cummings was a reliable on-base presence in the Bacharach lineup. He learned to be a good place hitter and a fine bunter. While most of the Bacharachs eventually moved on from Atlantic City, Cummings took full advantage of the way the Giants players were encouraged to blend into the Northside community, eventually becoming a longtime permanent resident and an Atlantic County employee.

While Henry Tucker brought most of his pitching staff from Jacksonville, he also added Tom Williams, a 20-year-old South Carolinian beginning a ten-year blackball career. Tucker's caravan also halted in Savannah, Georgia, to pick up the first-string catcher. Jim Deas, 21, at five feet, six inches and 148 pounds, was on the small side for a receiver and wasn't a great hitter. But he was fiery and tough, and lasted at high-level ball into the early 1920s as a backup and sometimes regular catcher who liked to be identified, even in the box score, by his nickname, "Yank."

The player who manned third base most of the time, Paul Mack, came from Charleston,

South Carolina. At 24 he was one of the older Bacharachs. Tucker did most of his recruiting off southern sandlots, so the team was remarkably young, and remarkably southern for its location in New Jersey. But to flesh out the team the Bacharachs also recruited reserve infielder William "Chick" Fuller, a New Yorker who at 26 had been playing black ball since 1908, and Dick Wallace, the regular second baseman, a Kentuckian who had been active since 1907. Wallace, only 33, was sometimes referred to in the newspapers as the "old man" of the team.[31]

Tucker, first the superscout and then field manager of the first Bacharach team, was about 40, a veteran of Atlantic City's dominant hotel and restaurant business for ten years or so. He had probably come straight from Jacksonville, where he had acquired a high school education at the Coopman Institute. In Atlantic City he eventually moved up to become proprietor of his own hotel for a time in the mid-1920s, partnering with Prince Baltimore, the owner of the Colored League's Manhattans, their baseball rivalry apparently forgiven or forgotten. Although much black baseball history lumps Tucker in with Tom Jackson as an "Atlantic City politician," Tucker doesn't seem to have been active in Northside Republican politics, as his partner constantly was. His name appeared in the newspapers only in connection with his ball team or his hotel, and the news was usually positive. In a preview of the 1918 season, the Daily Press portrayed Tucker as "very popular with his team and local fans on account of his sunny disposition. He is a firm believer in 'humane' treatment of players." By 1919 he had been noticed by the New York City sports correspondent for the Chicago Defender black weekly: "We have great respect for H. Tucker, Atlantic City, as a booking agent." He was involved with the Bacharach Giants in one way or another until the early 1920s.[32]

His partner Jackson, who was 50 when he thought up this living tribute to his political boss, was the front man, as for some time he had been one of Harry Bacharach's men in the black community. He had served a previous stint as a health inspector during the first Bacharach administration that ended in 1912, but "Henchman" to Bacharach was the term used by the New York Times that year when Jackson suffered that occasional

Napoleon "Chance" Cummings, one of the original Bacharach Giants in 1916 who played with the team for most of its years in Atlantic City, settled there and was a well-known member of the black community (National Baseball Hall of Fame and Library, Cooperstown, New York).

hazard of Atlantic City business and politics, an indictment. This was for running a gambling house, but he had lots of company at his arraignment in the county court, not only from ten other defendants from the gambling investigation, but from the city's power structure. The arrests of Jackson and his cohorts represented typical Atlantic City behavior at its relaxed, routine level. But the alleged gamblers' court appearances coincided with those of six former city councilmen who had been ensnared in a legendary corruption sting. They had taken bribes from an agent of the famous detective William J. Burns who had posed as a New York City contractor to induce them to vote for an ordinance authorizing the Boardwalk to be rebuilt out of concrete. The "Concrete Boardwalk" scandal, as the case became known, happened during Bacharach's first term as mayor, but he wisely had nothing to do with the scheme.[33]

When Jackson wasn't on the city payroll, he was involved in a variety of occupations. Starting as a waiter around the turn of the century, he dealt in liquor (before Prohibition), ran a billiard hall and sold real estate. He also tried his hand a few times at promoting boxing matches at the various sites known as Bacharach Park, not always successfully. His first attempt at a promotion was "marked by a near-riot," according to the *Daily Press*, when only 200 paying customers showed up, not enough to turn a profit. "Jackson waits for the crowd until nine o'clock, nine-fifteen, nine-thirty and then ten o'clock" before deciding to throw in the towel and start returning admissions. The refunds soon emptied the till, but there were still customers waiting to collect. It turned out that someone had dislodged a section of fence, allowing some of those who had exited with their money to re-enter surreptitiously, and "repeaters were collecting the refund time and again." The protests of the innocent ticketholders grew so loud that Jackson went into the red to make sure everyone went away whole, if not happy.[34]

However Jackson earned his daily wages, he was always out there on the Northside working for the Republican machine. A. Conrad Eckholm, a Boardwalk hotelier, complained in a letter to the *Daily Press* in 1920 about the difficult time he had pinning Jackson down for information on events scheduled for the Bacharachs' ballpark for a publication for the tourists. "The first time I called I was told he was at City Hall, and the second time I was told he was on the Northside attending to the registering of voters. As that was not on registration day, I did not understand what was meant." From the tenor of his letter, Eckholm seems to have been from the city's reform element, and perhaps he did not understand, or want to acknowledge, that success in Atlantic City politics required attention to the voters not just on registration day, but on all days. Although Jackson's political, sporting and gambling life had some ups and downs in his home city, he appears to have been well thought of in the wider world of black baseball. Although he did not accept it, in 1920 he was offered control of a travelling Cuban baseball team.[35]

The demise of the local league freed the Bacharachs to accept challenge games by out-of-town teams any time they wanted, and to travel away from the city for games. The offers came quickly—Loraine Melcher must have been receiving and making a lot of phone calls at City Hall that had nothing to do with city finance. By August the Giants were the team that had come from nowhere to impress everyone who played ball in Southern New Jersey and eastern Pennsylvania. The *Bridgeton* [New Jersey] *Evening News* which covered semi-pro ball in the area religiously, noted, "Those Bacharach Giants of Atlantic City are building up a reputation for themselves in their first season's playing in the north. They have been taking contests from virtually every team in this section of the country.... Some team!"[36]

Extensive research into newspapers of the time, conducted with the intention of assembling the most accurate account of the Bacharachs' seasons, has found 82 Giants games in 1916, of which the team won 67, lost 14 and tied one for an entirely dominating winning percentage of .827. By the Bacharachs' own count, they played 114 games, winning 98.[37] As newcomers to the area, the Bacharachs weren't as yet taking on the entire range of opponents in their baseball-crazy region, as their inflated won-lost record in 1916 demonstrates. Eventually, though, the Giants would play every type of team (even the occasional white major league club) in a region that included New Jersey, Eastern Pennsylvania, Delaware and the New York City metropolitan area. The Giants would also go on extended Southern and Midwestern road trips.

The opponents fell into several categories over the 14 seasons the team called Atlantic City home, with representatives of many of these groups on the 1916 schedule. First, there was the local opposition, all white clubs except for the Atlantic City Colored League opponents and the Atlantic City Giants. Even after the passing of the local black league the Bacharachs continued to play some of those teams, adding to their 15–2 league experience with another five wins in six games against the Rudolfs and a local black all-star team playing under the Big Six name. They also played squads representing nearby communities on the string of barrier islands that included Absecon and on the mainland just across the marshes away from the ocean.

The Pleasantville Regulars, a white town team just inland from the city, were constant opponents for the first two years of the Bacharachs' existence until the Giants' growing reputation enabled them to widen their scope. The two teams played at least seven times in 1916. The Giants won four times, the Regulars proving to be one of their toughest competitors that first year. Pleasantville was one of the few teams that could usually hit the Bacharachs' pitching, scoring 37 runs in the seven games. Overall, in the 82 discovered games, the Giants gave up an average of only three runs per game. They yielded more than six runs only five times, and two of those games were with Pleasantville. On August 13, Pleasantville scored nine runs off Giants pitching, a real rarity, but still lost, 10–9, when Shang Johnson won his own game in relief by launching an 11th-inning sacrifice fly. From the Bacharachs' side of things that score wasn't unusual. The team scored in double figures three times off the Regulars, usually having the number of Pleasantville's ace, lefty Wallace "Dump" Adams, who won only two of five decisions.

They also beat a local pickup white team, the Atlantic City Collegians, 7–1, on August 15. The college boys, drawn from other local teams, were easy—they made five errors and got only five hits off the Giants.

The Bacharachs also played white New Jersey teams from beyond the Atlantic City area, venturing within a 50-mile radius that first season to play Wildwood, another resort town down the coast, and inland to Hammonton, a Pine Barrens town along the Philadelphia railroad lines, as well as local baseball hotbeds Millville and Bridgeton. The Giants won four of these five games, losing only a 2–1 game on September 13 to Wildwood, even though Roberts threw a two-hitter. The Bacharachs played 38 games against New Jersey teams, and won 30 of them.

The Giants had expanded their horizons to the Philadelphia area only four games into the known season. The flat 60 miles that made Atlantic City's oceanside amusements so tempting to Philadelphians made its semi-pro and amateur baseball community irresistible to the Bacharachs. Baseball was, without question, the top sport in America in the early part of the twentieth century, and was already called the National Pastime. Philadelphia didn't necessarily have the biggest, hottest baseball culture of any U.S. city, but it was big, and it was hot. A Philadelphia newspaper estimated in 1910 that "on a Saturday in Philadelphia 50,000 men and boys either play or watch games." The surrounding countryside bloomed with baseball, too. The same paper declared in 1911 that "people in Pennsylvania, New Jersey, Delaware and Maryland are inoculated with baseball virus, and every city, town, village, hamlet and corner lot has a team."[38]

Saturday was the big baseball day around Philadelphia, since Sunday baseball was banned by the local Blue Laws. If a team wanted to play on a Sunday it had to go somewhere else, say, to Atlantic City when the reformers weren't holding sway. On Sunday, July 16, 1916, the *Philadelphia Inquirer*, one of several papers in the city to carry detailed local baseball coverage, carried box scores of 135 games played the day before among the upper-level clubs in its circulation area, which extended outside the city as much as 90 miles. That added up to 270 teams with about 2,500 men and boys (plus nine women, the lineup of the traveling Bloomer Girls team that lost a 3–2 squeaker to the Sunbury All-Stars).

On July 15 there was competition in the Philadelphia Suburban League, the Northeast Philadelphia League, the Delaware County League, the Delaware River League, the Montgomery County League, the Camden County League, the Lancaster Church League, the Penn-Jersey League, the Inter-County League and the Schuylkill Valley League.

Philadelphia baseball also included many teams sponsored by major businesses, primarily manufacturers, utilities, railroads and big retailers, particularly the downtown department stores. It wasn't unusual for a single big employer to operate an entire league for its employees (the Pennsylvania Railroad Motive Power League and the United Gas and Improvement League both had sets of games on July 15). Sometimes, as was the case at the Strawbridge and Clothier Department Store, a league existed for employees, "with various departments such as Credit, Retail, Clover, and White Sale represented, while the company's best players and imported 'ringers' represented the 'varsity' team."

The growth of business-backed sports teams for employees to play on (or to cheer for, in the cases of the outsider-dominated varsities) was part of the national growth of what came to be called "welfare capitalism," in which big business, under fire by progressive social and political leaders for anti-union activities, created fairly inexpensive fringe benefits such as athletic and recreation programs for workers and their families that "helped silence critics by demonstrating concern for labor, but more importantly placated potentially dissatisfied workers, built company loyalty, and simultaneously suppressed unionism."[39]

Good young players began their journey to professional baseball in these leagues. Minor and major leaguers whose full-time careers had ended came back to play here, sometimes for many more years, and occasionally full-fledged major leaguers on the outs with their team's management showed up on local rosters to make a few bucks while their professional disputes were being sorted out.

In the summer of 1916 Bacharach games uncovered in this search produced 15 with white Philadelphia neighborhood teams and three from Camden County, directly across the Delaware River in New Jersey and considered part of the bigger city's baseball universe. There were also the Media team from the Delaware County League directly west of Philadelphia and the Norristown Professionals from a town 20 miles northwest of the city. This group of teams proved to be even easier pickings than the New Jersey nines— the Giants won 24, lost only three and tied one.

Northern black players were used to playing against white teams. Actual integrated teams were in the future, but interracial play was accepted throughout the area. When the team had been the Duval Giants of Jacksonville, there had been no interracial competition, so this was a new thing to most of the Giants. Cummings maintained, though, that they weren't afraid: "We worked downtown [in Florida] with a whole lot of white fellas. And when we came up here and started playing ball with white boys, they were more scared of us than we were scared of them. Because we had such a hell of a ball club; we had a powerful ball club!"[40]

The Camden area teams were especially easy pickings for the Bacharachs. They played three white teams from the good-sized city of Camden and the smaller city of Gloucester next door, winning all six discovered games. The Giants had at least a 15–3–1 record against the Philadelphia neighborhood teams. They played 14 of them and beat them all at least once, except for the Tulpehocken Reds of the Germantown section of the city, who were behind 3–2 after the first inning, but held the Bacharachs scoreless the rest of the way for a 7–3 win on July 21 in the only game between the two teams. Other neighborhood teams, including Bridesburg, Bristol, East Philadelphia, Elwood, Frankford, the North Side Professionals, Pearce, the Philadelphia Professionals, Port Richmond, South Philadelphia, the West Philadelphia Giants and Wissinoming, were outclassed. Those teams lost a total of 13 games to the Bacharachs (South Philly twice) and were outscored by a collective 91 to 30. The Giants won three more from teams that like the Camden squads were within the Philadelphia baseball orbit although located outside the city. Norristown went down, 8–1, on July 22 and Media, the runaway 1916 champion in the crack Delaware County League, was swept in a September 25 doubleheader, 5–2 and 1–0.

The Giants were evenly matched against one Philadelphia team, however. The Logan Squares, one of the best clubs from the city at the time, played them even in 1916, each team winning two and battling to a 1–1 tie. The Logan Squares were owned by the powerful and wealthy James P. McNichol, a state senator and paving contractor who lived along Logan Square, one of the city's park-like neighborhoods. The team was in a sense a gift by the senator to his sons, three of whom, Edward, Frank and Daniel, were in the lineup. The first game between the two clubs, on July 8, was one of their best. Dilworth two-hit the Philadelphians, whose own hurler, Ad Swigler, was a perfect example of the importance of semi-pro ball to a good player who didn't quite have the ability to play professionally or, like Swigler, may have given up a shot at the highest level to happily play locally.

Adam Swigler was a Philadelphia high school sports star who in 1916 was still a student at the University of Pennsylvania, which he was attending on a baseball scholarship. He was a standout on the college baseball team and during the summers beginning in 1915 played ball on local teams. Either Swigler played for no pay to preserve his amateur status or no one at Penn cared, because his name could easily be found in the box scores and game accounts in the local newspapers.

Upon graduation he continued to play locally until signed by the New York Giants. He made one start in the majors in September 1917, gave up four runs (on seven hits and eight walks) in six innings and was the losing pitcher. In 1918 the Giants farmed him out, first to Nashville in the Southern Association, where he went 5–3 (but was still wild), and then to Newark in the International League when the Southern Association folded due to the loss of players to World War I. Swigler was 6–4 with Newark and was conquering his control problems when the season ended. On paper, at least, he seemed like a good prospect for the majors in 1919, but spring of that year found him working parttime as an assistant baseball coach at Penn, and he continued to pitch and play outfield and first base for Philadelphia semi-pro teams for many years after that. Swigler probably cut his nascent pro career short because he had an even better one available. He had graduated with a degree in dentistry and practiced in Philadelphia for the rest of his working life, playing ball and coaching on the side.

Swigler was on the mound for the Logan Squares again on July 15 in Atlantic City, this time shutting out the Bacharachs on just four hits. Nearly 50 years later, "Chance" Cummings still recalled the day: "they brought a little pitcher down here that we couldn't do anything with—Swigler; he had a spitter."[41] Logan Square went ahead in the series on August 26, winning 3–1 on neutral turf in Pleasantville, a game that saw only eight base hits between both teams. The Bacharachs finally produced some offense on September 17, scoring nine runs on 13 hits, four of them by Lundy. Johnson gave up only five hits, but with an unusual number of Giants errors (four), he yielded five runs. The fifth game showdown on October 1 in Atlantic City was another cliffhanger, which failed to produce a series winner. The two teams played ten innings to a 1–1 tie, Shang Johnson going the distance for the Giants, yielding only three hits. Swigler played first base, yielding the mound to a 21-year-old on the verge of becoming a long-term major leaguer. Rube Bressler, who had gotten into four games as a left-handed pitcher with the Athletics that season, was picking up a little extra post-season money pitching for the Logan Squares. Eventually converted to an outfielder-first baseman during a 19-year big league career, Bressler gave up seven hits in his ten innings against the Bacharachs.

In addition to being recognized as the South Jersey champions of 1916, the Giants also copped a mythical black championship by nearly sweeping two regional African American teams. They did sweep the Anchor City Giants, a team run by black Philadelphia sports figure J. Henry Sellars, five games to none. Except for a 5–4 win in July and back-to-back 4–3 victories in early September, the games weren't very close. Dilworth usually opposed the Anchors. He beat them four straight times in August and September, striking out 13 men once and ten in each of the other three starts.

The black Atlantic City Giants, whose desire to remain independent had brought the Bacharachs to the Shore in the first place, showed up on the schedule three times in September in what was originally supposed to be a five-game series. The first two games were close, Atlantic City winning the first, 5–4, and the Bacharachs the second, 6–3. But the Bacharachs then battered the other Giants 13–3 as Dilworth threw a three-hitter.

These teams never attained a higher level of competition, but three other African American opponents did, particularly two that, like the Giants, wound up in the black majors, the Negro Leagues, once those loops were formed in the 1920s. The Baltimore Black Sox, which had also just come into existence, visited on July 3 and 4, and were walloped both times. The Giants won the first game, 8–2. Lundy, Crump and Dilworth each got two hits. The Black Sox supposedly had lost for only the third time in 31 games, but it wasn't likely they had often seen a pitching performance like Dilworth's that day. He was said to have Baltimore "completely baffled," and struck out 16. On Tuesday, the holiday, the Bacharachs broke a 1–1 tie in the fourth inning and breezed to a 12–2 win. Paul Mack, Chance Cummings and Yank Deas each had two hits as Johnson breezed to another win.[42]

The Brooklyn Royal Giants, on the other hand, had been around since 1904, and they were not baffled two weeks later when they hit town and decisively defeated the local team, 8–5 on the 17th and 12–0 on the 18th. The games, sandwiched between the initial loss to the Logan Squares and the loss to the Tulpehocken team of Philadelphia, put the Bacharachs on a four-game losing streak, their longest of the season among the 82 discovered games.

The first game with the Royal Giants couldn't have been a showpiece—there were nine errors made in all, six by the Brooklyn team. But the Royals sprinted ahead 7–1 by

The Brooklyn Royal Giants met the Bacharach Giants in the Atlantic City club's first season, and eventually joined the Bacharachs in the Eastern Colored League. This 1916 Brooklyn team photograph includes six future Bacharachs: front row, Pearl Webster (second from left), Ernest Gatewood (center) and Richard "Lefty" Harvey (far right); second row, Andrew "Stringbean" Williams (far left), Bill Handy (second from right) and Johnny Pugh (far right). Brooklyn co-owner Nat Strong, a powerful and controversial figure in Negro League baseball, is at left in the top row (National Baseball Hall of Fame and Library, Cooperstown, New York).

the end of the third inning, and that was that. Their Dick "Lefty" Harvey mastered the Bacharachs on the 18th with a five-hit, nine-strikeout shutout. The third black team, the Philadelphia Red Caps (the players were purported to be railroad porters), never entered the Negro Leagues, but was considered a top-level team before league membership defined the best outfits. The Red Caps were soundly defeated, 11–2, on October 7.

The Bacharachs also had three games against a type of team that was very popular in those days, but has long since passed from existence. These were traveling teams, squads of fairly high caliber, usually without a home base but with some racial or other distinction that made them exotic to the mostly Caucasian middle- and working-class fan base in the towns and cities they visited. The most famous of such teams in the Bacharachs' era was the House of David from Benton Harbor, Michigan. The team represented a Christian religious sect that was well out of the Christian mainstream, and whose male members wore full beards.

The House of David hadn't become a nation-wide barnstorming attraction by 1916, although it would be a regular Bacharach opponent in coming years, but two fine representatives of the type visited Atlantic City in the last days of July. On July 24 the Giants eked out a 6–5 win over the Chinese University, a team which was not from China and whose players were not necessarily either Chinese or college students. But in an America which was more than 80 percent white, the roster was plenty exotic. The full name of the team was the "Chinese University of Hawaii," which did not exist and never has. The team's sponsors in Hawaii apparently thought that billing it as a college team would make it a more attractive attendance draw for its American college and professional opponents. The players were mostly Hawaiian, but their ethnicity was mixed. The best-known member, William "Buck" Lai, who went on to have a four-year minor league career and who played Eastern Seaboard semi-pro ball for years after that, was born in Hawaii, to a Chinese father and a Hawaiian mother.[43] The lineup at Bacharach Park featured two "Chinese" starters named Inman and Mark.

An account of the game claimed the crowd that day was the largest yet in Bacharach Park's first season of existence.[44] Perhaps the Giants were bedazzled by their first look at these "foreigners"—they made an egregious 11 errors, every starter but Cummings at first and Crockett in center booting at least one chance. The Chinese were ahead, 4–3, in the bottom of the seventh when Cummings' sacrifice fly tied the game. Then Crockett doubled home Lundy, who had walked, and successive singles by Crump and Tom Williams brought in Crockett with the sixth run (which proved the game-winner, since the Chinese scored again in the top of the ninth).

On July 26 the Bacharachs played the All Nations from New York City. This was not the famous All Nations team from the Midwest operated by J. L. Wilkinson, the future Hall of Fame owner of the Negro League Kansas City Monarchs. It was a separate and lesser East Coast squad, but structured in the same multi-ethnic manner so as to present a worldwide panorama of players. Although a double loser in Atlantic City (a 3–2 loss plus the defection of Fuller, their shortstop, to the Bacharachs), these All Nations seem to have accomplished their greater goal, with a lineup that included players named Mikami, Armendez, Kautines, Hong Long and Red Cloud. On August 20 the third traveling team, the Washington, D.C., All Stars, came to town and were beaten, 9–3, by the Giants.

The 1916 Bacharachs dominated their opponents—the average score in the discovered games was 7 to 3. The team batting average, .283, reflected the offensive half of that average, and the team earned run average, 2.08, supported the defensive half. The heart of the batting order, the numbers three, four and five hitters, were usually Lundy, Dilworth and Cummings. Cummings led the team in batting with a .364 average, drove in 74 runs, also a team high, and led the team in stolen bases with 17. Lundy was right behind him at .362 with 71 RBI and 12 steals. Dilworth, almost always in the lineup somewhere when not on the mound, hit .297 and was third in RBI with 54. Lundy was clearly the most explosive of the Bacharachs. He had a five-hit game June 18 against Camden City and three four-hit games, in a June 6 Atlantic City League game against the Manhattans (two of the hits were triples), August 23 against the Port Richmond Giants of Philadelphia and September 17 against the Logan Squares.

Crockett, usually in center field and hitting leadoff, underwent a late-season slump but still averaged .276. Mack put up a .289 average at third base and Dick Wallace hit .243 at second, while Deas, the main catcher, hit .260. Michael Tucker, Shang Johnson and Roy Roberts hit .306, .273 and .259 respectively in their roles as pitchers and outfielders, infielders and occasional backup catchers.

But the Bacharachs' really strong suit in 1916 was the pitching corps. Johnson was the ace of the staff, making 23 starts with two bullpen appearances, winning 20 games and losing only two with a minute 1.48 ERA. Dilworth made 21 starts and had four relief stints, winning 16 and losing only five. His ERA was 2.65. Roberts started 17 of his 22 games and went 13–3. His ERA wasn't as low as Johnson's, but it was very low, 1.75. Williams went 4–2 in six starts and Michael Tucker won all four of his starts.

Granted that the competition wasn't always first-rate, it's still remarkable how well the three main starters pitched. Dilworth struck out 16 men in a game on at least three occasions, but that wasn't his best—he fanned 17 men from Millville, New Jersey, on August 5 in the best Giants pitching performance of the season. The lone hit he allowed was a slow roller up the third base line. The end of that game gave Dilworth and the Bacharachs a chance for showboating similar to that later made popular by the legendary black pitcher Satchel Paige, who would call in his outfielders in exhibition games and proceed to strike out the side: "In the last round Adam Schwagle, who has great confidence in his own ability, was given an opportunity to show his skill. The Bacharach outfielders were called off the field; the third baseman played within half a dozen feet of the home plate, while Dilworth proceeded to whiff Schwagle on four pitched balls, the batter taking a healthy swing at each of them, fouling off the third."[45]

Roberts topped Dilworth for the most strikeouts in a discovered game, fanning 18 in an August 2 win over Bridesburg from Philadelphia after having already whiffed 16 against Frankford, another city team, on June 10. No one on the staff threw a no-hitter, but besides Dilworth's Millville gem, Roberts threw two one-hitters in the space of a week, July 6 against Hammonton and then on the 13th versus East Philadelphia.

Johnson doesn't seem to have piled up as high per-game strikeout totals as his two partners, nor achieved as many low-hit games, although the recovered games show him with a two-hitter and a three-hitter. All he did was win, earning the nickname "The Mainstay of the Mayors."[46]

Chapter 2

Surviving the Great War

1917

Being the champions of South Jersey was all right, but Jackson and Tucker clearly had more ambitious things in mind for the Bacharachs in their second season. First of all, the team had a new park that it didn't have to share, as it had had to do at Inlet Park, and where it wasn't a tenant of the city, as was the case at the Adriatic Avenue playground. The grounds were at Tennessee and Caspian Avenues, in the residential portion of the Northside. On the morning of the grand home opener on May 19, the *Atlantic City Daily Press* reported that "ground has been completely enclosed and a small army of carpenters are working overtime to have the stands up." The mayor, as might be expected, attended with the other four city commissioners and threw out the first ball before the Giants took on their keen 1916 rivals, the Logan Squares of Philadelphia. A number of Logan Squares rooters, including Senator McNichol himself, were also there.[1]

The Giants almost completely stopped playing local clubs (except for their continuing rivalry with Pleasantville) and instead booked more games against tougher competition in and around Philadelphia. What made the Bacharach ownership's intentions clear, though, was the number of high-level black teams they scheduled. To be fully recognized as a top-level team you have to play, and beat, the teams of that rank. The Bacharachs' won-lost record against these squads wasn't stellar in 1917, but it was decent and proved they could play with their well-known African American opponents.

The mining of contemporary newspapers for results, stories, and box scores turned up 102 games for this season, of which the Bacharachs won 60, lost 39 and tied 3, for a .606 winning percentage.

Besides the new ballpark, Jackson and Tucker had a number of renovations for the team itself in mind, and their plans had "necessitated a general change in the lineup" that portended "a generally stronger team."[2] But plans are what you have until something actually happens, and the Giants' success was seriously tempered by injuries and defections to other black clubs. Before league-imposed controls, players had what amounted to a nearly unrestricted free agency market. The Bacharachs shopped in that market themselves, of course, to replace some of the players they lost. And, although they almost completely stopped playing the local black teams, they used them instead as something of a farm system, adding stars from those clubs to their roster on a short-term basis.

By the end of the season the lineup of position players from 1916 had half-changed.

Reliable Cummings, who hit .275, led the team with 55 RBI and continued to be a base-running threat, was back at first. Lundy at shortstop, hitting .284, Crockett (.221) in the outfield and Deas at catcher remained from the inaugural season, but Lundy and Crockett were absent part of the time while Deas now shared the work behind the plate.

Dick Wallace, the 1916 second baseman, had moved on to the Lincoln Giants in New York City. The job was filled quite satisfactorily by the recruitment of McKinley "Bunny" Downs. Downs, who had turned 23 before the start of the season, was slight of stature, only about 5½ feet tall and 160 pounds. Nonetheless, his reputation was as "a hustler who always got the most from his talent." He was a native of Chattanooga who had started his professional career in the Midwest in 1915 and had played with the St. Louis Giants in 1916.[3] Downs, who hit .262, began the season as the Giants' leadoff man. However, Tucker dropped him down to second or lower in July when holes began to appear in the regular lineup. Downs was replaced at the top of the order by Elihu Roberts, another new Giant. Roberts, the son of a black doctor who had grown up in Atlanta and attended Morris Brown College there, was only 19 when he began playing left field in Atlantic City. No apparent relation to Roy Roberts, he played in nearly every discovered game, usually in left field, and hit .226. His top-level blackball career, most of it spent with the Bacharachs, lasted only until 1920. He became a permanent resident of Atlantic City, though, living there until his death in 1975.[4]

As the roster continued to turn over in favor of new players with some experience, Paul Mack, who hit .160 in a few games, fell by the wayside at third base in favor of Louis "Red" Miller. Miller joined the Giants in mid-June and hit .230. He was in his fourth year of professional baseball, most recently with the Brooklyn Royal Giants and Lincoln Giants of New York City, two of the top black teams in the East. At catcher the team brought in Burlin White, 22, in his third year, to share the position with Deas. White had been with the Chicago American Giants in 1916 where he was mostly kept on the bench by the presence of Bruce Petway, historically regarded as one of the best defensive catchers in black baseball. White was also regarded as a good defensive catcher, but failed to hit much.[5] In fact, Deas outhit him, although the results were meager in either case. Deas hit only .211 and White .148.

Most of the new Giants, in fact, weren't offensive powerhouses (and many of the returnees didn't have good years, either, as the Bacharachs hit only .228 as a team and scored an average of only a little more than four runs per game). Except for Downs, who had a long playing career before becoming a manager and front office executive, and White, who also became a manager after his defensive ability at the key position of catcher led to a moderately long playing career, most of these newcomers left the Bacharach Giants after just a few seasons, usually at about the time their days at black baseball's top level ended. It wouldn't be long before the Giants had constructed a much more solid foundation, but after their big break-in year, the roster was definitely in transition.

Even in cities such as Philadelphia and Atlantic City, where newspaper coverage of baseball below the major league level was extensive, there was very little in the papers other than game stories, usually no features about teams or individual players. So some men below the white major league level who had short careers, on white as well as black teams, left little behind other than their last names in box scores. Black baseball researchers are still trying to identify a Bacharach regular from this season more fully. His last name was Tomm (or Tomn, or Towns, depending on what box score is read), who joined the team in late June and held down center field until the end of the season.

The Giants' lineup began to fray after the game of June 13 when Frank Baynard, the original center fielder, and Lundy, the Giants' best player, left the team. Lundy came back after a month, but Baynard, hitting .306 in his 17 discovered games, stayed away all season. So long as the Bacharachs were going to venture outside their little world of South Jersey, things like this were going to happen to them. Sol White, a nineteenth century black baseball star who later became a journalist and wrote the definitive book on early Negro ball in 1908, unapologetically stated the case for the itinerant player: "the owner of a base ball team is in the business to make money for years to come, while the player is in the game to make the biggest rake off in the quickest time, never knowing just when he will have hard luck and fail to keep up a hot pace."[6]

Lundy and Baynard were lured away by blackball veteran John "Pop" Watkins. A catcher and first baseman in his playing days, which went back before the turn of the century, Watkins was known as a good scout of talent and developer of players with a multitude of contacts in both the black and white baseball worlds. In 1913 he had launched a team in a seemingly unusual spot for a black baseball venture. Watertown, New York, is near Lake Ontario, more than 300 miles north of New York City and nearly 400 north of Atlantic City. Even more unusual, the name of this team located almost in Canada was the Havana Red Sox.

Watkins may have had an "agent" in the Bacharach camp, put there by the Giants themselves. On June 13 Tucker started a new pitcher, Gifford McDonald, who had jumped the Havana Red Sox. McDonald, pitching against the tough Chester team from near Philadelphia, held it scoreless for six innings but was then lit up for seven runs in the seventh as the Bacharachs lost, 8–3. The *Daily Press* reported that Jackson and Tucker were not discouraged at McDonald's "blow-up" and intended to give him another chance. But a few days later McDonald, Lundy and Baynard were all headed north, and they were all in the lineup for the Red Sox on June 16 when Watkins' team played in Watertown.[7]

Jackson cancelled two games to give the Giants time to fill the holes.[8] Tomm was turned up to fill Baynard's spot in center and held it for the rest of the season, although he hit only .215. But so far as the middle infield went it was mostly a patch job with Downs switching between second and short. Except for William Clinton, who played most of the season for the Giants in the infield and outfield, hitting .211 in his only year in high-level baseball, Downs partnered with mostly unmemorable short-term replacements. There was one clear exception to the mediocre level of the new recruits, though. In the middle of July the Giants landed Bill Pettus.

Pettus was a very good hitter and was versatile. At one point or another in a 20-year career, Pettus played all the infield and outfield positions, and caught. A native Texan, he began in 1904 in the Southwest with teams primarily composed of whites and Hispanics, then moved into African American ball in 1909 in Kansas City. Pettus was almost always on the move between teams, frequently within the same season, playing often for the elite squads that would in future years become the core of the Negro Leagues. Negro Leagues historian James Riley says that at some times in Pettus' career "it requires a road map" to follow his peregrinations.⁹ In 1917 he was with four other outfits besides the Bacharachs. Pettus was the living embodiment, taken to an extreme, of Sol White's example of the man out to "make the biggest rake off in the quickest time."

Lundy was back in the lineup again a little more than a month later, playing shortstop and tripling in two runs in a 12-inning victory over the Logan Squares at Bacharach Park on July 22. He left unhappiness in his wake up in Watertown. The Red Sox were not drawing well and Watkins was threatening to move the team, hopefully to a better locale. In light of this, the Watertown newspaperman covering the Red Sox, who all season was given to fits of whimsy in his writing, characterized Lundy's departure as desertion: "His old team offered him his old position and Lundy was sorely tempted to accept it. He dug down into his jeans, found there a lone nickel and hopped the first train west, taking French leave, not having told 'Pop' or any of his fellow warriors that he was about to recuperate his health in other climes."[10]

If Lundy's departure shook up the Havana followers, they were in for a bigger shock the next day when McDonald, a longtime member of Watkins' teams and reportedly a close friend, packed up his wife and daughter and also headed south. The next day Watkins told the rest of the story—he had fired McDonald after the pitcher had been charged with shoplifting in a local clothing store and had been ordered to leave St. Lawrence County as part of his punishment. McDonald joined Lundy on the Bacharach Giants and became a starting pitcher again. But his acquisition wasn't a great investment. He went 2–8 in ten starts, including the June 13 pasting by Chester, although to be fair he lost a few close ones in which he pitched well enough to win. His late-inning meltdowns continued to be a problem in this era when starters were expected to go nine innings. Later in the season the *Daily Press* had discerned a pattern: "McDonald weakened in the same way that he has weakened in many other contests."[11]

Truthfully, though, for awhile almost anyone who had some promise as a pitcher was welcome to give the mound a try in Atlantic City, since the quality of the available staff was thin. The biggest problem was Arthur Dilworth's unavailability for most of the season. It's not clear what ailed him, an injury or an illness, but he made only four starts before September 2, when the "Giants Sick Man" beat the Logan Squares, 5–3.[12] All season long Dilworth was limited to ten pitching appearances, nine of them starts. He won seven and lost only one with a tiny 1.14 ERA, but his prolonged absence shifted a lot of responsibility to others, and no new pitcher emerged to step into his shoes. Tucker used 13 different starters for at least one game each. Other than Shang Johnson and Roy Roberts, no one had more than ten starts.

It also hurt that Roberts didn't join the team until the latter half of June. He was certainly expected—on June 13 the *Daily Press* mentioned that, with Johnson sent to the mound yet again, Jackson "hoped for the arrival of Roberts." On June 5, the day for men between 21 and 30 to present themselves to the newly-formed World War I draft boards, he registered in Jacksonville, which would have kept him home for awhile. His absence put a tremendous strain on Johnson, who started ten of the 21 recorded games until Roberts was available. The same *Daily Press* article that had Tom Jackson pining for Roberts also was upbeat about Johnson's workhorse abilities: "Hard work seems to improve his arm instead of weakening it." Together Roberts (26) and Johnson (30) made 56 of 97 recorded starts. Roberts went 16–10 with a 2.55 earned run average, and Johnson was 17–10 with a 1.79 ERA.[13]

After Johnson and Roberts and what could be gotten from Dilworth, the next-most effective starter was a recruit from another African American team in the city. The Rudolfs, Cyclones, Vandals and Atlantic City Giants had reconstituted the Colored League in late June.[14] Players from those teams were often found in the Bacharachs lineup, particularly when a starting pitcher was needed. Witherspoon of the Rudolfs was very effective. He made seven starts and two relief appearances, and went 6–2. He also pitched against the Bacharachs once, when they beat the Rudolfs, 6–2, on August 16. The Bacharachs also gave tryouts to two other local pitchers: Herman Gordon of the Cyclones, who won his only start, and Joe Forbes of the Big Six, who lost his two decisions but had the distinction of striking out his older brother, Frank Forbes of the Pennsylvania Red Caps from New York City, at Bacharach Park on July 5.[15] Other spot starters were Fred Wylie, who went 1–1 in two starts in July before heading for Pop Watkins' fold in Watertown, and Charlie "Red" Smith, in the middle of a four-year career at black baseball's top level, who was 2–2 in four starts.

Arch-rival Pleasantville and the Bacharachs played ten times in the recorded games, the Bacharachs winning six and losing three, with a tie. The highlight of the season series belonged to Johnson, who threw a perfect game with ten strikeouts on July 15, a 2–0 victory. The lowlight came the next day, when Wylie and Roberts were ripped for 19 hits in a 15–4 loss that featured an eight-run fifth inning for the Regulars. Or the lowlight might have come on June 5. Pleasantville had just scored the first run of the game in the top of the eighth when, with one on and none out, White chopped a pitch in front of home that Cesar Jamison, the regular African American umpire for the Giants' games, called a fair ball. Sherwood Risley, the Pleasantville manager, protested vigorously that the ball had struck White, making it either a foul strike if in foul territory or an out if fair. Jamison refused to change his call and Risley pulled his team off the field, somehow getting credit for a shortened victory instead of a well-deserved forfeit. The confusion spread to the stands. The *Daily Press* reported that "there were some negotiations between divers gentlemen of betting proclivities that needed to be settled."[16]

Except for the 15–4 blowout, all the games were reasonably close. Neither team won or lost by more than three runs. Among the other good games was the 3–3 tie on September 28 when Johnson and Dump Adams of the Regulars each threw a four-hitter, and the Bacharachs' 4–3 win on June 27. Down 3–0, the Giants went ahead on Tomm's RBI single in the bottom of the seventh and hung on in the ninth when former Atlantic City High School star Norman "Bees" Reeves doubled and stole third for Pleasantville, but was thrown out trying to steal home. A terrible tactical move, it must have been exciting anyway.

The Bacharachs seemed more interested in borrowing the Colored League's players than engaging its teams in match play. There are only two recorded games, a 7–4 win over the Vandal A.C. on June 4 and the 6–2 victory over the Rudolfs on August 4, in which Witherspoon pitched against the Giants. So far as local competition went, there was also an August 19, 5–2 win over the Atlantic City All-Stars, probably a white pickup team. The other two recorded local games showed a further mark of acceptance of the Giants in Atlantic City.

The Melrose Athletic Club, headquartered at the extreme northeast end of the city, up near the yacht basin, was an all-white aggregation. Even if one hadn't ever seen it play, the team's name alone would have identified its side of the racial divide. Some streets in the city changed their names as they passed through neighborhoods, and the spot of the name change could be an ethnic or racial divide. Mediterranean Avenue, a major thoroughfare paralleling the Boardwalk and the ocean, ran just two blocks from Bacharach Park, well inside the black Northside neighborhood. But as it proceeded to the northeast, toward the Absecon Inlet, its name changed to Melrose Avenue: "these street name changes created subtle boundaries that were observed by both races, especially blacks, who knew they weren't welcome in white neighborhoods, except as workers."[17]

The Melrose A.C. was the acknowledged 1917 white city champion. The Bacharachs were the acknowledged black champs because it was obvious they had risen above the level of the local competition. So in late September began a three-game series between the Melrose "Roses" and the Giants for the "city and South Jersey championship." The Bacharachs took the first game on the 23rd. Dilworth, now back in as fine a form as ever, opposed Dump Adams, the Pleasantville ace who also pitched for the Roses. Dilworth gave up six hits and struck out seven. The Giants scored three times in the third, assisted greatly by three of the six errors Melrose committed, and breezed to a 6–1 win. When the teams met again on the 26th, the "city and South Jersey" championship plan seemed to be in shambles. The Melrose manager couldn't get enough of his usual players to show up and "searched the highways and byways" for replacements. Mostly, he looked to Pleasantville, where he got three Regulars—Reeves, Raymond "Ike" Nelson and Terry Long—to bolster the Roses' lineup. Pitcher Jappy Christiansen of the Atlantic City Athletic Association team that had lost the white city title to Melrose, actually outpitched Shang Johnson. Christiansen gave up only three hits to Johnson's five, but the makeshift Roses again committed six errors and the Bacharachs won, 3–0, on unearned runs. There was no need for a third and final game, even if Melrose had been able to field a team.[18]

The Southern New Jersey teams from outside the immediate area continued to be fodder for the Bacharachs' won-lost record. They won seven in a row from this group, including a doubleheader from Hammonton and a single game from Vineland. The team from the nearby resort town of Wildwood came to Atlantic City twice for series in September. The Bacharachs won four in a row before Wildwood beat them, 6–2, on the September 21. The next day the Giants lost, 6–0, to Millville.

The Giants played 39 games against Philadelphia area teams, but two-thirds of them were equally divided between their main Philly opponent of 1916, the Logan Squares, and the teams of the Delaware County League, the top semi-pro circuit in Philadelphia baseball. In both cases, the Bacharachs held their own against the best the big city had to offer. The Logans visited Atlantic City 11 times for 13 games, and were the Giants' opponents for prime drawing doubleheaders on July 4 and Labor Day. The Philadelphia team, which of course couldn't play Sunday ball in its home town, came to the Shore eight times for Sunday games. Overall, the Bacharachs won five of the contests and lost six. Appropriately for such well-matched squads, there were two ties. The best game between the two teams was the second game on July 4, which went 18 innings and ended in a 1–1 tie. Johnson went the whole way for the Giants, striking out 20 and not giving up a hit until the seventh inning (and only six for the whole game). Frank McNichols, one of the senator's sons, also pitched a complete game, giving up 14 hits. The game was a double shutout through 14 innings. Each team scored one run in the 15th, and that was all.

The Logan Squares had no trouble finding former college stars and men with minor and major league experience. In Vince Molyneaux, who threw a 7–0 shutout in the first game against the Giants on May 19, the team had all three, although not in the order we would expect today. Molyneaux, a 28-year-old right-hander, was just finishing up at Villanova University in the Philadelphia area, and was less than two months away from his big league debut with the St. Louis Browns of the American League. He made seven relief appearances for the Browns that year and six more for the Boston Red Sox in 1918 before being shipped to the minors. But that wasn't his first tour of duty in professional ball. He had played the 1914 season with Jamestown, New York, in the Interstate League and in 1915 with London, Ontario, in the Canadian League. His 1915 season, in fact, was his second of the year—he had pitched for Villanova that spring, and would again in the 1916 spring baseball season. Today there's no way a career could unfold like this. The minor league seasons would have made Molyneaux ineligible for further intercollegiate ball.[19]

Ad Swigler, the eventual dentist who was to make his big league debut in September, opposed the Bacharachs the next day, a Sunday, but the Giants won, 4–1, as Johnson, the losing pitcher on the 19th, threw a four-hitter. Johnson, being run out to start as often as possible until Roy Roberts showed up, threw another four-hitter on June 3 but lost to the Logans, 1–0. The Philadelphia team stayed away for a month, but won the first July 4 game, 5–2, Swigler defeating Roberts, who gave up only five hits but did his "Wild Boy" act, walking eight.

On July 22 the Logan Squares were back for another Sunday game. Fans who might have said after the 18-inning July 4 game that "Johnson can't do THAT again," would have been partly right. This time he had to pitch only 12 innings, gaining a 7–6 win when Downs singled and scored on an error. This was Lundy's first game back from Watertown, which along with the Logans' presence might have helped account for the largest attendance of the season to that point at Bacharach Park. Lundy drove in two runs with a triple and hit the booted grounder that allowed Downs to score in the 12th.

Logan won again on July 29, 5–4, Swigler backed by a grand slam in the fifth off of the unfortunate Giff McDonald. Johnson threw a five-hitter to win, 5–2, on August 26, and then the Squares came back to the Shore for three games over the Labor Day weekend. Dilworth beat them, 5–3, on Sunday the 2nd, and Roberts threw two complete games on Labor Day. They weren't necessarily things of beauty—he lost the opener, 10–4, but won the nightcap, 9–4.

For the final two games, on September 16 and 30, the Logans brought in a once and future major league pitcher, left-hander Stan Baumgartner. Baumgartner pitched in parts of eight big league seasons in Philadelphia with both the Phillies and Athletics, and played semi-pro ball for top area teams when not in the majors or minors. He became a Philadelphia sportswriter after his playing days ended. He was matched up against Johnson both times, the first game ending in a 2–2, ten-inning tie, and the second a 4–2 Logan Squares win. Both Baumgartner and Johnson threw five-hitters, but the Philadelphians bunched three of theirs, together with an error and hit batsman, to score all their runs in the top of the sixth. The rally was interrupted, though, when University of Pennsylvania star Lou Martin, the Logan shortstop, disputed a third strike call and punched Cesar Jamison, the black umpire who regularly worked Bacharach games. "The local Ump resented the insult. He took a crack at Martin. [Logan third baseman Eddie] Lennox tried to act as peacemaker and as peacemakers do, received a blow intended for one of the belligerents."[20]

The Bacharachs did a little better against the teams of the Delaware County League, winning seven of 13, with no ties. Delaware County is immediately west of Philadelphia, and even in 1917 could have been considered a part of greater Philadelphia. The baseball league, founded in 1908, is still in existence as a men's amateur league. In its early days there was substantial pressure for the players to be paid. The league's original set of rules, while forbidding salaries during the season, allowed players to pocket a share of team profits after play was over. The dike between amateur and professional having been thus breached, it didn't take long for the league to become a haven for players whose professional careers were over, but who still wanted to play for at least a little pay. For example, pitcher George Mullin hurled for Chester after his 14-year big league career ended in 1915, and infielder Monte Cross, retired from the majors since 1907 and in his mid–40s, played for Media. Albert "Chief" Bender, the American Indian pitcher, and Bris Lord, an Upland native who had wrapped up an eight-year career as a big league outfielder, played for Upland.[21]

Beginning in 1915, with the defection of star third baseman Frank "Home Run" Baker from the Philadelphia Athletics to Upland after a contract dispute with Connie Mack, the league also became a sanctuary for disgruntled major leaguers who would jump their big league teams and play semi-pro ball. Players would use the presence of the league as a bargaining chip to get a better contract. Eventual Hall of Famer Grover Cleveland Alexander held out for $15,000 from the Phillies for 1917, threatening to go to the Delaware County League if he didn't get his price. Ban Johnson, the American League president, launched an investigation in mid-season when it was alleged that Baker, now with the New York Yankees, was trying to recruit big leaguers, including hitting star George Sisler, to jump to the league.[22]

As Neil Lanctot, a historian of Philadelphia baseball, puts it, "While the National Commission, the three-man governing body of major league baseball until 1920, outlawed any semipro teams harboring ineligible players who were still legally the property of organized baseball, local teams and leagues, most notably the Delaware County League, remained a haven for professional ballplayers."[23] The "outlawing," though, merely meant that organized baseball teams were banned from playing the semi-pros. This cost the semi-pros some games, but there were plenty of clubs on their own level, plus black teams such as the Bacharach Giants, more than ready to take up the slack.

The Giants played three Delaware County teams among the discovered games in 1917. They opened with Media on May 27, winning 5–4 when Banks, another Atlantic City Colored League product who played outfield early in the season, stole home with the winning run in the bottom of the ninth. The Giants went 4–2 with Media all year, their best performance against league teams. They split two games with J. G. Brill, a team sponsored by a company that manufactured trolley cars. The Giants went 2–3 with Chester, two of the losses coming on August 1, 7–0, and August 2, 7–1, when Baumgartner beat them in back-to-back starts, giving up only seven hits in the two games.

The remainder of the Philadelphia-area competition wasn't much more difficult for the Bacharachs than the New Jersey opposition. They went 7–1 against Philly neighborhood teams, beating Roxborough and Frankford twice and Wissahickon, Cadorna and Port Richmond once each. The sole loss to this group came on June 6, when Tucker, "badly in need of pitching," turned the mound over to two non-pitchers, Downs and Mack, and lost, 5–4, to Northeast Philadelphia.[24] From the New Jersey side of the Delaware River the Giants split a home and home series with the Camden Athletic Club, and Gloucester defeated them, 2–1, in 14 innings on August 13.

This season introduced the Giants to a powerful element of Philadelphia baseball, the teams sponsored by business and industry. Uncovered games show that in addition to the split with J. G. Brill, the Bacharachs defeated R. G. Dun (the mercantile agency that was a predecessor of Dun and Bradstreet), 14–3, on June 22, but lost, 2–1, on July 14 to J. B. Stetson (the company that introduced the cowboys' favorite, the Stetson hat), 2–1. There were also a pair of games on June 19–20 against a team representing Cressona, on a long road trip from its home base 160 miles away in Pennsylvania coal mining territory. The Giants won them both, 6–3 and 3–2.

The list of known games included six against two regional African American teams. The Giants swept four at the beginning of the season from the Peerless American Giants, a new team in the Philadelphia area, and put the Beaver Athletic Club of Wilmington, Delaware, away with no problems twice in September.

The Pennsylvania Red Caps, a team representing (but not necessarily including as players) Pennsylvania Station railroad porters from New York City, came to Bacharach Park on July 5–6. The Red Caps defeated the Bacharachs, 6–2, in the first game, a likely loss for the tired Giants, since the starting lineup was mostly the same players who had just finished the 27-inning marathon holiday doubleheader with the Logan Squares the day before. It was different the next day, though, when a five-run fourth inning backed Roy Roberts and, when he tired, Johnson, who pitched an inning and two-thirds of hitless relief two days after his 18-inning performance.

Although baseball historian James Riley characterizes them as a "marginal major-league team," the Red Caps were better than most local black teams such as the Peerless Giants.[25] There were no actual Negro major leagues until 1920, of course, but a squad's level of competition and the prior and subsequent careers of the players on its roster are considered by historians the benchmarks that separated the higher-class clubs from the rest. Although the Red Caps never joined one of the black major leagues, they were regarded as able to compete with the clubs that were soon to make up those circuits.

The Bacharachs strove to be recognized at this higher level, and in 1917 began to fill their schedule with opponents that would be members of the Negro National League when it was born in the Midwest in 1920 and the Eastern Colored League (of which the Giants were a charter member) when it was launched in 1923. Twenty-seven games against these eventual major league clubs have been found in 1917. The Bacharachs won only ten of them, and got soundly trounced in several of the losses, but this was the big step that had to be taken if the Giants were themselves to be considered more than a regional phenomenon.

The Bacharachs played five other future black major league teams that season. The first was the nearest, Hilldale of Darby, a suburb of Philadelphia. The Hilldale Athletic Club, founded in 1910, began as a team of African American teenagers indistinguishable from the teeming horde of amateur and semi-pro teams in Philadelphia. The team soon came under the control of Edward Bolden, a young, quiet and determined post office employee who by 1917 had recruited older, more experienced players, had the team playing on its own home field, Hilldale Park, and had made the team professional.[26]

Hilldale had its own park in Darby, and the games of June 21 and 23, sandwiched around the R. G. Dun game in Atlantic City, were two of the rare Giants road games among the recorded contests. On the 21st, Dan Johnson threw a four-hit shutout and with two hits joined Miller and Downs at the head of the offensive push that earned a 3–0 victory over Hilldale starter Frank "Doc" Sykes who, like the white Swigler, practiced dentistry when he wasn't throwing a spitball. Sykes and Johnson opposed each other again on the 23rd and the tables were turned. Sykes allowed only three hits and Johnson was touched up for five runs in the first five innings, all Hilldale needed for a 5–3 win.

On July 2 the Bacharachs played the first of nine games with, by early twentieth century standards, an exotic visitor, not as exotic as the Chinese University or the All Nations, but a better bunch of ballplayers. The Cuban Stars were one of two teams by that name. This one, owned by an aspiring young baseball entrepreneur named Alejandro Pompez, played on the East Coast and was often called the "Cuban Stars East" to differentiate it from its Midwestern counterpart, the "Cuban Stars West." Pompez's Stars didn't have a home city, although in later years they settled down in the New York metropolitan area. They travelled for all their games in 1917 and made three more visits to Atlantic City. By the end of the season the Stars had won five games, the Giants four.

That first game was close and exciting. The Bacharachs won, 7–6, when Clinton drove in Tomm in the bottom of the ninth inning with what would have been an extra-base hit if the game hadn't ended when Tomm crossed the plate. When the Cubans returned on July 26, the Bacharachs were in one of their short-handed modes. Downs, Johnson, White and Pettus were all temporarily absent, probably over in Philadelphia playing for Hilldale (of course, Pettus could also be said to be only temporarily present for most of his employers). In addition to the long-term defections such as Lundy's month-long fling with the Havana Red Sox and Baynard's permanent switch there, black baseball lineups were often disrupted on a short-term basis when players took advantage of an opportunity to play elsewhere for a little extra money. It's clear from tracking Hilldale box scores that Downs, Johnson and Pettus spent a good part of August with Hilldale, when they were missing from the Bacharachs. As black teams became more established, their owners and managers were able to put a stop to some of this activity, but this was early in the Bacharachs' existence and Jackson and Tucker probably hadn't developed enough clout yet to keep their players from straying. On this particular day the Cuban Stars walloped the Giants, 10–0, a shutout for Evelio Calderin. All the Bacharach absentees were back on the 27th, and while the Giants got only four hits, one was a Pettus home run in the second inning and one was a timely run-scoring hit by Cummings in the seventh that made a 4–3 win possible.

The two teams split again on August 9–10. Calderin again picked up the win on the 9th. Giff McDonald got one of his few Bacharach victories the following day, pitching a four-hit shutout and walking no one. The next meeting was a three-game series on August 20–22. Roberts and Calderin hooked up in a very good pitcher's duel, the Giants winning, 2–1, when Elihu Roberts threw what would have been the tying run out at the plate in the seventh. McDonald started for the Bacharachs the next day and couldn't blame hard luck for this 16–0 defeat. He gave up 12 hits and didn't survive the fifth inning. Julio Rojo, usually a catcher-outfielder, and in a few years a member of the Bacharachs, pitched a shutout. The Atlantic City team proved the next day that they could lose close, too. A combination of a single, an error, a walk, a wild pitch and a passed ball gave the Cuban team two runs in the first inning, and Leon of the Stars gave up two hits for a 2–1 victory. The final recorded game between the two teams on August 30 was a 2–0 Stars win as Calderin threw a four-hitter.

The season series with a third team, the Brooklyn Royal Giants, went a little better. The Bacharachs and the Brooklyn team had played at least two games in 1916 when the Royal Giants were one of only three black major league–quality teams that came to Atlantic City. This season the two teams played nine games, the Bacharachs winning five. The first game, on July 18, was a close one, tied 5–5 in the bottom of the ninth when Cummings got a timely hit to drive in Downs. The Royals' lineup featured one eventual member of the Baseball Hall of Fame, catcher–first baseman Louis Santop, and several solid players. In the fluid way that black baseball rosters worked, about half of the Royal Giants' starting lineup would be Bacharachs in a few years. Atlantic City made it two in a row over Brooklyn on the 20th with a 7–5 win.

The next time Brooklyn visited the shore, on August 14–15, the Royals won the first game, 4–3, in 11 innings when a pitch eluded Deas for a passed ball and let in the lead run for yet another of McDonald's hard-luck losses. He gave up only eight hits and at one point held Brooklyn scoreless for six straight innings. The next day Roy Roberts was matched up against Atlantic City resident Emerson Gray, who had a short tryout with the Bacharachs in mid–July. A two-run double by Miller in the sixth put the Bacharachs ahead to stay and they won, 5–3.

The Royal Giants returned to win, 7–5, on August 24. The *Daily Press* pronounced the game, which lasted three hours, as "listless" and the reporter, perhaps with a medical dictionary at his elbow, added a diagnosis: "Ennui was a common complaint at the Bacharach Park yesterday. The Bacharach Giants seemed to suffer the hookworm ailment in a most acute form, while the Brooklyn Royal Giants were in a less critical stage." Tucker was clearly not pleased, and after the game "gave a treatment for ankylostomiasis that was not taken with a teaspoon but, nevertheless, had something of the after-taste of cod liver oil. Some of the Giants were told that they would probably be sent back to the favorite haunt of the hookworm unless they shake some of their languor."[27]

When the Royals Giants returned in early September, the Bacharachs seem to have taken their physic. They beat the visitors, 3–1, on September 4 and 7–2 on the 5th. Dilworth gave up only two hits in the second game, the same number as he collected as a hitter. On the 6th, though, the Royal Giants swept a doubleheader, 5–4 and 5–3. The Bacharachs might have won the first game, except that in the first inning Tomm and Crockett collided in the outfield going for a fly ball in right-center when a catch would have ended the inning. Both were knocked out (although Crockett continued in the game), and the batter, Frank Earle, circled the bases, driving home two runners in front of him.

The fourth major black team to play the Bacharachs this season, the Lincoln Giants from New York, swept all five games, but the Lincolns were the class of the East Coast teams and the games were close, so the losers didn't need to hang their heads. The Lincolns had been playing since 1911 and were owned by a white man, James F. Keenan. They had a regular home park, Olympic Field in Harlem, and boasted the greatest black pitcher of the day, Joe Williams, a Texan who was part American Indian and went by the nicknames of "Cyclone" or "Smokey Joe." Williams, 32 years old this season, was not yet halfway through a 27-year career that eventually got him elected to the Hall of Fame. His only competition for best pitcher of the black baseball era is fellow Hall of Famer Satchel Paige. Williams pitched twice against the Bacharachs in 1917, beating them, 4–1, on July 12 and 5–3 in 11 innings on August 7. He gave up seven hits in the first game, but walked no one and struck out nine. In the second he gave up 13 hits in the 11 innings and was in and out of trouble, but "was wonderful in the pinches."[28]

The July 12 game was the third of a series at Bacharach Park. On July 10 the Bacharachs gave the game away in the tenth inning on lousy defense and apparent bonehead thinking. A double and two fielding errors filled the bases, and the lead runner, Blainey Hall, beat a throw home on Thomas' grounder for one run. Downs muffed a grounder by Dan Kennard and while unsuccessful attempts were made to get Thomas, and then Kennard, out when they rounded second and first, the two runners ahead of them dashed home for a 6–4 final. On the 11th the Giants pulled off a triple play but had few other highlights as the Lincolns won, 4–0.

The final game of the season between the two clubs was on August 8, the day after Williams' second victory, when the Lincolns scored two runs in each of the ninth and tenth innings to win, 7–5. The previous four high-level competitors, plus the Baltimore Black Sox of the 1916 season, would all wind up with the Bacharach Giants in the first East Coast Negro League, the Eastern Colored League, in 1923.

But the last top black team to come to Atlantic City, on August 27–28, was something more. The Chicago American Giants, generally regarded as the class of black baseball, included the Bacharachs in an Eastern barnstorming trip, and beat them, 5–4 and 4–0. The American Giants, in existence since 1911, were the brainchild of Andrew "Rube" Foster, once a star pitcher in independent black ball, then a manager and owner of the Giants. He later became president of the first successful black league, the Negro National League in 1920. Foster and Joe Cronin of the Washington Senators and Boston Red Sox of the white American League are the only Hall of Fame members to have performed as player, manager, club president and league president.

The two-game series was ballyhooed by the *Daily Press* as "the colored world series," which was the sort of claim that could be made before Negro Leagues were formed and all it took was a good team and some moxie for an owner to declare his squad the "cham-

The Lincoln Giants from New York City first began playing the Bacharachs in 1917 and were also charter members of the Eastern Colored League. This 1911 team photograph includes five future Bacharach Giants: front row, Bill Francis (left); second row, Dick Redding (far left) and John Henry Lloyd (center); third row, Bill Pettus (far left) and Spotswood Poles (far right) (National Baseball Hall of Fame and Library, Cooperstown, New York).

pion." Justifiably a "World Championship" or not, the Atlantic City fans loved the series, packing Bacharach Park.[29] The Bacharachs made good competition for the Chicagoans. Tom Johnson, the Chicago starter, and Roy Roberts each had a rough first inning on the 27th, giving up three and four runs respectively, but the game settled down to a long string of zeroes before the Bacharachs tied the score in the bottom of the eighth. However, Dick Redding, an ace starter who could also hit, pinch-hit for Johnson and drove in the winning run with a sacrifice fly in the top of the ninth. The Bacharachs' first-inning runs came on a blast by Pettus that was significantly aided by a lack of groundskeeping. His drive to left field got lost in tall grass and by the time it was found he had a three-run, inside-the-park homer. The next day former Bacharach Tom Williams, who also went by the nickname "Cyclone," at least when Joe Williams wasn't around, gave up only four scattered hits and a walk for his shutout.

There was one more type of team the Bacharachs played that season, with only one game in the category, but the opponent's very existence forecast a major upheaval for all of baseball that was just one season away. On July 17 the Giants played a team of U.S. Marines stationed at the Philadelphia Navy Yard. The Marine Corps team hadn't existed in 1916, nor would it exist for much longer. It was composed of enlistees who had answered the call to service in World War I, which the United States had officially entered on April 6. The team was good—it featured players such as Eddie Mahan, a Harvard University baseball player who had also been the star of the football team, and Mike Pasquarella, a local high school star who had played for Villanova.

The Bacharachs won, 8–6, after Roy Roberts came on in relief of young Emerson Gray. At the time the game was played, it was just another win over second-tier competition for the up-and-coming Giants. But by the spring of 1918 teams representing the military or vital defense industries came to dominate semi-pro schedules, including that of the Bacharachs. The war-time teams' rise naturally coincided with the temporary decline of the rest of semi-pro ball, and professional baseball for that matter, as the massive shift of manpower and resources to the war effort changed the face of baseball along with that of the entire nation.

1918

The United States had entered the war in 1917 as a result of Germany's resumption of unrestricted submarine attacks that threatened American lives and shipping, and the infamous "Zimmermann telegram." That was a coded message to German foreign officials in Mexico, intercepted by the British and passed on to the U.S., in which the German foreign minister attempted to persuade Mexico to enter the war on the side of Germany and its allies. The buildup of the U.S. armed forces through the institution of the Selective Service system took some time, however, and about 80 percent of the 2.8 million men drafted weren't inducted until 1918. Their departure, and the simultaneous movement into defense industry jobs that were an accepted substitute for military service, was a powerful drain on baseball rosters at all levels.

The major leagues closed their season a month early on Labor Day after league presidents and owners worried that continued play might be banned altogether by the government due to the Selective Service's "Work or Fight" dictum. This was a plan to encourage men not going into the military to take essential defense jobs on the home front. The Great War was on everyone's mind by the summer of 1918. Per-game attendance in the majors, which had already dropped 25 percent from 1916 in the first year of America's involvement in the war, dropped again until at 2,800 it was barely more than half of what it had been two years earlier. By 1918 the minor leagues had basically closed down. Nine leagues had begun play that spring, three less than had finished the previous season, and only one, the International League, completed its entire schedule.[30]

In Philadelphia, prospects for the kind of baseball-filled summers the city was used to enjoying were growing dim even in March. The Delaware County League decided to suspend for the season. President J. Borton Weeks declared his organization "has fallen victim to the Great War." The Camden County League also suspended in April. Even good news from local leagues was tempered. The announcement that the local district of the Patriotic Order of the Sons of America in Woodbury, New Jersey, would continue its baseball league also noted that "the war has cut a swath in baseball circles in amateur ranks as well as in semi and professional teams." Nearly 48,000 men were drafted from Philadelphia's 51 local draft boards. A count of the games reported in the encyclopedic sports section of the *Philadelphia Inquirer* that July shows the extent of the drop-off. The 270 teams in action in the paper's circulation area on Saturday, July 15, 1916, had declined to 164 on the comparable Saturday of July 6, 1918, and 114 on July 20 (it had rained, disrupting the schedule, on July 13).[31]

As was the case when the nation geared up for World War II a little more than 20 years later, the growth of Northern defense industries lured Southern workers, including blacks, and actually increased Negro baseball's fan base in major metropolitan areas. This put the African American version of the sport on the threshold of significant postwar expansion, when the first successful Negro League was formed. In Philadelphia, where Southern blacks poured in for industry jobs, the African American population increased 59 percent between the 1910 and 1920 censuses. This provided a comfortable fan base for Ed Bolden's Hilldale club, which realized a profit in 1918 despite the wartime disadvantages.[32]

Atlantic City, with no war industries to speak of, did not share in this permanent population boom. Atlantic County's entire population grew by only 12,000 (not quite 17 percent) between the 1910 and 1920 censuses, and the black population, most of which was in Atlantic City, increased by only about 1,800 (also a little less than 17 percent). The Bacharach Giants found it difficult both to keep players and find opponents, and suffered the financial malaise that afflicted higher levels of ball, nearly to a fatal extent in their case. The search for game accounts in 1918 turns up only 44 games. While there is always the likelihood that more were played, it is still likely that the schedule shrank considerably from the previous seasons. Like the major leagues, the Bacharach Giants suspended play after August.

The Bacharach roster was in a constant state of flux. The team employed 50 different players, 24 for only one game each. Lundy and Downs, along with John Reese, a fleet outfielder in his first year in top-level black baseball, split their time between the Giants and the more solvent Hilldale. Baynard played several games with the Pennsylvania Red Caps and Deas with the Lincoln Giants. (Although "Yank" caught more recorded games than any other Bacharach this season, he still hit only .198.)

Pettus, as usual, was almost everywhere in the region, with the Bacharachs, Hilldale, the Lincoln Giants and the Brooklyn Royal Giants. Shang Johnson made a couple of recorded appearances with the Bacharachs as a pitcher, and also played for Hilldale, the Royal Giants and the Red Caps. Chance Cummings was again a regular at first, hitting .297. Red Smith returned as a starting pitcher and played the field on occasion. He and Roy Roberts, along with two newcomers to the top level of blackball—George Robinson, known as the "Southern Bearcat," and Henry Howell, reportedly from Savannah—did the bulk of the pitching. They also did a lot of the hitting, with averages of .261, .273, .296 and .329, respectively. Dilworth had moved on for the time being, splitting his season between Hilldale and the Lincoln Giants.

Bill Handy, at age 29, was in his ninth season of top-ranked baseball, most it spent with the Royal Giants. He was acquiring the reputation as "the best [black] secondbaseman in the East during the '10s."[33] Except for an absence from the team for the first half of July, when he may have been injured or, more likely, had loaned himself to some other team (not Hilldale, for a change, though), he was the regular second baseman. Downs, when he was available to the Giants, moved over to shortstop, and sometimes to third. Handy appeared in 20 of the Giants games for which there are box scores and hit a tremendous .397. Downs, when available, was a key player, too, hitting .286 in 17 found games.

Handy helped anchor the Bacharach infield for three more years. This season also introduced Giants fans to another long-term asset, outfielder Elias "Country Brown" Bryant. An excellent outfielder with some power, Bryant, who for unknown reasons used the surname Brown during his playing days, was popular with fans for his on-field clowning, a practice begun by the earliest African American teams. Unlike the later black sensation, basketball's Harlem Globetrotters, the comedy routines were usually confined to times when the ball was not in play or the game had become one-sided. But Bryant reportedly was good at cutting it up from the coaching box, appearing at home plate with a shovel and pretending to dig an offending umpire's grave or getting into the batter's box on his knees (and sometimes getting a hit). The news stories of Bryant's time with the Bacharachs rarely include theatrics, but do account for a lot of base hits. In 1918 he hit .328 and led the team in runs batted in with 26, filling in at infield positions when not in the outfield.[34]

Weaving the rest of the lineup around the regulars proved a challenge, though. The short-term replacements were of all types. One of the best Negro League third basemen of the 1920s, Oliver Marcell, who started a long career with the Giants a few years later, played for them once in 1918, as did Bill Pierce, already a veteran first baseman. There were several of those players whose presence with the team, and in high-level black baseball period, was so fleeting that their first names are unknown. But in the last few weeks of the season the Bacharachs added a type player rarely ever seen in black baseball—whites.

In mid–August the *Daily Press* referred to the "reorganized Bacharach Giants," and they certainly were, in a way not often seen in semi-pro baseball in those days.[35] While Atlantic City thrived with de facto segregation, social interactions between the races were common. Apparently running short of black players, no doubt because there was a shortage of money to pay them, and existing in the midst of a pool of good white players, the Giants began recruiting them for their vacancies. One of them was Henry "Whitey" Gruhler, who at 17 was establishing himself as an infielder sought after by the better white teams in Atlantic City. He played third base for the Bacharachs against the white Melrose Athletic Club on August 18, and went one-for-three. Gruhler later went into journalism and became the sports editor of the *Atlantic City Daily Press*, where he used his regular column to advocate for the integration of baseball, having already done that himself in a small way. Like Gruhler, almost all of the white recruits were one- or two-game fill-ins. But Raymond "Ike" Nelson, a plumber from Pleasantville who was constantly sought after by semi-pro teams from the Shore to Philadelphia, joined the Giants in mid–August and played 11 games in left field, belting .351.

Two men who played with the Giants in 1918 wound up in the Army before the season ended. Roy Roberts left in August to report to Camp Dix in Central New Jersey.

Pearl Webster was an outfielder who played two games for the Bacharachs in May but spent the rest of the season with Hilldale, where he had played the year before. Webster also went into the Army and survived the actual war, but died in November 1919, five days after Armistice Day, during the Spanish Flu epidemic.

Despite the constant lineup changes, the Giants hit well, averaging .281 as a team and scoring six runs per game. This was a two-run-per-game increase over the anemic 1917 offense, although the pitching staff yielded nearly five runs per game, nearly a run and a half more than in 1917. Roberts led the hurlers, going 5–3 in eight starts that produced a 2.53 ERA. Robinson was 7–5 in 11 starts with a 2.75 ERA. Red Smith made eight starts and went 5–2, while Howell started six times and went 3–3.

Overall the Bacharachs continued to have a good record, winning 25 of the 44 found games, while losing 17 and tying two for a .595 winning percentage. There were only four recorded local games, all against the Melrose A.C., arch-rival Pleasantville having succumbed to the wartime shutdown. The Giants easily won all four from the Roses, 11–0 twice on July 25 and August 25, 6–3 on August 11, and 5–0 on August 18.

Likewise, there were only seven games against Philadelphia neighborhood and industrial teams, of which the Giants won six. The war could be blamed for most of this downturn, but the Bacharachs'

Raymond "Ike" Nelson, a longtime white semi-pro star in the Southern New Jersey-Philadelphia, who played many games against the Giants and a few for them in August 1918 when the team fell on financial hard times and recruited local white players to fill out its roster.

schedule took a major blow from the loss of the Logan Square team, which disbanded after the untimely death of Senator McNichol, its sponsor. Media was the only team from the suspended Delaware County League to make the trip to Atlantic City, and they beat the Giants, 3–0, on July 7 as Sid Agnew, a high school player who went on to a short minor league and a long Philadelphia semi-pro career, won a duel with Howell.

Among the wins, the Bacharachs took a raucous 11-inning, 12–11 game from the Indiana Boys Club of Philadelphia on June 2 in which the Giants had 23 hits, but had to come from five runs down in the eighth inning to keep their chances alive. They slaughtered Philadelphia U.G.I (United Gas Improvement, Inc., the city's natural gas company), 16–3, on June 9 when the Giants collected 21 hits, four by Bryant and three by Smith. They creamed Becker, Smith & Page, wallpaper manufacturers from Philadelphia, 12–2, on June 16, a three-hit day for Cummings and a six-hit win for Robinson. The Wissinoming team from Philadelphia went down twice on August 4 and 5 by scores of 6–4 and 13–7, when the Giants had entered their "reorganized" phase, but still had plenty of offense, and Roxborough, a tougher neighborhood squad from the city, fell 4–3 on August 11 in the second game of a three-team doubleheader, the Bacharachs having dispatched Melrose in the first game.

There were three recorded games against the Pennsylvania Red Caps early in the season. The Red Caps beat the Giants, 8–2, on May 25 and 6–4 on June 1, and the Bacharachs partially countered with a 10–4 win on May 31, another four-hit day for Bryant. The Giants also defeated the Wilmington Giants from nearby Delaware, 15–8, on July 6, when Howell had four hits and Deas three.

The Bacharachs continued to devote a large part of their schedule to top-flight black teams, the ones that would join them in the future Negro Leagues. An early-season story in the *Chicago Defender* predicted that the Giants would "play an important part in this year's Colored championship."[36] The "Colored championship" was still whatever the best teams defined it as, but however defined it was improbable that the Bacharach Giants would be part of it. Of the recorded games, they won seven, lost 11 and tied 1, an improvement over 1917 in this level of play but a record showing the need for still more improvement.

Despite the proximity of the two clubs and the constant shift of players from one roster to the other, the Giants played Hilldale only three times among the recorded games. They opened the season with the Philadelphia team at Darby on May 18 and lost badly, 21–5. Both teams took the short railroad hop to Atlantic City the next day and Hilldale won again, by a respectable 3–1. Doc Sykes defeated Robinson on the mound, and all three Hilldale runs were driven in by players (Downs, Pettus and Reese) who had been with the Bacharachs, would be with them yet in 1918, or both. The same thing, only worse, happened on June 20. Hilldale, with Webster, Downs, Pettus, Lundy, Reese and Judy Johnson all in its lineup, collected 17 hits which, coupled with seven errors by a weakened Bacharachs squad, enabled a 19–3 win.

The Bacharachs played the most games with the Cuban Stars, but unlike 1917, when the Giants almost achieved a season series split, this time the Stars won five of seven. A three-game series June 3–5 resulted in one Bacharach win, 5–3, as Lundy's four hits set up Roberts to be the winning pitcher. The Stars, however, took the other two games, 9–3 and 7–3. Another three-game series at Atlantic City June 17–19 produced the same result—one win for the Bacharachs by 11–3 as Lundy again had four hits and Cummings three in support of a Howell seven-hitter, but then 4–2 and 4–3 losses. The first loss on June 18 was sealed when the Cubans scored four runs in the second inning and held on. In the second loss on the 19th the *Daily Press* alluded that it was "owing to some good reason" that Lundy, Downs and Reese were not in the lineup. The reason was good enough for the three players and undoubtedly involved some money. They were over in Hilldale Park that day, playing for Hilldale against the crack Parkesburg, Pennsylvania, Iron Works team.[37] The Cuban Stars won again on July 12 when they took a 6–3 lead into the bottom of the ninth and survived a two-run Bacharach rally.

There were four games against the Brooklyn Royal Giants, split evenly. The Bacharachs won the first, 4–2, on June 11. Cummings stole third and scored on the catcher's throwing error and Downs then drove in two more runs, all in the first inning. The next day saw a 7–4 victory when three runs in the sixth broke a 4–4 tie and made Roberts the winning pitcher. The Royals came back in mid–July, though, and won, 13–2, on the 15th and 8–4 the next day. In this final game the Bacharachs were at the mercy of John Donaldson, who not only got the pitching win but hit safely twice. Donaldson, a Midwesterner who rarely played in the East, had come to the Royal Giants for a single season in his itinerant career. The *Daily Press* called him "the highest salaried colored twirler in the universe," and he may have been since he approached baseball employment with the theory that a star pitcher was the most important element to a team's success, and could name his own price and move along to any team that would pay it.[38] This was the view of employment that later would keep the great Satchel Paige both continuously employed as the best-paid player in black ball, and often on the move.

Smokey Joe Williams and the Lincoln Giants came to the Shore on June 24–25 and split the series. Outfielder Blainey Hall ripped a bases-loaded triple in a five-run ninth inning that gave the Lincolns a 9–5 win in the first game. The next day's contest might have been the best played at Bacharach Park all season. Robinson beat the legendary Williams, 2–1, Cummings and Howell each driving in a run early and the Bacharachs holding off a ninth-inning Lincoln rally.

Rube Foster's Chicago American Giants came around again as part of the late-season Eastern tour for games on July 29–30 and August 2. Even though the Bacharach roster had begun its end-of-season shuffle, the results were good for the Atlantic City team. The first game ended in a 4–4 tie, called when Pettus of the Bacharachs became ill following the ninth inning. No particular reason was given why the absence of a single player should have stopped the game, but it leads to speculation that perhaps the Bacharachs could suit up only nine men that day, and had no substitute for Pettus.

The Bacharach Giants won, 5–4, on the 30th, Johnson coming back to defeat Chicago star Frank Wickware. In the final game on August 2, Roberts won, 3–1, and had a shutout until the ninth inning. The highlight of this game, from a historical point of view, was the appearance of Foster himself, at age 38 and pretty rotund for an active player, making one of his last pitching appearances in a major black game. His starter left in the second inning after the Bacharachs scored two runs, and Rube put himself in to pitch through the sixth. He held the Bacharachs scoreless, and the *Daily Press* noted that "it was not his lack of ability to pitch that caused his retirement, but his lack of wind after he drove a double."[39]

Just as the country's mobilization for the Great War increased gradually to full force, the Bacharach's contribution—playing teams of soldiers, soldiers, sailors and war workers—took awhile to reach its maximum. The first war opponent, on May 30, was a field artillery regiment from Camp Dix, the military training base 60 miles to the northwest. The Giants won, 6–5, in a game that featured ten errors, a couple of which let in the winning runs in the ninth inning.

Two games with the Philadelphia Navy Yard Armed Guards produced a split decision. The Guards, with former minor leaguer Ray Fagan pitching, took the first game on June 23, 2–1. Fagan gave up only four hits and Roy Roberts only five, but three off Roberts came in the first inning when the Guards scored both their runs. In the follow-up on

June 30, Fagan again pitched and much of the rest of the Guards lineup was the same, but the Bacharachs smashed them, 13–2, anyway. Roberts might have had a shutout, but the Navy Yard team scored twice in the third inning while an argument raged over whether the batter had been hit by a pitch. Apparently no one thought to call time-out.

The final two games against wartime teams brought to the Shore a representative of the defense industry. The war industries fielded teams so strong that their presence, loaded with professional players working rather than fighting, began to give the major leagues the jitters. The major defense construction industries committed themselves early on to employee sports associations, copying the trend that pre-war industry and retail commerce had begun to provide as a popular employee benefit. But, as was the case with civilian firms, the temptation to gild the lily with professional players was too much to ignore. With draft-eligible major and minor leaguers having the option of going into defense work rather than the military, it wasn't hard to find jobs for them that allowed them to play on a company's "A Team" that played for employees' entertainment and publicity for the firm.

Bethlehem Steel formed an entire league of six company teams representing East Coast plants and attracted the most attention from the sporting press and angry major league officials. The company's operations show how defense baseball worked: "The rosters were initially filled out by local workers but a few old-time pros and failed minor leaguers were mixed in.... By the following year [1918] local plant executives started bringing in ringers to stock their clubs against league rivals. They hired professional scouts and managers to recruit the finest talent available."[40]

Ignoring the probability that their players defecting to the industrial leagues probably would have been lost to the military draft anyway, big league moguls claimed they were being robbed. What bothered them, in addition to the immediate decline in their leagues' competitive levels (which was going to happen anyway) was that their players, bound to their teams by the reserve clause in the standard player contract, now had a sanctioned way to jump. Who knew in 1918 how long the war would go on? These guys, who represented expensive investments, might not come back for years. In the meantime they would be playing for teams that could take a bite, however small, out of major league attendance.

Ban Johnson, the often outspoken president of the American League, spoke out again: "Some of them [the players gone to industrial teams] are patriotic. But if there any of them who are Class 1A [prime draft-eligible men], I hope Provost General Crowder yanks them from the shipyards and steel works by the coat collar and places them in cantonment to prepare for future events on the western front." F. C. Lane, the well-known writer for *Baseball Magazine*, took up the owners 'cause, claiming that players going into the defense plant leagues represented a danger to organized baseball: "Disguised in the false colors of patriotic service, it seeks to undermine the financial structure of organized baseball, and at the same time grossly outrages the spirit of military service."

But Ed Reulbach, a former star pitcher now an executive of the Submarine Boat Corporation in Newark and head of a shipyard league, countered that industrial ball was no danger to the majors. In the long run, he argued, industrial play would hone future major leaguers while also training them in solid construction jobs that would support them in the off-season. This, he said, would give them the leverage he lacked in his old days with the Chicago Cubs when, if he didn't like his yearly contract offer, "I nevertheless accepted it because I had no immediate prospect of being employed elsewhere." Of course, what Reulbach, who seems not to have shaken his employee mentality despite having become an executive, thought was a dandy improvement was just what Ban Johnson and his colleagues hated. At any rate, the defense business quickly declined after the war ended in November 1919, and major leaguers had to return to the folds of the teams they had left behind.[41]

Shipyards were the major defense industry in the area in which the Bacharachs played. The industry's "major league" on the East Coast was the Delaware River Shipyard League, which in 1918 had teams from eight yards in the Philadelphia and Wilmington areas. One Philadelphia team was from the Hog Island yard operated by American International Shipbuilding, which built merchant and transport craft there from 1917 until 1921. Hog Island, southwest of the city, reportedly got its name from early residents' practice of letting their swine run free, using the river to fence them in. The area was linked to the Pennsylvania mainland in the period after the war and remains an important site in the area's transportation system as the site of the Philadelphia International Airport.

The Hog Island baseball team was managed by Charles Albert Bender, a recently retired star pitcher for the Philadelphia Athletics and an alumnus of the crack Delaware County League. Bender, since he was half-American Indian, received the baseball nickname regularly bestowed on members of his race in those days: "Chief." He had a number of fine players at his disposal when he made out the Hog Island lineup. There was Hans Lobert, just retired at 35 after a 14-year big league career, at third. Johnny Castle, owner of 12 minor league seasons that included a cup of coffee with the Phillies in 1910, was in center field. The catcher was Mike Loan, who had played for Villanova College in Philadelphia and had a one-game major league career with the Phillies at the end of 1912. "Doc" Carris, assistant coach of the University of Pennsylvania team and a former Delaware County League manager with Media, played second.

Hog Island took the first game with the Giants, 3–2, on July 14. The game was tied going into the top of the ninth and Robinson had been pitching well for the Giants when a walk and two bunt singles filled the bases, and perennial area semi-pro Eddie Lennox blooped a single to left.

The shipbuilders' team returned on July 28 without some of the first game starters, who were sorely missed. The visitors scored two runs in the top of the first inning, but the Bacharachs took over with three runs in the second and two each in the next three innings. The Giants had 16 hits and the Hog Islanders committed eight errors as Atlantic City won, 13–2. Robinson got what he deserved this time, a win for a good pitching performance.

The 1918 Bacharach season was a strange, war-addled one, with old rivals disappearing, new ones popping up overnight, a churning roster and white guys on a colored team. As baseball gave way to the football season, the Great War was still on, many of its major battles remaining unfought. On the home front at Bacharach Park, despite a winning record, the summer campaign went badly. The *Bridgeton Evening News*, which covered Southern New Jersey baseball closely, noted on August 30 that "the Bacharach Giants have had a hard time keeping their heads above the water this summer, according to reports. Financially, the club has lost a lot of money and it completely collapsed last Saturday."[42]

Chapter 3

Under New Management

1919

The state of professional baseball had improved considerably by the spring of 1919. While the majors again had a shortened season, teams still played 140 of the usual 154 games and only about a week was cut out from each of the beginning and end of the year. The number of minor leagues increased to 14, and 13 made it all the way to the end of the season.[1] The Bacharach Giants didn't kick off their home season until Memorial Day, later than in their three previous years, but everything was looking up for them.

The failing franchise that had barely limped home the previous August had been revived by two treatments that rarely fail—money and connections. Two African Americans from New York City, both in the restaurant and entertainment business, had become the major investors in the team. One, John W. Connor, seemed to know just about everyone connected with black baseball on the East Coast due to his previous ownership of a New York team. Famous for constantly smoking big cigars and nicknamed "Uncle Jawn" by the other baseball men for his hearty mien, he was liked and trusted. The other new owner, Barron D. Wilkins, was an avid follower of sports, although he doesn't seem to have had much, if any, actual baseball experience. Still, he had a lot of money, and he seemed to know not just everyone in black baseball, but everyone else in New York's black community. It's not known who first sought out whom to bring the Atlantic City and New York men together, but it's abundantly clear that Connor and Wilkins didn't need to be dragged into the deal. They were highly enthusiastic, particularly Connor, who had something to prove.

He had been one of the earliest black baseball executives, founder of the Brooklyn Royal Giants in 1904. He used the club to some extent to publicize his Brooklyn restaurant, the Royal Café and Palm Garden, but he was serious about the sport. Sol White, the nineteenth-century player who became black baseball's first historian, named Connor one of the 12 greatest management figures in Negro baseball in 1927. In his 1907 history of blackball's accomplishments to date, White described Connor as playing "a noble part in keeping the game before the public. Like all true baseball men, he loved the game and went the limit for the 'grand old sport.'"[2]

Connor was a representative of what modern-day black baseball historian Michael Lomax describes as "a petit bourgeois of professionals and businessmen relying primarily for their livelihood on the black masses. They were primarily self-made men, of humble origins." The new black elite formed an ambitious middle class, and the more successful of them achieved upper-class status before World War I. Connor was born in Portsmouth, Virginia, the day after Christmas in 1875. The Portsmouth area on the Chesapeake Bay has several naval installations, so it was understandable that Connor joined the Navy during the Spanish-American War. There he became a ward-room steward on fighting ships, since the Navy, even as late as World War II, restricted its black seamen to non-combatant duties.[3]

After the war Connor took off for New York to seek his fortune, which he found. By 1900 he was living in Brooklyn at 176 Myrtle Street, the location of his Royal Café. Connor got in a little legal scrape in 1906 that landed him in the Brooklyn Magistrate's Court, where the reporter for the *Brooklyn Daily Eagle* wrote up his case in a tone that had all the condescending nature of a white writing about a Negro in those times. But it was probably a factual portrayal: "Connor is a bachelor negro, who wears the finest and the latest of clothing ... who caters to no one but the swellest of swell persons of his race, Pullman car conductors and head waiters."[4]

Harlem in Northern Manhattan was becoming predominantly black by the second decade of the twentieth century. Connor, like the good businessman he was, followed the trend. By 1908 he had moved the Royal Café to 71 West 135th Street, where it prospered. Connor offered music and dancing to differentiate his place from the run-of-the-mill saloons that were overrunning Harlem. He initiated teas from 2 p.m. into the evening where the advertised non-alcoholic refreshment could undoubtedly be supplemented with booze elsewhere on the premises, and where musicians and singers entertained. The cabaret, with John Connor's help, was being popularized in Harlem.[5]

Connor had been in court, by the way, for assaulting a police officer. Witnesses testified on his behalf that the officer had started it by knocking Connor on the head with his billy club. It appears that Connor was in no mood to put up with this treatment from a white man abusing his authority, and retaliated. This is how he reacted in his baseball career, too, and his attitude was crucial to his becoming an owner of the Bacharachs.

Barron D. Wilkins had interests that far exceeded the mere serving of meals and drinks, or the single sport of baseball, for that matter. He was a financial supporter and friend of the African American heavyweight boxing champion, Jack Johnson. He had put a $20,000 betting pool together for Johnson's July 4, 1910, fight in Reno against the white Jim Jeffries, which made Wilkins and his friends a lot of money when Johnson scored a technical knockout in the 15th round. At the time he bought into the Bacharach Giants, Wilkins ran the Exclusive Club in Harlem, which was just that—you had to be a member to get in.[6]

Wilkins also hailed from Portsmouth, born there in 1866. He lived with his family in Washington, D.C., for several years while young. But along with his brother Leroy, also well known in the Harlem nightclub business, he eventually made his way to the mecca of New York. Barron's first club was the Little Savoy on West 35th Street in Manhattan, a good spot for a black club before African Americans began to flood into Harlem. The Little Savoy was home to Jack Johnson when he was in town, and it attracted merrymakers, but also police attention. There was, for example, the problem of the 28-year-old white woman from New Jersey who was brought by horse-drawn cab to Roosevelt

Hospital in April 1904, in the last stages of a drug overdose, by two men who vanished after delivering her to the emergency room. It turned out she had been holed up at the Little Savoy, apparently selling her jewelry piece by piece to pay for the drugs that killed her.[7]

Wilkins escaped official action that time, but the Little Savoy was said to have "annoyed the police so much that it was raided scores of times." The authorities seemed to have succeeded in having Wilkins' liquor license revoked in 1910, but the judge hearing the case stayed the order after officials from legitimate black lodges and business associations went to bat for him, "all of them stating that Wilkins's was practically the only place in the city where colored people desirous of meeting and banqueting can be accommodated."[8]

When Wilkins, like Connor and so many other African American clubmen, pulled up stakes and went north to Harlem, he first relocated to 137th Street and Lenox Avenue. The police followed. Mary Sullivan, who eventually became a deputy police commissioner, first served as a groundbreaking woman New York police detective. In 1913 she was sent in Harlem to infiltrate an entertainment district that "teemed with clip joints, torrid dance halls, voodoo doctors, and cafes that were really recruiting grounds for disorderly houses." At Wilkins' place Detective Sullivan observed a floor show full of "grimy songs and fervid dancing," after which the attractive "high yellow" women performers fanned out through the audience to fleece drunken white middle-aged men of their money, while "brooding over the scene was the proprietor, Baron [sic] Wilkins, a gray-haired, benevolent-looking man who had the air of a kindly pastor taking a little tour through the Sunday-school room." Based on her observations, Wilkins' place was raided and he was charged and convicted, although the law never slowed him down for long.[9]

Wilkins had a lot of friends in high places and was politically important in Harlem, "swinging between the Democratic and Republican parties as the mood suited or as his private interests dictated." Perhaps the richest man in Harlem, he was well known for sharing his wealth: "his influence was built largely on his practice of extending a helping hand to those who required emergency financing." The African American filmmaker William Foster, who wrote for the black newspapers under the pseudonym "Juli Jones Jr.," said "the Barron lost over $150,000 in outside business," including backing the black song-and-dance team of Bert Williams and George Walker and financing a black music publication house. He probably also took a financial bath on the Bacharachs to some extent, but as Jones wrote, "he lost with a smile." He was also a soft touch for the Harlem lower class' individual hard-luck stories—that benevolent look on his face apparently was for real.[10]

The last and finest of Wilkins' establishments, the Exclusive Club, was located at 134th Street and Seventh Avenue. His entertainers and other employees were almost entirely black, but his high-rolling customers were largely white. He hired almost every important black pianist in the city at one time or another, including Duke Ellington, who played there with his Washingtonians in 1923. Konrad Bercovici, a European journalist, visited New York in the early 1920s and devoted a book to the city's various ethnic groups. To help illustrate Harlem, he visited the Exclusive Club: "It opens on week-days at about eleven o'clock P.M., officially, but the place really never gets started before one o'clock at night.... One must have his purse well garnished when visiting the place. A hundred-dollar-bill will not go very far and is not intended to do much service in this luxuriously fitted-out cabaret."[11]

Sol White said that Connor and Wilkins each invested $10,000 in the Bacharachs, the total being equal to about $260,000 today. White's numbers were probably reasonably accurate, since a reported $10,000 was spent improving Inlet Park to replace Bacharach Park as the Giants' home field, increasing its capacity to 3,500. The new investors incorporated the team, Wilkins as president and Connor as secretary-treasurer. Henry Tucker joined them as field manager and booking agent.[12] Tom Jackson was the odd man out and seemed none too happy about it. He registered the name "Bacharach Giants Athletic Club" with the state as a not-for-profit corporation with him as one of three trustees and its headquarters at his residence at 118 North New Jersey Avenue. Jackson's move for a time threatened to bar the new owners from using the team's name—they reportedly were considering a change to the "Colored Americans." But matters appear to have been worked out. The Connor-Wilkins outfit continued to play as the Bacharachs, and by June Jackson was back with the team when Tucker stepped down due to other business considerations. He was opening a hotel in Atlantic City, an effort that didn't appear to prosper since he was back with the team the following year.[13]

The *New York Age* speculated that Wilkins and Connor bought the team as a hedge against likely business losses that would be brought about by the advent of Prohibition, although it's clear it probably never occurred to them to cease to serve liquor at their establishments. The ongoing high-class party at the Exclusive Club is well documented, and the Royal Café was shut down for six months in late 1925 in the midst of an anti-booze campaign by Emory Buckner, the United States Attorney for Manhattan. For both men, buying into the Bacharachs had more to do with a deep sense of racial pride.[14]

This was particularly true for Connor, who had been pushed out of baseball in 1913 for challenging the white man who held an iron grip on New York semi-pro ball through its real estate. There were many good ball fields in and around the city, of course, but most were controlled by the Inter-City Baseball Association and Nathaniel C. "Nat" Strong, its president. Strong, a former sporting goods dealer, had become the semi-pro baseball king of New York. He seldom owned teams outright, but had dozens under his thumb as the result of his nearly indispensable booking service. If you did business with Strong, he would find you opponents for your lucrative weekend games and see to it that they were well advertised, for a ten percent share of the gate. The Inter-City Association eventually locked up prime playing sites throughout the area. A 1914 newspaper piece on Strong labeled him "King of the Bush Leaguers" and claimed he "directed" 5,000 semi-pro players in this way.[15]

Occasionally, a team owner would refuse to be "directed" by Strong, usually to the owner's eventual detriment. That's how Connor lost his Brooklyn Royal Giants in 1913. Connor didn't want to go to Strong for bookings, reasoning that there wasn't anything Strong could do for him that he couldn't do for himself, and besides, why give that ten percent to a white man when race men were providing the value? Strong retaliated by freezing the Royal Giants out of prime playing dates and forcing Connor to accept a fixed dollar guarantee, rather than a percentage of the gate, which could often be counted on to be higher than the guarantee. When the team failed financially, Strong bought it from Connor, probably at a bargain price.[16]

Getting back into baseball via Atlantic City was a perfect solution to Strong's barricade of New York, since Strong had no influence in South Jersey. Additionally the Bacharachs began to play games in New York at one of the few good locations not under Strong's control, the Dyckman Oval in Harlem. Having established themselves outside Strong's reach, Connor and Wilkins used their safe haven to execute a successful raid on the Royal Giants' roster. This venture probably gave Connor personal satisfaction, but more importantly it was the centerpiece of a total rebuilding of the tattered remnants of the squad from 1918. The Giants' brain trust replaced six of the eight regular position players—only Bill Handy at second and "Country Brown" Bryant in the outfield remained. They also turned over the entire pitching staff with the exception of stalwart Roy Roberts, although one of the "new" pitchers was very familiar—Shang Johnson had returned to the Bacharach fold.

The run on the Royal Giants supplied five key players, including two of the best ever to play with the Bacharachs. The signing of John Henry Lloyd in June made headlines. Lloyd had been renowned for years as the best shortstop in black baseball and even now, at age 35, he had no peer. Born in Palatka, Florida, in 1886, Lloyd soon was living with an aunt in Jacksonville, where he began playing baseball as a teenager, launching a long career that would see him on several Negro League teams, and eventually a member of the Baseball Hall of Fame.

Lloyd met with Wilkins and Connor and a roomful of others at a law office in Harlem on June 3 to enlist with the Bacharachs. William White, the *Chicago Defender*'s East Coast sports correspondent, was proud to point out that Lloyd had borrowed his pen to sign the contract. The news that the Bacharachs had gotten Lloyd not only excited the black sports world, it thrilled the fans down in Atlantic City. The day of the signing White "was talking over the phone with the bunch at Atlantic City. When they heard the news they jumped for joy and started singing 'Dear Old Pal of Mine.'"[17]

Lloyd was joined by the second-best pitcher on the Brooklyn squad, Dick Redding, who had spent most of the 1918 season with Brooklyn and, like Lloyd, had started 1919 there. Out of Georgia, Redding stood six feet, four inches tall and weighed more than 200 pounds. After a brief period with the Philadelphia Giants in 1911, when he was 21, he migrated to New York, where he and the fastball that got him nicknamed "Cannonball" thrived on the best blackball teams. Redding was a real workhorse, able to pitch both ends of a doubleheader and appear in relief of other pitchers between his own starts. By the end of the second decade of the 1900s, Redding and Joe Williams were considered the best two black pitchers in New York.

Two other immediate pickups from the Royals were Ernest Gatewood and Johnny Pugh. Gatewood, a decent hitter for a catcher although a slow runner like many at that position, was 28 and played in the New York and Philadelphia area for the better teams. Gatewood was the Bacharachs' primary catcher this season, and while he was not always in an Atlantic City uniform, he spent many seasons past 1919 with the team. Pugh had all the speed that Gatewood did not, but wasn't a strong hitter. However, his fielding ability at all three outfield positions made him a valuable starter or reserve, beginning in 1913 in East Coast ball. Pitcher Jesse Hubbard left Brooklyn in July to start regularly for Atlantic City, but was back with the Royal Giants by August.

The *Defender* saw the new Bacharach owners as striking a blow for race freedom, the force of the blow measured by how much it made Nat Strong squirm. Connor was quoted, and Wilkins confirmed, that when they met with Strong about the approaching season, the white promoter had told them "they were making things bad by offering these 'coons' more money." Strong was also reported to have used strong-arm methods to dissuade his players from jumping, although he obviously wasn't very successful. Strong also spread the word that Wilkins had welched on a debt owed to him, an assertion that Wilkins denied to the point of threatening to sue Strong for defamation of character.[18]

With Lloyd at short and the reliable Handy at second every day, replacing Lundy and Downs, who spent the year with Hilldale, the revolving door situation at third base was fixed with the signing of Fred Hutchinson. A 33-year-old veteran of Midwestern black baseball, Hutchinson, at 5 feet, 9 inches tall and weighing 175 pounds, had acquired the nickname "Pudge." He had a reputation as a good fielder with a strong arm and at one time or another played regularly at all the infield positions except first base. He had started the season with Jewell's ABCs in Indianapolis, but black baseball in that city was in a state of flux. The major team, Charles Isham ("C. I.") Taylor's ABCs, were dormant in 1919 after major player losses to the military the year before. Warner Jewell, an African American billiard hall proprietor, took over the team name and put together a squad. The dominance of well-moneyed black teams in this era of easy player movement was not just a regional phenomenon, however, and the Bacharachs succeeded in luring not only Hutchinson but three others away from Jewell.

The prize acquisition from Indianapolis was Ben Taylor. Like Lloyd an eventual member of the Hall of Fame, Taylor was the premier black first baseman of the era, "always a heads-up player" who was "an ideal man to have on a ballclub."[19] In addition to playing all year at first, this was the first of Taylor's several stints as a field manager. Taylor was the third of four baseball brothers from Anderson, South Carolina, who both played and managed at the top level of black baseball. All three younger brothers, Ben, Jim and Johnny, spent time on eldest C. I.'s Indianapolis team during their careers. As smart, slick and popular as Chance Cummings was, he was no match for Taylor. For the time being his services were not required by the new Bacharach management, and he signed with Hilldale.

The haul from Indianapolis also included the Giants' season-long center fielder, George Shively. A 26-year-old Kentucky native, Shively had been a C. I. Taylor man since 1911 and was the ABCs' regular left fielder. In addition to wide range in the outfield, he was a good contact hitter and bunter regarded as "one of the fastest men in baseball ... a 'desperate' base runner who commanded everyone's respect." A left-handed hitter, Shively was reputed to be very superstitious about his bats, and wouldn't let a right-handed hitter borrow one.[20]

It took awhile to settle on the left fielder. Tucker went through two men, J. W. "Gunboat" Thompson until mid–June and then Cecil "Sess" Johnson until mid–July, but neither hit well and both left the team. There was less player movement between the Bacharachs and Hilldale that season, but the one man who came the Giants' way was critical to their success. Spotswood Poles had been playing since 1909 in New York and Philadelphia. He had missed the entire 1918 season in the Army and had returned to Hilldale, his 1917 team, for the beginning of 1919. But in mid-July he appeared in a Giants uniform as Johnson's replacement. He was as fast as, or faster than, Shively and a dependable .300 hitter. He took over the leadoff spot in the batting order, dropping Shively to second. Johnny Pugh from the Royal Giants played right field on a regular basis until Bryant returned to the team from the Lincoln Giants in August, when Pugh was relegated to fourth outfielder status.

Gatewood did the bulk of the catching, replacing both Yank Deas and Burlin White, who had moved to Hilldale along with Lundy and Downs. In mid-season Gatewood got some relief as the Bacharachs signed one of the legendary figures in early twentieth century ball. George "Chappie" Johnson had been playing since 1896 and had acquired a reputation as a good teacher of younger players that occasionally got him work on the white side of professional baseball. At age 43 he was about finished as a player, but he caught in 28 games to give Gatewood relief behind the plate.

The top of the lineup was built to score runs. Poles hit .282 and scored 43 runs in 56 games. Shively hit .293 against all competition and scored 77 runs (with 26 stolen bases) in 78 games. Poles and Shively were often perched on the bases when Lloyd and Taylor came up, and they often scored. Lloyd drove in 72 runs and hit .312, but Taylor topped him with a .317 average and 79 RBI. After them, the output dropped off. The other two infielders, Handy at second and Hutchinson at third, hit .247 and .224, respectively. Of the other outfielders, Bryant hit .258 after joining the Bacharachs, by far the best of a light-hitting group (Pugh, the only other outfielder to see significant action for the Giants, hit only .206).

Gatewood started out well but, catching nearly every day until July, tailed off and finished at .189. Chappie Johnson, his main sub, hit .105. Some of the pitchers were better hitters than some of the position players. Shang Johnson hit .203 and Redding .217 over the full season, while Jesse Hubbard, who during his career also played a lot of outfield, batted .280.

The offensive production of five runs per game was good, but far from outstanding. However, the Bacharachs usually didn't need a lot of runs to win. The pitching staff was of the highest quality and gave up only an average of 2.7 runs per game with a team earned run average of 2.04. The staff threw 20 shutouts in 100 recorded starts in which pitching statistics are available.

Redding was the workhorse, starting 28 times and relieving 14 more. He won 22 games and lost ten. He had a minuscule ERA of 1.37 and struck out 209 batters in 275 innings. Roberts was the second-busiest pitcher, making 19 starts and seven relief appearances to go 13–4 with a 2.31 ERA. Dan Johnson was right behind him with 14 starts and seven relief jobs, in which he compiled a 10–3 record. Frank Wickware, a 31-year-old Kansan who had begun pitching in the Midwest in 1910, joined the team at the very end of July when Hubbard went back to the Royal Giants. Together they made 22 starts, 14 for Wickware and eight for Hubbard. Wickware went 9–6 and Hubbard 6–1 to complement the regular starters very nicely. Jim Jeffries, a left-hander in his seventh season at the top level, was the third player to come from Jewell's ABCs in Indianapolis and made seven starts, winning six and losing one, before heading back to Indianapolis. Arthur Dilworth made four starts early in the season and went 3–1.

The 20 shutouts were not always against lesser opponents—the Giants blanked Hilldale and the Detroit Stars from high-level black competition, as well as some good white all-star teams. In one eight-game stretch from July 5–14 the staff tossed eight straight shutouts against Pennsylvania and New Jersey semi-pro competition. Johnson threw three of them, including two- and three-hitters, and Redding threw a two-hitter. Roberts tossed a complete game three-hitter and got the win in a shared performance with Hubbard, who by himself threw two whitewashes, one a 16-strikeout no-hitter.

In 103 discovered games the Bacharachs won 73, lost 29 and tied one, an enviable winning percentage of .716. The look of the schedule under the new owners was different and more challenging, making the exemplary won-lost record look even better. Local games with Atlantic City area competition were mostly a thing of the past, replaced with better white teams made up of one-time major and minor leaguers and top semi-pros, pulled together by professional promoters and almost invariably labeled "all stars." The Bacharachs played five of these outfits (two of which had the same name) in 1919, winning 11 games and losing six.

The Giants opened their season with the first of these teams, the All-Nationals. The team name may have been borrowed from a post-season barnstorming squad of a few years earlier that consisted of actual major leaguers supplementing their incomes. The 1919 team, which hailed from New York City, was advertised as "reserve players of several of the big leagues," although a search of Baseball-Reference.com, a comprehensive professional baseball database, doesn't show any of the players who competed against the Giants as having played either major or minor league ball that year. The game dates of May 30–31 were well after the start of the professional season anyway, which in itself ought to mean the All-Nationals were not hot prospects.

Moreover, the team was billed as "Hal Chase's All-Nationals," which, if it didn't make people leery of the squad then, might well have a year later.[21] Chase, about to start his last year in the major leagues, was hailed at the time as the best-fielding first baseman in the majors, and could hit well, too. He also had another reputation that naggingly followed him around during his 15 years in the big leagues, that of someone happy to consort with gamblers to fix the outcome of games and "lie down" himself by withholding his best efforts. Although at age 36 Chase still was capable of playing well, he was at the end of his major league career. The rumors had caught up with him, and he was subsequently implicated in the complex plot to throw the 1919 World Series.

The baggage that came with the gregarious and well-connected Chase seems to have been delivered to the Bacharachs' door by Wilkins and Connor themselves. They were reportedly his personal friends (and of course, they were no strangers to gamblers and high rollers). Chase was present in the room the day Lloyd signed with the Giants, and shortly afterwards William White of the *Defender*, in praising Tucker's achievements as the booking agent for the team, noted that while Tucker and Chase had never met, "he [Chase] has been the boy behind the cause and has helped Tucker to succeed."[22]

Despite the shadow of Chase, from the perspective of history the two games with the Bacharachs look pretty ordinary. The Giants won the first, 7–0, Dick Redding throwing a four-hitter and striking out ten, the sort of performance he was capable of against anyone the Bacharachs played. The All-Nationals won the next day, 3–2, when Jack Warhop, who had won 69 games in an eight-year major league career that ended in 1915, and the only All-National that the average fan might have heard of, outpitched Roy Roberts, who lost a shutout in the ninth inning.

As soon as the All-Nationals left town, they were replaced at Inlet Park by the All-Americans. This was a Philadelphia-based team of some of the best semi-pros in the area pulled together by Art Summers, a long-time local baseball manager and all-around sports promoter in the city. Summers' team came to the Shore for two series in June and lost four of the five games to the Bacharachs. On June 1 Redding again threw a four-hitter, striking out eight this time. The All-Americans earned their sole victory the next day when Sam Lennox, from a Camden family that provided several semi-pro stars, drove in two runs in the top of the tenth inning off Johnson in relief for a 5–3 win. The June 3 game was tied 1–1 when Dilworth, who had yielded only four hits through eight innings, gave up a double to the leadoff batter in the ninth. Redding came on and retired the side on seven pitches, a groundout, a strikeout and a foul to the catcher, to earn a win when the Giants scored in the bottom of the ninth.

The Giants won both games easily when the All-Americans next came to Atlantic City on June 22–23. They knocked out 13 hits, three by Pugh, to support Roberts' six-hitter in a 9–2 win on the first day, and Johnson struck out eight and gave up seven hits for a 6–1 win on the second. On June 15 the Bacharachs defeated the Harry Davis All-Stars, a Philadelphia team named after, although probably not run by, a player-coach for Connie Mack's Athletics.

September brought the International League All-Stars, who were exactly what their name implied. Charley "Red" Dooin, a 15-year major league catcher who had managed the Phillies and who played semi-pro ball in Philadelphia and Atlantic City for years after the end of his pro career, had managed and played for the Reading Coal Barons in the International League in 1919. He put together a squad from his club and Newark and took them barnstorming after the minor league season ended. Nine of the 11 players who came to Atlantic City had been regulars during the season and another was a good-hitting reserve. Of the eight position players, four had hit over .300 at the minors' top rung and none, except for Dooin, had an average below .269. The three pitchers had been regular winners. One, Eddie Rommel of Newark, had gone 22–15 and was about to start a 13-year, 171-win career with the Athletics. Dooin and second baseman "Silent John" Hummel had already completed lengthy major league careers, and Rommel and seven others would reach the majors for at least a single season.

The All-Stars played four games on consecutive days beginning September 15, splitting the series with the Bacharachs. The visitors were so popular that the original three-game series was expanded to four.[23] The Stars won the opener, 3–2, in 10 innings. Rommel outpitched Wickware in what must have been a great game to watch. There were only 12 hits and 17 base runners in the entire contest, and no one committed an error. Rommel, a decent hitter for a pitcher who often played the field in exhibition games, knocked in the winning run in the top of the tenth.

The Giants won the next day, 2–0, thanks to their foresight in importing Cyclone

Joe Williams from the Lincoln Giants. Williams carried a no-hitter into the seventh inning and struck out nine. Dooin, known for being scrappy, "showed that old spark was still there. He had an altercation with the ump yesterday. Dooin also invited the austere gentleman 'outside.'"[24] It might have benefited Dooin to know that the umpire, Cesar Jamison, was the arbiter who had gone toe-to-toe with a complaining player in 1918 and hadn't hesitated to throw a retaliatory punch. Redding didn't have it in the third game and Roberts, in relief, had even less, while the Bacharachs made six errors and the All-Stars won, 14–1. The added fourth game belonged to the Giants, however, who won 7–3 and collected a cash bonus for winning the series.

The Bacharachs ended the season with five games against another International League team, the Stars (as opposed to the All-Stars), who were not as pure in their pedigree but still played good ball. The Giants won three of the five games, but the most important thing about this series was where it was played. For this series, Connor rented Ebbets Field from the Brooklyn National League club, whose season was over. The Bacharachs had played in a major league park before, Shibe Park in Philadelphia, but this was the first time a black team had taken the field at seven-year-old Ebbets, which was to be the Giants' part-time home for the next two years.

These Stars were salted heavily with top-level minor leaguers, several of whom had been in, or were going to, the majors. A major difference with this team, though, was the presence of current major leaguers worked into the lineup. The pitchers for the opening doubleheader on Sunday, October 19, were Dick Rudolph, a right-hander who had won 13 games with just a 2.17 ERA for the Boston Braves that year, and Johnny Enzman, 3–2 with a 2.28 ERA in 14 games for the Cleveland Indians.

The Bacharachs lost both of those games, the opener 7–4 to Rudolph when Redding got knocked out after just two innings. Comparisons between blackball stars and white major leaguers weren't common at this point in sports journalism, but John Henry Lloyd received a glowing one. The *Brooklyn Daily Eagle* reporter, after complimenting Stars shortstop Frank O'Rourke for his flashy fielding, added that "he had nothing on 'Old Man' Lloyd, however, that ancient performer uncovering some plays around short that would have caused 'Rabbit' Maranville, Dave Bancroft, et al, to kowtow some."[25] The Internationals took a seven-inning second game, 6–1. Enzman surprisingly won over Joe Williams, who gave up only five hits, one fewer than Enzman, but watched the Giants leave ten men on base.

The two teams were back again the following Sunday when Wickware threw a four-hit shutout for a 2–0 win. The second game of that day's doubleheader was called off in the third due to darkness with the Stars ahead, 2–0. The series picked up again on Sunday, November 2. This was pretty late in the year for baseball, and the International Stars had suffered some lineup turnover. Some of the earlier starters, including Rudolph and Enzman, were no longer available. This was helpful for Williams, who gave up seven runs on eight hits and a pair of walks, but got a 13–7 win. Redding recovered well from his earlier setback and pitched a three-hit shutout in the nightcap, which was called after five innings due to darkness.

The results of the two series against International League players, with some major leaguers thrown in, told a lot about how the Bacharachs had progressed. Their record against the teams of the future Negro Leagues, the launching of the first only a season away, confirmed this as the Giants had their first winning season against this tough group.

The Bacharach Giants' competition with their future Negro League rivals was also notable for who they played—or did not play, to be more precise. The Brooklyn Royal Giants and the Lincoln Giants from New York vanished from the schedule, reportedly at Strong's orders.[26] The Royal Giants' reluctance was understandable, given the player raids by Connor and Wilkins and Strong's determined retaliation attempts. But while Jim Keenan and Strong often had their differences, they had enough of a working relationship for the Lincolns to have participated in the "freeze out" of the Bacharachs after Connor and Wilkins bought them. This probably did not overly concern the Bacharach management. So far as Connor and Wilkins were concerned, Keenan and the Lincolns would have been just another piece of the white monopoly over New York black baseball.

The Bacharachs played most of their Negro League–level games against Hilldale and the Cuban Stars, and hosted the Detroit Stars for a two-game set in July. Ed Bolden's long history in black baseball included many instances when he cooperated with white promoters, and he was partners with one later in his career. But he had a public set-to with Strong in 1918 when the New Yorker tried to install a competitor to Hilldale near Hilldale Park, and couldn't be considered a pal of Strong's. The Giants and Hilldale played 12 single-game dates against each other during a nearly four-month period from the first week in June to the end of September. All the games were in the Philadelphia area or Atlantic City. It was like a subway series, with the railroad to the Jersey Shore standing in for the underground. The rail lines connected everything about the teams and their fans. Toward the end of the series, the *Philadelphia Inquirer* nailed down the relationship—the two teams were each other's "real rivals."[27]

The first Bacharach and Hilldale encounters were five games in back-to-back, home-and-home series from June 5–10. The Bacharachs took the first two games, on June 5 and 7, played at Hilldale Park. The Giants won the first, 9–2, with Redding throwing a five-hitter. In the second game the Giants won, 5–3, in 11 innings. Redding came back in relief of Roberts in the eighth and added three scoreless innings to his Hilldale-killing record. Overall, the hometown *Philadelphia Tribune* stated, Hilldale had "foozled away enough chances to win the game handily."[28]

Since the next game was on a Sunday, June 8, the show moved to the Shore for that contest and the following two. On Sunday Tom Williams, an original Bacharach Giant in 1916 who had been with Hilldale since 1918 and had been knocked out early in Hilldale's first-game loss, dominated his old team. Hilldale coasted to an 8–3 win. Arthur Dilworth hung in as the Bacharach starter until the seventh inning, when under the Hilldale onslaught he "sought a more secluded spot."[29] Hilldale was still rolling the next day, winning 5–2. Phil Cockrell tossed a complete game six-hitter, beating Redding. The rubber game the next day also went to Hilldale, 5–3, in 11 innings.

The teams got together again in late August back in Atlantic City. The first game on the 24th was great, Hilldale getting the only run in the top of the tenth to break up a double shutout. But before much of the game could be played, there was a fight. Spotswood Poles, who had left Hilldale for the Bacharachs in July, led off the bottom of the first. Before anything more of a baseball nature could happen, he dropped his bat and got into it with Deas, the Bacharach who had gone to Hilldale before the start of the season. The *Chicago Defender*, which referred to the contretemps as the "Poles-Yank Affair," passed on the intelligence that Deas "said something to Poles in whispered tones: then the battle began." The disagreement reportedly went back to when they were both with Hilldale, and it didn't help that they were "both very quick tempered." When they got into it at home plate the benches cleared and "after a football match between the two nines the two [Poles and Deas] were separated." But, "after a minute's rest they came together again." This time it took two city police detectives, aided by Atty. Isaac H. Nutter, a leader in the Atlantic City black community, to restore order. At this point each team had won four games, with four to go.[30]

Competition resumed with a three-game set on September 8, 11 and 13. The big crowds that had poured into the previous games had been noticed, and for the first game Bolden rented the Philadelphia Athletics' Shibe Park. The Hilldale-Bacharachs game was said to be the first time two black teams had met at Shibe, which had been open for ten years. Attendance was 5,000, with a large contingent of Atlantic City fans in attendance. Interestingly, the September 8 game was ballyhooed as the final one between the teams in 1919, the deciding game for the "colored championship" of the East, or of America, depending upon which newspaper account one read.[31] It may have been meant to be the decider in this made-up championship series, but given chances for more profitable gates, the teams kept playing. If it had been the deciding game, the Bacharach Giants would have put away the championship. They creamed Hilldale, 10–0, as the ever-available Redding pitched a three-hitter, allowing only seven base runners in all. Redding also got three hits, including a pair of triples, and scored three runs.

Then it was back out to the Shore, where the Bacharachs continued their success with a 4–3 win at Inlet Park on the 11th. The seemingly indefatigable Redding started and won for the Giants. Two days later the teams were in Darby at Hilldale Park, where the Giants' win streak continued, 5–2. Hilldale actually had a 2–1 lead going into the seventh inning, but Willis Flournoy fell apart in both pitching and on-the-field thinking. Dick Whitworth, who had relieved Bacharach starter Roy Roberts by the sixth, doubled. When Poles tried to bunt him to third, Flournoy made the disastrous decision to go for Whitworth instead of taking the easy out at first. Poles, who could fly on the bases, stole second and George Shively drove them both in. If there had been such a statistic as the save in blackball in 1919, that day it would have gone to an unusual candidate. Taylor, who seldom pitched in fast competition at that point in his career, put himself on the mound in the seventh inning and shut down Hilldale the rest of the way. Dick Lundy of Hilldale was the best overall performer of the day—he got four hits and reportedly starred at shortstop. Even though the so-called "championship" game of September 8 led to two more games and despite the Bacharachs being up 7–4 in the series, this was a profitable rivalry, and the teams played once more, in Darby on September 27, when Hilldale won, 7–2.

There had been talk at the beginning the season that Strong would see that the Cuban Stars also dropped the Bacharachs, since Stars owner Alex Pompez maintained a working relationship with Strong.[32] But the Stars played seven games against the Giants, the Bacharachs winning five. The first three were in a series at Inlet Park on June 24–26 that produced some good baseball and one strange ending.

The Giants were in control on the 24th, winning 10–2. They backed Redding with 11 hits, three by Taylor, off the Stars' Evelio Calderin. The Cubans won the second game of the series, 4–3, breaking a 1–1 tie when their pitcher Jose Suarez, a strong hitter, popped a three-run homer off of Roberts in the sixth inning. The third game was a spectacular pitchers' duel. Both Tom Williams, on loan from Hilldale, and Lucas Boada pitched in rainy weather and gave up only one hit apiece, and both teams were playing errorless ball behind them. Neither Williams nor Boada deserved to lose and, as it turned out, neither did on his own merits. With no score in the bottom of the seventh inning, Lloyd doubled and the rain increased, causing the umpire to halt the game. When the precipitation eased up, the ump restarted the game but the Cuban Stars refused to come back out and play, possibly because they thought the field was still too wet, or maybe because their business manager had already received their share of the gate receipts. The result was a forfeit to the Bacharachs.[33]

The Giants swept the next three-game series with the Stars, played at Atlantic City on July 22–24. In the opener Redding again defeated Calderin, 2–1, in 12 innings. Redding gave up only five hits, and scored both Bacharach runs after singling. The Giants won on the 23rd, 5–2, with Lloyd clearing the bases with a double. Hubbard threw a four-hitter. The next day the Bacharachs won, 7–4, Johnson getting the win. The team was behind, 5–2, until the bottom of the eighth inning, when it scored five times. The heart of the rally was a three-run wild pitch. With the bases loaded Juan Padron uncorked a wild one. As the *Daily Press*'s eyewitness recorded it, "[Firstbaseman Julio] Rojo got the ball and hurled it wild and the sphere was generally booted, and when the smoke cleared the trio of tallies were over."[34] The Stars made a single-game appearance in Atlantic City on August 4 and won this one, 9–3.

A Midwestern black club also visited again, not Rube Foster's American Giants this time, but the Detroit Stars. Despite being a new team, the Stars had beaten the American Giants head-to-head and "were in all probability the best team in the West that season."[35] Detroit visited Atlantic City for games on July 16 and 18, and split with the Bacharachs. The Stars won the opener, 6–3, scoring three runs in the top of the tenth, although the game ended with the tying run at bat for home team. Two days later Roberts tossed a three-hit shutout (although he gave up a whopping ten walks), barely besting John Donaldson, who gave up a run on four hits. The only run of the game was scored in the seventh—Pugh was safe at home on a play when top defensive catcher Bruce Petway dropped the throw that would have nailed the runner.

The involvement of New Yorkers Connor and Wilkins opened an important door to the Bacharachs. In 1919 Atlantic City was a good baseball town and Philadelphia was better, but if you could play in New York, the biggest, most famous city in the country that had a big neighborhood filling up with black folks, you could do really well. The Bacharach owners found such an opportunity in 1919 and linked up for ten games with a team owned by a man whose involvement with professional baseball was at least as unlikely as Harry Bacharach's.

Arthur Guy Empey was a Regular Army man who was recruiting for the National

Guard in New Jersey when a German submarine sank the British ocean liner *Lusitania* in 1915, moving the U.S. toward entering World War I. While it took the nation two more years to declare war on Germany, Empey did so right away, heading for England and joining the British army. He served in a machine gun company and was wounded at the Battle of the Somme in 1916. That ended Empey's soldiering days, but not his involvement in the Great War. He turned his experience in Europe into a novel, *Over the Top*, and then turned the book into a movie in which he played the lead role.

Empey, whose efforts to get re-involved in the war as an active participant failed due to his wounds, contributed what he could to the effort. In addition to public speaking appearances he edited "Treat 'Em Rough," the magazine published for the men of the Army's nascent tank corps, for which the phrase was a highly successful recruiting slogan and rallying cry. Employing striking first, and hard, as a means of victory, the Tank Corps' success on European battlefields made the phrase very popular in post-war America.

In early 1919 Empey, who had been a high school athlete, bought the Maroons, a semi-pro outfit from the Bronx, renamed them the "Treat 'Em Roughs," and used the squad to raise funds for war veterans, devoting the profits from some weekend doubleheaders toward artificial limbs for "returned heroes who are unable to buy them."[36] He forged an alliance with semi-pro promoter and manager Connie Savage, who controlled bookings at the Dyckman Oval, a multi-sport stadium located in Harlem. This alliance was also good for the Bacharachs, who by playing Empey's team had access to a good place to play ball that wasn't under Nat Strong's thumb. The city's black teams played often at the Oval, frequently against white opponents. Empey was a well-known figure on the New York entertainment scene, and it's entirely possible that he could have crossed paths with Connor and Wilkins. At any rate, he thought like they did in at least one respect. He told a *Defender* reporter, probably William White, that he would "join hands with Connors [sic]-Wilkins Co. to eliminate Strong and other magnates from the control of Eastern [black] semi-pro ball."[37]

The Treat 'Em Roughs was a mixture of professionals, semi-pros and collegians, with some former major leaguers and, as the white big league season drew to a close, present-day big leaguers looking for that extra payday. Marty Kavanagh, a five-year big leaguer through 1918 (and the Seton Hall College baseball coach), played first base, for example. But the heart of any semi-pro team was its pitching, and here the Treat 'Em Roughs excelled. Their number one starter at the beginning of the season was Jimmy Clinton, one of the best-known and possibly the best-paid pitcher in the New York area, despite a minimal pro career. Clinton worked in a bank during the day and pitched for many top-level semi-pro clubs. He reputedly was paid $75 a game (plus $25 a game in the winter for basketball). There was speculation his salary "must run as high as $15,000 a year."[38]

At the very end of July, Empey and Savage pulled off a real coup when Jeff Tesreau joined the team. Tesreau had been a big league mound star since 1912 and had won 115 games for the New York Giants, including seasons of 26 and 22 wins. He was stubborn, though, as stubborn as his manager, John McGraw. In 1918 McGraw sent Tesreau south to spring training at Marlin, Texas, in charge of an early contingent of pitchers, catchers and out-of-shape players. When McGraw arrived with the rest of the team, he asked Tesreau for an update not only on his charges' baseball progress but on their off-the-field activities (Marlin was a hot springs resort, although a fairly quiet one). Tesreau told McGraw that the players' lives after practice were their business, not their manager's. Thus began the deterioration of the relationship between McGraw and one of his dependable starting pitchers. Tesreau left the team in the middle of June and never played in the majors again. He took a wartime defense job with the Bethlehem Steel Company and pitched for one of the plant teams, then became the baseball coach at Dartmouth College. In the summer of 1919, though, he began an annual routine of coming back to New York to pitch semi-pro ball, this season for the Treat 'Em Roughs.

Enthusiasm for abolishing the Blue Laws that banned Sunday baseball in New York had been growing, and in 1919 Sunday ball was legalized, loosing a pent-up demand in the metropolis. The Bacharachs and Empey's team played each other 13 times between July 27 and October 5. Twelve of the games were in six highly profitable doubleheaders at Dyckman, where crowds of 7,000, 10,000 and 15,000 were reported, quite a turnout in a park that supposedly had a 4,500-seat official capacity. The Bacharachs were the host for the 13th game, at Inlet Park.

The Giants won seven of the 13 matches, beginning with the opening doubleheader on July 27. Redding threw a six-hit shutout and struck out 13 for a 6–0 win. The Bacharachs also won the second game, 8–4, the win going to Roberts. Tesreau turned in a four-hitter the second time the teams met on August 3, beating Redding, 2–1, before the Giants won the nightcap, 8–2, behind Hubbard's complete game. The Giants also swept the next doubleheader on August 10, 5–1 on a five-hitter by Wickware and 6–2 in 11 innings, Wickware winning again in relief. The teams split on September 21. Redding got the first-game win, 7–1, over Tesreau, but Clinton, whose pitching was mediocre at best in three straight earlier losses to the Bacharachs, hurled a one-hitter and won the nightcap, 6–2.

The Bacharachs were routinely roughing up the Treat 'Em Roughs, with six wins in the first eight games, several by commanding margins. But in the fluid world of semi-pro ball, things can change quickly. By the time the teams got together at Dyckman again in late September, the Roughs had a whole new look. The lineup no longer consisted of once-upon-a-time or future big leaguers. The white big leagues were finishing their season, freeing up current pros at the top of their games to round out their season's salaries with some of Guy Empey's money.

In the first such game on September 28, a vast overflow crowd of 10,000 came to see the matchup between Dick Redding and Carl Mays, who had pitched a six-hit win for the New York Yankees in his last white major league game of the year on the 26th. It wasn't until the following August that Mays became infamous for throwing the pitch that beaned and killed Cleveland Indians shortstop Ray Chapman. In 1919 he was just a well-known, front-line major league starter who had already won more than 20 games in a season twice. The Treat 'Em Roughs had been joined by two New York Giants players, pitcher Rube Benton and third baseman Heinie Zimmerman. Benton had pitched his last game of 1919 for the Giants three days before and like Mays would resume his major league career the next spring. But Zimmerman was permanently available. A close friend of teammate Hal Chase, he had been caught trying to bribe teammates to lose season-ending games, and his big league career was over.

The game on the 28th went 14 innings, with both Redding and Mays around for the end when the Bacharachs broke a 1–1 tie that had existed since the seventh inning with four runs in the top of the final frame. Redding struck out 12 men in his marathon performance, giving up 11 hits and walking only two. Poles, with three hits, and Shively and Bryant with two each, led the Giants' offense off Mays, who gave up only ten hits and pitched as well as Redding until things fell apart at the end. The first game lasted three hours and squeezed the second down to a brilliant six-inning contest that the Treat 'Em Roughs won on a 2–0 shutout by Benton. He and Wickware gave up only three hits each. The following day, a Monday, the only time the two teams didn't play on a Sunday, the Giants were the hosts and lost, 9–5, at Inlet Park. Marty Walsh, a brother of star major league hurler Ed Walsh, pitched decently for the New Yorkers and got the win, while Jeffries took the loss for the Bacharachs. Tesreau, who often played the outfield when not pitching, hit a single, double and triple and drove in four runs.

The Redding-Mays matchup of the previous Sunday was repeated a week later, on October 5, as the teams wrapped up their competition back at Dyckman in front of a crowd of 15,000. Both pitchers again went the nine-inning distance and Mays got a 1–0 win. He allowed the Bacharachs five hits and Redding gave up only six. The second game wasn't as thrilling, but it was good nonetheless. The Treat 'Em Roughs won, 4–3. Tesreau gave up 12 hits in the seven-inning contest, but got out of most of his jams. Wickware, who gave up only six hits, had a shutout until the fifth inning, when he was tagged for three runs, plus one in the sixth.

The rest of the recorded Bacharachs games in 1919 show them rolling over most of their regional and local competition. There was only one local game, a 10–0 drubbing of the black Atlantic City Giants on June 14. Other New Jersey teams fared little better. Hammonton and Vineland went down to defeat in single games, and Wildwood and the Paterson Giants each lost both of their contests. The Bacharachs beat Millville six times, although Millville did win once, 4–2, on July 19.

The Giants were quickly pulling away in quality from most of the teams in the region. The white and regional black teams were beginning to play the role for the Bacharachs that they came to play for the best black teams in the Negro Leagues era. Most of this competition offered a chance for a Bacharach win, and profits from the gate receipts. But then, there were the teams with former white major and minor leaguers, plus players who probably could have played at that level. They were real competition, no easier than playing most Negro League–quality teams.

The powerful shipyard teams were in this last category, although the Giants came out on top, winning three of the five discovered games in 1919. The first such opponent was New York Ship from Camden, on June 16–17. Roberts limited the shipbuilders to two runs. The Giants got 14 hits, three by Shively, every man in the lineup getting at least one, to win the first game, 7–2. The next day the Bacharachs scored a run in the bottom of the ninth to eke out a 10–9 win that featured a total of 28 hits and five errors. Dilworth slogged his way to a complete game, actually doing better and better after giving up seven runs in the first three innings. Merchant Ship from Bristol, Pennsylvania, run by Connie Mack's son, Earle, a minor league player and manager both before and after the war, came to town on August 11–12. The shipyard team won the opener, 4–0, as John "Mule"

Watson, who had appeared in 21 games with a 7–10 record for the Athletics in 1918, tossed a shutout. The next day, though, the Giants won, 6–4, by means of a three-run seventh inning. The Baltimore Dry Docks ventured north on September 9 and administered a 3–0 defeat.

The Giants' record of 17 wins, one loss and a tie in games against Philadelphia-area and other Pennsylvania teams showed the gap that was developing on the other end of the quality spectrum. They outscored their opponents by a total of 81–45 in the 19 games. The Philly neighborhood teams from Bridesburg, Overbrook, Roxborough and Wissinoming, from adjacent Gloucester, New Jersey, and from the Baldwin Locomotive Works in nearby Leiperville, Pennsylvania, each visited Atlantic City once and went home losers. The team from the Klein Chocolate Company in the Harrisburg area lost all three of its games, although each by a single run. What appear to have been two different teams representing Chester lost a total of four games. The Disston Saw Works battled to a 3–3 tie in Philadelphia on September 19, but the Bacharachs defeated them soundly the next time, 6–0, at the Athletics' Shibe Park. Wickware struck out 16, walked only one and had a no-hitter with two out in the ninth. But an inside pitch was shot down the line past Hutchinson, and the gem was gone. The reconstituted Logan Squares beat the Giants, 2–1, in Atlantic City on June 29 when reliable Ad Swigler four-hit the locals. But the Squares came back for a July 4 game and two more on the 5th and 6th and were slaughtered, 12–3, 6–0 and 12–0. Jesse Hubbard, new to the Bacharachs, threw a no-hitter in the final win.

The regional black teams went down in order, too. The Pennsylvania Red Caps came the closest, losing 9–7. The Bacharachs went to Camden on July 26 to play that city's Black Sox and won, 9–0. The Harlan Giants from Wilmington lost, 9–6, on September 4.

Grant Johnson had begun organized baseball in 1894, when he was 20. He had been the premier shortstop in black baseball in the first decade of the twentieth century, John Henry Lloyd's immediate predecessor as the acknowledged best at that key position. Now, at age 45, he was still playing short, although for the Pittsburgh Stars, a second-tier black team that despite its name was based in Buffalo, New York. A friendly, outgoing man, Johnson, who early in his career was called "Home Run Johnson" for his ability to hit the long ball even in the deadball era, was now called "Dad" by some of the younger players under his wing.[39]

The Stars arrived in Atlantic City for a pair of games on August 28–29. This time they had the temporary use of Joe "Cyclone" Williams, borrowed from the Lincoln Giants for the occasion. It didn't help on the 28th. Williams, as the *Daily Press* put it, "held no terrors for the home batters," who touched him for 11 hits, and the Bacharachs won, 6–2.[40] They repeated the performance the next day—Dan Johnson pitched a complete game six-hitter and the batters had 15 hits, three of them by Lloyd.

For six exciting days beginning on July 28, the Bacharachs played host at Inlet Park to a real traveling team that in addition to being tough competition stood as a sales pitch for, well, traveling. The Maxwell Motor Car Company (which became Chrysler) sent a team on the road that summer to hype the company's name. It had some marginal major leaguers from the last ten years in its lineup, and made it to Atlantic City on July 27, when it warmed up for the Giants by beating the Logan Squares. A five-game series was scheduled, but interest and attendance ran high and the Maxwells stayed for an extra contest. The teams split the series, three games each. The victory margins were one run twice, two runs twice and three and four runs once each. In the July 28 opener the Giants were behind, 6–3, in the bottom of the seventh inning, when Lloyd stepped up with the bases loaded and tripled to tie the game. Taylor singled him in for the winning run.

The Maxwells took the second game, 9–7, in 14 innings. This time the visitors came from behind, wiping out seven early Bacharach runs and tying it up 7–7 in the seventh inning. Six scoreless innings followed before the car team touched up Redding for three hits and the winning runs. Extra innings became the norm the next day, the 30th, when the Bacharachs won in ten, 4–3. The Maxwells had threatened seriously in the top of the inning when Redding, again in relief, fumbled a little grounder with the bases loaded. Cannonball managed to flip the ball to Gatewood for a force-out at home, despite the protests of the Maxwell team, and some spectators, that Gatewood's foot was about a foot off home plate.

The Maxwells won in 11 innings on July 31. The score again was 4–3. Redding was in his fifth inning of relief of Wickware when Angel Aragon, a Cuban native who had played 32 big league games over three years earlier in the decade but was a career .300 minor league hitter, knocked a homer over the left field fence for the game-winner. The visitors made it two in a row on August 1 by a 6–3 score as Ralph Comstock, who had hurled 40 major league games in his career, limited the Giants to six hits. Redding was totally in charge in the final game, allowing only six base runners in a complete-game 5–1 win.

Many times during the season the Bacharach Giants played teams with former or future major leaguers. On October 7 they went up against the real thing, the New York Giants on a post-season exhibition tour. The game was at Philadelphia's Shibe Park, to which a reported 1,500 Atlantic City fans, including Mayor Bacharach, travelled. The New Yorkers jumped ahead early but the Atlantic City team started to catch up, only to run out of innings and lose, 7–5.

1920

The leading black baseball men in the Midwest met in Kansas City in February 1920, for a momentous purpose, forming a Negro major league. A league had been tried in 1887, but was so short-lived that teams were left stranded hundreds of miles from home when it collapsed for lack of attendance. A cooperative association of black and Cuban clubs had been formed in the East in 1906, but it had existed mostly as a game-booking consortium, and had fallen apart by 1910. This new Negro National League, with the many-faceted Rube Foster in charge, had teams in the major cities of the Midwest. Only the Great Depression could kill it off 12 years later as all of professional baseball suffered along with its fans.

At the end of April, with the NNL firmly established, Foster journeyed East to protect its flank. The league had established rules to prevent the common player jumps between

Atlantic City in 1920, with the attractions that made the city a prime vacation location—the Boardwalk, Steeplechase Pier, the beach and man-powered rolling chairs—all on display (Atlantic City Heritage Collections, Atlantic City Free Public Library).

teams, which upset teams' stability and hurt the league's credibility with the public. But there was no National League team east of Dayton, Ohio. Without some sort of "no raiding" agreement with the top-flight Eastern teams such as the Bacharach Giants, the promises of the National League owners to each other wouldn't be enough to ward off raiding wars.

What Foster had to offer was an "associate membership" in the new league. Eastern independent teams could get preferential scheduling from the National League clubs, both in their home parks and on Midwestern barnstorming trips. In return they would respect league player contracts and would get the same consideration from NNL teams. Foster and Connor had been hard-headed baseball owners for a long time, and there were "complicated baseball matters that had been hanging fire for years" between them, as White of the *Chicago Defender* diplomatically put it. But Connie Savage of the Dyckman Oval played peacemaker at a meeting in New York City, and Connor bought into the plan for a $500 entrance fee. Savage's ambassadorial efforts weren't overlooked, either. Before the confab broke up Foster had agreed to showcase National League teams at the Oval when they came East.[41]

Foster's peace mission did not include offering an olive branch to every Eastern club—Foster had no love for Nat Strong, for one, agreeing with Connor that Strong's iron grip on a big part of East Coast ball was bad for the black race. Foster also didn't have a friend in Ed Bolden of Hilldale in Philadelphia. Bolden had signed away three regulars from Foster's Chicago American Giants three months before the National League established its reserve clause, but Foster still considered his roster to have been poached by Hilldale. Bolden, a highly organized and hard-headed executive, blasted Foster in an open letter in the *Philadelphia Tribune*, defending his signing of American Giants players. He also accused Foster of trying to undercut him in his own town by currying favor with the Madison Stars, a lesser Philadelphia black team. Bolden, whose "day job" was at a Philadelphia post office, could also write a mean letter: "Any of your Western Circuit that invade the East and ignore our club will be losing ready money, even should you be able to book them for every day of their stay.... We can make more money in a single day in New York than we can in a week at Detroit."[42]

But not being covered by the league's no-raiding policy, Bolden couldn't protect against player defections, and Dick Lundy and Yank Deas were soon on their way back to Atlantic City. They were in the lineup when the Bacharachs opened in New York City in early May. Not that the Hilldale owner didn't try to fight back—he sued both players in Pennsylvania courts for violating their contracts. Bolden failed to get a preliminary injunction in the Court of Common Pleas barring Lundy from playing for the Bacharachs, but did get one from a different judge in the same court restricting Deas. However, Lundy (who allegedly had signed contracts and accepted advance salary from Hilldale, the Bacharachs and another unidentified team), was in the end not restrained from changing teams, and Deas also switched when Bolden decided not to post a $2,000 bond required of him to continue pursuing the case.[43]

It was always good to have the fiery, hard-working Deas around, although he was now only the Giants' part-time catcher. But retrieving Lundy was essential, since John Henry Lloyd had left the team. Lloyd decided in the off-season to jump back to Strong's Brooklyn Royal Giants, and there was nothing Connor and Wilkins could do to stop him, since the Royals had no connection with the National League's reserve rules. As their partner Tom Jackson had said in 1916, "it's a poor trick that does not work both ways." Lundy's return was invaluable—he hit .297 overall in the discovered games, was second on the team in RBI, and pounded the pitches of the league-quality teams at a .354 rate.

Even with new controls over player movement among some teams, the Bacharachs again managed to turn over much of their lineup and pitching staff. Although he started the season with the Royal Giants, Bill Handy was back holding down second base by the first week in June, hitting .277. Country Brown Bryant hit .275 in left field and Johnnie Pugh, at .230, again was a utility outfielder. Redding was not only the ace of the pitching staff and occasional first baseman, he was now the team captain, which is to say field manager.

C. I. Taylor had returned to the fray, with his Indianapolis ABCs a charter member of the new league, and brother Ben had promptly left the Bacharachs to rejoin him. Connor went shopping in New York, where the reserve rules of course were not in effect. An acquisition from the city was likely to come at the expense of a white owner, Jim Keenan of the Lincoln Giants in this case. The player, Bill Pierce, was a slugger who had recently converted from catching to first base. He was 30 and had only five years of high-level play left in him. But he was still an everyday player and hit .305, led the team in doubles with 15, and drove in 54 runs. He wasn't Ben Taylor, but he was very good.

Across the infield Hutchinson was replaced at third by Oliver Marcell. One of the leading offensive and defensive infield stars of the 1920s, Marcell had a hot temper and fierce drive that made him a star, but which indirectly led to his premature decline. Marcell, a New Orleans native with the catchy nickname "Ghost," was 24 at the beginning of this season, already acquiring the reputation that got him picked in the 1950s as the best third baseman on two all-time blackball teams. His abilities are summed up by Jim Riley: "A rare gem afield, he could do everything. He was very fast, covered lots of territory, and possessed a quick and snappy arm.... Whether making spectacular plays to his left or to his right, or fielding bunts like a master, he delighted the fans." He could also hit, accumulating 122 base hits, the most for any Giant in the games for which 1920 box scores have been found. His .316 average, which led the team, also came with team leadership in runs scored (72) and RBI (64). The Ghost played with the Bacharachs for the bulk of the 1920s, teaming with Lundy to form a brilliant left side of the infield. But in 1930 with the Brooklyn Royal Giants, he got in a fight over a dice game with a teammate who bit off part of his nose. He continued to play, with a patch over the damaged portion of his face, but the humiliation of appearing on the field this way distracted him and soon led to his fall from top-level baseball.[44]

The fiery Oliver Marcell was the Giants third baseman from 1920 through 1922 and again from 1925 through 1928. This photograph was taken for his passport in 1920 before a team of Giants and others set sail for Cuba to play in the Winter League.

Deas split catching duties with one of the Bacharachs' first two Cuban players, Julio Rojo, who had spent four years with Alex Pompez's East Coast Cuban team. Although primarily a catcher, Rojo had speed and could play the outfield and infield. His versatility got him into 74 games for the Giants, in which he hit .246. Frank Mederos, a native of Havana, had played in the U.S. for ten years for various Latino teams. This was his last season in the States, and he covered center field until early September, hitting .262.

The Giants added two valuable outfielders during the second half of the season. Jesse Barbour, 32 (whose name usually showed up as Barber in box scores), had been playing for major black teams since 1910 and left Hilldale in July to take over right field, then center from Mederos. He had substantial foot speed and a good glove, and eventually put in 15 years at the top. In 49 recorded Bacharach games he hit .255. The outfield was further bolstered in September when George Shively, who had returned to Indianapolis with Ben Taylor, came back to the Giants in the season's last weeks, hitting .269 in 17 games. The only other semi-regular was 21-year-old Lewis Means, a rookie who played second in May until Handy arrived, then was used in the outfield until the middle of July. His playing time became very scarce, the hiring of Barbour and Shively contributing to Redding's decision to bench him although Means hit a decent .232, one of his better years in blackball.

The offense collectively hit .274 and scored an average of five and a half runs per game in the 134 for which results have been found, right in the range of the previous two years. But, as in 1919, the pitching, which allowed only three runs per game with a cumulative 2.06 ERA, was the strong point. It was the main reason the Bacharachs won 94 of those 134 games, lost 36 and tied four, for a .723 winning percentage. Redding and the rest of his staff were amazing. The Giants employed only five pitchers in the 128 games for which pitching data can be found, and one of them was Marcell, who threw some relief in a 12–0 rout of the Gimbel Brothers Department Store team from Philadelphia on July 3. The four-man starting rotation did everything else, including the occasional relief stint, although, including Marcell's appearance, Redding used relievers only 17 times in the discovered games. The complete game was the norm, and those 128 starts produced 111 of them.

Redding made 38 starts, including one of his signature feats of pitching both ends of a doubleheader, plus seven relief appearances. He was the workhorse of the staff, winning 27 games and losing 13. Like the rest of the lineup, the pitching staff had undergone radical changes. Although he would return to the Giants in a couple of years and be an important part of the staff, Roy Roberts went to the Brooklyn Royal Giants in 1920. Dan Johnson was pitching for the Pennsylvania Red Caps. Frank Wickware, who had been of substantial help in 1919, had gone back to Foster's Chicago American Giants.

Also winning 27 games for Redding's small but efficient staff was second-year pitcher Harold Treadwell. Treadwell, 23, was a submarining right-hander who made 34 starts with a 27–6 record. A native of Long Island, he had begun his top-level career with the Lincoln Giants and the Brooklyn Royal Giants in 1919. A third starter, Merven "Red" Ryan, so nicknamed for his dark red hair, began pitching in 1915, when he was 18, for the Pittsburgh Stars in Buffalo. He, too, had left Nat Strong's Royal Giants after the 1919 season to pitch for Connor and Wilkins, who were still picking off Strong's players, albeit at a slower rate than in the previous spring. Ryan, only 5 feet, 8 inches and 160 pounds, was a right-hander who "threw hard for his size, but utilized a knuckleball and a forkball."[45] He made 32 starts and seven relief appearances in 1920, going 22–11.

Andrew Williams, the fourth starter, weighed

Merven "Red" Ryan pitched for the Bacharachs in 1920 and 1921. This photograph was taken for his passport in 1920 before a team of Giants and others set sail for Cuba to play in the Winter League.

about as much as Ryan, but his bulk, if you could call it that, was strung out over a six-foot frame, earning him the nickname "Stringbean." He had been pitching professionally since 1914, beginning with the Royal Giants. Williams had pitched for teams in many places, St. Louis, Indianapolis, Philadelphia and Dayton among them, and the previous season had been with the Chicago American Giants before returning to the East to spend most of the remaining six years of his career with the Bacharachs. He made 25 starts, winning 16 and losing five. All four were decent hitters for pitchers and had fine years at bat this year, a .296 average for Williams, .279 for Ryan, .269 for Treadwell and .264 for Redding.

The Connor-Wilkins ownership team continued to make the Giants a first-class outfit right from the beginning of this season. At the beginning of April the team gathered back in Jacksonville for full-scale spring training at Barrs Field, which had just hosted the Brooklyn Dodgers (or Robins, as they were often called in those days). The Giants beat the local black team at least twice while there and shoved off for the North after the second win on April 18 to play other regional teams as tune-ups for the regular season, which began in New York City on May 2.

This Sunday doubleheader was at Dyckman Oval against a new, yet familiar, opponent. Guy Empey's Treat 'Em Roughs were still in existence, but Empey's close relationship with Connie Savage had ended. Jeff Tesreau, the former New York Giants pitcher, had stepped into the former soldier's boots. Tesreau was the manager, star pitcher and sometimes right fielder of Tesreau's Bears, stocked with players who, like Tesreau himself, had played for Empey in 1919.[46]

The Bacharachs played at least nine games at Dyckman, a few less than 1919, apparently because Connor and Savage had a disagreement over the all-important percentage of attendance money due to the Giants. Even so, continued heavy use of the Oval was significant to the Bacharachs' progress toward becoming a major force in black baseball, particularly when joined with the expanded use of Ebbets Field. Connor had continued his relationship with Charles Ebbets' white major league team, going from renting the ballpark for the late–1919 series against the International All-Stars, to going to Jacksonville in Brooklyn's wake in the spring, to playing 15 games at Ebbets in 1920. For the most part the Bacharachs reserved the big league park for the major league-level Negro teams. Inlet Park in Atlantic City still saw a lot of Bacharach action, but the team was looking much more cosmopolitan. Most importantly, in none of its major venues was it beholden to the powerful Nat Strong. Connor was obviously pleased. He promised the public that the Giants would be outfitted in brand new uniforms, since "we have been able to get Ebbets Field and we will look just as good as the Brooklyn Dodgers on that diamond."[47]

Besides the increased access to upscale ballparks (the Giants also played five games in the Philadelphia Athletics' Shibe Park), the major change in the 1920 season was an increased number of games against the most important opposition an aspiring top-level black team could have. The Bacharachs played 46 times against other black clubs that were already in the new Negro National League or, like the Giants themselves, were going to be in a black big league in the near future. Thirty-five of the contests were against the team's new colleagues from the Negro National League, including a 16-day road trip to the Midwest beginning July 31 during which the Bacharachs played the Detroit Stars, the

American Giants and the Indianapolis ABCs. The competition was hard—the team batting average for the games at the upper level was 29 points lower than the overall season mark, and the team ERA was a third of a run higher. But the results showed the Giants could be in the hunt—they won 25 of these games, lost 19 and played to two ties for a .568 record.

The Midwestern road trip wasn't auspicious from that point of view. Chicago, Detroit and Indianapolis finished first, second and fourth, respectively, in the NNL that year, and the Bacharachs only won four of 13 games. But the tour brought them plenty of positive publicity, even if the squad did leave Detroit under something of a cloud. It may also have produced a sizeable profit if the 20,000 people that reportedly turned out for an August 9 game against the American Giants is any indication of crowd sizes on the tour.[48]

The trip opened with five games in Detroit, and the Bacharachs won the first one, 4–2. Treadwell got the win, with relief help from Redding. Barbour had three hits for the Giants, including a double, and Handy had a home run and a single. Bill Gatewood of the Stars and Redding, the leading pitchers for both teams, each gave up seven hits in complete games the next day. But Detroit wiped out a three-run Giants lead in the bottom of the seventh with a rally that was capped by a two-run homer by future Hall of Fame outfielder Pete Hill, and won, 4–3.

The Bacharachs rebounded on August 2 with a 2–0 victory when Ryan tossed a six-hit shutout, topping former Giant Gifford McDonald, who pitched well but had the sort of bad luck that had plagued him in Atlantic City. Bill Holland, a 19-year-old who was the Stars' other key pitcher, outdueled Williams on the 3rd for a 2–1 Detroit win. Chick Harper, the right fielder, tripled in the winning run in the bottom of the fourth. The game of August 4 went into the books as a 6–4 Detroit win. Officially it was a forfeit when the Bacharachs got into a prolonged on-field argument and then walked off the field en masse, in the top of the ninth inning after Pierce pulled a hot shot down the third base line that the umpire called foul. The Detroit crowd wasn't pleased, and "it is thought by many of the fans that the longer they [the Bacharachs] stay away from Detroit the better the game will be."[49]

The Bacharachs were leaving town anyway, bound for Chicago for a six-game set with Rube Foster's American Giants that didn't go particularly well for them. They looked great in the August 7 opener in Gary, Indiana, an alternate American Giants venue just over the state line from Chicago, as they made ten hits, including a home run by Bryant, and Treadwell gave up only four hits in an 11–4 win. But then the action moved to the American Giants' home field, Schorling Park, and the Giants from the East lost four straight.

On August 8 Tom Williams, the former Bacharach who was pitching superbly for Foster's team, gave up seven hits as Chicago won, 7–3. The Bacharachs scored two runs in the top of the first inning and, as a *Chicago Whip* sportswriter put it, "assumed a chesty pose and began to turkey [sic] trot." But the American Giants tied the game in the bottom of that inning and went on from there. Cristobal Torriente, Chicago's future Hall of Fame outfielder, had three hits, and the Americans stole six bases off of Redding, Ryan and Rojo, the catcher. Marcell was taken to task by the *Chicago Defender* for misbehaving when he attempted to charge the mound after nearly being hit by a pitch, and then, when taunted by the home fans, "proceeded to make immoral movement with part of his body that would resemble a hoochy-coochy dancer."[50]

The game the next day wasn't decided until the bottom of the tenth inning when Chicago third baseman Dave Malarcher drilled a single to produce a 3–2 win. On August 10 Frank Wickware pitched a complete game for a 5–1 Chicago victory. The last of the four losses, on the 11th, was frustrating. The Bacharachs got 12 hits but could squeeze only four runs out of them. Redding gave up only six hits, but he and the rest of the team committed six errors to allow five Chicago runs. The finale on August 12 should have revived the teams' spirits. They won, 8–1, on a Stringbean Williams five-hitter that was backed up by 14 hits.

Two games in Indiana with the ABCs wrapped up the trip. The first, on August 14, was in Muncie, a secondary ABCs site 60 miles northeast of Indianapolis. ABCs veteran starter Dizzy Dismukes, relieved by Jim Jeffries, a Giant for part of 1919 while the ABCs were dormant, dueled Harold Treadwell. The three hurlers gave up only ten hits among them, but Indianapolis got six of them, usually with men on base, and won, 4–3. The Bacharachs scored their runs in a quiet rally in the seventh inning that consisted of four walks (three straight from a tiring Dismukes before he departed the mound) and a dropped line drive. The 3–2 lead only lasted moments as two future Hall of Famers put the ABCs ahead to stay. Twenty-three-year-old rookie Biz Mackey, who would go on to play and manage in the Negro Leagues until he was 50, tripled in a run and Oscar Charleston, arguably the best position player ever to play in the black leagues, singled him in to break the tie. The next day the ABCs won, 5–1, when Morris Williams, not one of the team's top starters, gave up only five hits and Charleston ripped Redding for three more hits. Redding gave up only seven hits all day, but the Giants made four errors.

Negro baseball travel could be arduous. Clearly traveling all night, the Bacharachs covered 500 miles in a day to show up in little Burnham, Pennsylvania, on August 16 to play the Standard Steel Works team from nearby Lewiston. The Giants' 3–2 loss, one of the few to local Pennsylvania teams that season, might reasonably be blamed on fatigue. Back on home turf at Inlet Park, the Bacharachs again engaged a Negro National League opponent. But this time, it was the Chicago Giants. They lacked the word "American" in their name, and were also distinguished from Rube Foster's team by their occupancy of last place. The Bacharachs pounced on these fellow Giants, winning four, losing one and playing to a rain-drenched tie.

The tie came first, on August 18 at Inlet Park. Chicago starter John Taylor, used to pitching with little offensive support, had held the Bacharachs to only four hits while Red Ryan had given up only three. The game was tied 2–2 after nine innings when it began to pour. The weather was much better the next day and the crowd at Inlet included many local dignitaries, including Harry Bacharach, out of office after declining to run for re-election earlier in the year. Bacharach may not have needed the team as a public relations appendage any more, but this didn't mean he had lost his affection for it. According to the *Atlantic City Gazette-Review*, "The ex-mayor was the most enthusiastic of the two thousand fans, taking a post beside the home team's bench and rewarding each player who secured a hit with a crisp greenback."[51] Bacharach went to his pocket often—the home team collected 11 hits, Brown, Redding, Handy and Pierce being double winners. Treadwell, meanwhile, gave up only six and the ex-mayor's men won, 9–3.

Williams and 42-year-old Walter Ball put on a dual pitching display on the 20th, and Chicago was actually ahead, 1–0, when the bottom of the ninth rolled around. The Bacharachs got two men on with one out and Stringbean came through with a two-run double, winning his own game. The teams played a Sunday doubleheader at Ebbets Field on August 22, and the Bacharachs won both games. Redding threw a shutout in the first game and Ryan scattered six hits in the nightcap, getting two of the Bacharachs' eight hits himself for an easy 4–1 win. Chicago won its only game of the series, 4–1, back in Atlantic City on the 24th, knocking Treadwell out with a four-run third inning after he had walked six and hit a batter.

Shortly thereafter the ABCs came to Atlantic City and stayed around for nine games in eight days. The Bacharachs won the opener at Inlet Park, 7–5, on August 30, with a super-aggressive base running show that featured three straight double steals. The ABCs won the next day, 3–1, though, when Bob Hudspeth, a 6½-foot-tall rookie first baseman backing up Ben Taylor, drilled a two-run single in the top of the ninth off Redding in relief. The teams continued to trade off wins as the Giants won, 7–4, on September 1 and Dicta Johnson, the other top ABCs starter in addition to Dismukes, outdueled Ryan for a 2–1 Indianapolis win the following day.

The Bacharachs knocked Dismukes out of the game in the first inning on September 3, and Treadwell gave up only six hits to preserve the early lead for a 5–3 victory. Almost predictably, the ABCs won the next day, 9–7, wiping out a comfortable Bacharach lead with a seven-run rush in the last two innings. The last game in Atlantic City, on the 5th, was a 4–4 tie, called due to darkness after ten innings. After seven games at Inlet Park, each team had won three games plus the tie. The last two games, a Labor Day doubleheader, were played at Ebbets Field in intermittent heavy showers. The weather and a trolley strike going on in Brooklyn held down attendance. The Bacharachs were not dismayed, however, and won both ends. Redding and Dismukes, the veteran pitching stars of both clubs, pitched complete games, the Bacharachs winning, 5–4, by scoring four runs in the bottom of the sixth inning, a rally capped by Rojo's pinch-hit, bases-loaded triple. Red Ryan breezed to a 4–1 win in the second game.

A month later the Chicago American Giants challenged the Bacharachs again while on an Eastern swing. All of the games were played at white major league parks, the first three at Shibe in Philadelphia. Chicago won the first two on October 6–7. It starts to get dark early in October on the East Coast, and the offensive explosions from both teams were outlasting daylight, the Americans ahead 11–10 when the game was called after six innings. The Bacharachs were cooled off considerably the next day by Chicago's Tom Johnson, who held them to five hits as the Americans won, 13–1. But Dick Redding changed the momentum decidedly on October 8 with a three-hit shutout for a 7–0 win.

The last four games between the two teams were a pair of Sunday doubleheaders at Ebbets Field. The car strike was settled, the rain didn't fall, and 7,000 people showed up, a good crowd for a black ballgame, especially one being played during football season. The Bacharach Giants swept the twin bill. Redding outdueled Dicta Johnson, giving up six hits and one walk and striking out eight for a 5–3 win. He also hit a triple, as did Barbour and Lundy. Ryan also pitched a six-hitter in the seven-inning second game and was supported by a Lundy homer as the Bacharachs won, 7–3.

The final matchups were a week later. The pitching was great—there were only 13 hits all day between both teams, but the ones that paid off all came off Chicago bats. Johnson shut the Bacharachs out, 2–0, in the first game, although Redding pitched better overall, giving up only two hits. Ryan also threw a two-hitter in the second game, which was stopped after six innings due to darkness. He was still a losing pitcher, though. Tom Williams allowed only four hits himself and produced a shortened shutout, 1–0.

There were also games against non–NNL competition—the Baltimore Black Sox, Cuban Stars and the Lincoln Giants. League politics took familiar rival Hilldale right off the Bacharachs' schedule. Foster and Bolden were feuding, Connor had aligned his club with Foster, and the "natural rivals" never met this year. Bolden had claimed in a September *Philadelphia Tribune* article that this wasn't his fault: "For some time the Hilldale management has endeavored to induce the Bacharachs to play a series at the big league park beginning October 4. Mr. Connors [sic] claims that because of a league agreement, he is unable to play Hilldale."[52] The two teams did go head-to-head on October 4, but only in the competition for attendance dollars. The Bacharachs were in Philadelphia at Shibe Park, defeating a somewhat ragtag all-star aggregation featuring Babe Ruth, while Hilldale was at the Phillies' park losing to another major league all-star team.

The Black Sox played home-and-home series with the Giants in September and October, and were beaten four times, only one game at all close. On September 19, before 8,000 fans at the Dyckman Oval, the Giants fell behind early in both games of a doubleheader, but then posted duplicate eight-run, fifth-inning rallies to put each contest out of reach. Redding won the opener, 13–5, and led off the big rally with a bases-empty home run, followed soon by Rojo's three-run double. Pierce socked three homers in the nightcap and Handy also hit one out to back Stringbean Williams in a 16–4 victory. On October 1 in Baltimore, Ryan threw a four-hit shutout and Deas hit a homer. The next day the Bacharachs won, 15–1. Treadwell started, got the win and also joined Handy in homering.

Alex Pompez's Cuban Stars came to Atlantic City for a three-game series beginning September 27 and managed to win one of the games. In the first game the Cubans scored three runs in the top of the ninth for a 4–3 win, largely due to the sudden inability of the Bacharach outfield to catch the ball. Bryant and Shively each allowed hits to go past them and Shively dropped a short fly. A better day arrived the next afternoon when Redding threw a four-hit shutout and two of six Cuban errors led to the Giants' two runs. An even better day arrived on the 29th, when the Giants scored one more run and Williams allowed only three hits as the Bacharachs won, 3–0.

The two doubleheaders against the Lincoln Giants had deep meanings. For one thing, they brought the Bacharachs, who avoided Nat Strong, up against a team owned by a sometime Strong ally. For another, while the Bacharachs had become the first blacks to play at Ebbets Field the previous fall, these games were the first at the Dodgers' park between two black teams. Jim Keenan's Lincoln Giants had been on the Bacharach Giants' schedule as recently as 1918, but that was before Connor and Wilkins owned the team and the Lincolns took part in Strong's "freeze out" of the Bacharachs.

In 1920 blackball fans in the city, egged on by the black weekly, the *New York Age*, began to push hard for a showdown between the two teams. In mid–June the *Age* reported a general agreement for a matchup. Plans then firmed up for a prime-time Sunday doubleheader. The two team's owners may not have had a great relationship, but both sides enjoyed making a profit, so there never seems to have been any doubt where the showdown would take place, since the Bacharachs had Ebbets Field at their disposal. The Lincolns' home field was at the Catholic Protectory Oval in the Bronx, which derived its name from being on the grounds of a church-run orphanage.

While the Connor-Strong feud percolated in the background, a long-festering dispute between the two teams' field managers and star pitchers was out in the open, fueling the excitement leading up to the game. Dick Redding and Cyclone Joe Williams of the Lincolns had pitched together for the Lincoln Giants in the team's earlier days. They both were stars, and a single roster was too small for both of them. Redding left the Lincolns and the aces became bitter rivals, to the extent that they refused to pose for a photo while shaking hands before the doubleheader.[53] Just as there was no question about in whose park these games would be played, there was no doubt which two pitchers would start the opener.

The ace black pitchers of the East, Joe Williams, left, and Dick Redding, the Bacharach Giants' leading hurler and manager, pointedly refused to pose shaking hands when the Bacharachs met Williams' Lincoln Giants in 1920 at the first game between two Negro teams at a white major league park. They later mellowed, though, as seen here (National Baseball Hall of Fame and Library, Cooperstown, New York).

Prior to the showdown doubleheader on July 11, the Lincolns had won 21 discovered games and had lost at least eight, playing mostly New York metropolitan area and suburban teams, plus several from New Jersey and Connecticut. The Bacharachs had won at least 40 discovered games and lost eight by July 11, and were on a roll with 13 straight wins and 25 of their last 26, most of them against Philadelphia and New York white semi-pro clubs.

There was an excellent crowd for the doubleheader by black baseball standards. Bacharach fans were reported to have come all the way from Atlantic City and Philadelphia. However, it's a mystery as to just how many patrons filed into Ebbets Field. According to the *Age*, the doubleheader drew 16,000 fans (the *Chicago Defender* reported 15,000), which if accurate would have produced a half-filled major league ballpark, a monster crowd for a black ballgame anywhere in the country at that time. But the *Brooklyn Daily Eagle*, which covered baseball at all levels in the borough, reported an attendance of only 6,000.[54] The *Eagle*'s number, while disappointing compared to the black papers' estimates, was still almost double the capacity of the Protectory Oval, confirming the wisdom of the decision to play at Ebbets Field.

No runs were scored by either team until the third inning, when the Bacharachs pushed one across. They picked up two more in the fourth, and "close pitching and clever fielding"produced no further scoring until the eighth. The Lincolns did rally in the top of the seventh, though. Outfielder Clarence "Fats" Jenkins tripled to lead off, and Joe Williams was so sure that at least one run was possible that he bolted off the bench to coach third base. But Redding got an out that didn't allow Jenkins to advance. Then he faced slugging Jules Thomas, and on a 2–2 count fired over a third strike. Redding got the next batter to ground to Marcell. He was out of the jam and was handed a crisp $20 bill by a front row fan as he returned to the dugout. The Bacharachs expanded their lead to 5–0 and in the top of the ninth, and Bryant made a running one-handed catch to take a likely triple away from Thomas and end the game. The *Daily Eagle* reported that the fans, still in a giving mood, showered Bryant with $100 in "coin and bills."[55]

The Bacharachs went ahead 3–2 in the second inning of the second game. Each team scored a pair in the third, with the Lincolns tying the contest up 5–5 with a run in the fourth. The Lincolns' Thomas struck again in the eighth, driving in the game-winning runs to give his team a 7–5 split of the doubleheader.

It was a great day. The crowd was large, excited and profitable for the Connor-Wilkins partnership and for Keenan. The doubleheader split provided no decisive bragging rights for either team, although Dick Redding definitely had a leg up on Joe Williams. There seemed nothing more sensible than to do the whole thing again, on August 29.

It was rainy on the day of the game, which also coincided with the first day of the transit strike. These events depressed attendance, but the *Age* still reported 10,000 fans on hand for a second Redding-Williams matchup (and, again, the *Daily Eagle* lowballed with a crowd of 6,200).[56] Again, it wasn't close. Redding threw another shutout, a three-hitter this time. The Bacharachs scored in the first, third and eighth innings for a 6–0 win. Lundy and Marcell each had two hits, Marcell's a double and triple. Bryant added another triple.

Before the second game, all likely Bacharach starters warmed up, keeping the crowd, and possibly the Lincolns, in suspense until Cesar Jamison announced the batteries. It was Redding again for the Bacharachs, going for back-to-back wins as the crowd went wild. The Cannonball, who had done this "Iron Man" thing before, appeared a little winded. He was touched for two runs in the top of the first inning. But the Bacharachs put this one away with five runs in the third, coming away with a 7–3 victory.

Of all the top-level black teams they played, the Bacharachs had losing records with only two, a close two wins versus three losses with the Detroit Stars and a 5–8 record with the American Giants. But they clobbered the lesser black teams they played, going 16–1–1 against them in the recovered games, starting with the two spring training wins in Jacksonville. The Giants' only loss was to the Madison Stars of Philadelphia, a club formed that season to challenge Hilldale but which, due to financial shortfalls, gradually evolved into a Hilldale farm club. The Stars beat the Bacharachs, 11–10, a wild game in which the Giants at one point held a 5–1 lead that steadily disintegrated even though Williams, Ryan and Redding were on the mound. Otherwise the Giants beat the Stars in their other three matchups.

Grant Johnson's Pittsburgh Stars managed an 8–8 tie on July 30 in Buffalo when darkness fell after ten innings. These Stars actually played the Bacharachs closely in all six games that season, losing 6–1, 1–0 (a Dick Redding shutout), 5–3, 3–1 and 3–0. The Pennsylvania Red Caps visited on July 6–7 and lost both games. The Portsmouth, Virginia, Giants lost three straight from June 17–19, a 3–2 defeat and two more definite losses, and Wade's Giants from Roanoke, Virginia, were soundly beaten, 11–4, on August 25.

The regional white semi-pro teams were no challenge any more either. The Bacharachs played 32 games against teams from the Philadelphia area and the rest of Pennsylvania and New Jersey, and won 27 of them, losing only four and tying one. For good measure they also defeated two teams from other states, the Albion, Michigan, Red Sox on August 5 in the middle of the Western road trip, and the Rex Athletic Club from Washington, D.C., on September 8. Most of the games weren't even close. The Giants scored an average of a little more than six runs per game against two for their opponents in the 34 contests. In the wins, the average score was basically 7–2.

The Bacharachs fell only to the Fleischer Yarn Co. of Philadelphia, 3–2, on June 25 (but they beat Fleischer soundly in two other games); rather unaccountably to Millville, a nearby New Jersey team they usually defeated, 2–1, on September 26; the Paterson Silk Sox, one of the better New York City–Northern New Jersey teams, 6–3, on October 23; and Standard Steel Works, 3–2, on August 16, the game near the end of the 500-mile trek back from Indiana. Philadelphia's Bridesburg club and the Giants played to a 0–0 ten-inning tie on September 23.

The Bacharachs' victims came from all varieties of semi-pro teams: the Philadelphia business and industrial teams (the J&J Dobson textile mill, Marshall E. Smith Sporting Goods, the Sun Oil refinery, the Aberfoyle yarn mill, Quaker City Rubber, the Gimbel Brothers and Lit Brothers department stores); town or neighborhood teams (the Camden Athletic Club, the Nativity Catholic Club, Home Run Baker's Upland team, the Southampton and Norristown Professionals, Cambridge, a team from the city of Scranton) and the "SPHAs," an acronym for the South Philadelphia Hebrew Association. The Association, a Jewish community group, had a great basketball team renowned in the East during hoop's early days. The baseball team was good, too, although not good enough to beat the Bacharach Giants. An old New Jersey rival, Vineland, also fell to the Giants, as did the Meadowbrook team from Newark in Northern New Jersey.

The toughest competition outside of Negro League–level teams came from the New York City semi-pro clubs and the teams from the World War I defense industries. The war was over but the sports teams were still in business, although this whole category of competition was going into decline as the drop in government orders for ships and steel and the need for professional players to find defense jobs had ended.

There were seven discovered games against Tesreau's Bears in 1920, and the Bears won five of them, giving Tesreau's team the best record against the Giants of any team they played more than once. The Bears were the Bacharachs' opening competition in the North after the spring training tour, and beat the Giants twice, 13–4 and 7–5, on May 2 at Dyckman. Errors were the bane of the Bacharachs in both games, particularly the second one, which they had led 5–2 at one time in what started out to be a fine matchup between Redding and Tesreau. The *Age* reporter singled out Grant Johnson, subbing at shortstop for an absent Lundy, as a chief culprit: "All through both games Home Run Johnson had shown that he was no shortstop," and at age 47 he wasn't able to handle the position at this high level of play, even though years ago he had been one of the best. Lundy, it turned out, had slipped away from the team after spring training to pursue a better opportunity, although Connor and Wilkins soon brought him back into the fold for the rest of the season.[57]

Lundy was back on May 9, fielding brilliantly at short in a doubleheader split with the Bears that crammed Dyckman with 7,500 fans.[58] In the first game Redding was supported by five runs in the third inning and four in the fourth and thereupon sent Treadwell in to coast to a 14–4 finish. Johnny Pugh, getting a lot of playing time early in the season, had four hits. Tesreau pitched the nightcap and gave up only six hits in an 8–4 win while Ryan was being raked for 13 hits. On the day, though, the Bacharachs were showing power—Bryant, Deas, Lundy and Rojo all homered.

The teams split again on May 23. Captain Redding had no other starters in mind than himself, and he scored a complete game five-hitter with nine strikeouts in the opener, which the Giants won, 4–2. The Cannonball pitched another compete game in the finale, but was victimized by Tesreau. Big Jeff didn't do the back-to-back starting routine, opting to pitch only in the second contest, but went the full 11 innings. Redding turned in ten, plus one batter in the bottom of the 11th. That was Tesreau. Big Jeff smacked a homer for a 4–3 Bears win.

It looked as if Giants-Bears doubleheaders might happen regularly at Dyckman, keeping the little ballpark full of excited fans. But Connor and Savage had their falling-out over money, and the teams don't seem to have played again until November 7 at the Oval. It was the very last game of the year for the Bacharachs, deep into the busy New York college and semi-pro football season. Still, 3,500 fans were reported to have seen another hotly contested game, which the Bears won, 5–4. Part of the Giants' team had drifted away to winter employment by then, but Connor recruited some very good replacements whose own teams had shut down for the season. Catcher Louis Santop and first baseman Toussaint Allen of Hilldale each hit home runs.

What was left of the Treat 'Em Roughs after Tesreau had picked over the roster gave the Bacharachs little trouble. The Giants swept all four games from Empey's team, 8–0 (the "Roughs" made eight errors) and 11–4 in an Ebbets Field doubleheader on May 16, 15–2 at Inlet Park on July 4 (the Giants had 19 hits, with four each for Lundy and Marcelle) and 8–0 the next day.

Heinie Zimmerman's Bronx Giants, who were the Bacharachs' main white competition for a short time early in the season, beat Connor and Redding's team twice in a May 30 Memorial Day doubleheader at their field, the Bronx Oval in the Hunts Point section of the borough. The Bronx team, allegedly aided by incompetent and/or biased umpiring, chased Ryan in the second inning and continued to score off Redding for a

10–4 first-game win. Two Bronx runs in the second game broke a 3–3 tie in the seventh.[59] Both teams went to Atlantic City the next day for the Bacharachs' home opener there. A reported 7,000 fans crowded into Inlet Park. The home team ripped off 12 hits, including triples by Means and Deas, to support Treadwell amply in a 15–6 win. The Bacharachs jumped right off to a three-run, first-inning lead in the second game and Ryan rationed out five hits over seven innings for a shortened 6–2 win. Back at the Bronx Oval for two final games on June 6, the Bacharachs won both, the opener 11–0 on a Redding shutout, and the second game a skin-tight 1–0 decision for Treadwell.

The Baltimore Dry Dock & Shipping Company had built 28 vessels for the government by the time its baseball time arrived in Atlantic City on July 12.[60] The Dry Docks had played and lost a single game to the Bacharachs in 1919. The game on the 12th kicked off three separate series in Atlantic City in the latter part of the 1920 season, plus another game at a neutral site, that totaled ten games. The Dry Docks, a member of the Delaware River Shipyard League, had several current or future major leaguers on the roster during the war, including eventual Hall of Fame pitcher Waite Hoyt, but the post-war big league membership was down to pitcher-manager Sam Frock, winner of 15 games over four seasons around 1910; Clarence "Lefty" Russell, a pitching phenom for Connie Mack's Athletics who had lost his mound career to a bad arm in 1912 and become a hard-hitting outfielder–first baseman, and Harvey Russell, no relation to Lefty, who had caught two years in the Federal League.

The Giants won six of the games, including an exciting opener. Baltimore went into the bottom of the ninth inning ahead 5–3, but a Bacharach rally produced three runs, the tying and winning ones on a long clutch double by pinch-hitter Rojo. Marcell had three hits and Bryant two on the 13th to back up Stringbean Williams for a 6–2 win. The Dry Docks came back in the last game of the series to win, 6–0.

The shipbuilders and the Giants met in Coatesville, Pennsylvania, on September 11, the Dry Docks running up an insurmountable 8–2 lead by the end of the fifth. Then it was back to Inlet Park for three games beginning September 13. Baltimore won again decisively that first day, 8–3. Although the Dry Docks had only one more hit than the Bacharachs, nine to eight, they "walloped the ball when it counted."[61] Pierce hit a ninth-inning home run for the Giants, when it in fact didn't count for much. Williams spun a no-hitter for six innings the next day, however, settling for a three-hit shutout. There was very little hitting on either side on the 15th, when Ryan gave up only four hits and Johnson of the Dry Docks five. The Bacharachs won, 2–1, when Marcell walked in the seventh inning, went all the way to third on a Brown sacrifice bunt when he spotted the base uncovered, and scored on a double by Lundy. Baltimore returned for three more games September 20–22, winning the first, 3–2, when Ryan and Frock, who was 37 years old, each hurled a three-hitter. The Bacharachs took the final two games, though, 6–1 on the 21st when Treadwell tossed his own three-hitter and 2–1 the next day when Redding threw a four-hitter.

Another Shipyard League team, Merchant Ship of Bristol, near Philadelphia, which had split two games with the Giants in 1919, lost a two-game series at Inlet Park on July 19–20. Williams four-hit Merchant Ship to win the first game, 4–1, and Lundy backed Ryan with three hits for a 5–1 win in the second. Bethlehem Steel, representing the company that had led the wartime industrial sports movement, split a pair of games with the Bacharachs on July 15–16, beating the Giants 5–3 and losing 5–4.

The team played a pair of white all-star teams in October after white organized baseball's season was over. A team called the All Leaguers fell on October 3 in Harrison, a small industrial city in Northern New Jersey with a ballpark left over from the Federal League of 1914 and 1915 which became a frequent site of semi-pro and black games. It's not clear just what league the All Leaguers represented, but they were no one special to Treadwell, who no-hit them in a 7–1 win.

The next day the Giants played the Babe Ruth All-Stars in Philadelphia. The team could have been called "Babe Ruth, a Handful of Big Leaguers and a Bunch of Underqualified Strangers." The *Philadelphia Inquirer* thought the bulk of the All-Stars roster might have been "composed of a lot of grammar school athletes—at least they performed like such."[62] The Bacharachs won, 9–4, but the game had a few highlights. It brought Redding and the New York Yankees' Carl Mays together again, but this was no repeat performance of their 14-inning duel in 1919. Mays was tagged for eight runs in six innings and gave way on the mound to Ruth himself, who pretty much stopped the Giants offense. The fans also got to see the Babe hit against the Cannonball, who got the slugger out the first two times but then surrendered a Ruthian homer.

The only traveling team included among the 134 Bacharach games discovered in 1920 was the House of David, which the Giants defeated in all three encounters. The first was at Shibe Park in Philadelphia on July 26, a 4–2 Bacharach win before 12,000 fans, Treadwell claiming a complete-game win. On the 28th the teams played at Inlet Park and Redding three-hit the Michigan visitors for a 3–1 win, allowing the *Atlantic City Daily Press*' sports headline writer to trot out the hackneyed phrase that followed the hirsute religious team wherever it went, whenever it lost—"B-Giants Trim Beards."[63]

The third game was played on August 28 at Ebbets Field, and the Bacharachs won decisively, 7–0. Sportswriters and fans at the games in Philadelphia and Atlantic City had remarked that the House of David pitcher, contrary to the sect's practice, was cleanshaven. It was explained that he was a fill-in for the sect's ace, Paul Mooney, who had a sore arm. But the Brooklyn fans on the 28th complained loudly when only about half of the Davids had beards and, to boot, they recognized the clean-shaven pitcher as Joe La Bate, a former Brooklyn high school hurler. The fans, who had paid regular Ebbets Field prices for their seats, became unruly, and half of them got up and left when the management promised them rain checks to future Dodgers games.[64]

The Cuban Winter League

Within two weeks of the final game against Tesreau's Bears, a team playing under the Bacharach Giants name arrived in Cuba to play in the winter league there. Cuban winter baseball was popular with both white major and minor league teams and the best black ones. The clubs visiting from the United States took on the island's best in what was called the American Series in November and early December. Then black players in some years would participate in the winter league itself. The winter league could only reliably count on two Cuban teams, Almendares and Havana, called the "eternal rivals." At least one other team was needed to keep things interesting, and in 1920–1921 the Bacharach Giants were going to be that club.

The Bacharach aggregation included only three actual Giants of the United States—Lundy, Redding and Ryan—plus Rojo, who was a Cuban native. But there were several men from other black teams, including the great Oscar Charleston and infielder Morton Clark of the ABCs; infielder Joe Hewitt of the Detroit Stars; outfielder Charlie Blackwell of the St. Louis Giants; catcher Louis Santop, first baseman Toussaint Allen and pitchers Willis Flournoy and Phil Cockrell of Hilldale; and infielder Recurvon Teran of the New York Cuban Stars. Edward B. Lamar, a veteran white organizer of American black teams, whose experience harked back to the late nineteenth century and included taking earlier teams to Cuba, was in charge. On paper this looked like a powerful team, "and it showed the wealthy status of the Cuban League when an entire team could be brought to Havana for a whole season."[65] But things fell apart. Key players shipped out back to the U.S. before the two-month schedule was over, and the team won only four of 15 games in the first half of the season. The second half of the Bacharachs' schedule was forfeited to Almendares and Havana.

Dick Lundy, an original Giant from Jacksonville, was a member of the team almost continually through 1928, starring at shortstop and often doubling as field manager. This photograph was taken for his passport in 1920 before a team of Giants and others set sail for Cuba to play in the Winter League.

Lundy returned to the U.S. in mid–December. Although in the future he would be a willing participant in Cuban winter ball, for now, at least, his opinion was that "Cuba may be all right for coacoanuts [sic], but not for ball players." By the New Year, Charleston, Blackwell, Cockrell, Hewitt, Ryan and Santop had all gone home. They were replaced by local talent, some of which was very good—catcher Victor Rodriguez of the Kansas City Monarchs and first baseman Augustin Parpetti of the Midwest's Cuban Stars, for example. But the situation in the three-team Cuban Winter League was summed up pithily by a *Chicago Defender* correspondent in late January: "The Almendares team beats the Havana Reds and the Bacharach Giants. The Reds beat the Giants and the Giants get beat every time they play."[66]

Chapter 4

Back Home in Atlantic City

1921

The Negro National League had finished its first year, and seven of the eight original teams were returning for 1921. Although Rube Foster had aggravated several of his colleagues with dictatorial actions as league president and his practice of taking ten percent of the gate for setting up games (as did his Caucasian enemy, Nat Strong), all the returning teams had made a profit and friendly relations reigned at the December 1920 league meeting. After replacement of the seventh-place Dayton Marcos with another Ohio team, the Columbus Buckeyes, expansion was in order. The league proper would continue to be composed of eight Midwest-based teams, but Foster had rounded up five new outfits to be associate members along with the Bacharachs.

As the Bacharachs had in 1920, each would pay a membership fee for the privilege of preferential scheduling with the actual league teams and protection against player raids from the league and associate members. Three of the teams, the Pittsburgh Keystones and the Tate Stars from Cleveland and a travelling All-Cuban squad that was a weaker version of the Midwestern and Eastern Cuban Stars, had only brief turns on the Negro major league stage. But the other two were longstanding successful Eastern clubs that would figure prominently in the black major leagues of the next decade or more.

One was the perennial Bacharach opponent from Baltimore, the Black Sox. The other was the Giants' natural rival, Hilldale, absent from their schedule in 1920 due to the restrictions imposed by Foster upon play with Ed Bolden's team. Bolden had decided that Hilldale would no longer keep itself out of league baseball and forked over his entry fee, now grown to $1,000 from the $500 that Connor and Wilkins had paid a year earlier. Bolden and Connor also settled their growing differences over player defections between their teams and appeared as the best of friends. Quincy Gilmore, the Kansas City Monarchs business manager, wrote a lengthy dispatch on the league meeting for the *Kansas City Sun* that included several tongue-in-cheek references to the goings-on. Connor and Bolden, he said, "arrived in the Convention City together, and not only stopped at the same hotel, but slept in the same bed. We just could not believe it, and to make sure, we had a flash light picture taken of the two big eastern magnets [sic] while they slept.... Negro base ball in the East is now due a great boon."[1]

The setup for 1921 propelled the Bacharachs into a higher level of play. Of 169 discovered games, 87 were against full or associate Negro National League clubs, the first time the Giants appear to have devoted half their schedule to the top-level black clubs. The Giants won 43 of these games and lost only 36 (with eight ties or no decisions), a respectable .544 winning percentage. Overall they went 103–56, with ten no-decisions, a .648 percentage.

Although the team was beset by injuries to its starters early in the year, the lineup from 1920 was kept largely intact. Marcell was back at third base, Handy at second and Lundy at shortstop . Marcell and Lundy tore things up offensively. Marcelle hit .322, led the team in runs scored with 76 and was third in RBI with 67. Lundy led all regulars at .329 and, despite missing some time with an injury, was among the runs scored and driven in leaders. Handy, in his last full season in high-level black ball, hit .285. Bill Pierce left the team for the Lincoln Giants, although he did make a doubleheader appearance in New York for the Bacharachs one Sunday in September. To replace him Connor signed Bill Pettus, a move described in the *Chicago Defender* as "a surprise to local fans as well as those throughout the country."[2] The real surprise, though, was that the peripatetic Pettus stuck around all season, hitting .310 and leading the team with eight home runs and 80 RBI. His playing with the Bacharachs all season long may have been a tribute

The 1921 Bacharach Giants, gathered around co-owner and business manager John W. Connor. Front row, left right, Julio Rojo, George Shively, Dennis Graham. Middle row, Oliver Marcell, Jimmy Fuller, Jim "Yank" Deas, Connor, John Harvey, Bill Handy (misidentified as "Williams") and Johnny Pugh. Back row, Benjamin Arnett Mitchell, Dick Redding, Maurice Busby, Gifford McDonald, Bill Pettus, Jesse Barbour, Elias "Country Brown" Bryant and Andrew "Stringbean" Williams (National Baseball Hall of Fame and Library, Cooperstown, New York).

to the relatively stringent enforcement of contracts in the new world of Negro baseball, although he presumably could have jumped to either the Lincoln or Brooklyn Royal Giants in New York City. They were not invited to be National League associates and so were not bound by any no-raiding agreements.

The three regular outfielders from 1920, George Shively (.309) in left, Jess Barbour (.293) in center and Country Brown Bryant (.307 and 75 RBI, second on the team) in right, all returned and provided a slugging outer defense to go with the productive infield. The team as a whole hit well, in fact, at a .287 mark that wasn't fattened on second-rate opponents, since the average against the league and top-level black independent teams was .275. The Giants averaged better than six runs per game in the discovered contests, better numbers than early in its existence when it was generally playing a lower quality of opponent.

Bryant spent a good bit of time at second base while Handy was absent for a couple of two-week stretches in June and September. The Bacharachs also got good fill-in production from a 24-year-old rookie, Richard Jackson, who also played second and a little outfield, hitting .247. Johnnie Pugh returned as a reserve outfielder and had a good year, batting .263. A new find, Dennis Graham, 24, was very useful. In his first season in high-level ball Graham, from Shaw University in North Carolina, was fast and often used as a defensive replacement. He usually took Bryant's place in right when Country played infield and pounded out a .325 average.

All three catchers, Yank Deas and Julio Rojo, the holdovers, and Ernest Gatewood, rejoining the team from the Brooklyn Royal Giants, also were pressed into service in both the infield and outfield. Rojo spent time at third, filling in for Marcell's move to short when Lundy missed more than a month with an injured ankle in May and June, and batted .262. Continuing to contribute key extra-base hits when games were close, he drove in 45 runs. Deas batted .237, creditable for him, and Gatewood hit .165.

Redding, who continued as field manager, was again the team's top pitcher. He made the most starts, 35, and added seven relief appearances. He won 24 games and lost 13, and had a 2.53 ERA, the best on the staff. His mates in the starting rotation, Red Ryan, Stringbean Williams and Harold Treadwell, all returned, but a plague of sore arms limited them to a total of 47 starts. Treadwell went 13–4, Ryan 12–5 and Williams 9–3.

The Bacharachs recruited a group of mostly journeymen pitchers to patch up the holes in the rotation as they occurred, although one of the substitutes was anything but ordinary in the long run. Jim "Nip" Winters was a tall, 22-year-old lefty who pitched sporadically for the Giants while also pitching and playing first base for Chappie Johnson's Norfolk Stars, a step down from major league blackball. He actually played against the Bacharachs in all four of their games with

Dick Redding's passport photograph in 1920 before a team of Giants and others set sail for Cuba to play in the Winter League.

Norfolk prior to his first recorded appearance with the Giants on July 10. Winters took the mound for the Bacharachs in 11 of the recorded games, eight of them starts, and had a 4–3 win-loss record. He stayed with the organization another year before going to Hilldale in 1923, where he became a star.

Henry "Long Tom" Richardson joined the club in early June, making 11 starts and six relief appearances with a 5–4 record and 3.12 ERA. A rookie this season, he went on to pitch until late in the 1930s, although usually with lesser quality teams. Benjamin Arnett Mitchell, who went by his middle name, was another product of the Jacksonville black baseball incubator. Born in 1895, he was of the same age as most of the core group of Duval Giants who had come north in 1916 to become the Bacharachs. He had played for the Jacksonville Red Caps, the city's entry in the Negro Southern League, a black minor league, in 1920, and this was his first year with a major team. A side-arming right-hander, Mitchell made seven starts and relieved six times, compiling a 4–4 record. Also on hand was a pair of lefties—Maurice Busby, who was a rookie at 29, made five starts, going 3–1, and Frank Harvey, finishing up his career at 34, started four times and went 1–1. The young Holsey Scranton Scriptus (Script) Lee, like Winters later a star with Hilldale, joined the Giants from Norfolk at the end of the season for some big series against both black and white major league opponents. He appeared in five games, four of them starts, but won only one of five decisions.

The Bacharachs began spring training in Jacksonville in late March and played their way north in April, taking on mostly Southern regional black teams along with a two-game series against the northward-bound St. Louis Giants of the NNL in early April and a four-game set with the Black Sox in Baltimore later that month. In the discovered games they handled the regional teams easily, winning 14 games from squads in Jacksonville; Brunswick, Georgia; Montgomery, Alabama; Atlanta; Greenville, South Carolina, and Richmond, losing only once to the Montgomery team, the Grey Sox, 7–3, on April 11.

The Bacharachs won, 7–1, over St. Louis in Montgomery on April 5 and played these other Giants to a 5–5 tie the next day. They took three of four from Baltimore, 9–3 and 14–4 in a doubleheader on April 24, and 4–1 the next day before losing, 4–1, on the 26th. They then went to Norfolk, Virginia, for two games with Chappie Johnson's Stars, winning 8–4 on the 28th and 16–8 on the 29th to finish out the Southern trip.

They beat Jeff Tesreau's Bears, 5–2 and 8–1, in a doubleheader at Dyckman Oval in New York on May 1, then began an extensive western swing against NNL competition that occupied the rest of the month. It didn't pay to open in Atlantic City too early—the tourists and seasonal black hotel and Boardwalk workers who swelled the local work force for the high season and provided part of the team's fan base didn't begin arriving in great numbers until Memorial Day.

By the time the Bacharachs hit the road, the injury jinx had begun to mess up manager Redding's plans. Lundy suffered his ankle injury during the second week in May, while Treadwell became ill and Harvey suffered a bout of arm soreness. The Giants went 9–9 against their big league competition out west and then dropped two in a row to Hilldale in Philadelphia as soon as they returned in early June. Williams and Redding were starting most games, and in addition Redding was throwing himself in as a late-inning reliever to no good end—he helped turn victory into defeat four times in late-inning one-run losses on the trip.

By the time the Giants returned home, injuries were healing and the pitching rotation had been augmented by the belated appearance of Red Ryan for the rest of the season. From June 5, the Ebbets Field opener, the found games have the Bacharachs playing at a near-.700 winning percentage, upping their percentage against Negro League-level teams to .544 and continuing their usual pattern of destroying the hopes of most of the regional semi-pro competition.

Reviving the strong rivalry with Hilldale made Ed Bolden's club a key part of the Bacharachs' schedule. The Giants played them 20 times in 1921, more than any other team except the Indianapolis ABCs, their opponent for 21 games. The Hilldale season series was predictably close—Hilldale won ten games and the Bacharachs nine, and there was a darkness-shortened no-decision. The first two games at Hilldale Park in Darby on June 2 and 4 didn't go well for the Bacharachs. Redding, still struggling to attain his usual high level of pitching, was knocked out in the fourth inning of an 8–6 loss on the 2nd that was brightened to some extent by home runs by Rojo and Bryant. Two days later Dick Whitworth shut the Giants out, 3–0.

Hilldale was the guest for the Ebbets Field opener on June 5. The Bacharachs continued to be down in the first game. Hilldale racked up 18 hits, 13 off of Redding in the first five innings, and won, 13–6. Redding was doing well, actually, until Louis Santop's three-run homer set off a nine-run fifth inning, after which he replaced himself on the mound. The second game was no masterpiece but Ryan, impeded by five Giant errors, including three by Bryant filling in at second base, held on for a five-inning, 6–5 victory.

The teams next met back at Ebbets Field a week later, and this time things clicked. The Bacharachs won the opener, 14–7. Redding and Phil Cockerell slogged their way through ugly complete games. There were a total of 28 hits, 15 by Hilldale, and 13 errors, eight by Hilldale. Despite another poor pitching performance, Redding starred at bat with a single and a homer. Matters calmed down in the nightcap when Williams tossed a seven-inning three-hitter and the Giants won, 5–1. In Atlantic City on June 20–21 the teams split a pair, Hilldale winning 4–3 the first day and the Giants 2–0 on the second as Ryan tossed a two-hit shutout. The next meeting was before a capacity crowd at Hilldale Park on June 25, when the home team knocked Ryan around with a five-run seventh inning and won, 11–6.

The Fourth of July fell on a Monday in 1921, allowing teams the golden opportunity to schedule a potentially lucrative Sunday doubleheader on the 3rd as well as the traditional holiday twin bill. The Bacharachs did this with an eye to attracting nearby Philadelphia fans, with Hilldale the visitors at Inlet Park for the Sunday games and their old semi-pro rivals, the Logan Squares, on the 4th. Hilldale and the Giants split on Sunday. The first game, with the veterans Redding and Whitworth pitching, seesawed back and forth. The Giants came from behind in the bottom of the eighth inning to tie the game and then pushed over the winner in the bottom of the tenth when Bryant singled in Marcell, who had singled and stolen second. The stands were packed and "persons with long green on the game—and there were many—felt like a fat man in a tight suit on a hot day," according to the *Daily Press*.³ Those inclined to bet on Hilldale should have recouped in the second game when Cockerell threw a five-hitter for a 5–1 win.

Bolden had leased a second Philadelphia area ballpark, across the Delaware River in Camden, to draw from a wider fan base, and the Bacharachs beat Hilldale there on July 6, 6–4. Lundy smacked a home run. The Giants also won back at Hilldale Park in Darby the next day, 5–1, thanks to a bases-loaded triple by Rojo in the top of the tenth inning.

The next meetings were four games in September, at Hilldale on September 22 and 24 and a doubleheader at Ebbets Field on the 25th. In the first game Marcell popped a three-run homer in the top of the first inning and the Bacharachs never trailed as Redding got a 4–3 win. Two days later Nip Winters threw a five-hitter, but one of the hits was a two-run homer by Hilldale third baseman Bill Francis and the Giants lost, 4–1. In the first game at Ebbets Field, Redding and Cockerell were on the mound again, as they had been three days before, and again Redding won, 4–3. Hilldale took the six-inning nightcap, though, 8–6.

There was no such thing as too much of the Bacharach-Hilldale competition, since fans always turned out to see them play. The teams met three more times in the very last days of the season. On October 22 at Hilldale, the Bacharachs knocked three home runs, by Bryant, Pettus and reserve outfielder Ralph Jefferson, but a tight game was blown open by Hilldale in the seventh inning when they scored four runs off Script Lee and won, 12–8. That was advertised as the last game of the season between the two teams, but a chance to play a doubleheader at Dyckman Oval on the 30th beckoned. Cockerell outpitched Winters in the first game, 7–2, and the autumn darkness descended in the third inning of what truly was the nightcap with Hilldale ahead, 2–1, but unable to get enough innings in to get a win.

The Bacharachs first took on the ABCs on the May Midwestern trip, splitting a four-game series in Indianapolis. They lost, 8–7, on May 21, losing in the bottom of the eighth when Redding, in one of his unfortunate relief appearances on the trip, gave up a run. The Cannonball picked himself to start the next day but lost, 5–3. The Bacharachs won on the 23rd and 24th, though, first by 9–3 and by 8–7 in the final game when poor ABC outfielding enabled the Bacharachs to score all their runs in the fifth, sixth and seventh innings.

Indianapolis came to Atlantic City in late July for four games. The Bacharachs won, 16–4, on July 24, when Winters threw a four-hitter and struck out 12 while the Giants pounded C. I. Taylor's pitching staff for 20 hits, and again on the 26th, 8–4. In between those games was a 3–2 thriller, the hero of which was ABCs star Biz Mackey, who tied the game with a home run in the ninth inning and then doubled and scored the winning run in the 11th. Redding and ABCs veteran Dizzy Dismukes each pitched a complete game. The final game on the 29th was tied 5–5 in the top of the ninth when "buckets of rain began to fall" and soon "the playing field resembled a lake."⁴

The ABCs were guests at one of the important Sunday Ebbets Field doubleheaders on July 31, and Redding hit his old form with a six-hitter as the Bacharachs won, 11–3. Rain washed out the second game at a 0–0 tie in the third. Even the *Brooklyn Daily Eagle*, whose crowd estimates for black games were usually on the conservative side, said 8,000 to 9,000 people attended, a great turnout by blackball standards.⁵

Then the two teams took off for Virginia, where they played five straight games in Norfolk and Richmond from August 1–5. The Bacharachs won the first and last of the set, and the ABCs took the middle three. On the 6th they split a doubleheader in Baltimore, winning the first game, 8–7, when Ben Taylor, still starring at first base for his brother's team, tried to stem a ninth-inning rally in relief but gave up a game-winning single to Lundy. The ABCs won the close nightcap, though, 6–5. Back in Atlantic City on August 7, the teams again split a doubleheader. The Bacharachs won, 3–1, another successful Redding outing against Dismukes, then lost, 7–1, when Dicta Johnson spun a six-hitter.

The action dropped south to Wilmington the next day and Indianapolis won, 3–0. The ABCs finally said goodbye on the 9th, losing 4–2 as Rojo broke a 2–2 tie with a pinch-hit single on Treadwell's behalf in the bottom of the eighth. Beginning on July 29 the two teams had played each other 14 times in 12 days, each winning six with two no-decisions. For the whole season's 21 games, the Bacharachs won ten and the ABCs nine, plus the two rained-out ties.

No recent season would have been complete without some hard-fought games against the Chicago American Giants. The recovered games show only one game between the two teams on the Bacharachs' early western swing, but it was a thriller. Redding had a three-hit shutout and a one-run lead going into the bottom of the ninth when Bingo DeMoss, the Chicago second baseman, doubled. DeMoss stole third and scored when Pettus dropped a throw at first on left fielder Jimmie Lyons' grounder. Lyons stole both second and third while Redding struck out the next batter, and then stole home, just beating Rojo's tag.

Chicago came east in October for 12 games, dominating the last month of the Bacharachs' schedule. The teams opened the month on October 1 in Harrison at the former Federal League park. Winters threw a shutout for a 4–0 win. The teams moved to the Dyckman Oval the next day and Dave Brown, a top Chicago starter, threw a two-hitter, besting Redding's six-hitter for a 6–3 American Giants win. Despite the fact that the sun goes down earlier and earlier as fall wears on and the ballparks didn't have lights, schedulers of blackball games usually tried to squeeze in a second game for the well-attended Sunday dates. This day, with a very large crowd by Dyckman standards, produced the usual outcome when a perfectly good 1–1 game had to be called off in the fourth inning.

Action resumed at the Bronx Oval in New York two Sundays later on October 16 with another doubleheader. Redding pitched for the Bacharachs, but his opposition was someone who usually just bedeviled other teams with his bat. Foster's starting rotation had been worked hard on this Eastern tour, and slugging outfielder Cristobal Torriente, who sometimes was a backup hurler, got the ball. He ate up four innings and was relieved by Dave Brown, who got credit for the 6–3 win. Becoming a pitcher didn't harm Torriente's hitting—he had an RBI single and a two-run homer. The hoped-for second game lasted three innings this time before it got dark with the Bacharachs ahead, 1–0.

The next day found the teams in Norfolk for the first of five games in the Virginia market. The Bacharachs won this first contest, 9–2. They had scored all their runs by the fourth inning and Red Ryan cruised to a five-hit win. Chicago won a doubleheader on

October 19, though, 8–5 and 6–5. It was on to Richmond on the 20th, where discord broke out on the field and the Bacharachs were awarded a forfeit. Chicago was ahead, 5–2, in the seventh when the Bacharachs scored three runs and had a man on third with two outs. These points were indisputable, but a long argument broke out as to whether the batter had touched second on his way to third, and the umpire declared him out on appeal. The question of who is where on the base paths when a retroactive out is declared is crucial in such a case, and all hell broke loose over whether the Bacharachs' fifth and tying run had crossed the plate before the batter missed second: "Then the fun began. The players argued back and forth as to whether two or three runs should be put up on the scoreboard. Representatives of each team implored the boy to put up either a '2' or a '3.' Nobody seemed to know which was right. Finally when Chicago refused to continue, the game was forfeited."[6] All appeared calm on the 21st when Chicago broke up a 1–1 tie with four runs in the fourth off of Phil Cockrell, who had joined the Bacharachs from Hilldale for these games, and finally won, 5–4.

The teams wound up their long set of games at Ebbets Field on October 23. Nip Winters and Chicago's Bill Holland each allowed only six hits, but the Bacharachs bunched theirs in the first inning to score three runs and win, 5–3. The Bacharachs were ahead in the attempted second game, 1–0, when it got dark in the third inning. Of the 13 games with Chicago, the Bacharachs won four (including the forfeit) and lost six, with three darkness-caused no-decisions. The American Giants were one of the few teams the Bacharachs couldn't master in 1921, but then few could—Foster's team had won its second straight Negro National League title.

The Giants played nine games with the Detroit Stars of the Negro National League, winning five of them. They split four games in Detroit on the May road trip. The first game on May 7 was the Stars' home opener at Mack Stadium. It was a definite hitters' day, although that was often the case at Mack, which recent research has shown to have had a minuscule right field (265 feet down the line, expanding to only 318 in right center).[7] Five pitchers were used by the two clubs and five home runs flew out. The Bacharachs hit three of them, by Lundy, Bryant and Handy. But all came with the bases empty, and the visitors were down, 9–8, in the top of the ninth inning with one out. They had the bases loaded, though, and Lundy launched a fly that might have tied things up, except right fielder Charley Hill threw Deas out trying to score from third to end the game.

The Bacharachs continued to hit the next day, with seven runs on ten hits that included a home run by Rojo and five doubles. Redding was on his game, allowing only three runs on seven hits. Mack Park's reputation as a place hitters loved had the batters smiling again on May 9 as Detroit won another 9–8 match. Pettus and Treadwell homered while Barber and Handy tripled, and the Giants went into the bottom of the ninth leading, 8–7. But the Stars beat up on Redding in one of his unfortunate relief appearances. Edgar Wesley, the Detroit first baseman, hit a home run to tie the game, and two singles and a sacrifice fly later the Stars had the winning run. The Giants evened the series at two-to-two by winning 7–4 on the 10th thanks to 13 hits, including homers by Lundy and Handy and a complete game from Stringbean Williams.

Detroit came to Atlantic City on September 1 and beat the Bacharachs, 7–5, before

2,000 fans at Inlet Park. It was an error-filled game that saw a total of nine miscues, five by the Giants. Redding sprinkled seven hits around the next day but shut off all Stars rallies and the Giants won, 3–0. A Sunday doubleheader up at Harrison on September 4 yielded a split. The Stars won the opener, 6–5, in 10 innings, and the Giants triumphed in the second game, 8–0, on a Redding three-hitter. The Stars returned to Inlet Park for a final game on September 10. Redding, who gave up five hits, and Bill Holland, who gave up only three, dueled mightily, but the Giants won, 1–0.

The other Negro National League team with whom the Bacharachs played several games was the Columbus, Ohio, Buckeyes. Nineteen twenty-one was the first of two seasons Columbus spent in big league black baseball, the other being 1935. Despite folding after this initial year Columbus played pretty well, finishing in sixth place in the eight-team league with a .444 winning percentage. The Buckeyes won four of 11 games with the Bacharachs, about as well as they did with their actual league competition. Their lineup wasn't star-studded, but they had some good players such as first baseman Bob Hudspeth and second baseman Clint Thomas. A key starter was former (and future) Bacharach Roy Roberts, who had left the non-league Brooklyn Royal Giants to play in the NNL. The star of the team was John Henry Lloyd, who had left the Royal Giants to play shortstop in Columbus and also manage.

The Bacharachs were the attraction in Columbus for the Memorial Day weekend. The Giants won the first game on Sunday, May 29, 7–4 in 13 innings. Redding and Roberts each went all the way. Two Giants hits and two Buckeyes errors produced three runs in the top of 13th to decide the game. Columbus pitcher George Britt pulled the old Dick Redding trick in the Monday holiday doubleheader, starting and winning both games, 8–7 and 7–6. Both were won in the bottom of the ninth inning, the second off Redding who, again, came up short in relief of Harvey. The Bacharachs bounced back the next day, though, winning 13–4 on the strength of 18 hits and six Columbus errors.

Seven games between the two teams in Atlantic City in mid–August produced five Bacharach wins. Redding and Roberts squared off again on August 10, and while Redding wasn't especially sharp, giving up 12 hits in eight innings, four Giants runs in the second inning and a couple more in the sixth stood up for a 6–5 win. Columbus won the next day, 5–2, when Willie Gisentaner threw a two-hitter. Ryan mastered the Buckeyes on the 12th, though, and the Giants won, 3–1.

The Giants and Buckeyes played three straight games, and tried to finish a fourth, on August 14–16. Redding was well over whatever had hampered his pitching earlier in the season—the *Daily Press* allowed as he had "dazzled his opponents in recent games with his sensational twirling."[8] He threw a five-hit shutout in the seven-inning first game of a Sunday doubleheader on the 14th. The Buckeyes were ahead 2–0 in the fifth inning of the second game, less than an inning away from claiming a victory, when rain washed out the contest. Ryan threw a four-hit shutout the next day and Dennis Graham got four hits as the Bacharachs won, 4–0.

Roy Roberts, getting a break from facing Redding, pitched against Richardson and got an 8–5 victory for Columbus on the 16th. Errors, which had hurt him against the Bacharachs back in May, helped him this time as the Buckeyes scored six times in the fifth inning. Pettus made two straight boots of ground balls, and Clint Thomas smashed a bases-loaded triple. The final contest was on August 19, when Ryan threw another fine game, a three-hitter, for a 3–2 Bacharach win.

The Bacharachs completed their season series with Baltimore with a 4–3 win on September 29, and also played a few games against two other league-level teams. The Cuban Stars of Havana, owned by Cuban baseball magnate Abel Linares, had been in the United States in the summer for years, and this season represented the city of Cincinnati in the NNL. The Bacharachs played one series with them there in mid-May, getting slaughtered, 17–2, in the opener and losing the second game, 6–5, before winning the third game, 2–1, behind Redding, who had a shutout until the bottom of the ninth. The Cleveland Tate Stars, another associate team, owned by Negro haberdasher George J. Tate, hosted the Giants in early May on the western trip. The Bacharachs beat them soundly, 17–2 and 9–2.

Interspersed with the sets of games with the American Giants in October were five games with an aggregation representing the Philadelphia Athletics. While the rosters of teams playing as major league clubs in the post-season could often be very low on actual big leaguers, these Athletics included a good representation of full- or part-time starters, including shortstop Chick Galloway, first baseman Ivy Griffin, catcher Gene Myatt, outfielder Paul Johnson and pitchers Eddie Rommel and Dave Keefe, along with several promising youngsters. On the other hand, this Athletics team was from the period after Connie Mack had sold off many of the stars from the A's early-1910s pennant winners. This roster had lost 100 games and finished dead last by 45 games. Nevertheless, the Athletics won four of the five games, which were played in cities and towns in New Jersey and Pennsylvania other than Philadelphia and Atlantic City. The only Bacharach win came in the last game on October 14, when the Giants unloaded on Rommel and aspiring minor leaguer Fred Heimach for 11 runs while Script Lee held the A's to four.

The only other category of team to give the Giants trouble in 1921 included the Pennsylvania clubs outside the Philadelphia area. These Bacharach opponents were usually among the groups of pushovers, but a particularly high-class bunch of opponents had been scheduled this season. The Parkesburg Iron Company west of Philadelphia sponsored a strong semi-pro team that sometimes played exhibitions against major league clubs. The PICOs played a pair of two-game series at Inlet Park, and there was a separate game at Parkesburg. Every game was a one- or two-run contest except the first one on June 14, which was a 13-inning, 2–2 tie. Each team had two wins. The American Chain Company team from York in central Pennsylvania was so good that two years later it actually entered a class B minor league. It visited Inlet in the middle of July and split a pair of one-run games with the Bacharachs. The Giants' 3–1 win featured a Treadwell three-hitter. A team from Tamaqua came to Atlantic City in June and beat the Bacharachs, 9–6.

All ten games found against New York City semi-pro teams in 1921 involved Tesreau's Bears. The Giants mostly played the Bears during Sunday doubleheaders at the Dyckman Oval, and the Giants won seven of the games. Many were slugfests—the Bacharachs averaged seven runs per game and the Bears nearly five.

The rest of the schedule was a walkover for the Bacharachs. Including the spring games, the team went 25–4 against regional black teams, losing more than once only to the traveling All Cubans team, which beat them twice in seven tries. Philadelphia area teams fared little better—the Bacharachs were 18–4–1 against them. The Giants won five of six from New Jersey teams outside Atlantic City, and the Philadelphia area and local competition dwindled to just one game, against a team fielded by the Ambassador Hotel. That game, on July 23, was a 5–1 Bacharach victory that in reality was totally one-sided. A pitching combination of Busby and Shively, the usual left fielder, held the hotel men to one hit, a bloop that fell among three fielders. Lundy, Pettus and Barbour sat out the game. Shortstop was manned in turn by Redding and Gatewood, a pitcher and catcher, and Treadwell, Richardson and Winters from the pitching staff took turns in the outfield.

1922

A major turn in the Bacharachs' fortunes was noted in the *New York Age* story of the October 16, 1921, battle with the Chicago American Giants, almost as a throwaway comment at the end. This particular game was played at the Bronx Oval, an athletic field on Southern Boulevard in the Hunts Point section of the South Bronx, five miles from downtown Harlem. Before the game, after the re-election aspirations of Mayor John F. Hylan were boosted, it was announced that the Giants were leaving Ebbets Field in 1922 for the Oval, an athletic field that had hosted baseball and other sports since at least the turn of the century. No reason was given, but it's likely that Ebbets Field didn't prove profitable enough for Connor and Wilkins. It was a 15-mile trolley ride from the team's base of fans in Harlem, and the Bronx site was much closer.

But when the 1922 season rolled around, the Bacharachs actually had the New York Oval, also a multi-purpose field best known for its professional soccer. It was on River Street in the Bronx, just across the East River from Harlem, and only a couple of blocks south of where the first Yankee Stadium would open two years later. This was the home of the New York Bacharach Giants because, for this one year, there were two Bacharach teams in the field, this one and a squad that revived Atlantic City as a Giants home base.

The event that apparently led to this division was the Pennsylvania Railroad's decision in 1921 to raze Atlantic City's Inlet Park in order to expand the adjacent rail yard. Wilkins was quoted that September to the effect that the Bacharachs were on the lookout for a new location at the Shore, but that the team wouldn't pull up stakes and leave.[9] He was correct, sort of, in that the version of the Bacharachs in which he had no financial interest would, after some initial difficulty, make Atlantic City once again a sole home base for the Giants. Wilkins' team, though, would never set foot in the city all season, and rarely played at all in Southern New Jersey, although they were sometimes spotted in Pennsylvania.

The void created by the loss of Inlet Park gave Tom Jackson and Henry Tucker the chance to get back into professional baseball. It was announced in mid-March that their aggregation, to be known as the "Original Bacharach Giants," would represent Atlantic City. Their news didn't exactly set the local sporting press's enthusiasm ablaze. *Daily Press* sports editor Louis Greenberg was pining for the Connor-Wilkins squad at the

Atlantic City's African American community had its own set of attractions, since it was barred from mixing with whites in many locations. The young women were riders on a parade float in 1922 sponsored by the black-owned Walls Bath House at "Chicken Bone Beach," the segregated beach. The men are Beach Patrol members assigned there (Atlantic City Heritage Collections, Atlantic City Free Public Library).

beginning of April, and didn't have much positive to say, or much at all, in fact, about the Jackson-Tucker "Originals." Greenberg, referring to the New York version as the "Bacharach X-Giants," (the team caps showed an x-shaped cross between a B and G) wrote that when Connor and Wilkins took over in 1919, "the squad was but a skeleton of the present wonder machine that has defeated every team it has met in a series with the exception of Rube Foster's American Giants," a statement that was mostly, if not entirely accurate. Those Giants, he continued, "have really been an asset to Atlantic City."[10]

On April 28 Greenberg noted that "no word has been heard as to what professional baseball will be played in Atlantic City with the exception of Tom Jackson and John Tucker's Bacharach Giants," who clearly weren't going to satisfy his sportswriter's desire to cover a top-flight team.[11] It's interesting, though, that the Connor-Wilkins group were being referred to as the X-Giants. The use of the X suffix in black baseball went all the way back to 1896 when the Cuban Giants, the first well-known professional black team, were challenged by a new outfit that lured away many of its best players. Coincidentally headed by E. B. Lamar Jr., the New York team's secretary in 1922, the new team had called itself the Cuban X-Giants to differentiate from the older team while still playing on the famous name.

With the Bacharachs split into two squads, the players from the 1921 roster had to pick sides, or just go somewhere else with more secure prospects. Four of the regulars—Marcell, Bryant, Shively and Rojo—along with most of the pitchers—Redding, Treadwell, Winters and Williams—opted to stay with the New York delegation. Lundy, who became the Atlantic City field manager, and Deas signed up with Jackson and Tucker. Jesse Barbour returned to the Midwest to play for the Detroit Stars. Pettus was on the move again, although not to become a migrating ballplayer. He joined the Richmond Giants, an apparent downward move except that he was now the team's manager. Bill Handy had been reported to be going to the Brooklyn Royal Giants, but didn't appear with them. In fact, his career at top-flight black ball had pretty much ended at age 33.

Both squads, therefore, had many holes to fill. Connor and Wilkins unquestionably pulled off the biggest coup, returning John Henry Lloyd to the Bacharach fold. Lloyd was at loose ends due to the demise of the Columbus Buckeyes team he had played for and managed. He not only filled the gaping shortstop hole left by Lundy, hitting .322 and leading the team in RBI (71, nearly one per game in which he's found), he also replaced Redding as the New Yorkers' field manager. First base was filled by the promising youngster Bob Hudspeth who, after an apprenticeship with C. I. Taylor's Indianapolis ABCs (where he had once beaten the Bacharachs with a late-inning pinch-hit), had distinguished himself in 1921 with Lloyd's Buckeyes. He was the regular first sacker for New York with a .317 average. Marcell was a strong presence at third base, as usual, and hit .299. Second base was primarily played by Dick Jackson, who had been an infield reserve the season before and this year hit a creditable .256.

Shively, at .271, was the regular in left field and Bryant, who hit .296, played right. Ramiro Ramirez, a stateside Cuban who been playing with East Coast Cuban teams since 1917, was picked up for center field. He hit .269. Warren Duncan, a rookie who hit .267, was the fourth outfielder. Julio Rojo did most of the catching, hitting .255. The pitching staff made the ordinarily weak pitcher's spot in the batting order extraordinary. Winters hit a scorching .333 and Treadwell was right behind him at .329. Williams hit .304 and Redding .227.

Redding went 10–10 in 25 discovered games, 19 of them starts, and was the only hurler with an ERA under 3.00 (at 2.59). Treadwell made 23 starts and ten relief appearances and was 13–10. Nip Winters didn't pitch as well as he hit this season, going 9–9 with a 4.39 ERA. Stringbean Williams, making only eight discovered starts, was 2–5. The staff was bolstered considerably by another former Columbus player who had come with manager Lloyd. Roy Roberts, an original Bacharach from Jacksonville, went 13–7 in 23 starts and four relief jobs.

The New Yorkers went 58–43, with four ties or no decisions in 105 discovered games, a .574 winning percentage. Most of their success, however, was against semi-pro white and lower-level black teams. This version of the Giants retained the Negro National League's associate membership, but went only 23–35–2 against that competition, a poor .397 winning percentage. The Giants had the disadvantage of playing few home games against Negro League–quality competition—few home games against anyone, actually, since of the 105 found games, only ten were at the New York Oval. Of eight top-level black opponents, only Hilldale played any games against the Bacharachs in New York.

The team set off on a Midwestern swing in May, playing at least 15 games in Cleveland, Detroit, Chicago and some other cities in Indiana that the ABCs were using as secondary sites. In July and August a 29-game tour against Negro National League teams and associate member squads took the Bacharachs all the way to Kansas City and St. Louis, as far west as a team could go in those days and still be in Negro League territory. In September and October there was a pair of series with Baltimore in the Black Sox's home territory.

Of the eight top opponents, the New York Bacharachs forged a winning record against only Hilldale. The teams played ten times, and the Bacharachs won six. The season series opened with a Decoration Day doubleheader at Hilldale Park in Darby. The Bacharachs hit the ball all over the place and won both games, although they were by no means showcase victories. The Giants broke a 6-6 tie in the opener with a run in the top of the sixth inning, then added three more in the seventh and one in the eighth. Hilldale came barreling back, though, and it took a good relief effort from Nip Winters to preserve an 11-10 victory. Marcell and Shively both homered, but Hilldale center fielder George Johnson hit two. The Bacharachs jumped all over Willis "Pud" Flournoy at the beginning of the second game for seven runs in the first two innings. Redding, although giving up 11 hits, including two more homers to Johnson, got a complete-game, 11-6 win.

Hilldale helped the Giants open their New York Oval season with a Sunday doubleheader on June 4 and took both games before an estimated 10,000 fans. Redding labored through a complete game in the opener, but gave up 18 hits. A 6-1 Bacharach lead began to evaporate in the sixth inning and Hilldale went on to an 8-6 win. Winters, Roberts and Treadwell shared the pitching in the nightcap and were awful. Hilldale smashed 21 hits and won, 19-4.

The teams played again on June 14-15, at the Hilldale alternate home site in Camden and then in Darby. Redding and Flournoy were again the starters in Camden, and the Giants scored two in the top of the eighth inning to tie the game at 3-3. Then heavy-hitting George Johnson, the first batter up in the bottom of the inning, hit one out of the park, and two subsequent runs ensured a 6-4 Hilldale win. The next day at Hilldale Park was better for the New Yorkers, especially Redding. The Cannonball relieved Treadwell in the fifth inning with a narrow Bacharach lead and pitched well the rest of the way as the Giants unloaded on Phil Cockrell and his relief, Connie Rector, to win, 9-5.

A pair of doubleheaders in early July completed the season series. The Giants won both ends of a Sunday doubleheader that was said to have again drawn 10,000 to the New York Oval on July 2. Redding in a complete game, then Winters, with Treadwell in relief, turned in good performances, Marcell got two hits in each game and Rojo three in the opener, and New York won, 4-2 and 4-3. On the Fourth of July the teams split at Hilldale Park. Hilldale won the first game, scoring four runs in the first inning and making that hold up for a 7-3 win. Each team got only seven hits in the second game, but the Bacharachs made theirs count for more and won, 5-1.

Given past difficulties with the Chicago American Giants, this year's result was a heartening five wins apiece in a pair of series in Chicago in May and August. The Bacharachs won three of the first five games, played in Chicago from May 20–24. The New York pitching was good—Treadwell threw a three-hitter in the opener for a 5–1 win, Redding won 7–3 on May 22, and Winters tossed a five-inning one-hitter on the 24th in a shortened game. Treadwell pitched a four-hitter on the 23rd, but lost to Juan Pardon's three-hitter, 2–0. The Chicago runs scored in the seventh inning when Rojo, trying to catch star outfielder Cristobal Torriente napping off third, fired the ball into left field instead. His errant throw was one of two instances when a Bacharach exhibited his least appealing on-field tendency. The other again involved Marcell's temperament, which got him tossed out of a 3–2, 11-inning loss on May 21. In the 11th inning the home plate umpire put a new ball in play. Marcell, apparently objecting to Chicago batters getting a new, white ball to hit with the game on the line, took it away from Winters on the mound, spit on it and bounced it in the dirt to destroy its pristine qualities before the ump gave him the heave-ho.[12]

Chicago turned the tables in the other five-game series from August 12–16, winning three games. Rojo was the hero in the first two contests, driving in the winning run in the 11th inning of a 5–4 win on August 12 with one of his three hits, and knocking in the winner the next day, too, in support of Treadwell's five-hitter. Chicago took the next two, 3–2 on the 14th, as Dave Brown edged Redding, and 7–3 on the 15th as Rojo, whose throwing from behind the plate was always adventurous, let in another run with a bad peg to third.

Chicago won the fifth and final game on August 16, one of the epic pitching battles in Negro Leagues history. Treadwell and American Giants starter Ed Rile had a dual shutout going through the top of the fifth when Brown relieved Rile. The double shutout went on, and on. New York couldn't get a runner near the plate. Chicago did twice, but Brown was thrown out by Bryant trying to score on a fly ball in the fifth, and left fielder Jimmy Lyons, who had won a game against the Bacharachs with a steal of home in 1921, failed to pull off the trick, this time in the 17th. Finally, in the bottom of the 20th inning, Torriente walked and was bunted to second. Dave Malarcher, the third baseman, drilled a single to score the Cuban star, and Chicago had a 1–0 win. Treadwell gave up only nine hits in his 19⅓ innings, struck out 12, walked seven and hit two batters.

Against the ABCs, the other major Negro League opponent, New York won five and lost six, with a tie. From May 11–17 on the first Western trip the teams played each other six times, the ABCs winning four games. The hitting outpaced the pitching on both sides—the ABCs averaged eight runs a game and the Bacharachs six. Treadwell got credit for both of the Giants wins, a five-hitter in the May 11 opening game between the two teams, which the Bacharachs won, 4–2, and a less artistic, 8–6 win in the second game of a May 14 doubleheader in which Bob Hudspeth produced three hits, one a triple, to boost the offense. Bacharach pitchers got ripped in two of the losses—Redding yielded 17 hits in the first game May 14 (although the ABCs won only 6–2), and Roberts persevered through an ugly 15-hit complete game on May 17 which the ABCs won, 17–8.

When the teams met in Indiana again July 23–27, the Bacharachs turned the tables, winning three and losing two, with a rain-shortened no-decision. Shively ripped three hits in two different games, but the Bacharach star of the series was Winters, who threw a no-hitter on July 26 in Kokomo. He struck out eight batters and walked four, giving up a sole unearned run when Duncan dropped a fly ball.

Otherwise, things did not go well against the other high-level black squads. The Cleveland Tate Stars was one of the lesser National League teams, but they whipped the Bacharachs soundly, once when the Giants were passing through Cleveland in late May and then in a five-game series in July. On May 29 the Bacharachs found themselves down 7–0 and couldn't catch up, losing 9–5. The July series in Cleveland featured several close games, but the Giants lost them all, getting solace only from a 6–6 tie on July 11. That possible solace was greatly diminished by the fact that New York had the potential winning run on base when it rained too hard in the top of the eighth inning to continue to play.

Likewise, the St. Louis Stars were spending the season in the NNL's second division, but they still took three of four when the Bacharachs journeyed there from July 30 through August 3. The Giants' win came in the first game of the series when Bryant singled in Marcell in the tenth inning for a 5–4 win. The Baltimore Black Sox, usually easy prey for a Bacharach team, won four of six in September and October. The Giants won one game each in a pair of three-game series. Hudspeth smacked four hits to lead a big offensive surge on September 16 to give Redding a 16–4 victory, and Redding tossed a six-hitter on October 22, riding another offense tide to a 10–1 win.

The Giants played the other two Negro National League first division teams besides Chicago and Indianapolis, with middling to poor results. They lost five of seven to the Detroit Stars on two Midwestern road trips, three straight at the end of May and another on July 16 before coming from behind, aided by a Hudspeth homer, for a 5–3 win on July 18. After losing by the same score the next day, they won the final game on the 20th, 9–4, cracking 15 hits, four by Marcell.

Given that the Kansas City Monarchs, like the ABCs, were in hot pursuit of the league's usual first place team, Chicago, the Giants' effort against them was commendable. New York won the first two of a five-game series at Kansas City, the farthest west any Bacharach team had ever travelled. In the August 5 opener, the first seven batters in the Giants order had at least one hit and the team won, 5–2. Winters threw a three-hitter and outpitched Bullet Joe Rogan, an eventual Hall of Famer, the next day for a 4–1 win. But the Monarchs took the rest of the series, 3–2, 11–0 and 4–3.

In the games against lesser competition, the Bacharachs had their way with all varieties of teams, running up an .814 winning percentage (35–8–2). The regional black squads contributed greatly to the Giants' dominance, as New York defeated them ten times with a single loss and one no-decision. Almost all of these discovered games were during the Giants' spring training in New Orleans, where they beat the Crescent Stars, the leading local black team, eight straight times, outscoring the Crescents, 65 to 33. The other discovered games were a 4–3 win over the Richmond Giants at Hilldale's park in Darby on August 19, a split of a doubleheader in Richmond on September 23, and a game at the New York Oval on June 11 when a merciful rain in the third inning halted a demolition of the Madison Stars of Philadelphia with the score already 7–1.

The New York Bacharachs went a combined 12–0 against semi-pro teams from towns in Pennsylvania, New Jersey and New York from outside New York City and Philadelphia.

These teams should have been pretty good—they represented companies that prided themselves on maintaining top-flight baseball programs (J. N. Barber of Trenton; Eagle Silk of Shamokin, Pennsylvania, and American Chain of York), good-sized cities (Hoboken and Scranton), smaller towns well-known for stocking their teams with good players from nearby cities (old rival Millville and the Huntingdon, Pennsylvania, Yellow Dogs), and the Ocean City Collegians from the resort town next door to Atlantic City (the closest the New York squad came to playing there). The Bacharachs beat them all, although many of the games were close.

Things were more difficult, although not extremely so, with the big city teams. Philadelphia area fans mostly saw the "Original" Bacharachs from Atlantic City, and the New York Bacharachs made few trips there. When they came to Philadelphia, they played only three of the best teams, with whom they went 3–3–1. Chester, always tough, continued to be so, winning two of the three found games, 7–5 on September 2, and a wild 11–10 contest two days later. Lloyd had tied that game at 10–10 with a homer in the top of the ninth inning, but two men well-known as Bacharach opponents from prior years combined for the winning run in the last of the inning. Sid Agnew reached based on an error and stole third, and Ad "Doc" Swigler drove him in with a single. The previous game on June 17 had also been tumultuous. Chester first chased starter Nate Jackson, and then Roy Roberts, from the mound in the second inning with six runs, and scored three more off Treadwell to lead 9–5 after four. But the Giants came back with three runs in the fifth and four in the eighth, and Treadwell hung on for a 12–10 victory.

An attempt to host South Philadelphia for the second game of a Sunday doubleheader at the New York Oval was rained out in the second inning with the visitors ahead, 3–0, but the Giants won a rematch on June 25, 6–2, as Marcell got four hits. The other game with a Philadelphia opponent was June 13, when the Nativity Catholic Club, on its way to becoming one of the pre-eminent semi-pro outfits in the city, won 7–4.

In New York the main opponent was the Bronx Giants. These Bacharachs took three of four from them in a pair of late-season doubleheaders, winning twice on September 24—4–0 when Redding threw a four-hitter and 11–8 in an untidy nightcap—then splitting on October 8, losing, 10–2, and winning, 5–2. The Giants played East New York twice. They won 4–0 in ten innings on June 24 when Redding five-hit the white team and Duncan and Marcell broke up a double shutout, each with a two-run hit. The Giants then lost, 8–7, in a very late game on October 28. Another Bronx team, the Yanks, were easily defeated on June 18, 11–0, when Roberts threw a five-hitter. September 10 featured a doubleheader win over a crack New York team, the Farmers, from that section of Queens, 14–3 and 7–2, as Williams and Roberts cruised to easy wins and the team had a total of 28 hits, six by Lloyd. This was the first time a Bacharach team played Farmers, but the rivalry would continue throughout the decade.

The only semi-pro team, other than Chester and Nativity, to achieve a winning record over the New York Bacharachs was the Canton, Ohio, Terminals, a railroad-connected team in that transportation hub city which took two of three from the Giants on July 13–15 when the team was on its way from Cleveland to Detroit on its mid-season trip to the Midwest.

The New York Bacharachs played a white major league all-star team twice, with excellent results, on October 14–15. The team was billed as the World Series Stars. It actually had a few standouts on its roster, primarily two pitchers from the Series-winning New York Giants and the team's shortstop and captain, Dave Bancroft. The rest of the squad was reportedly made up of area semi-pros, although Hank Gowdy, the veteran Boston Braves catcher, was the receiver for these two weekend games. Rosy Ryan had won 17 games as a swingman for the Giants' staff and had gotten a win in relief in the Series. He pitched against Treadwell in the first game on a Saturday in Dover, New Jersey, which the Bacharachs won, 5–4, in the bottom of the ninth. The Sunday game was in Harrison, a familiar neutral spot for the Bacharachs, and they won, 3–1, as Redding edged out Jack Scott, also a winner in the Series.

While the New York Bacharachs were able to take advantage of their Negro National League associate status to keep up rivalries with major black teams, the squad, seldom playing at its supposed home at the New York Oval, was pretty much a road team in 1922. Worse, the Original Bacharach Giants looked to be completely homeless for a time before the season began. With Inlet Park gone and summertime baseball continuing to be very active in Atlantic City, there was a serious shortage of places to play. At the Shore, the Giants could sometimes get the use of what was known as National Stadium at the city airport. Maps of the day show the airport property, which was between the Black Horse Pike, the southern route out of the city, and the system of bays between the island and the mainland, developed as more of a sports center than an airdrome, with tennis courts, grandstands and playing fields of several types.[13]

The Original Bacharachs opened their season on the road, then established themselves as the "adopted" home team of Wilmington, Delaware, 80 miles from Atlantic City but, more importantly, an easy 35-mile trip from Philadelphia, home of many of their opponents. In addition to a good location, Wilmington had an underutilized ballpark ready for the Bacharachs. The Harlan & Hollingsworth shipbuilding plant, owned by Bethlehem Steel at the onset of World War I, was among the yards fielding baseball teams in the highly competitive Delaware River Shipyard League. As was the case with the other defense industry teams, Harlan's roster included several professional players choosing work in a defense plant as an option to military duty. In 1918 Harlan landed "Shoeless Joe" Jackson of the Chicago White Sox, then regarded as one of the best hitters in the game. His reputation hadn't yet become perpetually darkened by being accused as one of the eight "Black Sox" who threw the 1919 World Series. Harlan turned out cargo ships and tankers during the war but, as was the case with the other big yards, both business and the availability of professional athletes declined thereafter. When shipyard teams were at their strongest, the company had built Harlan Field, a modern ballpark next to its plant which remained available to semi-pro and traveling black teams. In 1922 the Original Bacharachs booked it for 37 games, far more than they played at any other venue.

So the irony of the 1922 season was that there were two Bacharach Giants squads in the field, both of whom could trace their lineage to the team put together to honor Atlantic City Mayor Harry Bacharach, but the ball fans at the Shore never got to see one of them play at all and rarely caught sight of the other.

Dick Lundy and Yank Deas alone represented the Bacharachs of 1921 on this 1922 "original" team. Lundy had better years at bat, his average this season down to .276. But he was so well known as the face of the team it was often referred to as "Dick Lundy's Bacharach Giants." Deas, on the other hand, had one of his best years at the plate, hitting .266 while sharing the catching duties with a couple of others. The decisions of the bulk of the Bacharachs to go with the New York contingent opened up many opportunities, with 32 players getting into at least one game for the team. Some of the openings were offered to former Bacharach regulars. Chance Cummings, who had been playing a limited role with Hilldale, stuck behind Toussaint Allen at first base and Bunny Downs at second, returned as the regular first baseman. He was his old self, hitting .278, bunting, daring the opposition on the base paths and fielding smoothly at first. Frank Crockett, who hadn't played in high-level blackball since 1918, played outfield and hit .214.

Other openings were won by newcomers who not only played superbly in 1922 but stuck around the Negro Leagues for years thereafter. Ambrose Reid, a 23-year-old Georgian who had been a blacksmith before becoming a ballplayer, earned a full-time outfield spot, batting .292. He remained a Bacharach Giant for the rest of the decade. Sam Streeter, a short, stocky left-handed spitballer from Alabama, had broken in with a black team in Montgomery in 1920 at age 19 and had moved up to the Chicago American Giants for a short time in 1921, then joined Lundy's team to become a regular starter. This was his only season with the Bacharachs, one in which he was the staff leader with a 13–6 won-lost record and a 2.56 ERA. He went on to pitch in the Negro Leagues through 1936, and was one of the starting pitchers in the first Negro League All-Star Game in 1933.

The regular outfield that included Reid and Crockett was rounded out by Berdell Young, himself beginning a career that lasted most of the rest of the 1920s and included more years with the Bacharachs. Generally slotted down in the lineup, he nonetheless hit .291. Third base was turned over to Jack Davis, another rookie in black big-time baseball, whose .238 average nearly duplicated the team average of .237. Second base was up for grabs much of the season, but the two who played it most were Milton Lewis, a former Madison Star and Norfolk Star stepping up a notch to stick around as a utility man and sometimes starter with the Bacharachs for several more years, and Lewis Means, who had been a reserve with the team in 1920. Milton Lewis, who wound up with the longer career, hit .241 and began to show a little of the long ball power for which he became well known. Means batted .156. Willie Jones, who backed up Deas as catcher and also took some turns at second base, was one of the smallest catchers in black baseball. But he was a good fielder and adequate enough hitter (although he hit only .216 in 1922), to allow him to log 15 years in high-level black baseball.[14] He was a regular behind the plate for the Giants for most of the rest of the decade.

The pitching staff had to be completely reconstructed, since the entire 1921 starting rotation had chosen to go with the New York Bacharachs. Streeter was the main find, but two others without much in the way of previous or subsequent credentials were of great help to manager Lundy. Nate Johnson broke into big league blackball in 1922 with Atlantic City and dropped out two years later. But he went 11–6, with an excellent 2.11 ERA, as the most effective starter after Streeter. Joe "Jodie" Wheeler had come from the Baltimore Black Sox, another independent team outside the reach of the National League's player controls, to go 7–8. This was his only year with the Bacharachs—he returned to Baltimore in 1923 and played with a succession of lesser teams for six more years. Twelve other pitchers appeared in at least one game, but besides Charley Malloy, who made eight starts with a 3–2 record, the others came and went quickly.

Lundy's Bacharachs played .583 ball in 87 discovered games, winning 49 and losing 35 with three ties or no decisions. They did better than their New York brethren against Negro League–quality teams, although in a much smaller number of games, winning six of 13 decisions. Primarily they played lower-level competition than that which New York regularly faced, mostly taking on Philadelphia, New Jersey and Delaware semi-pro teams.

They did restore the Bacharach tradition of playing, and beating, Atlantic City teams. These Bacharachs, after playing in Wilmington and elsewhere in May and early June, made a much-ballyhooed "home opener" on June 21 with a doubleheader against the leading local white team, the Melrose Athletic Club. There were supposed to have been single games on June 20 and 21 at the airport stadium, but "Ole Jupiter Pluvius interfered with the attraction" on the first day—it rained, in other words—and both games were played the next day.[15]

Melrose was pretty well stocked. The perennial regional star Ike Nelson, who had played for the player-strapped Bacharachs at the end of 1918, was in left field and Walter Heckle, who had done the same, was at shortstop. Charley "Red" Dooin, the former Philadelphia Phillie who was now the Atlantic City High School coach, was in the outfield for the first game and at catcher, his old position, for the second. The Carmack brothers, well-known local stars, were there and some effort had gone into recruiting pitchers. Stanley Poploski, a veteran of Philadelphia semi-pro ball who had looks from major league teams in the past, was to pitch the first game, and Dick Lloyd, who had once pitched for the nearby Ocean City Collegians, would go in the second.

It was all to no avail. The Bacharach Giants shut out Melrose twice, 8–0 and 3–0. Nate Johnson gave up only three hits and Wheeler had a no-hitter going until the seventh and last inning of the second game when Dooin finally singled for Melrose. Crockett got three hits in the first game and Lewis three in the second, including a triple. Cummings got three over both games.

Very late in the season, on October 10, the Bacharachs beat the Kentucky Reds, 8–5, at the airport stadium. The Reds were not from Kentucky, the state, but from Kentucky Avenue, one of Atlantic City's state-named streets familiar later to Monopoly board game players. The northern end of Kentucky, like that portion of many of the other streets named after states, lay within the Northside African American neighborhood, and this team was black. Its pitcher was Emerson Gray, a local police officer who had pitched in the old Colored League, and occasionally for the Bacharachs and other higher-level black teams in earlier seasons. Even with Lundy, Cummings and Crockett sidelined with injuries, the Giants were able to run up a 6–0 lead after three innings and win, 8–5, in a seven-inning game.

The Original Bacharachs continued to mine the rich vein of semi-pro ball in the Philadelphia area, maintaining ties with several traditional opponents and adding some new ones. Twenty-three games with Philadelphia-area teams have been found, of which the Bacharachs won 12 and lost ten, with a tie. Four-game season series have been found with J & J Dobson, the textile maker's team; the South Philadelphia Hebrew Association

(SPHAs); and the Stenton Field Club, a long-time cricket and golf organization also playing baseball.

The Giants took a Sunday doubleheader from Dobson on July 30, two of the few games actually played in Atlantic City. The day belonged to the Bacharach pitchers, mostly Sam Streeter, who struck out ten and took a shutout into the ninth inning of the first game, a 4–3 win. He also pitched a scoreless ninth inning in the second game to save a 3–2 win for Wheeler. The two pitched a combined five-hitter. The two teams also played on June 19–20, first in Wilmington, where Malloy threw a three-hitter and the Giants had 19 hits for a 12–1 win, then in Philadelphia, where Lundy for some reason gave the ball to Deas, who rarely pitched, and who was knocked out in the second inning of a 13–3 defeat.

Herman "Chickie" Passon, mostly known as a basketball star, won two games for the SPHAs, a five-hitter on June 26 and a three-hitter on August 8. The Bacharachs won only one of the four games, when Nate Johnson threw his own five-hitter on June 30 for a 6–2 win at Harlan Field. The Giants had more success against Stenton, from the Mount Airy section of Philadelphia, winning a pair of games, 3–2 on July 7 and 4–1 on July 10, tying 4–4 when darkness fell in the seventh inning on July 24 and losing 2–0 on July 25.

Nativity was the team sponsored by a large Catholic parish in the Port Richmond section of Philadelphia. The parish team swept three games from the Giants, including a 6–4 win on September 16 in which the winning pitcher was right hander Harry "Socks" Seibold, a former major leaguer. The usually tough Chester team fell twice at home in a July 4 doubleheader, 8–4 and 11–1, and beat the Giants, 10–6, in Wilmington on July 28. The Bacharachs scored single-game victories over Germantown, Fleischer Yarn, Rockdale, the Sun Oil Company refinery and the Logan Athletic Club.

Outside the Philadelphia area the Bacharachs were 9–3–1 against other Pennsylvania teams, mostly local town outfits. There were some exceptions to that rule, the main one being the tough American Chain Co. team from York, which beat them twice. On May 26 Tom "Lefty" George, who at age 35 wasn't even close to the end of his pitching career (he was a regular in the minors until turning 46 and last appeared in a professional lineup at 57 during World War II), beat the Giants, 7–4. Six days later he won in relief, knocking in the winning runs with a double. The only other Pennsylvania teams the Bacharachs played more than once were the Cressona Tigers, from the heart of the state's anthracite coal mining territory northwest of Philadelphia, who were swept in a three-game series in May, and the Spring City–Royersford team from those adjacent towns, defeated twice plus a 4–4 tie. That game would also have been a Bacharach win had not a Spring City runner, sent to steal second, gone all the way around to score when the batter singled in the bottom of the ninth, just as it got too dark to play on. Individual games produced wins over the Pennsylvania Railroad team from Williamsport, Pottstown, Bristol and Bloomsburg, and a loss to Williamstown.

There are six found games with New Jersey teams: a split with American Bridge from Trenton and two doubleheaders with the Caven Point squad from Jersey City, a split on July 9 and a sweep on October 1. The Bacharachs' location in Wilmington put the Rex Athletic Club from Washington, D.C., within reach, and Johnson four-hit them on May 30 as part of a 9–3 Giants win. Wilmington was also the location for one of two games against a traveling Japanese All-Star team, which lost there, 12–4, on August 24 and later on September 14 in Baltimore by a 4–2 score. The visitors were said to be "students of the Imperial Japanese University" in Tokyo, although as the history of these types of teams shows, the farther the squad was from home, the more suspicious the high-flown claims of its origins.[16]

The Bacharach season ended at Harlan Field on October 14 when a white all-star team, the Combined Stars, featuring some familiar major league faces, including the Athletics' Eddie Rommel and the Phillies' Stan Baumgartner, defeated the Giants, 4–3.

These Bacharachs didn't make it to New York City very often. But unlike John Connor's New York version, this team had a positive relationship with the Nat Strong baseball empire, which brought them a prize opponent. The Bushwicks were regarded as one of the best, if not the best, semi-pro team in New York. Primarily owned by baseball entrepreneur Max Rosner, but with Strong as an influential investor, the team was located in Brooklyn's Bushwick neighborhood and played at Dexter Park, located on the Brooklyn-Queens borough boundary. Rosner owned the park and regularly filled it to capacity for Sunday doubleheaders against other top semi-pro teams and the better black teams either based in or visiting the East. The Bushwicks, as was the case with the Farmers and other top-flight semi-pro teams in New York, rarely if ever travelled. They played mostly Sunday doubleheaders, and if you wanted to take them on you went to their field, to be well-rewarded financially from the visitor's share of a healthy attendance that might be the biggest crowd you played before all season long.

Lundy's Bacharach Giants played two doubleheaders at Dexter in 1922, splitting them both. On August 13 they appeared before an estimated 9,000 fans. They lost, 14–6, in the opener but won the second game, 5–2, as Streeter outpitched Jeff Tesreau and Lundy had four hits. On September 3 Johnson struck out nine and four-hit the Bushwicks in the first game, 9–0. Tesreau, his Bears a thing of the past, pitched the Bushwicks to a 7–5 victory in the nightcap. On June 18 the Bacharach Giants beat the Bronx Giants, another familiar set of faces, 5–2, at the Bronx Oval.

The only common Negro League–quality opponent the Original Bacharachs shared with their New York counterparts was Hilldale, where such a long-standing bond existed that the Philadelphia team's affiliation with the Negro National League didn't prevent Ed Bolden from scheduling both teams. On the other hand, the lack of any obligation to Rube Foster and the National League opened the door again for a Bacharach team to play the New York City teams—the Brooklyn Royal Giants, the Cuban Stars East and the Lincoln Giants—connected to Nat Strong's booking operation and thus unacceptable opponents for the New York Bacharachs.

The Black Sox, who had dominated the Connor-Wilkins Giants in 1922, were a surprisingly easy opponent for Lundy's team, which defeated them four games out of six, including a five-hitter tossed by Stringbean Williams in the second game of a May 14 doubleheader, which the Bacharachs won, 5–2. It was Williams' only known appearance for the Atlantic City squad in 1922, although he pitched in several games for the New York team. Another game against the Black Sox, a 12-inning, 5–4 win in Wilmington on July 20, featured another fracas involving Yank Deas. He and Baltimore star Jud Wilson got into a scuffle at home plate. Wilson had overrun third base, was trapped off it and barreled into a tag by Deas. Wilson "knocked Yank down and fell on him at the plate. Several of the players on both teams got into the argument, and only the intervention of the police stopped the trouble."[17] The other Bacharach wins happened the next day, 6-3, and on August 31, 8-1. The Sox took the second game of the May 14 doubleheader, 7-3, and won 2-1 on September 1 when Talmadge Richardson threw a two-hitter.

Competition with Hilldale was limited to a two-game series on July 27-28. Sam Streeter, backed by three hits from Lundy and two each from Young and Deas, threw a four-hitter for an 8-4 win on the 27th. Nate Johnson was on a course to do even better the next day. He brought a no-hitter into the seventh inning when he experienced quite possibly his worst inning ever. Toussaint Allen, the Hilldale first baseman, broke up both the no-hitter and shutout with a triple, and a series of walks, hits, bunts and errors allowed eight runs to score as Hilldale won, 9-3.

These Bacharachs lost four of five discovered games against the New York City teams. The Brooklyn Royal Giants beat them, 6-2, on May 27. The Cuban Stars won, 9-8, on September 19 in Bridgeton, New Jersey, scoring the winning run in the bottom of the seventh, and last, inning. The Giants beat them ten days later, 6-1, in a five-inning game called by darkness. The Lincoln Giants took a doubleheader at their Catholic Protectory Oval in the Bronx on September 24 before 10,000 fans. They won the first game off Streeter, 3-2, with a run in the last of the ninth inning, and scored five runs in the third inning of the nightcap, including a home run by Wabishaw "Doc" Wiley, a sometime Bacharach in the past, to win, 6-2.

The Bacharachs' temporary move south to Delaware made the Richmond Giants a more accessible opponent, and eight games between the two clubs, all in Richmond or Wilmington, have been found. Bill Pettus, the former Bacharach first baseman, was still running the Richmond club, which won five of the games. Richmond won two of three in the first series at their Island Park May 8-10. Richardson, who hadn't yet moved up to Baltimore, threw a five-hitter against the Bacharachs on the 10th, gaining the distinction of having beaten them in 1922 pitching for two different teams. Richmond won again by 2-1 on June 28 in Wilmington when Pettus was trapped between third and home. Wheeler tagged him, but dropped the ball in the process, and Pettus ran home with the winning run. A four-game series back in Richmond from August 3-5 resulted in Bacharach wins the first two days and a Richmond sweep of a doubleheader on the 5th.

Richmond was a tough opponent for the Bacharachs, but was also a team that provided the Giants with several players from its roster. In this season alone the Bacharachs picked up two utility infielders, Tom Finley and Carl Perry, from the Richmond lineup. In 1923 they would take two pitchers, Arthur "Rats" Henderson and John Harper, who became the mainstays of the Bacharach starting staff. There's no record of how these transaction were handled, but Richmond, which belonged to no league, had no protection against roster raiding. Simple good will and the desire to keep up good relations with a regular opponent may have moved Jackson and Tucker to have paid for the services of their recruits. The other regional black team the Giants played, and defeated, was the Lincoln University varsity, a 10-3 victim on May 29.

Among the people attracted to the Giants in Wilmington were Joe Condon and Pete Cassidy, respectively the director and field manager of the city's best semi-pro team, sponsored by a major Catholic church, St. Thomas the Apostle. St. Thomas, or the "Saints," as the local papers called them, agreed to a best-of-five series with the Bacharachs, all of the games to be played at Harlan Field, for "the so-called championship of Wilmington."

The teams began to battle each other on July 8, but also had to battle a stretch of rainy weather. That first game was washed out in the bottom of the sixth inning, the Bacharachs' half of the inning, with victory within the Giants' damp grasp. They had started to rebound from a 5–2 deficit, had scored one run and had the bases loaded with two out when home plate umpire Josh Henry called the game off. "There was much wailing and gnashing of teeth among the men of Bacharach when 'Josh' Henry called things off, but 'Josh' had been soaked enough for one afternoon and thought he would duck before the downpour became violent—which it did," the *Wilmington Sunday Morning Star* reported.[18]

The competition resumed on July 22. The Bacharachs jumped out to a 3–0 lead, and it rained again, stopping play after four innings, one short of an official game. St. Thomas, who had a couple of injured starters, replaced them for the next game on August 7 with Sid Agnew, a long-time Bacharach rival, and Jake Munch from the crack Chester team. But the star of the Saints' 2–0 win was hometown pitcher Hawk Hayes, who gave up eight hits and no runs, besting Nate Johnson, who also pitched a complete game. On August 14, yet another soggy day, both Johnson and Nitchie of St. Thomas yielded just five hits each, but the Bacharachs also made five errors and lost, 6–3. The sweep ended the series, but neither side wanted to quit. The crowds for the first two games were reported as 2,000 and 2,500, despite the rain, and while estimates weren't available for the second pair of games, it appeared attendance was also healthy at them.

The Bacharachs challenged the Saints to a second series and spiced things up by offering a $1,000 side bet (the equivalent of nearly $14,000 today), a deal St. Thomas readily accepted. Maybe the lure of the money invigorated the Giants, or maybe they were glad it had stopped raining, but they turned things around immediately and won this second series, three games to one. Streeter kicked things off with a four-hit shutout on August 19, and there was just enough offense, mainly two doubles and a single by Jack Davis, to bring about a 2–0 win. Streeter was back on the mound two days later and was scored on in only one inning while a Deas home run paced a four-run second inning for a 6–3 win.

The Saints won, 2–0, on August 28, a game in which the winning pitcher, Manlove, and the combination of Wheeler and Lewis gave up only four hits each. Before 3,000 fans on September 2, the Bacharachs clinched this second "money" series with an 11–7 victory, roaring from behind with four runs in each of the seventh and eighth innings. Streeter was the winning pitcher in relief, giving him all three victories in the series.

But they still weren't finished. Labor Day, September 4, was right around the corner and the Giants and Saints celebrated with a split doubleheader. The games were divided between morning and afternoon, and so were the victories. St. Thomas ran up a 6–0 lead by the fifth inning of the morning game and won, 8–2. Streeter mastered the Saints again in the six-inning second game, allowing only three base runners, one each on a hit, a walk and an error. Crockett's two hits, one an RBI double, led a four-run Bacharach offense. The final match of this long season series was played on September 18, and St. Thomas won, 8–2, in a game described as "replete with errors, both of omission and commission on the part of both nines."[19] St. Thomas won the entire series (or string of three series, in fact), winning six games to the Bacharachs' four, with the early rain-soaked no-decision thrown in.

Given the ability of the New York squad to fill its schedule easily with the best black teams, the propensity for most of the best players from before the split to choose that team over the Atlantic City version and the wealth of Wilkins and Connor contrasted to the scuffling Jackson and Tucker had to do even to find a ball field to call home, one would have expected the Jersey Shore version to fold up at some point, leaving the team's name and legacy to the New Yorkers. But in fact, as of the end of October the Connor-Wilkins team would never play again. The scrabbling Atlantic City bunch would go on to carry the Bacharach name quite successfully for the rest of the decade. The decision to play in Wilmington, which allowed an adequate "home" schedule to be set up, quite possibly saved the franchise.

It isn't known exactly why the New Yorkers threw in the towel. The owners had plenty of money, especially Wilkins, but they may have tired of losing it in the competitive hotbed that was New York semi-pro baseball. The abandonment of their Ebbets Field deal and the limited number of games they played at the New York Oval after publicly making it their home field point toward a lack of success in drawing fans. Their poisonous relationship with the Nat Strong crew would also have limited their opportunities for play in the city. Wilkins, talking about the loss of Inlet Park, said the previous September that the Bacharachs were unlikely to move to New York because "there are too many teams in Manhattan already."[20] Although his version of the Bacharachs did, in fact, more or less become a New York team, he may have been right about the killing level of competition.

Wilkins seems not to have had any further interest in running a baseball team, but Connor kept his name in front of black baseball's magnates. Unable in the next few years to attend the meetings of the Negro National League and the Eastern Colored League, which had arisen on the East Coast and included the Atlantic City Bacharachs, he once sent 100 Havana cigars to be distributed among the attendees at their joint banquet. The *Chicago Defender* reported that "with a toast to the big-hearted New Yorker the baseball men and their friends listened to the speeches of the evening, puffing away enjoyably as the blue smoke and the aroma

Barron Wilkins, Harlem nightclub owner and political power, who was John Connor's co-owner (photographs and Prints Division, Schomburg Center for Research in Black Culture, The New York Public Library, Astor, Lenox and Tilden foundations).

of the cigars filled the room." But although Connor still technically held an associate membership in the National League, he never sponsored another team.[21]

In truth, neither Connor nor Wilkins had long to live. Barron was the first of the pair to die, making headlines as he went. Late on the night of May 24, 1924, Wilkins was taking the air on the sidewalk outside the Exclusive Club when Julius W. "Yellow Charleston" Miller rushed up to him, seeking help. Wilkins was a notorious soft touch for the down and out, and it was also known that "he often helped with money those in desperate need of eluding the police." Miller had just shot a man to death in a dice game in a nearby basement, and demanded $100 to make a getaway. Wilkins reportedly said he had no money and became the next victim, shot in the right side and head before Miller fled. The killer was arrested the next day across the Hudson River in Jersey City. Harlem residents immediately began to flock to the corner of Seventh Avenue and West 134th Street, where the shootings had taken place, and more than 500 of them were "weeping and wailing over the loss of the man many of them termed 'the finest man that ever lived.'" Miller, despite a claim of self-defense based on his fear that Wilkins was going for a pistol, was convicted of first degree murder in both deaths, and went to the electric chair at Sing Sing Prison in 1925. The police estimated that up to 70,000 people lined Seventh Avenue for Wilkins' funeral procession. Among the deceased's 16 pallbearers was John Connor, near the head of the procession.[22]

Connor suffered a stroke in late June 1926, and lingered until July 9, when he died at the Edgecombe Sanitarium, a Harlem hospital, of a cerebral hemorrhage at age 48. "I have talked to a goodly number of citizens, and I have yet to find one to make a discreditable remark about him," said the Rev. James W. Brown, pastor of the church where the funeral was held. Among Connor's pallbearers was Dick Redding.[23]

Chapter 5

In the Big Leagues

1923

With the initial success of the Negro National League in the Midwest, talk naturally arose about the chances of the Eastern teams having their own circuit. The *Atlantic City Daily Press* had reported at the beginning of the 1922 season that feelers were out for an eight-team organization that would include Atlantic City.[1] Eight months later the new league, officially the Mutual Association of Eastern Colored Baseball Clubs, known on the sports pages as the Eastern Colored League, was founded in Philadelphia, the headquarters of the main force behind the new league, Hilldale's Ed Bolden.

Bolden, the most astute team owner in Eastern blackball, was fed up with his National League associate membership, and fed up with Rube Foster, too. Bolden resented having to play top black Eastern competition with a team that organizationally had one hand tied behind its back (like the New York Bacharachs, he was barred from signing straying National Leaguers), and Hilldale did unusually poorly against this top level of competition. Hilldale also couldn't play the teams under Nat Strong's control, who were on Foster's "enemies' list." Connors was happy to have his Bacharachs avoid them, but Bolden, a master of "real politic" when it came to baseball relationships, had reached a détente with Strong.

Bolden also considered the NNL affiliation a money loser:

> Despite paying $1,000 for an associate membership, only four western teams had visited Hilldale Park during 1921 and 1922, while Hilldale had made a single costly western trip during 1922. Annoyed by high western travel expenses, Bolden noted in disgust that "we have received more money for a twilight engagement in Philadelphia, where the players could walk to the park, than a Sunday game in the West, with over a thousand miles' railroad fare to cover!"[2]

Bolden asked for his $1,000 deposit back so he could drop out of the NNL, but Foster wouldn't give it to him. A writer for the *Chicago Defender*, clearly inclined to tell Foster's side of things, alleged that Bolden had at first received his money back and was bent on raiding the NNL once free of its rules, but had relented and redeposited his fee. The league bylaws by then had changed (possibly because Foster could foresee Bolden coming back again), and Bolden could no longer recoup his money.[3]

All of this, plus agitation in the Eastern black sporting press, made a new Eastern league pretty much a given. The *New York Age* opined that "the fans want to see these teams mix it so that they can tell 'who's who' in the East." It also pointed out that excursion rail fares between Baltimore, Philadelphia, Atlantic City and New York weren't expensive (certainly not as expensive as a trip to Detroit, Chicago or Kansas City), thus reducing operating overhead for everyone.[4]

The New York contingent—Strong's Brooklyn Royal Giants, Jim Keenan's Lincoln Giants and Alex Pompez's Cuban Stars—joined up as did the Baltimore Black Sox and the surviving Bacharach team in Atlantic City. Although this was a "colored" league, three of the teams, the Brooklyn Royals, the Lincoln Giants and Baltimore, were white-owned, leading to criticism from those who liked to see the profits from black baseball go to black businessmen. But these were the best black teams on the East Coast, who had been playing each other for years, arrayed on a northeast-southwest axis only about 200 miles long. It was a setup that augured a successful league.

The Eastern Colored League was certainly a good deal for Tom Jackson and Henry Tucker's Bacharach Giants, reduced in 1922 not only to playing second fiddle to the New York Bacharachs in terms of player and opponent quality, but to being a fiddler wandering around without a permanent seat in the orchestra. The lack of a home field in Atlantic City was solved in the spring of 1923 with the aid of the team's "founding father," Harry Bacharach, and his brother Isaac, the congressman. The Bacharachs leased two city blocks of undeveloped residential real estate, about three acres, located in the Northside at North Tennessee and Caspian Avenues, from the Robinson Land Company. The Bacharachs paid the rent, $1,000 a year, with the team paying the real estate taxes. Upon this land, where the team had played in 1917 and 1918 in less grand surroundings, there rose a new version of Bacharach Park that belonged to the Giants, and which served them for five years, including their best seasons. The field had a grass infield, something missing at Atlantic City diamonds since Inlet Park had been torn down, was located on two streetcar lines for easy access, and eventually seated 10,000 fans, although only 7,000 seats had been built by the start of the home season on Decoration Day.[5]

To finance all this, Jackson and Tucker had taken on several partners, including Hammond Daniels, who was named president of the team. Daniels was a Northside businessman, 51 when he took over the Bacharachs' top position, who had emigrated to Atlantic City from Georgia in the very early twentieth century. From working in the hotel business and running pool and billiard halls, in the late 1910s Daniels graduated to the retail liquor business which, especially in Atlantic City, would seem to have ensured him a lifetime of profit.

Prohibition changed all that in 1920, of course. Daniels, as did so many liquor dealers in the city, instantly began advertising himself as a "soft drink" distributor. This either constituted a facile redirection of these men's businesses to keep up with the country's (official) changing mores, or quite possibly it was a relabeling of business as usual to keep government revenue agents at bay. Beginning in 1925 Daniels' annual listing in the Atlantic City directory omitted any mention of an occupation, although it's known he was an investor and officer in a Harlem real estate company. Whatever he did, he prospered at it. When he died in 1929 he left a bequest of $50,000, a share of the nation's wealth equivalent to $3.5 million today, as an educational fund for black children.[6]

John B. Dykes, a Northsider who graduated from running a pool room to becoming a lawyer who also ran real estate and insurance businesses and whose involvement in city Republican politics went all the way back to Louis Kuehnle's time, became the club treasurer. Charles B. Johnson, a leading officer of the city's black Elks lodge, an active Republican and proprietor of a "soft drink" saloon, was club secretary.[7]

The other new investors were three brothers who had come to Atlantic City from Barbados in the early 1900s. Duncan Weekes arrived shortly after the turn of the century when he was about 30 and started up a grocery in the Northside. His older brother, William, arrived in 1903 and a younger brother, Reginald, joined them in 1904. The 1905 New Jersey state census has all three families, including the wives and children of Duncan and Reginald, living with Duncan. Duncan and William both listed their occupations as tailors when they came to America, although Duncan soon opened his grocery store and, like so many others in the booming Atlantic City of the 1920s, got into real estate.

Reginald listed his occupation as "speculator" on the manifest of the S.S. Piemonte, the ship that brought him to the U.S., and he subsequently lived up to that self-description. Official records, city directories and family reminiscences have him running the Little Savoy Hotel on Baltic Avenue, and the New York Garage on North New Jersey Avenue that offered horse and buggy services and then switched to taxis, delivering ice and barbering. All three brothers were charged in 1920 with illegally selling liquor, caught in a roundup that, unusually, was conducted by county authorities, not the Federals. Eighty people, said to represent most of the saloon keepers in the city, were hauled into court. But little seems to have come of the cases after local law enforcement showed that it, too, could enforce the Volstead Act (although events of the Prohibition Era showed that while it could, it usually didn't).[8]

The Giants took out an advertisement in a municipal government trade journal in 1925 that listed William Weekes as team vice president and Reginald Weekes as assistant treasurer.[9] Originally, the brothers don't seem to have played prominent roles in the team's management, but in 1927 they teamed with Tom Jackson (who was Reginald's neighbor) to take over control of the Bacharachs and keep them playing during another of the team's periodic financial crises.

The influx of new partners successfully capitalized the ballpark improvements and paid for the acquisition of new players to upgrade the roster fractured by the 1922 split. But it also created a disorganized management structure, in which some of the investors felt quite at ease to dabble in team affairs, whether it might have been their responsibility or not. This led to situations such as the one that arose at the end of May 1924, when different factions in the Giants' front office booked them to play two different white semi-pro teams in the New York City borough of Queens on the same day. A solution to split the Giants' roster and play both games was rejected by the white home teams, which undoubtedly foresaw their gate receipts dropping as the Bacharachs fielded two inferior teams (while the Giants' management, of course, would reap two visitors' shares of the gate). Finally one game, against Corona, was scrubbed and the other, against College Point, was played.

John Henry Lloyd, field manager of the Bacharachs in 1924 and the team's representative on the road, was caught in the middle of the mess. Lloyd was not one to brook interference and confusion, and this incident contributed to his decision to leave the club after 1925. "The mystery to me," wrote Rollo Wilson in the *Courier*, "is how he ever managed to stick it out this season. Everyone has been allowed to boss the club and its unofficial managers have been legion."[10]

Until its new park was ready for the beginning of the 1923 season, the Bacharachs practiced in the city park at New York and Adriatic Avenues, where they had begun in 1916. There Tucker and field manager Lundy put together a competitive, but not championship-caliber, team. As might have been expected with the Bacharachs' step up into league play from 1922, when the Atlantic City contingent had practically fallen to the level of a regional black team, there was a lot of roster turnover. Lundy, who had a fine season, hitting .346 and second on the team with 73 RBI, was back at shortstop and Cummings, batting .271, was at first. Reid hit .305 and had a strong year in left field and at second base. Willie Jones continued to be the main catcher, although he hit only .195, and Frank Crockett played outfield for the first half of the season and hit .284. At age 30, this was his swan song in big league blackball.

Hilldale owner Ed Bolden had revamped his roster after the 1922 season, signing several stars, including John Henry Lloyd, and cutting loose second baseman Bunny Downs, third baseman Bill Francis and outfielder Chaney White. Daniels and Jackson stepped right in and signed all three. Second base was turned over to Downs, the former Bacharach, although he hit only .213 until leaving at the beginning of August for the Brooklyn Royal Giants. Reid then took over second. Third base went to Francis, a real veteran of the game. He had been playing with the best black teams since 1906, and had worn the uniforms of the Lincoln Giants, the Chicago American Giants and the Detroit Stars, among others. At age 44 he was all of five years older than the venerable Lloyd, who was being admired for his ability to star at an advanced age. Bolden may have decided that Francis was about done as a ballplayer, but the Bacharachs hadn't noticed that, or perhaps they couldn't do better at third. His veteran presence was in the lineup all season long, but he hit only .176. Another old-timer, Agustin Parpetti, a Cuban native who had played for the Giants'

John Henry Lloyd, considered one of the greatest Negro Leaguers, spent three stints with the Bacharach Giants and settled in Atlantic City to become a beloved "father figure" to black youngsters (John Henry "Pop" Lloyd Committee).

entry in the Cuban Winter League in 1920–1921, and who was now wrapping up his career in the United States at age 39, was the utility infielder and hit .282.

But the outfield was well stocked, with Reid, as accomplished and reliable as he was, only the third-best man out there. While the Downs and Francis acquisitions had barely plugged holes in the lineup, Chaney White was a real find. He had come up from his native Texas in 1919 to play for Hilldale and now, at age 29, continued to build an outstanding career as the Bacharachs' center fielder. He was a consistent high average hitter—he hit .320 for the Giants, and was fast and fearless on the bases. Nicknamed "Reindeer," he could sprint like one, and then slide, spikes up, into any infielder or catcher who tried to block his way to safety. A contemporary told Negro Leagues historian Jim Riley that Chaney was "built like King Kong but runs like Jesse Owens."[11]

Flanking him, sometimes in right field, sometimes in left, was Charlie Mason. The *Daily Press* almost constantly referred to him as the "Black Babe Ruth," and the nickname had a point—he was six feet, two inches tall, weighed 200 pounds, and could hit the ball a long way.

He led the Giants in discovered homers with 11 and RBI with 74, and hit .362. This was his first year in the black big leagues except for a "cup of coffee" with the New York Bacharachs at the end of the previous season.

Yank Deas began the season with the Bacharachs but soon left for the Richmond Giants. Eddie Huff, just starting out in high-level black baseball, was the second-string catcher behind Jones and hit .277.

With White, Reid, Lundy, Mason and Cummings producing well from the top of the batting order, the Bacharachs had some offense, but lack of production elsewhere in the infield and from catcher and most of the reserves held the team to an average of a little more than five runs per game in the found games. The team batting average was .261.

With the exception of Nate Johnson, who made 15 starts and went 6–5 in the discovered games (but with a 5.37 ERA), the pitching staff was completely turned over. The big pickup was a 26-year-old Virginian who had pitched for the Richmond Giants before signing with Atlantic City. Arthur Chauncey Henderson reportedly acquired the nickname "Rats" when he opened his lunchbox at work as a teenager and out popped one of those big rodents, hidden there by a prankster.[12] Henderson, a stocky right-hander, led the staff in starts (26) and relief appearances (ten), going 15–13 with a neat 2.41 ERA. He stayed around Atlantic City for most of the rest of the decade as a mainstay of the Bacharach pitching staff. John Harper, also from the Richmond Giants, was the second-busiest pitcher on the staff, going 11–11 in 21 starts and six relief jobs.

The other main starter was George Hubert Lockhart, 24. Lockhart, who often went by his middle name, arrived in Atlantic City a little later than his teammates every year because he was a college student and ballplayer, and later a college coach. A dependable and sometimes exemplary pitcher, he was in the Giants' rotation for six seasons as part of a long athletic career. The son of a Georgia farm family, Lockhart attended the all-black Talladega College in Alabama, where he excelled in his studies and starred for the baseball team, reportedly losing only one game in his collegiate career and throwing a no-hitter with 11 strikeouts against Morris Brown in 1922.[13]

Upon graduation Lockhart joined the faculty and coaching staff at Alabama State Normal School for Colored Students (now Alabama State University), where he remained for the rest of a long career as a gymnastics instructor and a coach of the baseball, football and basketball teams. So great was his reputation on campus that a new gymnasium was named after him in 1939, and the athletic department gives the annual Lockhart Award to its best all-around athlete.

Lockhart's all-around talents did not go unrecognized in the world of professional baseball. In addition to pitching and occasionally playing the outfield, he doubled as a sort of secretary for the club, handling administrative chores and team publicity. W. Rollo Wilson of the *Courier* took a liking to Lockhart, possibly because he enjoyed finding a player at least as literate as he was. His July 31, 1926, column credited Lockhart with solving a problem. Wilson related how he was trying to write something about the Bacharachs' current winning streak when a special from G. H. Lockhart saved me the effort on this enervating day. From the facile pen of the talented Lockhart drips: "Under the wise management of Dick Lundy, the Bacharachs have fought their way into the shining courts of baseball glory, coming up, up from the cellar to fill one of the choice seats so long occupied by clubs formerly considered in the running. TWELVE STRAIGHT LEAGUE GAMES have been won and the hosts of Lundy have been respecters of no clubs in the winning.... It's a wonderful team with a wonderful personnel, with every position well fortified. When all this ammunition is let loose on baseball humanity some souls must answer at the percentage judgment."[14]

In 1927 the *Courier* ran a feature on Lockhart, "An Unsung Hero," which gathered several laudatory quotes about him, including one from Ed Bolden: "He's a mighty good man. I wish I had a team of men like him." His former manager John Henry Lloyd said, "Lock is a great man to have on any team." The story bore no byline and, considering that Lockhart was doing the Bacharach PR, the suspicion arises that he wrote the piece himself. Nonetheless, the quotes from non-teammates stand to his credit.[15]

Pitcher Arthur "Rats" Henderson, mainstay of the Giants' pitching staff for most of the 1920s. Here is wearing the uniform of the Richmond Giants, where he played before signing with the Bacharachs (National Baseball Hall of Fame and Library, Cooperstown, New York).

Lockhart couldn't appear for the Bacharachs until mid–June in 1923, but still pitched in 21 of the discovered games, starting 16 of them with an 8–5 record and a 2.87 ERA. His arrival made one of the other starters, Lewis Hampton, surplus property, and the Giants sold him to Hilldale. He was 3–3 in nine games, six of them starts, but wasn't really pitching well (he had a 5.20 ERA). Thus the *Daily Press* reported that Hammond Daniels "was not at all pleased with Hampton's work last week [when he was knocked out in the first inning of a 7–5 loss to Hilldale] and therefore tied the can to him."[16]

Roy Roberts, only 28 but with a lot of innings on his arm, also came back from the 1922 New York version of the team. He made seven starts in the discovered games, winning two and losing four. Harold Treadwell, who spent most of the season with the Harrisburg Giants, a future ECL team but still playing independently in 1923, made three starts for the Bacharachs and went 1–1.

The rest of the 1922 New York Bacharachs scattered. Lloyd went to Hilldale to play and manage, and Winters joined him as an ace of the pitching staff. Marcell and Hudspeth joined the Lincoln Giants, Redding played for the Brooklyn Royal Giants, Rojo moved behind the plate for the Baltimore Black Sox, Shively went back to Indianapolis to rejoin the ABCs, and "Country Brown" Bryant joined the Washington Potomacs. "Original" Bacharachs of 1922 who didn't return to Atlantic City included Joe Wheeler, who went back to the Black Sox; Sam Streeter, who joined the Lincoln Giants; and Berdell Young, who dropped down a notch to play with the Philadelphia Giants, but who would come back up to big league-level ball, some of it with the Bacharachs, in a few years.

The Giants played .545 ball in all discovered games, winning 55 of 109 and losing 46 with eight ties or no-decisions. So far as the ECL went, they finished in the middle of the pack in this first season, bobbing around third and fourth place all season long.

The 1923 Bacharachs' season-opening team photograph from the *Atlantic City Daily Press*. Front row, left to right, Bill Francis, McKinley "Bunny" Downs, Frank Crockett, Willie Jones, Roy Roberts, Arthur "Rats" Henderson, Chaney White and Bill Webster. Back row, Jim "Yank" Deas, Lewis Hampton, Nate Johnson, Ambrose Reid, Napoleon Cummings, Charles "Johnny" Hobson, Dick Lundy, Charles Mason and co-owner and business manager Tom Jackson.

The league issued standings frequently for the major black newspapers and the team's local papers. On June 16 the Bacharachs were reported in fourth place with a 3–5 record. On July 7 they had risen to third at 6–8. In final standings they were fourth with a 19–23 record, Brooklyn having eased past them in the season's final weeks. Hilldale, at 32–17, ran away with the first league pennant, although the Cuban Stars, at 23–17, gave them a decent run for their money.

While the official standings had the Bacharachs playing 42 games, 52 matchups with ECL opponents have been discovered, of which the Giants won 24 and lost 26, with two ties. (The ties would not have been reported in the official standings, so the difference is actually eight games). This variance is, unfortunately, not that unusual in the history of Negro League standings. There were often no league statisticians or other officials at each game, and the league office had to depend upon reports from the teams themselves to compile standings and statistics. Of the six teams in the ECL only Hilldale, the Bacharachs, the Lincoln Giants and the Black Sox had their own ballparks—the Royal Giants and the Cuban Stars were "traveling" teams that had no home field. (Critics of the league, or of Nat Strong in particular, were always wondering how a man with dozens of fields at his disposal couldn't find one for his Royal Giants—perhaps, it was surmised, he cared more for the booking fees his empire produced than for the black team he actually owned.) This led to scheduled games not getting played due to bad weather or travel problems without an opportunity to reschedule. The official standings reported 49 official games played for Hilldale and Baltimore, 42 for the Bacharachs, 40 for the Cuban Stars, 38 for the Lincoln Giants and 36 for the Royal Giants. The less than accurate method of keeping standings and the inability of league officials to ensure that all scheduled games were played would lead to more than one season-ending dispute over who finished first in a Negro League season, although not this time in the ECL. Hilldale's success didn't leave anything to argue over.

Taking advantage of the inter-city rivalry with Hilldale, the Bacharach Giants played that team more than any other in the ECL, although some of the games were clearly noted as exhibitions or "special games" in the press and apparently didn't count in the final standings. Fifteen games between the two squads have been uncovered, of which the Giants won six and lost eight. There was one tie, possibly the best game of the bunch, when Lockhart and Phil Cockrell threw seven-inning double shutouts before it got too dark to play on September 26.

A reported 17,000 fans mobbed Hilldale Park on April 28 on Opening Day and saw a good game. Hilldale won, 4–2, after scoring three runs in the first inning off Lewis Hampton. The teams met again from June 3–6, the first three games at Bacharach Park and the last in Camden at Hilldale's alternate home site. Rats Henderson tossed a four-hitter in the first game for a 5–0 win. Downs got three hits off Nip Winters, and Lundy and Mason had two each. Hampton, with Henderson in relief, was successful the next day. According to the *Daily Press* on June 5, "Dame Luck" was on the Giants' side, although part of the luck appeared to be sage ball playing. Francis, on second base in the bottom of the seventh with the Bacharachs down a run, lingered in front of a ground ball to Lloyd at short, causing the star fielder to boot it, loading the bases. Chaney White tied the game with a sacrifice fly and Red Ryan, the Hilldale pitcher, balked in the winning run. Hilldale, however, easily won the last two games, 10–2 in the initial game (both Bacharach runs coming on a homer by "Babe Ruth" Mason) and 7–5 the next day, Hampton's farewell start when he let a 4–0 lead turn into a tie by the end of the first inning.

The teams split two games on July 1–2, the Giants winning, 8–3, when Mason drove in five runs, including three with another homer, and losing, 7–1, when Winters three-hit them. The July 2 loss was the first of five straight to Hilldale, the rest coming 7–6 and 9–4 in an August 15 doubleheader, 6–5 the next day and 6–4 on August 18. Hilldale followers were pleased to note that three of the losses were at the expense of Henderson, who had dominated them so thoroughly earlier in the season.

Harper tossed five shutout innings on September 19 before weakening in the final inning of a six-inning game in Wilmington, but Lundy had popped a three-run homer in the first inning and the Giants won, 5–4. The two teams played twice more on September 26–27 in Delanco and Roebling, New Jersey, two towns northeast of Philadelphia. The first game was the tie, frustrating for the Bacharachs because they scored four runs in the top of the eighth inning but it got too dark to complete the bottom of the eighth, requiring the game to revert to the 0–0 deadlock after seven. Hits were hard to come by the next day, too, as Harper and Ryan pitched twin three-hitters, but Hilldale errors helped the Giants win, 2–1.

The Bacharachs took the season series from the Lincoln Giants seven games to five, starting with a June 10 doubleheader sweep at the Lincoln's home Protectory Oval in the Bronx, followed by a 4–2 win in Atlantic City on the 12th when the Bacharachs scored twice to tie the game in the seventh inning and Mason drove in the two winning runs in the eighth. A pair of games at Bacharach Park on July 17–18 resulted in a split. In the first game, which the Lincolns won, 5–3, Oliver Marcell hit a three-run homer that got lost in the tall grass in deep right field. This happened again at least once more before the season was over. Bacharach Park might have been a good place to play ball, but regular mowing of the outfield would have enhanced the experience. Henderson four-hit the Lincolns for a 2–1 win. Sam Streeter, the erstwhile Bacharach, took the loss, one of five the Bacharachs hung on him this season. But in a July 22 doubleheader in the Bronx, Streeter actually got a win. He squeezed by, 5–4, in the opener when Bill Pierce, the former Bacharach, singled in Hudspeth, a New York Bacharach from 1922, in the bottom of the ninth. Left-hander Dave Brown led the Lincolns to victory in the second game, 4–1. Henderson defeated Streeter again, 5–2 on August 1 down in Atlantic City.

The Bacharachs were the visiting attraction at the Protectory Oval on Labor Day, September 3, and the rivals split. Although Atlantic City got 12 hits in the opener, three by White, Brown beat Henderson, 6–2. Lockhart benefited from a four-run Bacharach rally in the ninth inning of the nightcap, getting a 6–4 win. Mason and Huff each had three hits in that game. The next discovered meeting was on October 14 in the Bronx, where Henderson held onto a 4–0 lead after the first inning, the Bacharachs winning, 4–3, in the first game. But Bill Holland outdueled Harper, 2–1, in a seven-inning nightcap.

The Baltimore Black Sox was the other ECL team that the Bacharachs played most frequently, to a 6–6–1 draw. The season series was close all season long as the final record indicated. Neither team could get any particular traction. They opened against each other on Sunday, May 6, in Baltimore, splitting a doubleheader. Mason and Downs each had two hits in the first game, but a key contributor to the Giants' 6–4 win was Black Sox shortstop Ed Poles, who made two key errors in the same inning. The second game began with a bang, when Hampton gave up nine runs in the first, and the Sox coasted to a 15–9 victory. Since Hampton left that game early he was given the start the next day, too, but lost again, 6–5.

The Bacharachs walked all over the Black Sox in a Sunday doubleheader in Baltimore on July 15 by scores of 10–2 and 12–3. Henderson and Lockhart got easy wins, and the *Baltimore Afro-American* mocked the home team in print, comparing them to religious pacifists who, "overcome with a spirit of brotherly love, thereby deciding to henceforth do unto all men as they wished to be done unto."[17] But the spirit was fleeting—the Black Sox won the next day, 10–4.

A five-game series from August 5–8 at Bacharach Park produced, as usual, a perfectly balanced two wins for each team, and a tie. The highlight of the series was the last game, won by Baltimore, 1–0. Former Bacharach Arnett Mitchell won out over Lockhart in a game that had only ten total hits. A doubleheader on September 30 resulted in yet another split. Harper was backed by 16 runs in the first game, giving up only three. But Baltimore won the finale, 4–2.

As the traveling teams, the Cuban Stars and Royal Giants, played fewer league games overall, they also played the Bacharachs less often. Atlantic City went 3–4 with the Cubans. The Giants lost a three-game series from June 17–19 at Bacharach Park, 5–3, 10–5 and 8–5, but then won a doubleheader on July 8 in Baltimore, 9–7 and 5–4, and a game the next day, 5–4. Chaney White was the hitting star of that series. He had three hits in the first game, drove in the winning run in the second and the tying run in the final. The Cubans won the last discovered game, 8–5, in Atlantic City on July 10.

Only four games between Brooklyn and Atlantic City are among those discovered. The Royal Giants came to Atlantic City on July 23–24. They soundly defeated the Bacharachs, 10–0, the first day and led the second until the sixth inning, when the home team tied the game, going ahead in the seventh for a 10–7 win. On August 20–21, again at Bacharach Park, Brooklyn won the first game, 7–5, and Atlantic City the second, 9–6. Lockhart got the win and old pro Dick Redding was knocked out of the box early for the Royals.

The Giants played 11 games against black teams that weren't in a league, although one was just a year away from joining the ECL. The Washington Potomacs were bankrolled by George Robinson, an African American who owned the Roadside Hotel in Philadelphia, a well-known travel stop for blacks in those days of segregated travel accommodations. To build his new team Robinson hired Ben Taylor, who had left Indianapolis after his brother C. I.'s death and a subsequent argument with C. I.'s widow, Olivia, over who would control the ABCs. Taylor was the playing manager, holding down first base. The Potomacs started putting together a pretty good team, which included "Country Brown" Bryant and "Stringbean" Williams, and would win entry to the ECL the following season.

They played the Bacharachs as if they were already in the league, winning four of the nine confrontations. The teams split a four-game series at the white major league Washington Senators' Griffith Stadium that opened the Potomacs' home season from

May 10–13. The Potomacs, in fact, won the first two games, 5–2 and 5–4, Taylor hitting a homer in the second game. Hampton threw a less-than-model shutout the next day, giving up eight hits, but Mason homered and tripled to bring about a 3–0 win. Crockett, Lundy and White each had three hits in the final game, a wild 13–10 win for the Giants that was tied at ten runs each until the Bacharachs pushed three over in the last two innings.

Two games at Bacharach Park on June 25–26 resulted in Atlantic City wins. In the first game, a 10–1 victory, Lundy had five hits—he hit for the cycle and added another single. The second day both clubs were hitting, but the Giants won, 9–7. Roy Roberts apparently had grounded out as a pinch-hitter in the eighth, only to be struck by the throw to first, allowing two runs to score when the ball bounded away from Taylor. A Potomacs swing through the Bacharachs' home region produced wins over Atlantic City by 10–2 at Collingwood, Pennsylvania, on September 6, and 5–2 at Florence, New Jersey, closed out by a 7–1 Bacharach win at home on September 13 when Lockhart gave up only four hits.

Single-game victories have also been found with the team from Lincoln University, in Philadelphia, and the Richmond Giants (with Yank Deas and Arthur Dilworth in the visitors' lineup), both by 7–4 scores.

The reopened route to Nat Strong's New York City baseball empire forged by the Atlantic City version of the Bacharachs in 1922 produced six games with top-flight semi-pro talent, including two doubleheaders at the Bushwicks' Dexter Park. The Bacharachs were there for the opening of the Sunday doubleheader season, when 9,000 fans turned out to see the teams split. The Giants stormed from a 2–0 deficit in the opener with ten runs in the fifth and sixth innings, backing up Harper's pitching with three hits each from Cummings and Lundy, who included a homer and double in his production. Despite four more Lundy hits and four by Reid, the Bacharachs couldn't hold a lead and lost the second game, 9–6. A second Sunday doubleheader at Dexter on August 19 also produced a split. In September the Giants travelled to Farmers Oval in the Glendale section of Queens to play the Farmers, a semi-pro team on the Bushwicks' level, and split another doubleheader.

The team continued to play many games against semi-pro squads from the Philadelphia area, although the majority of the contests, 14 of 23, were played away from Bacharach Park. Sunday ball was still banned in Philadelphia, but the prized Sunday dates in Atlantic City were now by and large reserved for Eastern Colored League games. As had been the case in 1922, Philadelphia was no longer supplying cannon fodder for the Giants' record. The Bacharachs won only 9 of the 23 games, with 11 losses and three ties. The list of opponents was reduced to nine, only three of whom, regular rivals Chester and Camden and a new powerful team sponsored by Crane's Ice Cream, played the Bacharachs more than twice.

The Chester team, managed by its right fielder, Billy Whitman, a veteran semi-pro player and manager, also featured some other guys the Bacharachs had been seeing for a long time, including third baseman Buck Lai, who first played against them in 1916 with the "Chinese University of Hawaii," and Tony Pasquarella, an opponent with the Marine Corps team in 1917. Chester dominated the Giants, winning five of six discovered games. Mason hit a game-winning homer in the second meeting, on July 25, when Atlantic City won, 3–2. Herb Steen, the veteran semi-pro hurler, beat the Giants twice, once on a five-hitter and once when Chester backed him with 21 hits off of Harper and Henderson. The Bacharachs might have won another game, which was tied 4–4 in Chester on July 27, but they quit the field in protest in the eighth inning when the base umpire called Pasquarella out on a tag play at first, but then reversed his decision.

Camden was a different story. The Giants won four of five, including 5–0 on September 21 when Lockhart threw a four-hitter. High points of the other games against the Philly area teams were a double shutout of the South Philadelphia Hebrew Association on May 30, when Treadwell two-hit the SPHAs, 4–0, in the opener and Roberts three-hit them, 9–0, in the second game on Decoration Day, and a 16–4 beating of Kensington Congregational July 5 in which the Bacharachs piled up 25 hits, including four by Lundy.

The Giants had a one-run lead at Shetzline Park in Philadelphia as twilight began turning to darkness on June 23. The South Philadelphia team (from that neighborhood, not the SPHAs) was batting in the bottom of the eighth inning and the Bacharachs began stalling to get the game called. Henderson purposely walked the first two batters "after endless disputed decisions on balls and strikes," but Eddie Conahan, the home plate umpire, called the visitors' bluff by ordering Shetzline's lights turned on. Charlie Gault, the South Philly catcher, then dropped a surprise bunt and the first man to be walked scored to tie the game. The Bacharachs swarmed Conahan to protest the call, but Conahan, who may have had enough of the Giants, refused to call time and the winning run also sneaked home.[18]

Nine discovered games against teams from elsewhere in Pennsylvania and New Jersey, including some opponents from the Atlantic City area, showed those teams were still easy pickings for the Bacharachs. The contests produced eight wins and a single loss. That came on September 23 in a game which the Giants weren't supposed to be playing. What was supposed to have been the Atlantic City championship game between two white teams was left in doubt after a morning of rain that left the condition of the Sovereign Avenue grounds in the white section of the city a soggy mess. The Jeffries Athletic Club labored to make the field playable only to find that its opponent, the Melrose A.C., had abandoned the match on the assumption that no amount of work would get rid of so much water and mud. The Bacharachs had already called off their game at Bacharach Park, and so were available as fill-ins for Melrose. It would have been a nice touch if the Giants had won and become de facto champions of Atlantic City, but Jeffries beat them, 4–0, the first time in three games it had overcome the Giants that season.

Although the Bacharachs seldom returned to Delaware for games now that they had a new park in Atlantic City, they did go to Wilmington at least three times to play the Pennsylvania Railroad's Maryland Division team at Harlan Field. These two teams were definitely evenly matched. The Giants won the first game, 3–0, but the subsequent matches both ended in ties, 3–3 and 7–7, when darkness fell on the unelectrified Harlan.

One of the more interesting teams the Bacharachs played this season was the Middletown Cubans, sometimes advertised as the "All Cubans of Havana." Although some of the players, all with Spanish surnames, may well have been from Havana originally, they were playing for the Henriquez family, wealthy New Yorkers in the medical and real estate professions. Members of the family had been the backers for years of the Long Branch Cubans, a popular semi-pro team that originated in the New Jersey shore resort town of Long Branch, but shifted in and out of low-level minor leagues and represented different cities. In 1923 they were based in Middletown, New York, a small city in the Hudson Valley north of New York City, as part of the semi-pro Atlantic League. It's clear that the Cubans were not considered to be Negroes, since some of them, particularly Dolf Luque and Mike Gonzalez, went on to major league careers.[19] They played the Bacharachs five times in August and September. The Giants won three, including a 12–3 battering of Middletown on August 12 in which Chaney White had four hits and Mason two homers, and an 11-inning, 9–8 victory two days later won on Reid's bases-loaded single.

The Giants had re-established themselves in Atlantic City as a competitive team in a pioneering black major league. But not everything was rosy. Hammond Daniels told the *Daily Press* in October that "the season was anything but a financial success at home, but on foreign diamonds the Giants played to capacity gatherings all through the season." Daniels laid the lack of attendance to the very thing that made Atlantic City special, "too many counter attractions to buck against." The need to compete against the Shore's other fun had been a problem for the Giants before. Even back in 1916, Jackson had threatened to put the team on the road for all its games if attendance didn't improve. A shortage of paying customers would plague the team again before the 1920s were over and, in fact, it has been a recurring dilemma for anyone trying to run a professional baseball team in Atlantic City.[20]

1924

John Henry Lloyd had joined Hilldale as its shortstop and manager for 1923 after the New York City Bacharachs folded. In one big way his experience in Philadelphia couldn't have been better—Hilldale won the first Eastern Colored League pennant. But Lloyd was out of the lineup for about a month after injuring his knee on a slide into second base in mid–July. At the end of the season, Ed Bolden fired him. Never a true organization man, as his peripatetic roaming from team to team showed, Lloyd had run-ins with some of his players in 1923. Outfielder Clint Thomas was angry that Lloyd had intervened with Bolden to cancel a $150 a month pay raise that Bolden had promised him without Lloyd's consent. Young shortstop Jake Stephens chafed at being stuck behind the 39-year-old Lloyd, and *Courier* sportswriter W. Rollo Wilson revealed that "one of the new stars on the team has managerial designs and ... became a little messenger, sub rosa, from the clubhouse to the office." Wilson didn't name the player, but Frank Warfield, the Hilldale second baseman and a tough character (he was the teammate who later disfigured Oliver Marcell's nose), became the field manager as soon as Lloyd exited.[21]

This didn't stop Lloyd from being welcome back in Atlantic City, where he promptly signed up as playing manager, returning to the city and franchise for which he had starred in 1919. Of course, the Bacharachs already had a shortstop and field manager complete in one individual, the newly-emerged star Dick Lundy. Nonetheless, Lloyd seems to have assumed the managerial reins with no hard feelings. If Lundy had been at all disappointed in losing his official leadership role, he could hardly have been more pleased with Lloyd's other decision. After 17 years as a shortstop, Lloyd moved himself over to second base. Blocking the 23-year-old Stephens in Philadelphia was one thing—although he was probably the superior fielder, Stephens hadn't yet matured as a hitter. Lundy had everything and Lloyd graciously acknowledged it, passing the torch carried by the best shortstop in the Negro Leagues on to his successor right there at Bacharach Park. The presence of both men in the lineup formed the core of an intimidating batting order. The *Daily Press* labeled the combination of Lundy, Lloyd, Mason and Reid the Bacharachs' own "murderers' row," a term coined in 1918 for the New York Yankees lineup.[22]

Lloyd, who celebrated his 40th birthday that April 25, pounded the ball ferociously, leading the team with a .386 batting average and 90 RBI against all competition. Against expectations, the Bacharachs as a team hit better against Negro League and similar-level competition, at .281. Lloyd wasn't far off that pace—he hit .371 against those teams. His greatest hitting feat, 11 straight base hits, came against league competition. On June 29 he went four-for-four against the Potomacs, then did the same thing again to Washington's pitchers the next day, his hits including a home run. After a few days off he put himself back in the lineup for a July 4 doubleheader against the Harrisburg Giants and produced two doubles and a single in the first game before pitcher Kenneth "Ping" Gardner finally got him out his fourth time up. Although his consecutive hit streak was broken, Lloyd had not cooled down. He got three more hits in the nightcap. Lundy hit .348 for the season, leading the team in runs scored (105) and home runs (14), and was second with 86 RBI, four less than Lloyd).

Lloyd's change of positions also solved another pressing problem for the team. The next-most likely second baseman on the roster was Ambrose Reid, but the team had parted ways with the ancient Bill Francis, and Reid was needed at third base. Reid contributed a lot—he always hit well (.266 this season with 56 RBI, fourth-highest on the team), he rarely missed games due to injury and he wasn't inclined to take leave of the Bacharachs for what might seem like greener pastures with some other outfit. He was also versatile, and switched positions more than once in his Giants career not necessarily because he would play better at a different spot, but because it would help the team.

Cummings hit .257 this year, but as usual had plenty of walks and led the team in stolen bases with 21. With him back at first base, the infield was all set. So was the outfield at the start of the season. Chaney White shifted over to left field to replace Reid while Ramiro Ramirez, who had gone to the Baltimore Black Sox in 1923 after the demise of the New York Bacharachs, was brought in to play center. Ramirez contributed more with the glove than the bat—he hit just .222, although his 36 walks were tied with Lloyd for third-most on the team. Slugging Charley Mason continued to start in right field and batter pitchers, this year at a .345 rate. His eight triples led the team and his 11 homers were second only to Lundy, although he missed about a month of action beginning in the middle of August. His absence was met by moving Reid back to the outfield and putting Johnny George, signed after his release by the Harrisburg Giants, at third. George filled in adequately, hitting .221.

In the middle of June White left the team for Ben Taylor's Washington Potomacs.

He was replaced both in left field and the leadoff spot in the batting order by George Shively, who had gone from Indianapolis to Washington with Taylor but now was taking a final turn with the Bacharachs. The swap was described at the time as a case of both players being released and picked up by the other team, but Shively was in a Bacharach uniform mere days after White left, so it may have been a formal trade.[23] White was hitting .333 when he left, while Shively batted only .265 after joining the Giants, so the offensive drop-off accompanying the swap was noticeable, although the lineup had plenty of punch to make up the difference.

Willie Jones was back as one of the catchers, paired with Ernest Gatewood, back with the Giants for what would be the last four years of his Negro Leagues career. As usual, the Bacharachs didn't get much offense from the catching position. Gatewood hit .238 and Jones .216. Except for rotating his catchers, Lloyd used pretty much a set lineup every game when injuries or the need for an occasional day off didn't force a change. The only regular utilityman was Milton Lewis, back with Atlantic City after a year down with the Richmond Giants. Lewis got into about two-thirds of the games, often spelling Lloyd against non-league competition, and hit .223, although with five homers.

This Bacharach team had a potent offense. Its .276 team batting average and six runs per game represented levels achieved up until that time in the team's history only by the 1921 Giants, who had a nearly identical won-lost record to this squad. The 1924 Giants won 74 of 125 discovered games (including four ties or no-decisions) for a .612 won-lost percentage and went 33–31–2 (.516) against ECL competition.

Further progress was held back by the lack of a consistent starting rotation. The Bacharachs had several good pitchers, but almost none of them spent the entire year with the team. Rats Henderson hurt his arm on May 24 but returned to the rotation, only to jump the Bacharachs and the ECL's contract restrictions for a barnstorming team run by the venerable Chappie Johnson. He wound up making only ten starts, although they were excellent ones—he had a 6–3 won-lost record and a 2.26 ERA, continuing his high strikeout rate of seven per nine innings. Hubert Lockhart reported after his college year was over and started 18 times, winning 13 and losing 5 with a 3.05 ERA. Stringbean Williams began the season with the Potomacs, but after joining the Bacharachs on the Fourth of July again became a mainstay of the staff with a 1.97 ERA in 15 starts and a 10–4 record. Roy Roberts made eight starts, going 4–2. John Harper was back for the full season, with 14 very successful starts that resulted in a 12–3 mark and an ERA of 3.10.

But the returning staff started only slightly more than half of the discovered games. The rest of the load fell to newcomers who were journeymen. Otis "Lefty" Starks began the season with the Lincoln Giants, but made 12 starts and five relief appearances for the Bacharachs with a 6–7 record and a 4.02 ERA. Rookie Bill Nuttall likewise split his time between the rotation and the bullpen. His seven starts and five relief jobs resulted in a 4–4 record. Charlie Evans, another rookie, made seven starts, winning three and losing two in June and July.

Wayne Carr got into a salary dispute with his 1923 employer, the Black Sox, and quit the team in late April, although he went right back to work at Maryland Park. He signed with the Giants when they came to Baltimore to open the ECL season and made his first appearance for them on April 26, beating the Sox, 7–2. That may have been the high point of his year—he was only 2–3 for the Bacharachs, with a high ERA of 5.31, and was off the Atlantic City team, too, by the end of June. Arnett Mitchell, back with the Bacharachs from Baltimore, started six times and went 3–3. Johnny Hobson made eight starts with a 3–5 mark.

While Lloyd tended to start the same position players all the time, he seems to have spotted some of his starters to get the best ones more league starts. Henderson, with nine of ten starts against ECL teams, and Lockhart, 16 of 18, almost never pitched against anyone but league competitors.

Rollo Wilson of the *Courier* selected an ECL all-star team at the end of the season and four Giants were on it: Lloyd as manager, Lundy at shortstop, Mason in right field and Lockhart as a pitcher. Both catchers, Gatewood and Jones, as well as Lewis and Harper, were honorable mentions.[24]

The ECL had expanded to eight teams by adding the Potomacs and the Harrisburg Giants. Harrisburg, a two-year-old independent team, had, like the Bacharachs in signing Lloyd, improved itself in one single move by luring Oscar Charleston to be the slugging center fielder as well as the manager. The Potomacs, who had some good players, were inconsistent—Wilson called them the league's "mystery team" because "when they are good they are very, very good, but when they are bad they remind us of something Thomas Catt brought in."[25] The Potomacs and the two teams without home parks, the Royal Giants and the Cuban Stars, had sub-.400 winning percentages in league play. Hilldale again ran way with the pennant with a .676 percentage although Baltimore made a respectable run at the Philadelphians at .596. This left the Bacharachs, the Lincolns from New York, and Harrisburg stuck in the middle, all above .500 but not close to challenging for first or even second place. The three teams might have all been called Giants, but they weren't towering above anyone, except for the pygmies at the bottom of the standings.

After sweeping a three-game series from the Black Sox in late April, and taking two of three from Washington, the Bacharachs were in first place in early May. But then they lost four in a row to Harrisburg, Hilldale and the Lincoln Giants to finish the month in third at 5–5. The team hovered around .500 and fourth place for the rest of the season, finishing fourth with an official won-lost record of 30–29. The list of discovered games again shows a different outcome, with 32 wins, 30 losses and two no-decisions, a .548 winning percentage. Overall the Giants mastered most of their non-league opponents, going 41–16–2.

Despite the usual failure of the Eastern Colored League to play a balanced schedule (the number of decisions for each team ranged from 69 for Hilldale down to 41 for the perpetually traveling Brooklyn Royal Giants), the discovered Bacharachs games (likely all or nearly all of those played) have the team meeting six of their seven opponents between nine and 11 times each. Only the Royal Giants, predictably, show up less often (seven games). The Brooklyn team, in fact, was briefly expelled from the league in late May for failing to play scheduled league games. This continuing complaint against Nat Strong's team finally resulted in punitive action. Strong primarily refused to play the Lincoln Giants since the often-strained relations between him and Jim Keenan, competitors not just for the ECL title but for New York City baseball attendance dollars, had gotten worse. As Rollo Wilson, an acute observer of Strong over the years, put it, "he had no intention of forsaking that annual trip [to profitable game dates in New England] in order to conform to the mandates of men whom he felt were afraid of him. He had been the man of destiny of Eastern baseball for many years. But, like another man of destiny, he met his waterloo." Strong shortly apologized and promised to be a good league member, and the other owners relented and let the Royals stay in the league. Even though the Royals were a drag on the league, there was no sense in offending Strong, since a black team headed to his territory in New York for a Sunday doubleheader might still expect to be greeted by upwards of 10,000 fans, and take home a good share of the money they paid at the gate.[26]

The Bacharachs achieved their slightly-over-.500 record by playing more or less at the same level against everyone. They had winning marks against the three bottom teams, 6–2–1 against the Cuban Stars, 6–4–1 against the Potomacs and 4–3 versus the Royal Giants, played their closest rivals pretty much even (5–5 against the Lincoln Giants and 4–6 against Harrisburg) and had slight losing records to the top two squads (4–5 against Baltimore and 4–6 against Hilldale).

As might be imagined, it took good pitching to beat Hilldale, and the Bacharachs had it when they won against the league leaders. Hobson tossed a four-hitter in a 5–2 win on June 2, when the Giants loaded the bases on three straight Hilldale errors and then scored three times in the sixth inning. Lockhart gave up seven hits to win, 3–2, on August 3, the winning run scoring in the seventh inning when Shively singled, sped all the way to third on a sacrifice bunt by Cummings and scored on a Lundy single. Another 3–2 win on August 5 featured a six-hitter from Harper and a winning sacrifice fly by Mason in the eighth inning. Harper threw two crucial innings of shutout relief as the Giants scored in both the ninth and tenth innings for a come-from-behind 6–5 win on September 11. Two days later Harper pitched a good complete game, but lost, 3–0, when ex–Giant Nip Winters threw a two-hitter.

But when the pitching was poor, Hilldale battered the Giants by scores such as 13–3, 10–5, 8–1 and 13–9. One redeeming feature of the 13–9 loss at Hilldale Park was a home run by Reid, whose liner eluded left fielder Clint Thomas and got lost in the undergrowth in front of the fence, proving that there were places other than Bacharach Park where the groundskeeping could have stood improvement.

The Bacharachs swept the series in Baltimore on April 26–27 that began with Wayne Carr's debut by scores of 7–2, 6–4 and 10–7. After that, the Black Sox ruled this relationship. A 12-inning performance by Henderson on June 14, in which he gave up nine hits and struck out 16, resulted only in a 2–1 loss. Then the Sox took two in Atlantic City on July 15–16 by scoring late to wipe out Bacharach leads. The Giants took the final game of that series, 9–4, on July 18, but lost an excruciating doubleheader in Baltimore on September 24. Joe Strong outdueled Roberts, 2–1, in the opener and Bill Force beat Hobson in the second game, 3–2. The Giants almost tied the game in the top of ninth, scoring one run and having the ever-daring Cummings nipped at the plate on a sacrifice fly attempt.

The Lincoln Giants finished third, just above the Bacharachs, and a good run at them would have put Atlantic City one step higher in the standings. But the upper hand seesawed back and forth. The Lincolns decisively won an early doubleheader on May 25 at the Protectory Oval, 9–1 and 9–3, but the Bacharachs took two out of three in Atlantic City from June 9–11. Henderson threw a five-hitter in the first of the games for a 6–5 win and Lockhart a four-hitter the next day for a 6–5 victory. But the New York team won, 6–2, on the 11th, and again on July 11, 5–2.

The Bacharachs bounced back to sweep a doubleheader at the Protectory Oval on July 13. Milton Lewis socked a three-run, pinch-hit homer in the eighth inning of the first game to produce a 7–5 win, and Stark threw a seven-inning five-hitter in the rain-shortened nightcap. Johnny Harper one-hit the Lincolns for a 4–1 win in a five-inning twilight game that got started late at Bacharach Park on September 8. But 38-year-old Robert "Judy" Gans, the Lincoln manager who still pitched and played outfield on occasion, shut the Bacharachs down on four hits two days later, 9–1.

Although there were others making important contributions in the Harrisburg-Bacharach games, the outcome often seemed to hinge on the output of the biggest stars, Charleston for Harrisburg and Lloyd and Lundy for Atlantic City. A 9–5 Bacharach win in the first game of the July 4 doubleheader at Bacharach Park was the game in which Lloyd got the last three of his 11 straight base hits. The Atlantic City win before that, 10–3 on June 16, featured four hits by Lloyd, three by Lundy and six by everyone else in the lineup. Lundy homered twice on August 15 when the Bacharachs came roaring from behind to win, 7–6. Hubert Lockhart, though, took the laurels on August 24 when he threw a five-hitter in an 8–2 win.

Charleston was one of three Harrisburg Giants to triple when his men won the opening game with the Bacharachs, 5–4, on May 22. He had three hits and scored both of his team's runs on June 17 in a 2–1 win. The July 4 doubleheader was the first of a four-game series in Atlantic City, and Charleston produced a total of eight hits. Four of them, one a home run, led Harrisburg to a 6–1 win in the second game of the holiday doubleheader. Harrisburg also took the games on the 5th and 6th, rallying from a six-run deficit the first day to win, 7–6, and also triumphing, 8–4, in the last game when Charleston hit two homers and a single, and walked twice. The sixth Harrisburg victory occurred on August 14 when catcher Henry Jordan hit a sixth-inning, game-winning homer off Lockhart to put his team up, 3–2.

The up-and-down Potomacs fell behind early in the season series when the Bacharachs took two of three in Washington in the first three days of May. The first one was a slugfest in which the Giants, down 9–2 early, got 14 hits and eventually won, 14–10. On the last day of the series Chaney White got three hits to back up Henderson's complete game and the Giants won, 8–2. On May 2, despite a three-hit day by Mason, the Potomacs won easily, 8–4. In mid–June Washington broke a tie in the sixth inning with four runs and won, 9–8, but the Bacharachs won two games on June 29–30 in which hits rattled all over Bacharach Park. The Giants had 23 of them in the first game, four each by Lundy, Mason and Lloyd, in winning, 20–4. Lloyd followed up on the 30th with four more hits, the second batch in his hitting streak, and the Bacharachs won, 12–10.

The remaining five games were split. The Bacharachs won in mid–August, 6–2, and took a 6–5 thriller on September 7 in which Cummings was wild pitched home with the winning run by 20-year-old Washington starter Claude "Red" Grier. Grier, who had beaten the Bacharachs twice earlier in the season, including a four-hit shutout with nine strikeouts on July 17, was a good young pitcher due to play a major role in the Giants' future, and not by beating them, either. The other Potomacs-Bacharachs game, on July 19, was a 4–4 tie.

Atlantic City opened against the Royal Giants with a doubleheader on Decoration Day, May 30, before a large and lucrative crowd at Dexter Park in Brooklyn. Lockhart threw a three-hitter in the first game and Mason had four hits as the Bacharachs won, 12–1. But Brooklyn pitcher Willis "Pud" Flournoy turned the tables in the nightcap, allowing only two runs while the Royals scored nine off Hobson. The Bacharachs won two of three in a series at Atlantic City on July 28–30. Lockhart shut out the Royals in the opener, 4–0, but the venerable Cyclone Joe Williams won an 11-inning game for Brooklyn the next day, doubling in the winning run for a 3–2 victory. Roy Roberts defeated Williams on September 2, 4–3, but the Royals won the last discovered game, 3–2, on September 4, in 13 innings.

The last-place Cuban Stars were pretty easy pickings for the Giants, as they were for everyone else. The Bacharachs won a three-game series from them on June 23–25. They walloped 24 hits in the first game for a 20–0 victory as Henderson threw the shutout. They won the second, 3–2, rewarding Harper with a win for three innings of no-hit relief when Shively singled and scored as two Giants bunts in a row resulted in wild throws by the Cuban infielders. Henderson returned with a complete game win on the 25th, 9–3, as the Lundy-Lloyd partnership had seven hits. The Giants took two more on August 19–20 by scores of 8–7 and 7–6. Ramirez, not usually an outstanding hitter, won the first game with a two-run double, and Lewis hit his second game-winning, pinch-hit homer in the ninth inning the next day.

The Cuban Stars did manage to win one series, 14–4 and 10–7 in Atlantic City in mid–July, in which they collected 29 hits in the two games. The final game between the two teams, September 16 in Atlantic City, wound up a 6–6 tie, called by darkness.

In 1924 six of the best semi-pro teams in the area around Philadelphia banded together to form the Penn-Jersey League. The teams, Trenton and Camden in New Jersey, Chester from Delaware County, Pennsylvania, and Lit Brothers, South Philadelphia and Ascension from Philadelphia proper, were regular opponents of the Negro League clubs The Giants enjoyed a significant edge, going 18–11 against the semi-pro league teams.

Chester was the only Penn-Jersey team to win the majority of its games against the Bacharachs, five out of eight. Former major leaguers, of course, weren't unusual at this semi-pro level, but Chester boasted a pitcher with one of the majors' more unusual careers. Harry "Socks" Seibold, a Philadelphia native, had played ten games with the hometown Athletics as a shortstop in 1915, then became a pitcher for Connie Mack's club until 1919, although with little success. He dropped down to the Pacific Coast League in 1920 and 1921, then quit organized baseball to return to Philadelphia, where he played semi-pro ball, occasionally facing the Bacharachs. He went back to the Oakland Oaks in the PCL at the beginning of 1924 and pitched in an undistinguished way until the middle of June, when he jumped the team. The *Oakland Tribune* said he would be remembered there as "stepping to the mound occasionally to help the enemy increase their batting averages."[27] Seibold pitched semi-pro ball until 1928, when he returned to organized baseball and the majors in 1929. Despite being 33 years old and not having been in the big leagues for ten years, he pitched well for five more seasons. His exit from Oakland in 1924 brought him home just in time to face, and defeat, the Bacharachs, 7–2, in the seven-inning second game of a June 21 doubleheader. He threw even better on August 23, giving up only five hits. But the Giants won, 2–1, as Chester was held to six hits by Stringbean Williams.

The Giants played Trenton six times, winning five. Nuttall, who got three of his four wins against Penn-Jersey teams, beat Trenton twice, 8–3 on August 7 and 5–1 nine days later. Charlie Mason excelled against them as well getting three hits in a game twice and a home run to support Nuttall in his first win. In the sole loss to Trenton, the Bacharachs faced one of their oldest adversaries. Ad Swigler, the college ace who had forsaken a promising professional career to become a dentist in Philadelphia and play semi-pro ball, had first pitched against the Bacharachs for the Logan Squares back in 1916. Swigler was now the Trenton captain and, having always been a good hitter, primarily the first baseman. He wasn't a regular member of the starting rotation, and when he defeated a lower-level team the *Trenton Evening Times* described him as having "slowballed the Morgan batsmen into submission." But the demands of the Penn-Jersey pennant race had worn the Trenton pitching staff thin, and to keep the regular starters rested for league games Swigler was called to the mound on August 2. Given the circumstances, he was expected to throw a complete game against the Bacharachs, whatever the result. The game was regarded by the *Evening Times* as an "apparently lost cause," but Swigler threw all nine innings, gave up only six hits and struck out four, and Trenton won, 5–4.[28]

The Giants won four of six from the Camden Skeeters (the team's nickname referred to the mosquito, which some say is the unofficial New Jersey State Bird). Four of the games, two wins and both losses, were one- or two-run games. Ascension was sponsored by the Ascension of Our Lord Parish in the Kensington section of Philadelphia. It wasn't unusual to have a semi-pro team sponsored by a church, although it was certainly different that the pastor, the Rev. William J. Casey, was such a fan that he was known as the unofficial chaplain of Connie Mack's Athletics. But it was very unusual for Ascension to have had Babe Ruth in its lineup, which occurred on September 4, 1923, when Ruth dropped in after a Yankees-A's game as a favor to Father Casey.[29] Without any Ruthian assistance, Ascension was pretty easy pickings for the Bacharachs, who beat them three times in four tries, including a Harper four-hitter for a 5–1 win on August 28.

The team from the Lit Brothers Department Store split four games with the Giants in which every game was a one-run decision. The first game, at Bacharach Park on July 23, was a fundraiser for the Milk and Ice Fund sponsored by the *Daily Press*'s parent organization, which raised money to ensure that poor families got milk for their children and ice to keep it refrigerated. The Bacharachs won, 5–4, when Lundy stole home in the bottom of the tenth inning. On August 31 Lockhart outdueled former Atlantic City High School star Bill Pierson, a former Athletic, 2–1. The Giants played the sixth Penn-Jersey team, South Philadelphia, only once, but the game was memorable. Harper and South Phillie's Jimmie Burke threw a double shutout for eight innings, until Lundy led off the Bacharach ninth with a homer and Burke then let three more runs score.

Elsewhere in the region, the Giants were 6–2 with other Pennsylvania teams, taking two from Upland and winning the only contests against the Strawbridge and Clothier Department Store team from Philadelphia and the squad from Hanover, while splitting a pair each against York and Hazelton. They won six games with no defeats against New Jersey teams not in the Penn-Jersey League, although Glassboro forced a 4-4 tie on July 31. Among the defeated, in a doubleheader sweep on August 30, was a team named Elgawa. It sounded like an American Indian name, but the squad, from Millville, was made up of municipal utility workers, from the *Electric*, *Gas* and *Water* departments.

On the local scene, Pleasantville often provided the second game in doubleheaders in which the Bacharachs would face an ECL team in the first game. Three times these were two-park doubleheaders in which the Bacharachs would play an ECL team at Bacharach Park and then cross to the mainland to play a second game in Pleasantville. Although the Giants went 3-1-1 against Pleasantville, only two of the wins were blowouts. The Bacharachs had to work hard to win, 1-0, on September 14 as Williams and Walter Everham of Pleasantville dueled. An August 19 game resulted in a darkness-shortened 5-5 tie. Pleasantville's only win was a 14-3, six-inning laugher on July 29 that followed an 11-inning Bacharach loss to the Royal Giants. Willie Jones was the Bacharach starting pitcher and Stark, the pitcher, caught. Although these two had teamed up often between mound and plate, the reversal of positions caused problems—they "could not work together," as the *Daily Press* put it, and Jones gave up all of the Pleasantville runs in four innings.[30] In the only other discovered local game, the Giants beat the Jeffries Athletic Club, 5-0.

The Pennsylvania Railroad team from Wilmington was defeated, 8-1, on May 6. The Bushwicks were off the Giants' schedule, and less than a handful of discovered games against New York City semi-pros produced a split with the Farmers on May 4 and a 4-3 loss to the College Point team in the Bronx on May 28 to ex-major league pitcher Jack Warhop. The two regional black teams that opposed the Giants were slaughtered. The LeDroit Tigers of Washington, D.C., who had accompanied a group of black Elks from the Capitol on an excursion to the Shore, were beaten, 17-1, on May 18. The Bacharachs added insult to injury by turning a triple play on a liner to the pitcher by Johnnie Pugh, a former teammate. The St. Louis Giants were similarly dispatched, 18-0 and 19-0, when they hit town in August.

An aggregation called the McGinnis Minor League All-Stars, which seemed to be composed in part of Philadelphia semi-pros, including Swigler, lost a pair of shutouts to the Bacharachs in October, 4-0 and 8-0.

1925

The Bacharachs began 1925 with mostly the same lineup that had brought them to fourth place the season before. As the season went on, management took advantage of disaffection elsewhere in the league to pull off some coups that substantially revamped the club. The changes didn't do that much for the team this season—it finished in fourth place again—but the new Giants were to play key roles in the next two years when the Bacharachs dominated the Eastern Colored League and gave big Negro World Series scares to the Negro National League pennant winners.

The first big acquisition was actually a familiar, if not necessarily comforting, face. Oliver Marcell was in bad graces with the Lincoln Giants. Most of this was due to the Ghost just being himself: "he has been a storm center on the New York team for the past year. Possessed of an unusually quick temper, he became unpopular with local fans because of his readiness to argue and even fight with the umpires." He had also been involved as a possibly not-so-innocent bystander in a street murder in Harlem in late April. Benjamin Adair was gunned down at 3:25 in the morning while in the company of Marcell and two other Lincoln Giants, pitchers Dave Brown and Frank Wickware. No one was ever charged with the killing, but Brown, a leading pitcher, vanished immediately afterwards and never played in the black big leagues again. Marcell and Wickware, probably aided by the Lincolns' traveling schedule, weren't easy for the police to locate for questioning either, although both continued to play. A *Pittsburgh Courier* sports columnist claimed the affair had given baseball a black eye with its fans: "This fatal ending of the well known 'all night party' should serve as another warning to ball players that baseball is a business and each player should try to keep the sport on the pinnacle it now occupies by gentlemanly conduct on and off the field."[31]

But the Bacharachs, playing in a city where all-night parties were part of the local economy and being in need of a third baseman after cutting Bill Francis loose, were anxious to have Marcell back on the team. So anxious, in fact, that they traded for him twice. The first deal in early May sent two Bacharach starting pitchers, Roberts and Harper, to the Lincolns in exchange for Marcell. But Harper refused to report to New York and the trade was weirdly hung up—Marcell was playing for the Bacharachs and Roberts was pitching for the Lincolns, but Harper, who was ill, was at home in North Carolina and Lincoln Giants owner Jim Keenan was complaining to the league that the Bacharachs hadn't fulfilled their side of the bargain. *Courier* columnist Rollo Wilson, who was clearly becoming more and more fed up with the ECL's inability to police its internal affairs, wrote that Harper's refusal to report to New York was Keenan's problem: "The implied rule is 'Let the buyer beware.' But most anything can happen in this league."[32]

What happened was that the league commissioners (the owners) nullified the trade a month later, over Bacharach president Daniels' objections. But the Lincolns still wanted to unload Marcell and the Bacharachs still wanted him, so another arrangement was worked out. The Ghost stayed with Atlantic City and Roberts was returned to the Bacharachs, who then shipped Harper, who was now amenable to a trade, journeyman infielder Tom Finley, who had started the season as the third baseman, and slugging outfielder Charley Mason to the Lincolns.[33]

Mason's departure, the day after he collected four hits against a Philadelphia semi-pro team, the Passyunk Artisans, left the outfield short of power, but this was remedied in July when the Giants took advantage of the ire of George W. Robinson, owner of the ECL opponent Potomacs. Robinson's team, originally based in Washington, D.C., wasn't making money there and for the 1925 season moved to Wilmington. Despite leaving Washington, the team didn't change its nickname, making it the Potomacs on the Delaware.

Business wasn't good on that river, either. In July Robinson threw in the towel, but did not go meekly. He had for some time been angry at Ed Bolden, whom he accused of denying the Potomacs some choice playing dates when the ECL schedule was made up, mismanaging the supervision of umpires by hiring a white Philadelphia sportswriter instead of Rollo Wilson, and, again on the subject of white control of a Negro League, being entirely too close to Nat Strong. At the time Robinson unloaded all this in a letter to the *Pittsburgh Courier* in early August, he was also angry at a published statement from Bolden that Robinson had acted in an underhanded manner in refusing to sell any of his players to Hilldale as the Potomacs broke up. Robinson said that Bolden just couldn't meet his price, but as the team was parceled out around the ECL, the core of good players went to cities other than Philadelphia. The Bacharachs wound up with three of them.[34]

On July 16 "Country Brown" Bryant reappeared in a Bacharach uniform and remained a regular outfielder through the 1926 pennant-winning season. Claude "Red" Grier, a 21-year-old left-handed starter, came with Bryant. Grier was said to have a wide assortment of pitches and good control, and he helped anchor the Giants' starting staff for four seasons before his brief black big league career was over, a victim of poor training habits.[35]

Hammond Daniels teased the press and fans on July 22 when he stated that he "expected to sign one of the best-known outfielders in the game within the next 24 hours," but refused to give the player's name.[36] The man was present for duty for a doubleheader against the Baltimore Black Sox on July 26, and was none other than Chaney White, another Potomacs refugee returned to the Bacharach lineup. The pitching staff got another boost in July when Luther Farrell, a big lefty, was acquired from the Lincoln Giants. A good pitcher, he was an even better hitter, and took turns in the outfield when not on the mound. Berdell Young, cut by the Original Bacharachs in 1922 after part-time outfield duty, was brought back and also did much to bolster the outfield, particularly during the stretch after Mason was traded and until Bryant and White signed.

Not all the 1924 Bacharachs were welcomed back. The team cut its ties with George Shively in April when he wanted too much money. As manager Lloyd put it, "Shively wanted the ball park to play here, so we kept the ball park and let Shively do as he pleases." Big Milton Lewis, Lloyd's understudy at second base and a general handy utilityman, had never produced the offensive numbers that his six-foot, 200-pound frame seemed to promise, and he, too, was let go in April. Daniels, who never beat around the bush about a player's abilities, or lack thereof, was somewhat kind to Lewis: "Milton was a mighty fine boy and could drive the ball when he connected. But he was not connecting enough. We had to forget his fine social qualities in order to make a determined race for the Eastern Colored League pennant."[37]

Once the drawn-out trade for Marcell was finished, the Bacharachs had a stellar infield. Lloyd at second base had another outstanding season, leading the team with a .341 batting average and 92 runs batted in, tops on the Giants. Lundy hit .304, a little off his usual pace, but drove in 85 runs, second on the team, and led the Bacharachs in runs scored with 95. Marcell batted .317, hit at least nine home runs and had 62 RBI to rank third on the Giants. Cummings was his usual self. He batted .294 and was second in runs scored with 75 behind Lundy's 95.

Ambrose Reid, the only starting outfielder for the entire season, hit .250 and usually manned center field. After all the trades and signings, he was flanked by White in left at .338 and Bryant in right at .297. Reserves were Young, who batted .276; Jim "Bobo" Leonard, a pickup from the Lincoln Giants, who hit .243; and Farrell when he wasn't pitching. He batted .385 and showed plenty of extra-base power—he had a slugging percentage of at least .508.

Charley Mason was batting .341 when management decided that acquiring Marcell was worth offering him up. Willie Woods, who been with the Potomacs the previous season, was the other regular outfielder at the beginning of the year, but his light hitting (.208), plus an injury from an off-the-field fall, made him expendable when White and Brown came aboard. As in the previous season, Willie Jones and Ernest Gatewood shared the catching. Gatewood, who caught in 50 games, hit .267, very good for him. Jones caught 70 games, but only hit .229. Several of the pitchers besides Farrell gave themselves a lot of offensive help. Grier batted .289, Rats Henderson .242 and Arnett Mitchell .214.

Overall the Bacharachs batted .283 and averaged a little more than five runs per game. As in past years, though, the pitching kept the team from being exceptional. The pitchers had a cumulative ERA of 3.77 and allowed about four and a half runs per game. Henderson again was the workhorse and as close to being an ace as anyone on the staff. He made 28 starts, mostly against ECL competition, added nine relief appearances, and went 18–12 with a 3.77 ERA that matched the team average. But nobody else hit double figures in wins, although Grier and Farrell likely would have if they had been on the team all season. In ten starts Grier went 8–3 with a 3.65 ERA, and in seven starts and three relief jobs Farrell went 5–3 with a nice 2.96 ERA. After reporting from Talladega College in May, Lockhart made 11 starts and had a 3.65 ERA, winning three and losing six. Mitchell went 7–7 in 14 starts with a 4.19 ERA. Roy Roberts was 3–5 in 10 starts, although he had a very creditable 3.01 ERA. Henry Gillespie, who had been pitching for the regional Philadelphia Giants, was signed as a starter at the beginning of the season, but was released after eight starts and a 4–3 record. He and Bill Nuttall, who also started the season with the Bacharachs, wound up with the Lincoln Giants.

This season the *Courier*'s Wilson let fans vote for the ECL all-stars by sending in written ballots. Two hundred twenty-one of them did so, and Lloyd and Lundy repeated as manager and shortstop, respectively. White was the top left fielder and Henderson was picked as a pitcher. Judy Johnson of Hilldale, one of the early Negro League electees to the Baseball Hall of Fame, was picked as the third baseman with 113 votes, but Marcell was right on his heels with 108, no other ECL third sacker having gotten any votes at all.[38]

The official ECL standings had the Bacharach Giants at 26 wins and 26 losses, six games behind third-place Baltimore, at the end of the season. To account for the inevitable differences in games played, it had been decided that only the first ten contests between any two of the teams would count toward the standings, the rest being "exhibition games." The search for Bacharach league games in 1925 turned up 74, with 36 wins, 36 losses and two ties. So any way the Giants' season is looked at, this was a .500 team at Negro League level competition. The overall discovered record, as usual, was better, 70–52–5, a .574 winning percentage.

In every Bacharach season the team's record against non-league level opponents was better, sometimes substantially so, than its mark against the Negro League and other tougher squads, which is to be expected. That is the main reason, for the statistically minded, that player stats against all levels of competition and league-level teams are included for each season. Before the Bacharachs entered the ECL in 1923, they had some impressive annual batting and pitching spreads between the two categories of discovered games, and overall averaged 20 percentage points better in batting per season against the lesser teams. The pitchers were even better, with an earned run average of more than one run less. Beginning with league play in 1923, though, the spread got tighter. The composite batting average against the lower-level teams was only seven points higher, and the pitchers' ERA only six-tenths of a run better.

The demands of keeping a league schedule had a lot to do with these changes. The share of discovered games against Negro League teams jumped from around 50 percent before and in the first year of the ECL, up to nearly 80 percent by 1927. While the games against local competition might well constitute the largest share of the undiscovered games (league games usually got reported in at least one major black newspaper), it is also pretty clear that fewer game dates were available to play the small town and city neighborhood teams after league play and travel between ECL cities was taken into account. Also, there may well have been fewer of the lesser teams around by the end of the 1920s, at least those talented enough to reasonably take on a Negro League team. For example, the number of games the Bacharachs played against Philadelphia semi-pro squads each season declined somewhat during the ECL years, but the actual number of opponents sank into the mid to low single digits. And those teams appear to have been strong ones, their lineups showing some of the same names over and over again—like Ad Swigler or Stan Baumgartner, for example—who could be found playing for one or more top-flight teams each year.

In the ECL, Hilldale was again the league champion with a 45–13 record, although the Harrisburg Giants hung closely behind most of the season, finally finishing 6½ games behind. The season was again rife with disputes, George Robinson not being the only dissatisfied party. Bill Dallas, Bolden's pick for umpiring supervisor, was not a strong choice, seemingly made more to spur coverage of the league by major white newspapers than to instill discipline among the arbiters and those who would disagree with their decisions. One figure who often vehemently opposed the umps was Baltimore playing manager John Beckwith, described that year as "belligerent and incorrigible." In early August Beckwith assaulted an umpire in Harrisburg who had made several bad calls in a previous Black Sox game. He was suspended by the league, although he was its leading home run hitter.[39]

Despite an attempt to set up a balanced 70-game schedule for each team, no one reached that total, and the number of official games varied from 58 for Hilldale to 33 for the ever-recalcitrant Royal Giants. Part of the shortfall was due to the folding of the Potomacs, who were not replaced as the league went on after late July with only seven teams. But a pre-season story in the *Courier* about the development of the league schedule made the frank point that while a balanced schedule would be desirable, "with the clubs paying top salaries to players and with practically only one day per week at the respective cities being a paying proposition, the owners can ill afford to pass up lucrative bookings with independent clubs in their adjacent vicinity."[40]

The Bacharachs did well in the 74 discovered games against all their ECL opponents except first-place Hilldale and second-place Harrisburg, which beat them a combined 20 times against only 11 Giants victories. Atlantic City opened well against Hilldale on May 14 when Henderson three-hit the Philadelphia team, gaining a 2-1 win over Nip Winters' seven-hitter. But for the season Hilldale won ten of 14 games, beginning right away on May 16 when Henderson lost a 7-3 decision. Rats had eight decisions against Hilldale, but only three of them were victories. He won the third game between the two teams, on May 21, in relief when the Giants scored three runs in the ninth inning on Hilldale fielding lapses to win, 8-6, and beat Winters a second time by a 2-1 score, this time in 12 innings, on August 9.

But a close game turned into a rout on June 11 when Henderson gave up six runs in the eighth inning in an 11-4 loss. Another showdown with Winters on June 28 resulted in another good set of pitching performances. Henderson gave up four hits and Winters seven, but Hilldale won, 3-2. Veteran outfielder Otto Briggs drove in the winning runs in the seventh inning on July 30 to tag Henderson with a 5-4 defeat, and he won, 8-1, on August 20.

The only other Bacharach win occurred on September 23 when Red Grier got a seven-inning, 5-1 win. Grier took a 5-2 loss, though, on August 10 when Phil Cockrell not only outpitched him but collected three hits. In general, the Giants just could not hit Hilldale pitching, and were outscored in the season series, 68 runs to 37. They were held to two or fewer runs in nine of the 14 games, including a 1-0 loss on August 22 when Mitchell, who had given up only six hits, was victimized by a bad throw by catcher Jones. A good throw to the plate had stopped Briggs in his tracks between third and home in the first inning, but Jones' attempt to nail Briggs as he retreated sailed into left field, letting in the only run of the game. Mitchell lost twice more, 7-2 in the second game of a doubleheader on June 28, and 6-1 on September 22, and Roberts was defeated, 6-1, on September 24.

Eighteen games with the Harrisburg Giants produced seven wins, ten losses and a tie. The season series opened in Harrisburg in mid-May. The Bacharachs lost the first game, 12-7, on May 18 when Mitchell, who "had nothing after the sixth" gave up seven runs over the next two innings.[41] Henderson gained a 5-4 win the next day, backed by home runs by Lundy, Mason and himself, but Oscar Charleston and Dick Jackson, who had developed hitting skills since his utilityman stint with the Bacharachs at the beginning the decade, homered off Bill Nuttall on the 20th to give the home team a 4-3 victory.

The next meeting a month later, also on the road, produced two Harrisburg wins to one for the Bacharachs. Mason supported Mitchell with three hits in an 8-3 win on June 12. But that followed a 6-4 loss on June 8 in which Harrisburg scored all its runs in the sixth through eighth innings and an 11-inning offensive donnybrook on June 10 in which the Bacharachs got 20 hits and Harrisburg 19. Atlantic City scored seven runs in the first inning and led 10-4 going into the bottom of the ninth, but the home team scored 11 times in its final three turns at bat.

The win one-lose two pattern repeated itself over the July 4 weekend when the

Bacharachs lost, 3–2, on the 3rd and split a doubleheader, winning 3–2 and losing 9–1, on the holiday, and again in the middle of the month when two losses, 5–4 on July 12 and 8–3 on the 15th, were followed by another hitters' battle. This time the two teams had a total of 30 hits and the Bacharachs won, 13–9. A three-game series at the end of August resulted in a 7–6 loss on the 28th in which a three-run ninth-inning rally fell short, and a 4–3 loss and 2–2 tie called in the seventh inning due to darkness the next day.

The Bacharachs finally had a successful series when they swept three games split between the two cities. Grier won the first, 9–2, on September 8 in Harrisburg, and a 7–6 victory followed back in Atlantic City the next day plus an 8–2 win there on the 10th. Mitchell won that game in relief and Marcell, who collected four hits, won a new pair of pants from a local clothing store for being the game's outstanding batsman.[42]

Despite finishing behind the Black Sox, the Bacharachs handled them fairly easily in the season's series, winning eight and losing five. They had 20 hits in the opener on May 24, with Mason collecting four and Jones and Henderson three each. Henderson wasn't very sharp, giving up 12 hits, but the Giants won, 14–8. On June 14 they split a doubleheader. Lundy tripled and scored the game's only run while Henderson threw a seven-hit shutout. Despite a homer by Young, the Black Sox won the second game, 5–2. A July 26 doubleheader resulted in another split. Marcell had four hits and Lundy three in the opener as the Bacharachs won, 13–8. Baltimore's Bob McClure and Henderson put on a pitching exhibition in the nightcap, which was won, 2–1, by the Sox when Beckwith, about a week short of his outburst and suspension, sent himself up as a pinch-hitter in the seventh inning and homered.

Lundy was the hero for the Atlantic City home crowd on August 3 when he broke a 2–2 tie by tripling home a run and then stealing home. But the next day Beckwith and Oscar "Heavy" Johnson homered in the ninth inning for a 7–3 Baltimore win. Trautwein Brothers, the same clothiers that later provided Marcell with a pair of pants, bestowed a new suit on Bryant on August 19 when his three hits led the Giants to a 10–9 win.[43] Luther Farrell picked up a 4–3 win in the first game of a doubleheader in Baltimore on August 23, but George Britt pitched a five-hit shutout for the Black Sox in the second game, which they won, 5–0. The teams moved to Richmond, Virginia, the next day, and this time Henderson shut out the Sox, 6–0. The third straight shutout between the two teams occurred on September 15, when Farrell was the winning pitcher again and Lloyd's four hits led the offense to a 5–0 win. The last game, on September 18, also the Bacharachs' last home game, belonged to the Black Sox. McClure outdueled Lockhart, 3–2, although Lundy homered for the Giants.

The New York Cuban Stars, who finished in sixth place, won five of the ten games played against the Bacharachs while the Giants won four and there was a tie. The Bacharachs backed Henderson with 17 hits, three by Lloyd, in the first game of a May 30 doubleheader for a 9–6 win. The tie, at 3–3, happened in the second game when darkness enveloped the neutral field in Jersey City, New Jersey. The Cubans were the hitting stars when the teams next met at Bacharach Park on June 22, getting 20 of them to win, 12–3. The next day, though, Lundy, Cummings and Gatewood each had three hits as the Giants scored six runs in the seventh inning for a 13–7 win.

After all of that offense, the season series settled down into mostly well-pitched games. The Stars won both games of a short series in Atlantic City on July 27–28. Farrell yielded only four hits on the first day, but one of them was a grand slam homer to future Hall of Famer Martin Dihigo and the Bacharachs lost, 6–1. Dihigo, who was as likely to show up on the mound as at a position, pitched the next day and gave up only six hits as the Giants lost again, 8–5.

Red Grier, who gave up only one run and Willie Jones, who had three hits, were the stars on August 17 as the Bacharachs won, 3–1. They lost by inches the next day, though, 5–4. Farrell hit a long drive to right in the bottom of the ninth that, had it cleared the fence, would have tied the game. But it hit the top of the wall for a double, and no one could drive him in. The Cubans' last visit to Bacharach Park at the end of September produced another series split. Grier won his own game, 3–2, with an RBI single in the seventh inning on the 29th, but Oscar Levis pitched a four-hitter on the 30th as the Stars won, 4–1.

Atlantic City took four of six from the Brooklyn Royal Giants, as usual the team that played the fewest league games. The two teams were opposed on May 3 in Jersey City as 4,000 fans came out to see a Bacharach sweep generated by Mason. The first game was won, 5–4, as he hit a two-run homer, and the second, 4–2, on the strength of his two-run triple. Henderson threw good games for the other two wins. He tossed a one-hit, six-inning shutout for a rain-shortened 3–0 victory on May 30 and won, 4–2, on July 7. The Bacharach losses to the Royal Giants came 8–4 on May 15 and 7–6 on July 6.

The Lincoln Giants had a terrible season and finished in last place (of the seven teams that finished the year) with only seven wins and 39 losses. The Bacharachs dominated them, too, although not by as large a margin as the rest of the league, winning five of eight. This was due to the Lincolns getting off to a great start on April 26, sweeping a doubleheader at the Protectory Oval. Dave Brown's last big league game before he became a fugitive was a seven-hitter for a 6–1 win. The Bacharachs were ahead in the second game until Bob Hudspeth, their former teammate, homered in the eighth to tie the score and Rich Gee singled in a run in the bottom of the ninth for a 4–3 win.

Thereafter the Bacharachs won nearly all the time. Grier was the winning pitcher on July 20 in an 11–2 game. Farrell won in relief the next day, 7–6, when he homered to start a four-run ninth-inning rally. Hits flew around little Protectory Oval in an August 2 doubleheader. White, Lundy and Marcell each homered once and Bryant hit two as the Bacharachs won the first game, 10–8. They followed with a 13–6 nightcap victory. A September 6 doubleheader at Protectory was split, the former Bacharach Bill Nuttall getting a 4–3 win in the first game and Farrell a win by the same score in the second. Always a threat at bat, Farrell singled in Lloyd in the top of the ninth for the winning run.

The Bacharachs had opened their season on April 19 in Dexter Park, Brooklyn, against the Bushwicks, on a day when the American flag in center field hung at half mast in memory of Brooklyn Dodgers owner Charles F. Ebbets, who had died the day before. The Giants won, 6–3, although starting pitcher Roberts' control was at its worst—he gave up three walks and four wild pitches in addition to four hits in 2⅓ innings. But Henderson took over and held Bushwick scoring to three runs in the third inning. Meanwhile the Giants went ahead with two runs in the fourth. It was the beginning of a successful season with the New York semi-pro teams, against whom the Giants won nine of 14, with a tie. The Bushwicks were the only squad that gave them consistent trouble, including sweeping a doubleheader on July 5. The first game went 13 innings, getting most exciting near the end. Nuttall and former white big leaguer Leon Cadore were in an extended pitchers' duel when the Bushwicks tied the score at 3–3 in the bottom of the 12th. The Bacharachs went ahead, 4–3, in the top of the 13th, but second baseman Joe Weiss drilled a two-run single off Nuttall to give the home team a 5–4 win. Farrell gave up six hits and struck out eight in the first game of two on September 20 as the Giants won, 6–1, but a 28-hit second game went the Bushwicks' way, 12–10.

The Giants took two doubleheaders from the Farmers, 4–1 and 14–8 on June 21, Lloyd homering in both games, and 7–2 and 8–4 on August 16, when Marcell, Bryant and Leonard each homered. A doubleheader with the Bay Ridge team in Brooklyn on September 13 resulted in a Bacharach sweep, 3–2 in 14 innings and 6–2 in six as it got dark, and they played a 2–2 tie on October 4 stopped by rain in the sixth inning. The Yonkers Caseys, a new opponent from that suburban city just north of the New York, fell 10–2 on August 11, and Heinie Zimmerman's College Point team from Queens won, 5–4, on July 9. Roberts, the veteran Negro Leaguer, actually outpitched Jimmy Clinton, the white semi-pro vet, but the Giants' fielding let him down.

Competition from the Philadelphia area consisted mostly of a long series of games with the Camden Skeeters. The ambitious Penn-Jersey semi-pro league of 1924 was not back in action, but the Skeeters were. They played the Bacharachs an extremely competitive season series—each team won five games, and there were two ties. Socks Seibold, still on his extended hiatus from white pro ball, outpitched Mitchell for a 7–4 win on April 25. Playing in unseasonable Shore heat on June 7 that had the fans doffing their coats (baseball was still a dress-up occasion for spectators in 1925), everyone in the Bacharach lineup got at least one hit, 16 in all, and Lockhart cruised to a 10–1 win.[44] Six days later, though, Jim "Lefty" York, who had been a spot starter and reliever for the Chicago Cubs in 1921, was the winner for Camden, 11–5.

Down 6–2 on July 13, the Bacharachs, paced by Lundy's four hits, scored four times in the seventh inning to tie the game and put across a winning run in the bottom of the ninth. Camden then swept a two-game series at its field on July 17–18, 5–2 and 5–4. Another game in Camden on July 29 looked to be in the Giants' pocket, but four Skeeters runs in the bottom of the ninth tied it at 5–5, and it was too dark to keep playing. Seven runs in the seventh inning, with a bases-loaded triple by Cummings the key hit, brought about an 8–7 victory on August 8. Typical for a season series where no team ever had a lead of more than two games, the Giants and Skeeters split a September 19 doubleheader. Grier shut out Camden in the first game, 3–0, and York shut out the Bacharachs in the second, 1–0. The Bacharachs won the first game of a doubleheader on October 3 that wrapped up the series by 7–3, and the second game resulted in a 3–3 tie. The Giants took all five discovered games against other Philadelphia teams, including three from Lit Brothers and one each from the Passyunk Artisans and the SPHAs.

Games with more far-flung white Pennsylvania teams resulted in a 2–2 split with Allentown, a 15–4 win from Easton on May 22, and a win and a loss against Hazelton. The results against New Jersey teams were similarly mixed, with wins over Glassboro,

Vineland and Wildwood, but losses to Hammonton (usually an easy mark), Trenton, Salem (a new opponent) and the Doherty Silk Sox from Paterson. In that game Chickie Passon, a regular pitcher for the SPHAs, made his debut with the high-level Doherty team and gained a 6–1 win.

Local Atlantic City teams continued to be easy pickings. The Bacharachs beat the Ocean City Collegians twice and Pleasantville, Melrose, the Atlantic City Police and the Morris Guards once each.

The 1925 season featured single games against opponents of the type that the Giants didn't usually play. On April 29 the team went to Harrisburg not for an ECL game but to play the Harrisburg Senators of the white Class B New York–Pennsylvania League. The Bacharachs beat the home team, 10–6, Gillespie not only getting the win but also three hits, one a triple.

The *Daily Press* headline on September 4 summed up the other game: "Bacharach Giants Conquer Bloomer Girls in Comedy." The New York Bloomer Girls, one of several women's regional touring teams, primarily played semi-pro teams, barnstorming around much in the way of the black teams of the day. These Bloomer Girls usually had men at catcher, pitcher and shortstop to begin the game although one of their stars, Helen Demarest, pitched the final three innings against Atlantic City. Their leadoff hitter, Ethel Condon, was reportedly 15 years old this season (she is said to have lied about her age to get on the team), and played women's baseball in the New York area into the early 1950s.[45]

Manager Lloyd used most of his pitching staff—in the field. Roberts played first base, Henderson second and Mitchell third. Lockhart was in center field and Grier in right. Bryant caught (and did many of his comedy routines). Jones, one of the usual catchers, played shortstop. Reid, Lundy and Gatewood did the pitching. Lloyd assigned himself to left field, where he should have had an unobstructed view of the festivities: "The B-Giants would give the girls any number of runs they desired to an inning and then tie the count in their half. In the ninth, with the game already won with a one-run margin, Henderson could resist the temptation no longer and leaned on one of Miss Demarest's benders for a homer."

"A good time was had by all," the *Daily Press* reported.[46]

Chapter 6

The Championship Seasons

1926

Atlantic City was booming. Hundreds of thousands of tourists arrived noisily and expectantly by train, bus and car from the mainland in the tourist season. Hundreds to thousands of cases of liquor arrived quietly and illegally by boat all the time. Chamber of Commerce types were smiling broadly, while revenue agents were gnashing their teeth.

It seemed that every summer weekend brought a new record for tourists. Business leaders estimated a half-million arrived over a rainy Fourth of July weekend and guessed that 100,000 more had been scared away by the weather. A regular non-holiday weekend in early August over which the sun shone was said to have already shattered the Fourth of July mark. A conservative estimate put the crowd at "well over half a million." A real estate article in the *Daily Press* put the assessed value of all Atlantic City real estate at $302 million, with beachfront property going from $5,000 to $10,000 (or $65,000 to $130,000 today) per linear foot.[1]

The annual Easter Day stroll on the Boardwalk, a custom allowing people, particularly women, to parade in their latest finery, drew a quarter of a million participants. Someone in the Businessmen's League of Atlantic City had the bright idea in 1920 to hold a beauty pageant in September to stimulate post–Labor Day tourism. By 1922 the winner was being called "Miss America" and the pageant attracted international attention. Norma Smallwood of Oklahoma, a Cherokee who was the first American Indian to win, was 1926's Miss America.

Atlantic City also had another national distinction—in 1924 a journalist said it was "known in prohibition circles as the wettest town in the United States." The writer described encountering a drinking establishment that looked exactly as the most comfortable of such establishments had appeared before 1920, where he got a good dark beer for 20 cents. "Plainly," he wrote, "Volstead had never been here."[2]

A syndicated series by writer William P. Helm Jr. claimed "it has been carefully estimated that there are from 250 to 300 open saloons, cafes and cabarets where liquor is sold in Atlantic City." But Helm was more interested in the booze traffic through the beaches of the city and nearby towns. "An average week ... sees from 3,000 to 5,000 cases ... brought ashore" from storage ships kept anchored beyond the 12-mile limit beyond which U.S. authorities, primarily the Coast Guard, had jurisdiction. Fast motor boats set out from shore, usually between the hours of midnight and 4 a.m., and brought the cases

"The Pageantry of Atlantic City in a Single Picture," taken in 1929 by Clifton Adams (Atlantic City Heritage Collections, Atlantic City Free Public Library).

in to be offloaded quickly onto truck and touring cars that carried them to Philadelphia, where further distributions were made. Helm claimed that liquor traffic through Atlantic City was "highly systematized," run by a syndicate that took its orders from New York City bootleggers. He said the syndicate had an office, which it took no pains to conceal, two blocks off the Boardwalk where "the illegal traffic is conducted in much the same manner as a legitimate business."[3]

All of this, of course, would not have been possible without the winks and nods of Atlantic City and County officials. But in 1926 Harry Bacharach was not one of them. He had decided against running for re-election to the city commission in 1920 at the behest of his wife, who was in poor health since the death of their young daughter. He tended to the various family business interests after that, although he did make a comeback attempt in the commission election of 1924. His ticket of aspiring commissioners was up against that of his successor, Edward L. Bader. This put county political leader Enoch Johnson on the spot, since his endorsement would most likely determine the winner, and both Bacharach and Bader had been members of his political machine. Johnson went for Bader, whose ticket won, but not before the conclusion of a campaign in which neither side shrank from slinging mud and whatever else was handy at the opposition. Bader, in a likely attempt to undercut Bacharach's popularity with the Northside black community, accused Bacharach of being soft on the Ku Klux Klan, which had a public presence in Southern New Jersey. This was an unusual charge to lodge against a Jew. Bacharach, running as a reform candidate, constantly accused the Bader administration of corruption, and particularly campaigned against "protected vice." Atlantic City being what it was, that wasn't a strange charge at all.[4]

Former Mayor Bacharach's Giants started their banner year with some setbacks, the biggest of which occurred before spring training. Rumors that were flying at the end of the 1925 season that manager and star second baseman John Henry Lloyd, dissatisfied with the way the Bacharachs were being run by what he considered a disorganized group of owners, would leave the club to manage the Lincoln Giants. W. Rollo Wilson, the *Pittsburgh Courier* columnist, wrote in September that Lloyd "does not intend to return to the Bees another year" and that a hydra-headed management system that had developed under Hammond Daniels was to blame. Wilson's column also contained pithy summaries of each Eastern Colored League team in the just-concluding season. The Bacharachs, he said, had "too many cooks."[5]

A *Baltimore Afro-American* story back in July 1925 quoted Lloyd as disparaging the organization of the entire league, but he may have been thinking closer to home when he said "the whole outfit will not be worth a picyune [sic] until men that know baseball are in charge." While in Atlantic City the issue of whether or not Lloyd would return was portrayed as being in doubt until just before the start of the 1926 season, the *New York Age* had stated confidently in early January that negotiations between Lloyd and Jim Keenan, the owner of the Lincolns, had been going on for months and that Lloyd was definitely going to Keenan's team. The Bacharachs claimed that, although Lloyd's contract with the team had expired the previous October, he was bound to them anyway by the rules against unregulated player movement. Lloyd contended, however, that his contract with the Giants was as a manager, and anyway the club had breached it in 1925, in a manner he never specified. A majority of the league's owners, acting as its ruling commission, let him go to New York.[6]

Field leadership reverted back to Dick Lundy, who, with the exception of the large hole Lloyd left at second, put much the same team on the field as in 1925. Three of the four members of the high-class infield were back. Lundy was again at shortstop, leading the team in batting (.343), runs scored (83), hits (141), doubles (15), RBI (84) and walks (50). Marcell hit .276 at third base and drove in 54 runs. Although a pre-season story on the Giants described Cummings uncharitably as having "reached the pinnacle and is on his way down," Chance hit a reliable .282. Often batting high up in the order ahead of Lundy and the other sluggers, he scored 64 runs. Second base was turned over to Romando "Cheno" Garcia, a Cuban playing his first year in the U.S. He was no Lloyd (but then, few were), hitting only .225. But he was a good fielder (the *Daily Press* described him as "young, small and wiry") playing most every day at his main position and occasionally spelling Marcell and Lundy.[7]

Chaney White became the center fielder on a daily basis. He was also a permanent fixture in the showcase number three spot in the batting order, finishing second to Lundy in hitting (.324), runs (82), hits (135), doubles (13) and RBI (75). Luther Farrell played right field when he wasn't pitching, and his power sometimes displaced Lundy from the cleanup spot. Farrell led the Giants in home runs with seven and was third on the team with 64 RBI while batting .282. Ambrose Reid was the primary left fielder, walking 43 times to supplement his .249 batting average and scoring 69 runs. "Country Brown" Bryant was still with the team, although clearly past his prime. He was a utility fill-in all over the infield and outfield, but his batting average dropping drastically to .186. In August the team picked up outfielder Maurice "Eggie" Dallard, who had been cut loose by the Black Sox for "breaking training rules," particularly the one about excessive drinking. Lundy snapped Dallard right up and the manager's strict but even-tempered approach to discipline extracted a .319 average in 12 games until Dallard contracted a throat infection and was lost for the rest of the season.[8] McKinley "Jack" Wallace logged the first season of a short Negro League career when he was signed as a utilityman in June, July and August while Garcia, Marcell and Farrell were out the lineup for short periods. He hit .221.

Willie Jones, who hit .225, was back to do the majority of the catching, as was the 36-year-old Ernest Gatewood, who backed him up and hit .238. In August, when Gatewood was out for a spell, the Giants picked up Joe Lewis from the Lincoln Giants to back up Jones. Lewis, in the midst of a 16-year career as a blackball catcher, hit .209.

The pitching staff was improved primarily by having a full year each of Red Grier and Farrell, particularly Grier, who moved past Rats Henderson to become the ace of the staff. Grier appeared in 42 games, 34 of them starts, threw 26 complete games (five of them shutouts), and had a 21–13 won-lost record with a 2.92 ERA. He struck out 224 batters in 283 innings. Henderson made 28 starts among his 37 games and completed 22. He won 15 and lost 11 and had a 2.69 ERA. Roy Roberts, 10–5 in 26 appearances, including 19 starts; Farrell, 7–5 in 17 games with 13 starts; Hubert Lockhart, 7–6 in 18 games, 15 of them starts; and Alonzo Mitchell, who had a 4–5 record in 13 games, eight of them starts, formed the rest of the rotation (and the bullpen).

Alonzo, only 21, was the younger brother of Arnett Mitchell, who had pitched for three years for Atlantic City, most recently in the previous season. A right-hander like his brother, Alonzo was in his rookie year in the black big leagues, but would stick around as a player and manager until 1940. Good-hitting Bacharach teams in the ECL years had been held back by a lack of good pitching, but this was no longer a problem.

Rollo Wilson of the *Courier* dropped in at Bacharach Park in early September and found the Giants' lineup and pitching staff sound throughout. As for Lundy's management, "the boys all like him and he never rides them. If they have brains he allows them to be used, and while he is absolutely the manager, he welcomes suggestions from anyone competent to make them."[9]

In the offseason the ECL had added a new team, the Newark Stars, to replace the ill-fated Potomacs and bring the league back to eight teams. But the poorly-funded Stars folded at the end of June after only 11 league games, ten of them losses. For a time it seemed that the main function of the Stars was to occupy last place so the Bacharachs wouldn't tumble into it. On the road for most of May, the Giants lost their first three games against league opponents and won only two for the month. At the end of May, Lundy's men were in seventh place with a 2–7 record. The team's performance improved in June, when it went 7–5. This brought its winning percentage up to .429, just good enough for sixth place.

But everything changed with the turn of the calendar to July 1. Beginning with a win over Harrisburg to even up a two-game series, the Bacharachs reeled off a reported 13 straight ECL wins by July 25 and vaulted all the way to second place. The 6–5 win that day, in which Roberts won his own decision in relief by singling in the game-winning run in bottom of the ninth inning, was against the Cuban Stars, the only team ahead of the Giants in the ECL. The Stars won the next day, 5–4, in 11 innings to break an overall 17-game Bacharach winning streak. But the Giants took the last game of the series on July 27, 9–1, to move into a first place tie. The race was on.

Stewart B. Thorbahn, covering the team for the *Daily Press*, said when the Giants beat Harrisburg on July 19 that the home town team "looks like the class of the league and is bound for the top of the Eastern Colored League."[10] As well as the team played, the road to the pennant was hardly unobstructed. The Cubans stayed hot and Hilldale, not quite the team it had been in previous years but still very good, cruised right in the Bacharachs' wake. Then, in August, after Lloyd's Lincoln Giants cooled and fell out of contention, Harrisburg caught fire and moved commandingly into second place. But the Bacharachs got hot, too, with nine straight discovered wins between August 15 and September 4. In the standings published September 12 they were comfortably 34 percentage points ahead of Harrisburg.

But it never paid to get too comfortable about anything in the ECL. As usual, the sought-for balanced schedule with each team playing an equal number of games was in disarray. The collapse of Newark was the first thing to screw up the 1926 schedule, but all of the forces that prevented or discouraged some of the other teams to keep to the plan were again present. Each team was supposed to play 60 games, and in the September 12 standings dependable Hilldale had 57 decisions to the Bacharachs' 54. The Black Sox had played 46 games and Harrisburg 42, relatively close to their full schedules. But Brooklyn, as usual, had ditched a number of league games and had only 20 decisions (and only four wins). The other full-time road team, the Cuban Stars, and the Lincoln Giants, who purportedly would rather play at home in the Bronx on Sundays, whoever the opponent might be, had logged only 39 games.

The season as scheduled was supposed to end on September 15, and at that point the Bacharachs would win the pennant. But the commissioners (the owners, that is) decided to extend play until the 26th to try to get in as many unplayed games as possible. Hilldale, with three games left and four more losses than Atlantic City, had little chance to catch up. But if the Bacharachs were to go into a slump in their last six games, it was at least mathematically possible for Harrisburg or the Cubans to catch them, if they somehow could squeeze in enough league games in the 11 extra days. Since the number of games played by the ECL teams was never even in any season, the pennant was determined by winning percentage, not total games won, and a hot team with a smaller schedule could theoretically triumph.

The Giants were extremely unhappy with this turn of events. Bryant suggested the team get a court injunction against the league and "Marcell, Gatewood and several other members of the club nod their heads." Jones said that "everybody knows that we have won the pennant." As it turned out, even with the extra days the Bacharachs had, in fact, finished first. Very few additional games were played before the league relented and Ed Bolden announced that the flag belonged to Atlantic City. The Giants' winning percentage of .629 (34–20) topped Harrisburg by 34 percentage points, Hilldale by 43 and the Cubans by 46.[11]

This put the Bacharachs into the third Negro World Series, but it wasn't clear which Negro National League team they would be playing. The Kansas City Monarchs, winners of the first half of the NNL's split season, seemed to have the second half wrapped up, too, which would have automatically given them the title. But the Chicago American Giants came on fast in September and won the second half when the St. Louis Stars beat the Monarchs on September 12. Chicago then defeated Kansas City in a playoff series for the opportunity to go against the Bacharachs. The Monarchs had gone ahead four games to three in the best-five-of-nine series, but the American Giants won the last two games by shutouts, 1–0 and 5–0, to take the pennant.

The American Giants were the team of the famous Rube Foster, but he was not around to lead them into the Series. Growing signs of mental instability had led to a breakdown in late August, and Foster had been committed to a psychiatric hospital in Chicago as the season was coming to an end. Dave Malarcher, the veteran third baseman, took over as manager. "We won it for Rube," some of the players said of the pennant play-off.[12]

The best-of-nine World Series actually included 11 full games, all nine possible decisions and two nine-inning games that ended in ties when it got too dark to play. The first of the ties was the opener, October 1 at Bacharach Park. Rats Henderson and Rube Curry, who had bolted Hilldale following a salary dispute in the spring and signed with Chicago, dueled effectively. Chicago scored a run in the second inning when shortstop Stanford "Jambo" Jackson, the eighth-place hitter, laid down a squeeze bunt and Henderson made a wild throw to the plate. The Bacharachs went ahead, 2–1, in the bottom of the fourth. Lundy's single drove in White all the way from first when the throw to the plate bounced over the catcher's head, and Farrell singled in Lundy. Jackson struck again in the sixth, though, driving in two runs with a hit and putting Chicago ahead again. Farrell tied the game at 3–3 with a home run in the bottom of the seventh. Atlantic City might have been in the lead at that point, but Lundy had been thrown out trying to steal second just before Farrell's wallop. Farrell had another chance to win the game in the eighth. Relief pitcher Willie Foster, Rube's half-brother and a star left-hander, came in with two men on and two out and walked Lundy intentionally to load the bases. Farrell, a left-handed hitter, didn't hit lefties very well, and he didn't hit Foster at all, striking out to end the rally. Soon it was too dark to continue.

An estimated 5,000 fans saw the first game, and 4,000 were there the next day as Chicago scored seven runs in the second inning and hung on for dear life for a 7–6 win. The Bacharachs disintegrated in every possible way in the fatal inning. Grier, the starter, and Lockhart gave up five hits and the Giants made four errors, a combination of wild throws, a dropped throw and a missed grounder. The Bacharachs scored three times in the bottom of the sixth to draw within one run when Garcia drove in two runs with a bases-loaded single and Reid knocked in another with a drive to the right field wall. But an attempt by Garcia to score the tying run turned into a "two men on third" double play. Cheno prudently retreated back to the base in the face of a good throw to the plate, only to find Lockhart, the trailing runner, also heading there. Lockhart beat it back to second and was tagged out. Garcia tried to sneak home while that was going on, and was thrown out there.

Some games in a Negro World Series were traditionally held in cities other than those of the two contesting teams in order to stimulate attendance. In this series the teams moved south to Baltimore on October 3 for what turned out to be an historic Negro Leagues game. Grier hadn't gotten out of the second inning the day before and Lundy decided that he hadn't spent so much energy that he couldn't start again. Grier could indeed start, and he could finish, and he allowed no hits along the way. He walked five batters and there was one Bacharach error, but his no-hitter was the first in Negro World Series history. The American Giants threatened to score only in the fifth, when they loaded the bases on two walks and an error, but Grier got left fielder Sandy Thompson to ground back to him.

The Bacharachs scored ten runs, four in the first inning off starter Webster McDonald on RBI singles by Marcell and Lundy and a throwing error by Malarcher that let in two more. They put six runs over in the sixth inning. Reid, Cummings and Jones drove in runs with hits, Reid scored on an error, White hit a sacrifice fly and Lundy stole home, kicking the ball out of catcher John Hines' hand to avoid an out.

Then it was on to Philadelphia for two games in Baker Bowl, the park of the white major league Phillies. The stay in Philadelphia was supposed to be for only one game, but the game on October 4 resulted in the second nine-inning tie, which was replayed the following day. Henderson again got the no-decision for Atlantic City, and Willie Foster also pitched a complete game for Chicago. The American Giants held a 3–0 lead going into the bottom of the fifth, when the Bacharachs scored four times with two out. Garcia scored on a throwing error, White knocked in two runs with a single, and Lundy tripled Chaney home. Chicago tied the game in the seventh when Jackson and second baseman Charlie Williams beat out bunts. A sacrifice moved them into scoring position and Jackson was let in on a passed ball by Jones.

The Bacharachs went up two games to one the next day at Baker Bowl with a 7–5 win. Mitchell pitched a complete game four-hitter, substantially marred by three errors by his defense. Atlantic City was shut out by Curry for the first four innings and was down by three runs when the offense exploded for six runs in the top of the fifth inning to go ahead and stay there. Mitchell himself and Lundy were the top Bacharach hitters with three hits each. Mitchell included a triple among his hits and Lundy a double.

The series went back to Atlantic City on October 6, and the Bacharachs backed Grier's six-hit pitching performance with 11 hits, good for 17 total bases, to win, 6–4, and take a big three games to one lead in the Series. Chaney White was ill, so Mitchell, the winning pitcher the day before, was put in left field for his strong bat and Ambrose Reid moved to center. It was as if the starting lineup hadn't been disrupted—Reid had four hits, including a triple, and Mitchell singled and scored a run. The game was tied 2–2 after four innings, but the Bacharachs scored single runs in their next four times up.

After a two-day travel break, the Series finished in Chicago. Lockhart and Foster started and were both still around in the ninth inning, with the game tied, 4–4. The Bacharachs had been down, 4–2, but got back into the game in the top of the eighth when White tripled in Marcell, who had singled, and Joe Lewis, a right-handed hitter, pinch-hit for Farrell. Using the platoon advantage against Foster, the southpaw, worked as Lewis hit a sacrifice fly. But Foster set the Bacharachs down without any scoring in the top of the ninth. Lockhart got the first out in the bottom of the inning, but Malarcher singled through the box and Lundy pulled his starter in favor of Rats Henderson. Henderson got the second out, but Malarcher stole second during the at-bat. Hines singled to him in with the winning run, 5–4.

Henderson, more than any other Giant, put his team on the verge of the Series title on the 10th. Pitching through a rainy mist that didn't lift until the eighth inning, he three-hit Chicago for a 3–0 victory, the fourth Bacharach win. He struck out seven and walked only two batters. Henderson and George Harney, who along with Foster and Curry was one of Chicago's best starters, had a double shutout going until the top of the eighth, when Atlantic City scored all its runs. Bryant, replacing Reid in left field for this game, led off with a single. Cummings laid down one of his signature sacrifice bunts, but was safe when the throw was juggled. Chicago decided to walk Marcell intentionally but the strategy backfired. Cummings was doing his daredevil act, taking a big lead off second, and when Jackson cut in behind him White knocked the ball right through the big hole created by the shortstop's move to his left. Further, the hit got past Thompson in left, and all three runners scored.

This left the Bacharach Giants up four games to two in the Series, looking for one more win in three possible remaining games to become the black champions. They are still looking. The American Giants won, 6–3, on October 11, scoring all their runs by the sixth inning off of Grier and then withstanding a Bacharach rally in the eighth off of Curry that produced all three Atlantic City runs. Chicago tied the Series on the 13th with a 13–0 blowout that featured a seven-run, fourth-inning whaling of Henderson. Rats gave up seven hits, some on infield rollers, but others belted to the outfield. Roberts finished the game in his first pitching turn in the Series, and gave up six more runs.

Lockhart and Foster were the pitchers in the final game, another double shutout destined to be decided in the last half-inning. The Bacharachs had several chances to score. They loaded the bases in the top of the first with two out, but Foster struck out Cummings to kill that rally. They did the same in the seventh, but White flied out. Frustratingly, the team got ten hits, three by Marcell, but couldn't convert any of them into a single run.

Lockhart yielded only five hits and a single walk, and Chicago never mounted a serious threat until the bottom of the ninth. Then Gardner singled, Malarcher bunted him to second and Thompson singled to center. The ball took a bad hop away from Chaney White, and while he was retrieving it Gardner made it home with the game's only run and the championship.

Although the Series outcome was disappointing in the extreme, there was no denying that the Bacharachs had a fine season and could play with the best Negro League teams. In the discovered games the Giants played .594 ball during the regular season, including both games that counted in the standings and exhibitions, winning 38 and losing 26 with two ties. In fact, the American Giants were one of only two black teams to defeat them in a season series. The other was Harrisburg which, if the perpetually out-of-whack ECL

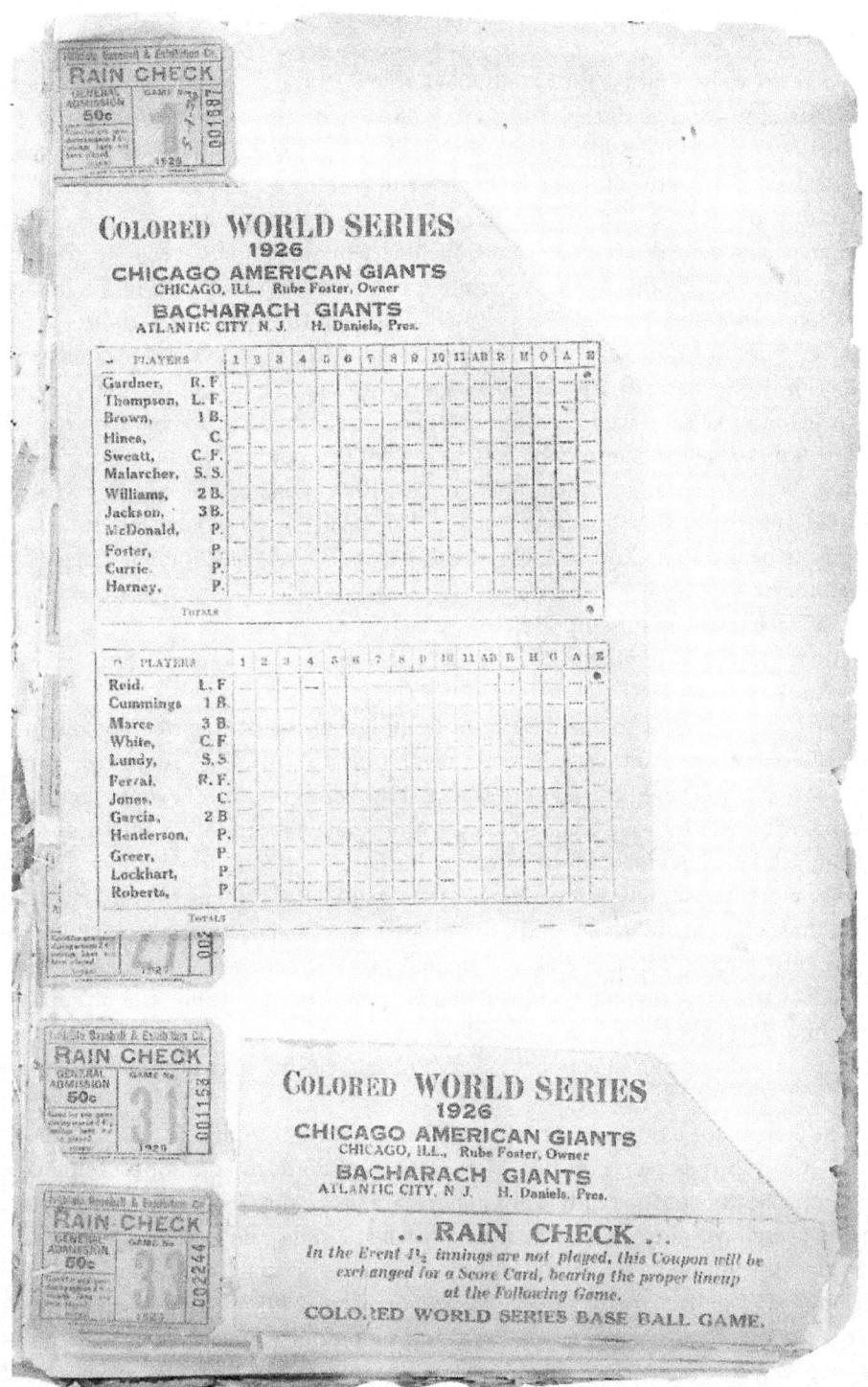

Program and ticket stubs from one of the 1926 Negro World Series games played in Atlantic City between the Bacharach Giants and the Chicago American Giants (Lawrence D. Hogan).

schedule had provided more opportunities, might have made a stronger run at Atlantic City.

There are only eight meetings found between Atlantic City and Harrisburg in 1926, and Harrisburg won five of them, including a sweep of a two-game series on May 7–8 when the Bacharachs were still finding themselves. Grier was outdueled by Harrisburg's Ping Gardner, 2–1, on the 7th, the Bacharach run coming on a Farrell homer. Farrell hit another four-bagger the next day but Henderson was off his game and Atlantic City lost, 9–4. Harrisburg won three more games in June when Atlantic City was beginning to improve. The Pennsylvania team took another two-game series on June 16–17. In the first game Henderson and Samuel Cooper had double no-hitters and shutouts going at Bacharach Park until the seventh inning, when all the game's runs were scored. Unfortunately for the Bacharachs, Henderson yielded three hits in that inning which, combined with an error and a sacrifice fly, gave Harrisburg three runs. The Bacharachs loaded the bases with no outs in the bottom of the inning, but Cooper held them to only two runs. The next day's game was a pitcher's duel, too. Darltie Cooper of Harrisburg gave up four this and Grier six, and the visitors won, 4–3. Harrisburg was the last team to defeat the Bacharachs before their July winning streak began, by 4–0 on June 30, when Charles Corbett threw a shutout.

The Bacharachs ground up Harrisburg as part of the July surge that put them into the pennant race, beating them 11–5 on July 1, 4–1 on the 18th (a Grier four-hitter) and 8–3 on the 19th.

The Cuban Stars, who also had eight found games with Atlantic City, might have wanted to play them even less, since they won only two of them. Alejandro Pompez's team was one of the beneficiaries of the Giants' slow start on May 18, when seven Giants errors contributed to a 7–6 Cubans victory. Unfortunately for the Stars, they didn't return to Bacharach Park again until July, when the Bacharachs won four out of five. On July 7, the 6–2 victory had some extracurricular excitement. After Cubans starter Juan Mirabel buzzed three straight pitches around Cummings' head, Chance lost his temper and threw his bat at the pitcher. Mirabel picked it up and threw it back at Cummings, prompting several Bacharachs to run onto their field and fling more bats at the hurler, not, apparently, hitting him. Everyone cooled off and apologized after the game. The next day Cummings drove in the winning run in support of Roy Roberts' six-hitter as the Giants won again, 6–4.

The Stars made a three-game visit to Atlantic City in late July. The Bacharachs eked out a 6–5 win in the opener on July 25 as Gatewood doubled and Roberts singled him home in the bottom of the ninth. The Cuban team broke the Giants' 13-game league and 17-game overall winning streaks the next day when Lundy called in four pitchers in the top of the 11th inning to try to hold off the visitors, who nonetheless scored four runs for a 5–4 win. The Bacharachs resumed winning on the 27th, though, when Grier's five-hitter and good offense produced a 9–1 win and a temporary first-place tie with the Stars. This was the Bacharachs' first taste of the top spot all season long. As the Giants pulled away from the pack they beat the Stars twice more, 6–6 on August 19 in 11 innings, and 3–0 the following day when Grier gave up only three hits, the same number he collected himself as a batter.

Fourteen games with archrival Hilldale produced a split. The season opener before 10,000 fans at Hilldale Park was lost, 5–4, in the tenth inning when Hilldale third baseman Judy Johnson, an eventual Hall of Famer, poled a double into the overflow crowd in center field to drive in the winning run. Johnson thus atoned for three earlier fielding errors that had kept the Giants in the game. Hilldale won, 6–4, on May 14, and there is no record of the two teams meeting again until June 9, when Lundy hit a two-run homer in the first inning to establish a lead the Bacharachs never lost in winning, 7–4, at home. In Wilmington on June 11, former Giant Red Ryan and Henderson dueled into the tenth inning when Hilldale won, 3–2, on Giants errors. The same pitchers hooked up again on July 4 at Bacharach Park. This game went 11 innings and produced the same score, except this time Atlantic City had the upper hand after Farrell homered. So far as is known, the Bacharach management didn't give out bonuses for individual performances, but in this case they didn't have to—the game-ending blow "netted the clouter himself a tidy sum in the form of bills and change, which literally rained upon him as he was carried about the park on the shoulders of players and friends."[13]

The Bacharachs also won a three-game series from August 6–9 in Atlantic City and Wilmington. Reid got three hits to lead the offense to a 6–4 win in the first game. Lundy doubled home Marcell after his walk to score the only run in the second game on the 8th. Henderson, who gave up six hits, got the victory. Hilldale's Phil Cockrell lost the game, his temper and $100, the amount he was fined after getting into an argument with base umpire Lou Pieka and slugging him. Cockrell did gain something from the interchange—a sore spot of his own from a thump by a policeman who rushed onto the field to drag him out of the fray.[14] Hilldale slugged back as a team the next day, scoring all its runs in the first four innings for an 8–6 win.

At Hilldale Park and again in Wilmington, a series on August 12–14 tilted Hilldale's way. The Philadelphia team won the first game, 4–3, for its starter, Script Lee, and scored another one-run victory the next day, 3–2. Mitchell won the final game for the Bacharachs with a seven-inning, 5–0 shutout. Roberts gave up only three hits and participated in an eighth-inning rally on August 24 that produced a 3–2 Giants win. The teams met last on September 11 in a doubleheader at Hilldale. The Bacharachs won the first game easily, 11–2. Farrell and Jones each had three hits and Henderson gave up only four, with eight strikeouts. Lockhart spun a one-hitter in the nightcap, but the lone run he gave up was enough for Hilldale's win, since Cockrell threw a four-hit shutout.

There also was a split against John Henry Lloyd's Lincoln Giants, the other team that made a run at the pennant, with each team winning four discovered games. The opening game of a Sunday doubleheader on June 9 at the Protectory Oval in New York City broke the season-opening losing streak with league teams as Grier carried a no-hitter into the ninth inning before giving up three hits. Lundy collected three of his own and White homered. The Lincolns won the second game, 11–7, with a nine-run assault of Roberts, Mitchell and Grier in the sixth inning. Lloyd hit a grand slam on June 6 to lead his team to 9–6 win in the first game of another Sunday doubleheader at the Oval, although Grier picked up a 5–1 victory in the second game.

The next meeting was during the Bacharachs' streak, at Bacharach Park, and the Lincolns were victims 11 and 12 in the July winning streak, 7–3 on the 21st as Farrell struck out 14, and 2–1 on the 22nd as Marcell drove in both runs in support of Grier's four-hit, 13-strikeout performance. The Lincolns managed to disrupt the Bacharachs' upward trajectory on August 1 with a doubleheader sweep. Arthur "Rube" Chambers, a 19-year-old southpaw, shut out Atlantic City in the first game, 4–0. The Lincolns won the second game, 7–5, but almost were awarded a forfeit when Marcell was thrown out of the game after arguing with the umpires but refused to leave the field. The umps had actually declared a forfeit when Jim Keenan, the owner of the New York team, talked them out of it, possibly figuring an easy win wasn't worth aggravating his Sunday crowd by shutting down play.

The vagaries of ECL scheduling were such that the Bacharachs played one of their longest season series against the Brooklyn Royal Giants, the team that played the fewest league games. Although several of these contests were likely exhibitions that didn't count in the standings, the matchup was beneficial to the Bacharachs, who won ten in a row from the Royals. The first two were a sweep of a June 21–22 series, highlighted by Grier winning his own game, 3–2, on the 22nd with a two-run double while giving up only four hits and striking out nine. Another visit by Brooklyn to Bacharach Park on July 12–13 produced two more Atlantic City victories, 8–6 and 4–3. A three-game series in late August meant three more Bacharach wins, 5–2 on the 23rd, 4–1 on the 24th, and 6–0 on the 26th when Grier gave up only four hits and Dallard homered.

Henderson struck out eight and also gave up only four hits on September 3 for a 2–1 win, and Roberts topped him the next day with a two-hitter and a 5–1 victory. The pennant was in the bag and the pressure off in a four-game series in mid–September. The Bacharachs won the first game of a September 19 doubleheader, 6–3, as 36-year-old Brooklyn field manager Dick Redding, responsible for so many wins in Atlantic City's early seasons, started himself, but gave himself the hook after giving up four runs in the first two innings. Younger pitchers Connie Rector and Bill Holland combined for a 6–0 Royals win in the second game, and Brooklyn went on to take the game on September 20, 6–2, and the next day, 9–3. Redding proved he wasn't washed up in that last game, giving up only six hits over ten innings.

The Giants won eight games against the Black Sox, losing five and tying two. The Bacharachs won the first game of a doubleheader in Baltimore on May 23, 8–6, by scoring three runs in the top of the ninth inning, but suffered a 7–3 defeat in the second game. June games against Baltimore helped the Giants get back on track. They won, 8–3, on June 1, 7–3 on June 7 (Roberts the pitcher gave up five hits and Farrell, as an outfielder, had four), and 13–2 in the first game of a June 27 doubleheader. Baltimore won, 8–5, on June 24 despite Lundy's four hits, including a home run, and 8–5 in the second game on the 27th.

Mild-mannered Ben Taylor, the Black Sox manager, earned his team a forfeit on August 4 at Bacharach Park when he raged at home plate umpire Emerson Grey over whether a ball was fair or foul. The game had been tied, 4–4, in the tenth inning. Baltimore made five errors the next day and Grier gave up only four hits and struck out 13 as the Giants won, 6–1. An August 15 doubleheader in Baltimore produced an 11-inning, 5–4 win for Atlantic City when Marcell tripled in Cummings for the winning run. The second game was a 6–6 tie, called because of darkness after six innings. The Black Sox took a 6–5 game in 12 innings on September 7, but Grier, hot as usual, gave up only three hits and struck out seven the next day for an 8–0 win. Darkness caused an 8–8 tie after six innings on September 13 and, in a loosely-played warm-up for the World Series, Baltimore beat the Bacharachs, 14–13, at home on September 26.

The majority of the Bacharach games against non–Negro League opponents came against their rivals in the new Interstate League, an interesting and possibly unique organization that combined three ECL squads and three of the better white semi-pro teams in the region. The Interstate included the Bacharachs, Hilldale and the Harrisburg Giants, as well as Camden, Chester and Allentown. Leagues with both white and black teams weren't new, although they weren't commonplace. The California Winter League had already included teams of top black players for 15 years. In the case of the Interstate League, having the three ECL teams in two leagues at the same time was interesting, but one twist made it even more so. The games among the three ECL teams scheduled for their own league were also part of the Interstate schedule. So when any of the three white teams played one another, or one of them played one of the black teams, there was a win and a loss to be added to the Interstate standings. But when two of the black teams competed, the game counted in both the Interstate and the ECL.

If the white teams had been just run-of-the-mill semi-pro outfits, the ECL teams would have dominated them. But Chester, Camden and Allentown had gone out looking for the best white talent they could get in the region around Philadelphia, and had found quite a bit of it. Their rosters included some of the best-known names from that area's semi-pro ranks, many with professional experience in the white majors. Some of them also played with the highly competitive Brooklyn semi-pro teams, and most were already familiar to the Bacharachs. The Camden Skeeters were run by Lou Schaub, a semi-pro veteran. His pitching staff included the ever-present Socks Seibold; Jim "Lefty" York, who had 42 big league games under his belt; and Rube Chambers (not the black pitcher). Chambers was nicknamed "The Milkman" because that was his regular job, and although he never played professional ball he was a star for years in the semi-pro ranks.[15] The infield included Jake Munch, who had played for Connie Mack's Athletics in 1918; Tony Citrano, who had a five-year minor league career before World War I; and Buck Lai, the native Hawaiian who played in the minors, in Philadelphia and New York and with the traveling Chinese University team before the war.

Chester was managed by Harry Passon, a sporting goods store owner and organizer of the South Philadelphia Hebrew Association sports teams. His brother Herman "Chickie" Passon, a longtime player for the SPHAs and other teams, was on his pitching staff, as was Herb Steen, who had played in the International League in 1922, and Bill Durbin, a three-sport star at Swarthmore College who pitched semi-pro ball for years. The outfield included Howard Lohr, who had two short stints in the majors prior to the war, then played into his forties on the East Coast semi-pro circuit.

The Allentown Dukes were named after their owner, Ernest "Duke" Landgraf, a longtime minor league club owner who used the money from the sale of his most recent club in Syracuse to build a stadium and establish a team in Allentown. The most prominent member of the Dukes was Claude Hendrix, a right-handed pitcher. Hendrix's ten-year major league career, which included 144 wins, had ended abruptly in 1920 when he was implicated in a gambling plot to throw a game involving his current team, the Chicago

Cubs. Hendrix was never charged, nor officially suspended from organized baseball, but the grand jury investigation into the 1920 Cubs game turned up the Black Sox scandal, and Hendrix, along with others, became persona non grata in the majors. He settled in Allentown, where he bought a restaurant and started a second baseball career outside organized ball.[16]

The Interstate League's leaders released an ambitious first-half schedule that was to run through July 3, but the league didn't make it that far. Allentown was losing money and Landgraf, who said he had lost $30,000 on baseball in the city since beginning in 1923, shut the Dukes down in the middle of June.[17]

The Bacharachs also stopped playing Chester after the league fell apart, but continued a close rivalry with Camden for the rest of the season, winning seven of 16 games. Led by White's three hits, the Giants broke a four-all tie in the fifth inning and won, 9–4, on May 17. They unloaded 19 hits, including five by Cummings, and won, 15–1, on June 2. Roberts (six hits) and Chambers (five) both pitched well on June 25 as the Bacharachs won, 5–2. Roberts excelled again on June 29 and York was bombed in a 10–2 Atlantic City win. White made one of his infrequent pitching appearances in the second game of a doubleheader on July 3. The Skeeters got only six hits off of him and he beat Chambers again, 3–2. A lopsided 17–7 win on July 24 was the Bacharachs' 16th straight victory during their ECL pennant surge. The team collected 19 hits, four by Lundy and three each by Cummings and Gatewood. Lockhart, the winning pitcher, hit a home run. Lockhart also won the second game of a September 11 doubleheader, 3–1, in the last matchup of the year between these squads.

The Skeeters' wins began with a 10–5 victory in the first meeting on May 6, followed by a five-run rally in the ninth inning on May 22 for a 9–8 win. Dick Richards was the winning pitcher over Farrell on June 14, 3–2. Willie Pratt of Camden gave up only two runs on June 28 and Lockhart pitched eight shutout innings. Unfortunately, this was after having given up four runs in the first inning, so Camden won.

Hendrix, who had joined Camden after the Dukes went out of business, was the winning pitcher in the first game of that July 3 doubleheader, by a 9–5 score. The Skeeters gained a forfeit on July 30 when, with the game tied 1–1 and the evening getting dark, Lundy got into a prolonged argument with umpire Eddie Conahan about Conahan's pitch calling and pulled the Giants off the field in the sixth inning. Three straight Skeeters wins came on August 3, 8–3, with Johnny Carr throwing a four-hitter, 8–5 on September 9 with Chambers getting a win, and the first game on September 11, when Seibold tossed a shutout, topping Henderson's four-hitter in a 1–0 duel.

The season series with Chester, which the Giants won, 4–3–1, began with a 3–3 tie on May 12. The Bacharachs next won games on May 24–25 by identical 6–3 scores. Roberts threw a four-hitter in the first game and Farrell treated himself to a win in the second with a tie-breaking home run. Chester won two in a row, on May 29, 5–3, and June 10, 3–1, Chester's Bill Halas topping Mitchell. A June 19 doubleheader resulted in a split. Jack Wallace doubled and scored the winning run on a dropped fly ball as the Giants took the first game, 6–5. Chester pushed over its winning run in the ninth inning in the second game and won, 4–3. Farrell gave up seven hits and struck out 12 in the last game on June 20 in a 3–1 win.

The Bacharachs were in the process of sweeping Allentown, having won 3–0 on May 10 (Farrell struck out 11) and 6–1 on May 11 (a three-hitter for Roberts), then 11–7 on May 30, when a June 13 doubleheader, among the last games the Dukes ever played, rolled around. The Giants won the opener, peppering the outfield of Bacharach Park with 25 hits. They kept up their attack in the second game, but Allentown got the idea, too, and took the nightcap, 20–19. The doubleheader featured a total of 56 runs and 71 hits, and the only pitcher who could point with any sort of pride was Lockhart, who pitched seven good innings in the opener.

In a few other discovered games with other New Jersey teams, the Bacharachs beat East Orange, 7–2; tied 2–2 with Trenton; won three from the nearby Ocean City Rivieras, and defeated the Atlantic City Police, 11–0, in a five-inning game that Reid pitched. Newton Coal of Philadelphia went down, 6–1, and Parkesburg Iron from that Pennsylvania town was beaten twice, 3–2 and 6–3.

Trips to New York to play the top-level semi-pros there resulted in four losses in six games. Henderson had thrown five no-hit innings against the Bushwicks on April 18 but Lundy replaced him with Grier, who promptly gave up four runs in the sixth. The Bushwicks' Herb Steen, who soon was also pitching for Chester, was touched for a couple of runs, but the home team won, 4–2. A week later a game with Bay Ridge in Brooklyn resulted in an 8–6 loss. The Bacharachs had a 6–0 lead after six innings, but Grier gave up six runs in the seventh. A doubleheader with Bay Ridge on August 29 resulted in a split. Mitchell threw a four-hit shutout in the first game, 2–0, and Bay Ridge won the second, 5–4. A doubleheader with the Farmers in Queens on May 2 was also split, a 10–6 win in the first game and a 10–5 loss in the second.

1927

Having wrested the Eastern Colored League pennant away from Hilldale in 1926, the Bacharachs prepared to defend it. The ECL decided in 1927 on a split-season format, ideally designed to create different winners of the first and second halves and a crowd-pleasing playoff to determine who would go to the Negro World Series. The Giants took all the fun out of this scheme, though, winning both halves of the schedule, although not without some difficulty, and again battling the Chicago American Giants in October for the black baseball championship.

The Bacharachs had an overall winning percentage of .616, including the World Series, in 127 discovered games, and played .611 ball during the regular season against Negro League opponents, winning 55 games, losing 35 and tying one.

Much of the lineup and the pitching rotation contained the familiar faces of the previous season, although some roles changed, largely due to injuries, illness or, in one case, the recovery from a disability. Eggie Dallard, whose promising start with the Bacharachs was shortened due to illness the previous September, was back and moved from the outfield to first base. Dallard had a powerful hot streak early in the season and although he cooled off to an eventual .286 average, he was adept at drawing a walk, leading the team with 53. He settled into the second spot in the batting order and was among the run-scoring leaders. Dallard was needed at first because the longtime Giants regular there, Chance Cummings, had his contract sold to the Lincoln Giants.[18] Cummings, who turned 34 that June, was now on the down side of his career, as the *Daily Press* had noted a little prematurely before the 1926 season, Dallard was six years younger, although he probably didn't remind anyone of Frank Chance in the field—he made 28 errors.

But Cummings' departure may have mostly been due to a falling-out with his manager, Dick Lundy, a fellow original Bacharach. Despite their ties going all the way back to the Duval Giants, Cummings said the two never got along well, and that Lundy was jealous of Chance, his popularity with the fans ("I was the talk of the town everywhere I went"), his rivalry with his manager as a sharp dresser, and the fact that sometimes Lundy had to come to him for a short-term loan to keep up his appearances. According to Cummings, things had come to a head in the October 9 game of the 1926 World Series. Chicago had a man on second in the bottom of the ninth inning in a tie game and Cummings walked to the mound to advise Rats Henderson, the relief pitcher, to walk batter Johnnie Hines and pitch to the weaker-hitting next batter. Lundy, who was at shortstop, came over and countermanded that advice—"See, he didn't want to take advice from me—anybody but me"—and Hines singled to give the American Giants one of the wins they eventually used to take the Series.[19]

Cheno Garcia, the good-field, light-hitting second baseman, was not back, also having been peddled to the Lincolns. After an early-season experiment with 38-year-old Bill Handy didn't work out, second was turned over to Milton Lewis. Lewis had been released by the Giants in 1925, when club president Hammond Daniels characterized him as a player who had some ability but didn't have the overall skill to play in the black majors. A year with the regional Philadelphia Giants seems to have remedied many of Lewis' shortcomings, though. He hit .300 and led the team in home runs with 12. Lewis was the exact opposite of Garcia—he was a physically large player who wasn't very graceful as an infielder (the *Daily Press* described him as "awkward and ungainly"), but he certainly had learned how to hit and despite his defense could "gladden the heart of any manager."[20]

Manager Lundy continued to be his own best overall offensive and defensive contributor, starring at shortstop, batting .338 and leading the team with 98 RBI. Oliver Marcell was as good, if not better than ever, at third, hitting .310. Dallard, Lewis, Lundy and Marcell played most of the games at their respective positions. Late in the season Lewis was shifted to first base in place of Dallard when the usual first sacker was out with an injury, and second base was taken over by the only reserve to log any sort of substantial time in the field. Bill Wagner, a good fielder but light hitter who had been with the Brooklyn Royal Giants since 1922, hit .247 in 25 games.

Willie Jones, whose average popped up to .286 this year, caught nearly every day upon rejoining the team in late May after finishing a college semester. Joe Duncan, in apparently his only year in the Negro Leagues, was a very adequate backup, hitting .277. Ernest Gatewood, at age 36, caught some games in April and May, but then left the team and the Negro Leagues forever. Lewis Means, the light-hitting utility man who had last been with the Bacharachs in 1922 before moving to the NNL, got behind the plate briefly early in the season.

Chaney White was back in center field on a daily basis and had a great season. He hit .311, led the team in runs (97) and doubles (18) in the discovered games, and was second to Lundy in RBI with 85. He was flanked by some valuable additions to the rest of the outfield. Ambrose Reid was back in left field, but missed most of June. When in the lineup, though, he was his dependable self, hitting .274. Luther Farrell played some outfield, but spent as much of his time pitching. Wherever he was in the field he was still at home in the batters' box, hitting .306.

Clarence "Scally" Smith had broken into the Negro Leagues in 1921 with the short-lived Columbus Buckeye franchise in the Negro National League, and then had gone to the Detroit Stars, where he could be relied upon almost annually for a better than .300 batting average. Signed by the Bacharachs to bolster their outfield, he hit exactly .300, dividing a full season between left field and right. The outfield was also bolstered by the return of a former Bacharach doing the Luther Farrell routine. Jesse James "Mountain Man" Hubbard played right field in about half of the Giants' games, but pitched the rest of the time. He had broken into high-level black ball with Atlantic City in 1919 before going to the Royal Giants through 1926. Although he hit only .267 this season, like Dallard he displayed excellent plate discipline and his keen eye in time earned him the leadoff spot in the batting order. In keeping with his colorful given name and nicknames, Hubbard stood out in a crowd. He was over six feet and 200 pounds in size and, "handsome and a sharp dresser, Hubbard was a ladies' man and had a lasting preference for big cigars and bigger Cadillacs."

A right-handed pitcher, Hubbard had suffered an arm injury in 1925 with Brooklyn, and upon his recovery had turned himself into a man of guile, rather than speed, on the mound. He reportedly developed sidearm and submarine deliveries to vary his original overhand motion and threw "junkball" pitches to set off what remained of his fastball.[21] His presence in the Bacharach rotation, as was the case with Farrell's move from being nearly a full-time outfielder, was required to make the starting staff whole again.

Grier, the Giants' leading pitcher the season before and the owner of the World Series no-hitter, barely pitched at all in 1927. He arrived in the spring with a sore arm and reportedly out of shape, and can only be found pitching in seven games with a 2–2 record and a 5.09 ERA.[22] Despite all of his promise and early success, this was Grier's next-to-last season in the Negro Leagues. He was finished after 1928, when the Bacharachs let him go to Baltimore. Rats Henderson was in his usual fine form as a regular starter and reliever in the pinch when he developed arm trouble again. Although in 24 games (17 starts) he went 12–6 with a 3.05 ERA, he rarely pitched after the middle of July and didn't appear at all in the World Series.

Despite these setbacks the Bacharachs had strong pitching. Farrell made 32 starts in the discovered games with a 20–14 record and a 3.43 ERA. Hubbard started 21 games, winning 13 and losing seven with a 3.80 ERA. The veteran Roy Roberts went 12–6 in 19 starts and 12 relief jobs. Hubert Lockhart, no longer a college student but now a college coach, still needed to arrive late, but once with the Giants made 16 starts and went 8–6. The Bacharachs took another chance on the journeyman Henry Gillespie, who had pitched part of a season with them in 1925, and got pretty good return. He made 11 starts and went 4–6. As was often the case with a Bacharach Giants team, the pitching was good, but not great, but that wasn't a critical problem since it was backed by such a potent offense. The team batting average in the found games was .293 and the OBP .387, and this wasn't accomplished by feasting on the semi-pros. The team actually hit better against league-level completion. The Giants averaged six runs per game, the first time that had been done since 1921.

While the Giants continued to dominate the ECL on the field, Atlantic City had another major force in the league, the new president. While Ed Bolden of Hilldale is clearly due the lion's share of the credit for bringing the league together in the first place, his presidency for its first four years of operation had come under increasing criticism. Some of it derived from Hilldale's domination of the league, particularly when it won the first three pennants, and may have been tinged by more than a little jealousy. More substantial criticisms were of his inability to enforce discipline among the players, particularly involving altercations with umpires, and his equally ineffective control over Nat Strong, whose general lack of cooperation disrupted the ECL schedule and diminished revenues in what should have been a strong New York City market.

Bolden, while continuing to sit as a league commissioner via his control of Hilldale, stepped down from the presidency in January 1927. The job went to Atty. Isaac H. Nutter, a leading African American lawyer and political figure in Atlantic City. Nutter, 48 years old, had earned a law degree from Howard University in 1901. After working as a waiter and factory worker, he was steered by a friend to Atlantic City, where he started practicing law in 1907. He soon became a force in establishing the Atlantic City Republican machine's hold on the black Northside community, but his work did not only involve playing the insider political game. He served Harry Bacharach as a mayoral citizen advisor. Walter Edge, owner of the *Atlantic City Daily Press*, while New Jersey governor, recruited him as head of the Department of Negro Welfare and Employment Bureau, commonly known as the "Migrant Board," to ease the transition into Northern life of the flood of African Americans from the South who came to the state for war industry jobs during World War I.[23]

But Nutter was more than willing to take on the political establishment in support of his race. In 1908 he represented Winfield F. Cozart, a black newspaper correspondent, in a complaint before the Interstate Commerce Commission alleging discriminatory railroad accommodations. In 1921 he criticized the national Republican party for rules changes that would potentially dilute black Southern representation at the party's next national convention: "It smacks of 'Lily White' tendencies."[24]

Late in his career as a lawyer Nutter claimed to have represented 54 murder defendants and obtained acquittals for all but two, which stretches one's credulity.[25] However, he clearly was widely sought after as a criminal defense attorney, and a detailed, if possibly biased, account of one of his cases shows why. In 1936 Enoch "Nucky" Johnson's longtime rule over corruption that permeated Atlantic City politics brought about a full-scale Federal investigation that earned Johnson four years in prison, also resulting in convictions for several local figures. One of the defendants, club owner Leroy Williams, was defended by Nutter. Williams was suspected of being one of the kingpins of the city's numbers betting business, and was charged with income tax evasion. Out of cases against 45 defendants, there were only four acquittals, and Williams' was one of them.

The Federal after-action report on the entire investigation only grudgingly credits Nutter with obtaining the not guilty verdict. The writers allowed as how the jurors may have been swayed more by an obvious lack of knowledge about tax cases on the part of Nutter and his fellow defense counsel than by a lack of evidence, and so returned a "sympathy" not guilty verdict. A possibly poor grasp of tax law would not deter Nutter, however. As the report states:

Isaac H. Nutter, an Atlantic City attorney and political figure on both the local and state level, who served as president of the Eastern Colored League in 1927 and 1928.

> Nutter's summation was the most unusual that had been heard in the District Court. All the charms and voodoos for which negroes are noted were brought into play. Nutter carried a rabbit's foot in his pocket throughout the trial and put his hand in his pocket to hold it several times during the summation. Once when he brought his fist down upon the jury rail to emphasize a point, his cuff links flew off and everyone thought he had dropped a pair of dice. After the case was over he admitted that when Attorney Smith had started his summation, he walked behind Smith and dropped salt to "hex" him. During his own summation, Nutter avoided completely discussing the evidence of the case, but made an evangelistic appeal like a preacher at a revival meeting. It worked like a charm, for after deliberating nine hours the jury found the defendant not guilty.

Although having vexed (or possibly hexed) the prosecution at this trial, Nutter turned out to be a significant help to the Feds. Williams refused to pay his legal bill, and in return Nutter went to the investigators he had so recently stymied. "From that time on," the Federal after-action report states, "Nutter became the most important factor in producing evidence to break up the numbers syndicate and to compel them to testify to the payment of protection money. He continued to give the Government information and to use his influence with witnesses to compel them to tell the truth right up until the time that [Enoch] Johnson was tried and convicted."[26]

Nutter followed the Bacharach Giants' fortunes, but his only previous public act regarding the team had happened in 1919, when he and two Atlantic City police officers rushed onto the field at Inlet Park to restore order after fans started jumping out of the stands to join in an altercation between the Bacharachs and Hilldale. Getting the fans to sit down and the players to resume playing that day was easier than keeping the ECL on an even keel in 1927. As the year dawned, the league, which had never successfully replaced the Potomacs to become an eight-team loop again, was in danger of dropping to a group of six. Jim Keenan, with a profitable home grounds in the Bronx, but fed up with what he saw as a disadvantageous schedule (which so far as he was concerned favored his enemy Nat Strong) announced in December that he was taking the Lincoln Giants out of the league. Keenan relented in January and the Lincolns stayed in the ECL, but in June they resigned again, this time for good.

At the beginning of the season Keenan had signed hard-hitting Cuban outfielder

Alonzo Montalvo, who had been playing for the Midwestern version of the Cuban Stars team (not connected with Pompez's ECL Cuban Stars) in the Negro National League. Montalvo was in a salary dispute with Augustin Molina, the owner of the NNL team, and had been left off that team's reserve list over the winter, probably accidentally. So, at least technically, Montalvo was a free agent and Keenan signed him. The NNL protested vigorously and the other ECL owners supported them—Montalvo was banned from playing in league games. Keenan accepted this decision briefly. But upon considering what home games at the Catholic Protectory Oval were drawing and his ability to offer visiting teams gate shares of up to $1,000 for a Sunday doubleheader, he decided that "the league will need the Lincoln Giants more than the Lincolns will need the league."[27]

Keenan based his stand at least in part on principle, but he may have been perfectly happy to avoid paying traveling expenses for the Lincolns to play in other ECL parks where the chances of a good gate were slim. Although the Great Depression was more than two years away from its recognized beginning, some sections of the economy were stagnant, and African Americans were unduly affected by the slump.

The common perception of economic conditions in America was that the boom times of the 1920s benefited all segments of society until the stock market crash of late 1929 brought on the Great Depression. But there had been a manufacturing slump in 1927, particularly in industries that produced iron and steel, automobiles, lumber and woolen goods (the sort of items manufactured in northern cities where Negro Leagues clubs played). The slump amounted to nothing more than a leveling-off of growth. But the slowdown cost jobs, and the cities' black populations, consigned to less-skilled jobs and often the more recently hired, were especially vulnerable. As one review of the period described the situation, "The Great Depression of the 1930s began for black workers by the end of 1926. 'The last to be hired, the first to be fired,' Negroes experienced widespread unemployment as early as 1927, and by 1929, about one-fifth of all blacks employed in industry had been thrown out of work."[28]

The story was similar in many black major league cities: In Philadelphia, a study reported that "there has been a decrease in general employment, [and] Negroes have suffered more in proportion than whites," and there was a 24 percent unemployment rate among blacks. In Cleveland, the Urban League's job placement program could place only 30 percent of its job applicants, as opposed to nearly 75 percent in 1924. The closing of the Ford auto plants in Detroit in 1927 for retooling as the new Model A replaced the Model T put workers on both sides of the color line out of work, but for blacks it was especially bad. The Urban League job placement program's success rate in 1927 was only slight more than half of the previous year's results.[29]

While Atlantic City, having no industries, was immune from the manufacturing slump, employment for blacks in the Shore's hotel industry, a mainstay of the Northside economy, was declining. In the past, headwaiters would literally hire African American men off the street at good wages to meet the tourist demand in their dining rooms. Now, in the late 1920s, food service jobs were starting to go to whites, particularly women. It was speculated that the shift involved their willingness to work for lower wages, and "there was less social friction between the guest of the hotel and the employee."[30]

All this in turn suppressed Negro Leagues attendance, and the leagues reacted by cutting back. In January the ECL owners mirrored the decision of their brothers in the Negro National League in the Midwest to lower team payroll caps from $3,000 to $2,700 per month and limit rosters to 14 (the NNL went with 16). In July the ECL decided to move several games promised to Norfolk, Virginia, back north to cut travel expenses.[31]

The Bacharach Giants were one of the suffering teams. In April the Bacharach Athletic Association, the parent organization for the team, was in bankruptcy court with debts of $30,000 and an outstanding judgment of $6,800 in favor of team president Hammond Daniels and fellow owner John B. Dykes. The Giants' season was disrupted temporarily in mid–June when the team was thrown out of Bacharach Park. A well-played 4–3 loss to Hilldale on June 21 brought many fans back out on the afternoon of the 22nd, hoping for an exciting repeat performance. But they were turned away on the orders of Congressman Isaac Bacharach, Harry's brother. The Giants played at the park at the Congressman's sufferance, since he leased the grounds, considered undeveloped residential housing land, from a local land company for their use. The deal was that Bacharach would pay the Robinson Land Company $1,000 per year, and the Giants would pay the property taxes, about $5,000 annually. The taxes had remained unpaid for 1927 and Bacharach, his patience exhausted, took the drastic step of padlocking the gates. The Giants went on the road to Philadelphia, Camden and Mount Holly, New Jersey, for a few days, and returned home on June 26 to their familiar home grounds with a new, but very familiar, team president.[32]

While they were away, Tom Jackson had organized a new board of directors of himself and the three Weekes brothers, Reginald, Duncan and William, to replace Daniels, Dykes, Charles Johnson and Henry Tucker, and had found the money for the real estate taxes. Jackson, his local government career over with Harry Bacharach out of office, was now in real estate, but his desire to be a baseball "magnate" was unchecked. This was the second time since 1922 he had stepped in at a time of trouble to keep the Bacharachs in Atlantic City.[33]

The Giants played well from the beginning of the season and were usually in first or second place whenever first-half ECL standings were published. The Baltimore Black Sox were their chief competition, leading the Bacharachs until late in the season. Both teams played well, but the Giants finished with a 28–17 record and a .622 winning percentage. The Black Sox finished 23–17 and .575. As usual, the number of games each team played varied, but the five- game differential between the first- and second-place teams was entirely in the win column, and it's not likely that the Black Sox would have won all five of their unplayed games.

The chronic imbalance in the league schedule became a definite issue at the end of the second half, however. The Bacharachs started fast and kept going, finishing at .581 with 25 wins and 18 losses. Statistically, they were dogged by the Cuban Stars who, although as usual playing fewer games, had a winning percentage good enough in September to be in first place temporarily. But while the Stars' smaller number of decisions (less than half of those owned by the Bacharachs) allowed them somewhat absurdly to have a claim on first, their late-season losing streak affected their percentage even more, and that team finished fourth.

The Harrisburg Giants also had played fewer league games in the second half, 29 to

Atlantic City's 43, but in percentage the teams were nearly neck and neck. Harrisburg claimed to have won at the wire with 17 wins and 12 losses. That would give them a .586 mark, five percentage points better than the Bacharachs, thus setting up a playoff. Jackson and the Weekes brothers adamantly refused to give up on the second-half flag. They based their claim on their team having played many more games, and the fact that at least one of the victories Harrisburg claimed was a forfeit from Baltimore, which hadn't shown up for a game in Harrisburg. Precedent, such as it was in the matter of ECL standings, wasn't particularly on the Bacharachs' side on the first point, but as to the second argument, cancelled games often occurred. The usual practice if they couldn't be replayed was to ignore them in the standings. President Nutter convened a meeting in Philadelphia to settle the matter, but no one from Harrisburg showed up to argue for the pennant, and it was awarded again to Atlantic City.[34]

The Negro National League had also played a split season, the Chicago American Giants winning the first half and the Birmingham Black Barons the second. Chicago easily swept four straight in the league playoff series and again became the Bacharachs' opponent in the Negro World Series. The Series opened in Chicago on October 1, a Saturday. The Giants arrived a few days early for practice and a little sightseeing. Lundy, in addition to anchoring the infield and managing the team, also had his byline on all the stories in the *Daily Press* from the Western swing. On September 30, after a tour of Chicago's high points, including the stockyards, where "we got a glimpse of some of the material we eat in our hot dogs and such," he proclaimed the Bacharachs "full of the old ginger."[35]

However, the dose of Chicago did not agree with the Bacharachs. They lost four straight games there, none of them close, and when the two teams headed east Chicago was only one game short of winning the best-of-nine series. Luther Farrell actually allowed fewer hits, eight, in the opener than the 13 Atlantic City made off of Chicago ace left-hander Willie Foster. But, as Lundy (or his ghostwriter put it) "our bingles were usually poled out with second and third base unoccupied."[36] Two doubles and a single off Farrell in the third inning produced three runs, and the American Giants were ahead the rest of the way, winning 6–2. Hubbard was raked for 11 hits and was removed with no one out in the fourth inning the next day, October 2, leaving with the Bacharachs behind by four runs. Lockhart was pounded for five runs in the fifth and the final score was 11–1.

"What I have to tell tonight is nothing to write home about," began Lundy's October 3 dispatch, but Atlantic City readers on the 4th could read about how American Giants right-hander George Harney shut out their team on four hits while Hubbard, Roberts and Lockhart gave up ten hits and the Giants made four errors (two by Lundy).[37] The final score was 7–0. The outcome of the fourth game was no less ugly. Farrell pitched a complete game again, but this time he gave up 11 hits which, combined with four more Bacharach errors, allowed Chicago to score nine runs. Farrell's triple and an error on the throw to the infield in the second inning scored the only Atlantic City run.

Three days passed before the fifth game of the series at Bacharach Park. The Bacharachs needed to win five straight games to take the Series, and that task was insurmountable. But they came close to pulling it off, buoyed by strong support from the home fans. Fay Young reported in the *Chicago Defender* that "the club went back home disgusted and ashamed, but William Russell, the man who owns the big restaurant, tendered them a banquet. The boys were told that the fans were with them.... No town in the whole universe would have rallied to the Bees as did these seashore folks. They guaranteed the boys anything they needed to win—money and support." Regarding the money, Young specified that "each game when a player made a two base hit or one for three bases his cap was filled with coin. A home run meant twenty-five or more dollars." Prominent Atlantic City residents, including political boss Enoch Johnson and Ike Nutter himself, were putting up a reported several hundred dollars as a pool available to the Giants if they came back and won the Series.[38]

The weather was cold and damp on October 8, but it didn't bother Farrell, who became the second Negro Leagues pitcher, and the second Bacharach, to throw a Series no-hitter. Farrell's game wasn't as spectacular as Red Grier's had been in the previous Series. One difference, beyond Farrell's or anyone's control, was the darkness immediately preceding a downpour that turned the contest into a seven-inning game. Also, he gave up two runs, although both were at least partly the fault of Bacharach errors, plus one of five walks. Foster was sharp for the American Giants and gave up only four hits in six innings. But three of them, by Lewis, Smith and Jones, drove in two runs in the bottom of the second. Then a double play attempt resulted in a wild throw that allowed Jones to score the third, and winning, run.

The rain continued overnight, and it was still raining when Game Six was supposed to start the next afternoon. The contest proceeded the afternoon of October 10. Except for perhaps the game before, it was the best of the Series, although nobody won. Darkness produced a ten-inning, 1–1 tie. Lockhart, who pitched a complete game, gave up only five hits. Three American Giants hurlers gave up eight. The only runs of the game came on solo home runs. Chicago first baseman Jim Brown hit his in the sixth inning to negate the lead produced by Milt Lewis. Lewis, who had been left out of the Series lineup in favor of Wagner's better glove at second, had in turn moved in at first, sending Dallard to the outfield. His blow, a reported 200 feet past the right field fence, "was probably the longest clout ever made at the Bacharach Park."[39]

Farrell turned in another winning performance in the seventh game (or the eighth, if the tie is counted). He gave up six hits and a single unearned run in the fourth inning, when the game was still close. The Bacharachs blew things open in the bottom of the fifth with five runs that featured a sacrifice fly by the winning pitcher and a two-run double by Hubbard, playing right field. The Atlantic City comeback continued the next day, on October 12, with a 6–5 win. Smith doubled to lead off the bottom of the eighth and had gotten to third when Jones beat out an infield hit. Reid, pinch-hitting for Wagner, hit a long sacrifice fly to center. Hubbard went all the way and only gave up six hits, having real trouble only with Chicago third baseman and manager Dave Malarcher, who drove in three runs with a pair of hits.

The Bacharach comeback couldn't be sustained, though. Lockhart started on the 13th and was "duck soup for the boys from the shores of Lake Michigan," going out in the second, when Chicago was opening up a five-run lead. The final score was 11–4. The American Giants, in the last discovered game between them and the Atlantic City Bacharachs, had won another World Series.[40]

The American Giants were the only Negro Leagues team to post a winning record against the Bacharachs in 1927 in the discovered games, although the season series against Harrisburg ended in a 12–12 tie. Harrisburg won the first game of a two-game series as Bacharach Park on May 6 when Henderson gave up all his runs in the first inning and lost, 4–1. Lundy hit a two-run homer in the bottom of the tenth inning the next day, though, for a 5–3 win. Darltie Cooper, a right-hander who had been the winning pitcher for Harrisburg on the 6th, was the winner again on May 15, 4–3, when Oscar Charleston homered in the eighth. His blow was reported to have cleared the right field fence by 20 feet and sailed completely over adjacent South Carolina Avenue.[41] Harrisburg also won another squeaker at home on May 21 when Oscar "Heavy" Johnson, another powerful hitter on a team that had several, hit a bases-loaded single in the tenth inning to bring about a 5–4 victory. The two teams traveled to Richmond for a series in mid-June (some of the games originally scheduled for Norfolk), and Harrisburg continued its dominance. The Bacharachs did win the first contest on June 13, Henderson outpitching Cooper for a 3–2 win. But Atlantic City lost a doubleheader on the 15th, 11–2 and 4–3.

The two teams of Giants traded winning streaks all season long, and it was the Bacharachs' turn to be dominant right after the Richmond series. Back home at Bacharach Park, they won three in a row. On June 16 Harrisburg's Earl Gurley was pitching well until after he tripled in the top of the third. The *Daily Press* sportswriter surmised he may have been tired out from his trip around the bases, because he opened the bottom of the inning with two walks and a hit batter, and then Dallard hit a grand slam to produce the winning margin in a 6–2 win. Other than clearing the right field wall, this blow in no way resembled Charleston's a month earlier. Dallard's fly ball hit an interior brace that held up the wall and somehow was imparted sufficient spin to carry it up in the air and over the fence. Lundy followed later in the game with a similarly unheroic homer to right that was lost in a collection of "old broken down chairs" allowed to accumulate in fair territory.[42] Hubbard had three hits and scored the winning run in the seventh inning the next day as Henderson picked up a 7–5 win, and White's three hits on the 18th helped Roberts to a 4–3 relief win.

Then it was Harrisburg's turn during a Fourth of July holiday series at home, sweeping all four games before the Bacharachs could get out of town. A doubleheader on the Fourth gave Harrisburg 5–4 and 9–6 wins. Charleston again got a game-winning hit, this time an 11th-inning single off of Farrell, to assure a 6–5 win on July 5 and Heavy Johnson homered to help Harrisburg to a 4–2 win on July 6.

Five days later the rivalry picked up back in Atlantic City. This time the Bacharachs swept all four games. Farrell allowed only five hits on July 11 and Hubbard collected three as the Bacharachs won easily, 7–1. Hubbard got three more hits the next day to back Roberts in a 7–3 win. Henderson threw a five-hitter on the 13th and White stole home on a double steal for the winning run in a 4–3 game. The game on the 14th was held at Bradley Beach, another seaside resort north of Atlantic City that the ECL was trying to cultivate as a site for its games. White came through again with a game-winning single in the bottom of the ninth as the Bacharachs won, 6–5.

A month later, again at Bacharach Park, the home team unloaded on Harrisburg, winning 20–5 with 23 hits in support of Farrell's complete game. Smith had five hits and Lewis and Lundy four each, Lewis' haul including a homer. Lewis hit another home run the next day, as did Smith in a four-run, seventh-inning rally that made a 5–4 win possible. The two Bacharachs each homered again on the 16th in a 9–4 win.

The opposing teams immediately left for Harrisburg where, true to form, the home team swept that series. Harrisburg had many of the best hitters in the Negro Leagues at that time and three of them, John Beckwith, Charleston and Herbert "Rap" Dixon, hit successive two-out singles in the bottom of the ninth off of Lockhart to bring about a 6–5 win. On August 19 Harrisburg took a doubleheader to wrap up the season series. Walter "Rev" Cannady hit a grand slam in the opening game as Harrisburg won, 8–5, a preliminary to a 10–4 second-game win.

The Cuban Stars, the Bacharachs' other rival in the season's second half, were also tough opponents. Atlantic City won seven of 13 discovered games. The Stars, whose status as one of two teams in the ECL without a home park made things tough on both the players and the league's schedulers, tried in 1927 to establish themselves in Newark. They opened there before 3,200 fans on May 1 against the Bacharachs, who swept a doubleheader, 3–2 and 7–4. The Giants continued to keep ahead of the Stars a little more than a month later in Atlantic City. They won 6–5 on June 6, the game featuring four home runs, two by the Cubans' Martin Dihigo, an eventual Hall of Famer, and one by Dallard. Arthur Dilworth, an original Bacharach Giant who had remained in Atlantic City, took a turn as home plate umpire this day. In his new role he was no longer the "Mighty Dilworth," as he had been known as a strikeout artist in the early days. The *Daily Press* noted his presence behind the plate and remarked only that the umpiring was "far from satisfactory." Dihigo, who pitched as well as played field positions, took the mound and struck out ten Giants on the 7th as the Cubans won, 7–4. Henderson excelled in a 9–1 win the following day. This game was halted for awhile when a pony, which had been grazing nearby, wandered into right field, possibly looking for some of the unmowed grass for which the park was known. "Man O' War," as the *Daily Press* writer labeled the beast, "refused to be shooed off the diamond despite the fact that the shooing was done in Spanish, English and profane." Finally Tom Jackson and pitcher Henry Gillespie took matters in hand and led the pony out of the park.[43]

The Stars won a doubleheader in Newark on July 17, 6–3 in the first game despite four hits from Marcell, and 5–4 in a seven-inning second game. The Giants took two of three at Bacharach Park a week later. Henderson pitched a six-hit shutout and Lewis popped a pair of doubles and a single in an 8–0 win on July 24. Dihigo hit a game-winning home run in the 12th inning the next day, but the Cubans' 7–6 win wasn't secured until Lundy's answering drive to right in the bottom of the inning flew out of the park two feet foul, and he then flied out to center. Dihigo could occasionally make a mistake, and his error on the 26th allowed Marcell to score the winning run, 8–7. While making a run at the Giants in late August, the Stars took two of three at Bacharach Park, winning 6–5 on August 22 and 2–1 on the 24th, victories flanking a 4–1 Bacharach win that featured a Hubbard complete game on the 23rd.

Hilldale was, as usual, one of the most frequent Bacharach opponents, but the Giants handled the Philadelphia club easily this season, with 14 discovered wins, nine losses and a tie. Atlantic City wiped out Hilldale, 10–0, when the teams first met on April 17. The pitching staff was still getting into shape, so Lundy used Henderson, Roberts and Farrell for three innings each, and together they produced a two-hitter. A short series in the middle of May resulted in a split—the Bacharachs won, 5–2, on May 12, Henderson getting the win and Dallard hitting a home run. Then Nip Winters, with a three-hitter and a home run of his own, outpitched Grier, in one of his few starts, for a 4–2 win. The teams split again on May 23–24 in Norfolk. The Giants, with Henderson pitching and Lewis hitting a homer, won the first game, 6–2. Hilldale scored five runs in the second inning on the 24th and won, 7–5.

The Bacharachs won a slugfest in Wilmington on June 10, 12–10. The hitting festivities included successive home runs in the third inning by White, Hubbard and Dallard. But Winters tossed a five-hitter on June 20 at Bacharach Park and Hilldale won, 4–3. The Bacharachs won three of four in a series beginning June 23. Henderson only gave up five hits and Dallard and Jones had three hits each for an 8–3 win at Hilldale Park. The series moved to nearby Mount Holly, New Jersey, the next day, when Red Ryan tossed his own five-hitter and Hilldale won, 8–1. On June 25 the Giants swept a doubleheader back at Hilldale Park. The first game, a 16–0 win, was a star turn for Farrell, who gave up only five hits while pitching and drove in six runs as a batter with a home run and single. Smith and Marcell had four hits each. The ball kept flying in the second game, although some of the shots were now being hit by Hilldale off Roberts. He was awarded an 8–6 win, though, thanks to three Bacharach homers, two by Hubbard and another by Dallard.

Three discovered meetings in July went mostly Hilldale's way, although the Bacharachs pounded 16 hits on July 3 and won, 15–5. In a short series at Hilldale Park the home team won twice, 11–10 on July 21 and 5–3 on the 23rd. The first game went ten innings and the Giants seemed to have it sewed up when they scored three runs in the top of that inning. But Hilldale came back with four runs in the bottom of the tenth, scoring the winning run without depending on hits. Dallard's wild throw let in two runs to tie the game, and Hilldale shortstop Jake Stephens sneaked home from third with the winning run when the Giants unwisely tried for an out at second after Dallard's throw had been corralled. Despite three hits, including a homer from Lewis, Winters beat the Giants again, outpitching Roberts on the 23rd.

The two teams didn't go long without playing each other, and met again on August 7–9 at Bacharach Park in a series featuring good pitching. Phil Cockrell of Hilldale gave up only five hits on the 7th, one of them another Milt Lewis home run, and earned a 4–1 win. The missing Giants offense manifested itself the next day in the form of 19 hits for a 10–1 win, as Farrell yielded seven in a complete game. Hubbard held Hilldale to four hits in the final game while Marcell drove in three runs for a 4–2 victory.

Farrell beat Hilldale again on August 21, 3–2 in 13 innings. He went all the way, giving up only seven hits and striking out 11, and scored the winning run when he walked and came around on a throwing error by third baseman Judy Johnson. The offensive outbursts that characterized many Bacharach-Hilldale games this season arrived again on the 25th when the team from Darby won, 22–12. Hilldale had 25 hits and the Giants 20, five of them by Lewis.

The Bacharachs won the first two of a three-game series in mid–September. The ever-versatile Farrell pitched a two-hitter and hit two home runs on the 11th in a 4–1 win, and Hubbard gave up only five hits the next day as the Giants won, 3–1, and clinched the second-half ECL pennant. With the pressure off Atlantic City, Hilldale won the next day, 11–4. A late-season doubleheader on September 25 produced a 10–8 Bacharach win and a 7–7 tie.

Although the Baltimore Black Sox pursued the Bacharachs closely for the first-half ECL title, they didn't play very well against the Giants in their discovered season series games. Atlantic City won 11 and lost only four. After Baltimore won the first game of a doubleheader, 6–4, on May 22, the Bacharachs reeled off four straight wins, including a 5–3 victory in the second game that day and a sweep of a late June series. Henderson's five-hitter and Marcell's three hits on June 27 led to a 6–2 win. Hubbard started a three-run rally with a home run in the eighth inning the next day and the Giants won, 11–9. Farrell's three hits, one a home run, backed Lockhart on the 29th in a 9–4 win.

Baltimore won easily, 11–3, in Atlantic City on July 27, but when the teams moved to Bradley Beach the next day Farrell threw a shutout and struck out nine in a 14–0 win. A few days later the Giants swept a two-game series, winning 11–6 on August 2, while Hubbard's four-hit shutout ensured a 2–0 victory the next day.

The Black Sox and Bacharachs played back-to-back doubleheaders on September 4, a Sunday, and September 5, Labor Day, and split both of them. The first doubleheader was in Baltimore, where the Sox scored five runs in the bottom of the ninth inning off of Farrell to come from behind, 8–7, while Hubbard mastered them again in a seven-inning second game, winning 3–2. The teams stopped before nine innings because they had to get to Atlantic City. They covered the 150 miles and were ready to play again the following afternoon. Grier, making a little comeback late in the season, surprised with a six-hitter and a 4–3 win. Bob McClure of the Sox, though, threw a 6–0 shutout in the finale. The Giants scored eight runs in the third inning the next day, still at Bacharach Park, and won, 15–7. They wrapped up the season series the next afternoon with a 6–5 win that featured a Lundy home run.

The Brooklyn Royal Giants also offered little trouble throughout the season. The Bacharachs won six of nine discovered meetings, beginning with a 14–8 trouncing of the Royals on May 8 that featured four hits by Lundy, including a grand slam. The Bacharachs also won the next day, 3–2. It was a battle of the old-timers on the mound as Roy Roberts, the 33-year-old original Giant, outpitched his former manager and rotation partner, 37-year-old Dick Redding. Brooklyn won the final game of the series on the 10th, 8–7, when center fielder Chester Brooks had one of his best days at the plate. In five times up he got five hits, including a homer and triple, scored two runs and drove in six.

Atlantic City then won three straight, beginning with a 9–4 decision on June 12, following up with a 7–5 win on July 20 and a 5–4 victory on August 4 when White stole home for the winning run in the bottom of the tenth inning. Brooklyn took two of its three wins in a series at the end of August. The Bacharachs could get only four hits off right-hander Bill Holland on the 28th and lost, 3–2. Hubbard pitched a good game the next day and also hit an inside-the-park home run as Atlantic City won, 9–3. A disputed ball four call in the top of the tenth inning on August 30 led to the winning run for the

Royal Giants in a 9–8 game. According to the *Daily Press*, left fielder Sonny Arnold took a pitch on a 3–2 count that the umpire seemed to call strike three. But Arnold protested and teammate Chino Smith ran out on the field and gave the ump a shove. "The Royals chewed the rag plenty and all of a sudden the arbiter said he meant for Arnold to take his base." Umpire intimidation was nothing new in the ECL, but this time it was eminently successful for Brooklyn, as Arnold soon scored on a hit.[44]

The Bacharachs played the Lincoln Giants six times in six days before the Lincolns dropped out of the league, and won five of the games. Farrell chalked up a 6–3 win on May 28, and Henderson and Hubbard won a doubleheader at the Protectory Oval the next day, 12–7 and 4–2, respectively. Two days later the teams were in Atlantic City as the Bacharachs collected 14 hits in support of Farrell and won, 13–3. The Lincolns got their sole discovered win on June 1, 7–4, but Henderson allowed only seven hits and Dallard socked a three-run homer to star in a 6–3 win on the 2nd.

Four games with regional black teams resulted in four Bacharach wins, although one was a forfeit. With Atlantic City trailing the Philadelphia Giants by a run on April 18, Jesse Hubbard was called out when trying to score on a passed ball with two out in the bottom of the tenth inning. But the ball rolled out of the glove of the tagging defender and plate umpire Louie Plaket reversed his call. The Philadelphians were headed off the field, though, under the impression they had won. They refused to heed Plaket's order to return, and a 9–9 tie became a Bacharach victory. There was no such drama the next day—the Bacharachs pounded 18 hits and won, 14–2. Chappie Johnson's Stars, the veteran baseball showman's current team, came to Bacharach Park on April 24 and were beaten, 8–3. On September 21, with the Giants tuning up for the World Series, Henderson, Hubbard and Roberts combined for a six-hit, 6–0 shutout of the Washington Potomacs, which had adopted the name of the former ECL club.

The Camden Skeeters continued to be a prime semi-pro opponent, actually topping the Giants in the discovered games this season, four to three. Camden won the first meeting on April 23, 7–0, when Jack Stewart pitched a five-hit shutout. Then the Bacharachs battered the Skeeters twice in a row, 16–5 on April 30 and 16–6 on June 11. The Giants got 21 hits in each game and Hubbard breezed to a pair of victories. The Skeeters won three of the final four found games, 9–4 on June 22, 12–4 on July 2, and 15–5 on July 30. Atlantic City's other win was 7–5 on July 1, when three runs in the seventh inning brought the team from behind to make a winner of Roy Roberts.

Other competition against Philadelphia-area teams was minimal, at least in the discovered games. The Bacharachs beat the Curley Athletic Club and teams from the Wentz-Olney, North Philadelphia, Kensington and Lamott neighborhoods. They split a pair with the team from the Harrowgate section of the city.

Elsewhere in New Jersey outside Camden, there were wins over old reliable opponents Millville (8–4 on August 10), Pleasantville (a four-hit shutout by Lockhart on September 3 in which Lundy had four hits), Bridgeton (6–4 on September 10) and the Ocean City Collegians (7–2 on August 13). The Northern New Jersey powerhouse Paterson Silk Sox were a tougher opponent, going down to the Bacharachs, 3–2, on August 6. By accident or design Lockhart seems to have been the "New Jersey" starter for the Giants, getting four of the five wins. There are only three discovered games with New York City semi-pro teams, a split with the Farmers (a 14–7 win on June 5 and a 2–1 loss on July 10), and a 5–3 win over the Bushwicks on June 19, in which Farrell allowed only four hits.

In late October after the Negro World Series, Earle Mack, the son of Athletics manager Connie Mack and a coach for his father's team, put together a post-season all-star team of white American Leaguers to play a five-game series against the Bacharachs. It was a powerful squad. Harry Heilmann, a Detroit Tiger who had led the majors in 1927 with a .398 batting average, was in right field. Fellow Tiger Heinie Manush, who had led the majors in batting the previous year, was in center. Practically every position was manned by someone who had hit more than .300 in the white majors in the season just ended. Four of the five Athletics starting pitchers—Lefty Grove, Rube Walberg, Eddie Rommel and Jack Quinn—made up the pitching staff. Not to be outdone, the Bacharachs recruited heavily and were to have Oscar Charleston, John Beckwith and Rev Cannady from the heavy-hitting Harrisburg Giants lineup, and Phil Cockrell and Nip Winters from Hilldale's pitching in their lineup.

This series might have gone down in baseball history as one of the most important matchups of pre-integration black and white big leaguers, except that it rained. Late October was pushing luck for baseball weather in the Northeast, and while college football could be played in the wet mire that accumulated on the region's athletic fields, baseball couldn't. The vaunted series was limited to a single game, in Atlantic City on October 21. The AL Stars won, 3–0, on the strength of a two-hitter by Quinn. The *Daily Press* referred to him as "Old Jack," and by baseball standards, at age 43, he *was* old. Not that he was finished, by any means. A spitballer among the 17 big league hurlers allowed to keep using their money pitch after it was banned in 1920, he had run up a 15–10 record for Mack in 1927 with a 3.26 ERA. He won 18 games in 1928 and continued to pitch in the majors until he was 49. After all the delayed games, Charleston was the only non-Bacharach in the Atlantic City lineup and he, like nearly everyone else, went hitless. Only Jones, the catcher, and Farrell, the losing pitcher, could reach Old Jack for a hit.

Chapter 7

Down in the Standings, and Out of the City

1928

The Eastern Colored League pennants of 1926 and 1927 were the last that the Bacharach Giants would win. On the other hand, no other team would win any more ECL banners, either, since the league collapsed in the middle of the 1928 season. Prospects for even beginning play in the spring were dim, as poor attendance beset many teams, including the Giants, due to economic conditions in the African American communities and the lack of respect for the league from fans fed up with its scheduling problems, player-umpire squabbles and the continuing arguments among the owners.

The early onset of bad economic times for America's urban blacks left the black baseball owners out on a limb regarding their players. They were paying them salaries based upon what could have been afforded a few years before when financial conditions were better, but now those outlays were pinching team profits, or making them impossible to achieve. In other lines of business the solution would have been layoffs, or replacing the higher-paid workers with less experienced, lower-paid ones. But in professional sports the players are the product, and to discharge them would have been a sure way to disaffect the fans. The ECL's solution to its financial imbalance had been to institute a $2,700 monthly team salary cap in 1927.

This had left the players understandably unhappy, and there were accusations that some of them weren't giving their best. Rollo Wilson wrote that he observed players "'dogging' it day after day. These men are thieves in effect. They were robbing their boss of his money and they were depriving him of the services which he had bought. By their actions they drove fans away from the ball parks." Hubert Lockhart, the Bacharach pitcher who spent his off-season teaching and coaching at Talladega College, and whom Wilson had lauded more than once for his brains and writing ability, stepped up as a spokesman for the players. He told the *Baltimore Afro-American* that ballplayers were "slaves." Their contracts, he said, "are merely useless pieces of paper so far as the individual players are concerned," because when push came to shove owners would "sing the blues and point to depleted treasuries" as an excuse for not honoring them fully. There were some good owners (he mentioned John Dykes of the Bacharachs as an example), but Lockhart was looking to create a players' union to protect him and his fellows.[1]

The unsettled situation in the East brought about the early withdrawal from the

ECL of the Harrisburg Giants and Brooklyn Royal Giants. Getting rid of Nat Strong wasn't necessarily a bad thing, but the next defection was definitely disastrous. Ed Bolden had been in poor health and had lost control of his Hilldale club while recuperating, but he returned in the spring by ousting the management that had taken over the team during his absence. Hilldale was still facing a multi-year financial deficit, however, and Bolden decided that he could make more money on the independent circuit than in a league.

That left the Bacharachs, Baltimore Black Sox and Lincoln Giants, plus the Cuban Stars, whose lack of a home park promised to keep contributing to the endemic scheduling chaos. However, a replacement team from Philadelphia, the Tigers, was organized and found home grounds in that city. The addition of the Tigers as a fifth ECL team was deemed sufficient to allow the league to proceed to open its season, which it did on April 29. The ECL's resurrection by President Nutter and others surprised many in black baseball who had believed it dead. A *Baltimore Afro-American* headline on April 28 captured their surprise: "Is Eastern League Dead or Fooling? Body, Last Week Reported Dead, Now Said to Be Alive and Kicking."

But two months later the organization fell apart for good. Sensing, as Bolden had, that more profitable bookings could be had outside of the constraints of a league schedule, Alex Pompez and Jim Keenan took their Cuban Stars and Lincoln Giants, respectively, out of the league. No amount of first aid could staunch this much bleeding. *Baltimore Afro-American* writer Bill Gibson succinctly summed up the league's six-year history:

> A child of Edward Bolden, Hilldale pilot, and spasmodically fed by the owners of seven clubs, the Eastern League always remained rather a puny thing, never developing the robustness and virility of its relative, the National League. The league led a sort of see-saw existence, assuming an ascendancy or soaring to minor heights on the wind of certain powers behind the throne who dictated to large measure the policies of its administration.[2]

Even before its players had gathered for spring training, the Bacharachs had undergone some major changes of their own—a new owner and a new ballpark. Isaac W. "Ike" Washington had taken over the debt-ridden team. Wilson of the *Courier* noted that among other things, having Washington as the sole man in charge would eliminate "all the warring factors [sic]" that had driven the Bacharachs into bankruptcy and caused the embarrassing lockout at Bacharach Park the previous season. Tom Jackson, bought out with the rest of the owners, remained with the club as the Bacharachs' business manager.[3]

Washington, a 41-year-old Louisiana native, had been in Atlantic City since at least 1914, when he was a partner in a pool hall. He was married until after World War I to Sarah Spencer Washington, who after their divorce parlayed a small beauty parlor into a half-million-dollar cosmetics company and became a longtime community leader in the Atlantic City African American community. While both continued to live and do business in the Northside, Sarah seems to have washed Ike out of her hair, so to speak—he barely gets a passing mention, if that, in her several biographies.[4]

When Washington registered for the draft in 1917 he listed his occupation as a hotel bellman. As was the case with so many other arrivals in Atlantic City, he worked his way up in the city's main business, catering to the tourists. A succession of city directories has him running a restaurant in 1924, and in the saloon and "soft drink" business by 1926. He then is found running nightclubs in the Northside, the Blue Kitten Cabaret in

1927–1928 and the Palais Orient and Gaiety Nite Club in 1929. Then, like others who had arrived as stable members of the middle class (including Jackson and the Bacharachs), he got into the booming real estate market, a less strenuous way to make money.[5]

Washington had another source of income that involved no heavy lifting, although occasionally it may have made him sweat. He was one of the city's leaders of the numbers betting business, which worked much like today's state lotteries, except that then it was illegal. Washington and his brother Edward were arrested in March of 1929 for running a numbers operation. This brush with the law did not seem to discourage Ike, though, and he was still in business in 1939 when caught up in the massive Federal investigation into all things illegal in Atlantic City that finally sent the powerful political boss Enoch "Nucky" Johnson to prison. Washington was charged with evading income taxes on his numbers profits, nabbed in the same dragnet as Leroy Williams. Unlike Williams, though, he did not have Isaac Nutter for a lawyer, and while Williams walked away from the courthouse a free man, Washington served four months in jail.[6]

As to a ballpark for 1928, the five-year lease negotiated by Congressman Bacharach on the property at Tennessee and South Carolina Avenues had expired and new grounds were acquired north of that site. The grounds along Absecon Boulevard, the northern access to the island, had been a kennel and dog track. In the late summer of 1926 it had hosted the famous heavyweight boxer Jack Dempsey, training for the September bout in Philadelphia in which he lost his title to Gene Tunney. Turning the track into a baseball field took some doing—the infield, the area in the middle of the oval track, was also to be the baseball infield, but it was graced by a small lake. The lake had to be filled and its former banks graded down to make a flat surface. This, and the construction of additional seating that brought total capacity to 11,000 customers, took some doing and kept the Giants on the road until Memorial Day.[7]

Washington made a dramatic statement of purpose to Rollo Wilson just before the season began that made him sound tough and in charge: "The boys are going to subscribe to my rules and live up to them or they are going to be off the payroll.... We do not expect to make any money this year but we are building for the years to come."[8]

Dick Lundy was back as field manager and shortstop, leading the team in RBI with 76 and placing second in batting average at .362. Several mainstays of the previous year's pennant winner were also back and hitting, particularly Chaney White in center field at .342, and Luther Farrell, who hammered the ball to the tune of a .318 average with seven home runs while splitting his time between pitching and the outfield.

Two factors associated with the league's breakup also changed the Giants' roster, primarily for the better. The first was the invariable interest of league teams in the players of the teams that had dropped out of the organization and put themselves outside the roster raiding rules. Black baseball was well known for this sort of poaching, although the white majors had been quite capable of this when a new, rival big league formed and immediately went after men from established loops' rosters. The American League poached National Leaguers in 1901, for example, and in 1914 and 1915 the renegade Federal League raided both the NL and the American League.

The target in this case was Keenan's Lincoln Giants, once they had left the ECL. For a non-league owner trying to keep the desirable part of his team, forsaking league protection was the equivalent of throwing fresh bait into shark-infested waters. In this case the first fin sighted was coming from the direction of Atlantic City. The Bacharachs gobbled up George "Tank" Carr to play first base and Clarence "Fats" Jenkins for the outfield. Nutter defended the Bacharachs and, by extension, all league teams who picked over the rosters of the departed squads: "Every player on every club which has withdrawn from the league is the property of the league and it will continue to sign such men as are wanted by its members."[9]

Though in signing Jenkins and Carr the team profited from the free-for-all that ensued in the player contract market, it was reportedly denied an even better prize. Rollo Wilson reported in March that the great outfielder Oscar Charleston, plus reliable starting pitcher Darltie Cooper, had been allotted to the Bacharachs when Harrisburg dropped out of the league, but both instead signed with Hilldale. Since Bolden had also taken his team out of the ECL, there was no way to enforce the promise to Atlantic City.[10]

Carr, a switch-hitter standing six feet, two inches and weighing 230 pounds, had played in the Negro National League's first season in 1920 and had been with Hilldale since 1923 until traded to the Lincolns earlier in 1928. He hopped to the Bacharachs at the end of May and hit .328 with significant power for the Giants. While Carr's physique justified his nickname, Jenkins was anything but overweight. In fact, he was a lithe two-sport black major leaguer. He spent his winters as a guard and floor captain on the Harlem Renaissance basketball team and has a spot in the National Basketball Hall of Fame, since the Rens were one of the pioneer hoop squads inducted by the Hall. A left-handed slap hitter whose speed made him a likely candidate to beat out an infield hit, Jenkins joined the Bacharachs in the first week in June, played left field on a daily basis and led the team in batting at .381.

The other factor freeing up players for moves among teams was the willingness of some owners to cut regulars loose. Money, or the lack of it, to pay salaries, had something to do with this, making some players dissatisfied and their bosses happy to be rid of what they considered malcontents. Although details are slim, Clint Thomas, a star outfielder for Hilldale since 1923, seems to have fallen out of favor with Bolden, who released him in mid–July. (Hilldale had a surplus of outfielders, having picked up Charleston and Rev Cannady from the Harrisburg Giants when that team dropped out of the ECL.) Thomas immediately signed with Atlantic City, took over right field and hit .348 for the remainder of the season. To sort out its now-crowded outfield, the Bacharachs released Eggie Dallard, who was said to be allowing his "fiery temper" to interfere with his playing. His .195 batting average probably had something to do with the move also.[11]

The outfield was full of .300 hitters but the infield had to be patched together a bit because Oliver Marcell missed two months with a broken hand. Marcell still hit .298 and covered third in his usual exemplary fashion when healthy, however. His absence was covered by Carr and Ambrose Reid, who had shifted positions yet again to become the regular second baseman, since Milt Lewis had left the team in mid–June. Reid didn't have one of his better years, hitting .256, but as usual he made himself handy. When Carr temporarily moved to third, he was replaced by a familiar face. Nap Cummings returned to the Giants for a final go-round, filling in a first base and sometimes at second, ripping the ball at a .297 rate. Reid was also backed up at second by Jimmy Shields, a college player who hit .282 as a sub and also pitched. Willie Jones, with a startlingly productive .314 batting average, split the catching with new acquisition Johnny Cason, a .222 hitter most recently a Brooklyn Royal Giant during a ten-year career in high-level blackball.

It was a good team, with an overall .581 winning percentage (54–39–4) in 97 discovered games and almost a .500 mark (32–33–3) against current or former ECL teams plus three Negro National League teams they played at the end of the season. The Bacharachs certainly could hit, nearly .300 as a team and another six-run-a-game offense. Wilson thought "the Bees have at last hit their true stride.... They have the best infield hereabouts. No outfield is better. They have smart moundsmen and two real catchers. What else do they need?"[12]

But as had been the case in the past when hard-hitting Bacharach teams had to settle for good, but not outstanding, records, there was a lack of pitching depth. Farrell went 16–8 with a 3.30 ERA in 21 starts and seven relief appearances, and Rats Henderson, making 21 appearances, 16 of them starts, went 10–4, although his ERA rose to 4.05. But Red Grier's meteoric career had flamed out, Jesse Hubbard had moved on to the Baltimore Black Sox, Roy Roberts was released in early June, and Hubert Lockhart, still showing up late in the spring after his college duties were over, was less effective and less used, going 4–3 in 13 games, eight of them starts. Kenneth "Ping" Gardner, a submarining right-hander, had been pitching in high-level black ball since 1919 with mixed results. Signed from the defunct Harrisburg franchise, he made 20 starts for the Bacharachs in 1928, but had only a 7–14 won-lost record and was rung up for a 5.42 ERA. The right-handed journeyman Alonzo Mitchell returned to the Giants but didn't pitch well, with a 5.76 ERA, although he won four games. Shields made nine starts and went 6–3 with a very good 2.61 ERA. Curtis Green, a journeyman in the middle and late 1920s who also played outfield, made six starts and won three of them, but was mostly successful against lesser competition.

With the Eastern teams free to schedule their own games once the ECL had collapsed, the Bacharachs played nearly three-fifths of their contests with the teams that began the season in the ECL, against only two of those opponents, the Baltimore Black Sox and Hilldale, with 20 games against each in the discovered games.

Things went better against the Black Sox, from whom the Bacharachs won 12, while losing seven and tying one. Baltimore swept the first meeting, a doubleheader in its Maryland Park, on May 6. Norman Yokely, the Sox ace, threw a three-hit shutout for a 2–0 win in the first game, negating fine pitching by Farrell. Home runs by outfielders Herbert "Rap" Dixon and Christopher Columbus "Crush" Holloway led the home team to an 8–6 victory in the second game, shortened to six innings by darkness. Dallard scored all three runs, driven in twice by Farrell, the next day in Richmond as Alonzo Mitchell gained a 3–2 win.

The teams split a two-game series at Bacharach Park on June 1–2. Lockhart's four-hitter produced a 7–2 Giants victory in the first game, but Yokely struck again the next day, holding a shutout until the ninth inning as Baltimore eventually won, 7–2. The Bacharachs took two out of three in New Jersey on June 12, 13 and 15. Rookie Baltimore pitcher Bernalle "Bun" Hayes took a no-hitter into the eighth inning but weakened substantially, although not enough to keep the Sox from winning, 6–5. The next day the

Giants scored three runs in the fifth inning on a collection of hits, walks and Sox errors and gained a 5–3 win for Farrell. Lockhart continued to handle the Black Sox with ease, pitching a five-hitter on the 15th as the Giants won, 5–2, at the sister Jersey Shore resort town of Wildwood. The two teams then headed for Baltimore, where the Sox won two close ones. Yokely won his third game over the Bacharachs, 3–2, in the opener, and Baltimore also copped the nightcap, 4–2.

July meetings almost all went the Giants' way as they won eight of the ten games, starting with a 21–1 slaughter of Baltimore on July 9 in Atlantic City. Farrell pitched a complete game even though he spent plenty of time cooling off on the bench while the Bacharachs pounded 23 hits. On the other hand, four of the hits were his, allowing him to keep loose running the bases. Cummings led the team with five hits. Rain intervened in the seventh inning the following day to bring about a 4–4 tie.

What was essentially a six-game series in three cities linked the teams from July 15–19, beginning with a doubleheader in Baltimore. Lundy had three hits in the first game to help Ping Gardner win, 5–4, over Jesse Hubbard. Then Yokely won his fourth game over the Bacharachs, 8–3. The series moved to Richmond on the 16th. There Jenkins drove in the winning run with a double (the last of his four hits) in the ninth inning, the win going to Henderson. The Bacharachs got 16 hits the next day, including a home run by Marcell. Still in Richmond, they won, 9–4. On the 18th Thomas tripled in two runs in the fifth inning to give the Giants the edge needed to finally hand a loss to Yokely, 6–5. Farrell got the win. The final game was in Norfolk on July 19, where the Bacharachs won a 15–11 slugfest for their fifth win in this far-flung matchup. Back at home at the end of July, the Bacharachs beat with Sox, 5–1, on the 30th as Shields pitched a two-hitter. Henderson followed up with a three-hitter the next day as the Giants won, 10–0.

Hilldale, however, was an entirely different situation with the Philadelphia team winning 11 games and losing seven to Atlantic City, with two ties. The first two wins, in Durham, North Carolina, on April 17–18, weren't a fair fight. Hilldale had been left high and dry for a couple of spring training exhibition games by the inability of another team to join them, so the "Bacharach All-Stars" were born with several Giants starters missing, replaced by Hilldale players. The full Hilldale squad won, 2–0 and 9–1, although Farrell's six-hitter in the opener made the slapped-together squad very respectable.

With both squads fully assembled and the season into gear, a May 31 contest at Hilldale Park produced an 11-inning, 8–8 tie halted by darkness. A set of five games between June 3–9 produced two Bacharach wins and three for Hilldale. Four Philadelphia errors helped the Bacharachs to a 5–2 win on the 3rd, Farrell getting the victory. Nineteen hits, four by Dallard, propelled the team to a 12–6 win at Hilldale Park on the last day. In between, however, Hilldale swept a doubleheader on June 5 at Bacharach Park when Darltie Cooper outpitched Gardner, 4–2, in the first game and Porter Charleston, a youngster from Texas in his second season with the club, threw a three-hit shutout in the second contest. The third Hilldale win came the next day, 8–5.

While July had brought much good fortune to the Giants playing the Black Sox, no such streak existed that month with Hilldale, which won four of seven games (one of which was a rain-shortened no-decision). That event came in the second game of a July 1 doubleheader with the Bacharachs ahead, 3–1, in the second inning. Cooper had won the first game, 2–1, when Gardner wild-pitched the winning run home in the seventh. The Giants won on the next two days. Porter Charleston, an uneven starter, was belted in an 11–1 loss on the 2nd, Farrell getting the win and Lundy and Jones each getting three hits.

Reid launched a ninth-inning sacrifice fly in the July 3 game that brought home the winning run, 3–2. Henderson pitched a five-hitter, but Hilldale starter Joe Strong was doing even better until Otto Briggs yanked him in the bottom of the seventh after a leadoff walk and two straight balls to the next batter. The Bacharachs scored all their runs off reliever Phil Cockrell, and the *Daily Press* criticized Hilldale manager Otto Briggs for the switch. The reporter ventured, however, that Strong may have lost more than just his control: "Judy Johnson [Hilldale's third baseman] was caught with some emory paper in his glove, and Strong is known as the emory ball pitcher."[13] The rest of July belonged to Hilldale, which had 21 hits on July 12 and won, 20–4; pulled out a 4–3 win on July 21 on a ninth-inning home run by Oscar Charleston; and won, 3–1, on July 26 when Cooper pitched a four-hitter.

The Bacharachs rebounded in August to win three of the last five games in the season series, 10–4 in Darby on August 4 when White and Thomas had three hits each and Carr hit a home run; 11–3 in the second game of a doubleheader the next day at Bacharach Park; and 4–2 there in the last discovered meeting on August 7 on a Gardner three-hitter. Hilldale won the first game of the August 5 doubleheader, 4–2, behind another good pitching turn by Cooper, and 8–3 on the 6th.

Discovered games against other Eastern black teams are few and far between. The most were five with the Lincoln Giants, all on Sundays at their Protectory Oval in the Bronx. Jim Keenan was loathe to have his team play anywhere else on Sundays, one of the lesser scheduling problems that had faced the ECL. The Lincolns won four of the five games, starting with a sweep of an April 29 doubleheader, 4–2 and 10–3. The first game was a home run derby in the little Oval, with two by losing pitcher Farrell and three by the Lincolns. The Lincolns won there again on May 20, 14–7, despite two homers by White. The Bacharachs finally got a win in the first game of a doubleheader on July 29. Farrell gave up seven hits and Carr delivered three for the offense as the Bacharachs won, 6–3. The venerable John Henry Lloyd, now moved over to the less demanding first base at age 44, but still with a live bat, got four hits in the second game to pace a 10–7 Lincoln win.

The Brooklyn Royal Giants don't show up in the discovered games until the very end of the season at Bacharach Park, when they came in for a four-game series beginning September 9. A doubleheader that day produced a split. The Royal Giants won the opener, 6–4. Dick Redding, still pitching at 38, gave up 15 hits but, as the *Daily Press* put it, "used his noodle rather than his arm to win the ball game. He took things quite easy when there was no one on the cushions. But once there was a man on the sacks he tightened."[14] The Bacharachs continued to hit in the second game, with 12 safeties, but turned them into a few more runs and won, 6–3. Shields pitched a six-hit shutout on the 10th as Atlantic City won, 2–0. But Gardner was shelled in the final game, which Brooklyn won, 12–5, to split the three-day series.

There are only three discovered games each with the New York Cubans and the

Harrisburg Giants. The Bacharachs won two close ones in a row against the Cubans, 7–6 on June 18 when they made an early lead stand up, and 8–7 the next day when Reid broke a tie with an RBI single in the bottom of the ninth. The Bacharachs swept three games with Harrisburg in late June, winning 10–5 on June 25 at Bacharach Park as Carr homered and Cummings had three hits, and 9–2 the next day when Farrell gave up six hits and racked up three, including a home run, for himself. The third win two days later, on neutral ground in Parkesburg, Pennsylvania, was by a 6–3 score.

There are only two discovered games with the Philadelphia Tigers, the new team that fleshed out the ECL briefly at the beginning of the season. The Bacharachs won them both, 10–6 on May 5, and 5–2, the Giants' ECL home opener, on May 30.

For the first time since 1922 a Bacharach squad went west to play Negro National League teams during the regular season. The results, at least until the Giants got to St. Louis, weren't bad. They started in Detroit and lost two of three to the Stars, 9–2 on August 11 and 9–6 on the 13th, but won, 9–7, on the 12th on the strength of a three-run go-ahead rally in the eighth inning. Four games with the Chicago American Giants, their World Series opponents the past two seasons, also produced a split. The first game, on August 20, was easy for the Bacharachs as Henderson threw a six-hitter and they won, 13–0. Then things got difficult, and Chicago won 4–2 and 5–0 the next two days. Fats Jenkins closed out the series on August 23 with a ninth-inning, game-winning hit as the Bacharachs left Chicago with a 3–2 victory.

The St. Louis Stars were the best team in the NNL that season, with a strong, young lineup that included future Negro League stars such as center fielder James "Cool Papa" Bell, first baseman George "Mule" Suttles, shortstop Willie Wells and pitcher Ted Trent. They don't seem to have been impressed by the Bacharachs, sweeping a four-game game series from August 25 to 28 by scores of 9–7, 5–4, 14–3 and 6–1.

Atlantic City played two regional black teams in 1928, taking two out of three from the St. Louis Giants and winning the single game with Santop's Bronchos, a team run by former Hilldale star catcher Louis Santop.

There were few struggles with the white teams on the Bacharach schedule. They won 11 of 13 discovered games with Philadelphia-area teams. Harrowgate managed a split of four games. Atlantic City won, 6–4, on June 23 and 9–7 in the first game of a doubleheader on June 24, while the Philadelphia squad won, 7–0, on May 26 and 4–0 in the second game on June 24. The Giants took two games from Kensington Congregational in May, 7–5 in 12 innings on the 12th and 4–1 on the 18th. West Philadelphia went down, 7–1, on July 25. The Philadelphia Elks, who had collected several of city's regular semipro standouts, couldn't translate those acquisitions into wins against the Bacharachs, who beat them, 7–2, on May 30 and 7–6, twice, in a July 8 doubleheader that featured a total of 51 hits.

Stan Baumgartner, the former white major league hurler now pitching for the Corley Catholic Club, dueled with Farrell on August 1 in a game that the Bacharachs won, 5–1, although Baumgartner gave up only five hits to Farrell's four. Chester came to Bacharach Park on September 3 and lost a doubleheader, 9–1 and 6–0. Farrell in the first game and Shields in the second each pitched five-hitters.

There were three doubleheaders in New York with the Farmers, resulting in three wins for each team. The Bacharachs swept on May 13, 13–8 in the first game, in which Farrell and Dallard both homered, and 6–1 in the second when Farrell, now on the mound, struck out seven. The Farmers swept two on June 10, the first 1–0. Chad See, a former major league outfielder and minor league pitcher, gave up only two hits, winning his own game with a sacrifice fly off of Green, who allowed only three hits. The score of the second game was 9–6. The teams split the final twin bill on July 22. The Bacharachs won the opener, 11–6, but lost the nightcap, 7–4.

Other white semi-pro opponents were the Trenton Young Italian Americans, who hung in with the Giants for 11 innings in Trenton before losing, 7–6, and the Lancaster, Pennsylvania, Eighth Ward team. It came to Wildwood for a game on June 16 but instead became the center of a farce. The team wasn't a regular Bacharach opponent and may have miscalculated the Giants' strength. In addition, many of its best players did not make the trip to the Shore. As a result the Bacharachs were ahead, 19–0, when the game was mercifully stopped and declared a no-decision in the fourth inning. William "Doc" Lambert, the Giants' booking agent, took the field to announce that tickets sold for the game would be honored at the Giants' next appearance in Wildwood, as the team would not take money under "false pretenses."[15]

Two local opponents were dispatched easily. The Atlantic City Police Department's team fell, 8–4, on May 29, and 9–1 on June 27, and Ocean City was beaten, 8–2, on July 29. A House of David team played at Bacharach Park on July 11 and was beaten badly, 20–10. The Giants had 25 hits, five each by Lundy and Carr. Shields pitched and coasted along, giving up 17 hits.

As well as the Giants played, lack of attendance and a resulting shortage of revenue at Atlantic City home games continued to be a serious problem. Washington sent the team on the road for the second half of July, in the apparent hope that its absence from Bacharach Park would make the local fans' hearts grow fonder. The *Daily Press* reported that Washington's efforts "seemed almost futile. Excellent attractions have been booked and some thrilling games have been played, but the attendance has been poorer than during any season heretofore." Washington sent the team out of town again in late August, on the Midwestern swing to NNL territory, for the same reason, and meant to close Bacharach Park for the year, keeping the Giants on the road for as long as possible. Despite that decision they did return to Atlantic City in September, but the final opinion of the *Daily Press* was that "the new park, so conscientiously renovated and altered to the purpose of baseball by Washington, did little or nothing to enhance the popularity of the great team. The attendance during the entire season was nothing short of miserable."[16]

1929

The Eastern Colored League was barely dead when the African American sportswriters who had covered it, banded together as the Eastern Sport Writers Association, called for another try. A lengthy argument on behalf of the association, calling for the return of league ball, appeared in the *New York Amsterdam-News* on August 15, 1928, under the byline of Romeo L. Dougherty, the *News* sports editor and association president. An identical piece was published in the *Pittsburgh Courier* three days later with the byline of W. Rollo Wilson, *Courier* columnist and association vice president. Ignoring that one of the country's leading black sports journalists (or perhaps two of them, since this was an association product) had his byline on someone else's work, the article made a strong case that a well-organized league was the only way to curry the favor of disaffected and disappearing fans of Eastern black baseball: "The public will never again patronize 'independent' baseball as it did in the days before it knew the association brand of the game. Owners are losing money, players are recalcitrant, fans are dissatisfied. The game and the men interested in it and the men who make their living by it need a strong, well-balanced circuit which will protect all of those involved." The sportswriters also knew just who they wanted to lead this movement—it was time for Ed Bolden to step up again, "because Ed Bolden means more to baseball than baseball can ever mean to Ed Bolden.... We draft him and designate him as ... the one individual, perhaps, who can work order out of the present chaos."[17]

Sure enough, shortly after the New Year there was a meeting in Philadelphia to form the American Negro League, and Bolden was elected president. The new league "offered several promising contrasts to the Eastern Colored League. Its racial composition differed substantially from its predecessor with the involvement of only two white owners, James Keenan and George Rossiter (of the Baltimore Black Sox), compared to four at the inception of the ECL." Bolden was given broader powers than he or Nutter had in the old ECL, and punishments for attacks on umpires or other players were increased. To keep a lid on salaries, rosters were limited to 14 players at the beginning of the season, with expansion to 16 per team by July. Rollo Wilson was made league secretary, an important nod to the sportswriting fraternity.[18]

Five teams that had been regular members of the ECL—the Bacharachs, Hilldale, the Lincoln Giants, the Black Sox and the Cuban Stars—were in the ANL, along with one team joining its first major league. The Homestead Grays were no newcomers to professional baseball, though, nor was the owner and manager, Cumberland Willis Posey, Jr. Posey's best sport as an athlete was basketball, in which he starred both in college and professionally. His real talents lay in organization, and he ran a professional basketball squad and dabbled in promoting football and boxing, as well as getting involved in local politics in the borough of Homestead, a steel-manufacturing center adjacent to Pittsburgh. An outfielder in baseball, he joined a local semi-pro team in 1911 and was soon running it.

Posey gradually built the Grays into a regional powerhouse, taking advantage of a geographical vacuum between the Eastern Colored League, which extended no farther west than Philadelphia, and the Negro National League, which only occasionally had teams in central and northern Ohio. The Grays were plenty good enough to have been in either league, but Posey was extremely canny and kept the Grays out of league affiliations. By remaining independent the team could sign players away from the leagues, while the salaries Posey could afford to pay seldom resulted in defectors. And he didn't have to share control of his regional booking empire.

Posey's decision to bring the Grays into the ANL was probably a vote of confidence in the league being on a more organized basis than its predecessor, and in Bolden's leadership. But the two men couldn't have been more different. Bolden was reserved and businesslike. Although he disdained the violence that sometimes erupted in black games, Posey the field manager could raise hell with an umpire along with the best of them, and wasn't above pulling his team off the field and forfeiting a game if angry enough. A workmanlike writer with many connections in the sporting world, Posey wrote a regular column for the hometown *Courier*. He was never afraid to criticize other black sporting magnates, and it is possible that the only sportsman he ever totally agreed with was the one he saw in his mirror each morning.

Prior to joining the ANL, Posey used his position as an "outsider" to the Negro Leagues, albeit one with plenty of clout, to give pointed and probably unwelcome advice. For example, in 1927 he mocked a statement calling for a five-year ban on contract jumpers by league officials who were simultaneously failing to deal with player rowdyism and sub-standard umpiring:

> This is not worth the ink it took to write it. Five years from now five-sixths of the magnates now in Organized Negro baseball will have followed the paths of C. I. Taylor or "Rube" Foster [both dead, possibly in part due to the physical and mental stress of running teams and a league], or will be broke, if they keep building up defenses against players and each other instead of getting fair umpires and getting rid of the rowdies on the club and in the stands and give the people a chance to see baseball played.[19]

From 1929 on, the Grays were usually affiliated with a league, at least as an associate member. Shortly after the second Negro National League was founded in the East in the mid–1930s, the Grays began to dominate it, and have gone down in history as one of the strongest franchises in the Negro Leagues. Posey remained in black baseball until his death in 1946, and is one of five Negro Leagues owners voted into the National Baseball Hall of Fame.

Baltimore won both halves of the split season and undisputed possession of the ANL pennant with healthy competition from Posey's Grays, the Lincoln Giants and Hilldale. Two clubs were never in the running. The Bacharachs were one of them, actually finishing last in the season's second half behind the equally woebegone Cuban Stars. The Giants' offensive powerhouse that had been built over the past few years was partially dismantled, and the pitching was worse than ever. In the discovered games against league opponents, the Bacharachs won only 20, lost 44 and tied two, a dismal .313 winning percentage.

Ike Washington had promised a serious shakeup if things didn't go well in 1928, but the big changes didn't occur until 1929. As Washington had predicted, the team didn't make money in 1928, which was nothing new for Atlantic City baseball in that period. The wreck of the ECL, coupled with continuing low attendance at Bacharach Park, may have produced more red ink than he had expected, and perhaps led to the shedding of some regulars. Tensions that arose from the previous year, though, were clearly responsible for much of the upheaval.

When Washington was introducing himself to the black baseball press in March of 1928 he placed a lot of responsibility for team building on his manager and star player, Dick Lundy: "If there are any dissatisfied men he will be the negotiator and if he can't bring them into line, there are plenty others who are waiting for a chance to show what they can do." By the middle of the season, though, there were rumors that Lundy himself was in the owner's doghouse, along with Oliver Marcell, and that both might quit the team.[20]

They lasted the season, but Washington's first big offseason move for 1929 was to trade Lundy even-up for Ben Taylor, the Baltimore manager. On paper, the swap was a one-sided one in favor of the Black Sox. Taylor, an eventual Hall of Famer, had a sterling reputation as a manager. He was credited with improving the Sox after becoming manager there in 1926 and had done well as the field boss of the Bacharachs in 1919 before returning to Indianapolis to rejoin his brother C. I.'s team. But he was traded for a man who was both the Giants' manager and star player, and at age 40 Taylor wasn't expected to be much more than a part-timer at first base. Lundy, meanwhile, was only 30 and was definitely still a regular shortstop. Taylor, who had a home and business interests (reportedly a shoe shine parlor and a pool hall) in Baltimore, hemmed and hawed for awhile about reporting to the Bacharachs, but eventually signed a one-year contract for what was reported to be a hefty raise over his Black Sox salary. When the trade was first announced, Washington said diplomatically it would be the best for all concerned. The owner was quite satisfied with the deal, even if it looked one-sided from the outside. What Washington was looking for was a strong and steady veteran hand to run the Bacharachs, and he thought he had found his man. All three Taylor brothers who managed in the Negro Leagues, C. I., Ben and Jim, were regarded as among the most superlative handlers of players in black baseball.[21]

Once Taylor had taken charge of the Giants the team pulled off another headline trade with the Black Sox that also seemed lopsided in Baltimore's favor. But Taylor got the player he wanted, and may have gotten rid of a man he didn't want. Leaving Atlantic City were Oliver Marcell and catcher Johnny Cason. Arriving were catcher Macajah "Mack" Eggleston, right-handed pitcher Bob McClure and shortstop Bill Lindsey. Baltimore had also acquired second baseman Frank Warfield over the winter, and the addition of him, Marcell and Lundy to future Hall of Famer Jud Wilson at first gave the Black Sox the best infield in the league.

McClure, Lindsey and Cason weren't the focus of the trade, which boiled down to Taylor acquiring Eggleston, who had served with him in black baseball for years, and who was described as Ben's "first lieutenant ... always valuable to the House of Taylor." Marcell, on the other hand, had been his usual hard-to-handle self in 1928. In the middle of the season he had gotten into a fight with Doc Lambert, a well-known athletic trainer who also served as a booking contact for the team, furthering his reputation as the antithesis of the ideal Ben Taylor–type ballplayer.[22]

Two regulars from 1928, first baseman Tank Carr and pitcher Ping Gardner, were lost from the beginning of the season until June 24 when the league suspended them for reporting late. They had been playing with a black team in the California Winter League and then had taken a side-trip to Honolulu. Early-season absenteeism had been a problem in the Eastern Colored League, and one of the marks against its leadership had been its ineffectual handling of these situations. The ANL's organizers meant for their new league to be stricter in handing out discipline to players. Unfortunately for the Giants, this was one case when the punishment (one day of suspension for each late day in reporting) held firm.

Nagging injuries bothered Chaney White, Ambrose Reid and Willie Jones during the season. Reid's sore arm kept him out of the lineup often, although as a super utility man he managed to play six different field positions. But the most serious loss was the defection of Luther Farrell, who left the team in the middle of May, depriving the Bacharachs of their best pitcher and one of their strongest sluggers. Farrell wasn't lured away by a lucrative promise from another top black team. The uniform for which he traded his Giants jersey was the blue of the Atlantic City Police Department which, not coincidentally, was fielding one of the top semi-pro teams in the Southern New Jersey area at the time. Although local government jobs were long recognized as plums in Atlantic City, since they insured year-round employment even after the tourists had gone home, Farrell's leaving the Bacharachs for such a position can be seen as a strong clue to the precariousness of the team's financial situation.[23]

In July a *Daily Press* reporter presented an interview with Ben Taylor in which the manager was "trying his utmost to recall the day or night he had smashed a mirror, walked under a ladder, had a cross-eye girl give him the once over, have a black cat run across his path or have someone put the curse of Michael Feeney on him," so bad had been the Bacharachs' luck with injuries and defections. "We've had lots of luck, but mostly bad," Taylor concluded. Chaney White was overheard at a home game explaining the season-long problem to Atlantic City Postmaster Al Perkins, a big Bacharachs fan, as follows: "When we're hitting the pitchers are going bad. When the pitchers [*sic*] settin' 'em down we're not hitting."[24]

The Bacharach starting outfield of White, Fats Jenkins and Clint Thomas played almost every day, with Reid available as an occasional replacement. It was the best part of the team that year. Jenkins hit .356, which led the team, and was second in runs scored with 75. White, despite his nagging injury, hit .353 and drove in 68 runs, both runner-up totals. Thomas narrowly led in both those departments with 76 runs and 69 RBI, and hit .343 to boot.

First base should have been all set with Carr playing it. But his late arrival and subsequent suspension, plus a benching by Taylor in July for not being in playing shape, limited him to less than half of the team's games, although he hit .328 when in the lineup. Taylor put himself in the lineup most of the time when Carr wasn't playing and hit a very creditable .313 in his last season as an active ballplayer. Reid, who batted .293, also played several games at first and at second, although that spot mostly belonged to Wilson "Connie" Day, another Ben Taylor colleague on the Indianapolis, Harrisburg and Baltimore teams. Day was regarded as one of the best infield gloves of his day, "one of the best ground ball men in the game."[25] Never a great hitter, even in his prime (he was now 31), he batted only .233 for the Bacharachs.

Lindsey, obtained in the Marcell trade, became Lundy's replacement at shortstop while rookie Jesse Walker, a 17-year-old Texan beginning a long career as a player and manager, took over from Marcell. Taylor switched their positions on July 13 for the rest of the season, but either at third or short they were regulars all season long, although failing the very difficult test of measuring up to the men they replaced. Lindsey hit .285

and Walker .226, and while neither had much power, they could work a walk and got on base frequently. They were the team's top run scorers behind the outfield triumvirate. Taylor opened the season with Bobby Williams, a seasoned, 33-year-old veteran of both the Negro National and Eastern Colored Leagues, at shortstop, but he failed to hit and was replaced by Lindsay at the end of May.

Eggleston and Jones split the catching about equally, with Eggleston also filling in at third base and Jones occasionally in the outfield. Eggleston hit .235 for the year and Jones .240.

The pitching staff was woebegone. Rats Henderson was only 31 years old, but he was coming off of another bout of arm trouble and reportedly had added a bit too much weight to his already rotund frame. Despite those problems he was still the best pitcher on the Bacharach staff once Farrell had decamped, going 11–13 with a 5.26 ERA.[26] McClure had some excellent years with Baltimore, but they had been in the middle of the decade. Now, at age 38, he posted a 5.41 ERA, with eight wins and 11 losses. Gardner might have done the Giants more good on the beach in Honolulu than on the mound in Atlantic City—he had a 7.40 ERA and a 4–9 won-lost mark. Jimmie Shields fell off sharply from his rookie year, with a 5.82 ERA. Opportunities went to others, but no one could step up. While Alonzo Mitchell won both his decisions in seven games, his ERA was 5.76. Joe Cade, a rookie, made ten starts for a 2–5 mark and a big 6.30 ERA.

This was the recipe for a second-division team—too many light-hitting journeymen and rookies in key positions and an eminently hittable pitching staff that in 102 discovered games gave up an average of seven runs per game.

The Giants achieved their dismal .313 winning percentage against the rest of the ANL by getting trounced in season series with Baltimore, Homestead and the Lincoln Giants, while playing .500 ball against fellow second-division occupants Hilldale and the Cuban Stars. Their worst experience was with the Black Sox, who won 14 of 17 discovered games. The Bacharachs didn't fare too badly after the middle of June, but their early-season schedule was loaded with Baltimore games, and the Sox won the first nine meetings.

Many of the best players in the league had been Bacharachs at one time or another, and the Sox had several that especially haunted the Giants in this poor season. Red Ryan, for example, shut them out, 8–0, in the second game of a doubleheader on May 12 and won again, 10–4, on June 16. Nip Winters got the win on September 4 when a five-run rally in the seventh inning produced a 9–4 Baltimore victory. That rally included a home run by Dick Lundy, who more than once made the off-season trade that had sent him from Atlantic City a painful experience. In addition to that timely hit, he doubled in the tying run on April 23 when the Sox won, 4–3, and had three hits in an 8–6 win at Bacharach Park on June 18. That was the first Atlantic City appearance as Black Sox for both Lundy and Marcell, who also got a hit, and the *Daily Press* noted they both "gave splendid accounts of themselves." Among the other notable losses to Baltimore was a 21–4 pasting on April 24 in which the Sox had 18 hits and five homers down in Richmond, and a doubleheader in Baltimore on August 18 in which Script Lee threw a four-hitter in an 8–4 win and the other game was forfeited to Baltimore with the score 7–2 in the seventh inning after a prolonged Bacharach argument over the use of a discolored ball.[27]

The Bacharach wins came on June 20 at home, 8–7, when Lindsay singled in the winning run in the bottom of the ninth; 13–7 on July 9 in a comedy of errors that included six boots by the Sox and most of the runs scored off Henderson being unearned because of Giants outfield errors, and 12–4 in Baltimore on September 3.

If the Black Sox bedeviled the Bacharachs with some ghosts from their past, Cumberland Posey's Homestead Grays were practically running a haunted house. The Grays won nine of 12 discovered games, and the winning pitcher in five of them had figured prominently in Bacharach history. Joe Williams, Dick Redding's mound opponent in the first black games at Ebbets Field in 1921 while a Lincoln Giant and an occasional Bacharach hire for big exhibition games, was still pitching at age 44, and doing it pretty well. He picked up three wins over the Giants in 1929: 14–2 on May 5; 5–4 on June 27 when Homestead wiped out a four-run Atlantic City lead in the late innings; and 4–3 on August 11 when he struck out 11 batters in the first game of a doubleheader.

Sam Streeter, the left-hander who had anchored the pitching staff of the Atlantic City version of the Bacharachs in 1922, threw a two-hitter for a 4–1 win in the second game on August 11 and pitched a ten-inning complete game win on June 26. The score was 5–4, the winning run coming on a single by Charlie Mason, a regular Bacharach outfielder in the mid-'20s until traded to the Lincoln Giants for Marcell.

The Bacharach victories included an 11–2 win in the second game of the June 27 doubleheader; a 14–10 victory at Forbes Field, the Pittsburgh Pirates' home park that the Grays sometimes rented for home games (in which Walker had three hits, including two triples); and a 7–4 win at Bacharach Park on August 26 when McClure not only got the win but hit safely three times, as did White.

Owner Jim Keenan had signed some of the best hitters in the Negro Leagues for his Lincoln Giants in 1929. John Henry Lloyd was still the playing manager and had at his disposal such batting stars as John Beckwith, George Scales, Charles "Chino" Smith and Bob Hudspeth. So meetings between the Lincolns and the Bacharachs tended to be slugfests, although the New York City team won ten, while Atlantic City won only three and one was a tie. The Bacharachs scored an even 100 runs in the 14 discovered games, an average of seven per game, but gave up 128, a per-game average of nine.

The few Bacharach wins showed a potent offense, but the weak pitching was exposed even more than usual by the Lincolns' hitting. Atlantic City won, 18–9, on June 24 at the Protectory Oval, banging out 18 hits as Gardner staggered nine innings for the win, giving up 13 hits himself. The second game of a July 3 doubleheader at Bacharach Park was a 14–9 Atlantic City win. The Bacharachs jumped right off with seven runs in the bottom of the first inning. But the Lincolns matched that in the fourth inning and were ahead, 9–8, when the home team rallied for the lead in the seventh. The explosive hitting was just a continuation of the first game that day, which the Lincolns won, 18–9. This time the Bacharachs had a 9–8 lead after five innings, but were swept away by ten more Lincoln runs. The score of the other Bacharach win was modest by the standards of this season series, 7–6 on July 16. Down 6–4, Atlantic City scored three runs in the seventh to take the lead, then Fats Jenkins made a game-saving catch in the outfield in the ninth.

Low-scoring Bacharach-Lincoln games were at a premium. The Lincolns' Bill Holland won a 3–1 decision over Joe Cade in Atlantic City on July 2, and Jimmie Everett threw a two-hitter and beat the Bacharachs, 4–1, on July 15. The Lincolns' ace, Cornelius "Connie" Rector, and Henderson had a double shutout going at the Protectory Oval, a rare thing at that little park, on September 8 when another figure from the Bacharachs' past, catcher Julio Rojo, tripled in the bottom of the ninth and Rector singled him in for the sole run of the game.

The Bacharachs were actually ahead of Hilldale in the season series of discovered games, six to four, until the Darby team swept the last three games at the end of August. Any ANL team playing the Giants in the last two months of the season was almost sure to better its record—beginning with a loss on August 11 Atlantic City nosedived, going only 2–16 from there to the end of play.

But while things were better, the Giants stepped right off with a 13–7 win in Philadelphia on May 10, their 14 hits being greatly aided by eight Hilldale errors. After being five-hit by Hilldale's Phil Cockrell the next day in a 15–1 loss and beaten by Martin Dihigo's seven-hitter, 5–2, on June 7, the Bacharachs picked up a second win, 4–3, on June 11. Lindsay won the game in the bottom of the ninth with a sacrifice fly that was so deep to center field that Oscar Charleston, who caught it, flipped it over the fence instead of trying to throw the winning run out at the plate.

Jenkins was the hitting star on the Fourth of July with six hits in a doubleheader, including two home runs. The Bacharachs took the second game easily, 19–9, but lost the first, 9–6. They also won two out of three in the next series, which rotated from Philadelphia to Atlantic City from July 19–21. Henderson, supported by a six-run second inning, got a 7–2 win in the first game. Hilldale was completely in charge the next day, winning 13–1, but the Bacharachs backed a good performance by Gardner and won the finale, 5–2. The crowd that day, estimated at 3,000, was said to have been the biggest one of the season at Bacharach Park to date. Considering the place seated about 11,000, this was a commentary on the difficulty the Giants were having drawing fans at home.

On August 4 the Bacharachs played Hilldale in Brooklyn at Dexter Park, home of the crack semi-pro Bushwicks, and drew 15,000 fans, five times what had seen the two teams play in Atlantic City two weeks before. Henderson allowed only two hits and Carr banged out four as the Giants won, 4–0. A return engagement at Dexter, the last discovered game between the two teams, drew another 15,000 fans on August 25. This one went to Hilldale, 8–4, on the strength of a six-run rally in the fourth inning that was started by a Dihigo homer. Hilldale had also won the two previous games of the series, 6–2 on the 23rd and 11–4 on the 24th, both four-hit performances by Joe Strong and Darltie Cooper.

The Cuban Stars, the only ANL team to finish with a worse record than the Bacharachs, were also the only team from which the Giants won a season series, albeit narrowly (5–4–1). The first meeting was another of those very profitable days at Dexter Park on May 30. An estimated 7,500 fans saw Atlantic City sweep a Decoration Day doubleheader, 4–2 and 13–6. Henderson got the opening game win. Jenkins had four hits and Thomas three at Bacharach Park on June 3 to pace an 11–4 win, and Jenkins hit safely five times and White four when the Cubans were defeated, 9–8, on June 22. Lindsay doubled in two runs in the bottom of the ninth on July 23 to give Shields a 5–4 win.

The Stars beat the Bacharachs only once in the first part of the season, 8–6, in

Atlantic City when Jose Fernandez, pinch-hitting with a bandaged thumb, socked a two-run double in the top of the 11th inning. Then the Stars won all three meetings in August, including a three-hit shutout by Basilio Rosell on August 30 as the Cubans shared in the advantages of the deep, season-ending Bacharach slump.

As usual, games against white semi-pro teams bolstered the Bacharach record, to the tune of a .583 winning percentage (21–15) outside the league. Surprisingly the Bushwicks of Brooklyn, ordinarily a tough opponent for even Negro League teams, were easy pickings—the Giants won seven of nine games against them at Dexter Park, including the first five discovered meetings. The wins included two straight Sunday doubleheader sweeps on June 9 and July 7. In the second pair White had six hits, three per game, and Thomas had four, including a homer. Sunday, July 28, was a day for hitting—the Bacharachs collected 19 hits, four by Lindsay, and Henderson pitched well as the Giants won the first game, 13–2. The Bushwicks started Jimmy Ring, who had just wrapped up a 12-year white major league career, in the nightcap, though. The Brooklyn team backed his six-hit shutout with 22 of their own for a 17–0 win. Shields outpitched Ring on August 4 in a 6–5 win in which White got three hits, then topped constant opponent Stan Baumgartner, 5–3, on September 1, backed by four hits from Lindsay. That was the second game of a doubleheader. The Bushwicks won the opener, 7–3, with Ring again the winner.

Elsewhere in New York the Bacharachs looked more like the struggling team they were, losing a doubleheader to the Springfields of Long Island City in late May and to the Bay Parkways of Brooklyn in late September. They did sweep the Farmers of Queens on June 30, 6–4 behind Henderson and 5–3 behind McClure, who beat Johnny Enzman. He was the former major leaguer who had pitched for a white all-star team against the Bacharachs in late 1919 in the first games at Ebbets Field featuring a black team. Thomas ripped eight straight hits in the two games, including a home run and triple.

For a change the Giants weren't generally successful with Philadelphia area teams, going only 3–6 against them. This was due completely to their inability to defeat the crack South Philadelphia squad, which won four straight before the Bacharachs finally took one. This was surprising, given the Giants' success against the Bushwicks, since half of the starting lineup of each team was composed of the same players. Sunday ball was still illegal under Pennsylvania's Blue Laws, but it was in its 11th season of being welcome in New York. The entire South Philadelphia outfield—Howard Lohr, Eddie Gerner and Cupie Dean—plus third baseman Buck Lai, played in Philly during the week. Then they traveled to Brooklyn on summer Sundays for the best-attended baseball show in New York outside of Yankee Stadium, Ebbets Field and the Polo Grounds, the Lord's Day doubleheaders at Dexter Park.

One South Philadelphia regular who stayed home on Sunday was Ad Swigler, the dentist who had been competing against the Bacharachs since 1916 with the old Logan Square squad. Once a formidable pitcher, now a first baseman at age 33, Swigler still swung a mean bat. His double in the bottom of the ninth on May 15 drove in Lohr and Gerner for a 4–2 win. The Bacharachs didn't beat South Philadelphia until the last discovered meeting on August 17, when Eggleston drove four hits and Taylor three to back Shields in a 6–3 victory.

Teams in New Jersey and Pennsylvania outside Philadelphia were easy pickings—the Bacharachs won six of nine against them, plus one from the Agathons of Massillon, Ohio, on August 13 on the way home from playing Homestead in Cleveland. They also beat a House of David traveling team, 6–1, at Bacharach Park on July 13.

On September 6 there was a showdown at Bacharach Park as the Giants played the Police Department team, with their former ace Luther Farrell hurling for the lawmen against Tom Albright. Both men were pitching well and the Police had a 2–0 lead going into the bottom of the seventh. But the Giants loaded the bases and Lindsay came through with a single that tied the game. In the bottom of the eighth the Bacharachs managed to get Thomas on third and Taylor to second. When Taylor took a daring lead, the Police Department catcher tried to pick him off. As the *Daily Press* described the result, the shortstop "bopped the play and while he played with the pellet Thomas scored" for a 3–2 Bacharach victory.[28]

The ANL had lived up to many of its goals in 1929. It had increased the number of African Americans on its umpiring staff (including Cesar Jamison, the Bacharachs' umpire in residence in Atlantic City in the team's early years), compliance with the official schedule and cooperation among the owners. But attendance was still down, finances were still a serious problem around the league, and 1929 would be the ANL's only season. Posey had already let it be known that the Grays were dropping out to play independently again when four of the six owners, including Washington, met in Philadelphia in February 1930 to dissolve the league in the face of "declining economic prospects of urban blacks, who increasingly found baseball more a luxury than a necessity."[29]

The early years of the Great Depression were a very difficult time for black baseball. The Negro National League in the Midwest went out of business after the 1931 season and an attempted new league, the East-West League, broke up partway through its first season in 1932. That year the only black league that could claim major league status was the Negro Southern League, which before that season had been regarded as a minor league.

Many of the prominent black teams made it through the lean years playing independent ball, eventually becoming members of the reconstituted Negro National League, now in the East, and the Negro American League in the Midwest and South. But the Bacharach Giants were not among them. Washington fired Ben Taylor, his hoped-for savior, in October 1929. "I didn't like the way Ben ran the club," Washington was quoted. "Our club failed to show anything worthwhile under his direction." Taylor did not go quietly. He told the *Baltimore Afro-American* that his discharge was news to him, but Washington's statement didn't really matter because he had been on a one-year contract and had no intention of going back to Atlantic City. He charged Washington with being no help in running the team and with being late with the players' final paychecks. But Taylor also zeroed in on the big problem—practically no one was coming to Bacharach Park: "a crowd of three or four hundred was average. You can readily see, then, that no man can make any money out of baseball there."[30]

Ike Washington certainly couldn't, and in March 1930 he acknowledged the obvious and disbanded the team. He had a long-shot plan to keep going but came to his senses, telling Rollo Wilson that "I meant to have a club and was gonna borrow the money to finance it, if necessary, but a couple ball players stuck me for a hundred dollars each [by taking advance money and then going to play elsewhere] and that cured me."[31]

"It looks as though the resort will be without professional baseball after fifteen years," the *Courier* had reported that spring. Rollo Wilson, it turned out, had written the epitaph for the Bacharachs at the Shore the previous fall: "Personally, I wonder if baseball has ever paid in Atlantic City. I doubt if it ever will. Folks go there to bask in the sun and loaf on the beach and boardwalk. Baseball is something they can get plenty of at home and they feel that any daylight hours away from the sun and surf is wasted time."[32] Although night baseball became possible, casino gambling came to the Boardwalk in 1978, and the state of affairs Wilson described has for the most part remained the case. No Negro League team ever again made the city its home, and a new ballpark built in 1998 for minor league baseball lost its team 11 seasons later.

After Atlantic City

Harry Passon had played against the Bacharach Giants before World War I and had managed the Chester team that that had opposed them in the hybrid Interstate League in 1926. Now, in 1931, he owned them. He owned the name, at least, having seized upon this recently popular brand for his own black team. Passon is much better known to sports historians as an original organizer and player for one of the best early professional basketball teams, the SPHAs (sponsored by the South Philadelphia Hebrew Association). But he was an all-around sports entrepreneur, running semi-pro baseball teams and a sporting goods business with fellow SPHA figure Eddie Gottlieb, who became a major figure in pro basketball and a power behind the scenes in Negro baseball.

Passon owned the Philadelphia Giants, the regional black team, in the mid–1920s and reconstituted the Bacharachs in that city in 1931, using his Passon Field at 48th and Spruce Streets as the home park. This was during the three seasons in which the East did not have a Negro League, so the Bacharachs joined Hilldale, the Homestead Grays and the Baltimore Black Sox, along with some significant new teams such as the Pittsburgh Crawfords and the New York Black Yankees, in playing each other and white semi-pro teams on an independent basis. Although the team was often referred to as the "Atlantic City Bacharach Giants," it had no connection to Atlantic City any longer, except to play an occasional road game there.

The roster was a mix of familiar Negro League names and young prospects. The vets were mostly nearing the end of their careers, but some of the youths became well known in black baseball later in the 1930s and into the 1940s, including one who became a major league Hall of Famer after white baseball was integrated. Others came and went with barely a ripple. The Bacharachs' makeup closely resembled that of a white minor league team in that period, when those franchises were often independently owned and mixed their few rising stars in with journeymen and retreads. The Giants, in fact, had become a version of one of the types of teams they had often feasted on in the past, the regional black squad.

Otto Briggs, one of the first Hilldale stars as an outfielder in the late 1910s, managed the new Giants and played until he was into his 40s. In 1932 he had supervised a former star still older than himself, the seemingly indestructible John Henry Lloyd, now 48. George "Tank" Carr showed up at first base for a few years in his late 30s. Roy Roberts, an original Bacharach Giant, pitched for Passon's club in 1932 at age 38. In 1934 Mack Eggleston again wore a Giants uniform at 37, Jesse Hubbard was there at 38, and Luther Farrell, he of the World Series no-hitter, was on the roster at age 40.

On the other hand, outfielder Ed Stone, who went on to play Negro League ball through 1950 and made two appearances in the black showcase East-West All-Star Game, spent most of the early 1930s with the Bacharachs. Terris McDuffie, who likewise had a long career as a Negro League pitcher with East-West appearances, was with the team in 1932. Gene Benson, another All-Star who played outfield for the Philadelphia Stars, the successor to Hilldale as the prime team in that city, also graced the Bacharach roster during Passon's ownership.

The best young player to use the Bacharachs as a springboard was a local schoolboy who joined in 1937 as a fresh-faced 15-year-old. Roy Campanella had been catching for a neighborhood team in Philadelphia until noticed by the Bacharachs, who needed a catcher and signed him on his family's condition that his baseball be worked in around school. Campanella was a Bacharach only for a short time, though. The Washington Elite Giants of the Negro National League came through town with a catching shortage and manager Raleigh "Biz" Mackey, one of the best catchers professional baseball has ever produced, talked young Roy into giving up his job with the Bacharachs to join the NNL as perhaps its youngest player ever. He was a Negro League star through the war years and in 1946 became one of the first blacks recruited for the Brooklyn Dodgers organization. He was promoted to the Dodgers in 1948 and was the team's regular catcher until being paralyzed in an off-season auto accident and forced to retire in 1957. He was elected to the Hall of Fame in 1969.[33]

Passon entered the Bacharachs into the second Negro National League for the 1934 season, a move that was driven both by his entrepreneurial bent and the ever-present politics of the black leagues. Cumberland Posey in Pittsburgh was a staunch league member but was also ever-protective of his Western Pennsylvania fiefdom. He saw danger in a new alliance between Ed Bolden, who had rejuvenated his ownership career with the Philadelphia Stars, and Gottlieb, Passon's business partner, who was not only a part-owner of the Stars but a booking agent. Posey looked over at the Eastern Seaboard and saw an alliance between the Bolden/Gottlieb duo and Nat Strong, still operating in New York City, as a threat to his business. His answer was to recruit the Bacharachs to become a second Philadelphia team, thus diluting the Stars' influence. But Bolden and Gottlieb succeeded in blocking the Bacharachs' application for a full membership, although the team was admitted as an associate member. Continued pressure by Posey and Passon succeeded in the Giants getting a full membership for the second half of the season. But the team finished near the bottom of the second-half standings and Passon threw in the towel in the off-season, withdrawing from the NNL and selling the team to Malcolm McGowan. The Bacharachs played on as non-league opponents for Negro League teams in the East and made frequent appearances in Brooklyn to play the Bushwicks and the other top-level white semi-pro teams until the beginning of World War II.

While the Bacharach Giants were on the decline, the man from whom they had taken their name was making a comeback in the bare-knuckle sport known as Atlantic City politics. Harry Bacharach had been appointed a New Jersey public utilities commissioner after giving up the mayorship in 1920 and seemed content to work at that job and in the family businesses that included real estate, banking and insurance. But in 1930 another of the city's periodic anti-vice crusades put the current mayor, Anthony M. Ruffo Jr., in the spotlight. Ruffo was under indictment for what a cynic might characterize as business as usual at the Shore—he was charged with steering municipal insurance contracts to companies in which he held a financial interest. A jury had found him not guilty of four of the charges in early June, but ten more were pending when fate excused Ruffo from standing again at the bar of justice, at least the temporal one in Atlantic City. On June 23 his auto, carrying himself, a New Jersey legislator and two women, was struck and demolished by a locomotive at a crossing just outside the city, killing everyone in the car.

Enoch "Nucky" Johnson, Atlantic City political boss (center), shakes hands with John Henry Lloyd, far left, at a banquet in the late 1930s honoring Lloyd, manager of the Johnson Stars, a local semi-pro squad that followed the city's tradition of naming teams after political leaders. Arthur "Rats" Henderson, a former Bacharach pitcher who settled in Atlantic City after his Negro League career and pitched for the Johnson Stars, is between Lloyd and Johnson (Atlantic City Heritage Collections, Atlantic City Free Public Library).

After a short period of public respect for the late mayor, during which political machinations went on behind the scenes, Bacharach emerged from a bevy of potential replacements with the backing of not only Enoch Johnson's Republican machine but also the leaders of Atlantic City's much smaller Democratic Party. In tune with the ongoing campaign against vice, one of the new mayor's first major moves was to ask for help from big-city police departments in the region, particularly Philadelphia and New York, to sweep the city for criminals and "other undesirables" and run them out of town, as well as having a newly-appointed "crime commission" compile a list of undesirables who would be kept under surveillance should they decide to take the bracing salt air at the Boardwalk. This was no mere public relations campaign—the year before Boardwalk hotels had been hosts to a major meeting of organized crime figures, including a Chicago contingent led by Al Capone.[34]

Although Atlantic City was $40 million in debt during the early years of the Depression, Bacharach and local financial leaders cut deals with its bondholders and the city worked its way out of the hole while continuing to be a vibrant vacation destination. Bacharach led a publicity campaign that helped the city's tourism business fight off the Depression. He himself signed a puff piece on the city's wonderfulness for the *Washington Post* just prior to the 1935 season. He called his city "America's Bagdad-by-the-Sea." Bacharach resigned as mayor that summer, though, citing health concerns that made it impossible to continue to serve both the city and the state utilities board. He served on the state board until 1941 and then became the managing director of the trade association for the state's utilities. He died at age 73 in 1947. His *New York Times* obituary identified him as Atlantic City's "number one booster."[35]

A few Bacharach Giants were among the mayor's constituents during the early 1930s. Napoleon Cummings was a bartender in the city at one point, then an investigator for the county detective bureau. He was still an Atlantic City resident when he died in 1974. Another original Bacharach, Arthur Dilworth, also stayed at the Shore. Farrell, of course, did a stretch with the police department during that period and Rats Henderson worked for Beyda & Co., which sold linens at its store on the Boardwalk.

In 1932 the most renowned ex–Giant, John Henry Lloyd, made Atlantic City his year-round home.

Epilogue

The Northside had been Lloyd's home since at least 1920—he shows up in the U.S. Census in January that year living with his first wife, Anna, in an apartment at 1 Brooklyn Avenue, listing his occupation as "athlete" and his business as "baseball."[1] But Lloyd was often out of town in a time when black players frequently played a winter season in Florida or the Caribbean in addition to summertime in the northern United States. Anna reportedly often travelled with him, including to destinations outside the U.S., but they always seem to have come back to the Shore to claim it as their more or less official residence.

That changed when Anna Lloyd died suddenly in September 1931, and when Lloyd finally retired from Negro League ball after the following season with Passon's no-longer-Atlantic City Bacharach Giants. She was buried in the Atlantic City Cemetery in nearby Pleasantville, and Lloyd settled down at age 48 to become a full-time resident of Mayor Bacharach's city.

The economic future Lloyd faced was a common one for many ex-ballplayers in those days, who had no particular job skills other than playing ball. He went from batting cleanup in the top levels of black baseball to just cleaning up, first as a janitor in the Atlantic City post office and then in city schools. He clearly was welcome, though. The post office position was one that likely could not have been gotten without the aid of a political connection. Lloyd's third wife, Nan, recalled that her husband's benefactor was none other than Enoch "Nucky" Johnson, still riding high at the top of the Atlantic City political machine. This being Atlantic City, Lloyd also did something for the leader in return, becoming playing manager of the amateur baseball team, the Johnson Stars, that publicized the machine leader's attachment to the city's African American populace, just as the original Bacharach Giants had served to advertise Mayor Bacharach. After Johnson went to prison in 1941, State Sen. Francis S. "Hap" Farley took over the Atlantic City machine. The politically-blessed baseball team became known, naturally, as the Farley Stars, although Lloyd retired soon after the name change, finally hanging up his spikes at age 58.[2]

Although the Johnson Stars were many rungs below the level at which Lloyd had excelled for so many years, his attitude toward hard work that had made him so admired and sought after as a Negro Leaguer still stood out. Max Manning, later a star Negro Leagues pitcher with the Newark Eagles, grew up in Pleasantville and played for the Stars as a youngster. He had this to say about his mentor: "In my opinion, Pop Lloyd was one of the finest human beings I ever met. He was such a gracious kind of fellow, humble, kind, and gentle. He didn't drink, didn't smoke, didn't curse; he was really a role model."[3]

Lloyd's upstanding and straightforward manner served him well in his next job, which was as janitor at an Atlantic City elementary school on Indiana Avenue. The group that Lloyd could influence was growing ever younger, from veteran Negro Leaguers to aspiring players like Manning and now elementary school boys. This was the bunch, though, upon which Lloyd had the most impact. His biographer, Wes Singletary, describing the post-war era when the city went into a deep decline, says that

> In an era of constant, unrelenting racism, depression and war, many of Atlantic City's children lacked the guidance necessary to avoid pitfalls that surely awaited them.... Lloyd happily stepped into this void, showing many of these kids the difference between right and wrong, teaching them the hard truth that no one owed them anything, and that it would be up to each one of them to make of their lives what they could, good or bad.

Naturally, Lloyd, who had acquired the nickname "Pop" since his playing days, used sports to attract and instruct the youngsters. He is known to have kept a bucket of used baseball gloves in the janitor's room, hauling it out and passing around the mitts as he taught the kids how to play ball.[4]

Lloyd became an institution in Atlantic City, his current efforts on behalf of the children appreciated and his past exploits as a star ballplayer not allowed to be forgotten. As a young man, Henry "Whitey" Gruhler had been one of the better semi-pro players in the area and was among the whites recruited to play for the Bacharach Giants at the end of the 1918 season when the team was in financial straits and had lost many of its starters. Gruhler went into journalism and eventually became the *Atlantic City Daily Press* sports editor. He paid attention to the Negro Leagues, even though his paper no longer had a home team to cover, and would laud Lloyd in his "Press Box" columns, going so far as to stump for him in print when managerial vacancies showed up on Negro Leagues teams. So well-respected was Lloyd in Atlantic City that in 1949 the city built a ballpark in a public park on the Northside, where the Johnson Stars had played in their day, and named it John Henry Lloyd Stadium. Pop, wiping tears from his eyes, told the crowd that "I hope the young men, not only of Atlantic City but of the entire nation, will benefit from what I have tried to give the youth of America. And I promise that this day, more than anything else, inspires me to continue to live righteously, so that I may justify the confidence you kind folks have shown in me."[5]

Lloyd died in 1964. Atlantic City itself, its decline as a beach resort having arrived as television and the freedoms brought by the automobile proved to be tough competition, and the economic resuscitation from casino gambling on the Boardwalk still in the future, was doing poorly itself. Among its many casualties of governmental neglect was John Henry Lloyd Stadium. Northern New Jersey college professor Lawrence D. Hogan had been one of the producers of a video on black baseball in the 1980s and had interviewed the elderly Gruhler in the grandstand at the stadium. Gruhler's recollections of watching the Negro Leaguers were informative and touching (he breaks into tears at one point), and made it into the final cut of the documentary. But the condition of the park disturbed Hogan, as it already was bothering people in Atlantic City who had known Lloyd.

The local press described the sorry state of the stadium in 1991: "The fence is falling

Dedication of John Henry "Pop" Lloyd Stadium in 1949. Lloyd, working as a janitor at a city school, introduced many boys to baseball and served as a role model for them. His popularity in the community led to the building of a local baseball park in his honor (Atlantic City Heritage Collections, Atlantic City Free Public Library).

down. Future Pop Lloyds who want to slide into second base risk sliding into broken beer bottles." A *New York Times* writer a year later was even more specific in describing the stadium's ruination: "It's not much of anything now—a shabby brick grandstand, a cheap corrugated steel roof curling up on itself like the fingers of an angry fist, blown-out windows and trash and weeds down where the grandstand meets Indiana and Huron Avenues."[6]

Max Manning, Lloyd's baseball student on the Johnson Stars, was also interviewed by Hogan and his team the day Whitey Gruhler spoke to the cameras. Manning's pitching career had ended when his arm gave out just as integration beckoned with a shot at formerly all-white Organized Baseball. Instead he went back to college (he had dropped out in the late 1930s to play professional ball) and began a second career as an educator in Pleasantville, his home town. Erudite and a good organizer, Manning eventually became president of the Negro League Baseball Players Association, the benevolent association for those veterans.

He also became the first president of the new Committee to Restore Pop Lloyd Stadium, a non-profit organization founded in 1991 with a goal of raising thousands of dollars to bring the ballpark up to the standards of the man for whom it was named. The key source of funds was herself an Atlantic City institution. Redenia Gilliam-Mosee was an African American who had grown up in Atlantic City. A community planning professor at Rutgers University, she returned to the city in 1978 to work for the Bally's Casino firm developing employee training courses. She became an influential executive in the city's casino industry, which, crucial to the Pop Lloyd Stadium restoration effort, paid a share of its profits to a governmental fund used to revitalize the moribund community. Gilliam-Mosee "had complete control of government allocations from community development money. If you were involved in something she had a real interest in, you were golden." As it happened, Gilliam-Mosee was acquainted with Max Manning and came to be a believer in restoring the stadium.[7]

With funds from Bally's, the development fund and local sources, the field was repaired and rededicated in 1995. Then Michael Everett, a former Atlantic City school teacher who with his wife Kathy Whitmire came to be the organizers of the public Pop Lloyd events, posed a suggestion to the Stadium committee after the park had been reopened: "You obviously need to reinvent yourself because you can't continue to call yourself the Committee to Restore Pop Lloyd Stadium—10 years from now people will ask you 'aren't you done yet?'"[8]

By this time the Committee was well into its further goals, which included a long-term plan to promote not only the memory of Lloyd, but black baseball in general through a series of educational programs, humanitarian awards to national and local figures, and a lecture series. Accordingly, the group changed its name to the John Henry "Pop" Lloyd Committee. It began an annual celebration that grew to include a day-long sports symposium, an awards banquet at which local high schoolers were honored for academic achievement and living Negro Leaguers were introduced, and the awarding of a college scholarship in Max Manning's name. The weekend would end with a commemorative Sunday morning service at the Asbury Methodist Church, where Pop and Nan Lloyd were members, and where older parishioners still remember him.

The first humanitarian award recipient in 1993 was to be tennis great Arthur Ashe, who was also to have been the keynote speaker. The occasion was dimmed considerably when Ashe, who had contracted AIDS through a blood transfusion in the 1980s, died shortly before the event. The day was saved by the appearance of Arnold Rampersad, Ashe's friend and co-author of his memoir *Days of Grace*. Besides the sadness, Hogan recalls, the episode left the Lloyd Committee with "awe and gratitude for [Ashe's] willingness to come to us even as he knew he was near death" and "pride in what we were setting out to do that had attracted this tremendous person to our effort."[9]

The Committee subsequently gave out 75 more awards through 2012, to athletes such as Baseball Hall of Fame members Willie Mays, Bob Feller, Monte Irvin and Larry Doby; Negro Leaguers Manning, John "Buck" O'Neil, Minnie Minoso and Emilio Navarro; stars of other sports such as Olympians John Carlos, Donna DeVarona, Kathy Kusner and Willye Brown White; pro footballers Calvin Hill and George Taliaferro, and black basketball star John Isaacs. Congressmen Floyd Flake and John Lewis have been honored as have major league baseball executives Fay Vincent, Leonard Coleman and Bill White and nationally-known entertainers such as singer Dionne Warwick, dancer Savion Glover (a descendant of original Bacharach Giant Dick Lundy), actress Cicely Tyson and Peter Yarrow of the folk trio Peter, Paul and Mary.

The list is quite varied, but there are common themes qualifying the recipients—sports and community service. "We looked for more than an elite athlete," Everett says.

"We tried to stick with our baseball roots, but then we looked at the culture in which Negro League baseball was played and extended that to athletes who contributed to those roots, and who contributed to the youth of America. Then we expanded it to cultural people."[10]

After 20 consecutive Pop Lloyd celebrations, though, the committee did not hold its usual weekend in October of 2013. Operations had been hampered in recent years by two shortages. One was financing, as the recession that began in 2008 and competition for Atlantic City casinos from legalized gambling in nearby states began to dry up contributions. While the gambling and tourism economy at the Shore can improve, the other shortage, of former Negro Leagues players, an increasingly rare group as death winnows their irreplaceable ranks, is irreversible.

In addition, the Lloyd Committee decided to reorganize. Both Belinda Manning, Max Manning's daughter who succeeded him as president of the committee, and Everett, the chief organizer, stepped down from their positions in 2013. Speaking for himself, Everett says that "I can't do all of it, and if I continue to do all of it, there will come a time when I can't." He decided it was better to go through the tribulations of change while he and the other committee veterans can help with the transition. There are long-term plans to continue the committee's work, possibly including its large historical and education collection held at nearby Richard Stockton College, in city government's plans to develop a downtown arts and historic district. However the Pop Lloyd legacy lives on, according to Everett, "What's critical is that we continue to embrace the values engendered by this sport, because it speaks volumes to young people today, baseball being the vehicle to teach about perseverance, dignity, pride, overcoming adversity and social justice."[11]

* * *

Even though actual segregated black baseball is of another period, those who both admire its success against the odds and see in it values that pertain to this, or any, era are always ready to strike another blow for it. So it was in early October 2013 that Mike Everett drove over to the Atlantic City Cemetery.

The cemetery, actually inland in Pleasantville, is the burial location of three black baseball stars. John Henry Lloyd was laid to rest there in 1964 and Max Manning in 2003, both of their graves well-marked by headstones. But black baseball researchers established some time ago that the cemetery also contains the grave of one of the earliest black professionals. Clarence Williams was a catcher for the first fully professional African American team, the Cuban Giants, in 1886, and went on to play and manage black teams into the early twentieth century. Williams died in Atlantic City in 1934 and was interred in a grave without a stone. Exactly where in the cemetery he was buried, though, was a mystery. Cemetery records give a section and number for his grave, but the maps of the older section of the place aren't always helpful in finding specific interments.

Everett, who as the local blackball historian had been to the cemetery in the past to look for Williams' grave, concluded that it was time to look again. Williams' grave was supposedly marked by a round clay marker with the number 192. The section of the cemetery was known, and finding the spot should have been a cinch. However, there are several markers with the same number, and others with their numbered tops sheared off, probably by lawn mowers.

Frustration was setting in when Everett returned to the cemetery office for a consultation with recently appointed Superintendent Jim Williams. It turned out that the superintendent was very familiar with Pop Lloyd's gravesite and intrigued that another old ballplayer was in his cemetery. He immediately took up the search and, through the use of his maps, careful measurements and the sort of "inside baseball" type of things a superintendent knows about his own cemetery, pinned down Williams' plot. The discovery makes the old catcher's grave eligible for a program operated by the Society for American Baseball Research's Negro Leagues Committee that places headstones on the unmarked graves of black ballplayers. Once Williams gets his marker in 2015 he will join the company of two old teammates, Sol White, buried on Staten Island in New York City, and Frank Grant, in Clifton, New Jersey, whose graves were recently marked by the program.

Given that the history of Negro baseball is infused with the inequality between the races that existed in the late nineteenth and early twentieth centuries, it's a predictable footnote that many of its outstanding players, discriminated against in the rest of their lives as they had been in baseball, lived marginal existences after retiring from the game and died in relative (or actual) obscurity. The Negro Leagues Baseball Grave Marker Project, run by Dr. Jeremy Krock, an Illinois anesthesiologist, has so far marked nearly 30 graves around the country. The graves identified and on the waiting list for markers along with Williams are two former Bacharach Giants, Elias "Country Brown" Bryant and Bill Francis.

The history of black baseball nearly died out after the Negro Leagues finally went out of business in 1960 once major league integration was well along. A first wave of historians tracked down surviving players and executives and the spouses of the deceased in the mid-1960s, wrote the first Negro League histories and were followed in turn by others. The effort, which now includes statisticians, symposium organizers, scholarship givers and live people who haunt cemeteries, goes on. It's a contradiction, but a welcome one, that as Negro League history moves further into the past, there are probably more people involved in preserving and publicizing it than ever. They operate not just out of a sense of nostalgia, but with the knowledge that success in the face of discrimination has a lesson for all of us.

Appendix A: Game Log

Race: Race of opponent *(B=black, W=white, Mx=mixed race)*
W/L: Includes ties (T) in regulation games and no decisions (ND) in less than 5 innings

1916 Bacharach Giants (67–14–1)

Date	Opponent	Race	W/L	Score	Location
8-May	Vandal Athletic Club (Atlantic City)	B	W	12–2	Atlantic City
12-May	Atlantic City Cyclones	B	W	15–5	Atlantic City
18-May	Manhattan (Atlantic City)	B	W	15–3	Atlantic City
21-May	Elmwood (Philadelphia)	W	W	12–7	Atlantic City
22-May	Rudolph (Atlantic City)	B	W	13–2	Atlantic City
25-May	Vandal Athletic Club (Atlantic City)	B	W	3–2	Atlantic City
26-May	Camden City (NJ)	W	W	9–0	Atlantic City
28-May	Atlantic City Cyclones	B	W	9–7	Atlantic City
29-May	Vandal Athletic Club (Atlantic City)	B	W	12–5	Atlantic City
31-May	Atlantic City Cyclones	B	L	2–1	Atlantic City
3-Jun	Big Six (Atlantic City)	B	W	13–0	Atlantic City
4-Jun	Wissinoming (Philadelphia)	W	W	6–1	Atlantic City
6-Jun	Manhattan (Atlantic City)	B	W	10–1	Atlantic City
8-Jun	Rudolph (Atlantic City)	B	W	5–3	Atlantic City
9-Jun	Frankford (Philadelphia)	W	W	4–0	Atlantic City
10-Jun	Atlantic City Cyclones	B	W	10–2	Atlantic City
12-Jun	Vandal Athletic Club (Atlantic City)	B	W	8–2	Atlantic City
15-Jun	Atlantic City Cyclones	B	W	10–2	Atlantic City
18-Jun	Camden (NJ)	W	W	12–2	Atlantic City
23-Jun	Manhattan (Atlantic City)	B	W	16–11	Atlantic City
24-Jun	Pleasantville (NJ)	W	W	14–3	Pleasantville
26-Jun	Rudolph (Atlantic City)	B	L	4–3	Atlantic City
29-Jun	Vandal Athletic Club (Atlantic City)	B	W	7–5	Atlantic City
1-Jul	West Philadelphia Giants	W	W	10–1	Atlantic City
3-Jul	Baltimore Black Sox	B	W	8–2	Atlantic City
4-Jul	Baltimore Black Sox	B	W	12–2	Atlantic City
6-Jul	Hammonton (NJ)	W	W	12–0	Atlantic City
8-Jul	Logan Squares (Philadelphia)	W	W	2–0	Atlantic City
11-Jul	Anchor Giants (Philadelphia)	B	W	9–1	Atlantic City
12-Jul	Anchor Giants (Philadelphia)	B	W	5–4	Atlantic City
13-Jul	East Philadelphia	W	W	2–0	Atlantic City
14-Jul	Rudolf (Atlantic City)	B	W	8–1	Atlantic City
15-Jul	Logan Squares (Philadelphia)	W	L	2–0	Atlantic City
17-Jul	Brooklyn Royal Giants	B	L	8–5	Atlantic City
18-Jul	Brooklyn Royal Giants	B	L	12–0	Atlantic City
21-Jul	Tulpehocken Reds (Philadelphia)	W	L	7–3	Atlantic City
22-Jul	Norristown (PA)	W	W	8–1	Atlantic City
24-Jul	Chinese University	Mx	W	6–5	Atlantic City
26-Jul	All-Nations	Mx	W	3–2	Atlantic City
28-Jul	Atlantic City (Big Six) All-Stars	B	L	3–2	Atlantic City
29-Jul	Ocean City (NJ)	W	L	1–0	Ocean City
30-Jul	Bristol (PA)	W	W	8–2	Atlantic City
31-Jul	Atlantic City (Big Six) All-Stars	B	W	4–2	Atlantic City
1-Aug	Pearce Athletic Assoc. (Philadelphia)	W	W	4–3	Atlantic City

Date	Opponent	Race	W/L	Score	Location
2-Aug	Bridesburg (Philadelphia)	W	W	7–1	Atlantic City
5-Aug	Millville (NJ)	W	W	9–0	Millville
7-Aug	North Side Professionals (Philadelphia)	W	W	9–0	Atlantic City
8-Aug	Philadelphia Professionals	W	W	11–6	Atlantic City
9-Aug	Big Six (Atlantic City)	W	W	4–3	Atlantic City
11-Aug	Big Six (Atlantic City)	W	W	14–1	Atlantic City
12-Aug	Pleasantville (NJ)	W	L	4–2	Pleasantville
13-Aug	Pleasantville (NJ)	W	W	10–9	Atlantic City
14-Aug	Gloucester (NJ)	W	W	9–3	Atlantic City
15-Aug	Atlantic City Collegians	W	W	7–1	Atlantic City
16-Aug	Anchor Giants (Philadelphia)	B	W	5–2	Camden
17-Aug	Bridgeton (NJ)	W	W	8–3	Bridgeton
19-Aug	Camden City (NJ)	W	W	6–2	Camden
19-Aug	Anchor Giants (Philadelphia)	B	W	8–2	Camden
20-Aug	Washington All-Stars (D.C.)	W	W	9–3	Atlantic City
21-Aug	Big Six (Atlantic City)	W	W	13–6	Atlantic City
23-Aug	Port Richmond Giants (Philadelphia)	W	W	7–2	Atlantic City
24-Aug	Ocean City Giants (NJ)	W	W	5–3	Ocean City
26-Aug	Logan Squares (Philadelphia)	W	L	3–1	Pleasantville
27-Aug	Pleasantville (NJ)	W	L	6–5	Atlantic City
29-Aug	South Philadelphia	W	W	4–1	Atlantic City
2-Sep	Camden City (NJ)	W	W	11–6	Camden
4-Sep	Pleasantville (NJ)	W	W	10–4	Atlantic City
4-Sep	Pleasantville (NJ)	W	L	8–7	Pleasantville
7-Sep	Anchor Giants (Philadelphia)	B	W	4–3	Atlantic City
10-Sep	Wildwood (NJ)	W	W	2–1	Atlantic City
13-Sep	Wildwood (NJ)	W	L	2–1	Wildwood
17-Sep	Logan Squares (Philadelphia)	W	W	9–5	Atlantic City
18-Sep	Atlantic City Giants	B	L	5–4	Atlantic City
19-Sep	Atlantic City Giants	B	W	6–3	Atlantic City
20-Sep	South Philadelphia	W	W	7–6	Atlantic City
22-Sep	Atlantic City Giants	W	W	13–3	Atlantic City
25-Sep	Media (PA)	W	W	5–2	Atlantic City
25-Sep	Media (PA)	W	W	1–0	Atlantic City
30-Sep	Camden Athletic Club (NJ)	W	W	7–6	Camden
1-Oct	Logan Squares (Philadelphia)	W	T	1–1	Atlantic City
7-Oct	Philadelphia Red Caps	B	W	11–2	Darby, PA
8-Oct	Pleasantville (NJ)	W	W	8–3	Atlantic City

1917 Bacharach Giants (60–39–3)

Date	Opponent	Race	W/L	Score	Location
17-May	Peerless American Giants (Philadelphia)	B	W	8–0	Philadelphia
19-May	Logan Squares (Philadelphia)	W	L	7–0	Atlantic City
20-May	Logan Squares (Philadelphia)	W	W	4–1	Atlantic City
21-May	Roxborough (Philadelphia)	W	W	13–2	Atlantic City
22-May	Roxborough (Philadelphia)	W	W	4–2	Atlantic City
24-May	Pleasantville (NJ)	W	L	5–2	Atlantic City
25-May	Peerless American Giants (Philadelphia)	B	W	4–3	Atlantic City
25-May	Peerless American Giants (Philadelphia)	B	W	6–4	Atlantic City
27-May	Media	W	W	5–4	Atlantic City
30-May	Hammonton (NJ)	W	W	13–4	Atlantic City
30-May	Hammonton (NJ)	W	W	5–2	Atlantic City
31-May	Peerless American Giants (Philadelphia)	B	W	8–6	Philadelphia
1-Jun	Peerless American Giants (Philadelphia)	B	W	6–2	Philadelphia
2-Jun	Frankford (Philadelphia)	W	W	3–1	Atlantic City
3-Jun	Logan Squares (Philadelphia)	W	L	1–0	Atlantic City
4-Jun	Vandal Athletic Club (Atlantic City)	W	W	7–4	Atlantic City
5-Jun	Pleasantville (NJ)	W	L	1–0	Atlantic City
6-Jun	Northeast Philadelphia	W	L	5–4	Atlantic City
9-Jun	Cressona (PA)	W	W	6–3	Atlantic City
10-Jun	Cressona (PA)	W	W	3–2	Atlantic City
12-Jun	Chester (PA)	W	W	4–1	Atlantic City
13-Jun	Chester (PA)	W	L	8–3	Atlantic City
17-Jun	J.G. Brill (PA)	W	L	9–1	Atlantic City

Date	Opponent	Race	W/L	Score	Location
21-Jun	Hilldale	B	W	3–0	Darby, PA
22-Jun	R.G. Dunn (Philadelphia)	W	W	14–4	Atlantic City
23-Jun	Hilldale	B	L	5–3	Darby, PA
24-Jun	Wissahickon (Philadelphia)	W	W	9–4	Atlantic City
27-Jun	Pleasantville (NJ)	W	W	4–3	Atlantic City
1-Jul	Media (PA)	W	W	5–3	Atlantic City
2-Jul	Cuban Stars	B	W	7–6	Atlantic City
4-Jul	Logan Squares (Philadelphia)	W	T	1–1	Atlantic City
4-Jul	Logan Squares (Philadelphia)	W	L	5–2	Atlantic City
5-Jul	Pennsylvania RR Red Caps	B	L	6–2	Atlantic City
6-Jul	Pennsylvania RR Red Caps	B	W	7–5	Atlantic City
8-Jul	Media (PA)	W	L	4–3	Atlantic City
9-Jul	Media (PA)	W	L	2–1	Atlantic City
10-Jul	Lincoln Giants	B	L	6–4	Atlantic City
11-Jul	Lincoln Giants	B	L	4–0	Atlantic City
12-Jul	Lincoln Giants	B	L	4–1	Atlantic City
13-Jul	Cadorna (Philadelphia)	W	W	12–2	Atlantic City
14-Jul	J.B. Stetson (Philadelphia)	W	L	2–1	Atlantic City
15-Jul	Pleasantville (NJ)	W	W	2–0	Atlantic City
16-Jul	Pleasantville (NJ)	W	L	15–4	Atlantic City
17-Jul	Marine Corps (Philadelphia)	W	W	8–6	Atlantic City
18-Jul	Brooklyn Royal Giants	B	W	6–5	Atlantic City
20-Jul	Brooklyn Royal Giants	B	W	7–5	Atlantic City
22-Jul	Logan Squares (Philadelphia)	W	W	7–6	Atlantic City
23-Jul	Pleasantville (NJ)	W	W	6–5	Atlantic City
24-Jul	Pleasantville (NJ)	W	W	4–1	Atlantic City
25-Jul	Frankford (Philadelphia)	W	W	11–2	Atlantic City
26-Jul	Cuban Stars	B	L	10–0	Atlantic City
27-Jul	Cuban Stars	B	W	4–3	Atlantic City
29-Jul	Logan Squares (Philadelphia)	W	L	5–4	Atlantic City
30-Jul	Port Richmond (Philadelphia)	W	W	6–5	Atlantic City
31-Jul	Chester (PA)	W	W	6–3	Atlantic City
1-Aug	Chester (PA)	W	L	7–0	Atlantic City
2-Aug	Chester (PA)	W	L	7–1	Atlantic City
5-Aug	Vineland (NJ)	W	W	2–0	Atlantic City
6-Aug	Pleasantville (NJ)	W	W	8–6	Atlantic City
7-Aug	Lincoln Giants	B	L	5–3	Atlantic City
8-Aug	Lincoln Giants	B	L	7–5	Atlantic City
9-Aug	Cuban Stars	B	L	7–2	Atlantic City
10-Aug	Cuban Stars	B	W	5–0	Atlantic City
12-Aug	J.G. Brill (PA)	W	W	4–0	Atlantic City
13-Aug	Gloucester (NJ)	W	L	2–1	Atlantic City
14-Aug	Brooklyn Royal Giants	B	L	4–3	Atlantic City
15-Aug	Brooklyn Royal Giants	B	W	5–3	Atlantic City
16-Aug	Rudolf (Atlantic City)	B	W	6–2	Atlantic City
19-Aug	Atlantic City All-Stars	W	W	5–2	Atlantic City
20-Aug	Cuban Stars	B	W	2–1	Atlantic City
21-Aug	Cuban Stars	B	L	16–0	Atlantic City
22-Aug	Cuban Stars	B	L	2–1	Atlantic City
24-Aug	Brooklyn Royal Giants	B	L	7–5	Atlantic City
25-Aug	Camden Athletic Club (NJ)	W	L	3–0	Camden
26-Aug	Camden Athletic Club (NJ)	W	W	8–0	Atlantic City
26-Aug	Logan Squares (Philadelphia)	W	W	5–2	Atlantic City
27-Aug	Chicago American Giants	B	L	5–4	Atlantic City
28-Aug	Chicago American Giants	B	L	4–0	Atlantic City
31-Aug	Cuban Stars	B	L	2–0	Atlantic City
2-Sep	Logan Squares (Philadelphia)	W	W	5–3	Atlantic City
3-Sep	Logan Squares (Philadelphia)	W	W	9–4	Atlantic City
3-Sep	Logan Squares (Philadelphia)	W	L	10–4	Atlantic City
4-Sep	Brooklyn Royal Giants	B	W	3–1	Atlantic City
5-Sep	Brooklyn Royal Giants	B	W	7–2	Atlantic City
6-Sep	Brooklyn Royal Giants	B	L	5–4	Atlantic City
6-Sep	Brooklyn Royal Giants	B	L	5–3	Atlantic City
9-Sep	Wildwood (NJ)	W	W	2–1	Atlantic City
10-Sep	Wildwood (NJ)	W	W	9–1	Atlantic City
14-Sep	Beaver Athletic Club (Wilmington, DE)	B	W	7–1	Atlantic City

Date	Opponent	Race	W/L	Score	Location
14-Sep	Beaver Athletic Club (Wilmington, DE)	B	W	6–0	Atlantic City
16-Sep	Logan Squares (Philadelphia)	W	T	2–2	Atlantic City
19-Sep	Wildwood (NJ)	W	W	2–1	Atlantic City
20-Sep	Wildwood (NJ)	W	W	6–0	Atlantic City
21-Sep	Wildwood (NJ)	W	L	6–2	Atlantic City
22-Sep	Millville (NJ)	W	L	6–0	Millville
23-Sep	Melrose Athletic Club (Atlantic City)	W	W	6–1	Atlantic City
25-Sep	Media (PA)	W	W	5–2	Atlantic City
25-Sep	Media (PA)	W	W	1–0	Atlantic City
26-Sep	Melrose Athletic Club (Atlantic City)	W	W	3–0	Atlantic City
28-Sep	Pleasantville (NJ)	W	T	3–3	Atlantic City
30-Sep	Logan Squares (Philadelphia)	W	L	4–2	Atlantic City
2-Oct	Pleasantville (NJ)	W	W	5–2	Atlantic City

1918 Bacharach Giants (25–17–2)

Date	Opponent	Race	W/L	Score	Location
18-May	Hilldale	B	L	21–5	Darby, PA
19-May	Hilldale	B	L	3–1	Atlantic City
25-May	Pennsylvania and Reading RR (Philadelphia)	B	L	8–2	Atlantic City
26-May	Camden Athletic Club (NJ)	W	W	9–0	Atlantic City
30-May	Camp Dix (NJ)	W	W	6–5	Atlantic City
31-May	Pennsylvania RR Red Caps	B	W	10–4	Atlantic City
1-Jun	Pennsylvania RR Red Caps	B	L	6–4	Atlantic City
2-Jun	Indiana Boys Club (Philadephia)	W	W	12–11	Atlantic City
3-Jun	Cuban Stars	B	L	9–3	Atlantic City
4-Jun	Cuban Stars	B	W	5–3	Atlantic City
5-Jun	Cuban Stars	B	L	7–3	Atlantic City
9-Jun	Philadelphia United Gas Improvement	W	W	16–3	Atlantic City
11-Jun	Brooklyn Royal Giants	B	W	4–2	Atlantic City
12-Jun	Brooklyn Royal Giants	B	W	7–4	Atlantic City
16-Jun	Becker, Smith & Page (Philadelphia)	W	W	12–2	Atlantic City
17-Jun	Cuban Stars	B	W	11–3	Atlantic City
18-Jun	Cuban Stars	B	L	4–2	Atlantic City
19-Jun	Cuban Stars	B	L	4–3	Atlantic City
20-Jun	Hilldale	B	L	19–3	Darby, PA
23-Jun	Philadelphia Navy Yard Armed Guards	W	L	2–1	Atlantic City
24-Jun	Lincoln Giants	B	L	9–5	Atlantic City
25-Jun	Lincoln Giants	B	W	2–1	Atlantic City
29-Jun	Millville (NJ)	W	W	7–4	Millville
30-Jun	Philadelphia Navy Yard Armed Guards	W	W	13–2	Atlantic City
4-Jul	Marines Radio Station (NJ)	W	W	11–0	Atlantic City
5-Jul	Wilmington (DE) Giants	B	L	10–3	Atlantic City
6-Jul	Wilmington (DE) Giants	B	W	15–8	Atlantic City
7-Jul	Media (PA)	W	L	3–0	Atlantic City
10-Jul	Newark (International League)	W	ND	0–2	Atlantic City
12-Jul	Cuban Stars	B	L	6–5	Atlantic City
14-Jul	Hog Island (Philadelphia)	W	L	3–2	Atlantic City
15-Jul	Brooklyn Royal Giants	B	L	13–2	Atlantic City
16-Jul	Brooklyn Royal Giants	B	L	8–4	Atlantic City
25-Jul	Melrose Athletic Club (Atlantic City)	W	W	11–0	Atlantic City
28-Jul	Hog Island (Philadelphia)	W	W	12–2	Atlantic City
29-Jul	Chicago American Giants	B	T	4–4	Atlantic City
30-Jul	Chicago American Giants	B	W	5–4	Atlantic City
2-Aug	Chicago American Giants	B	W	3–1	Atlantic City
4-Aug	Wissinoming (Philadelphia)	W	W	6–4	Atlantic City
5-Aug	Wissinoming (Philadelphia)	W	W	13–7	Atlantic City
11-Aug	Melrose Athletic Club (Atlantic City)	W	W	6–3	Atlantic City
11-Aug	Roxborough (Philadelphia)	W	W	4–3	Atlantic City
18-Aug	Melrose Athletic Club (Atlantic City)	W	W	5–0	Atlantic City
25-Aug	Melrose Athletic Club (Atlantic City)	W	W	11–0	Atlantic City

1919 Bacharach Giants (73–29–1)

Date	Opponent	Race	W/L	Score	Location
30-May	All-Nationals	W	W	7–0	Atlantic City
31-May	All-Nationals	W	L	3–2	Atlantic City
1-Jun	All-Americans (Philadelphia)	W	W	6–1	Atlantic City
2-Jun	All-Americans (Philadelphia)	W	L	5–3	Atlantic City
3-Jun	All-Americans (Philadelphia)	W	W	2–1	Atlantic City
5-Jun	Hilldale	B	W	9–2	Darby, PA
7-Jun	Hilldale	B	W	5–3	Darby, PA
8-Jun	Hilldale	B	L	8–3	Atlantic City
9-Jun	Hilldale	B	L	5–2	Atlantic City
10-Jun	Hilldale	B	L	5–3	Atlantic City
12-Jun	Wissinoming (Philadelphia)	W	W	8–1	Atlantic City
14-Jun	Atlantic City Giants	B	W	10–0	Atlantic City
15-Jun	Harry Davis All-Stars (Philadelphia)	W	W	11–1	Atlantic City
16-Jun	New York Ship (Camden, NJ)	W	W	7–2	Atlantic City
17-Jun	New York Ship (Camden, NJ)	W	W	10–9	Atlantic City
18-Jun	Bridesburg (Philadelphia	W	W	8–0	Atlantic City
21-Jun	Roxborough (Philadelphia)	W	W	8–3	Atlantic City
22-Jun	All-Americans (Philadelphia)	W	W	9–2	Atlantic City
23-Jun	All-Americans (Philadelphia)	W	W	6–1	Atlantic City
24-Jun	Cuban Stars	B	W	10–2	Atlantic City
25-Jun	Cuban Stars	B	L	4–3	Atlantic City
26-Jun	Cuban Stars	B	W	0–0 forfeit	Atlantic City
27-Jun	Pennsylvania RR Red Caps	B	W	9–7	Atlantic City
29-Jun	Logan Squares (Philadelphia)	W	L	2–1	Atlantic City
4-Jul	Logan Squares (Philadelphia)	W	W	12–3	Atlantic City
5-Jul	Logan Squares (Philadelphia)	W	W	6–0	Atlantic City
6-Jul	Logan Squares (Philadelphia)	W	W	12–0	Atlantic City
7-Jul	Paterson Giants (NJ)	W	W	8–0	Atlantic City
8-Jul	Paterson Giants (NJ)	W	W	4–0	Atlantic City
11-Jul	Overbrook (Philadelphia)	W	W	13–0	Atlantic City
12-Jul	Leiperville (PA; Baldwin Locomotive Works)	W	W	9–0	Atlantic City
13-Jul	Chester (PA)	W	W	2–0	Atlantic City
14-Jul	Chester (PA)	W	W	2–0	Atlantic City
16-Jul	Detroit Stars	B	L	6–3	Atlantic City
17-Jul	Millville (NJ)	W	W	5–2	Millville
18-Jul	Detroit Stars	B	W	1–0	Atlantic City
19-Jul	Millville (NJ)	W	L	4–2	Millville
22-Jul	Cuban Stars	B	W	2–1	Atlantic City
23-Jul	Cuban Stars	B	W	5–2	Atlantic City
24-Jul	Cuban Stars	B	W	7–4	Atlantic City
25-Jul	Millville (NJ)	W	W	5–1	Atlantic City
26-Jul	Camden Black Sox (NJ)	B	W	9–0	Camden
27-Jul	Treat 'Em Roughs (New York City)	W	W	8–4	New York City
27-Jul	Treat 'Em Roughs (New York City)	W	W	6–0	New York City
28-Jul	Maxwell Motor Car (Detroit)	W	W	8–6	Atlantic City
29-Jul	Maxwell Motor Car (Detroit)	W	L	9–7	Atlantic City
30-Jul	Maxwell Motor Car (Detroit)	W	W	4–3	Atlantic City
31-Jul	Maxwell Motor Car (Detroit)	W	L	4–3	Atlantic City
1-Aug	Maxwell Motor Car (Detroit)	W	L	6–3	Atlantic City
2-Aug	Maxwell Motor Car (Detroit)	W	W	5–1	Atlantic City
3-Aug	Treat 'Em Roughs (New York City)	W	W	8–2	New York, NY
3-Aug	Treat 'Em Roughs (New York City)	W	L	2–1	New York, NY
4-Aug	Cuban Stars	B	L	9–3	Atlantic City
7-Aug	Millville (NJ)	W	W	4–3	Atlantic City
8-Aug	Millville (NJ)	W	W	5–1	Atlantic City
9-Aug	Millville (NJ)	W	W	6–5	Millville
10-Aug	Treat 'Em Roughs (New York City)	W	W	5–1	New York, NY
10-Aug	Treat 'Em Roughs (New York City)	W	W	6–2	New York, NY
11-Aug	Merchant Ship (Bristol, PA)	W	L	4–0	Atlantic City
12-Aug	Merchant Ship (Bristol, PA)	W	W	6–4	Atlantic City
16-Aug	Klein Chocolate (Elizabethtown, PA)	W	W	3–1	Millville
18-Aug	Klein Chocolate (Elizabethtown, PA)	W	W	2–1	Harrisburg, PA
24-Aug	Hilldale	B	L	1–0	Atlantic City
26-Aug	Hilldale	B	W	7–1	Atlantic City
27-Aug	Hilldale	B	W	5–2	Atlantic City

Date	Opponent	Race	W/L	Score	Location
28-Aug	Pittsburgh Stars (Buffalo, NY)	B	W	6–2	Atlantic City
29-Aug	Pittsburgh Stars (Buffalo, NY)	B	W	8–2	Atlantic City
30-Aug	Klein Chocolate (Elizabethtown, PA)	W	W	1–0	Atlantic City
31-Aug	Klein Chocolate (Elizabethtown, PA)	W	W	3–2	Atlantic City
2-Sep	Chester Athletic Club (PA)	W	W	5–3	Atlantic City
3-Sep	Chester Athletic Club (PA)	W	W	10–1	Atlantic City
4-Sep	Harlan Giants (Wilmington, DE)	B	W	9–6	Atlantic City
5-Sep	Wildwood (NJ)	W	W	2–0	Atlantic City
7-Sep	Wildwood (NJ)	W	W	9–0	Atlantic City
8-Sep	Hilldale	B	W	10–0	Shibe Park
9-Sep	Baltimore Dry Docks	W	L	3–0	Atlantic City
11-Sep	Hilldale	B	W	4–3	Atlantic City
12-Sep	Vineland (NJ)	W	W	8–6	Vineland
13-Sep	Hilldale	B	W	5–2	Darby, PA
14-Sep	Morse Dry Dock (Brooklyn)	W	L	8–7	Brooklyn, NY
14-Sep	Morse Dry Dock (Brooklyn)	W	W	8–0	Brooklyn, NY
15-Sep	International League All-Stars	W	L	3–2	Atlantic City
16-Sep	International League All-Stars	W	W	2–0	Atlantic City
17-Sep	International League All-Stars	W	L	14–1	Atlantic City
18-Sep	International League All-Stars	W	W	7–2	Atlantic City
19-Sep	Disston (Philadelphia)	W	T	3–3	Philadelphia
21-Sep	Treat 'Em Roughs (New York City)	W	L	6–2	New York, NY
21-Sep	Treat 'Em Roughs (New York City)	W	W	7–1	New York, NY
22-Sep	Hammonton (NJ)	W	W	6–2	Atlantic City
24-Sep	Gloucester (NJ)	W	W	5–4	Atlantic City
27-Sep	Hilldale	B	L	7–2	Darby, PA
28-Sep	Treat 'Em Roughs (New York City)	W	L	2–0	New York, NY
28-Sep	Treat 'Em Roughs (New York City)	W	W	5–1	New York, NY
29-Sep	Treat 'Em Roughs (New York City)	W	L	9–5	Atlantic City
5-Oct	Treat 'Em Roughs (New York City)	W	L	4–3	New York, NY
5-Oct	Treat 'Em Roughs (New York City)	W	L	1–0	New York, NY
7-Oct	New York Giants	W	L	7–5	Shibe Park
11-Oct	Disston (Philadelphia)	W	W	6–0	Shibe Park
19-Oct	International League Stars	W	L	7–4	Ebbets Field
19-Oct	International League Stars	W	L	6–1	Ebbets Field
26-Oct	International League Stars	W	W	2–0	Ebbets Field
2-Nov	International League Stars	W	W	13–7	Ebbets Field
2-Nov	International League Stars	W	W	3–0	Ebbets Field

1920 Bacharach Giants (94–36–4)

Date	Opponent	Race	W/L	Score	Location
13-Apr	Jacksonville (FL)	B	W	6–3	Jacksonville
18-Apr	Jacksonville (FL)	B	W	6–1	Jacksonville
2-May	Tesreau's Bears (New York City)	W	L	13–4	New York, NY
2-May	Tesreau's Bears (New York City)	W	L	7–5	New York, NY
9-May	Tesreau's Bears (New York City)	W	W	14–4	New York, NY
9-May	Tesreau's Bears (New York City)	W	L	8–4	New York, NY
16-May	Treat 'Em Roughs (New York City)	W	W	8–0	Ebbets Field
16-May	Treat 'Em Roughs (New York City)	W	W	11–4	Ebbets Field
23-May	Tesreau's Bears (New York City)	W	W	4–2	New York, NY
23-May	Tesreau's Bears (New York City)	W	L	4–3	New York, NY
24-May	Madison Stars (Philadelphia)	B	W	6–3	Philadelphia
25-May	Madison Stars (Philadelphia)	B	W	8–1	Philadelphia
30-May	Bronx Giants (New York City)	W	L	10–4	Bronx, NY
30-May	Bronx Giants (New York City)	W	L	6–3	Bronx, NY
31-May	Bronx Giants (New York City)	W	W	15–6	Atlantic City
31-May	Bronx Giants (New York City)	W	W	6–2	Atlantic City
1-Jun	Sun Oil (Philadelphia)	W	W	6–0	Atlantic City
2-Jun	Sun Oil (Philadelphia)	W	W	5–3	Atlantic City
3-Jun	Pittsburgh Stars (Buffalo, NY)	B	W	6–1	Atlantic City
6-Jun	Bronx Giants (New York City)	W	W	11–0	Bronx, NY
6-Jun	Bronx Giants (New York City)	W	W	1–0	Bronx, NY
7-Jun	Madison Stars (Philadelphia)	W	L	11–9	Atlantic City
8-Jun	Madison Stars (Philadelphia)	W	W	7–1	Atlantic City

Appendix A: Game Log

Date	Opponent	Race	W/L	Score	Location
9-Jun	Pittsburgh Stars (Buffalo, NY)	B	W	1–0	Atlantic City
10-Jun	Pittsburgh Stars (Buffalo, NY)	B	W	5–3	Atlantic City
11-Jun	Southampton Professionals (Philadelphia)	W	W	8–4	Atlantic City
17-Jun	Portsmouth (VA) Giants	B	W	3–2	Atlantic City
18-Jun	Portsmouth (VA) Giants	B	W	7–2	Atlantic City
19-Jun	Portsmouth (VA) Giants	B	W	9–5	Atlantic City
20-Jun	Upland (PA)	W	W	2–0	Atlantic City
21-Jun	Quaker City Rubber (Philadelphia)	W	W	5–1	Atlantic City
22-Jun	Quaker City Rubber (Philadelphia)	W	W	3–0	Atlantic City
23-Jun	Vineland (NJ)	W	W	7–1	Vineland
24-Jun	Camden Athletic Club (NJ)	W	W	8–0	Atlantic City
25-Jun	Fleischer Athletic Club (Philadelphia)	W	L	3–2	Atlantic City
28-Jun	Cambridge C.C. (Philadelphia)	W	W	8–1	Atlantic City
29-Jun	South Philadelphia Hebrew Association	W	W	6–4	Atlantic City
30-Jun	Norristown Professionals (PA)	W	W	9–0	Atlantic City
1-Jul	Norristown Professionals (PA)	W	W	6–0	Atlantic City
2-Jul	J & J Dobson (Philadelphia)	W	W	6–3	Atlantic City
3-Jul	Gimbel Brothers (Philadelphia)	W	W	12–0	Atlantic City
4-Jul	Treat 'Em Roughs (New York City)	W	W	15–2	Atlantic City
5-Jul	Treat 'Em Roughs (New York City)	W	W	8–0	Atlantic City
6-Jul	Pennsylvania RR Red Caps	B	W	7–3	Atlantic City
7-Jul	Pennsylvania RR Red Caps	B	W	5–2	Atlantic City
8-Jul	Fleischer Athletic Club (Philadelphia)	W	W	10–1	Atlantic City
9-Jul	Fleischer Athletic Club (Philadelphia)	W	W	5–0	Atlantic City
9-Jul	Pittsburgh Stars (Buffalo, NY)	B	W	3–1	Atlantic City
11-Jul	Lincoln Giants	B	W	5–0	Ebbets Field
11-Jul	Lincoln Giants	B	L	7–5	Ebbets Field
12-Jul	Baltimore Drydocks	W	W	6–5	Atlantic City
13-Jul	Baltimore Drydocks	W	W	6–2	Atlantic City
14-Jul	Baltimore Drydocks	W	L	6–0	Atlantic City
15-Jul	Bethlehem Steel	W	L	5–3	Atlantic City
16-Jul	Bethlehem Steel	W	W	5–4	Atlantic City
17-Jul	Lit Brothers (Philadelphia)	W	W	8–6	Atlantic City
19-Jul	Merchant Ship (Bristol, PA)	W	W	4–1	Atlantic City
20-Jul	Merchant Ship (Bristol, PA)	W	W	5–1	Atlantic City
21-Jul	Nativity Catholic (Philadelphia)	W	W	9–3	Atlantic City
22-Jul	Nativity Catholic (Philadelphia)	W	W	9–3	Atlantic City
23-Jul	Aberfoyle (Chester, PA)	W	W	7–0	Atlantic City
25-Jul	Upland (PA)	W	W	6–4	Atlantic City
26-Jul	House of David	W	W	4–2	Shibe Park
27-Jul	M.E. Smith (Philadelphia)	W	W	4–0	Atlantic City
28-Jul	House of David	W	W	3–1	Atlantic City
29-Jul	Pittsburgh Stars (Buffalo, NY)	B	W	3–0	Buffalo
30-Jul	Pittsburgh Stars (Buffalo, NY)	B	T	8–8	Niagara Falls
31-Jul	Detroit Stars	B	W	4–2	Detroit
1-Aug	Detroit Stars	B	L	4–3	Detroit
2-Aug	Detroit Stars	B	W	2–0	Detroit
3-Aug	Detroit Stars	B	L	2–1	Detroit
4-Aug	Detroit Stars	B	L	6–4	Detroit
5-Aug	Albion (MI) Red Sox	W	W	8–5	Albion
7-Aug	Chicago American Giants	B	W	11–4	Chicago
8-Aug	Chicago American Giants	B	L	7–3	Chicago
9-Aug	Chicago American Giants	B	L	3–2	Chicago
10-Aug	Chicago American Giants	B	L	5–1	Chicago
11-Aug	Chicago American Giants	B	L	5–4	Chicago
12-Aug	Chicago American Giants	B	W	8–1	Chicago
14-Aug	Indianapolis ABCs	B	L	4–3	Muncie, IN
15-Aug	Indianapolis ABCs	B	L	5–1	Indianapolis
16-Aug	Standard Steel Works (Burnham, PA)	W	L	3–2	Burnham
18-Aug	Chicago Giants	B	T	2–2	Atlantic City
19-Aug	Chicago Giants	B	W	9–3	Atlantic City
20-Aug	Chicago Giants	B	W	2–1	Atlantic City
22-Aug	Chicago Giants	B	W	7–0	Ebbets Field
22-Aug	Chicago Giants	B	W	4–0	Ebbets Field
24-Aug	Chicago Giants	B	L	4–1	Atlantic City
25-Aug	Wade's Giants (Roanoke, VA)	B	W	11–4	Atlantic City

Date	Opponent	Race	W/L	Score	Location
26-Aug	J & J Dobson (Philadelphia)	W	W	4–0	Atlantic City
27-Aug	J & J Dobson (Philadelphia)	W	W	6–0	Atlantic City
28-Aug	House of David	W	W	7–0	Ebbets Field
29-Aug	Lincoln Giants	B	W	6–0	Ebbets Field
29-Aug	Lincoln Giants	B	W	7–3	Ebbets Field
30-Aug	Indianapolis ABCs	B	W	7–5	Atlantic City
31-Aug	Indianapolis ABCs	B	L	3–1	Atlantic City
1-Sep	Indianapolis ABCs	B	W	7–4	Atlantic City
2-Sep	Indianapolis ABCs	B	L	2–1	Atlantic City
3-Sep	Indianapolis ABCs	B	W	5–3	Atlantic City
4-Sep	Indianapolis ABCs	B	L	9–7	Atlantic City
5-Sep	Indianapolis ABCs	B	T	4–4	Atlantic City
6-Sep	Indianapolis ABCs	B	W	5–4	Ebbets Field
6-Sep	Indianapolis ABCs	B	W	5–1	Ebbets Field
8-Sep	Rex Athletic Club (Washington, D.C.)	W	W	11–5	Washington, D.C.
11-Sep	Baltimore Drydocks	W	L	12–5	Coatesville, PA
12-Sep	Upland (PA)	W	W	9–8	Atlantic City
13-Sep	Baltimore Drydocks	W	L	8–3	Atlantic City
14-Sep	Baltimore Drydocks	W	W	7–0	Atlantic City
15-Sep	Baltimore Drydocks	W	W	2–1	Atlantic City
16-Sep	Scranton (PA)	W	W	9–3	Atlantic City
19-Sep	Baltimore Black Sox	B	W	13–5	New York, NY
19-Sep	Baltimore Black Sox	B	W	16–4	New York, NY
20-Sep	Baltimore Drydocks	W	L	3–2	Atlantic City
21-Sep	Baltimore Drydocks	W	W	6–1	Atlantic City
22-Sep	Baltimore Drydocks	W	W	2–1	Atlantic City
23-Sep	Bridesburg (Philadelphia)	W	T	0–0	Philadelphia
26-Sep	Millville (NJ)	W	L	2–1	Millville
27-Sep	Cuban Stars	B	L	4–3	Atlantic City
28-Sep	Cuban Stars	B	W	2–0	Atlantic City
29-Sep	Cuban Stars	B	W	3–0	Atlantic City
1-Oct	Baltimore Black Sox	B	W	5–0	Baltimore
2-Oct	Baltimore Black Sox	B	W	15–1	Baltimore
3-Oct	Meadowbrooks (Newark, NJ)	W	W	12–1	Harrison, NJ
3-Oct	All Leaguers	W	W	7–1	Harrison, NJ
4-Oct	Babe Ruth All-Stars	W	W	9–4	Shibe Park
6-Oct	Chicago American Giants	B	L	11–10	Shibe Park
7-Oct	Chicago American Giants	B	L	13–1	Shibe Park
8-Oct	Chicago American Giants	B	W	7–0	Shibe Park
10-Oct	Chicago American Giants	B	W	5–3	Ebbets Field
10-Oct	Chicago American Giants	B	W	7–3	Ebbets Field
17-Oct	Chicago American Giants	B	L	2–0	Ebbets Field
17-Oct	Chicago American Giants	B	L	1–0	Ebbets Field
23-Oct	Paterson (NJ) Silk Sox	W	L	6–3	Harrison, NJ
7-Nov	Tesreau's Bears (New York City)	W	L	5–4	New York, NY

1921 Bacharach Giants (103–56–10)

Date	Opponent	Race	W/L	Score	Location
28-Mar	Jacksonville (FL)	B	W	9–3	Jacksonville
31-Mar	Brunswick (GA)	B	W	9–3	Brunswick
1-Apr	Brunswick (GA)	B	W	7–2	Brunswick
2-Apr	Brunswick (GA)	B	W	13–4	Brunswick
5-Apr	St. Louis Giants	B	W	7–1	Montgomery
6-Apr	St. Louis Giants	B	T	5–5	Montgomery
7-Apr	Atlanta	B	W	4–0	Atlanta
8-Apr	Atlanta	B	W	12–4	Atlanta
9-Apr	Atlanta	B	W	7–3	Atlanta
10-Apr	Montgomery (AL) Grey Sox	B	W	11–0	Montgomery
11-Apr	Montgomery (AL) Grey Sox	B	L	7–3	Montgomery
12-Apr	Greenville (SC)	B	W	19–8	Greenville
13-Apr	Greenville (SC)	B	W	27–2	Greenville
18-Apr	Brooklyn Slides (Richmond Giants)	B	W	5–0	Richmond
19-Apr	Brooklyn Slides (Richmond Giants)	B	W	2–1	Richmond
20-Apr	Brooklyn Slides (Richmond Giants)	B	W	11–3	Richmond

Date	Opponent	Race	W/L	Score	Location
21-Apr	Brooklyn Slides (Richmond Giants)	B	W	15–3	Richmond
24-Apr	Baltimore Black Sox	B	W	9–3	Baltimore
24-Apr	Baltimore Black Sox	B	W	14–4	Baltimore
25-Apr	Baltimore Black Sox	B	W	4–1	Baltimore
26-Apr	Baltimore Black Sox	B	L	4–1	Baltimore
28-Apr	Norfolk Giants	B	W	8–4	Norfolk
29-Apr	Norfolk Giants	B	W	16–8	Norfolk
1-May	Tesreau's Bears (New York City)	W	W	5–2	New York, NY
1-May	Tesreau's Bears (New York City)	W	W	8–1	New York, NY
3-May	Cleveland Tate Stars	B	W	17–2	Cleveland
4-May	Cleveland Tate Stars	B	W	9–2	Cleveland
7-May	Detroit Stars	B	L	9–8	Detroit
8-May	Detroit Stars	B	W	7–3	Detroit
9-May	Detroit Stars	B	L	9–8	Detroit
10-May	Detroit Stars	B	W	7–4	Detroit
15-May	Chicago American Giants	B	L	2–1	Chicago
16-May	Cincinnati Cuban Stars	B	L	17–2	Redlands Park
17-May	Cincinnati Cuban Stars	B	L	6–5	Redlands Park
19-May	Cincinnati Cuban Stars	B	W	2–1	Redlands Park
21-May	Indianapolis ABCs	B	L	8–7	Indianapolis
22-May	Indianapolis ABCs	B	L	5–3	Indianapolis
23-May	Indianapolis ABCs	B	W	9–3	Indianapolis
24-May	Indianapolis ABCs	B	W	8–7	Indianapolis
29-May	Columbus Buckeyes	B	W	7–4	Columbus
30-May	Columbus Buckeyes	B	L	8–7	Columbus
30-May	Columbus Buckeyes	B	L	7–6	Columbus
31-May	Columbus Buckeyes	B	W	13–4	Columbus
2-Jun	Hilldale	B	L	8–6	Darby, PA
4-Jun	Hilldale	B	L	3–0	Darby, PA
5-Jun	Hilldale	B	W	6–5	Ebbets Field
5-Jun	Hilldale	B	L	13–6	Ebbets Field
6-Jun	Tesreau's Bears (New York City)	W	W	11–3	Atlantic City
7-Jun	Tesreau's Bears (New York City)	W	W	12–4	Atlantic City
8-Jun	J & J Dobson (Philadelphia)	W	W	8–0	Atlantic City
9-Jun	Logan Squares (Philadelphia)	W	W	8–1	Atlantic City
10-Jun	Fleischer Yarn (Philadelphia)	W	W	7–1	Atlantic City
11-Jun	Fleischer Yarn (Philadelphia)	W	L	8–3	Atlantic City
12-Jun	Hilldale	B	W	14–7	Ebbets Field
12-Jun	Hilldale	B	W	5–1	Ebbets Field
13-Jun	Bridesburg (Philadelphia)	W	W	11–7	Atlantic City
14-Jun	Parkesburg Iron (Parkesburg, PA)	W	W	9–8	Atlantic City
15-Jun	Cressona (PA)	W	W	11–5	Atlantic City
16-Jun	Marshall E. Smith (Philadelphia)	W	L	8–5	Atlantic City
17-Jun	Parkesburg Iron (Parkesburg, PA)	W	T	2–2	Atlantic City
18-Jun	Norfolk Giants	B	W	5–3	Atlantic City
19-Jun	Tesreau's Bears (New York City)	W	W	12–3	New York City
19-Jun	Tesreau's Bears (New York City)	W	L	8–5	New York City
20-Jun	Hilldale	B	L	4–3	Atlantic City
21-Jun	Hilldale	B	W	5–0	Atlantic City
22-Jun	Tamaqua (PA)	W	L	9–6	Atlantic City
23-Jun	Chester (PA)	W	W	8–7	Atlantic City
24-Jun	Chester (PA)	W	W	17–3	Atlantic City
25-Jun	Hilldale	B	L	11–6	Darby, PA
26-Jun	Norfolk Giants	B	W	6–5	New York, NY
26-Jun	Norfolk Giants	B	L	9–2	New York, NY
29-Jun	Marshall E. Smith (Philadelphia)	W	W	6–4	Atlantic City
2-Jul	All Cubans	B	W	13–2	Ebbets Field
2-Jul	All Cubans	B	W	4–3	Ebbets Field
3-Jul	Hilldale	B	W	6–5	Atlantic City
3-Jul	Hilldale	B	L	4–1	Atlantic City
4-Jul	Logan Squares (Philadelphia)	W	W	4–1	Atlantic City
4-Jul	Logan Squares (Philadelphia)	W	L	8–7	Atlantic City
6-Jul	Hilldale	B	W	6–4	Camden
7-Jul	Hilldale	B	W	5–1	Darby, PA
10-Jul	Tesreau's Bears (New York City)	W	L	9–7	New York, NY
10-Jul	Tesreau's Bears (New York City)	W	L	10–4	New York, NY

Appendix A: Game Log

Date	Opponent	Race	W/L	Score	Location
11-Jul	Parkesburg Iron (Parkesburg, PA)	W	W	2–1	Atlantic City
12-Jul	Parkesburg Iron (Parkesburg, PA)	W	L	4–3	Atlantic City
13-Jul	Madison Stars (Philadelphia)	B	W	5–4	Atlantic City
14-Jul	Pennsylvania Red Caps	B	W	6–0	Atlantic City
17-Jul	Tesreau's Bears (New York City)	W	W	4–3	New York, NY
17-Jul	Tesreau's Bears (New York City)	W	W	10–8	New York, NY
18-Jul	American Chain (York, PA)	W	W	3–1	Atlantic City
19-Jul	American Chain (York, PA)	W	L	2–1	Atlantic City
21-Jul	All Cubans	B	W	11–7	Atlantic City
22-Jul	All Cubans	B	L	3–1	Atlantic City
23-Jul	Ambassador Hotel, Atlantic City	W	W	5–1	Atlantic City
24-Jul	Indianapolis ABCs	B	W	16–4	Atlantic City
25-Jul	Indianapolis ABCs	B	L	3–2	Atlantic City
26-Jul	Indianapolis ABCs	B	W	8–4	Atlantic City
27-Jul	Fleischer Yarn (Philadelphia)	W	W	12–3	Phillies Park
28-Jul	All Cubans	B	L	13–10	Atlantic City
29-Jul	Indianapolis ABCs	B	T	5–5	Atlantic City
30-Jul	Chester (PA)	W	W	2–0	Atlantic City
31-Jul	Indianapolis ABCs	B	W	14–3	Ebbets Field
31-Jul	Indianapolis ABCs	B	ND	0–0	Ebbets Field
1-Aug	Indianapolis ABCs	B	W	7–1	Norfolk
2-Aug	Indianapolis ABCs	B	L	13–8	Norfolk
3-Aug	Indianapolis ABCs	B	L	7–5	Richmond
4-Aug	Indianapolis ABCs	B	L	4–2	Richmond
5-Aug	Indianapolis ABCs	B	W	7–1	Richmond
6-Aug	Indianapolis ABCs	B	W	8–7	Westport, MD
6-Aug	Indianapolis ABCs	B	L	6–5	Westport, MD
7-Aug	Indianapolis ABCs	B	W	3–1	Atlantic City
7-Aug	Indianapolis ABCs	B	L	7–1	Atlantic City
8-Aug	Indianapolis ABCs	B	L	3–0	Wilmington, DE
9-Aug	Indianapolis ABCs	B	W	4–2	Atlantic City
10-Aug	Columbus Buckeyes	B	W	6–5	Atlantic City
11-Aug	Columbus Buckeyes	B	L	5–2	Atlantic City
12-Aug	Columbus Buckeyes	B	W	3–1	Atlantic City
13-Aug	Parkesburg Iron (Parkesburg, PA)	W	L	3–1	Parkesburg
14-Aug	Columbus Buckeyes	B	W	9–0	Atlantic City
14-Aug	Columbus Buckeyes	B	ND	2–0	Atlantic City
15-Aug	Columbus Buckeyes	B	W	4–0	Atlantic City
16-Aug	Columbus Buckeyes	B	L	8–5	Atlantic City
18-Aug	Donovan-Armstrong (Philadelphia)	W	W	7–6	Atlantic City
19-Aug	Columbus Buckeyes	B	W	3–2	Atlantic City
20-Aug	J & J Dobson (Philadelphia)	W	W	3–2	Philadelphia
23-Aug	Elmer (NJ)	W	W	4–1	Elmer
24-Aug	Philadelphia Old-Timers	W	W	12–0	Philadelphia
25-Aug	All Cubans	B	W	21–7	Atlantic City
26-Aug	All Cubans	B	W	9–8	Atlantic City
27-Aug	J & J Dobson (Philadelphia)	W	W	4–1	Philadelphia
29-Aug	Logan Squares (Philadelphia)	W	W	10–2	Philadelphia
30-Aug	Wildwood (NJ)	W	W	13–0	Wildwood
31-Aug	Elmer (NJ)	W	W	4–2	Elmer
1-Sep	Detroit Stars	B	L	7–5	Atlantic City
2-Sep	Detroit Stars	B	W	3–0	Atlantic City
4-Sep	Detroit Stars	B	W	8–0	Harrison, NJ
4-Sep	Detroit Stars	B	L	6–5	Harrison, NJ
8-Sep	Elmer (NJ)	W	L	6–4	Mount Holly, NJ
10-Sep	Detroit Stars	B	W	1–0	Atlantic City
11-Sep	Orange Athletic Association (NJ)	W	W	4–3	New York City
11-Sep	Orange Athletic Association (NJ)	W	W	8–2	New York City
12-Sep	Norristown Professionals (PA)	W	W	8–5	Norristown
13-Sep	South Philadelphia Hebrew Association	W	T	3–3	Philadelphia
20-Sep	Fleisher Yarn (Philadelphia)	W	W	7–5	Philadelphia
22-Sep	Hilldale	B	W	4–3	Darby, PA
24-Sep	Hilldale	B	L	4–1	Darby, PA
25-Sep	Hilldale	B	W	4–3	Ebbets Field
25-Sep	Hilldale	B	L	8–6	Ebbets Field
29-Sep	Baltimore Black Sox	B	W	4–3	Wilmington, DE

Date	Opponent	Race	W/L	Score	Location
1-Oct	Chicago American Giants	B	W	4–0	Harrison, NJ
2-Oct	Chicago American Giants	B	T	1–1	New York, NY
2-Oct	Chicago American Giants	B	L	3–1	New York, NY
4-Oct	Philadelphia Athletics	W	L	3–1	Mount Holly, NJ
5-Oct	Philadelphia Athletics	W	L	8–7	Reading, PA
7-Oct	Philadelphia Athletics	W	L	6–3	Trenton
12-Oct	Chester (PA)	W	L	10–2	Chester
13-Oct	Philadelphia Athletics	W	L	5–1	Elmer, NJ
14-Oct	Philadelphia Athletics	W	W	11–4	Bridgeton, NJ
16-Oct	Chicago American Giants	B	ND	1–0	Bronx, NY
16-Oct	Chicago American Giants	B	L	6–3	Bronx, NY
17-Oct	Chicago American Giants	B	W	9–2	Norfolk
19-Oct	Chicago American Giants	B	L	8–5	Norfolk
19-Oct	Chicago American Giants	B	L	6–5	Norfolk
20-Oct	Chicago American Giants	B	W	5–5 forfeit	Richmond
21-Oct	Chicago American Giants	B	L	5–4	Richmond
22-Oct	Hilldale	B	L	12–8	Darby, PA
23-Oct	Chicago American Giants	B	W	5–3	Ebbets Field
23-Oct	Chicago American Giants	B	ND	1–1	Ebbets Field
30-Oct	Hilldale	B	ND	2–1	New York, NY
30-Oct	Hilldale	B	L	7–2	New York, NY

1922 Bacharach Giants (Atlantic City) (49–35–3)

Date	Opponent	Race	W/L	Score	Location
8-May	Richmond Giants	B	L	9–3	Richmond
9-May	Richmond Giants	B	W	3–2	Richmond
10-May	Richmond Giants	B	L	8–2	Richmond
14-May	Baltimore Black Sox	B	W	5–2	Baltimore
14-May	Baltimore Black Sox	B	L	7–3	Baltimore
19-May	Cressona (PA) Tigers	W	W	8–6	Wilmington (DE)
20-May	Cressona (PA) Tigers	W	W	4–2	Wilmington (DE)
21-May	Cressona (PA) Tigers	W	W	8–4	Pottsville (PA)
25-May	American Chain (York, PA)	W	L	7–4	Wilmington (DE)
27-May	Brooklyn Royal Giants	B	L	6–2	Wilmington (DE)
29-May	Lincoln University (Philadelphia)	B	W	10–3	Wilmington (DE)
30-May	Rex Athletic Club (Washington, D.C.)	W	W	9–3	Wilmington (DE)
1-Jun	American Chain (York, PA)	W	L	6–3	York
3-Jun	Willliamsport Pennsylviania R.R.	W	W	3–1	Williamsport
8-Jun	Rockdale (PA)	W	W	3–0	Wilmington (DE)
9-Jun	Royersford (PA)	W	W	9–1	Wilmington (DE)
10-Jun	Sun Oil (Philadelphia)	W	W	4–2	Wilmington (DE)
12-Jun	Williamstown (PA)	W	L	8–6	Williamstown
15-Jun	Bloomsburg (PA)	W	W	15–1	Bloomsburg
16-Jun	Germantown (Philadelphia)	W	W	8–4	Philadelphia
17-Jun	American Bridge (Trenton)	W	L	4–0	Trenton
18-Jun	Bronx Giants (New York City)	W	W	5–2	Bronx, NY
19-Jun	J & J Dobson (Philadelphia)	W	W	12–1	Wilmington (DE)
20-Jun	J & J Dobson (Philadelphia)	W	L	13–3	Philadelphia
21-Jun	Melrose Athletic Club (Atlantic City)	W	W	8–0	Atlantic City
21-Jun	Melrose Athletic Club (Atlantic City)	W	W	3–0	Atlantic City
22-Jun	American Bridge (Trenton)	W	W	7–6	Wilmington (DE)
23-Jun	Logan Athletic Club (Philadelphia)	W	W	7–2	Wilmington (DE)
26-Jun	South Philadelphia Hebrew Association	W	L	6–2	Philadelphia
28-Jun	Richmond Giants	B	L	2–1	Wilmington (DE)
30-Jun	South Philadelphia Hebrew Association	W	W	6–2	Wilmington (DE)
2-Jul	Pottstown (PA)	W	W	3–2	Pottstown
4-Jul	Chester (PA)	W	W	8–4	Chester
4-Jul	Chester (PA)	W	W	11–1	Chester
6-Jul	Nativity Catholic Club (Philadelphia)	W	L	7–1	Wilmington (DE)
7-Jul	Stenton Field Club (Philadelphia)	W	W	3–2	Wilmington (DE)
8-Jul	St. Thomas (Wilmington, DE)	W	L	5–3	Wilmington (DE)
9-Jul	Caven Point (Jersey City)	W	W	6–4	Jersey City
9-Jul	Caven Point (Jersey City)	W	L	1–0	Jersey City
10-Jul	Stenton Field Club (Philadelphia)	W	W	4–1	Philadelphia

Date	Opponent	Race	W/L	Score	Location
11-Jul	Nativity Catholic Club (Philadelphia)	W	L	5–3	Philadelphia
13-Jul	Spring City-Royersford (PA)	W	W	1–0	Spring City
20-Jul	Baltimore Black Sox	B	W	5–4	Wilmington (DE)
21-Jul	Baltimore Black Sox	B	W	6–3	Wilmington (DE)
22-Jul	St. Thomas (Wilmington, DE)	W	ND	3–0	Wilmington (DE)
24-Jul	Stenton Field Club (Philadelphia)	W	T	4–4	Philadelphia
25-Jul	Stenton Field Club (Philadelphia)	W	L	2–0	Wilmington (DE)
26-Jul	Hilldale	B	W	8–4	Camden
28-Jul	Chester (PA)	W	L	10–6	Wilmington (DE)
29-Jul	Hilldale	B	L	9–3	Darby (PA)
30-Jul	J & J Dobson (Philadelphia)	W	W	4–3	Atlantic City
30-Jul	J & J Dobson (Philadelphia)	W	W	3–2	Atlantic City
3-Aug	Richmond Giants	B	W	3–2	Richmond
4-Aug	Richmond Giants	B	W	10–2	Richmond
5-Aug	Richmond Giants	B	L	8–4	Richmond
5-Aug	Richmond Giants	B	L	10–4	Richmond
7-Aug	St. Thomas (Wilmington, DE)	W	L	2–0	Wilmington (DE)
8-Aug	South Philadelphia Hebrew Association	W	L	5–1	Philadelphia
10-Aug	Spring City-Royersford (PA)	W	T	4–4	Spring City
13-Aug	Bushwicks (Brooklyn)	W	W	5–2	Brooklyn, NY
13-Aug	Bushwicks (Brooklyn)	W	L	14–6	Brooklyn, NY
14-Aug	St. Thomas (Wilmington, DE)	W	L	6–3	Wilmington (DE)
17-Aug	Fleischer Yarn (Philadelphia)	W	L	9–4	Philadelphia
18-Aug	South Philadelphia Hebrew Association	W	L	9–3	Wilmington (DE)
19-Aug	St. Thomas (Wilmington, DE)	W	W	2–0	Wilmington (DE)
21-Aug	St. Thomas (Wilmington, DE)	W	W	6–3	Wilmington (DE)
24-Aug	Japanese All-Stars	W	W	12–4	Wilmington (DE)
28-Aug	St. Thomas (Wilmington, DE)	W	L	2–0	Wilmington (DE)
31-Aug	Baltimore Black Sox	B	W	8–1	Wilmington (DE)
1-Sep	Baltimore Black Sox	B	L	2–1	Wilmington (DE)
2-Sep	St. Thomas (Wilmington, DE)	W	W	11–7	Wilmington (DE)
3-Sep	Bushwicks (Brooklyn)	W	W	9–0	Brooklyn, NY
3-Sep	Bushwicks (Brooklyn)	W	L	7–5	Brooklyn, NY
4-Sep	St. Thomas (Wilmington, DE)	W	W	4–0	Wilmington (DE)
4-Sep	St. Thomas (Wilmington, DE)	W	L	8–2	Wilmington (DE)
14-Sep	Japanese All-Stars	W	W	4–2	Baltimore
16-Sep	Nativity Catholic Club (Philadelphia)	W	L	6–4	Philadelphia
18-Sep	St. Thomas (Wilmington, DE)	W	L	6–2	Wilmington (DE)
19-Sep	Cuban Stars	B	L	9–8	Bridgeton (NJ)
24-Sep	Lincoln Giants	B	L	3–2	Bronx, NY
24-Sep	Lincoln Giants	B	L	6–2	Bronx, NY
29-Sep	Cuban Stars	B	W	6–1	Wilmington (DE)
1-Oct	Caven Point (Jersey City)	W	W	6–5	Jersey City
1-Oct	Caven Point (Jersey City)	W	W	13–1	Jersey City
8-Oct	Bristol (PA)	W	W	9–6	Bristol
10-Oct	Kentucky Reds (Atlantic City)	B	W	8–5	Atlantic City
14-Oct	Combined All Stars	W	L	4–3	Wilmington (DE)

1923 Bacharach Giants (55–46–8)

Date	Opponent	Race	W/L	Score	Location
22-Apr	Egg Harbor (NJ)	W	W	16–1	Egg Harbor
28-Apr	Hilldale	B	L	4–2	Darby, PA
29-Apr	Bushwicks (Brooklyn)	W	W	10–2	Brooklyn, NY
29-Apr	Bushwicks (Brooklyn)	W	L	9–6	Brooklyn, NY
6-May	Baltimore Black Sox	B	W	6–4	Baltimore
6-May	Baltimore Black Sox	B	L	15–9	Baltimore
7-May	Baltimore Black Sox	B	L	6–5	Baltimore
10-May	Washington Potomacs	B	L	5–2	Washington, D.C.
11-May	Washington Potomacs	B	L	5–4	Griffith Stadium
12-May	Washington Potomacs	B	W	3–0	Griffith Stadium
13-May	Washington Potomacs	B	W	13–10	Griffith Stadium
23-May	Crane's Ice Cream (Philadelphia)	W	W	9–0	Philadelphia
30-May	South Philadelphia Hebrew Association	W	W	6–0	Atlantic City
30-May	South Philadelphia Hebrew Association	W	W	8–0	Atlantic City

Appendix A: Game Log

Date	Opponent	Race	W/L	Score	Location
31-May	Lincoln University (Philadelphia)	B	W	7–4	Atlantic City
1-Jun	Pennsylvania RR, Maryland Div. (Wilmington, DE)	W	W	3–0	Wilmington (DE)
3-Jun	Hilldale	B	W	5–0	Atlantic City
4-Jun	Hilldale	B	W	5–4	Atlantic City
5-Jun	Hilldale	B	L	10–2	Atlantic City
6-Jun	Hilldale	B	L	7–5	Camden
10-Jun	Lincoln Giants	B	W	8–5	Bronx, NY
10-Jun	Lincoln Giants	B	W	7–6	Bronx, NY
12-Jun	Lincoln Giants	B	W	4–2	Atlantic City
13-Jun	Crane's Ice Cream (Philadelphia)	W	L	11–7	Vineland
14-Jun	Crane's Ice Cream (Philadelphia)	W	T	4–4	Philadelphia
17-Jun	Cuban Stars	B	L	5–3	Atlantic City
18-Jun	Cuban Stars	B	L	10–5	Atlantic City
19-Jun	Cuban Stars	B	L	8–5	Atlantic City
22-Jun	South Philadelphia	W	L	8–7	Philadelphia
24-Jun	Nativity Catholic Club (Philadelphia)	W	L	3–2	Atlantic City
25-Jun	Washington Potomacs	B	W	10–1	Atlantic City
26-Jun	Washington Potomacs	B	W	9–7	Atlantic City
1-Jul	Hilldale	B	W	8–3	Atlantic City
2-Jul	Hilldale	B	L	7–1	Atlantic City
3-Jul	Lit Brothers (Philadelphia)	W	L	2–0	Atlantic City
4-Jul	Lit Brothers (Philadelphia)	W	L	4–2	Atlantic City
5-Jul	Kensington Congregational (Philadelphia)	W	W	16–4	Philadelphia
8-Jul	Cuban Stars	B	W	9–7	Baltimore
8-Jul	Cuban Stars	B	W	5–4	Baltimore
9-Jul	Cuban Stars	B	W	5–4	Atlantic City
10-Jul	Cuban Stars	B	L	8–5	Atlantic City
11-Jul	Atlantic City Post Office	W	W	3–1	Atlantic City
15-Jul	Baltimore Black Sox	B	W	10–2	Baltimore
15-Jul	Baltimore Black Sox	B	W	12–3	Baltimore
16-Jul	Baltimore Black Sox	B	L	10–4	Baltimore
17-Jul	Lincoln Giants	B	L	5–3	Atlantic City
18-Jul	Lincoln Giants	B	W	2–1	Atlantic City
19-Jul	Chester (PA)	W	L	7–1	Millville, NJ
20-Jul	Germantown (Philadelphia)	W	T	5–5	Philadelphia
21-Jul	Tuckerton (NJ)	W	W	8–0	Tuckerton
22-Jul	Lincoln Giants	B	L	4–1	Bronx, NY
22-Jul	Lincoln Giants	B	L	5–4	Bronx, NY
23-Jul	Brooklyn Royal Giants	B	L	10–0	Atlantic City
24-Jul	Brooklyn Royal Giants	B	W	10–7	Atlantic City
25-Jul	Chester (PA)	W	W	3–2	Atlantic City
26-Jul	Chester (PA)	W	L	17–7	Atlantic City
27-Jul	Chester (PA)	W	L	4–4 forfeit	Chester
1-Aug	Lincoln Giants	B	W	5–2	Atlantic City
3-Aug	Pennsylvania RR, Maryland Div. (Wilmington, DE)	W	T	3–3	Wilmington
4-Aug	Chester	W	L	5–3	Chester
5-Aug	Baltimore Black Sox	B	ND	4–0	Baltimore
5-Aug	Baltimore Black Sox	B	L	8–2	Baltimore
6-Aug	Baltimore Black Sox	B	L	8–7	Atlantic City
7-Aug	Baltimore Black Sox	B	W	3–1	Atlantic City
8-Aug	Baltimore Black Sox	B	W	1–0	Atlantic City
9-Aug	Spring City (PA)	W	W	5–4	Spring City
10-Aug	Wildwood	W	W	6–0	Wildwood
11-Aug	Camden	W	W	4–1	Camden
12-Aug	Middletown Cubans	B	W	12–3	Atlantic City
13-Aug	Middletown Cubans	B	L	4–2	Atlantic City
14-Aug	Middletown Cubans	B	W	9–8	Atlantic City
15-Aug	Hilldale	B	L	7–6	Camden, NJ
15-Aug	Hilldale	B	L	9–4	Woodbury, NJ
16-Aug	Hilldale	B	L	6–5	Darby, PA
17-Aug	Chester	W	L	3–2	Chester
18-Aug	Hilldale	B	L	6–4	Darby, PA
19-Aug	Bushwicks	W	L	7–6	Brooklyn, NY
19-Aug	Bushwicks	W	W	9–4	Brooklyn, NY

Date	Opponent	Race	W/L	Score	Location
20-Aug	Brooklyn Royal Giants	B	L	7–5	Atlantic City
21-Aug	Brooklyn Royal Giants	B	W	9–6	Atlantic City
23-Aug	Pennsylvania RR, Maryland Div. (Wilmington, DE)	W	T	7–7	Wilmington (DE)
24-Aug	Germantown (Philadelphia)	W	T	2–2	Philadelphia
28-Aug	Middletown (NY) Cubans	B	L	6–4	Atlantic City
30-Aug	Baltimore Black Sox	B	L	4–2	Wilmington, DE
31-Aug	Wildwood (NJ)	W	W	6–3	Wildwood
1-Sep	Camden (NJ)	W	W	10–4	Camden
3-Sep	Lincoln Giants	B	L	6–2	Bronx, NY
3-Sep	Lincoln Giants	B	W	6–4	Bronx, NY
4-Sep	Middletown (NY) Cubans	B	W	7–3	Atlantic City
6-Sep	Washington Potomacs	B	L	10–2	Collingwood, PA
7-Sep	Washington Potomacs	B	L	5–2	Florence, NJ
13-Sep	Washington Potomacs	B	W	7–1	Atlantic City
14-Sep	Jeffries Athletic Club (Atlantic City)	W	W	5–0	Atlantic City
14-Sep	Jeffries Athletic Club (Atlantic City)	W	W	9–3	Atlantic City
16-Sep	Farmers (New York City)	W	W	7–4	Queens, NY
16-Sep	Farmers (New York City)	W	T	5–5	Queens, NY
19-Sep	Hilldale	B	W	5–4	Wilmington, DE
20-Sep	Camden (NJ)	W	L	3–2	Atlantic City
21-Sep	Camden (NJ)	W	W	5–0	Atlantic City
23-Sep	Jeffries Athletic Club (Atlantic City)	W	L	4–0	Atlantic City
25-Sep	Richmond Giants	B	W	7–4	Atlantic City
26-Sep	Hilldale	B	T	0–0	Delanco, NJ
27-Sep	Hilldale	B	W	2–1	Roebling, NJ
29-Sep	Camden (NJ)	W	W	4–3	Camden
30-Sep	Baltimore Black Sox	B	W	16–3	Baltimore
30-Sep	Baltimore Black Sox	B	L	4–2	Baltimore
4-Oct	Hilldale	B	W	2–1	Phillies Park
14-Oct	Lincoln Giants	B	W	4–3	Bronx, NY
14-Oct	Lincoln Giants	B	L	2–1	Bronx, NY

1924 Bacharach Giants (74–47–4)

Date	Opponent	Race	W/L	Score	Location
21-Apr	Hanover (PA)	W	W	9–2	Hanover
23-Apr	York (PA)	W	W	5–2	York
24-Apr	York (PA)	W	L	8–7	York
26-Apr	Baltimore Black Sox	B	W	7–2	Baltimore
27-Apr	Baltimore Black Sox	B	W	6–4	Baltimore
27-Apr	Baltimore Black Sox	B	W	10–7	Baltimore
28-Apr	Hazelton (PA)	W	W	11–1	Atlantic City
29-Apr	Hazelton (PA)	W	L	8–4	Atlantic City
1-May	Washington Potomacs	B	W	14–10	Washington, D.C.
2-May	Washington Potomacs	B	L	8–4	Washington, D.C.
3-May	Washington Potomacs	B	W	8–2	Washington, D.C.
4-May	Farmers (New York City)	W	W	11–9	Queens, NY
4-May	Farmers (New York City)	W	L	4–3	Queens, NY
5-May	Trenton	W	W	7–2	Trenton
6-May	Pennsylvania RR, Maryland Div. (Wilmington, DE)	W	W	8–1	Wilmington (DE)
7-May	Ascension (Philadelphia)	W	L	9–4	Philadelphia
9-May	Waco Athletic Club (Camden)	W	W	7–0	Atlantic City
18-May	LeDroit Tigers (Washington, D.C.)	B	W	17–1	Atlantic City
22-May	Harrisburg Giants	B	L	5–4	Harrisburg
23-May	Trenton	W	W	11–3	Trenton
24-May	Hilldale	B	L	4–3	Darby, PA
25-May	Lincoln Giants	B	L	9–1	Bronx, NY
25-May	Lincoln Giants	B	L	9–3	Bronx, NY
28-May	College Point (New York City)	W	L	4–3	Queens, NY
30-May	Brooklyn Royal Giants	B	W	12–1	Brooklyn, NY
30-May	Brooklyn Royal Giants	B	L	9–2	Brooklyn, NY
1-Jun	Hilldale	B	L	13–3	Atlantic City
2-Jun	Hilldale	B	W	5–2	Atlantic City

Appendix A: Game Log

Date	Opponent	Race	W/L	Score	Location
3-Jun	Hilldale	B	L	10–5	Atlantic City
4-Jun	Woodbury (NJ)	W	W	8–1	Woodbury
8-Jun	Lit Brothers (Philadelphia)	W	L	4–3	Atlantic City
9-Jun	Lincoln Giants	B	W	3–2	Atlantic City
10-Jun	Lincoln Giants	B	W	6–5	Atlantic City
11-Jun	Lincoln Giants	B	L	6–2	Atlantic City
14-Jun	Baltimore Black Sox	B	L	2–1	Baltimore
15-Jun	Washington Potomacs	B	L	9–8	Washington, D.C.
16-Jun	Harrisburg Giants	B	W	10–3	Harrisburg
17-Jun	Harrisburg Giants	B	L	2–1	Harrisburg
19-Jun	Chester (PA)	W	L	8–7	Vineland, NJ
21-Jun	Chester (PA)	W	W	6–3	Chester
21-Jun	Chester (PA)	W	L	7–2	Chester
22-Jun	Ascension (Philadelphia)	W	W	4–3	Atlantic City
23-Jun	New York Cuban Stars	B	W	20–0	Atlantic City
24-Jun	New York Cuban Stars	B	W	3–2	Atlantic City
25-Jun	New York Cuban Stars	B	W	9–3	Atlantic City
29-Jun	Washington Potomacs	B	W	20–4	Atlantic City
30-Jun	Washington Potomacs	B	W	12–10	Atlantic City
3-Jul	Chester (PA)	W	L	9–7	Millville, NJ
4-Jul	Harrisburg Giants	B	W	9–5	Atlantic City
4-Jul	Harrisburg Giants	B	L	6–1	Atlantic City
5-Jul	Harrisburg Giants	B	L	7–6	Atlantic City
6-Jul	Harrisburg Giants	B	L	8–4	Atlantic City
11-Jul	Lincoln Giants	B	L	5–2	Atlantic City
12-Jul	Camden (NJ)	W	W	8–1	Camden
13-Jul	Lincoln Giants	B	W	7–5	Bronx, NY
13-Jul	Lincoln Giants	B	W	3–1	Bronx, NY
15-Jul	Baltimore Black Sox	B	L	11–9	Atlantic City
15-Jul	Pleasantville (NJ)	W	W	13–5	Pleasantville
16-Jul	Baltimore Black Sox	B	L	8–5	Atlantic City
16-Jul	Pleasantville (NJ)	W	W	9–5	Atlantic City
17-Jul	Washington Potomacs	B	L	4–0	Wilmington, DE
18-Jul	Baltimore Black Sox	B	W	9–4	Atlantic City
19-Jul	Hilldale	B	L	13–9	Darby, PA
19-Jul	Washington Potomacs	B	T	2–2	Wilmington, DE
21-Jul	New York Cuban Stars	B	L	14–4	Atlantic City
22-Jul	New York Cuban Stars	B	L	10–7	Atlantic City
23-Jul	Lit Brothers (Philadelphia)	W	W	5–4	Atlantic City
26-Jul	South Phillies (Philadelphia)	W	W	4–0	Philadelphia
27-Jul	Ascension (Philadelphia)	W	W	8–4	Atlantic City
28-Jul	Brooklyn Royal Giants	B	W	4–0	Atlantic City
29-Jul	Brooklyn Royal Giants	B	L	3–2	Atlantic City
29-Jul	Pleasantville (NJ)	W	L	14–3	Pleasantville
30-Jul	Brooklyn Royal Giants	B	W	10–4	Atlantic City
31-Jul	Glassboro (NJ)	W	T	4–4	Glassboro
1-Aug	Wildwood (NJ)	W	W	6–2	Wildwood
2-Aug	Trenton	W	L	5–4	Trenton
3-Aug	Hilldale	B	W	3–2	Atlantic City
4-Aug	Hilldale	B	L	8–1	Atlantic City
5-Aug	Hilldale	B	W	3–2	Atlantic City
6-Aug	St. Louis Giants	B	W	18–0	Atlantic City
7-Aug	Trenton	W	W	8–3	Atlantic City
8-Aug	Trenton	W	W	7–6	Atlantic City
9-Aug	Camden (NJ)	W	L	5–4	Camden
10-Aug	Camden (NJ)	W	W	7–3	Atlantic City
11-Aug	Chester (PA)	W	W	4–3	Atlantic City
12-Aug	Chester (PA)	W	L	7–2	Atlantic City
13-Aug	St. Louis Giants	B	W	19–0	Atlantic City
14-Aug	Harrisburg Giants	B	L	3–2	Harrisburg
15-Aug	Harrisburg Giants	B	W	8–7	Harrisburg
16-Aug	Trenton	W	W	5–1	Trenton
17-Aug	Washington Potomacs	B	L	9–3	Atlantic City
18-Aug	Washington Potomacs	B	W	6–2	Atlantic City
19-Aug	Cuban Stars	B	W	8–7	Atlantic City
19-Aug	Pleasantville (NJ)	W	T	5–5	Pleasantville

Date	Opponent	Race	W/L	Score	Location
20-Aug	Cuban Stars	B	W	7–6	Atlantic City
21-Aug	Strawbridge and Clothier (Philadelphia)	W	W	10–6	Philadelphia
23-Aug	Chester (PA)	W	W	2–1	Chester
23-Aug	Chester (PA)	W	L	9–1	Chester
24-Aug	Harrisburg Giants	B	W	8–2	Atlantic City
28-Aug	Ascension (Philadelphia)	W	W	5–1	Philadelphia
29-Aug	Bridgeton (NJ)	W	W	7–6	Bridgeton
30-Aug	Elgawa (Millville, NJ)	W	W	6–3	Millville
30-Aug	Elgawa (Millville, NJ)	W	W	4–3	Millville
31-Aug	Lit Brothers (Philadelphia)	W	W	2–1	Atlantic City
1-Sep	Upland (PA)	W	W	5–0	Atlantic City
1-Sep	Upland (PA)	W	W	6–1	Atlantic City
2-Sep	Brooklyn Royal Giants	B	W	4–3	Atlantic City
4-Sep	Brooklyn Royal Giants	B	L	3–2	Atlantic City
6-Sep	Camden (NJ)	W	W	6–4	Camden
7-Sep	Washington Potomacs	B	W	6–5	Atlantic City
8-Sep	Lincoln Giants	B	W	4–1	Atlantic City
10-Sep	Lincoln Giants	B	L	9–1	Atlantic City
11-Sep	Hilldale	B	W	6–5	Atlantic City
12-Sep	Lit Brothers (Philadelphia)	W	L	2–1	Philadelphia
13-Sep	Hilldale	B	L	3–0	Darby, PA
14-Sep	Jeffries Athletic Club (Atlantic City)	W	W	5–0	Atlantic City
14-Sep	Pleasantville (NJ)	W	W	1–0	Atlantic City
15-Sep	New York Cuban Stars	B	W	5–1	Atlantic City
16-Sep	New York Cuban Stars	B	T	6–6	Atlantic City
22-Sep	Camden (NJ)	W	W	4–3	Atlantic City
23-Sep	Camden (NJ)	W	L	4–3	Atlantic City
28-Sep	Baltimore Black Sox	B	L	2–1	Baltimore
28-Sep	Baltimore Black Sox	B	L	3–2	Baltimore
10-Oct	McInnis Minor League All-Stars	W	W	4–0	Philadelphia
11-Oct	McInnis Minor League All-Stars	W	W	8–0	Philadelphia

1925 Bacharach Giants (70–52–5)

Date	Opponent	Race	W/L	Score	Location
19-Apr	Bushwicks (Brooklyn)	W	W	6–3	Brooklyn, NY
22-Apr	Morris Guards (Atlantic City)	W	W	5–1	Atlantic City
25-Apr	Camden (NJ) Skeeters	W	L	7–4	Camden
26-Apr	Lincoln Giants	B	L	6–1	Bronx, NY
26-Apr	Lincoln Giants	B	L	4–3	Bronx, NY
29-Apr	Harrisburg Senators	W	W	10–6	Harrisburg
3-May	Brooklyn Royal Giants	B	W	5–4	Jersey City, NJ
3-May	Brooklyn Royal Giants	B	W	4–2	Jersey City, NJ
9-May	Pleasantville (NJ)	W	W	12–1	Pleasantville
10-May	New York Cuban Stars	B	W	9–6	Jersey City, NJ
10-May	New York Cuban Stars	B	T	3–3	Jersey City, NJ
14-May	Hilldale	B	W	2–1	Darby, PA
15-May	Brooklyn Royal Giants	B	L	8–4	Atlantic City
16-May	Hilldale	B	L	7–3	Darby, PA
18-May	Harrisburg Giants	B	L	12–7	Harrisburg
19-May	Harrisburg Giants	B	W	5–4	Harrisburg
20-May	Harrisburg Giants	B	L	4–3	Harrisburg
21-May	Hilldale	B	W	8–6	Philadelphia
22-May	Easton (PA)	W	W	15–4	Easton
24-May	Baltimore Black Sox	B	W	14–8	Baltimore
26-May	Wilmington Potomacs	B	L	11–6	Philadelphia
27-May	Glassboro (NJ)	W	W	6–2	Woodbury, NJ
30-May	Brooklyn Royal Giants	B	W	3–0	Brooklyn, NY
31-May	Doherty Silk Sox (Paterson, NJ)	W	L	6–1	Clifton, NJ
1-Jun	Wilmington Potomacs	B	W	6–4	Wilmington, DE
3-Jun	Wilmington Potomacs	B	W	7–1	Wilmington, DE
6-Jun	Trenton	W	L	9–4	Trenton
7-Jun	Camden (NJ) Skeeters	B	W	10–1	Atlantic City
8-Jun	Harrisburg Giants	B	L	6–4	Harrisburg
10-Jun	Harrisburg Giants	B	L	15–14	Harrisburg

Appendix A: Game Log

Date	Opponent	Race	W/L	Score	Location
11-Jun	Hilldale	B	L	11–4	Darby, PA
12-Jun	Harrisburg Giants	B	W	8–3	Carlisle, PA
13-Jun	Camden (NJ) Skeeters	W	L	11–5	Camden
14-Jun	Baltimore Black Sox	B	W	1–0	Baltimore
14-Jun	Baltimore Black Sox	B	L	5–2	Baltimore
20-Jun	Passyunk Artisans (Philadelphia)	W	W	12–7	Philadelphia
21-Jun	Farmers (New York City)	W	W	4–1	Queens, NY
21-Jun	Farmers (New York City)	W	W	14–8	Queens, NY
22-Jun	New York Cuban Stars	B	L	12–3	Atlantic City
23-Jun	New York Cuban Stars	B	W	13–7	Atlantic City
25-Jun	Wilmington Potomacs	B	W	7–2	Atlantic City
27-Jun	Lit Brothers (Philadelphia)	W	W	4–3	Philadelphia
28-Jun	Hilldale	B	L	3–2	Jersey City, NJ
28-Jun	Hilldale	B	L	7–2	Jersey City, NJ
30-Jun	Wilmington Potomacs	B	W	5–4	Atlantic City
1-Jul	Melrose Athletic C;lub (Atlantic City)	W	W	5–2	Atlantic City
2-Jul	Allentown (PA) Dukes	W	L	5–3	Allentown
3-Jul	Harrisburg Giants	B	L	6–4	Harrisburg
4-Jul	Harrisburg Giants	B	L	9–1	Harrisburg
4-Jul	Harrisburg Giants	B	W	3–2	Harrisburg
5-Jul	Bushwicks (Brooklyn)	W	L	5–4	Brooklyn, NY
5-Jul	Bushwicks (Brooklyn)	W	L	8–4	Brooklyn, NY
6-Jul	Brooklyn Royal Giants	B	L	6–4	Atlantic City
7-Jul	Brooklyn Royal Giants	B	W	4–2	Atlantic City
9-Jul	College Point (New York City)	W	L	5–4	Queens, NY
12-Jul	Harrisburg Giants	B	L	5–4	Lancaster, PA
13-Jul	Camden (NJ) Skeeters	W	W	7–6	Atlantic City
15-Jul	Harrisburg Giants	B	L	8–3	Atlantic City
16-Jul	Harrisburg Giants	B	W	13–9	Atlantic City
17-Jul	Camden (NJ) Skeeters	W	L	5–2	Camden
18-Jul	Camden (NJ) Skeeters	W	L	5–4	Camden
20-Jul	Lincoln Giants	B	W	11–2	Atlantic City
21-Jul	Lincoln Giants	B	W	7–6	Atlantic City
22-Jul	Ocean City (NJ) Collegians	W	W	3–1	Ocean City
23-Jul	Ocean City (NJ) Collegians	W	W	6–0	Ocean City
24-Jul	Salem (NJ)	W	L	3–2	Salem
26-Jul	Baltimore Black Sox	B	W	13–8	Baltimore
26-Jul	Baltimore Black Sox	B	L	3–1	Baltimore
27-Jul	New York Cuban Stars	B	L	6–1	Atlantic City
28-Jul	New York Cuban Stars	B	L	8–5	Atlantic City
29-Jul	Camden (NJ) Skeeters	W	T	5–5	Camden
30-Jul	Hilldale	B	L	5–4	Philadelphia
1-Aug	Lit Brothers (Philadelphia)	W	W	5–1	Philadelphia
2-Aug	Lincoln Giants	B	W	10–8	Bronx, NY
2-Aug	Lincoln Giants	B	W	13–6	Bronx, NY
3-Aug	Baltimore Black Sox	B	W	4–2	Atlantic City
4-Aug	Baltimore Black Sox	B	L	7–3	Atlantic City
6-Aug	Hammonton (NJ) Peaches	W	L	4–2	Hammonton
8-Aug	Camden (NJ) Skeeters	W	W	8–7	Camden
9-Aug	Hilldale	B	W	2–1	Atlantic City
10-Aug	Hilldale	B	L	5–2	Atlantic City
11-Aug	Yonkers (NY) Caseys	W	W	10–3	Yonkers
15-Aug	Allentown (PA) Dukes	W	W	7–2	Allentown
15-Aug	Allentown (PA) Dukes	W	W	9–1	Allentown
16-Aug	Farmers (New York City)	W	W	7–2	Queens, NY
16-Aug	Farmers (New York City)	W	W	8–4	Queens, NY
17-Aug	New York Cuban Stars	B	W	3–1	Atlantic City
18-Aug	New York Cuban Stars	B	L	5–4	Atlantic City
19-Aug	Baltimore Black Sox	B	W	10–9	Atlantic City
20-Aug	Hilldale	B	L	8–1	Darby, PA
22-Aug	Hilldale	B	L	1–0	Darby, PA
23-Aug	Baltimore Black Sox	B	W	4–3	Baltimore
23-Aug	Baltimore Black Sox	B	L	5–0	Baltimore
24-Aug	Baltimore Black Sox	B	W	6–0	Richmond, VA
28-Aug	Harrisburg Giants	B	L	7–6	Williamsport, PA
29-Aug	Harrisburg Giants	B	T	2–2	Harrisburg

Date	Opponent	Race	W/L	Score	Location
29-Aug	Harrisburg Giants	B	L	4–3	Harrisburg
31-Aug	South Philadelphia Hebrew Association	W	W	6–5	Atlantic City
1-Sep	Vineland (NJ)	W	W	4–2	Vineland
2-Sep	Wildwood (NJ)	W	W	11–5	Wildwood
3-Sep	New York Bloomer Girls	W	W	11–8	Atlantic City
6-Sep	Lincoln Giants	B	L	4–3	Bronx, NY
6-Sep	Lincoln Giants	B	W	4–3	Bronx, NY
7-Sep	Hazelton (PA)	W	W	7–4	Hazelton
7-Sep	Hazelton (PA)	W	L	10–3	Hazelton
8-Sep	Harrisburg Giants	B	W	9–2	Harrisburg
9-Sep	Harrisburg Giants	B	W	7–6	Atlantic City
10-Sep	Harrisburg Giants	B	W	8–2	Atlantic City
12-Sep	Allentown (PA) Dukes	W	L	12–6	Allentown
13-Sep	Bay Ridge (Brooklyn)	W	W	3–2	Brooklyn, NY
13-Sep	Bay Ridge (Brooklyn)	W	W	6–2	Brooklyn, NY
14-Sep	Lit Brothers (Philadelphia)	W	W	7–0	Philadelphia
15-Sep	Baltimore Black Sox	B	W	5–0	Atlantic City
18-Sep	Baltimore Black Sox	B	L	3–2	Atlantic City
19-Sep	Camden (NJ) Skeeters	W	W	3–0	Camden
19-Sep	Camden (NJ) Skeeters	W	L	1–0	Camden
20-Sep	Bushwicks (Brooklyn)	W	L	12–10	Brooklyn, NY
20-Sep	Bushwicks (Brooklyn)	W	W	6–1	Brooklyn, NY
22-Sep	Hilldale	B	L	6–1	Woodbury, NJ
23-Sep	Hilldale	B	W	5–1	Mount Holly, NJ
24-Sep	Hilldale	B	L	6–1	Darby, PA
25-Sep	Atlantic City Police	W	W	6–0	Atlantic City
29-Sep	New York Cuban Stars	B	W	3–2	Atlantic City
30-Sep	New York Cuban Stars	B	L	4–1	Atlantic City
3-Oct	Camden (NJ) Skeeters	W	W	7–3	Camden
3-Oct	Camden (NJ) Skeeters	W	T	3–3	Camden
4-Oct	Bay Ridge (Brooklyn)	W	T	2–2	Brooklyn, NY

1926 Bacharach Giants (67–48–6)

Date	Opponent	Race	W/L	Score	Location
18-Apr	Bushwicks (Brooklyn)	W	L	4–2	Brooklyn, NY
25-Apr	Bay Ridge (Brooklyn)	W	L	8–6	Brooklyn, NY
1-May	Hilldale	B	L	5–4	Darby, PA
2-May	Farmers (Queens)	W	W	10–6	Queens, NY
2-May	Farmers (Queens)	W	L	10–5	Queens, NY
6-May	Camden (NJ) Skeeters	W	L	10–5	West Chester, PA
7-May	Harrisburg Giants	B	L	2–1	Harrisburg
8-May	Harrisburg Giants	B	L	9–4	Harrisburg
9-May	Lincoln Giants	B	W	8–2	Bronx, NY
9-May	Lincoln Giants	B	L	11–7	Bronx, NY
10-May	Allentown (PA) Dukes	W	W	3–0	Atlantic City
11-May	Allentown (PA) Dukes	W	W	6–1	Atlantic City
12-May	Chester (PA)	W	T	3–3	Chester
14-May	Hilldale	B	L	6–4	Wilmington
17-May	Camden (NJ) Skeeters	W	W	9–4	Atlantic City
18-May	New York Cuban Stars	B	L	7–6	Atlantic City
22-May	Camden (NJ) Skeeters	W	L	9–8	Camden
23-May	Baltimore Black Sox	B	W	8–6	Baltimore
23-May	Baltimore Black Sox	B	L	7–3	Baltimore
24-May	Chester (PA)	W	W	6–3	Atlantic City
25-May	Chester (PA)	W	W	6–3	Atlantic City
29-May	Chester (PA)	W	L	5–3	Chester
30-May	Allentown (PA) Dukes	W	W	11–7	Allentown
1-Jun	Baltimore Black Sox	B	W	8–3	Atlantic City
2-Jun	Camden (NJ) Skeeters	W	W	15–1	Camden
6-Jun	Lincoln Giants	B	L	9–6	Bronx, NY
6-Jun	Lincoln Giants	B	W	5–1	Bronx, NY
7-Jun	Baltimore Black Sox	B	W	7–3	Atlantic City
9-Jun	Hilldale	B	W	7–4	Atlantic City
10-Jun	Chester (PA)	W	L	3–1	Atlantic City

Appendix A: Game Log

Date	Opponent	Race	W/L	Score	Location
11-Jun	Hilldale	B	L	3–2	Wilmington, DE
13-Jun	Allentown (PA) Dukes	W	W	14–2	Allentown
13-Jun	Allentown (PA) Dukes	W	L	20–19	Allentown
14-Jun	Camden (NJ) Skeeters	W	L	4–3	Atlantic City
16-Jun	Harrisburg Giants	B	L	3–2	Atlantic City
17-Jun	Harrisburg Giants	B	L	4–3	Atlantic City
19-Jun	Chester (PA)	W	W	6–5	Chester
19-Jun	Chester (PA)	W	L	4–3	Chester
20-Jun	Chester (PA)	W	W	3–1	Atlantic City
21-Jun	Brooklyn Royal Giants	B	W	9–4	Atlantic City
22-Jun	Brooklyn Royal Giants	B	W	3–2	Atlantic City
24-Jun	Baltimore Black Sox	B	L	8–5	Atlantic City
25-Jun	Camden (NJ) Skeeters	W	W	5–2	Atlantic City
26-Jun	Newton Coal (Philadelphia)	W	W	6–1	Philadelphia
27-Jun	Baltimore Black Sox	B	W	13–2	Baltimore
27-Jun	Baltimore Black Sox	B	L	8–5	Baltimore
28-Jun	Camden (NJ) Skeeters	W	L	4–2	Atlantic City
29-Jun	Camden (NJ) Skeeters	W	W	10–2	Atlantic City
30-Jun	Harrisburg Giants	B	L	4–0	Atlantic City
1-Jul	Harrisburg Giants	B	W	11–5	Atlantic City
2-Jul	Ocean City (NJ) Rivieras	W	W	8–3	Ocean City
3-Jul	Camden (NJ) Skeeters	W	L	9–5	Camden
3-Jul	Camden (NJ) Skeeters	W	W	3–2	Camden
4-Jul	Hilldale	B	W	3–1	Atlantic City
7-Jul	New York Cuban Stars	B	W	6–2	Atlantic City
8-Jul	New York Cuban Stars	B	W	6–4	Atlantic City
12-Jul	Brooklyn Royal Giants	B	W	7–6	Atlantic City
13-Jul	Brooklyn Royal Giants	B	W	4–3	Atlantic City
17-Jul	Parkesburg Iron (Parkesburg, PA)	W	W	3–2	Parkesburg
18-Jul	Harrisburg Giants	B	W	4–1	Atlantic City
19-Jul	Harrisburg Giants	B	W	8–3	Atlantic City
21-Jul	Lincoln Giants	B	W	7–3	Atlantic City
22-Jul	Lincoln Giants	B	W	2–1	Atlantic City
24-Jul	Camden (NJ) Skeeters	W	W	17–7	Camden
25-Jul	New York Cuban Stars	B	W	6–5	Atlantic City
26-Jul	New York Cuban Stars	B	L	5–4	Atlantic City
27-Jul	New York Cuban Stars	B	W	9–1	Atlantic City
30-Jul	Camden (NJ) Skeeters	W	L	1–1 forfeit	Chester
1-Aug	Lincoln Giants	B	L	4–0	Bronx, NY
1-Aug	Lincoln Giants	B	L	7–5	Bronx, NY
3-Aug	Camden (NJ) Skeeters	W	L	12–4	Atlantic City
4-Aug	Baltimore Black Sox	B	W	4–4 forfeit	Atlantic City
5-Aug	Baltimore Black Sox	B	W	6–1	Atlantic City
6-Aug	Hilldale	B	W	6–4	Wilmington, DE
7-Aug	East Orange (NJ)	W	W	7–2	Newark, NJ
8-Aug	Hilldale	B	W	1–0	Atlantic City
9-Aug	Hilldale	B	L	8–6	Atlantic City
11-Aug	Trenton	W	T	2–2	Trenton
12-Aug	Hilldale	B	L	4–3	Darby, PA
13-Aug	Hilldale	B	L	3–2	Wilmington, DE
14-Aug	Hilldale	B	W	5–0	Darby, PA
15-Aug	Baltimore Black Sox	B	W	5–4	Baltimore
15-Aug	Baltimore Black Sox	B	T	6–6	Baltimore
19-Aug	New York Cuban Stars	B	W	6–5	Atlantic City
19-Aug	Atlantic City Police	W	W	11–0	Atlantic City
20-Aug	New York Cuban Stars	B	W	3–0	Atlantic City
23-Aug	Brooklyn Royal Giants	B	W	5–2	Atlantic City
24-Aug	Brooklyn Royal Giants	B	W	4–1	Atlantic City
24-Aug	Hilldale	B	W	3–2	Atlantic City
26-Aug	Brooklyn Royal Giants	B	W	6–0	Atlantic City
28-Aug	Parkesburg Iron (Parkesburg, PA)	W	W	6–3	Parkesburg
29-Aug	Bay Ridge (Brooklyn)	W	W	2–0	Brooklyn, NY
29-Aug	Bay Ridge (Brooklyn)	W	L	5–4	Brooklyn, NY
30-Aug	Ocean City (NJ) Rivieras	W	W	10–0	Ocean City
31-Aug	Ocean City (NJ) Rivieras	W	W	3–2	Ocean City
3-Sep	Brooklyn Royal Giants	N	W	2–1	Atlantic City

Appendix A: Game Log

Date	Opponent	Race	W/L	Score	Location
4-Sep	Brooklyn Royal Giants	N	W	5–1	Atlantic City
7-Sep	Baltimore Black Sox	N	L	6–5	Atlantic City
8-Sep	Baltimore Black Sox	N	W	8–0	Atlantic City
9-Sep	Camden (NJ) Skeeters	W	L	8–5	Atlantic City
11-Sep	Camden (NJ) Skeeters	W	L	1–0	Camden
11-Sep	Camden (NJ) Skeeters	W	W	3–1	Camden
13-Sep	Baltimore Black Sox	B	T	8–8	Baltimore
18-Sep	Hilldale	B	W	11–2	Darby, PA
18-Sep	Hilldale	B	L	1–0	Darby, PA
19-Sep	Brooklyn Royal Giants	B	W	6–3	Brooklyn, NY
19-Sep	Brooklyn Royal Giants	B	L	6–0	Brooklyn, NY
20-Sep	Brooklyn Royal Giants	B	L	6–2	Atlantic City
21-Sep	Brooklyn Royal Giants	B	L	9–3	Atlantic City
26-Sep	Baltimore Black Sox	**B**	L	14–13	Baltimore

1926 Negro World Series

Date	Opponent	Race	W/L	Score	Location
1-Oct	Chicago American Giants	B	T	3–3	Atlantic City
2-Oct	Chicago American Giants	B	L	7–6	Atlantic City
3-Oct	Chicago American Giants	B	W	10–0	Baltimore
4-Oct	Chicago American Giants	B	T	4–4	Phillies Park
5-Oct	Chicago American Giants	B	W	7–5	Phillies Park
6-Oct	Chicago American Giants	B	W	6–4	Atlantic City
9-Oct	Chicago American Giants	B	L	5–4	Chicago
10-Oct	Chicago American Giants	B	W	3–0	Chicago
11-Oct	Chicago American Giants	B	L	6–3	Chicago
13-Oct	Chicago American Giants	B	L	13–0	Chicago
14-Oct	Chicago American Giants	B	L	1–0	Chicago

1927 Bacharach Giants (77–48–2)

Date	Opponent	Race	W/L	Score	Location
17-Apr	Hilldale	B	W	10–0	Atlantic City
18-Apr	Philadelphia Giants	B	W	9–9	Atlantic City
19-Apr	Philadelphia Giants	B	W	14–2	Atlantic City
23-Apr	Camden (NJ) Skeeters	W	L	7–0	Camden
24-Apr	Chappy Johnson's Stars	B	W	8–3	Atlantic City
30-Apr	Camden (NJ) Skeeters	W	W	16–5	Camden
1-May	New York Cuban Stars	B	W	3–2	Newark, NJ
1-May	New York Cuban Stars	B	W	7–4	Newark, NJ
6-May	Harrisburg Giants	B	L	4–1	Harrisburg
7-May	Harrisburg Giants	B	W	5–3	Harrisburg
8-May	Brooklyn Royal Giants	B	W	14–8	Atlantic City
9-May	Brooklyn Royal Giants	B	W	3–2	Atlantic City
10-May	Brooklyn Royal Giants	B	L	8–7	Atlantic City
12-May	Hilldale	B	W	5–2	Darby, PA
14-May	Hilldale	B	L	4–2	Darby, PA
15-May	Harrisburg Giants	B	L	4–3	Atlantic City
21-May	Harrisburg Giants	B	L	5–4	Harrisburg
22-May	Baltimore Black Sox	B	L	6–4	Baltimore
22-May	Baltimore Black Sox	B	W	5–3	Baltimore
23-May	Hilldale	B	W	6–2	Norfolk
24-May	Hilldale	B	L	7–4	Norfolk
28-May	Lincoln Giants	B	W	6–3	Mount Holly, NJ
29-May	Lincoln Giants	B	W	12–7	Bronx, NY
29-May	Lincoln Giants	B	W	4–2	Bronx, NY
30-May	Harrowgate (Philadelphia)	W	W	11–1	Atlantic City
31-May	Lincoln Giants	B	W	13–3	Atlantic City
1-Jun	Lincoln Giants	B	L	7–4	Atlantic City
2-Jun	Lincoln Giants	B	W	6–3	Atlantic City
5-Jun	Farmers (Queens)	W	W	14–7	Queens, NY
6-Jun	New York Cuban Stars	B	W	6–5	Atlantic City
7-Jun	New York Cuban Stars	B	L	7–4	Atlantic City

Appendix A: Game Log

Date	Opponent	Race	W/L	Score	Location
8-Jun	New York Cuban Stars	B	W	9–1	Atlantic City
10-Jun	Hilldale	B	W	12–10	Wilmington, DE
11-Jun	Camden (NJ) Skeeters	W	W	16–6	Camden
12-Jun	Brooklyn Royal Giants	B	W	9–4	Atlantic City
13-Jun	Harrisburg Giants	B	W	3–2	Richmond
15-Jun	Harrisburg Giants	B	L	11–2	Richmond
15-Jun	Harrisburg Giants	B	L	4–3	Richmond
16-Jun	Harrisburg Giants	B	W	6–3	Atlantic City
17-Jun	Harrisburg Giants	B	W	7–5	Atlantic City
18-Jun	Harrisburg Giants	B	W	4–3	Atlantic City
19-Jun	Bushwicks (Brooklyn)	W	W	5–3	Brooklyn, NY
20-Jun	Hilldale	B	L	4–3	Atlantic City
22-Jun	Camden (NJ) Skeeters	W	L	9–4	Camden
23-Jun	Hilldale	B	W	8–3	Darby, PA
24-Jun	Hilldale	B	L	8–1	Mount Holly, NJ
25-Jun	Hilldale	B	W	16–0	Darby, PA
25-Jun	Hilldale	B	W	8–6	Darby, PA
26-Jun	North Philadelphia	W	W	4–2	Atlantic City
27-Jun	Baltimore Black Sox	B	W	6–2	Atlantic City
28-Jun	Baltimore Black Sox	B	W	11–9	Atlantic City
29-Jun	Baltimore Black Sox	B	W	9–4	Atlantic City
30-Jun	Lamott (Philadelphia)	W	W	4–2	Philadelphia
1-Jul	Camden (NJ) Skeeters	W	W	7–5	Atlantic City
2-Jul	Camden (NJ) Skeeters	W	L	12–4	Camden
3-Jul	Hilldale	B	W	15–5	Atlantic City
4-Jul	Harrisburg Giants	B	L	5–4	Lancaster, PA
4-Jul	Harrisburg Giants	B	L	9–6	Harrisburg
5-Jul	Harrisburg Giants	B	L	6–5	Harrisburg
6-Jul	Harrisburg Giants	B	L	4–2	Harrisburg
7-Jul	Harrowgate (Philadelphia)	W	L	15–14	Philadelphia
10-Jul	Farmers (Queens)	W	L	2–1	Queens, NY
11-Jul	Harrisburg Giants	B	W	7–1	Atlantic City
12-Jul	Harrisburg Giants	B	W	7–3	Atlantic City
13-Jul	Harrisburg Giants	B	W	4–3	Atlantic City
14-Jul	Harrisburg Giants	B	W	6–5	Asbury Park, NJ
15-Jul	Kensington Congregational (Philadelphia)	W	L	7–4	Philadelphia
17-Jul	New York Cuban Stars	B	L	6–3	Newark, NJ
17-Jul	New York Cuban Stars	B	L	5–4	Newark, NJ
20-Jul	Brooklyn Royal Giants	B	W	7–5	Atlantic City
21-Jul	Hilldale	B	L	11–10	Darby, PA
23-Jul	Hilldale	B	L	5–3	Darby, PA
24-Jul	New York Cuban Stars	B	W	8–0	Atlantic City
25-Jul	New York Cuban Stars	B	L	7–6	Atlantic City
26-Jul	New York Cuban Stars	B	W	8–7	Atlantic City
27-Jul	Baltimore Black Sox	B	L	11–3	Atlantic City
28-Jul	Baltimore Black Sox	B	W	11–0	Atlantic City
30-Jul	Camden (NJ) Skeeters	W	L	15–5	Camden
2-Aug	Baltimore Black Sox	B	W	11–6	Atlantic City
3-Aug	Baltimore Black Sox	B	W	2–0	Atlantic City
4-Aug	Brooklyn Royal Giants	B	W	5–4	Atlantic City
6-Aug	Paterson (NJ) Silk Sox	W	W	3–2	Asbury Park, NJ
7-Aug	Hilldale	B	L	4–1	Atlantic City
8-Aug	Hilldale	B	W	10–1	Atlantic City
9-Aug	Hilldale	B	W	4–2	Atlantic City
10-Aug	Millville (NJ)	W	W	8–4	Millville
13-Aug	Ocean City (NJ) Collegians	W	W	7–2	Ocean City
14-Aug	Harrisburg Giants	B	W	20–5	Atlantic City
15-Aug	Harrisburg Giants	B	W	5–4	Atlantic City
16-Aug	Harrisburg Giants	B	W	9–4	Atlantic City
17-Aug	Harrisburg Giants	B	L	6–5	Harrisburg
19-Aug	Harrisburg Giants	B	L	8–5	Harrisburg
19-Aug	Harrisburg Giants	B	L	10–4	Harrisburg
21-Aug	Hilldale	B	W	3–2	Atlantic City
22-Aug	New York Cuban Stars	B	L	6–5	Atlantic City
23-Aug	New York Cuban Stars	B	W	4–1	Atlantic City
24-Aug	New York Cuban Stars	B	L	2–1	Atlantic City

Date	Opponent	Race	W/L	Score	Location
25-Aug	Hilldale	B	L	22–12	Darby, PA
28-Aug	Brooklyn Royal Giants	B	L	3–2	Atlantic City
29-Aug	Brooklyn Royal Giants	B	W	9–3	Atlantic City
30-Aug	Brooklyn Royal Giants	B	L	9–8	Atlantic City
3-Sep	Pleasantville (NJ)	W	W	6–0	Pleasantville
4-Sep	Baltimore Black Sox	B	L	8–7	Baltimore
4-Sep	Baltimore Black Sox	B	W	3–2	Baltimore
5-Sep	Baltimore Black Sox	B	W	4–3	Atlantic City
5-Sep	Baltimore Black Sox	B	L	6–0	Atlantic City
6-Sep	Baltimore Black Sox	B	W	15–7	Atlantic City
7-Sep	Baltimore Black Sox	B	W	6–5	Atlantic City
10-Sep	Bridgeton (NJ)	W	W	6–4	Bridgeton
11-Sep	Hilldale	B	W	4–1	Atlantic City
12-Sep	Hilldale	B	W	3–1	Atlantic City
13-Sep	Hilldale	B	L	11–4	Atlantic City
17-Sep	Corley Catholic Club (Philadelphia)	W	W	8–3	Philadelphia
21-Sep	Washington Potomacs	B	W	6–0	Atlantic City
24-Sep	Wentz-Olney (Philadelphia)	W	W	8–7	Philadelphia
25-Sep	Hilldale	B	W	10–8	Allentown, PA
25-Sep	Hilldale	B	T	7–7	Allentown, PA
21-Oct	American League Stars	W	L	3–0	Atlantic City

1927 Negro World Series

Date	Opponent	Race	W/L	Score	Location
1-Oct	Chicago American Giants	B	L	6–2	Chicago
2-Oct	Chicago American Giants	B	L	11–1	Chicago
3-Oct	Chicago American Giants	B	L	7–0	Chicago
4-Oct	Chicago American Giants	B	L	9–1	Chicago
8-Oct	Chicago American Giants	B	W	3–2	Bacharach Park
10-Oct	Chicago American Giants	B	T	1–1	Bacharach Park
11-Oct	Chicago American Giants	B	W	8–1	Bacharach Park
12-Oct	Chicago American Giants	B	W	6–5	Bacharach Park
13-Oct	Chicago American Giants	B	L	11–4	Bacharach Park

1928 Bacharach Giants (54–38–4)

Date	Opponent	Race	W/L	Score	Location
17-Apr	Hilldale	B	L	2–0	Durham, NC
18-Apr	Hilldale	B	L	9–1	Durham, NC
29-Apr	Lincoln Giants	B	L	4–2	Bronx, NY
29-Apr	Lincoln Giants	B	L	10–3	Bronx, NY
5-May	Philadelphia Tigers	B	W	10–6	Philadelphia
6-May	Baltimore Black Sox	B	L	2–0	Baltimore
6-May	Baltimore Black Sox	B	L	8–6	Baltimore
7-May	Baltimore Black Sox	B	W	3–2	Richmond
12-May	Kensington Congregational (Philadelphia)	W	W	7–5	Philadelphia
13-May	Farmers (Queens)	W	W	13–8	Queens, NY
13-May	Farmers (Queens)	W	W	6–1	Queens, NY
18-May	Kensington Congregational (Philadelphia)	W	W	11–4	Philadelphia
20-May	Lincoln Giants	B	L	14–7	Bronx, NY
24-May	Atlantic City Police	W	W	8–4	Atlantic City
26-May	Harrowgate (Philadelphia)	W	L	7–0	Philadelphia
30-May	Philadelphia Elks	B	W	7–2	Atlantic City
30-May	Philadelphia Tigers	B	W	5–2	Atlantic City
31-May	Hilldale	B	T	8–8	Darby, PA
1-Jun	Baltimore Black Sox	B	W	7–2	Atlantic City
2-Jun	Baltimore Black Sox	B	L	7–2	Atlantic City
3-Jun	Hilldale	B	W	5–2	Atlantic City
5-Jun	Hilldale	B	L	4–3	Atlantic City
5-Jun	Hilldale	B	L	5–0	Atlantic City
7-Jun	Hilldale	B	L	8–5	Darby, PA
8-Jun	Santop's Bronchos (Philadelphia)	B	W	2–0	Atlantic City
9-Jun	Hilldale	B	W	12–6	Darby, PA

Date	Opponent	Race	W/L	Score	Location
10-Jun	Farmers (Queens)	W	L	1–0	Queens, NY
10-Jun	Farmers (Queens)	W	L	9–6	Queens, NY
12-Jun	Baltimore Black Sox	B	L	6–5	Atlantic City
13-Jun	Baltimore Black Sox	B	W	5–3	Atlantic City
15-Jun	Baltimore Black Sox	B	W	5–2	Wildwood, NJ
16-Jun	Lancaster (PA) 8th Ward	W	ND	19–0	Wildwood, NJ
17-Jun	Baltimore Black Sox	B	L	3–2	Baltimore
17-Jun	Baltimore Black Sox	B	L	4–2	Baltimore
18-Jun	New York Cuban Stars	B	W	7–6	Atlantic City
19-Jun	New York Cuban Stars	B	W	8–7	Atlantic City
23-Jun	Harrowgate (Philadelphia)	W	W	6–4	Philadelphia
24-Jun	Harrowgate (Philadelphia)	W	W	9–7	Atlantic City
24-Jun	Harrowgate (Philadelphia)	W	L	4–0	Atlantic City
28-Jun	Harrisburg Giants	B	W	10–5	Atlantic City
26-Jun	Harrisburg Giants	B	W	9–2	Atlantic City
27-Jun	Atlantic City Police	W	W	9–1	Atlantic City
30-Jun	Harrisburg Giants	B	W	6–3	Parkesburg, PA
1-Jul	Hilldale	B	L	2–1	Atlantic City
1-Jul	Hilldale	B	ND	3–1	Atlantic City
2-Jul	Hilldale	B	W	11–1	Atlantic City
3-Jul	Hilldale	B	W	3–2	Atlantic City
4-Jul	St. Louis Giants	B	W	11–4	Atlantic City
4-Jul	St. Louis Giants	B	W	9–1	Atlantic City
5-Jul	St. Louis Giants	B	L	13–9	Atlantic City
7-Jul	Trenton Young Italian Americans	W	W	7–6	Trenton
8-Jul	Philadelphia Elks	W	W	7–6	Atlantic City
8-Jul	Philadelphia Elks	W	W	7–6	Atlantic City
9-Jul	Baltimore Black Sox	B	W	21–1	Atlantic City
10-Jul	Baltimore Black Sox	B	T	4–4	Atlantic City
11-Jul	House of David	W	W	20–10	Atlantic City
12-Jul	Hilldale	B	L	20–4	Darby, PA
15-Jul	Baltimore Black Sox	B	W	5–4	Baltimore
15-Jul	Baltimore Black Sox	B	L	8–3	Baltimore
16-Jul	Baltimore Black Sox	B	W	4–3	Richmond
17-Jul	Baltimore Black Sox	B	W	9–4	Richmond
18-Jul	Baltimore Black Sox	B	W	6–5	Richmond
19-Jul	Baltimore Black Sox	B	W	15–11	Norfolk
21-Jul	Hilldale	B	L	4–3	Darby, PA
22-Jul	Farmers (Queens)	W	W	11–6	Queens, NY
22-Jul	Farmers (Queens)	W	L	7–4	Queens, NY
25-Jul	West Philadelphia	W	W	7–1	Philadelphia
26-Jul	Hilldale	B	L	3–1	Philadelphia
28-Jul	Ocean City (NJ) Collegians	W	W	8–2	Ocean City
29-Jul	Lincoln Giants	B	W	6–3	Bronx, NY
29-Jul	Lincoln Giants	B	L	10–7	Bronx, NY
30-Jul	Baltimore Black Sox	B	W	5–1	Atlantic City
31-Jul	Baltimore Black Sox	B	W	10–0	Atlantic City
1-Aug	Corley Catholic Club (Philadelphia)	W	W	5–1	Philadelphia
4-Aug	Hilldale	B	W	10–4	Darby, PA
5-Aug	Hilldale	B	L	4–2	Darby, PA
5-Aug	Hilldale	B	W	11–3	Darby, PA
6-Aug	Hilldale	B	L	8–3	Atlantic City
7-Aug	Hilldale	B	W	4–2	Atlantic City
11-Aug	Detroit Stars	B	W	9–7	Detroit
12-Aug	Detroit Stars	B	L	9–2	Detroit
13-Aug	Detroit Stars	B	L	9–6	Detroit
20-Aug	Chicago American Giants	B	W	13–0	Chicago
21-Aug	Chicago American Giants	B	L	4–2	Chicago
22-Aug	Chicago American Giants	B	L	5–0	Chicago
23-Aug	Chicago American Giants	B	W	3–2	Chicago
25-Aug	St. Louis Stars	B	L	9–6	St. Louis
26-Aug	St. Louis Stars	B	L	14–3	St. Louis
27-Aug	St. Louis Stars	B	L	5–4	St. Louis
28-Aug	St. Louis Stars	B	L	6–1	St. Louis
3-Sep	Chester (PA)	W	W	9–1	Atlantic City
3-Sep	Chester (PA)	W	W	6–0	Atlantic City

Date	Opponent	Race	W/L	Score	Location
4-Sep	New York Cuban Stars	B	L	5–2	Atlantic City
9-Sep	Brooklyn Royal Giants	B	L	6–4	Atlantic City
9-Sep	Brooklyn Royal Giants	B	W	6–3	Atlantic City
10-Sep	Brooklyn Royal Giants	B	W	2–0	Atlantic City
11-Sep	Brooklyn Royal Giants	B	L	12–5	Atlantic City

1929 Bacharach Giants (41-59-2)

Date	Opponent	Race	W/L	Score	Location
14-Apr	Jersey City Red Sox	W	L	16–2	Jersey City
23-Apr	Baltimore Black Sox	B	L	4–3	Richmond
24-Apr	Baltimore Black Sox	B	L	21–4	Richmond
28-Apr	Lincoln Giants	B	T	8–8	Bronx, NY
4-May	Homestead Grays	B	L	7–6	Forbes Field
5-May	Homestead Grays	B	L	16–1	Cleveland
5-May	Homestead Grays	B	L	14–2	Cleveland
10-May	Hilldale	B	W	13–7	Philadelphia
11-May	Hilldale	B	L	13–1	Philadelphia
12-May	Baltimore Black Sox	B	L	6–4	Baltimore
12-May	Baltimore Black Sox	B	L	8–0	Baltimore
15-May	South Phillies (Philadelphia)	W	L	4–2	Philadelphia
16-May	Wentz-Olney (Philadelphia)	W	L	12–8	Philadelphia
26-May	Springfields (Queens)	W	L	7–4	Queens, NY
26-May	Springfields (Queens)	W	L	10–8	Queens, NY
30-May	New York Cuban Stars	B	W	4–2	Brooklyn, NY
30-May	New York Cuban Stars	B	W	13–6	Brooklyn, NY
2-Jun	New York Cuban Stars	B	L	8–6	Atlantic City
3-Jun	New York Cuban Stars	B	W	11–4	Atlantic City
7-Jun	Hilldale	B	L	5–2	Philadelphia
9-Jun	Bushwicks (Brooklyn)	W	W	6–5	Brooklyn, NY
9-Jun	Bushwicks (Brooklyn)	W	W	8–4	Brooklyn, NY
11-Jun	Hilldale	B	W	4–3	Atlantic City
12-Jun	South Phillies (Philadelphia)	W	L	5–4	Philadelphia
16-Jun	Baltimore Black Sox	B	L	8–6	Baltimore
16-Jun	Baltimore Black Sox	B	L	10–4	Baltimore
17-Jun	Baltimore Black Sox	B	L	18–3	Baltimore
18-Jun	Baltimore Black Sox	B	L	8–6	Atlantic City
19-Jun	Baltimore Black Sox	B	L	13–3	Atlantic City
20-Jun	Baltimore Black Sox	B	W	8–7	Atlantic City
21-Jun	New York Cuban Stars	B	T	7–7	Philadelphia
22-Jun	New York Cuban Stars	B	W	9–8	Darby, PA
23-Jun	Lincoln Giants	B	L	12–11	Bronx, NY
23-Jun	Lincoln Giants	B	L	8–2	Bronx, NY
24-Jun	Lincoln Giants	B	W	18–9	Bronx, NY
26-Jun	Homestead Grays	B	L	5–4	Atlantic City
27-Jun	Homestead Grays	B	L	5–4	Atlantic City
27-Jun	Homestead Grays	B	W	11–2	Atlantic City
29-Jun	Bradley Beach (NJ)	W	W	4–0	Bradley Beach
30-Jun	Farmers (Queens)	W	W	6–4	Queens, NY
30-Jun	Farmers (Queens)	W	W	5–3	Queens, NY
1-Jul	Lincoln Giants	B	L	8–4	Atlantic City
2-Jul	Lincoln Giants	B	L	3–1	Atlantic City
3-Jul	Lincoln Giants	B	L	18–9	Atlantic City
3-Jul	Lincoln Giants	B	W	14–9	Atlantic City
4-Jul	Hilldale	B	L	9–6	Darby, PA
4-Jul	Hilldale	B	W	19–9	Darby, PA
7-Jul	Bushwicks (Brooklyn)	W	W	7–5	Brooklyn, NY
7-Jul	Bushwicks (Brooklyn)	W	W	4–3	Brooklyn, NY
8-Jul	Baltimore Black Sox	B	L	10–2	Atlantic City
9-Jul	Baltimore Black Sox	B	W	13–7	Atlantic City
13-Jul	House of David	W	W	8–1	Atlantic City
14-Jul	Lincoln Giants	B	L	15–9	Bronx, NY
14-Jul	Lincoln Giants	B	L	14–12	Bronx, NY
15-Jul	Lincoln Giants	B	L	4–1	Atlantic City
16-Jul	Lincoln Giants	B	W	7–6	Atlantic City

Date	Opponent	Race	W/L	Score	Location
17-Jul	South Phillies (Philadelphia)	W	L	10–9	Philadelphia
19-Jul	Hilldale	B	W	7–2	Philadelphia
20-Jul	Hilldale	B	L	13–1	Darby, PA
21-Jul	Hilldale	B	W	5–2	Atlantic City
23-Jul	New York Cuban Stars	B	W	5–4	Atlantic City
28-Jul	Bushwicks (Brooklyn)	W	W	13–2	Brooklyn, NY
28-Jul	Bushwicks (Brooklyn)	W	L	17–0	Brooklyn, NY
29-Jul	Holmesburg (Philadelphia)	W	W	10–2	Philadelphia
30-Jul	Frankford Collegians (Philadelphia)	W	L	5–4	Philadelphia
1-Aug	Red Bank (NJ)	W	W	7–0	Red Bank
3-Aug	Bradley Beach (NJ)	W	W	2–1	Bradley Beach
4-Aug	Hilldale	B	W	4–0	Brooklyn, NY
4-Aug	Bushwicks (Brooklyn)	W	W	6–5	Brooklyn, NY
5-Aug	South Phillies (Philadelphia)	W	L	7–0	Philadelphia
9-Aug	Homestead Grays	B	W	14–10	Forbes Field
11-Aug	Homestead Grays	B	L	4–3	Cleveland
11-Aug	Homestead Grays	B	L	4–1	Cleveland
13-Aug	Massillon (OH) Agathons	W	W	10–3	Canonsburg, PA
15-Aug	Viscose Silk Rayoneers (Lewiston, PA)	W	L	6–3	Lewistown, PA
17-Aug	South Phillies (Philadelphia)	W	W	6–3	Atlantic City
18-Aug	Baltimore Black Sox	B	L	7–2	Baltimore
18-Aug	Baltimore Black Sox	B	L	8–4	Baltimore
19-Aug	New York Cuban Stars	B	L	16–4	Bradley Beach, NJ
20-Aug	Highstown (NJ)	W	W	4–1	Highstown
23-Aug	Hilldale	B	L	6–2	Philadelphia
24-Aug	Hilldale	B	L	11–4	Philadelphia
24-Aug	Holmesburg (Philadelphia)	B	W	5–3	Philadelphia
25-Aug	Hilldale	B	L	8–4	Brooklyn, NY
26-Aug	Homestead Grays	B	W	7–4	Atlantic City
27-Aug	Homestead Grays	B	L	8–0	Atlantic City
28-Aug	Homestead Grays	B	L	11–6	Atlantic City
29-Aug	New York Cuban Stars	B	L	5–3	Atlantic City
30-Aug	New York Cuban Stars	B	L	4–0	Atlantic City
31-Aug	Woodbury (NJ)	W	W	13–12	Woodbury
1-Sep	Bushwicks (Brooklyn)	W	L	7–3	Brooklyn, NY
1-Sep	Bushwicks (Brooklyn)	W	W	5–3	Brooklyn, NY
2-Sep	Baltimore Black Sox	B	L	10–4	Baltimore
3-Sep	Baltimore Black Sox	B	W	12–4	Baltimore
4-Sep	Baltimore Black Sox	B	L	9–4	Richmond
6-Sep	Atlantic City Police	W	W	3–2	Atlantic City
8-Sep	Lincoln Giants	B	L	1–0	Bronx, NY
8-Sep	Lincoln Giants	B	L	13–4	Bronx, NY
15-Sep	Jersey City Red Sox	W	W	8–3	Jersey City
15-Sep	Jersey City Red Sox	W	L	10–3	Jersey City
22-Sep	Bay Parkways (Brooklyn)	W	L	1–0	Brooklyn, NY
22-Sep	Bay Parkways (Brooklyn)	W	L	11–0	Brooklyn, NY

Appendix B: Rosters

1916

	TG	P	C	1B	2B	3B	SS	LF	CF	RF	PH	PR	RP
Banks	11	0	0	0	0	0	0	4	2	5	0	0	0
Crockett, Frank	69	1	1	0	0	4	1	8	55	1	0	0	0
Crump, Willis (Shorty)	43	0	1	0	6	2	11	12	1	12	0	0	0
Cummings, Napoleon (Chance)	70	0	1	69	0	0	0	1	0	0	0	0	1
Davis	1	0	0	0	0	0	0	0	0	1	0	0	0
Deas, James Alvin (Yank)	64	0	58	0	1	1	0	2	1	2	0	0	1
Dilworth, Arthur	67	20	3	1	0	0	0	38	8	1	0	0	4
Fuller, William W. (Chick)	33	0	0	0	0	2	30	0	0	1	0	0	0
Gunn, J.H.	2	0	2	0	0	0	0	0	0	0	0	0	0
James, William (Nux)	8	0	0	0	8	0	0	0	0	0	0	0	0
Johnson, Daniel Spencil (Shang, Dan, Gatling Gun)	54	24	6	0	1	0	0	5	4	14	2	0	2
Lundy, Richard Benjamin (Dick, King Richard, Geronimo)	66	0	2	0	1	48	17	0	0	0	0	0	2
Mack, Paul	38	0	4	0	5	16	10	3	0	3	0	0	1
O'Neil	3	0	0	0	2	0	0	0	1	0	0	0	0
Price	1	0	0	0	0	0	0	1	0	0	0	0	0
Roberts, Leroy (Roy, Everready)	49	16	0	1	9	0	1	2	4	19	0	0	4
Short	1	0	1	0	0	0	0	0	0	0	0	0	0
Tucker, Michael	22	5	0	0	0	1	0	0	0	17	0	0	1
Wallace, Richard Felix (Dick, Noisy)	49	0	0	0	43	1	4	1	1	0	0	0	0
Williams, Thomas (Wrist, Tom)	17	6	3	1	0	0	0	2	0	6	0	0	0

1917

	TG	P	C	1B	2B	3B	SS	LF	CF	RF	PH	PR	RP
Banks	11	0	0	0	0	0	0	2	2	7	0	0	0
Baynard, James Howard (Frank)	17	0	0	0	0	0	0	0	16	1	0	0	0
Briggs, Otto (Mirror)	1	0	0	0	0	0	0	0	1	0	0	0	0
Brodie, Milledge T.	1	1	0	0	0	0	0	0	0	0	0	0	0
Clinton, William	69	0	0	0	15	22	4	1	0	28	2	0	0
Crockett, Frank	22	0	0	0	0	0	1	0	1	21	0	0	0
Cummings, Napoleon (Chance)	90	0	0	90	0	0	0	0	0	0	0	0	0
Deas, James Alvin (Yank)	43	0	37	0	0	1	0	0	0	6	0	0	0
Dilworth, Arthur	19	9	0	1	0	0	0	5	1	0	2	0	1
Downs, McKinley (Bunny)	70	0	1	1	59	2	8	0	0	2	0	0	0
Fisher	2	1	0	0	0	0	0	0	0	1	0	0	0
Forbes, Joseph (Joe)	3	2	0	0	0	0	0	0	0	0	1	0	0
Franklin	6	0	0	0	0	0	5	0	2	0	0	0	0
Fuller, William W. (Chick)	4	0	0	0	4	0	0	0	0	0	0	0	0
Gedschem	1	0	0	0	0	1	0	0	0	0	0	0	0
Gordon, Herman Evan	2	1	0	0	0	0	0	0	0	1	0	0	0
Gould, Jr., Lafayette	5	0	0	0	0	0	0	0	3	3	0	0	0
Gray, Emerson	1	1	0	0	0	0	0	0	0	0	0	0	0
Handy, William Oscar (Bill, Scream, Buck, Duckbreast)	2	0	0	0	2	0	0	0	0	0	0	0	0
James, William (Nux)	1	0	0	0	1	0	0	0	0	0	0	0	0
Johnson, Daniel Spencil (Shang, Dan, Gatling Gun)	36	28	0	0	0	0	0	0	0	3	1	0	4
Lundy, Richard Benjamin (Dick, King Richard, Geronimo)	68	0	0	0	0	0	68	0	1	0	0	0	0
Mack, Paul	7	0	0	0	1	0	0	0	0	6	0	0	0
Mays, Horace	1	1	0	0	0	0	0	0	0	0	0	0	0
McDonald, Gifford Van Horn (Iron Man)	11	10	0	0	0	0	0	0	1	1	0	0	0
Miller, Louis Lee (Red, Shorty)	65	0	0	1	1	63	0	0	0	0	0	0	1
Murphy, W. Charles (Speedball)	2	1	0	0	0	0	0	0	0	0	0	0	1

(1917)

	TG	P	C	1B	2B	3B	SS	LF	CF	RF	PH	PR	RP
Oliver, Jr., Hudson J. (Huddy)	2	0	0	0	1	0	1	0	0	0	0	0	0
Pettus, William Thomas (Zack, Bill)	12	0	6	0	0	2	2	0	0	2	0	0	0
Roberts, Elihu(e) D.	92	0	0	0	0	6	0	87	0	0	0	0	0
Roberts, Leroy (Roy, Everready)	40	26	0	0	3	0	0	0	0	3	2	0	6
Smith, R. (Red)	15	4	0	0	0	0	0	0	0	10	0	0	1
Thomas	1	0	0	0	0	0	0	0	1	0	0	0	0
Tomm (Town)	73	0	0	0	1	0	2	0	70	1	1	0	0
Tucker, Michael	1	0	0	0	0	0	0	0	0	0	0	0	1
Wallace, Richard Felix (Dick, Noisy)	12	0	0	0	9	0	0	0	0	3	0	0	0
White, Burlin	66	0	57	2	0	0	0	0	0	5	2	0	0
Wilson, Frank (Chink)	9	1	0	0	1	0	8	0	0	0	0	0	0
Witherspoon	9	7	0	0	0	0	0	0	0	0	0	0	3
Wylie, Fred Lewis (The Atlanta Surprise)	7	2	0	0	0	0	2	0	0	1	1	0	2

1918

	TG	P	C	1B	2B	3B	SS	LF	CF	RF	PH	PR	RP
Albritton, Alexander C. (Alex)	2	2	0	0	0	0	0	0	0	0	0	0	0
Baynard, James Howard (Frank)	16	0	3	0	0	0	0	4	10	0	0	0	0
Bowden, Cicero	3	0	2	0	0	0	0	0	0	1	0	0	0
Bryant, Elias (Country Brown)	31	1	1	0	0	1	8	3	3	16	0	0	0
Burton, W. (Shorty, Billy)	14	0	5	0	0	0	1	0	1	8	0	0	0
Carney	1	0	0	0	0	0	0	0	0	1	0	0	0
Crockett, Frank	1	0	0	0	0	0	0	0	1	0	0	0	0
Cummings, Napoleon (Chance)	28	0	0	28	0	0	0	0	0	0	0	0	1
Davis, Jack	1	0	0	0	0	0	1	0	0	0	0	0	0
Deas, James Alvin (Yank)	23	0	15	0	0	0	0	10	1	0	0	0	0
Downs, McKinley (Bunny)	17	0	0	0	3	5	11	1	0	0	0	0	0
Edwards, James (Smokey)	1	0	0	0	0	0	0	0	1	0	0	0	0
Farrell	1	0	0	0	0	0	0	0	1	0	0	0	0
Fiall, Jr., Thomas Vivian (Tom)	2	0	1	0	1	0	0	0	0	0	0	0	0
Fields,	1	0	0	0	0	0	0	0	0	1	0	0	0
Forman,	2	0	0	0	2	0	0	0	0	0	0	0	0
Gregory	1	0	0	0	1	0	0	0	0	0	0	0	0
Gruhler, Henry (Whitey)	1	0	0	0	0	1	0	0	0	0	0	0	0
Gunn, J.H.	4	4	0	0	0	0	0	0	0	0	0	0	0
Handy, William Oscar (Bill, Scream, Buck, Duckbreast)	20	0	0	0	15	3	2	0	0	1	0	0	0
Harris	1	0	0	0	0	0	0	0	0	1	0	0	0
Harrison	1	0	0	0	0	1	0	0	0	0	0	0	0
Heckle, Walter	1	0	0	0	1	0	0	0	0	0	0	0	0
Hogan	1	0	0	0	0	0	0	0	1	0	0	0	0
Howell, Henry Reese	21	6	3	1	0	10	0	3	1	0	0	0	1
Johnson, Daniel Spencil (Shang, Dan, Gatling Gun)	2	2	0	0	0	0	0	0	0	0	0	0	0
Johnson, Jr., George Washington (Dibo, Junior)	5	0	0	1	0	3	1	0	0	0	0	0	0
Jones	1	0	0	0	0	0	0	0	1	0	0	0	0
Lundy, Richard Benjamin (Dick, King Richard, Geronimo)	8	0	0	0	0	1	8	0	0	0	0	0	0
Marcell, Oliver Hazzard (Ghost)	1	0	0	0	0	0	1	0	0	0	0	0	0
Mason	1	0	0	0	0	0	1	0	0	0	0	0	0
Mays, Horace	1	1	0	0	0	0	0	0	0	0	0	0	0
Moore	2	0	0	2	0	0	0	0	0	0	0	0	0
Mott	1	0	0	0	0	0	1	0	0	0	0	0	0
Nelson, Raymond (Ike)	11	0	0	0	0	0	0	11	0	0	0	0	0
Pettus, William Thomas (Zack, Bill)	3	0	0	1	2	0	0	0	0	0	0	0	0
Pierce, William Herbert (Big Bill, Bonehead)	1	0	0	1	0	0	0	0	0	0	0	0	0
Ray, Arthur	1	0	0	0	0	0	1	0	0	0	0	0	0
Reese, John Edward (Speedboy)	15	0	0	0	0	0	0	0	15	0	0	0	0
Roberts, Elihu(e) D.	11	0	0	0	8	0	0	1	0	2	0	0	0
Roberts, Leroy (Roy, Everready)	13	7	0	3	1	0	0	0	0	0	1	0	1
Robinson, George Washington (Sis, The Southern Bearcat)	15	7	0	0	0	0	0	0	0	5	0	0	3
Rogers	1	0	0	0	0	1	1	0	0	0	0	0	0
Shadrick,	1	0	1	0	0	0	0	0	0	0	0	0	0
Smith, C. (Red)	1	0	1	0	0	0	0	0	0	0	0	0	0
Smith, R. (Red)	28	8	3	0	3	9	3	0	3	1	0	0	0
Warmack, Sam	1	0	0	0	0	1	0	0	0	0	0	0	0
Webster, Pearl Franklyn (Speck)	2	0	0	0	0	0	0	2	0	0	0	0	0
Wiley, Wabishaw Spencer (Doc, Bill)	1	0	0	0	0	0	0	1	0	0	0	0	0

1919

	TG	P	C	1B	2B	3B	SS	LF	CF	RF	PH	PR	RP
Baynard, James Howard (Frank)	3	0	0	0	0	0	0	2	0	1	0	0	0
Bryant, Elias (Country Brown)	34	0	0	1	0	0	0	7	1	25	2	0	0
Deas, James Alvin (Yank)	3	0	3	0	0	0	0	0	0	0	0	0	0
Dilworth, Arthur	6	4	0	0	0	0	0	0	1	0	1	0	0
Earle, Charles Babcock (Peles, Frank)	5	0	0	0	0	0	0	1	5	0	0	0	0
Edwards, James (Smokey)	4	1	1	0	0	0	0	0	0	0	2	0	0
Forbes, Frank Lindsey (Strangler, Iron Man)	6	0	0	0	0	4	0	0	1	1	0	0	0
Gatewood, Ernest E.	70	0	67	0	0	2	0	0	0	2	1	0	0
Handy, William Oscar (Bill, Scream, Buck, Duckbreast)	89	0	0	0	88	0	1	0	0	0	0	0	0
Hubbard, Jesse James (Mountain Man)	8	7	0	0	0	0	0	0	0	1	0	0	2
Hutchinson, Fred (Hutch, Pug)	88	0	0	0	0	83	5	0	0	0	0	0	0
Jeffries, James Courtney (Jim)	7	7	0	0	0	0	0	0	0	0	0	0	0
Johnson, Cecil Leon (Sess)	15	0	0	0	0	0	0	14	1	0	0	0	0
Johnson, Daniel Spencil (Shang, Dan, Gatling Gun)	23	14	0	0	0	0	0	2	0	0	0	0	7
Johnson, Jr., George (Chappie, Rat)	28	0	28	0	0	0	0	0	0	0	0	0	0
Lloyd, John Henry (Pop)	84	0	0	0	1	0	83	0	0	0	0	0	0
Lundy, Richard Benjamin (Dick, King Richard, Geronimo)	1	0	0	0	0	0	0	1	0	0	0	0	0
Miller, Louis Lee (Red, Shorty)	1	0	0	0	0	0	0	1	0	0	0	0	0
Parks, Joseph B. (Joe, Bill)	2	0	0	0	0	0	0	0	1	1	0	0	0
Pierce, William Herbert (Big Bill, Bonehead)	1	0	1	0	0	0	0	0	0	0	0	0	0
Poles, Spottswood (Spot)	56	0	0	0	0	0	0	31	28	0	0	0	0
Pugh, John (Johnny)	70	1	0	1	0	0	0	10	1	57	2	0	0
Redding, Richard (Cannonball, Dick)	44	25	0	3	0	1	1	0	0	0	2	0	13
Roberts, Leroy (Roy, Everready)	24	18	1	0	1	0	0	0	0	0	0	0	5
Shively, George Anner (Rabbit)	78	0	0	0	0	0	0	23	54	4	0	0	0
Taylor, Benjamin Harrison (Ben)	87	0	0	87	0	0	0	0	0	0	0	0	1
Thompson, J.W. (Gunboat, Fred)	13	0	0	0	0	0	0	6	0	7	0	0	0
Whitworth, Richard Henderson (Dick)	1	0	0	0	0	0	0	0	0	0	0	0	1
Wickware, Frank Ellis (Red Ant, Big Red, Smiley)	16	10	0	0	0	0	0	0	0	0	0	1	5
Wiley, Wabishaw Spencer (Doc, Bill)	5	0	5	0	0	0	0	0	0	0	0	0	0
Williams, Joseph (Smokey Joe, Cyclone)	2	2	0	0	0	0	0	0	0	0	0	0	0
Williams, Thomas (Wrist, Tom)	2	2	0	0	0	0	0	0	0	0	0	0	0

1920

	TG	P	C	1B	2B	3B	SS	LF	CF	RF	PH	PR	RP
Barbour [Barber], Jesse Bernard (Phantom, Jess)	49	0	0	0	3	1	0	1	19	28	0	0	0
Bryant, Elias (Country Brown)	95	0	0	0	0	0	1	64	1	29	0	1	0
Carroll	1	0	0	0	0	0	0	0	0	1	0	0	0
Deas, James Alvin (Yank)	36	0	33	0	0	0	0	0	2	1	0	0	0
Handy, William Oscar (Bill, Scream, Buck, Duckbreast)	88	0	0	0	82	0	6	0	0	0	0	0	0
Lundy, Richard Benjamin (Dick, King Richard, Geronimo)	91	0	0	0	0	0	89	0	0	2	0	0	0
Marcell, Oliver Hazzard (Ghost)	97	0	0	1	0	96	0	0	0	0	0	0	1
Means, Lemuel Lewis (Lou)	45	0	0	0	13	0	0	0	1	31	0	0	0
Mederos, Jesus (Frank, Lico)	69	0	0	1	0	0	0	0	66	1	1	0	0
Pierce, William Herbert (Big Bill, Bonehead)	99	0	1	88	7	2	3	0	0	0	0	0	0
Pugh, John (Johnny)	41	0	1	2	0	0	0	21	2	12	2	1	0
Redding, Richard (Cannonball, Dick)	48	28	0	9	0	0	0	0	0	0	5	0	6
Rojo, Domingo Julio (Clown)	74	0	50	3	1	3	5	1	4	5	4	0	0
Ryan, Merven John (Red, Jabao)	32	26	0	0	0	0	0	0	0	0	0	1	5
Shively, George Anner (Rabbit)	17	0	0	0	0	0	0	15	2	0	0	0	0
Smith, R. (Red)	22	0	21	1	0	0	0	0	0	0	0	0	0
Thomas, Julian R. (Jules, Jack, Home Run)	7	0	0	0	0	0	0	0	7	1	0	0	0
Treadwell, Harold E.	32	26	0	1	0	0	0	2	1	0	1	1	2
Williams, Andrew (Stringbean)	24	20	0	0	0	0	0	0	0	1	0	2	1

1921

	TG	P	C	1B	2B	3B	SS	LF	CF	RF	PH	PR	RP
Barbour [Barber], Jesse Bernard (Phantom, Jess)	86	0	0	0	2	0	3	1	80	0	1	0	0
Bryant, Elias (Country Brown)	103	0	0	0	22	3	1	23	9	51	0	0	0
Busby, Maurice (Lefty)	5	5	0	0	0	0	0	0	0	0	0	0	0
Cockrell [Williams], Phillip (Fish)	1	0	0	0	0	0	0	0	0	0	1	0	0
Crump, Willis (Shorty)	1	0	0	0	1	0	0	0	0	0	0	0	0
Deas, James Alvin (Yank)	41	0	40	1	0	1	0	0	0	0	0	0	0
Fuller, James (Jimmy)	1	0	1	0	0	0	0	0	0	0	0	0	0
Gatewood, Ernest E.	29	0	17	4	0	5	1	1	1	0	0	0	0
Graham, Dennis Wilson (Peaches)	59	0	0	0	1	0	0	1	3	40	12	1	0

(1921)

	TG	P	C	1B	2B	3B	SS	LF	CF	RF	PH	PR	RP
Handy, William Oscar (Bill, Scream, Buck, Duckbreast)	78	0	1	0	73	0	4	1	0	1	0	0	0
Harvey, John Henry (Howling Harvey, Little Pitch)	6	4	0	0	0	0	0	0	0	2	0	0	0
Jackson, Jr., Richard Alvin (Dick, Workie)	29	0	1	0	10	1	14	0	0	2	1	0	0
Jefferson, Ralph Tennyson	8	0	0	0	0	0	0	6	2	0	0	0	0
Johnson, Daniel Spencil (Shang, Dan, Gatling Gun)	2	1	0	0	1	0	0	0	0	0	0	0	0
Johnson, Jr., George Washington (Dibo, Junior)	1	0	0	0	0	0	0	1	0	0	0	0	0
Lee, Sr., Holsey Scranton (Script)	5	4	0	0	0	0	0	0	0	0	0	0	1
Lundy, Richard Benjamin (Dick, King Richard, Geronimo)	74	0	0	1	0	0	73	0	0	0	0	0	0
Lyons, James Henry (Jimmy)	1	0	0	0	0	0	0	1	0	0	0	0	0
Marcell, Oliver Hazzard (Ghost)	105	0	0	0	0	87	19	0	0	0	0	0	0
McDonald, Gifford Van Horn (Iron Man)	3	1	0	0	0	0	0	0	0	0	0	0	2
Miller, Louis Lee (Red, Shorty)	1	0	0	0	1	0	0	0	0	0	0	0	0
Mitchell, Benjamin Arnett [Ernest] (Hooks)	12	6	0	0	0	0	0	0	0	0	0	0	6
Mungin [Mongin], Samuel (Sam, Polly)	3	0	0	0	3	0	0	0	0	0	0	0	0
Pettus, William Thomas (Zack, Bill)	103	0	0	102	0	0	0	1	0	0	0	0	0
Pierce, William Herbert (Big Bill, Bonehead)	2	0	0	0	0	0	0	0	1	1	0	0	0
Pugh, John (Johnny)	41	0	0	0	1	2	0	11	2	20	4	2	0
Reavis, Al W.	2	2	0	0	0	0	0	0	0	0	0	0	0
Redding, Richard (Cannonball, Dick)	38	31	0	0	0	1	1	1	0	0	0	0	4
Richardson, Henry Layton (Long Tom)	17	10	0	0	0	1	0	0	0	1	0	0	6
Rojo, Domingo Julio (Clown)	86	0	60	5	0	15	0	0	1	4	3	1	1
Ryan, Merven John (Red, Jabao)	23	14	0	0	0	0	0	0	1	1	1	0	5
Shively, George Anner (Rabbit)	83	0	0	0	0	0	0	66	11	3	1	0	2
Suttles, George (Mule)	1	0	1	0	0	0	0	0	0	0	0	0	0
Torriente y Torrienti, Cristobal (Carlos)	1	0	0	0	0	0	0	0	1	0	0	0	0
Treadwell, Harold E.	28	16	0	0	0	0	0	0	1	0	2	1	8
Williams, Andrew (Stringbean)	16	9	0	0	0	0	0	1	0	2	0	0	4
Winters, James Henry (Nip, Jesse)	9	5	0	0	0	0	0	0	0	1	0	0	3
Woods, William J. (Willie)	1	0	0	1	0	0	0	0	0	0	0	0	0

1922

	TG	P	C	1B	2B	3B	SS	LF	CF	RF	PH	PR	RP
Brown, Arnold (Buck)	18	0	0	0	6	5	6	0	1	0	0	0	0
Childs	1	1	0	0	0	0	0	0	0	0	0	0	0
Cramer	1	1	0	0	0	0	0	0	0	0	0	0	0
Crockett, Frank	72	1	0	0	1	0	0	15	52	1	2	0	0
Cummings, Napoleon (Chance)	67	0	0	67	0	0	0	0	0	0	0	0	0
Davis, Jack	73	0	0	0	1	72	0	0	0	0	0	0	0
Deas, James Alvin (Yank)	51	1	40	8	0	0	0	1	0	0	2	0	0
Ermy	1	0	0	0	1	0	0	0	0	0	0	0	0
Finley, John Thomas (Tom)	11	0	0	0	8	0	2	0	0	1	0	0	0
Hairstone, James Burton (J.B., Harry)	6	0	0	0	0	0	0	1	5	0	0	0	0
Harris	5	3	0	0	0	0	0	0	0	0	0	0	2
Johnson, Nate (Speedboy)	22	18	0	0	0	0	0	1	0	0	0	1	2
Jones, William (Fox, Bill, Willie)	41	0	20	0	16	1	3	0	0	1	1	0	0
Jordan, Henry (Hen)	1	0	1	0	0	0	0	0	0	0	0	0	0
Kyle, Andy	6	5	0	0	0	0	0	0	0	0	0	0	1
Lewis, Milton	27	3	0	0	21	0	0	0	0	0	0	0	3
Lloyd	1	1	0	0	0	0	0	0	0	0	0	0	0
Lundy, Richard Benjamin (Dick, King Richard, Geronimo)	66	0	0	0	0	0	66	0	0	0	0	0	0
Malloy, Charles	10	8	0	0	0	0	0	0	0	0	0	0	2
Mason, Charles (Corporal, Suitcase)	1	1	0	0	0	0	0	0	0	0	0	0	0
Means, Lemuel Lewis (Lou)	33	0	9	3	20	1	0	0	0	1	0	0	0
O'Neill, Charles	17	0	17	0	0	0	0	0	0	0	0	0	0
Patterson	4	1	0	0	0	0	0	0	0	0	1	0	2
Penn	2	0	0	2	0	0	0	0	0	0	0	0	0
Perry, Carlisle (Cash, Carl, Native Son)	5	0	0	0	5	0	0	0	0	0	0	0	0
Reid, Ambrose Leevolia (Ambrose)	75	0	0	0	0	0	2	55	17	1	0	0	0
Richardson, Henry Layton (Long Tom)	1	0	0	0	0	0	0	0	0	0	0	0	1
Smith, Jake	39	0	0	0	2	0	0	3	6	24	3	0	1
Streeter, Samuel (Lefty, Sam)	24	17	0	0	0	0	0	0	0	1	1	0	5
Wheeler, Joseph (Jodie)	25	18	0	0	0	0	0	0	0	0	0	0	7
Williams, Andrew (Stringbean)	1	1	0	0	0	0	0	0	0	0	0	0	0
Young, Berdell	58	0	0	2	0	0	0	5	2	47	2	0	0

1922 *(New York City Bacharach Giants Roster)*	TG	P	C	1B	2B	3B	SS	LF	CF	RF	PH	PR	RP
Blane	1	0	0	0	0	0	0	0	0	0	0	0	1
Bryant, Elias (Country Brown)	67	0	0	0	17	6	0	18	3	27	0	0	0
Crain, John	1	0	1	0	0	0	0	0	0	0	0	0	0
Davis	1	0	1	0	0	0	0	0	0	0	0	0	0
Duncan, Warren	55	0	0	0	0	0	0	28	2	25	0	0	0
Gray, Emerson	9	0	9	0	0	0	0	0	0	0	0	0	0
Hairstone, James Burton (J.B., Harry)	1	0	1	0	0	0	0	0	0	0	0	0	0
Holland	1	0	0	0	0	0	0	0	0	1	0	0	0
Hudspeth, Robert (Highpocket)	76	0	0	75	1	0	0	0	0	0	0	0	0
Hutchinson, Fred (Hutch, Pug)	2	0	0	0	2	0	0	0	0	0	0	0	0
Jackson, Jr., Richard Alvin (Dick, Workie)	57	0	0	1	54	1	0	0	0	0	0	1	0
Jenkins, Clarence Reginald (Fats)	2	0	0	0	0	0	0	2	0	0	0	0	0
Jones, William (Fox, Bill, Willie)	2	0	0	0	0	0	0	0	0	2	0	0	0
Lloyd, John Henry (Pop)	73	0	0	0	3	0	70	0	0	0	0	0	0
Lundy, Richard Benjamin (Dick, King Richard, Geronimo)	3	0	0	0	0	0	3	0	0	0	0	0	0
Marcell, Oliver Hazzard (Ghost)	72	0	0	0	0	70	2	0	0	0	0	0	0
Mason, Charles (Corporal, Suitcase)	2	0	0	0	0	0	0	2	0	0	0	0	0
McIntyre	1	1	0	0	0	0	0	0	0	0	0	0	0
Means, Lemuel Lewis (Lou)	1	0	0	0	0	0	0	1	0	0	0	0	0
O'Neill, Charles	10	0	10	0	0	0	0	0	0	0	0	0	0
Ramirez, Ramiro (Rome)	65	0	0	0	0	0	0	3	61	0	1	1	0
Redding, Richard (Cannonball, Dick)	24	15	0	0	1	0	0	1	1	0	1	0	5
Reid, Ambrose Leevolia (Ambrose)	1	0	0	0	0	0	0	1	0	0	0	0	0
Roberts, Leroy (Roy, Everready)	21	17	0	0	0	0	0	0	0	0	0	0	4
Rojo, Domingo Julio (Clown)	62	0	60	0	2	1	0	0	0	1	0	0	0
Shively, George Anner (Rabbit)	65	0	0	0	0	0	0	29	13	27	0	0	0
Smith	3	2	0	0	0	0	1	0	0	0	0	0	0
Treadwell, Harold E.	28	20	0	0	0	0	0	0	0	0	1	0	7
Williams, Andrew (Stringbean)	10	7	0	0	0	0	0	0	0	0	0	0	3
Winters, James Henry (Nip, Jesse)	22	13	0	0	1	0	0	0	0	3	0	0	5
York, James Henry (Jim)	5	0	5	0	0	0	0	0	0	0	0	0	0

1923	TG	P	C	1B	2B	3B	SS	LF	CF	RF	PH	PR	RP
Allen, Jr., Major Robert	1	0	0	0	1	0	0	0	0	0	0	0	0
Carter, Clifford	1	1	0	0	0	0	0	0	0	0	0	0	0
Crockett, Frank	26	0	0	0	0	0	0	0	22	4	1	0	0
Crump, Willis (Shorty)	2	0	0	0	2	0	0	0	0	0	0	0	0
Cummings, Napoleon (Chance)	79	0	0	74	5	0	0	0	0	0	1	0	0
Deas, James Alvin (Yank)	8	0	7	0	0	0	0	0	0	1	0	0	0
Denis	1	1	0	0	0	0	0	0	0	0	0	0	0
Downs, McKinley (Bunny)	50	0	0	0	47	0	0	0	4	0	0	0	1
Francis, William Henry (Billy)	81	0	0	0	0	81	0	0	0	0	0	0	0
Gisentaner, William (Lefty)	6	1	0	0	0	0	0	0	1	4	0	0	0
Hampton, Lewis	12	7	0	0	0	0	0	1	0	1	1	0	2
Harper, John	28	18	0	0	0	0	0	0	1	3	1	0	5
Henderson, Arthur Chauncey (Rats)	33	23	0	0	1	0	0	0	0	0	0	0	9
Hobson, Charles Johnson (Johnny)	1	0	0	0	0	0	0	0	0	0	1	0	0
Huff, Jr., Edward C. (Eddie)	36	0	21	0	0	0	0	0	0	10	5	0	0
Hughes	1	0	1	0	0	0	0	0	0	0	0	0	0
Johnson, Nate (Speedboy)	17	13	0	0	0	0	0	0	0	0	2	0	2
Jones, William (Fox, Bill, Willie)	71	0	63	0	1	0	0	0	0	4	3	1	0
Lockhart, George Hubert (Prof)	27	16	0	0	0	1	0	0	1	4	0	1	4
Lundy, Richard Benjamin (Dick, King Richard, Geronimo)	80	0	0	0	0	0	78	0	0	1	1	0	0
Marlin	1	1	0	0	0	0	0	0	0	0	0	0	0
Mason, Charles (Corporal, Suitcase)	85	0	0	0	0	0	0	56	2	28	0	0	0
McLloyd	1	1	0	0	0	0	0	0	0	0	0	0	0
Parpetti, Agustin (Pulpita)	24	0	0	12	6	0	0	1	0	5	2	0	0
Price	1	0	0	0	0	0	0	0	0	1	0	0	0
Ramirez, Ramiro (Rome)	4	0	0	0	0	0	0	3	1	0	0	0	0
Reid, Ambrose Leevolia (Ambrose)	76	0	0	1	26	6	9	10	11	14	2	0	1
Roberts, Leroy (Roy, Everready)	11	7	0	1	0	0	0	0	0	3	0	0	0
Robinson, George Washington (Sis, The Southern Bearcat)	1	0	0	0	0	0	0	0	0	0	0	0	1
Smith, R. (Red)	11	1	0	0	1	0	0	1	0	8	0	0	1
Thompson	7	0	0	0	0	0	0	2	1	4	0	0	0

(1923)

	TG	P	C	1B	2B	3B	SS	LF	CF	RF	PH	PR	RP
Treadwell, Harold E.	2	2	0	0	0	0	0	0	0	0	0	0	0
Webster, William (West)	6	0	6	0	0	0	0	0	0	0	0	0	0
White, Chaney Leonard (Reindeer)	73	1	1	0	0	0	0	18	49	3	2	0	0
Wright, Joseph	1	0	0	0	0	0	0	1	0	0	0	0	0

1924

	TG	P	C	1B	2B	3B	SS	LF	CF	RF	PH	PR	RP
Bryant, Elias (Country Brown)	2	0	0	0	0	2	0	0	0	0	0	0	0
Capenemzi	1	0	0	0	0	0	0	0	1	0	0	0	0
Carr, Wayne	10	8	0	0	0	0	0	0	0	0	0	0	2
Carter, Clifford	2	0	0	0	0	0	0	0	0	0	0	0	2
Cummings, Napoleon (Chance)	110	0	0	109	0	0	0	0	0	0	0	0	0
Dallard, Maurice Julius (Eggie, Morris)	2	0	2	0	0	0	0	0	0	0	0	0	0
Estrada, Oscar	1	0	0	0	0	0	0	0	0	0	0	0	1
Evans, W.P.	10	7	1	0	0	0	0	0	0	0	1	0	1
Gatewood, Ernest E.	70	0	68	0	0	1	0	0	0	0	1	0	0
George, John	32	0	0	0	0	32	0	0	0	0	0	0	0
Hampton, Lewis	1	1	0	0	0	0	0	0	0	0	0	0	0
Harper, John	18	14	0	0	0	0	0	0	0	0	0	0	4
Henderson, Arthur Chauncey (Rats)	12	10	0	0	0	0	0	0	0	0	0	0	2
Hobson, Charles Johnson (Johnny)	9	9	0	0	0	0	0	0	0	0	0	0	0
Johnson	1	0	0	0	0	0	0	0	1	0	0	0	0
Jones, William (Fox, Bill, Willie)	56	1	51	0	0	0	0	0	0	4	0	0	0
Lewis, Milton	71	0	0	0	33	1	2	8	2	11	14	0	0
Lindsay, Clarence Holmes (C.H.)	2	0	0	0	0	0	2	0	0	0	0	0	0
Lloyd, John Henry (Pop)	105	0	0	5	90	1	11	0	0	1	0	0	0
Lockhart, George Hubert (Prof)	24	18	0	0	0	0	0	0	1	1	0	0	4
Lowell	1	0	0	0	0	0	0	0	0	0	0	0	1
Lundy, Richard Benjamin (Dick, King Richard, Geronimo)	104	0	0	0	2	103	0	0	0	0	0	0	1
Mason, Charles (Corporal, Suitcase)	82	0	0	0	0	0	0	25	10	49	2	0	0
Mitchell, Benjamin Arnett [Ernest] (Hooks)	10	6	0	0	0	0	0	0	0	0	2	0	2
Nuttal, H. (Bill)	12	7	0	0	0	0	0	0	0	0	0	0	5
Raines, Lawrence Glenn Hope (Larry)	1	0	0	0	0	0	0	0	1	0	0	0	0
Ramirez, Ramiro (Rome)	98	0	0	0	0	0	0	14	79	4	1	0	0
Reid, Ambrose Leevolia (Ambrose)	113	0	0	0	0	79	0	31	0	4	1	0	0
Roberts, Leroy (Roy, Everready)	8	8	0	0	0	0	0	0	0	0	0	0	0
Shively, George Anner (Rabbit)	77	0	0	0	0	0	0	14	19	44	0	0	0
Starks, Otis (Lefty)	18	11	1	0	0	0	0	0	0	0	2	0	4
Thompson	1	1	0	0	0	0	0	0	0	0	0	0	0
White, Chaney Leonard (Reindeer)	34	0	0	0	0	0	0	28	5	0	1	0	0
Williams, Andrew (Stringbean)	19	15	0	0	0	0	0	0	0	0	3	0	1

1925

	TG	P	C	1B	2B	3B	SS	LF	CF	RF	PH	PR	RP
Bryant, Elias (Country Brown)	64	0	1	1	2	4	0	8	0	51	0	0	0
Burnett, Fred (Tex)	1	0	0	0	0	0	0	0	0	0	1	0	0
Clark, Maceo Richard	2	2	0	0	0	0	0	0	0	0	0	0	0
Cummings, Napoleon (Chance)	120	0	0	119	1	0	0	0	0	0	0	0	0
Farrell, Luther Alaner (Buck, Red, Fats, Lefty)	26	13	0	0	0	0	0	0	4	2	7	0	1
Finley, John Thomas (Tom)	24	0	0	0	2	19	1	2	0	0	0	0	0
Gatewood, Ernest E.	64	0	54	2	0	0	0	0	0	2	5	0	1
Gillespie, Henry	13	10	0	0	0	0	0	0	0	1	1	0	1
Grier, Claude Bonds (Red)	16	14	0	0	0	0	0	0	0	1	0	0	2
Henderson, Arthur Chauncey (Rats)	43	32	0	0	1	0	0	0	0	1	1	0	10
Jones, William (Fox, Bill, Willie)	76	0	72	0	0	0	1	0	0	0	3	0	0
Leonard, James (Bobo, Bull)	48	0	0	0	0	0	0	20	25	1	2	0	0
Lewis, Milton	1	0	0	0	1	0	0	0	0	0	0	0	0
Lloyd, John Henry (Pop)	120	0	0	4	111	1	3	1	0	0	0	0	0
Lockhart, George Hubert (Prof)	22	17	1	0	0	0	0	0	0	1	1	0	3
Lundy, Richard Benjamin (Dick, King Richard, Geronimo)	120	0	0	0	0	0	118	0	0	0	1	0	1
Marcell, Oliver Hazzard (Ghost)	104	0	0	1	0	101	1	0	0	0	1	0	0
Mason, Charles (Corporal, Suitcase)	35	0	0	0	0	0	0	2	1	31	0	0	0
Mitchell, Benjamin Arnett [Ernest] (Hooks)	33	19	0	0	0	0	1	0	0	1	3	2	0	7
Nuttal, H. (Bill)	8	7	0	0	0	0	0	0	0	0	0	0	2
Reid, Ambrose Leevolia (Ambrose)	108	3	0	0	7	1	0	21	72	4	0	0	1
Roberts, Leroy (Roy, Everready)	20	16	0	2	0	0	1	0	0	0	0	0	2

(1925)

	TG	P	C	1B	2B	3B	SS	LF	CF	RF	PH	PR	RP
Walsh	1	0	0	0	0	0	0	0	1	0	0	0	0
Waters, Theodore Francis Mullen (Ted)	1	0	0	0	0	0	0	0	0	0	1	0	0
White, Chaney Leonard (Reindeer)	51	0	0	0	0	0	0	39	3	9	0	0	0
Wilson, Benjamin (Benny)	3	0	0	0	0	0	0	1	1	1	0	0	0
Woods, William J. (Willie)	31	0	0	0	0	0	0	0	17	14	0	0	0
Young, Berdell	54	0	0	0	0	0	0	38	7	9	0	0	0

1926

	TG	P	C	1B	2B	3B	SS	LF	CF	RF	PH	PR	RP
Bryant, Elias (Country Brown)	75	0	0	0	3	14	1	15	0	42	6	0	0
Cummings, Napoleon (Chance)	108	0	0	108	0	0	0	0	0	0	0	0	0
Dallard, Maurice Julius (Eggie, Morris)	12	0	0	0	0	0	0	9	0	4	0	0	0
Farrell, Luther Alaner (Buck, Red, Fats, Lefty)	94	13	0	0	0	0	0	9	2	69	2	0	4
Garcia, Romando (Cheno)	108	0	0	0	98	6	6	0	0	0	0	0	0
Gatewood, Ernest E.	53	0	50	0	1	0	0	0	0	0	3	0	0
Grier, Claude Bonds (Red)	50	35	0	0	1	0	0	1	0	0	7	0	7
Henderson, Arthur Chauncey (Rats)	38	28	0	0	0	0	0	1	0	0	0	0	9
Johnson	1	1	0	0	0	0	0	0	0	0	0	0	0
Jones, Sr., Robert Leo (Fox)	1	0	1	0	0	0	0	0	0	0	0	0	0
Jones, William (Fox, Bill, Willie)	73	0	69	0	0	0	0	0	0	1	4	0	0
Lewis, Joseph Herman (Joe, Sleepy)	18	0	16	0	0	0	0	0	0	0	2	0	0
Lockhart, George Hubert (Prof)	21	15	0	0	0	0	0	0	1	0	1	1	3
Lundy, Richard Benjamin (Dick, King Richard, Geronimo)	113	0	0	0	0	0	111	0	1	0	2	0	0
Marcell, Oliver Hazzard (Ghost)	103	0	0	0	1	100	0	0	0	0	1	0	0
Mitchell, Alonzo (Monty, Fluke)	23	7	0	0	0	0	0	7	0	1	2	1	5
Reid, Ambrose Leevolia (Ambrose)	111	1	0	10	3	1	1	85	11	3	0	0	0
Roberts, Leroy (Roy, Everready)	29	18	0	1	0	0	0	1	0	1	2	1	6
Robinson	1	0	0	0	0	0	0	1	0	0	0	0	0
Wallace, McKinley (Jack)	33	0	0	0	20	0	0	3	2	8	0	1	0
White, Chaney Leonard (Reindeer)	108	1	0	0	0	0	0	2	103	1	0	0	2

1927

	TG	P	C	1B	2B	3B	SS	LF	CF	RF	PH	PR	RP
Charleston, Oscar McKinley (Charlie)	1	0	0	0	0	0	0	1	0	0	0	0	0
Cooper, Samuel (Sam)	1	0	0	0	0	0	0	0	0	0	0	0	1
Dallard, Maurice Julius (Eggie, Morris)	102	0	4	93	1	1	0	3	0	0	0	0	0
Duncan, (Joe)	29	0	27	0	1	0	0	0	0	0	1	0	0
Farrell, Luther Alaner (Buck, Red, Fats, Lefty)	78	31	0	0	0	0	1	15	3	16	6	0	11
Gatewood, Ernest E.	9	0	8	0	0	0	0	0	0	0	1	0	0
Gillespie, Henry	20	10	0	0	0	0	0	4	0	3	0	0	4
Grier, Claude Bonds (Red)	12	6	0	0	1	0	0	0	0	0	4	0	1
Handy, William Oscar (Bill, Scream, Buck, Duckbreast)	4	0	0	0	3	0	0	0	0	0	0	0	0
Henderson, Arthur Chauncey (Rats)	26	17	0	0	0	0	0	0	0	0	2	0	7
Hubbard, Jesse James (Mountain Man)	98	22	0	0	0	0	0	5	2	65	3	1	3
Jones, William (Fox, Bill, Willie)	84	0	79	2	2	0	1	0	0	0	0	0	0
Lewis, Milton	104	0	1	17	84	1	0	2	0	0	2	0	1
Lockhart, George Hubert (Prof)	26	16	0	0	0	0	0	1	0	0	1	0	8
Lundy, Richard Benjamin (Dick, King Richard, Geronimo)	112	0	0	0	0	1	110	1	0	0	0	0	1
Marcell, Oliver Hazzard (Ghost)	112	0	0	0	1	111	0	0	0	0	0	0	0
Means, Lemuel Lewis (Lou)	13	0	11	2	0	0	0	0	0	0	0	0	0
Reid, Ambrose Leevolia (Ambrose)	77	0	0	6	15	4	6	43	2	0	5	0	1
Roberts, Leroy (Roy, Everready)	31	18	0	0	0	0	0	0	0	0	0	0	13
Smith, Clarence (Scally)	101	0	0	0	0	5	0	51	2	44	1	0	0
Wagner [Pop Turner], Bert (Billy)	25	0	0	0	21	1	4	0	0	0	0	0	0
White, Chaney Leonard (Reindeer)	120	1	0	0	0	0	0	1	117	3	0	0	0
Williams	2	0	2	0	0	0	0	0	0	0	0	0	0

1928

	TG	P	C	1B	2B	3B	SS	LF	CF	RF	PH	PR	RP
Blackwell, Charles H. (Rucker)	6	0	0	0	0	0	0	0	0	6	0	0	0
Carr, George Henry (Tank)	64	0	0	48	0	14	0	0	0	2	1	0	0
Cason, John	46	0	45	0	0	0	0	0	0	0	2	0	0
Chew	1	0	0	0	1	0	0	0	0	0	0	0	0
Collier, Bob	4	0	2	0	0	0	0	0	0	1	1	0	0
Cummings, Napoleon (Chance)	36	0	0	24	8	0	0	0	0	0	4	0	0
Dallard, Maurice Julius (Eggie, Morris)	38	0	2	1	0	0	0	11	3	22	0	0	0

(1928)

	TG	P	C	1B	2B	3B	SS	LF	CF	RF	PH	PR	RP
Daniels, Fred	1	0	0	0	0	0	0	0	0	0	0	0	1
Farrell, Luther Alaner (Buck, Red, Fats, Lefty)	53	21	0	0	0	0	0	1	0	19	8	0	6
Gardner, Kenneth Fuller (Ping)	27	18	0	0	1	0	0	0	0	0	2	0	6
Green, Curtis (Cornelius)	23	6	0	9	0	0	0	3	0	1	2	0	2
Grier, Claude Bonds (Red)	1	0	0	0	0	0	0	0	0	0	1	0	0
Henderson, Arthur Chauncey (Rats)	22	16	0	0	0	0	0	1	0	0	0	0	5
Jackson, Jack	3	0	0	0	0	0	0	0	1	2	0	0	0
Jenkins, Clarence Reginald (Fats)	67	0	0	0	0	0	0	64	3	0	0	0	0
Jones, William (Fox, Bill, Willie)	42	0	40	0	0	0	0	0	0	0	2	0	0
Lackey, Obie Ezekiel	1	0	0	0	0	0	1	0	0	0	0	0	0
Lewis, Joseph Herman (Joe, Sleepy)	1	0	1	0	0	0	0	0	0	0	0	0	0
Lewis, Milton	26	0	0	8	17	0	0	0	0	0	1	0	0
Lockhart, George Hubert (Prof)	13	8	0	0	0	0	0	0	0	0	0	0	5
Lundy, Richard Benjamin (Dick, King Richard, Geronimo)	77	0	0	0	0	0	77	0	0	0	0	0	1
Marcell, Oliver Hazzard (Ghost)	50	0	0	0	0	48	0	0	1	0	1	0	0
Mitchell, Alonzo (Monty, Fluke)	14	6	0	0	0	0	0	1	0	0	1	0	6
Moore, Clarence L. (C.L., Cool Breeze, Dago)	1	0	0	1	0	0	0	0	0	0	1	0	0
Reid, Ambrose Leevolia (Ambrose)	76	0	0	0	45	20	3	5	0	3	1	0	0
Shields, James D. (Jaydee)	39	8	0	0	17	5	6	0	0	0	1	1	1
Stanley, John Wesley (Neck)	3	2	0	0	0	0	0	0	0	1	0	0	0
Thomas, Clinton Cyrus (Hawk, Clint)	34	0	2	0	0	0	0	0	1	31	0	0	0
Thorpe, Clarence Jim	1	0	0	0	0	0	0	1	0	0	0	0	0
White, Chaney Leonard (Reindeer)	78	0	0	0	0	0	0	1	77	0	0	0	0

1929

	TG	P	C	1B	2B	3B	SS	LF	CF	RF	PH	PR	RP
Albright, Thomas (Pistol Pete)	11	4	0	0	1	0	0	0	0	0	0	0	7
Briggs, Otto (Mirror)	2	0	0	0	0	0	0	0	0	2	0	0	0
Brown, Malcolm Elmore Arnold (Scrappy)	1	0	0	0	0	0	1	0	0	0	0	0	0
Cade, Joe	18	8	0	0	0	0	0	0	0	1	2	0	7
Carr, George Henry (Tank)	34	0	1	31	0	0	0	0	0	1	1	0	0
Coleman, Gilbert	3	0	0	0	0	0	0	0	0	3	0	0	0
Cooper, Samuel (Sam)	12	5	0	0	0	0	0	0	0	0	0	0	7
Craddock, William [Walter]	2	1	0	0	0	0	0	0	0	1	0	0	0
Day, Wilson C. (Connie)	76	0	0	0	76	0	0	0	0	0	0	0	0
Downs, McKinley (Bunny)	2	0	0	0	0	0	2	0	0	0	0	0	0
Eggleston, Macajah Marchand (Mack, Egg)	82	0	50	0	4	17	0	2	0	8	5	0	1
Farrell, Luther Alaner (Buck, Red, Fats, Lefty)	9	3	0	0	0	0	0	0	0	6	0	0	1
Gardner, Kenneth Fuller (Ping)	16	13	0	0	0	0	0	0	0	0	0	1	3
Green, Curtis (Cornelius)	1	0	0	0	0	1	0	0	0	0	0	0	0
Hall, Perry	1	0	0	0	0	1	0	0	0	0	0	0	0
Henderson, Arthur Chauncey (Rats)	37	25	0	0	0	0	0	0	0	2	2	1	8
Hoyt, Dana	1	0	0	0	0	0	0	0	1	0	0	0	0
Jefferson, Ralph Tennyson	2	0	0	0	0	0	0	0	2	0	0	0	0
Jenkins, Clarence Reginald (Fats)	76	0	0	0	0	0	0	63	2	11	0	0	0
Jones, William (Fox, Bill, Willie)	60	0	53	0	1	0	0	0	0	3	5	0	0
Kerry	1	0	0	0	0	0	0	0	0	0	1	0	0
Lindsay, William Hudson (Red)	83	0	0	0	0	44	41	0	0	0	0	0	3
Mason, Charles (Corporal, Suitcase)	3	0	0	0	0	0	0	3	0	0	0	0	0
McClure, Robert E. (Bob, Big Boy)	36	17	0	0	0	0	0	0	0	1	1	0	17
Miller	1	1	0	0	0	0	0	0	0	0	0	0	0
Mitchell, Alonzo (Monty, Fluke)	11	4	0	0	0	0	0	0	0	0	3	1	3
Reid, Ambrose Leevolia (Ambrose)	70	2	0	21	19	6	0	5	1	11	8	0	1
Roberts, Leroy (Roy, Everready)	3	1	0	0	0	0	0	0	0	0	0	0	2
Shields, James D. (Jaydee)	37	15	0	0	5	0	2	1	0	1	1	1	13
Stevens, Frank L. (Lefty)	1	0	0	0	0	0	0	0	0	0	0	0	1
Taylor, Benjamin Harrison (Ben)	56	0	0	50	0	1	0	0	0	0	9	0	0
Thomas, Clinton Cyrus (Hawk, Clint)	79	0	0	0	0	0	0	23	11	47	1	0	0
Walker, Jesse T. (Hoss, Selassie, Deuce, Aussa)	77	0	0	0	0	30	45	2	0	0	0	0	0
White, Chaney Leonard (Reindeer)	85	0	0	0	0	0	0	0	81	3	1	0	0
Williams, Robert Lawns (Bobby)	19	1	0	0	0	6	12	0	0	0	1	0	0

Appendix C: Batting and Pitching Statistics by Year

Batting

1916

All Games	Games	AB	R	H	D	T	HR	RBI	W	SB	SAC	E	AVG.	SLUG.
Banks	11	42	10	13	0	0	0	9	3	0	0	0	.310	.310
Crockett, Frank	69	283	57	78	4	3	1	46	16	3	1	12	.276	.322
Crump, Willis (Shorty)	43	136	24	27	3	0	1	14	11	2	2	15	.199	.243
Cummings, Napoleon (Chance)	70	292	75	106	5	4	3	74	16	17	2	21	.363	.438
Davis	1	5	3	3	0	0	0	3	0	0	0	0	.600	.600
Deas, James Alvin (Yank)	64	235	39	61	5	0	1	34	7	0	1	21	.260	.294
Dilworth, Arthur	67	269	54	80	5	2	0	54	15	8	5	8	.297	.331
Fuller, William W. (Chick)	33	135	25	25	1	1	0	12	10	1	8	10	.185	.207
Gunn, J.H.	2	9	1	2	0	1	0	0	0	0	1	0	.222	.444
James, William (Nux)	8	26	5	7	1	1	0	3	5	0	0	2	.269	.385
Johnson, Daniel Spencil (Shang)	54	194	32	53	3	2	1	30	10	3	1	3	.273	.325
Lundy, Richard Benjamin (King Richard)	66	268	79	97	9	1	1	72	26	12	3	30	.362	.414
Mack, Paul	38	152	34	44	3	3	2	24	13	3	2	16	.289	.388
O'Neil	3	7	1	3	0	0	0	2	1	0	0	0	.429	.429
Price	1	4	0	0	0	0	0	0	0	0	0	0	.000	.000
Roberts, Leroy (Roy)	49	170	24	44	4	0	0	20	6	4	1	14	.259	.282
Short	1	1	0	0	0	0	0	0	0	0	0	1	.000	.000
Tucker, Michael	22	72	16	22	1	0	0	15	6	1	0	3	.306	.319
Wallace, Richard Felix (Dick)	49	185	28	45	2	0	0	24	9	4	4	21	.243	.254
Williams, Thomas (Tom)	17	62	7	12	1	0	0	4	2	0	1	3	.194	.210
		2,547	514	722	47	18	10	440	156	58	32	180	.283	.328

League-Level Opponents	Games	AB	R	H	D	T	HR	RBI	W	SB	SAC	E	AVG.	SLUG.
Crockett, Frank	5	20	1	3	0	0	0	1	0	0	0	3	.150	.150
Crump, Willis (Shorty)	5	17	5	2	1	0	0	3	3	1	0	1	.118	.176
Cummings, Napoleon (Chance)	5	19	8	5	0	0	0	4	2	3	0	2	.263	.263
Deas, James Alvin (Yank)	3	13	3	4	0	0	0	5	0	0	0	2	.308	.308
Dilworth, Arthur	5	18	4	2	0	0	0	1	3	1	1	1	.111	.111
Fuller, William W. (Chick)	1	4	3	1	0	0	0	2	2	0	0	0	.250	.250
James, William (Nux)	2	6	0	3	0	0	0	1	1	0	0	0	.500	.500
Johnson, Daniel Spencil (Shang)	3	13	0	3	0	0	0	1	0	0	0	0	.231	.231
Lundy, Richard Benjamin (King Richard)	5	17	6	4	1	0	0	5	3	1	0	1	.235	.294
Mack, Paul	4	15	1	3	1	1	0	2	1	0	0	3	.200	.400
Roberts, Leroy (Roy)	3	8	0	1	0	0	0	0	0	0	0	0	.125	.125
Short	1	1	0	0	0	0	0	0	0	0	0	1	.000	.000
Wallace, Richard Felix (Dick)	2	7	3	2	0	0	0	2	0	0	1	0	.286	.286
Williams, Thomas (Tom)	3	12	2	1	0	0	0	1	1	0	0	1	.083	.083
		170	36	34	3	1	0	28	16	6	2	14	.200	.229

1917

All Games	Games	AB	R	H	D	T	HR	RBI	W	SB	SAC	E	AVG.	SLUG.
Banks	11	42	8	11	0	0	0	6	3	1	1	1	.262	.262
Baynard, James Howard (Frank)	17	72	6	22	0	0	0	7	0	0	0	1	.306	.306
Briggs, Otto (Mirror)	1	5	0	0	0	0	0	0	0	0	0	0	.000	.000
Brodie, Milledge T.	1	3	0	1	0	0	0	0	0	0	0	0	.333	.333
Clinton, William	69	242	30	51	1	1	0	21	14	5	3	20	.211	.223
Crockett, Frank	22	86	10	19	0	0	0	6	3	0	0	0	.221	.221
Cummings, Napoleon (Chance)	90	346	51	95	3	1	0	55	22	15	7	20	.275	.289
Deas, James Alvin (Yank)	43	147	19	31	3	0	0	13	7	1	3	8	.211	.231
Dilworth, Arthur	19	58	5	13	2	1	1	9	1	0	2	2	.224	.345
Downs, McKinley (Bunny)	70	286	44	75	5	0	1	29	26	12	3	20	.262	.290
Fisher	2	3	0	1	0	0	0	1	0	0	0	0	.333	.333
Forbes, Joseph (Joe)	3	4	0	3	0	0	0	2	1	0	0	2	.750	.750
Franklin	6	23	0	0	0	0	0	0	0	0	0	4	.000	.000
Fuller, William W. (Chick)	4	18	2	2	0	0	0	0	0	0	0	1	.111	.111
Gedschem	1	4	0	1	0	0	0	0	0	0	0	1	.250	.250
Gordon, Herman Evan	2	6	1	2	0	0	0	0	1	1	0	0	.333	.333
Gould, Jr., Lafayette	5	21	0	3	0	0	0	1	0	0	0	0	.143	.143
Gray, Emerson	1	1	0	0	0	0	0	0	0	0	0	0	.000	.000
Handy, William Oscar (Bill)	2	9	0	3	1	0	0	0	0	0	0	0	.333	.444
James, William (Nux)	1	4	0	0	0	0	0	0	0	0	0	1	.000	.000
Johnson, Daniel Spencil (Shang)	36	117	12	22	0	0	0	10	4	2	0	7	.188	.188
Lundy, Richard Benjamin (King Richard)	68	268	37	76	11	1	0	45	19	6	3	43	.284	.332
Mack, Paul	7	25	5	4	0	0	0	3	3	0	0	0	.160	.160
Mays, Horace	1	4	3	3	0	0	0	2	1	0	0	0	.750	.750
McDonald, Gifford Van Horn (Iron Man)	11	31	4	4	0	0	0	1	5	0	1	2	.129	.129
Miller, Louis Lee (Red, Shorty)	65	269	41	62	7	1	1	23	19	5	6	19	.230	.275
Murphy, W. Charles (Speedball)	2	4	1	2	0	0	0	0	0	0	0	0	.500	.500
Oliver, Jr., Hudson J. (Huddy)	2	8	0	1	0	0	0	0	2	0	0	0	.125	.125
Pettus, William Thomas (Bill)	12	50	10	12	1	0	1	7	4	0	0	5	.240	.320
Roberts, Elihu(e) D.	92	363	45	82	5	1	0	36	38	6	6	17	.226	.245
Roberts, Leroy (Roy)	40	111	8	26	1	0	0	12	6	1	3	8	.234	.243
Smith, R. (Red)	15	60	4	11	2	0	0	3	1	2	1	1	.183	.217
Thomas	1	3	0	0	0	0	0	0	0	0	0	0	.000	.000
Tomm (Town)	73	265	30	57	4	0	0	24	21	9	5	8	.215	.230
Tucker, Michael	1	4	0	0	0	0	0	0	0	0	0	0	.000	.000
Wallace, Richard Felix (Dick)	12	41	7	6	1	0	0	3	5	2	2	3	.146	.171
White, Burlin	66	203	10	30	2	0	0	12	12	2	3	10	.148	.158
Wilson, Frank (Chink)	9	29	4	5	1	0	0	0	5	1	0	8	.172	.207
Witherspoon	9	22	1	6	1	0	0	3	1	0	0	0	.273	.318
Wylie, Fred Lewis (The Atlanta Surprise)	7	21	2	4	1	0	0	2	1	0	2	6	.190	.238
		3,278	400	746	52	6	4	336	225	71	51	218	.228	.251

League-Level Opponents	Games	AB	R	H	D	T	HR	RBI	W	SB	SAC	E	AVG.	SLUG.
Clinton, William	22	76	9	14	1	0	0	5	6	3	1	9	.184	.197
Crockett, Frank	3	11	3	2	0	0	0	1	2	0	0	0	.182	.182
Cummings, Napoleon (Chance)	28	105	9	19	1	0	0	11	9	7	7	4	.181	.190
Deas, James Alvin (Yank)	17	58	6	12	3	0	0	4	3	1	3	5	.207	.259
Dilworth, Arthur	4	9	0	2	0	0	0	1	0	0	1	0	.222	.222
Downs, McKinley (Bunny)	16	67	8	17	1	0	1	6	5	2	2	3	.254	.313
Fisher	1	0	0	0	0	0	0	1	0	0	0	0	.000	.000
Forbes, Joseph (Joe)	1	0	0	0	0	0	0	0	1	0	0	0	.000	.000
Franklin	2	7	0	0	0	0	0	0	0	0	0	2	.000	.000
Fuller, William W. (Chick)	2	9	2	2	0	0	0	0	0	0	0	0	.222	.222
Gordon, Herman Evan	1	3	1	1	0	0	0	0	1	1	0	0	.333	.333
Gould, Jr., Lafayette	3	10	0	2	0	0	0	1	0	0	0	0	.200	.200
Handy, William Oscar (Bill)	2	9	0	3	1	0	0	0	0	0	0	0	.333	.444
James, William (Nux)	1	4	0	0	0	0	0	0	0	0	0	1	.000	.000
Johnson, Daniel Spencil (Shang)	11	33	2	6	0	0	0	3	1	1	0	2	.182	.182
Lundy, Richard Benjamin (King Richard)	18	71	10	24	5	0	0	6	9	2	0	12	.338	.408
Mack, Paul	1	3	0	0	0	0	0	0	0	0	0	0	.000	.000
McDonald, Gifford Van Horn (Iron Man)	6	20	2	3	0	0	0	1	3	0	1	2	.150	.150
Miller, Louis Lee (Red)	24	101	8	18	4	1	1	6	5	1	4	6	.178	.267

League-Level Opponents	Games	AB	R	H	D	T	HR	RBI	W	SB	SAC	E	AVG.	SLUG.
Murphy, W. Charles (Speedball)	1	2	0	1	0	0	0	0	0	0	0	0	.500	.500
Pettus, William Thomas (Bill)	5	22	3	5	1	0	1	3	0	0	0	2	.227	.409
Roberts, Elihu(e) D.	28	109	10	27	2	0	0	7	16	2	2	6	.248	.266
Roberts, Leroy (Roy)	15	38	4	12	1	0	0	3	4	0	2	6	.316	.342
Smith, R. (Red)	7	28	2	4	0	0	0	0	1	2	1	0	.143	.143
Tomm (Town), 18BRG	28	97	10	20	0	0	0	9	9	5	3	3	.206	.206
Wallace, Richard Felix (Dick)	3	12	0	1	0	0	0	0	2	0	0	0	.083	.083
White, Burlin	15	38	1	5	0	0	0	3	2	0	1	6	.132	.132
Wilson, Frank (Chink)	3	7	3	1	1	0	0	3	0	0	0	4	.143	.286
Wylie, Fred Lewis (The Atlanta Surprise)	3	8	0	3	1	0	0	2	0	0	2	6	.375	.500
		957	93	204	22	1	3	73	82	27	30	79	.213	.248

1918

All Games	Games	AB	R	H	D	T	HR	RBI	W	SB	SAC	E	AVG.	SLUG.
Albritton, Alexander C. (Alex)	2	6	1	1	0	0	0	0	0	1	1	1	.167	.167
Baynard, James Howard (Frank)	16	64	7	17	1	0	0	7	6	1	2	4	.266	.281
Bowden, Cicero	3	11	2	4	0	0	0	1	0	0	1	1	.364	.364
Bryant, Elias (Country Brown)	31	128	26	42	2	1	0	26	8	2	2	18	.328	.359
Burton, W. (Shorty)	14	65	9	17	1	0	0	9	4	2	1	2	.262	.277
Carney	1	3	1	1	0	0	0	0	0	0	0	0	.333	.333
Crockett, Frank	1	4	0	1	0	0	0	0	0	0	0	0	.250	.250
Cummings, Napoleon (Chance)	28	118	17	35	2	0	0	23	8	6	1	4	.297	.314
Davis, Jack	1	4	1	1	0	0	0	0	0	0	0	1	.250	.250
Deas, James Alvin (Yank)	23	86	10	17	1	0	0	12	11	0	0	6	.198	.209
Downs, McKinley (Bunny)	17	70	13	20	2	0	0	9	5	1	1	3	.286	.314
Edwards, James (Smokey)	1	4	0	1	0	0	0	0	0	0	0	1	.250	.250
Farrell	1	3	1	1	0	0	0	1	0	0	0	0	.333	.333
Fiall, Jr., Thomas Vivian (Tom)	2	3	0	0	0	0	0	0	1	0	0	0	.000	.000
Fields	1	3	0	0	0	0	0	0	0	0	0	0	.000	.000
Forman	2	5	1	1	0	0	0	0	2	0	0	2	.200	.200
Gregory	1	5	2	2	0	0	0	2	0	0	0	3	.400	.400
Gruhler, Henry (Whitey)	1	3	0	1	0	0	0	0	1	0	0	0	.333	.333
Gunn, J.H.	4	13	2	2	0	0	0	2	3	0	0	1	.154	.154
Handy, William Oscar (Bill)	20	73	24	29	4	0	0	19	9	2	1	10	.397	.452
Harris	1	3	0	0	0	0	0	0	1	0	0	0	.000	.000
Harrison	1	0	0	0	0	0	0	0	0	0	0	0	.000	.000
Heckle, Walter	1	3	0	0	0	0	0	0	0	0	0	0	.000	.000
Hogan	1	3	0	0	0	0	0	0	0	0	0	0	.000	.000
Howell, Henry Reese	21	85	14	28	1	0	0	19	2	1	3	10	.329	.341
Johnson, Daniel Spencil (Shang)	2	7	0	1	0	0	0	0	0	0	0	1	.143	.143
Johnson, Jr., George Washington (Dibo)	5	18	1	3	0	0	0	1	1	0	0	3	.167	.167
Jones	1	2	1	0	0	0	0	0	1	0	0	0	.000	.000
Lundy, Richard Benjamin (King Richard)	8	31	4	11	0	0	0	6	1	2	1	4	.355	.355
Marcell, Oliver Hazzard (Ghost)	1	4	0	0	0	0	0	0	0	0	0	1	.000	.000
Mason	1	3	0	0	0	0	0	0	0	0	0	2	.000	.000
Mays, Horace	1	4	2	2	0	0	0	0	0	0	0	0	.500	.500
Moore	2	7	1	2	0	0	0	2	0	0	0	1	.286	.286
Mott	1	3	1	1	0	0	0	0	1	0	0	0	.333	.333
Nelson, Raymond (Ike)	11	37	10	13	1	0	0	7	6	0	1	0	.351	.378
Pettus, William Thomas (Bill)	3	13	1	4	0	0	0	1	2	0	0	3	.308	.308
Pierce, William Herbert (Big Bill)	1	4	0	0	0	0	0	0	0	0	0	0	.000	.000
Ray, Arthur	1	4	1	1	0	0	0	1	0	0	0	0	.250	.250
Reese, John Edward (Speedboy)	15	62	19	17	2	0	0	9	8	3	0	0	.274	.306
Roberts, Elihu(e) D.	11	39	6	9	0	0	0	2	3	0	0	3	.231	.231
Roberts, Leroy (Roy)	13	33	5	9	0	0	0	1	2	1	1	0	.273	.273
Robinson, George Washington (Sis)	15	54	13	16	0	0	0	5	4	0	1	3	.296	.296
Rogers	1	5	2	2	0	0	0	2	0	0	0	0	.400	.400
Shadrick, 18BAG—c	1	1	0	1	0	0	0	0	0	0	0	4	1.000	1.000
Smith, C. (Red)	1	3	0	1	0	0	0	0	0	0	0	3	.333	.333
Smith, R. (Red)	28	111	22	29	2	0	0	16	5	0	1	8	.261	.279
Warmack, Sam	1	4	0	0	0	0	0	0	0	0	0	1	.000	.000
Webster, Pearl Franklyn (Speck)	2	8	4	2	0	0	1	2	1	1	0	0	.250	.625
Wiley, Wabishaw Spencer (Doc, Bill)	1	4	0	0	0	0	0	0	0	0	0	0	.000	.000
		1,226	225	345	19	1	1	185	96	23	18	104	.281	.301

Appendix C: Batting and Pitching Statistics by Year

League-Level Opponents	Games	AB	R	H	D	T	HR	RBI	W	SB	SAC	E	AVG.	SLUG.
Baynard, James Howard (Frank)	9	35	4	8	1	0	0	2	3	0	1	2	.229	.257
Bryant, Elias (Country Brown)	14	58	8	20	1	0	0	11	2	1	1	5	.345	.362
Burton, W. (Shorty)	6	27	2	6	0	0	0	2	0	0	0	1	.222	.222
Cummings, Napoleon (Chance)	14	54	4	14	1	0	0	7	5	3	1	0	.259	.278
Davis, Jack	1	4	1	1	0	0	0	0	0	0	0	1	.250	.250
Deas, James Alvin (Yank)	13	45	3	7	0	0	0	4	7	0	0	5	.156	.156
Downs, McKinley (Bunny)	9	38	6	11	1	0	0	5	4	1	0	0	.289	.316
Edwards, James (Smokey)	1	4	0	1	0	0	0	0	0	0	0	1	.250	.250
Handy, William Oscar (Bill)	13	47	13	14	2	0	0	6	6	2	1	8	.298	.340
Howell, Henry Reese	10	35	6	10	1	0	0	3	2	1	2	5	.286	.314
Johnson, Daniel Spencil (Shang)	2	7	0	1	0	0	0	0	0	0	0	1	.143	.143
Johnson, Jr., George Washington (Dibo)	3	12	1	2	0	0	0	0	1	0	0	3	.167	.167
Lundy, Richard Benjamin (King Richard)	5	20	2	7	0	0	0	2	0	1	1	2	.350	.350
Mason	1	3	0	0	0	0	0	0	0	0	0	2	.000	.000
Nelson, Raymond (Ike)	3	12	1	4	0	0	0	2	0	0	0	0	.333	.333
Pettus, William Thomas (Bill)	3	13	1	4	0	0	0	1	2	0	0	3	.308	.308
Reese, John Edward (Speedboy)	7	29	6	4	1	0	0	2	3	1	0	0	.138	.172
Roberts, Elihu(e) D.	5	16	0	4	0	0	0	1	0	0	0	0	.250	.250
Roberts, Leroy (Roy, Eveready)	4	10	3	3	0	0	0	0	0	0	0	0	.300	.300
Robinson, George Washington (Sis)	6	18	0	1	0	0	0	0	0	0	1	0	.056	.056
Smith, C. (Red)	1	3	0	1	0	0	0	0	0	0	0	3	.333	.333
Smith, R. (Red)	9	33	6	5	1	0	0	2	2	0	0	2	.152	.182
Webster, Pearl Franklyn (Speck)	2	8	4	2	0	0	1	2	1	1	0	0	.250	.625
		531	71	130	9	0	1	52	38	11	8	44	.245	.267

1919

All Games	Games	AB	R	H	D	T	HR	RBI	W	SB	SAC	E	AVG.	SLUG.
Baynard, James Howard (Frank)	3	7	1	1	0	0	0	1	1	0	0	0	.143	.143
Bryant, Elias (Country Brown)	34	124	13	32	4	0	0	15	6	5	3	1	.258	.290
Deas, James Alvin (Yank)	3	6	0	1	0	0	0	0	2	0	0	0	.167	.167
Dilworth, Arthur	6	18	2	4	0	0	0	1	0	0	0	1	.222	.222
Earle, Charles Babcock (Frank)	5	23	3	4	0	0	0	3	3	1	1	0	.174	.174
Edwards, James (Smokey)	4	5	0	1	0	0	0	1	0	0	0	0	.200	.200
Forbes, Frank Lindsey (Strangler)	6	28	2	6	1	0	0	3	1	1	0	1	.214	.250
Gatewood, Ernest E.	70	249	22	47	3	1	0	27	7	2	5	6	.189	.209
Handy, William Oscar (Bill)	89	377	68	93	12	5	2	44	25	6	11	15	.247	.321
Hubbard, Jesse James (Mountain Man)	8	25	6	7	1	0	1	3	2	0	0	0	.280	.440
Hutchinson, Fred (Hutch, Pug)	88	357	36	80	5	4	3	37	17	2	8	14	.224	.286
Jeffries, James Courtney (Jim)	7	21	3	5	0	0	0	2	2	1	0	0	.238	.238
Johnson, Cecil Leon (Sess)	15	47	10	10	2	0	0	3	4	1	1	0	.213	.255
Johnson, Daniel Spencil (Shang)	23	64	4	13	1	0	0	3	3	0	1	1	.203	.219
Johnson, Jr., George (Chappie)	28	86	4	9	0	0	0	2	4	0	4	1	.105	.105
Lloyd, John Henry (Pop)	84	345	48	111	15	6	1	72	26	12	8	18	.322	.409
Lundy, Richard Benjamin (King Richard)	1	3	0	1	0	0	0	0	1	0	0	0	.333	.333
Miller, Louis Lee (Red)	1	4	0	0	0	0	0	0	0	0	0	0	.000	.000
Parks, Joseph B. (Joe)	2	11	0	0	0	0	0	0	0	0	0	1	.000	.000
Pierce, William Herbert (Big Bill)	1	4	0	0	0	0	0	0	0	0	0	0	.000	.000
Poles, Spottswood (Spot)	56	248	43	70	6	3	1	27	19	9	3	6	.282	.343
Pugh, John (Johnny)	70	272	28	56	8	4	0	26	13	7	5	6	.206	.265
Redding, Richard (Cannonball)	44	120	13	26	1	2	1	9	2	1	2	7	.217	.283
Roberts, Leroy (Roy)	24	68	4	9	0	1	0	2	2	0	1	2	.132	.162
Shively, George Anner (Rabbit)	78	345	77	101	5	3	1	35	24	26	6	2	.293	.333
Taylor, Benjamin Harrison (Ben)	87	347	57	110	14	5	3	79	33	8	4	15	.317	.412
Thompson, J.W. (Gunboat)	13	49	5	9	0	0	0	3	3	1	0	2	.184	.184
Whitworth, Richard Henderson (Dick)	1	1	0	0	0	0	0	0	0	0	0	0	.000	.000
Wickware, Frank Ellis (Red Ant)	16	42	3	4	2	0	0	1	3	2	0	1	.095	.143
Wiley, Wabishaw Spencer (Doc)	5	15	3	1	0	0	0	3	1	0	0	0	.067	.067
Williams, Joseph (Smokey Joe)	2	8	1	1	0	0	0	1	1	0	0	0	.125	.125
Williams, Thomas (Tom)	2	5	0	0	0	0	0	0	0	0	0	0	.000	.000
		3,324	456	812	80	34	13	400	207	86	63	100	.244	.301

League-Level Opponents	Games	AB	R	H	D	T	HR	RBI	W	SB	SAC	E	AVG.	SLUG.
Baynard, James Howard (Frank)	2	6	1	1	0	0	0	1	1	0	0	0	.167	.167
Bryant, Elias (Country Brown)	6	19	1	3	0	0	0	0	0	0	0	0	.158	.158

Appendix C: Batting and Pitching Statistics by Year

League-Level Opponents	Games	AB	R	H	D	T	HR	RBI	W	SB	SAC	E	AVG.	SLUG.
Dilworth, Arthur	2	3	0	0	0	0	0	0	0	0	0	0	.000	.000
Earle, Charles Babcock (Frank)	1	5	1	1	0	0	0	0	1	0	0	0	.200	.200
Edwards, James (Smokey)	1	2	0	0	0	0	0	0	0	0	0	0	.000	.000
Forbes, Frank Lindsey (Strangler)	2	9	1	3	1	0	0	2	1	0	0	0	.333	.444
Gatewood, Ernest E.	20	74	5	9	1	1	0	3	2	0	0	2	.122	.162
Handy, William Oscar (Bill)	23	99	20	26	5	2	1	13	7	1	3	4	.263	.384
Hubbard, Jesse James (Mountain Man)	2	6	1	1	0	0	0	0	1	0	0	0	.167	.167
Hutchinson, Fred (Hutch, Pug)	23	98	11	21	0	1	2	11	3	0	3	4	.214	.296
Jeffries, James Courtney (Jim)	1	2	0	0	0	0	0	0	0	0	0	0	.000	.000
Johnson, Cecil Leon (Sess)	4	10	2	0	0	0	0	0	2	0	0	0	.000	.000
Johnson, Daniel Spencil (Shang)	5	13	0	4	1	0	0	2	0	0	0	1	.308	.385
Johnson, Jr., George (Chappie)	6	18	2	4	0	0	0	1	0	0	2	2	.222	.222
Lloyd, John Henry (Pop)	23	99	12	36	3	1	0	23	7	4	3	7	.364	.414
Parks, Joseph B. (Joe)	2	11	0	0	0	0	0	0	0	0	0	1	.000	.000
Poles, Spottswood (Spot)	14	68	13	23	3	2	0	8	4	2	1	1	.338	.441
Pugh, John (Johnny)	20	78	5	14	2	2	0	5	2	4	2	1	.179	.256
Redding, Richard (Cannonball)	13	43	10	13	1	2	1	7	1	0	1	1	.302	.488
Roberts, Leroy (Roy)	9	21	0	1	0	0	0	0	1	0	1	0	.048	.048
Shively, George Anner (Rabbit)	21	93	16	19	1	0	0	4	7	2	2	1	.204	.215
Taylor, Benjamin Harrison (Ben)	23	95	10	25	2	3	0	17	8	3	1	1	.263	.347
Thompson, J.W. (Gunboat, Fred)	3	9	0	0	0	0	0	0	0	0	0	1	.000	.000
Whitworth, Richard Henderson (Dick)	1	1	0	0	0	0	0	0	0	0	0	0	.000	.000
Wickware, Frank Ellis (Red Ant)	2	6	1	1	1	0	0	1	0	0	0	0	.167	.333
Wiley, Wabishaw Spencer (Doc)	1	2	0	0	0	0	0	0	1	0	0	0	.000	.000
Williams, Thomas (Tom)	1	2	0	0	0	0	0	0	0	0	0	0	.000	.000
		892	112	205	21	14	4	98	49	16	19	25	.230	.298

1920

All Games	Games	AB	R	H	D	T	HR	RBI	W	SB	SAC	E	AVG.	SLUG.
Barbour [Barber], Jesse Bernard (Phantom)	49	196	38	50	3	1	0	13	18	7	1	5	.255	.281
Bryant, Elias (Country Brown)	95	345	53	95	6	5	1	36	26	12	7	10	.275	.330
Carroll	1	1	0	0	0	0	0	0	0	0	0	0	.000	.000
Deas, James Alvin (Yank)	36	122	19	33	0	1	1	20	10	2	1	7	.270	.311
Handy, William Oscar (Bill)	88	310	56	86	8	5	3	42	39	14	3	16	.277	.365
Lundy, Richard Benjamin (King Richard)	91	340	65	101	11	4	3	60	30	16	4	33	.297	.379
Marcell, Oliver Hazzard (Ghost)	97	386	72	122	7	5	1	64	24	13	10	19	.316	.368
Means, Lemuel Lewis (Lou)	45	151	29	35	2	0	1	11	16	6	2	12	.232	.265
Mederos, Jesus (Frank)	69	237	28	62	6	3	1	26	20	7	3	13	.262	.325
Pierce, William Herbert (Big Bill)	99	354	54	108	15	5	4	54	34	8	3	19	.305	.410
Pugh, John (Johnny)	41	135	30	31	2	2	2	13	18	5	2	4	.230	.319
Redding, Richard (Cannonball)	48	129	15	34	4	2	0	15	7	3	1	8	.264	.326
Rojo, Domingo Julio (Clown)	74	236	39	58	5	1	0	31	17	13	4	14	.246	.275
Ryan, Merven John (Red)	32	86	7	24	2	0	0	8	3	1	0	2	.279	.302
Shively, George Anner (Rabbit)	17	67	11	18	0	1	0	8	6	3	1	3	.269	.299
Smith, R. (Red)	22	70	4	13	2	0	0	3	2	2	3	2	.186	.214
Thomas, Julian R. (Jules)	7	27	2	3	0	0	0	1	0	0	0	2	.111	.111
Treadwell, Harold E.	32	108	18	29	0	0	1	13	1	0	1	3	.269	.296
Williams, Andrew (Stringbean)	24	71	7	21	1	1	0	5	2	1	1	2	.296	.338
		3,371	547	923	74	36	18	423	273	113	47	174	.274	.333

League-Level Opponents	Games	AB	R	H	D	T	HR	RBI	W	SB	SAC	E	AVG.	SLUG.
Barbour [Barber], Jesse Bernard (Phantom)	29	114	18	27	3	1	0	5	10	5	0	4	.237	.281
Bryant, Elias (Country Brown)	40	137	20	33	3	1	1	10	13	6	2	6	.241	.299
Deas, James Alvin (Yank)	11	34	5	6	0	0	1	5	3	0	1	4	.176	.265
Handy, William Oscar (Bill)	38	121	19	29	4	2	3	11	20	7	3	6	.240	.380
Lundy, Richard Benjamin (King Richard)	37	130	24	46	4	1	3	19	14	8	1	13	.354	.469
Marcell, Oliver Hazzard (Ghost)	40	146	20	40	2	2	1	11	14	2	5	8	.274	.336
Means, Lemuel Lewis (Lou)	10	33	3	8	1	0	0	1	0	3	0	3	.242	.273
Mederos, Jesus (Frank)	24	81	6	16	2	1	1	5	3	1	1	4	.198	.284
Pierce, William Herbert (Big Bill)	40	132	18	38	5	3	2	18	15	3	2	5	.288	.417
Pugh, John (Johnny)	14	37	4	3	0	0	1	2	4	3	1	3	.081	.162
Redding, Richard (Cannonball)	24	56	8	15	3	2	0	6	3	0	1	4	.268	.393
Rojo, Domingo Julio (Clown)	31	85	9	12	1	1	0	4	10	1	1	5	.141	.176
Ryan, Merven John (Red)	15	33	4	7	1	0	0	3	1	1	0	1	.212	.242

Appendix C: Batting and Pitching Statistics by Year

League-Level Opponents	Games	AB	R	H	D	T	HR	RBI	W	SB	SAC	E	AVG.	SLUG.
Shively, George Anner (Rabbit)	8	26	2	7	0	1	0	1	5	3	1	3	.269	.346
Smith, R. (Red)	5	16	0	0	0	0	0	0	0	0	1	2	.000	.000
Thomas, Julian R. (Jules)	5	19	1	2	0	0	0	1	0	0	0	1	.105	.105
Treadwell, Harold E.	8	29	4	10	0	0	1	2	0	0	0	0	.345	.448
Williams, Andrew (Stringbean)	10	30	2	10	1	0	0	2	1	0	0	1	.333	.367
		1,259	167	309	30	15	14	106	116	43	20	73	.245	.326

Cuban Winter League Batting, 1920-21	Games	AB	R	H	D	T	HR	RBI	W	SB	SAC	E	AVG.	SLUG.
Allen, Sr., Toussaint L'Ouverture (Tom)	7	19	1	3	0	0	1	4	1	0	0	1	.158	.316
Arumi, Joaquin	4	15	2	3	0	0	0	0	0	0	1	3	.200	.200
Barbour [Barber], Jesse Bernard (Phantom)	1	3	0	1	1	0	0	0	0	1	1	0	.333	.667
Blackwell, Charles H. (Rucker)	6	27	5	9	1	1	0	4	1	1	0	2	.333	.444
Bryant, Elias (Country Brown)	1	4	0	1	0	0	0	0	0	0	1	0	.250	.250
Campos yToledo, Francisco (Tatica)	2	6	1	0	0	0	0	0	1	0	0	1	.000	.000
Casanas	1	2	0	0	0	0	0	0	0	0	0	0	.000	.000
Charleston, Oscar McKinley (Charlie)	6	22	6	9	1	0	0	5	5	2	0	0	.409	.455
Clark, Morten Avery (Specs)	11	50	6	15	1	0	0	5	4	3	2	5	.300	.320
Clemente, Miguel	4	16	1	3	1	0	0	1	0	0	1	1	.188	.250
Cockrell [Williams], Phillip (Fish)	6	10	4	0	0	0	0	0	2	0	0	0	.000	.000
Flournoy, Willis Jefferson (Pud)	5	10	0	0	0	0	0	0	0	0	1	1	.000	.000
Handy, William Oscar (Bill)	1	1	0	0	0	0	0	0	2	0	1	0	.000	.000
Hewitt, Joseph William (Joe)	5	19	3	2	0	0	0	0	1	3	2	1	.105	.105
Jenkins, Clarence Reginald (Fats)	1	3	1	1	1	0	0	0	0	0	0	0	.333	.667
Lundy, Richard Benjamin (King Richard,	2	7	1	0	0	0	0	0	2	0	0	0	.000	.000
Marcell, Oliver Hazzard (Ghost)	1	4	0	0	0	0	0	0	0	0	0	1	.000	.000
Martinez, Magdaleno (Maleno)	7	27	4	4	0	0	0	3	3	0	0	0	.148	.148
Mirabal, Juanelo (Juan)	3	13	0	1	0	0	0	0	0	0	0	1	.077	.077
Parpetti, Agustin (Pulpita)	7	30	0	7	0	0	0	3	0	1	0	2	.233	.233
Pedroso, Eustaquio (Bombin)	3	13	0	2	0	0	0	0	1	0	1	4	.154	.154
Pierce, William Herbert (Big Bill)	1	4	1	2	0	0	0	0	0	0	0	0	.500	.500
Redding, Richard (Cannonball)	9	26	1	9	1	0	0	2	6	0	0	0	.346	.385
Rodriguez yValera, Vicente Jose (El Loco)	7	27	2	6	0	0	0	3	2	1	0	4	.222	.222
Rodriquez, A.	2	5	1	2	0	0	0	0	0	0	0	0	.400	.400
Rodriquez, Jose Agustin (Frijolito)	2	8	0	0	0	0	0	0	1	0	0	0	.000	.000
Rojo, Domingo Julio (Clown)	2	4	1	2	0	0	0	1	0	0	1	0	.500	.500
Ryan, Merven John (Red	4	13	1	2	0	0	0	3	0	0	0	0	.154	.154
Santop [Loftin], D. Louis (Top)	7	23	2	10	2	1	1	4	4	1	1	1	.435	.739
Teran, Julian (Recurvon, Julio)	6	22	1	5	2	0	0	1	0	1	1	0	.227	.318
Valdes, Severino	6	26	2	5	0	0	0	0	4	3	0	0	.192	.192
Villarin, M.	3	12	0	1	0	0	0	0	1	0	0	3	.083	.083
		471	47	105	11	2	2	39	41	17	14	31	.223	.268

1921

All Games	Games	AB	R	H	D	T	HR	RBI	W	SB	SAC	E	AVG.	SLUG.
Barbour [Barber], Jesse Bernard (Phantom)	86	376	71	110	18	5	1	44	18	10	4	10	.293	.375
Bryant, Elias (Country Brown)	103	398	65	122	13	5	5	75	23	9	12	12	.307	.402
Busby, Maurice (Lefty)	5	13	1	0	0	0	0	0	0	0	0	0	.000	.000
Cockrell [Williams], Phillip (Fish)	1	1	0	0	0	0	0	0	0	0	0	0	.000	.000
Crump, Willis (Shorty)	1	4	0	1	0	0	0	1	0	0	0	0	.250	.250
Deas, James Alvin (Yank)	41	131	14	31	2	0	0	15	6	1	2	4	.237	.252
Fuller, James (Jimmy)	1	2	1	1	0	0	0	1	1	0	0	0	.500	.500
Gatewood, Ernest E.	29	79	9	13	0	0	0	3	8	1	0	4	.165	.165
Graham, Dennis Wilson (Peaches)	59	169	29	55	3	1	0	23	8	3	4	7	.325	.355
Handy, William Oscar (Bill)	78	270	39	77	13	4	5	43	24	2	8	22	.285	.419
Harvey, John Henry (Howling Harvey)	6	7	1	1	0	0	0	0	0	0	0	0	.143	.143
Jackson, Jr., Richard Alvin (Dick)	29	77	8	19	0	2	1	11	3	0	2	8	.247	.338
Jefferson, Ralph Tennyson	8	31	1	4	0	0	1	4	0	0	0	1	.129	.226
Johnson, Daniel Spencil (Shang)	2	5	1	0	0	0	0	0	0	0	1	1	.000	.000
Johnson, Jr., George Washington (Dibo)	1	5	0	0	0	0	0	0	0	1	0	0	.000	.000
Lee, Sr., Holsey Scranton (Scrip)	5	13	1	1	0	0	0	0	0	0	0	0	.077	.077
Lundy, Richard Benjamin (King Richard,	74	283	51	93	10	5	3	55	17	10	4	36	.329	.431
Lyons, James Henry (Jimmy)	1	4	0	0	0	0	0	0	0	0	0	0	.000	.000

238 Appendix C: Batting and Pitching Statistics by Year

All Games	Games	AB	R	H	D	T	HR	RBI	W	SB	SAC	E	AVG.	SLUG.
Marcell, Oliver Hazzard (Ghost)	105	407	76	131	13	10	3	67	36	10	14	30	.322	.425
McDonald, Gifford Van Horn (Iron Man)	3	5	0	0	0	0	0	0	0	0	0	0	.000	.000
Miller, Louis Lee (Red)	1	3	1	1	0	0	0	1	0	0	0	1	.333	.333
Mitchell, Benjamin Arnett [Ernest] (Hooks)	12	25	0	7	0	0	0	0	1	0	0	3	.280	.280
Mungin [Mongin], Samuel (Sam)	3	8	0	4	1	0	0	1	1	1	0	0	.500	.625
Pettus, William Thomas (Bill)	103	400	75	124	12	5	8	80	40	6	9	21	.310	.425
Pierce, William Herbert (Big Bill)	2	4	1	0	0	0	0	0	1	0	1	0	.000	.000
Pugh, John (Johnny)	41	114	21	30	3	3	1	18	14	2	4	5	.263	.368
Reavis, Al W.	2	3	1	2	0	0	0	0	1	0	0	0	.667	.667
Redding, Richard (Cannonball)	38	109	12	16	4	3	1	11	4	0	2	4	.147	.266
Richardson, Henry Layton (Long Tom)	17	37	1	11	0	0	0	5	1	0	1	2	.297	.297
Rojo, Domingo Julio (Clown)	86	279	54	73	11	6	5	45	24	9	3	11	.262	.398
Ryan, Merven John (Red)	23	50	2	11	0	0	0	2	1	0	5	2	.220	.220
Shively, George Anner (Rabbit)	83	320	73	99	4	2	1	34	40	8	10	8	.309	.344
Suttles, George (Mule)	1	4	0	1	0	0	0	0	0	0	0	0	.250	.250
Torriente yTorrienti, Cristobal (Carlos)	1	4	1	1	0	0	0	1	0	0	0	0	.250	.250
Treadwell, Harold E.	28	71	14	16	1	1	1	9	6	0	0	1	.225	.310
Williams, Andrew (Stringbean)	16	32	9	15	1	2	0	6	1	1	0	1	.469	.625
Winters, James Henry (Nip)	9	18	4	6	0	0	0	5	3	0	3	0	.333	.333
Woods, William J. (Willie)	1	4	2	3	0	0	0	1	0	0	0	1	.750	.750
		3,765	639	1,079	109	54	36	561	282	74	89	196	.287	.373

League-Level Opponents	Games	AB	R	H	D	T	HR	RBI	W	SB	SAC	E	AVG.	SLUG.
Barbour [Barber], Jesse Bernard (Phantom)	58	250	46	69	13	3	0	22	13	10	3	8	.276	.352
Bryant, Elias (Country Brown)	62	225	36	61	11	1	3	40	17	7	12	8	.271	.369
Cockrell [Williams], Phillip (Fish)	1	1	0	0	0	0	0	0	0	0	0	0	.000	.000
Deas, James Alvin (Yank)	18	48	4	8	2	0	0	6	4	0	2	2	.167	.208
Fuller, James (Jimmy)	1	2	1	1	0	0	0	1	1	0	0	0	.500	.500
Gatewood, Ernest E.	11	28	4	7	0	0	0	3	6	1	0	1	.250	.250
Graham, Dennis Wilson (Peaches)	32	79	14	26	3	1	0	12	5	3	4	2	.329	.392
Handy, William Oscar (Bill)	53	180	24	49	9	4	3	28	20	2	6	13	.272	.417
Harvey, John Henry (Howling Harvey)	2	2	0	0	0	0	0	0	0	0	0	0	.000	.000
Jackson, Jr., Richard Alvin (Dick)	16	36	1	6	0	1	1	7	0	0	2	5	.167	.306
Jefferson, Ralph Tennyson	3	10	1	1	0	0	1	2	0	0	0	0	.100	.400
Johnson, Daniel Spencil (Shang)	1	4	1	0	0	0	0	0	0	0	1	1	.000	.000
Johnson, Jr., George Washington (Dibo)	1	5	0	0	0	0	0	0	1	0	0	0	.000	.000
Lee, Sr., Holsey Scranton (Script)	1	2	0	0	0	0	0	0	0	0	0	0	.000	.000
Lundy, Richard Benjamin (King Richard)	47	177	36	60	7	5	3	40	13	8	4	23	.339	.486
Marcell, Oliver Hazzard (Ghost)	63	232	46	75	9	6	1	40	24	8	13	14	.323	.427
McDonald, Gifford Van Horn (Iron Man)	3	5	0	0	0	0	0	0	0	0	0	0	.000	.000
Miller, Louis Lee (Red)	1	3	1	1	0	0	0	1	0	0	0	1	.333	.333
Mitchell, Benjamin Arnett [Ernest] (Hooks)	5	9	0	2	0	0	0	0	0	0	0	1	.222	.222
Mungin [Mongin], Samuel (Sam)	3	8	0	4	1	0	0	1	1	1	0	0	.500	.625
Pettus, William Thomas (Bill)	64	239	46	71	10	4	5	55	30	5	8	19	.297	.435
Pierce, William Herbert (Big Bill)	2	4	1	0	0	0	0	0	1	0	1	0	.000	.000
Pugh, John (Johnny)	21	50	8	12	1	2	0	6	6	0	4	1	.240	.340
Reavis, Al W.	1	0	0	0	0	0	0	0	0	0	0	0		
Redding, Richard (Cannonball)	28	82	8	12	3	2	1	9	3	0	2	3	.146	.268
Richardson, Henry Layton (Long Tom)	7	11	0	4	0	0	0	0	1	0	1	0	.364	.364
Rojo, Domingo Julio (Clown)	57	182	34	47	7	4	5	33	18	8	3	9	.258	.423
Ryan, Merven John (Red)	14	33	1	5	0	0	0	2	1	0	3	2	.152	.152
Shively, George Anner (Rabbit)	51	192	48	56	3	2	0	13	30	7	9	6	.292	.328
Suttles, George (Mule)	1	4	0	1	0	0	0	0	0	0	0	0	.250	.250
Treadwell, Harold E.	15	38	7	5	0	1	1	4	3	0	0	1	.132	.263
Williams, Andrew (Stringbean)	10	22	4	11	1	0	0	4	1	0	0	1	.500	.545
Winters, James Henry (Nip)	6	13	3	4	0	0	0	4	3	0	1	1	.308	.308
		2,176	375	598	80	36	24	333	201	61	79	122	.275	.378

1922

All Games	Games	AB	R	H	D	T	HR	RBI	W	SB	SAC	E	AVG.	SLUG.
Brown, Arnold (Buck)	18	61	4	11	1	0	0	5	3	0	0	5	.180	.197
Childs	1	3	0	1	0	0	0	0	0	0	0	0	.333	.333
Cramer	1	3	0	0	0	0	0	0	0	0	0	0	.000	.000
Crockett, Frank	72	281	37	60	8	1	0	21	21	2	5	7	.214	.249

Appendix C: Batting and Pitching Statistics by Year

All Games	Games	AB	R	H	D	T	HR	RBI	W	SB	SAC	E	AVG.	SLUG.
Cummings, Napoleon (Chance)	67	252	51	70	6	2	0	39	21	7	4	13	.278	.317
Davis, Jack	73	261	38	62	6	2	1	34	15	13	3	19	.238	.287
Deas, James Alvin (Yank)	51	173	31	46	3	3	1	24	5	3	4	3	.266	.335
Ermy	1	4	0	1	0	0	0	0	0	0	0	0	.250	.250
Finley, John Thomas (Tom)	11	39	1	7	0	0	0	1	2	0	0	3	.179	.179
Hairstone, James Burton (J.B.)	6	20	1	1	0	0	0	0	1	1	0	0	.050	.050
Harris	5	14	0	3	0	0	0	1	0	0	0	2	.214	.214
Johnson, Nate (Speedboy)	22	67	9	12	1	1	1	6	2	1	0	7	.179	.269
Jones, William (Willie)	41	125	17	27	6	1	2	12	13	3	3	8	.216	.328
Jordan, Henry (Hen)	1	4	0	1	0	0	0	0	0	0	0	0	.250	.250
Kyle, Andy	6	17	3	6	0	0	1	2	0	0	0	0	.353	.529
Lewis, Milton	27	87	11	21	3	1	2	12	5	0	2	5	.241	.368
Lloyd	1	1	0	0	0	0	0	0	3	0	0	0	.000	.000
Lundy, Richard Benjamin (King Richard)	66	239	47	66	10	2	3	49	25	9	5	26	.276	.372
Malloy, Charles	10	22	2	5	0	0	0	0	2	0	1	2	.227	.227
Mason, Charles (Corporal)	1	1	1	1	0	0	0	1	0	0	0	1	1.000	1.000
Means, Lemuel Lewis (Lou)	33	96	14	15	2	0	0	5	11	1	3	8	.156	.177
O'Neill, Charles	17	51	4	7	0	0	0	2	6	1	1	2	.137	.137
Patterson	4	7	1	2	0	0	0	0	0	0	0	3	.286	.286
Penn	2	4	0	0	0	0	0	0	0	0	0	1	.000	.000
Perry, Carlisle (Cash)	5	17	2	3	0	0	0	2	0	0	0	1	.176	.176
Reid, Ambrose Leevolia (Ambrose)	75	281	47	82	10	2	2	42	18	5	7	9	.292	.363
Richardson, Henry Layton (Long Tom)	1	1	0	0	0	0	0	0	0	0	0	0	.000	.000
Smith, Jake	39	128	21	29	5	1	2	14	12	1	2	3	.227	.328
Streeter, Samuel (Sam)	24	67	9	12	1	0	0	6	3	0	0	3	.179	.194
Wheeler, Joseph (Jodie)	25	55	3	3	0	0	0	0	7	1	0	4	.055	.055
Williams, Andrew (Stringbean)	1	3	1	1	1	0	0	1	0	0	0	0	.333	.667
Young, Berdell	58	199	26	58	11	6	0	39	10	4	0	2	.291	.407
		2,583	381	613	74	22	15	318	185	52	40	137	.237	.300

League-Level Opponents	Games	AB	R	H	D	T	HR	RBI	W	SB	SAC	E	AVG.	SLUG.
Brown, Arnold (Buck)	1	2	0	0	0	0	0	0	0	0	0	0	.000	.000
Cramer	1	3	0	0	0	0	0	0	0	0	0	0	.000	.000
Crockett, Frank	16	65	13	14	4	0	0	3	4	0	1	2	.215	.277
Cummings, Napoleon (Chance)	15	57	9	15	1	1	0	9	5	2	2	7	.263	.316
Davis, Jack	17	57	5	14	2	0	0	4	3	0	0	7	.246	.281
Deas, James Alvin (Yank)	11	36	10	12	0	3	0	6	1	1	0	1	.333	.500
Finley, John Thomas (Tom)	3	11	0	2	0	0	0	0	1	0	0	1	.182	.182
Hairstone, James Burton (J.B.)	3	12	0	0	0	0	0	0	0	0	0	0	.000	.000
Harris	1	4	0	2	0	0	0	1	0	0	0	1	.500	.500
Johnson, Nate (Speedboy)	7	22	2	2	0	0	0	0	1	1	0	2	.091	.091
Jones, William (Willie)	8	22	2	3	1	0	0	2	2	1	0	1	.136	.182
Jordan, Henry (Hen)	1	4	0	1	0	0	0	0	0	0	0	0	.250	.250
Lewis, Milton	3	9	0	4	2	0	0	0	0	0	0	0	.444	.667
Lloyd,	1	1	0	0	0	0	0	0	3	0	0	0	.000	.000
Lundy, Richard Benjamin (King Richard)	17	59	9	16	2	1	0	11	8	3	1	5	.271	.339
Mason, Charles (Corporal)	1	1	1	1	0	0	0	1	0	0	0	1	1.000	1.000
Means, Lemuel Lewis (Lou)	11	33	5	6	0	0	0	1	4	0	1	4	.182	.182
O'Neill, Charles	3	8	0	1	0	0	0	0	2	0	0	0	.125	.125
Patterson	1	1	0	1	0	0	0	0	0	0	0	1	1.000	1.000
Penn	1	1	0	0	0	0	0	0	0	0	0	1	.000	.000
Perry, Carlisle (Cash)	2	7	1	2	0	0	0	2	0	0	0	1	.286	.286
Reid, Ambrose Leevolia (Ambrose)	17	61	11	16	3	0	0	9	6	0	2	1	.262	.311
Smith, Jake	8	23	5	4	0	0	0	2	5	0	0	0	.174	.174
Streeter, Samuel (Sam)	5	16	4	5	1	0	0	4	0	0	0	1	.313	.375
Wheeler, Joseph (Jodie)	1	3	0	0	0	0	0	0	1	0	0	1	.000	.000
Williams, Andrew (Stringbean)	1	3	1	1	1	0	0	1	0	0	0	0	.333	.667
Young, Berdell	9	36	4	12	1	2	0	11	0	0	0	0	.333	.472
		557	82	134	18	7	0	67	46	8	7	38	.241	.298

1922 (New York City Bacharach Giants)

All Games	Games	AB	R	H	D	T	HR	RBI	W	SB	SAC	E	AVG.	SLUG.
Blane	1	0	0	0	0	0	0	0	0	0	0	0	.000	.000
Bryant, Elias (Country Brown)	67	253	29	75	10	2	0	32	12	7	9	13	.296	.352

1922 (New York City Bacharach Giants)

All Games	Games	AB	R	H	D	T	HR	RBI	W	SB	SAC	E	AVG.	SLUG.
Crain, John	1	2	0	0	0	0	0	0	0	0	0	0	.000	.000
Davis	1	3	0	0	0	0	0	0	0	0	0	0	.000	.000
Duncan, Warren	55	202	25	54	6	1	0	21	8	4	4	6	.267	.307
Gray, Emerson	9	21	4	5	1	0	0	2	4	1	1	2	.238	.286
Hairstone, James Burton (J.B.)	1	1	0	0	0	0	0	0	0	0	0	0	.000	.000
Holland	1	4	1	1	0	0	0	1	0	0	0	0	.250	.250
Hudspeth, Robert (Highpocket)	76	312	47	99	10	6	6	54	18	4	3	18	.317	.446
Hutchinson, Fred (Hutch, Pug)	2	7	1	2	1	0	0	0	0	0	0	1	.286	.429
Jackson, Jr., Richard Alvin (Dick)	57	215	30	55	8	3	0	24	7	6	2	11	.256	.321
Jenkins, Clarence Reginald (Fats)	2	6	2	3	0	0	0	1	1	1	1	0	.500	.500
Jones, William (Willie)	2	9	2	2	0	0	0	1	0	0	0	0	.222	.222
Lloyd, John Henry (Pop)	73	311	59	100	18	2	6	71	16	9	8	14	.322	.450
Lundy, Richard Benjamin (King Richard)	3	11	4	4	1	1	0	3	0	1	0	0	.364	.636
Marcell, Oliver Hazzard (Ghost)	72	291	55	87	12	4	1	36	24	4	15	13	.299	.378
Mason, Charles (Corporal)	2	7	0	1	0	0	0	1	0	0	0	0	.143	.143
McIntyre	1	5	0	3	0	0	0	0	0	0	0	0	.600	.600
Means, Lemuel Lewis (Lou)	1	4	0	0	0	0	0	0	0	0	0	0	.000	.000
O'Neill, Charles	10	39	3	7	0	0	0	4	0	0	0	5	.179	.179
Ramirez, Ramiro (Rome)	65	234	30	62	6	1	0	25	18	4	5	4	.265	.299
Redding, Richard (Cannonball)	24	66	6	15	1	0	0	7	0	0	2	2	.227	.242
Reid, Ambrose Leevolia (Ambrose)	1	4	1	1	0	0	0	0	0	0	0	0	.250	.250
Roberts, Leroy (Roy)	21	56	9	14	2	0	0	6	3	1	0	0	.250	.286
Rojo, Domingo Julio (Clown)	62	204	32	52	7	2	2	31	21	4	6	8	.255	.338
Shively, George Anner (Rabbit)	65	277	53	75	9	0	0	30	20	4	4	5	.271	.303
Smith	3	9	2	1	0	0	0	0	1	0	0	1	.111	.111
Treadwell, Harold E.	28	82	12	27	2	0	0	9	3	0	2	2	.329	.354
Williams, Andrew (Stringbean)	10	23	1	7	0	0	0	1	0	0	0	0	.304	.304
Winters, James Henry (Nip)	22	51	5	17	2	0	0	5	2	0	1	1	.333	.373
York, James Henry (Jim)	5	9	1	0	0	0	0	0	2	0	1	0	.000	.000
		2,718	414	769	96	22	15	365	160	50	64	106	.283	.351

League-Level Opponents	Games	AB	R	H	D	T	HR	RBI	W	SB	SAC	E	AVG.	SLUG.
Blane	1	0	0	0	0	0	0	0	0	0	0	0	.000	.000
Bryant, Elias (Country Brown)	52	193	21	55	10	2	0	24	9	7	8	10	.285	.358
Crain, John	1	2	0	0	0	0	0	0	0	0	0	0	.000	.000
Davis	1	3	0	0	0	0	0	0	0	0	0	0	.000	.000
Duncan, Warren	39	138	12	28	4	1	0	9	6	1	4	4	.203	.246
Gray, Emerson	3	7	2	1	1	0	0	1	3	1	1	2	.143	.286
Hairstone, James Burton (J.B.)	1	1	0	0	0	0	0	0	0	0	0	0	.000	.000
Hudspeth, Robert (Highpocket)	56	223	30	67	8	3	4	34	15	2	3	12	.300	.417
Hutchinson, Fred (Hutch)	2	7	1	2	1	0	0	0	0	0	0	1	.286	.429
Jackson, Jr., Richard Alvin (Dick)	41	155	21	36	7	1	0	14	5	6	1	8	.232	.290
Jenkins, Clarence Reginald (Fats)	2	6	2	3	0	0	0	1	1	1	1	0	.500	.500
Jones, William (Willie)	2	9	2	2	0	0	0	1	0	0	0	0	.222	.222
Lloyd, John Henry (Pop)	56	233	39	70	15	0	1	43	11	8	7	11	.300	.378
Lundy, Richard Benjamin (King Richard)	3	11	4	4	1	1	0	3	0	1	0	0	.364	.636
Marcell, Oliver Hazzard (Ghost)	53	209	30	56	10	2	1	26	17	3	12	9	.268	.349
Mason, Charles (Corporal)	2	7	0	1	0	0	0	1	0	0	0	0	.143	.143
Means, Lemuel Lewis (Lou)	1	4	0	0	0	0	0	0	0	0	0	0	.000	.000
O'Neill, Charles	4	13	0	2	0	0	0	0	0	0	0	2	.154	.154
Ramirez, Ramiro (Rome)	46	165	18	43	6	1	0	15	10	1	4	3	.261	.309
Redding, Richard (Cannonball)	22	63	6	13	1	0	0	6	0	0	2	2	.206	.222
Reid, Ambrose Leevolia (Ambrose)	1	4	1	1	0	0	0	0	0	0	0	0	.250	.250
Roberts, Leroy (Roy)	12	32	6	7	1	0	0	4	2	1	0	0	.219	.250
Rojo, Domingo Julio (Clown)	51	166	25	45	7	2	2	27	17	4	5	7	.271	.373
Shively, George Anner (Rabbit)	48	201	37	57	7	0	0	25	15	3	3	3	.284	.318
Treadwell, Harold E.	21	62	5	17	0	0	0	4	1	0	2	2	.274	.274
Williams, Andrew (Stringbean)	6	10	1	4	0	0	0	0	0	0	0	0	.400	.400
Winters, James Henry (Nip)	18	41	4	12	1	0	0	3	1	0	1	1	.293	.317
York, James Henry (Jim)	3	5	1	0	0	0	0	0	0	0	1	0	.000	.000
		1,970	268	526	80	13	8	241	113	39	55	77	.267	.333

1923

All Games	Games	AB	R	H	D	T	HR	RBI	W	SB	SAC	E	AVG.	SLUG.
Allen, Jr., Major Robert	1	4	2	1	0	0	0	1	1	0	0	1	.250	.250
Carter, Clifford	1	2	0	0	0	0	0	0	0	0	0	0	.000	.000
Crockett, Frank	26	95	16	27	1	1	0	10	8	2	0	3	.284	.316
Crump, Willis (Shorty)	2	5	1	0	0	0	0	0	0	1	0	1	.000	.000
Cummings, Napoleon (Chance)	79	284	26	77	2	0	0	36	19	5	4	18	.271	.278
Deas, James Alvin (Yank)	8	22	0	1	0	0	0	0	0	0	1	2	.045	.045
Denis	1	4	2	2	0	0	0	0	0	0	0	1	.500	.500
Downs, McKinley (Bunny)	50	188	26	40	4	2	0	26	11	1	3	14	.213	.255
Francis, William Henry (Bill)	81	284	50	50	1	0	1	19	48	3	7	12	.176	.190
Gisentaner, William (Lefty)	6	14	4	2	0	0	0	0	3	0	0	0	.143	.143
Hampton, Lewis	12	20	3	6	0	0	0	3	0	0	1	0	.300	.300
Harper, John	28	76	5	12	0	0	0	4	5	0	0	1	.158	.158
Henderson, Arthur Chauncey (Rats)	33	82	7	9	0	0	0	2	7	2	3	8	.110	.110
Hobson, Charles Johnson (Johnny)	1	1	0	1	0	0	0	1	0	0	0	0	1.000	1.000
Huff, Jr., Edward C. (Eddie)	36	101	15	28	1	0	1	14	5	0	1	5	.277	.317
Hughes	1	4	1	2	0	0	0	0	0	0	0	0	.500	.500
Johnson, Nate (Speedboy)	17	40	4	8	1	0	0	3	0	0	0	1	.200	.225
Jones, William (Willie)	71	220	27	43	4	0	0	17	12	0	4	6	.195	.214
Lockhart, George Hubert (Prof)	27	76	6	12	2	0	0	3	5	0	0	4	.158	.184
Lundy, Richard Benjamin (King Richard)	80	309	60	107	8	4	4	73	15	4	1	32	.346	.437
Marlin	1	0	0	0	0	0	0	0	0	0	0	0	.000	.000
Mason, Charles (Corporal)	85	326	68	118	10	4	11	74	17	6	3	7	.362	.518
McLloyd	1	3	0	0	0	0	0	0	0	0	0	0	.000	.000
Parpetti, Agustin (Pulpita)	24	78	9	22	0	0	0	6	2	0	0	6	.282	.282
Price	1	3	0	0	0	0	0	0	1	0	0	0	.000	.000
Ramirez, Ramiro (Rome)	4	12	3	2	0	0	0	1	3	0	1	1	.167	.167
Reid, Ambrose Leevolia (Ambrose)	76	282	44	86	7	0	0	39	17	3	3	18	.305	.330
Roberts, Leroy (Roy)	11	21	5	6	0	0	0	4	2	0	0	0	.286	.286
Robinson, George Washington (Sis	1	1	1	0	0	0	0	0	0	0	0	0	.000	.000
Smith, R. (Red)	11	41	4	6	0	0	0	3	3	0	0	1	.146	.146
Thompson	7	23	7	4	2	0	0	2	7	1	0	2	.174	.261
Treadwell, Harold E.	2	4	0	0	0	0	0	0	0	0	0	1	.000	.000
Webster, William (West)	6	12	2	2	0	0	0	0	4	0	0	1	.167	.167
White, Chaney Leonard (Reindeer)	73	272	52	87	6	2	0	41	20	4	3	5	.320	.357
Wright, Joseph	1	3	0	0	0	0	0	0	0	0	0	0	.000	.000
		2,912	450	761	49	13	17	382	215	32	35	151	.261	.305

League-Level Opponents	Games	AB	R	H	D	T	HR	RBI	W	SB	SAC	E	AVG.	SLUG.
Carter, Clifford	1	2	0	0	0	0	0	0	0	0	0	0	.000	.000
Crockett, Frank	15	56	10	17	1	1	0	9	5	2	0	3	.304	.357
Crump, Willis (Shorty)	2	5	1	0	0	0	0	0	0	1	0	1	.000	.000
Cummings, Napoleon (Chance)	46	165	17	41	2	0	0	19	8	2	3	14	.248	.261
Deas, James Alvin (Yank)	6	15	0	0	0	0	0	0	0	0	1	2	.000	.000
Downs, McKinley (Bunny)	32	120	14	27	2	1	0	16	5	1	2	11	.225	.258
Francis, William Henry (Bill)	50	171	25	26	1	0	0	6	33	1	2	7	.152	.158
Gisentaner, William (Lefty)	4	11	1	1	0	0	0	0	1	0	0	0	.091	.091
Hampton, Lewis	8	11	2	1	0	0	0	1	0	0	1	0	.091	.091
Harper, John	17	44	2	5	0	0	0	3	3	0	0	1	.114	.114
Henderson, Arthur Chauncey (Rats)	23	56	7	8	0	0	0	2	7	2	1	6	.143	.143
Huff, Jr., Edward C. (Eddie)	22	66	13	20	0	0	1	10	5	0	0	2	.303	.348
Johnson, Nate (Speedboy)	8	14	0	1	0	0	0	0	0	0	0	0	.071	.071
Jones, William (Willie)	43	130	17	25	2	0	0	9	8	0	3	4	.192	.208
Lockhart, George Hubert (Prof)	16	43	5	7	1	0	0	3	4	0	0	3	.163	.186
Lundy, Richard Benjamin (King Richard)	47	175	35	58	5	2	2	39	9	3	0	27	.331	.417
Mason, Charles (Corporal)	51	196	40	73	7	3	9	48	10	4	3	4	.372	.577
Parpetti, Agustin (Pulpita)	12	36	3	10	0	0	0	5	2	0	0	5	.278	.278
Ramirez, Ramiro (Rome)	1	3	1	1	0	0	0	0	0	0	0	0	.333	.333
Reid, Ambrose Leevolia (Ambrose)	44	158	22	49	3	0	0	22	8	2	2	15	.310	.329
Roberts, Leroy (Roy)	5	6	2	1	0	0	0	0	1	0	0	0	.167	.167
Robinson, George Washington (Sis)	1	1	1	0	0	0	0	0	0	0	0	0	.000	.000
Smith, R. (Red)	7	29	4	5	0	0	0	3	3	0	0	1	.172	.172
Thompson	2	9	2	2	0	0	0	1	1	0	0	0	.222	.222
Treadwell, Harold E.	1	1	0	0	0	0	0	0	0	0	0	1	.000	.000
Webster, William (West)	2	2	0	0	0	0	0	0	3	0	0	0	.000	.000

League-Level Opponents	Games	AB	R	H	D	T	HR	RBI	W	SB	SAC	E	AVG.	SLUG.
White, Chaney Leonard (Reindeer)	44	166	33	57	6	2	0	29	10	2	2	4	.343	.404
Wright, Joseph	1	3	0	0	0	0	0	0	0	0	0	0	.000	.000
		1,694	257	435	30	9	12	225	126	20	20	111	.257	.306

1924

All Games	Games	AB	R	H	D	T	HR	RBI	W	SB	SAC	E	AVG.	SLUG.
Bryant, Elias (Country Brown)	2	8	3	4	0	0	0	2	1	0	0	0	.500	.500
Capenemzi	1	4	1	1	0	0	0	0	0	0	0	0	.250	.250
Carr, Wayne	10	25	2	4	0	0	0	0	0	0	1	2	.160	.160
Carter, Clifford	2	2	1	0	0	0	0	0	1	0	0	0	.000	.000
Cummings, Napoleon (Chance)	110	408	76	105	6	0	0	38	37	21	16	12	.257	.272
Dallard, Maurice Julius (Eggie)	2	7	0	1	0	0	0	1	0	0	0	0	.143	.143
Estrada, Oscar	1	1	0	1	0	0	0	0	0	0	0	0	1.000	1.000
Evans, W.P.	10	20	2	5	1	0	0	2	1	0	0	2	.250	.300
Gatewood, Ernest E.	70	231	25	55	8	0	0	23	10	2	4	12	.238	.273
George, John	32	113	15	25	2	0	0	6	13	0	3	7	.221	.239
Hampton, Lewis	1	3	1	0	0	0	0	0	1	0	0	0	.000	.000
Harper, John	18	45	4	6	0	1	0	3	3	1	3	0	.133	.178
Henderson, Arthur Chauncey (Rats)	12	36	7	9	0	0	0	3	1	0	0	4	.250	.250
Hobson, Charles Johnson (Johnny)	9	29	1	5	0	0	0	1	0	0	0	0	.172	.172
Johnson	1	4	1	3	1	0	0	0	0	0	0	0	.750	1.000
Jones, William (Willie)	56	176	17	38	5	1	2	14	14	0	4	9	.216	.290
Lewis, Milton	71	215	19	48	4	0	5	36	6	1	1	8	.223	.312
Lindsay, Clarence Holmes (C.H.)	2	9	0	0	0	0	0	0	0	0	0	0	.000	.000
Lloyd, John Henry (Pop)	105	383	63	148	15	5	2	90	36	9	9	31	.386	.467
Lockhart, George Hubert (Prof)	24	71	8	18	2	0	0	6	0	0	3	4	.254	.282
Lowell	1	3	0	1	0	0	0	0	0	0	0	2	.333	.333
Lundy, Richard Benjamin (King Richard)	104	408	105	142	12	7	14	86	39	17	5	48	.348	.515
Mason, Charles (Corporal)	82	328	79	113	13	8	11	73	24	3	5	5	.345	.534
Mitchell, Benjamin Arnett [Ernest] (Hooks)	10	19	1	6	0	0	0	2	0	0	0	1	.316	.316
Nuttal, H. (Bill)	12	26	1	3	0	0	0	0	1	0	3	2	.115	.115
Raines, Lawrence Glenn Hope (Larry)	1	4	0	1	0	0	0	0	0	0	0	0	.250	.250
Ramirez, Ramiro (Rome)	98	342	48	76	7	0	1	37	36	4	14	5	.222	.251
Reid, Ambrose Leevolia (Ambrose)	113	413	68	110	8	3	2	56	27	6	11	25	.266	.315
Shively, George Anner (Rabbit)	77	325	55	86	4	1	1	30	24	4	4	5	.265	.292
Starks, Otis (Lefty)	18	41	4	5	1	0	0	1	4	0	1	4	.122	.146
Thompson	1	5	0	2	0	0	0	1	0	0	0	1	.400	.400
White, Chaney Leonard (Reindeer)	34	138	32	46	5	1	1	20	8	5	5	0	.333	.406
Williams, Andrew (Stringbean)	19	51	11	12	0	0	1	4	1	0	1	0	.235	.294
		3,917	651	1,082	94	28	40	536	288	73	93	194	.276	.345

League-Level Opponents	Games	AB	R	H	D	T	HR	RBI	W	SB	SAC	E	AVG.	SLUG.
Carr, Wayne	7	17	1	3	0	0	0	0	0	0	1	0	.176	.176
Carter, Clifford	2	2	1	0	0	0	0	0	1	0	0	0	.000	.000
Cummings, Napoleon (Chance)	66	248	44	61	3	0	0	21	23	16	13	9	.246	.258
Evans, W.P.	4	7	0	1	0	0	0	0	0	0	0	0	.143	.143
Gatewood, Ernest E.	39	133	13	27	3	0	0	12	3	1	4	10	.203	.226
George, John	15	51	4	10	0	0	0	2	3	0	2	2	.196	.196
Harper, John	13	27	3	3	0	1	0	1	3	1	3	0	.111	.185
Henderson, Arthur Chauncey (Rats)	10	31	7	8	0	0	0	2	1	0	0	4	.258	.258
Hobson, Charles Johnson (Johnny)	7	23	1	4	0	0	0	1	0	0	0	0	.174	.174
Jones, William (Willie)	35	106	12	26	4	1	0	10	8	0	4	8	.245	.302
Lewis, Milton	40	110	9	26	3	0	3	18	6	0	1	3	.236	.345
Lloyd, John Henry (Pop)	63	237	42	88	12	2	1	54	19	7	8	17	.371	.451
Lockhart, George Hubert (Prof)	20	54	6	15	1	0	0	6	0	0	3	3	.278	.296
Lowell	1	3	0	1	0	0	0	0	0	0	0	2	.333	.333
Lundy, Richard Benjamin (King Richard)	67	267	58	90	8	4	8	55	20	14	4	35	.337	.487
Mason, Charles (Corporal)	54	223	54	74	8	3	8	47	13	3	3	4	.332	.502
Mitchell, Benjamin Arnett [Ernest] (Hooks)	6	9	0	3	0	0	0	1	0	0	0	1	.333	.333
Nuttal, H. (Bill)	6	11	0	1	0	0	0	0	1	0	1	1	.091	.091
Raines, Lawrence Glenn Hope (Larry)	1	4	0	1	0	0	0	0	0	0	0	0	.250	.250
Ramirez, Ramiro (Rome)	58	200	28	47	4	0	1	27	26	3	11	5	.235	.270
Reid, Ambrose Leevolia (Ambrose)	68	253	40	73	7	1	1	39	12	4	10	15	.289	.336
Roberts, Leroy (Roy)	3	7	0	0	0	0	0	0	0	0	0	3	.000	.000

League-Level Opponents	Games	AB	R	H	D	T	HR	RBI	W	SB	SAC	E	AVG.	SLUG.
Shively, George Anner (Rabbit)	45	193	35	58	1	1	1	21	13	4	3	3	.301	.332
Starks, Otis (Lefty)	10	21	3	2	0	0	0	0	1	0	1	2	.095	.095
White, Chaney Leonard (Reindeer)	23	95	19	33	2	1	0	12	4	4	3	1	.347	.389
Williams, Andrew (Stringbean)	10	25	8	7	0	0	0	2	0	0	0	0	.280	.280
		2,357	388	662	56	14	23	331	157	57	75	128	.281	.346

1925

All Games	Games	AB	R	H	D	T	HR	RBI	W	SB	SAC	E	AVG.	SLUG.
Bryant, Elias (Country Brown)	64	246	44	73	3	0	3	43	22	8	4	7	.297	.346
Burnett, Fred (Tex)	1	2	0	0	0	0	0	0	0	0	0	0	.000	.000
Clark, Maceo Richard	2	1	0	0	0	0	0	0	2	0	0	0	.000	.000
Cummings, Napoleon (Chance)	120	503	75	148	10	0	1	52	29	8	13	17	.294	.320
Farrell, Luther Alaner (Red)	26	65	9	25	3	1	1	12	5	0	1	3	.385	.508
Finley, John Thomas (Tom)	24	90	13	26	2	0	2	12	4	5	2	7	.289	.378
Gatewood, Ernest E.	64	210	29	56	5	1	1	25	11	2	2	3	.267	.314
Gillespie, Henry	13	27	6	10	0	3	0	2	1	0	1	0	.370	.593
Grier, Claude Bonds (Red)	16	45	5	13	0	0	0	3	1	0	3	2	.289	.289
Henderson, Arthur Chauncey (Rats)	43	120	15	29	4	1	2	11	5	0	5	7	.242	.342
Jones, William (Willie)	76	258	28	59	3	2	2	24	15	1	8	10	.229	.279
Leonard, James (Bobo)	48	148	17	36	4	0	1	14	14	2	5	4	.243	.291
Lewis, Milton	1	1	0	0	0	0	0	0	0	0	0	0	.000	.000
Lloyd, John Henry (Pop)	120	451	67	154	14	7	5	92	41	16	12	12	.341	.437
Lockhart, George Hubert (Prof)	22	66	5	16	3	0	0	3	2	0	1	3	.242	.288
Lundy, Richard Benjamin (King Richard)	120	460	95	140	17	3	8	85	47	7	6	30	.304	.407
Marcell, Oliver Hazzard (Ghost)	104	391	68	124	11	6	9	62	33	5	8	11	.317	.445
Mason, Charles (Corporal)	35	138	29	47	1	3	4	28	12	8	4	3	.341	.478
Mitchell, Benjamin Arnett [Ernest] (Hooks)	33	84	10	18	2	0	0	4	7	0	0	4	.214	.238
Nuttal, H. (Bill)	8	24	2	6	1	0	0	0	2	0	1	1	.250	.292
Reid, Ambrose Leevolia (Ambrose)	108	408	65	102	9	1	2	40	36	3	14	11	.250	.292
Roberts, Leroy (Roy)	20	50	7	14	0	1	0	7	2	0	0	4	.280	.320
Walsh	1	2	0	0	0	0	0	0	0	0	0	0	.000	.000
Waters, Theodore Francis Mullen (Ted)	1	1	0	0	0	0	0	0	0	0	0	0	.000	.000
White, Chaney Leonard (Reindeer)	51	207	37	70	9	2	3	33	12	0	2	1	.338	.444
Wilson, Benjamin (Benny)	3	15	1	1	0	0	0	1	0	0	0	0	.067	.067
Woods, William J. (Willie)	31	130	9	27	1	1	0	5	1	2	1	1	.208	.231
Young, Berdell	54	196	27	54	3	3	2	26	13	8	6	3	.276	.352
		4,339	663	1,248	105	35	46	584	317	75	99	144	.288	.360

League-Level Opponents	Games	AB	R	H	D	T	HR	RBI	W	SB	SAC	E	AVG.	SLUG.
Bryant, Elias (Country Brown)	36	129	24	35	1	0	2	21	18	5	4	5	.271	.326
Burnett, Fred (Tex)	1	2	0	0	0	0	0	0	0	0	0	0	.000	.000
Cummings, Napoleon (Chance)	73	295	39	83	5	0	1	24	19	7	10	11	.281	.308
Farrell, Luther Alaner (Buck)	19	42	6	16	2	1	1	8	3	0	1	3	.381	.548
Finley, John Thomas (Tom)	15	54	8	10	1	0	1	4	4	4	0	5	.185	.259
Gatewood, Ernest E.	31	90	5	22	2	0	0	11	5	2	1	2	.244	.267
Gillespie, Henry	9	17	4	5	0	2	0	1	0	1	0	0	.294	.529
Grier, Claude Bonds (Red)	11	32	2	9	0	0	0	3	0	0	3	1	.281	.281
Henderson, Arthur Chauncey (Rats)	33	89	9	19	3	1	1	7	4	0	5	7	.213	.303
Jones, William (Willie)	52	172	20	46	3	2	2	20	11	1	8	7	.267	.343
Leonard, James (Bobo)	29	81	5	19	3	0	0	4	10	1	5	1	.235	.272
Lloyd, John Henry (Pop)	71	252	43	84	8	5	3	55	32	13	10	6	.333	.440
Lockhart, George Hubert (Prof)	10	23	2	4	2	0	0	1	1	0	0	1	.174	.261
Lundy, Richard Benjamin (King Richard)	71	259	53	71	12	2	5	43	38	6	6	19	.274	.394
Marcell, Oliver Hazzard (Ghost)	62	214	38	69	6	3	3	28	25	4	6	6	.322	.421
Mason, Charles (Corporal)	24	88	16	27	0	2	3	16	11	6	4	3	.307	.455
Mitchell, Benjamin Arnett [Ernest] (Hooks)	18	40	6	5	1	0	0	1	5	0	0	2	.125	.150
Nuttal, H. (Bill)	3	10	1	3	1	0	0	0	1	0	0	1	.300	.400
Reid, Ambrose Leevolia (Ambrose)	61	232	36	57	7	1	1	19	26	1	7	9	.246	.297
Roberts, Leroy (Roy)	4	10	0	1	0	0	0	0	1	0	0	2	.100	.100
Waters, Theodore Francis Mullen (Ted)	1	1	0	0	0	0	0	0	0	0	0	0	.000	.000
White, Chaney Leonard (Reindeer)	30	116	18	38	6	2	1	15	6	0	1	0	.328	.440
Wilson, Benjamin (Benny)	3	15	1	1	0	0	0	1	0	0	0	0	.067	.067
Woods, William J. (Willie)	16	66	2	10	0	0	0	1	0	2	1	0	.152	.152
Young, Berdell	34	118	15	31	1	3	1	16	12	6	6	3	.263	.347
		2,447	353	665	64	24	25	298	233	58	79	94	.272	.348

1926

All Games	Games	AB	R	H	D	T	HR	RBI	W	SB	SAC	E	AVG.	SLUG.
Bryant, Elias (Country Brown)	75	236	41	44	3	2	2	10	22	8	5	6	.186	.242
Cummings, Napoleon (Chance)	108	422	64	119	5	5	1	52	28	5	13	21	.282	.325
Dallard, Maurice Julius (Eggie)	12	47	11	15	0	0	1	7	4	0	1	0	.319	.383
Farrell, Luther Alaner (Red)	94	319	48	90	8	4	7	64	28	3	8	3	.282	.398
Garcia, Romando (Cheno)	108	356	50	80	4	1	1	33	40	7	11	22	.225	.250
Gatewood, Ernest E.	53	151	18	36	2	1	0	15	11	0	1	1	.238	.265
Grier, Claude Bonds (Red)	50	115	18	35	5	0	0	10	16	0	3	7	.304	.348
Henderson, Arthur Chauncey (Rats)	38	108	10	18	3	0	0	5	5	0	0	9	.167	.194
Johnson	1	0	0	0	0	0	0	0	0	0	0	1	.000	.000
Jones, Sr., Robert Leo (Fox)	1	2	0	1	0	0	0	0	0	0	0	0	.500	.500
Jones, William (Willie)	73	222	21	50	10	2	2	29	23	2	6	7	.225	.315
Lewis, Joseph Herman (Sleepy)	18	43	3	9	2	0	0	3	6	0	1	2	.209	.256
Lockhart, George Hubert (Prof)	21	57	8	16	1	0	1	6	2	0	0	2	.281	.351
Lundy, Richard Benjamin (King Richard)	113	411	83	141	15	5	5	84	50	11	3	30	.343	.440
Marcell, Oliver Hazzard (Ghost)	103	369	59	102	9	1	2	54	47	2	10	21	.276	.322
Mitchell, Alonzo (Fluke)	23	43	6	10	0	1	0	1	1	0	2	1	.233	.279
Reid, Ambrose Leevolia (Ambrose)	111	422	69	105	7	3	2	53	43	1	5	9	.249	.294
Roberts, Leroy (Roy)	29	60	10	11	1	1	0	7	4	0	0	0	.183	.233
Robinson	1	1	0	0	0	0	0	0	4	0	0	0	.000	.000
Wallace, McKinley (Jack)	33	104	15	23	1	1	1	12	12	2	2	5	.221	.279
White, Chaney Leonard (Reindeer)	108	417	82	135	13	9	2	75	33	7	9	5	.324	.412
		3,905	616	1,040	89	36	27	520	379	48	80	152	.266	.328

League-Level Opponents	Games	AB	R	H	D	T	HR	RBI	W	SB	SAC	E	AVG.	SLUG.
Bryant, Elias (Country Brown)	41	121	21	19	2	1	1	7	12	5	2	0	.157	.215
Cummings, Napoleon (Chance)	61	237	32	58	2	3	1	25	21	5	5	11	.245	.291
Dallard, Maurice Julius (Eggie)	7	28	6	9	0	0	1	3	3	0	0	0	.321	.429
Farrell, Luther Alaner (Red)	47	154	24	47	7	1	4	36	18	1	4	2	.305	.442
Garcia, Romando (Cheno)	60	192	23	44	2	0	0	14	20	4	9	11	.229	.240
Gatewood, Ernest E.	28	72	7	15	1	1	0	4	5	0	1	1	.208	.250
Grier, Claude Bonds (Red)	35	79	9	21	2	0	0	7	13	0	1	7	.266	.291
Henderson, Arthur Chauncey (Rats)	25	81	7	11	2	0	0	3	3	0	0	6	.136	.160
Jones, William (Willie)	45	130	12	30	5	1	1	17	14	1	5	5	.231	.308
Lewis, Joseph Herman (Sleepy)	9	20	1	4	0	0	0	1	1	0	0	1	.200	.200
Lockhart, George Hubert (Prof)	8	19	3	7	1	0	0	2	1	0	0	1	.368	.421
Lundy, Richard Benjamin (King Richard)	62	221	49	74	11	2	2	42	29	4	2	23	.335	.430
Marcell, Oliver Hazzard (Ghost)	58	201	38	55	4	1	2	30	34	1	7	14	.274	.333
Mitchell, Alonzo (Fluke)	10	14	3	2	0	0	0	0	0	0	1	1	.143	.143
Reid, Ambrose Leevolia (Ambrose)	63	238	29	55	6	1	1	33	22	1	3	6	.231	.277
Roberts, Leroy (Roy)	11	23	3	5	0	0	0	3	1	0	0	0	.217	.217
Wallace, McKinley (Jack)	18	51	10	11	0	1	1	6	9	1	2	4	.216	.314
White, Chaney Leonard (Reindeer)	63	239	41	67	7	4	1	31	20	1	6	2	.280	.356
		2,120	318	534	52	16	15	264	226	24	48	95	.252	.313

1927

All Games	Games	AB	R	H	D	T	HR	RBI	W	SB	SAC	E	AVG.	SLUG.
Charleston, Oscar McKinley (Charlie)	1	3	0	0	0	0	0	0	0	0	0	0	.000	.000
Cooper, Samuel (Sam)	1	1	0	0	0	0	0	0	0	0	0	0	.000	.000
Dallard, Maurice Julius (Eggie)	102	406	79	116	8	3	8	52	53	5	5	28	.286	.379
Duncan, (Joe)	29	94	13	26	1	0	0	8	2	0	2	3	.277	.287
Farrell, Luther Alaner (Red)	78	235	44	72	12	3	6	43	19	0	3	11	.306	.460
Gatewood, Ernest E.	9	27	4	6	2	0	0	3	1	1	0	1	.222	.296
Gillespie, Henry	20	52	11	14	0	0	1	3	3	0	1	1	.269	.327
Grier, Claude Bonds (Red)	12	20	2	8	0	0	0	5	1	0	0	1	.400	.400
Handy, William Oscar (Bill)	4	11	2	6	1	0	0	3	1	0	0	0	.545	.636
Henderson, Arthur Chauncey (Rats)	26	59	6	11	1	0	0	5	5	0	2	4	.186	.203
Hubbard, Jesse James (Mountain Man)	98	344	65	92	12	4	7	48	37	3	3	7	.267	.387
Jones, William (Willie)	84	276	40	79	6	1	1	35	27	4	9	12	.286	.326
Lewis, Milton	104	387	60	116	17	1	12	76	25	0	3	22	.300	.442
Lockhart, George Hubert (Prof)	26	58	5	11	1	0	0	3	2	0	1	4	.190	.207
Lundy, Richard Benjamin (King Richard)	112	441	78	149	15	5	7	98	44	6	9	32	.338	.442
Marcell, Oliver Hazzard (Ghost)	112	423	65	131	10	4	2	70	42	7	10	22	.310	.366

Appendix C: Batting and Pitching Statistics by Year

All Games	Games	AB	R	H	D	T	HR	RBI	W	SB	SAC	E	AVG.	SLUG.
Means, Lemuel Lewis (Lou)	13	34	3	8	1	1	0	4	2	0	1	1	.235	.324
Reid, Ambrose Leevolia (Ambrose)	77	303	52	83	6	3	2	29	24	5	9	9	.274	.333
Roberts, Leroy (Roy)	31	71	11	14	0	1	0	4	0	0	2	7	.197	.225
Smith, Clarence (Scally)	101	390	79	117	11	5	2	57	33	4	9	9	.300	.369
Wagner [Pop Turner], Bert (Billy)	25	85	12	21	2	1	0	6	7	1	3	4	.247	.294
White, Chaney Leonard (Reindeer)	120	485	97	151	18	1	5	85	45	10	7	4	.311	.384
Williams	2	6	1	2	0	0	0	0	0	0	0	0	.333	.333
		4,211	729	1,233	124	33	53	637	373	46	79	182	.293	.376

League-Level Opponents	Games	AB	R	H	D	T	HR	RBI	W	SB	SAC	E	AVG.	SLUG.
Cooper, Samuel (Sam)	1	1	0	0	0	0	0	0	0	0	0	0	.000	.000
Dallard, Maurice Julius (Eggie)	77	310	62	85	5	2	7	36	42	3	4	20	.274	.371
Duncan, (Joe)	13	35	7	8	1	0	0	1	1	0	1	1	.229	.257
Farrell, Luther Alaner (Red)	57	169	35	49	10	1	6	30	15	0	2	6	.290	.467
Gatewood, Ernest E.	8	24	4	5	1	0	0	3	1	1	0	1	.208	.250
Gillespie, Henry	13	35	10	12	0	0	1	2	2	0	0	1	.343	.429
Grier, Claude Bonds (Red)	8	10	1	3	0	0	0	0	1	0	0	0	.300	.300
Handy, William Oscar (Bill)	3	9	2	6	1	0	0	3	1	0	0	0	.667	.778
Henderson, Arthur Chauncey (Rats)	26	59	6	11	1	0	0	5	5	0	2	4	.186	.203
Hubbard, Jesse James (Mountain Man)	75	267	51	69	10	2	6	36	33	3	2	5	.258	.378
Jones, William (Willie)	65	220	34	62	6	1	1	30	23	1	7	6	.282	.332
Lewis, Milton	79	292	42	84	11	0	9	61	21	0	2	18	.288	.418
Lockhart, George Hubert (Prof)	18	36	4	8	1	0	0	3	1	0	0	3	.222	.250
Lundy, Richard Benjamin (King Richard)	85	328	60	114	12	5	7	84	40	5	7	21	.348	.479
Marcell, Oliver Hazzard (Ghost)	85	321	50	103	8	4	2	58	32	7	8	15	.321	.389
Means, Lemuel Lewis (Lou)	12	33	3	8	1	1	0	4	2	0	1	1	.242	.333
Reid, Ambrose Leevolia (Ambrose)	55	215	40	59	2	3	2	22	21	4	8	8	.274	.340
Roberts, Leroy (Roy)	25	54	7	10	0	1	0	3	0	0	2	5	.185	.222
Smith, Clarence (Scally)	74	290	61	92	9	5	2	45	23	1	7	5	.317	.403
Wagner [Pop Turner], Bert (Billy)	12	41	6	9	0	0	0	1	3	1	2	2	.220	.220
White, Chaney Leonard (Reindeer)	89	360	79	119	13	1	5	67	36	10	7	3	.331	.414
Williams	2	6	1	2	0	0	0	0	0	0	0	0	.333	.333
		3,115	565	918	92	26	48	494	303	36	62	125	.295	.387

1928

All Games	Games	AB	R	H	D	T	HR	RBI	W	SB	SAC	E	AVG.	SLUG.
Blackwell, Charles H. (Rucker)	6	20	5	5	0	0	1	6	4	0	0	1	.250	.400
Carr, George Henry (Tank)	64	244	56	80	7	3	5	52	27	3	0	13	.328	.443
Cason, John	46	153	8	34	1	0	0	10	17	3	0	6	.222	.229
Chew	1	4	0	0	0	0	0	0	0	0	0	0	.000	.000
Collier, Bob	4	10	0	1	0	0	0	0	0	0	0	1	.100	.100
Cummings, Napoleon (Chance)	36	128	25	38	0	2	0	15	9	1	1	5	.297	.328
Dallard, Maurice Julius (Eggie)	38	149	25	29	0	1	1	11	18	2	1	4	.195	.228
Daniels, Fred	1	0	0	0	0	0	0	0	0	0	0	0	.000	.000
Farrell, Luther Alaner (Red)	53	148	25	47	2	2	7	27	17	0	2	5	.318	.500
Gardner, Kenneth Fuller (Ping)	27	64	7	10	0	0	0	3	2	0	1	1	.156	.156
Green, Curtis (Cornelius)	23	69	10	18	1	0	0	7	3	0	4	1	.261	.275
Grier, Claude Bonds (Red)	1	1	0	0	0	0	0	0	0	0	0	0	.000	.000
Henderson, Arthur Chauncey (Rats)	22	55	2	5	1	0	0	3	1	0	2	3	.091	.109
Jackson, Jack	3	8	0	1	0	0	0	0	0	0	1	0	.125	.125
Jenkins, Clarence Reginald (Fats)	67	270	65	103	8	2	1	34	29	8	3	3	.381	.437
Jones, William (Willie)	42	140	16	44	4	2	0	20	11	0	1	5	.314	.371
Lackey, Obie Ezekiel	1	3	1	1	0	0	0	0	0	0	0	1	.333	.333
Lewis, Joseph Herman (Sleepy)	1	3	0	2	0	0	0	0	0	0	0	0	.667	.667
Lewis, Milton	26	96	12	26	1	0	0	10	2	0	0	6	.271	.281
Lockhart, George Hubert (Prof)	13	30	4	6	1	0	1	2	3	0	1	1	.200	.333
Lundy, Richard Benjamin (King Richard)	77	290	51	105	12	3	3	76	24	9	1	25	.362	.455
Marcell, Oliver Hazzard (Ghost)	50	191	32	57	5	2	1	25	12	1	6	10	.298	.361
Mitchell, Alonzo (Fluke)	14	23	4	4	0	0	0	1	2	0	0	0	.174	.174
Moore, Clarence L. (C.L)	1	2	0	1	0	0	0	0	0	0	0	0	.500	.500
Reid, Ambrose Leevolia (Ambrose)	76	312	48	80	6	1	1	25	21	5	2	26	.256	.292
Shields, James D. (Jaydee)	39	131	18	37	2	1	0	6	8	0	0	16	.282	.313
Stanley, John Wesley (Neck)	3	5	0	0	0	0	0	0	1	0	0	0	.000	.000
Thomas, Clinton Cyrus (Clint)	34	135	24	47	4	4	1	27	9	3	3	0	.348	.459

Appendix C: Batting and Pitching Statistics by Year

All Games	Games	AB	R	H	D	T	HR	RBI	W	SB	SAC	E	AVG.	SLUG.
Thorpe, Clarence Jim	1	3	0	1	0	0	0	0	0	0	0	0	.333	.333
White, Chaney Leonard (Reindeer)	78	313	73	107	4	8	3	53	25	6	3	5	.342	.435
		3,000	511	889	59	31	25	413	245	41	32	138	.296	.362

League-Level Opponents	Games	AB	R	H	D	T	HR	RBI	W	SB	SAC	E	AVG.	SLUG.
Blackwell, Charles H. (Rucker)	3	9	1	2	0	0	1	4	0	0	0	0	.222	.556
Carr, George Henry (Tank)	50	188	40	57	6	2	4	39	21	3	0	12	.303	.420
Cason, John	32	99	3	24	1	0	0	6	11	3	0	6	.242	.253
Collier, Bob	3	6	0	0	0	0	0	0	0	0	0	1	.000	.000
Cummings, Napoleon (Chance)	24	77	14	19	0	1	0	6	4	0	1	4	.247	.273
Dallard, Maurice Julius (Eggie)	27	104	16	23	0	1	0	7	14	2	1	3	.221	.240
Daniels, Fred	1	0	0	0	0	0	0	0	0	0	0	0	.000	.000
Farrell, Luther Alaner (Red)	39	101	18	35	1	2	6	21	13	0	2	3	.347	.574
Gardner, Kenneth Fuller (Ping)	21	48	4	7	0	0	0	2	2	0	1	1	.146	.146
Green, Curtis (Cornelius)	13	32	4	5	1	0	0	0	1	0	1	0	.156	.188
Grier, Claude Bonds (Red)	1	1	0	0	0	0	0	0	0	0	0	0	.000	.000
Henderson, Arthur Chauncey (Rats)	17	38	2	4	1	0	0	3	1	0	2	2	.105	.132
Jackson, Jack	2	5	0	0	0	0	0	0	0	0	1	0	.000	.000
Jenkins, Clarence Reginald (Fats)	50	203	42	74	5	2	0	15	18	7	3	3	.365	.409
Jones, William (Willie)	34	114	14	39	3	2	0	17	6	0	1	5	.342	.404
Lewis, Milton	18	62	7	17	1	0	0	6	1	0	1	5	.274	.290
Lockhart, George Hubert (Prof)	10	20	1	4	0	0	0	1	2	0	1	1	.200	.200
Lundy, Richard Benjamin (King Richard)	57	208	37	74	12	3	3	55	19	9	1	21	.356	.486
Marcell, Oliver Hazzard (Ghost)	37	135	19	36	3	2	1	15	8	1	6	8	.267	.341
Mitchell, Alonzo (Fluke)	12	18	2	4	0	0	0	1	1	0	0	0	.222	.222
Moore, Clarence L. (C.L.,)	1	2	0	1	0	0	0	0	0	0	0	0	.500	.500
Reid, Ambrose Leevolia (Ambrose)	57	233	32	56	5	1	0	16	18	5	2	23	.240	.270
Shields, James D. (Jaydee)	27	89	15	29	1	0	0	3	5	0	0	14	.326	.337
Stanley, John Wesley (Neck)	1	0	0	0	0	0	0	0	1	0	0	0	.000	.000
Thomas, Clinton Cyrus (Clint)	27	105	20	35	4	3	0	19	8	3	3	0	.333	.429
White, Chaney Leonard (Reindeer)	56	225	58	81	4	7	3	40	17	6	3	5	.360	.480
		2,122	349	626	48	26	18	276	171	39	29	117	.295	.368

1929

All Games	Games	AB	R	H	D	T	HR	RBI	W	SB	SAC	E	AVG.	SLUG.
Albright, Thomas (Pistol Pete)	11	13	0	3	0	0	0	0	0	0	0	0	.231	.231
Briggs, Otto (Mirror)	2	7	1	1	0	0	0	0	0	0	0	0	.143	.143
Brown, Malcolm Elmore Arnold (Scrappy)	1	5	1	1	0	0	0	0	0	0	0	0	.200	.200
Cade, Joe	18	25	4	5	1	0	0	2	3	0	0	4	.200	.240
Carr, George Henry (Tank)	34	122	21	40	1	0	0	21	13	6	1	6	.328	.336
Coleman, Gilbert	3	10	0	1	0	0	0	0	0	0	0	1	.100	.100
Cooper, Samuel (Sam)	12	21	2	7	0	0	0	2	1	0	0	1	.333	.333
Craddock, William [Walter]	2	8	1	1	0	0	0	0	0	0	0	0	.125	.125
Day, Wilson C. (Connie)	76	275	36	64	4	2	1	30	15	0	6	14	.233	.273
Downs, McKinley (Bunny)	2	8	0	1	0	0	0	0	0	0	0	0	.125	.125
Eggleston, Macajah Marchand (Mack)	82	268	31	63	5	2	4	37	30	6	9	15	.235	.313
Farrell, Luther Alaner (Red)	9	30	6	7	0	1	0	2	4	0	1	2	.233	.300
Gardner, Kenneth Fuller (Ping)	16	31	3	5	0	0	0	1	2	0	0	3	.161	.161
Green, Curtis (Cornelius)	1	5	0	1	0	0	0	0	0	0	0	0	.200	.200
Hall, Perry	1	2	0	2	0	0	0	1	0	0	0	0	1.000	1.000
Henderson, Arthur Chauncey (Rats)	37	81	9	15	1	0	0	4	6	0	2	10	.185	.198
Hoyt, Dana	1	4	0	2	0	0	0	2	0	0	0	0	.500	.500
Jefferson, Ralph Tennyson	2	6	0	1	0	0	0	0	0	0	0	0	.167	.167
Jenkins, Clarence Reginald (Fats)	76	303	75	108	8	2	2	45	39	8	0	5	.356	.416
Jones, William (Willie)	60	192	22	46	6	3	0	21	17	1	3	4	.240	.302
Kerry	1	1	0	0	0	0	0	0	0	0	0	0	.000	.000
Lindsay, William Hudson (Red)	83	319	50	91	7	3	3	53	29	3	9	31	.285	.354
Mason, Charles (Corporal, Suitcase)	3	13	1	2	1	0	0	0	0	0	0	0	.154	.231
McClure, Robert E. (Bob)	36	65	5	10	0	0	0	3	4	0	1	6	.154	.154
Miller	1	1	0	0	0	0	0	0	0	0	0	0	.000	.000
Mitchell, Alonzo (Fluke)	11	15	4	7	2	0	0	2	0	0	0	2	.467	.600
Reid, Ambrose Leevolia (Ambrose)	70	242	38	71	6	2	2	38	14	3	2	9	.293	.360
Roberts, Leroy (Roy)	3	4	1	0	0	0	0	0	0	0	0	1	.000	.000
Shields, James D. (Jaydee)	37	66	12	12	1	0	0	4	4	0	1	3	.182	.197

Appendix C: Batting and Pitching Statistics by Year

All Games	Games	AB	R	H	D	T	HR	RBI	W	SB	SAC	E	AVG.	SLUG.
Stevens, Frank L. (Lefty)	1	2	0	0	0	0	0	0	0	0	0	0	.000	.000
Taylor, Benjamin Harrison (Ben)	56	176	19	55	6	0	2	37	15	1	3	10	.313	.381
Thomas, Clinton Cyrus (Clint)	79	309	76	106	14	5	7	69	30	21	4	4	.343	.489
Walker, Jesse T. (Hoss)	77	248	42	56	5	4	2	27	25	2	3	20	.226	.302
White, Chaney Leonard (Reindeer)	85	343	71	121	14	4	3	68	20	6	2	9	.353	.443
Williams, Robert Lawns (Bobby)	19	51	4	10	1	0	0	3	4	1	4	9	.196	.216
		3,271	535	915	83	28	26	472	275	58	52	168	.280	.346

League-Level Opponents	Games	AB	R	H	D	T	HR	RBI	W	SB	SAC	E	AVG.	SLUG.
Albright, Thomas (Pistol Pete)	7	4	0	1	0	0	0	0	0	0	0	0	.250	.250
Briggs, Otto (Mirror)	2	7	1	1	0	0	0	0	0	0	0	0	.143	.143
Brown, Malcolm Elmore Arnold (Scrappy)	1	5	1	1	0	0	0	0	0	0	0	0	.200	.200
Cade, Joe	12	13	2	4	1	0	0	2	2	0	0	4	.308	.385
Carr, George Henry (Tank)	21	77	16	28	1	0	0	17	11	5	0	4	.364	.377
Coleman, Gilbert	2	5	0	0	0	0	0	0	0	0	0	0	.000	.000
Cooper, Samuel (Sam)	9	19	2	6	0	0	0	2	1	0	0	1	.316	.316
Day, Wilson C. (Connie)	47	172	21	38	2	2	1	18	6	0	2	9	.221	.273
Eggleston, Macajah Marchand (Mack)	53	160	17	37	3	1	3	21	21	3	6	12	.231	.319
Farrell, Luther Alaner (Red)	7	23	5	5	0	1	0	1	3	0	1	2	.217	.304
Gardner, Kenneth Fuller (Ping)	11	21	3	4	0	0	0	1	2	0	0	2	.190	.190
Hall, Perry	1	2	0	2	0	0	0	1	0	0	0	0	1.000	1.000
Henderson, Arthur Chauncey (Rats)	26	57	6	12	1	0	0	4	3	0	2	9	.211	.228
Jenkins, Clarence Reginald (Fats)	54	213	56	81	7	2	2	33	28	4	0	4	.380	.460
Jones, William (Willie)	36	114	12	27	4	0	0	11	8	1	1	2	.237	.272
Kerry	1	1	0	0	0	0	0	0	0	0	0	0	.000	.000
Lindsay, William Hudson (Red)	55	208	30	57	5	3	2	34	22	2	5	19	.274	.356
McClure, Robert E. (Bob)	25	35	3	8	0	0	0	3	3	0	0	4	.229	.229
Mitchell, Alonzo (Fluke)	8	10	2	4	0	0	0	0	0	0	0	0	.400	.400
Reid, Ambrose Leevolia (Ambrose)	47	149	27	40	4	1	1	24	10	2	1	6	.268	.329
Roberts, Leroy (Roy)	1	2	0	0	0	0	0	0	0	0	0	0	.000	.000
Shields, James D. (Jaydee)	24	32	8	6	0	0	0	3	2	0	0	2	.188	.188
Stevens, Frank L. (Lefty)	1	2	0	0	0	0	0	0	0	0	0	0	.000	.000
Taylor, Benjamin Harrison (Ben)	32	89	9	26	3	0	2	18	9	1	1	6	.292	.393
Thomas, Clinton Cyrus (Clint)	48	191	44	59	7	2	4	44	16	8	1	0	.309	.429
Walker, Jesse T. (Hoss)	47	143	30	34	2	4	1	17	14	0	1	14	.238	.329
White, Chaney Leonard (Reindeer)	58	233	48	82	10	4	2	54	15	6	2	7	.352	.455
Williams, Robert Lawns (Bobby)	11	27	3	5	1	0	0	1	3	1	1	6	.185	.222
		2,014	346	568	51	20	18	309	179	33	24	113	.282	.354

Pitching

1916

All Games	App.	GS	CG	SHO	IP	H	RS	ER	BB	K	WP	HB	WON	LOST	PCT.	ERA	RPG
Crockett, Frank	1	1	0	0	6.0	8	6	4	1	5	0	0	1	0	1.000	6.00	9.00
Cummings, Napoleon (Chance)	1	0	0	0	1.0	3	2	1	0	1	0	0	0	0	.000	9.00	18.00
Dilworth, Arthur	25	21	17	2	176.7	124	69	52	48	215	4	3	16	5	.762	2.65	3.52
Johnson, Daniel Spencil (Shang)	25	23	18	1	189.0	126	63	31	45	164	1	7	20	2	.909	1.48	3.00
Lundy, Richard Benjamin (King Richard)	2	0	0	0	5.0	4	0	0	0	2	2	0	0	0	.000	0.00	0.00
Mack, Paul	1	0	0	0	1.0	0	0	0	0	1	0	0	0	0	.000	0.00	0.00
Roberts, Leroy (Roy)	22	17	14	3	149.0	80	41	29	37	221	1	6	13	3	.813	1.75	2.48
Tucker, Michael	5	4	3	0	37.3	28	21	14	11	19	0	2	4	1	.800	3.38	5.06
Williams, Thomas (Tom)	6	6	6	0	54.0	44	21	12	10	48	0	0	4	2	.667	2.00	3.50
	72		**58**	**6**	**619.0**	**417**	**223**	**143**	**152**	**676**	**6**	**18**	**58**	**13**	**.817**	**2.08**	**3.24**

League-Level Opponents	App.	GS	CG	SHO	IP	H	RS	ER	BB	K	WP	HB	WON	LOST	PCT.	ERA	RPG
Dilworth, Arthur	4	4	4	0	36.0	32	19	15	11	32	1	0	3	1	.750	3.75	4.75
Johnson, Daniel Spencil (Shang, Dan, Gatling Gun)	1	1	1	0	9.0	7	2	2	4	7	0	0	1	0	1.000	2.00	2.00
Williams, Thomas (Wrist, Tom)	1	1	1	0	9.0	9	8	6	3	3	0	0	0	1	.000	6.00	8.00
	6		**6**	**0**	**54.0**	**48**	**29**	**23**	**18**	**42**	**1**	**0**	**4**	**2**	**.667**	**3.83**	**4.83**

1917

All Games	App.	GS	CG	SHO	IP	H	RS	ER	BB	K	WP	HB	WON	LOST	PCT.	ERA	RPG
Brodie, Milledge T.	1	1	1	0	9.0	4	1	1	0	6	0	0	1	0	1.000	1.00	1.00
Dilworth, Arthur	10	9	6	2	71.0	48	15	9	22	54	0	2	7	1	.875	1.14	1.90
Downs, McKinley (Bunny)	1	0	0	0	6.0	5	0	0	0	0	2	0	0	0	.000	0.00	0.00
Fisher	1	1	0	0	0.0	0	0	0	1	0	0	1	0	1	.000	0.00	0.00
Forbes, Joseph (Joe)	2	1	0	0	7.0	7	2	2	4	5	1	0	0	2	.000	2.57	2.57
Gordon, Herman Evan	1	1	1	0	9.0	3	2	2	5	3	1	2	1	0	1.000	2.00	2.00
Gray, Emerson	1	0	0	0	3.0	6	4	3	0	3	0	0	0	0	.000	9.00	12.00
Johnson, Daniel Spencil (Shang)	34	30	20	5	291.7	211	96	58	30	228	1	4	17	10	.630	1.79	2.96
Mack, Paul	1	1	0	0	2.0	7	5	4	0	1	0	0	0	1	.000	18.00	22.50
Mays, Horace	1	1	1	0	9.0	10	4	3	4	7	1	3	1	0	1.000	3.00	4.00
McDonald, Gifford Van Horn (Iron Man)	10	10	6	1	77.0	78	51	36	30	43	1	3	2	8	.200	4.21	5.96
Miller, Louis Lee (Red)	1	0	0	0	4.0	6	3	2	1	2	0	0	0	0	.000	4.50	6.75
Murphy, W. Charles (Speedball)	2	1	0	0	10.0	9	5	5	2	9	0	1	1	0	1.000	4.50	4.50
Roberts, Leroy (Roy, Eveready)	34	26	21	2	247.3	190	111	70	79	163	4	10	16	10	.615	2.55	4.04
Smith, R. (Red)	5	4	3	0	39.0	38	20	13	4	25	0	2	2	2	.500	3.00	4.62
Tucker, Michael	1	0	0	0	2.0	4	3	3	2	0	0	0	0	0	.000	9.00	13.50
Wilson, Frank (Chink)	1	1	1	0	9.0	9	1	1	0	4	0	0	1	0	1.000	1.00	1.00
Witherspoon	9	7	0	0	54.0	44	20	14	14	44	0	2	6	2	.750	2.33	3.33

Appendix C: Batting and Pitching Statistics by Year

	App.	GS	CG	SHO	IP	H	RS	ER	BB	K	WP	HB	WON	LOST	PCT.	ERA	RPG
Wylie, Fred Lewis (The Atlanta Surprise)	4	2	2	0	28.0	28	13	9	4	20	0	2	1	1	.500	2.89	4.18
		97	62	10	878.0	707	358	233	200	619	10	29	56	38	.596	2.39	3.67

1918

League-Level Opponents	App.	GS	CG	SHO	IP	H	RS	ER	BB	K	WP	HB	WON	LOST	PCT.	ERA	RPG
Dilworth, Arthur	2	1	1	0	12.0	4	4	2	3	10	0	2	1	1	.500	1.50	3.00
Fisher	1			0	0.0	0	2	1	1	0	0	1	0	1	.000	0.00	0.00
Forbes, Joseph (Joe)	1	1	0	0	2.0	2	1	1	4	3	1	1	0	1	.000	4.50	4.50
Johnson, Daniel Spencil (Shang)	11	9	7	1	80.7	71	34	17	13	64	1	2	3	5	.375	1.90	3.79
McDonald, Gifford Van Horn (Iron Man)	5	5	4	0	43.0	48	26	19	22	20	1	2	1	4	.200	3.98	5.44
Miller, Louis Lee (Red)	1	0	0	0	4.0	6	3	3	1	2	0	0	0	0	.000	4.50	6.75
Murphy, W. Charles (Speedball)	1	0	0	0	6.0	5	3	3	1	2	0	0	0	0	.000	4.50	4.50
Roberts, Leroy (Roy)	13	10	7	0	95.3	73	49	32	39	49	4	9	5	5	.500	3.02	4.63
Smith, R. (Red)	1	1	0	0	3.0	8	7	5	0	3	0	2	0	1	.000	15.00	21.00
Wylie, Fred Lewis (The Atlanta Surprise)	1	0	0	0	6.0	9	5	3	2	9	0	0	0	0	.000	4.50	7.50
	28		19	2	252.0	226	134	85	86	162	7	19	10	18	.357	3.04	4.79

All Games	App.	GS	CG	SHO	IP	H	RS	ER	BB	K	WP	HB	WON	LOST	PCT.	ERA	RPG
Albritton, Alexander C. (Alex)	2	2	1	0	12.0	11	10	6	8	7	0	0	1	0	1.000	4.50	7.50
Bryant, Elias (Country Brown)	1	1	1	1	7.0	3	0	0	0	9	0	1	1	0	1.000	0.00	0.00
Cummings, Napoleon (Chance)	1	0	0	0	0.7	3	3	1	1	0	0	0	0	0	.000	13.50	40.50
Howell, Henry Reese	8	6	6	0	64.0	71	47	32	10	29	0	3	3	3	.500	4.50	6.61
Johnson, Daniel Spencil (Shang)	2	2	1	0	15.3	17	10	5	0	10	0	0	1	1	.500	2.93	5.87
Mays, Horace	1	1	1	0	9.0	10	7	6	2	4	0	0	1	0	1.000	6.00	7.00
Roberts, Leroy (Roy)	9	8	7	0	67.7	60	27	19	11	52	2	3	5	3	.625	2.53	3.59
Robinson, George Washington (Sis)	14	11	8	1	101.3	94	44	31	16	48	0	2	7	5	.583	2.75	3.91
Smith, R. (Red)	8	8	8	2	61.0	52	29	19	10	56	0	5	5	2	.714	2.80	4.28
	39		33	4	338.0	321	177	119	58	215	2	10	24	14	.615	3.17	4.71

1919

League-Level Opponents	App.	GS	CG	SHO	IP	H	RS	ER	BB	K	WP	HB	WON	LOST	PCT.	ERA	RPG
Cummings, Napoleon (Chance)	1	0	0	0	0.7	3	3	1	1	0	0	0	0	0	.000	13.50	40.50
Howell, Henry Reese	6	5	5	0	50.0	59	40	27	8	25	0	0	3	2	.600	4.86	7.20
Johnson, Daniel Spencil (Shang, Dan, Gatling Gun)	2	2	1	0	15.3	17	10	5	0	10	0	0	1	1	.500	2.93	5.87
Roberts, Leroy (Roy, Eveready)	5	4	3	0	31.7	26	12	8	10	19	2	3	3	1	.750	2.27	3.41
Robinson, George Washington (Sis)	6	4	2	0	35.3	35	18	14	8	10	0	2	1	3	.250	3.57	4.58
Smith, R. (Red)	3	3	3	0	27.0	27	14	10	5	12	0	5	0	2	.000	3.33	4.67
	18		14	0	160.0	167	95	65	32	76	2	10	8	9	.471	3.66	5.34

All Games	App.	GS	CG	SHO	IP	H	RS	ER	BB	K	WP	HB	WON	LOST	PCT.	ERA	RPG
Dilworth, Arthur	4	4	1	0	31.3	28	19	14	8	21	0	0	3	1	.750	4.02	5.46
Edwards, James (Smokey)	1	1	0	0	5.0	10	8	5	1	2	0	0	0	1	.000	9.00	14.40

1920

All Games

	App.	GS	CG	SHO	IP	H	RS	ER	BB	K	WP	HB	WON	LOST	PCT.	ERA	RPG
Hubbard, Jesse James (Mountain Man)	9	8	4	2	60.7	39	18	15	15	45	2	2	6	1	.857	2.23	2.67
Jeffries, James Courtney (Jim)	8	7	3	1	54.0	46	21	16	13	25	0	0	6	1	.857	2.67	3.50
Johnson, Daniel Spencil (Shang)	21	14	11	4	134.0	105	37	26	26	89	0	0	10	3	.769	1.75	2.49
Pugh, John (Johnny)	1	1	0	0	7.0	9	4	3	1	4	0	0	0	0	.000	3.86	5.14
Redding, Richard (Cannonball)	42	28	21	5	275.3	184	61	42	42	209	1	1	22	10	.688	1.37	1.99
Roberts, Leroy (Roy)	26	19	12	4	163.7	118	57	42	61	140	0	5	13	4	.765	2.31	3.13
Taylor, Benjamin Harrison (Ben)	2	0	0	0	2.7	3	1	1	1	0	0	0	0	0	.000	3.37	3.37
Whitworth, Richard Henderson (Dick)	1	1	0	0	3.0	3	1	1	0	1	0	0	0	0	.000	3.00	3.00
Wickware, Frank Ellis (Red Ant)	19	14	11	3	134.3	87	36	32	30	96	1	2	9	6	.600	2.14	2.41
Williams, Joseph (Smokey Joe)	2	2	2	0	15.0	13	13	7	4	17	1	1	1	1	.500	4.20	7.80
Williams, Thomas (Tom)	2	2	2	1	16.0	4	0	0	2	12	0	0	1	0	1.000	0.00	0.00
	100		**67**	**20**	**902.0**	**649**	**276**	**204**	**204**	**664**	**5**	**11**	**71**	**28**	**.717**	**2.04**	**2.75**

League-Level Opponents

	App.	GS	CG	SHO	IP	H	RS	ER	BB	K	WP	HB	WON	LOST	PCT.	ERA	RPG
Dilworth, Arthur	1	1	0	0	6.3	8	7	6	2	5	0	0	0	1	.000	8.53	9.95
Edwards, James (Smokey)	1	1	1	0	5.0	10	8	5	1	2	0	0	0	0	.000	9.00	14.40
Hubbard, Jesse James (Mountain Man)	1	1	1	0	9.0	4	2	2	1	6	2	0	1	0	1.000	2.00	2.00
Jeffries, James Courtney (Jim)	1	1	0	0	5.0	4	2	2	1	1	0	0	1	0	1.000	3.60	3.60
Johnson, Daniel Spencil (Shang)	5	4	2	0	27.0	29	15	11	6	17	0	1	2	0	1.000	3.67	5.00
Redding, Richard (Cannonball)	12	8	7	1	99.3	63	21	15	15	63	1	2	7	4	.636	1.36	1.90
Roberts, Leroy (Roy)	9	6	6	1	45.3	38	20	16	21	37	3	2	2	2	.500	3.18	3.97
Taylor, Benjamin Harrison (Ben)	1	0	0	0	2.0	3	1	1	1	3	0	0	0	0	.000	4.50	4.50
Whitworth, Richard Henderson (Dick)	1	1	0	0	3.0	3	1	1	0	1	0	0	0	0	.000	3.00	3.00
Wickware, Frank Ellis (Red Ant)	2	0	1	0	13.0	5	1	1	1	10	0	2	2	0	1.000	0.69	0.69
Williams, Thomas (Tom)	1	1	0	0	7.0	1	0	0	0	3	0	0	0	0	.000	0.00	0.00
	24		**14**	**1**	**222.0**	**168**	**78**	**60**	**49**	**148**	**3**	**4**	**15**	**8**	**.652**	**2.43**	**3.16**

All Games

	App.	GS	CG	SHO	IP	H	RS	ER	BB	K	WP	HB	WON	LOST	PCT.	ERA	RPG
Marcell, Oliver Hazzard (Ghost)	1	0	0	0	2.0	1	0	0	0	0	1	0	0	1	.000	0.00	0.00
Redding, Richard (Cannonball, Dick)	44	37	35	11	341.3	225	109	76	39	204	2	6	27	11	.711	2.00	2.87
Ryan, Merven John (Red, Jabao)	39	32	30	4	289.7	201	93	62	45	137	0	2	22	11	.667	1.93	2.89
Treadwell, Harold E.	36	34	28	6	279.7	185	105	80	50	167	4	5	27	6	.818	2.57	3.38
Williams, Andrew (Stringbean)	26	25	18	6	214.7	164	56	40	15	99	2	0	16	5	.762	1.68	2.35
	128		**111**	**27**	**1,127.3**	**776**	**363**	**258**	**149**	**607**	**8**	**13**	**92**	**33**	**.736**	**2.06**	**2.90**

League-Level Opponents

	App.	GS	CG	SHO	IP	H	RS	ER	BB	K	WP	HB	WON	LOST	PCT.	ERA	RPG
Redding, Richard (Cannonball, Dick)	19	16	15	5	141.3	106	52	39	20	69	1	5	11	6	.647	2.48	3.31
Ryan, Merven John (Red, Jabao)	17	12	11	2	112.0	80	31	24	27	48	0	1	8	3	.727	1.93	2.49
Treadwell, Harold E.	11	11	7	0	77.3	61	37	29	18	30	3	1	6	5	.545	3.37	4.31
Williams, Andrew (Stringbean)	13	12	8	1	105.7	90	36	26	5	30	1	0	5	4	.556	2.21	3.07
	51		**41**	**8**	**436.3**	**337**	**156**	**118**	**70**	**177**	**5**	**7**	**30**	**18**	**.625**	**2.43**	**3.22**

Appendix C: Batting and Pitching Statistics by Year

Cuban Winter League Pitching, 1920–21

	App.	GS	CG	SHO	IP's	HA	RS	ER	BB	K	WP	HB	WIN	LOST	PCT.	ERA	RPG
Cockrell [Williams], Phillip (Fish)	1	0	0	0	1.3	1	0	0	1	0	0	0	0	0	.000	0.00	0.00
Flournoy, Willis Jefferson (Pud)	5	4	2	0	27.0	31	26	19	17	16	0	0	0	4	.000	6.33	8.67
Redding, Richard (Cannonball)	8	8	7	0	67.0	47	29	20	25	32	0	0	1	5	.167	2.69	3.90
Rodriquez, A.	1	0	0	0	6.0	6	3	2	3	4	0	0	0	1	.000	3.00	4.50
Ryan, Merven John (Red)	4	3	3	0	28.7	21	10	6	6	13	0	1	3	0	1.000	1.88	3.14
	4	15	12	0	130.0	106	68	47	52	65	0	1	4	10	.286	3.25	4.71

1921

All Games

	App.	GS	CG	SHO	IP	H	RS	ER	BB	K	WP	HB	WON	LOST	PCT.	ERA	RPG
Busby, Maurice (Lefty)	5	5	1	0	40.3	31	20	15	4	20	0	0	3	1	.750	3.35	4.46
Cockrell [Williams], Phillip (Fish)	3	3	3	0	13.0	11	6	4	0	0	0	0	1	1	.500	2.77	4.15
Harvey, Frank (Lefty)	2	2	2	0	14.0	7	11	9	0	14	0	0	1	1	.500	5.79	7.07
Harvey, John Henry (Howling Harvey)	4	4	0	0	13.3	14	12	8	13	8	2	1	1	1	.500	5.40	8.10
Johnson, Daniel Spencil (Shang)	1	1	0	0	2.7	10	5	4	0	2	0	0	0	0	.000	13.50	16.87
Lee, Sr., Holsey Scranton (Script)	5	4	2	0	26.3	34	29	25	12	21	0	0	1	4	.200	8.54	9.91
McDonald, Gifford Van Horn (Iron Man)	3	1	0	0	7.3	9	7	7	2	1	0	2	0	0	.000	8.59	8.59
Mitchell, Benjamin Arnett [Ernest] (Hooks)	13	7	4	0	78.3	75	42	30	20	50	0	0	4	4	.500	3.45	4.83
Reavis, Al W.	2	2	0	0	6.7	12	11	8	2	2	0	0	1	1	.500	10.80	14.85
Redding, Richard (Cannonball)	42	35	30	5	316.0	294	119	89	52	150	1	0	24	13	.649	2.53	3.39
Richardson, Henry Layton (Long Tom)	17	11	6	1	89.3	96	45	31	12	45	0	0	5	4	.556	3.12	4.53
Rojo, Domingo Julio (Clown)	1	0	0	0	3.3	5	5	5	2	2	0	0	0	0	.000	13.50	13.50
Ryan, Merven John (Red)	24	17	12	2	156.7	145	78	60	32	53	7	3	12	5	.706	3.45	4.48
Shively, George Anner (Rabbit)	2	0	0	0	7.3	3	2	1	0	2	0	0	1	0	1.000	1.23	2.45
Treadwell, Harold E.	26	16	14	2	174.3	160	79	63	34	80	0	0	13	4	.765	3.25	4.08
Williams, Andrew (Stringbean)	17	14	7	0	98.0	104	59	49	19	28	0	5	9	3	.750	4.50	5.42
Winters, James Henry (Nip)	11	8	4	1	67.7	49	26	21	29	35	0	0	4	3	.571	2.79	3.46
		130	85	11	1,114.7	1059	556	429	233	513	10	11	80	45	.640	3.46	4.49

League-Level Opponents

	App.	GS	CG	SHO	IP	H	RS	ER	BB	K	WP	HB	WON	LOST	PCT.	ERA	RPG
Cockrell [Williams], Phillip (Fish)	3	3	3	0	13.0	11	6	4	0	0	0	0	1	1	.500	2.77	4.15
Harvey, Frank (Lefty)	2	2	2	0	14.0	7	11	9	0	14	0	0	1	1	.500	5.79	7.07
Harvey, John Henry (Howling Harvey)	2	2	0	0	5.3	6	7	5	8	3	1	0	0	0	.000	8.44	11.81
Lee, Sr., Holsey Scranton (Script)	1	1	0	0	4.7	6	7	7	4	1	0	0	0	0	.000	13.50	13.50
McDonald, Gifford Van Horn (Iron Man)	3	1	0	0	7.3	9	7	7	2	2	0	2	0	0	.000	8.59	8.59
Mitchell, Benjamin Arnett [Ernest] (Hooks)	5	2	1	0	25.7	26	14	10	7	15	0	0	1	1	.500	3.51	4.91
Reavis, Al W.	1	1	0	0	1.0	4	6	3	2	0	0	0	0	0	.000	27.00	54.00
Redding, Richard (Cannonball)	29	25	22	4	229.7	226	93	72	44	106	1	0	17	11	.607	2.82	3.64
Richardson, Henry Layton (Long Tom)	7	5	2	0	31.0	42	28	18	11	12	0	0	1	3	.250	5.23	8.13
Rojo, Domingo Julio (Clown)	1	0	0	0	3.3	5	5	5	2	2	0	0	0	0	.000	13.50	13.50
Ryan, Merven John (Red)	15	11	8	2	101.0	90	42	30	23	39	0	3	8	3	.727	2.67	3.74
Treadwell, Harold E.	14	7	6	0	88.3	89	52	42	25	38	0	0	6	3	.667	4.28	5.30
Williams, Andrew (Stringbean)	13	11	4	1	72.0	87	56	46	19	16	0	5	5	3	.625	5.75	7.00
Winters, James Henry (Nip)	8	7	4	1	56.3	34	18	14	20	28	0	2	4	2	.667	2.24	2.88
		78	52	8	652.7	642	352	272	167	277	2	10	44	30	.595	3.75	4.85

1922

All Games

	App.	GS	CG	SHO	IP	H	RS	ER	BB	K	WP	HB	WON	LOST	PCT.	ERA	RPG
Childs	1	1	0	0	7.0	5	3	2	2	3	0	0	0	1	.000	2.57	3.86
Cramer	1	1	1	0	6.0	3	2	1	1	1	1	2	2	0	1.000	1.50	3.00
Crockett, Frank	1	1	0	0	6.7	9	4	3	3	2	0	0	1	0	1.000	4.05	5.40
Deas, James Alvin (Yank)	1	1	0	0	2.0	5	4	2	2	2	0	1	0	1	.000	9.00	18.00
Harris	7	5	2	0	37.0	36	24	17	15	35	0	0	2	4	.333	4.14	5.84
Johnson, Nate (Speedboy)	19	17	16	2	145.3	98	51	34	51	107	5	9	11	6	.647	2.11	3.16
Kyle, Andy	5	4	3	0	35.0	23	9	7	8	26	0	3	0	4	.000	1.80	2.31
Lewis, Milton	6	3	1	0	22.3	30	16	11	5	9	0	1	0	4	.000	4.43	6.45
Lloyd	2	1	0	0	9.7	9	5	2	6	3	0	0	1	0	1.000	1.86	4.66
Malloy, Charles	10	8	3	0	54.7	53	38	27	23	49	1	0	3	2	.600	4.45	6.26
Mason, Charles (Corporal)	1	1	0	0	2.7	9	5	4	1	1	0	0	0	0	.000	13.50	16.87
McAttall	1	1	1	0	6.0	10	10	8	3	2	0	2	0	1	.000	12.00	15.00
Patterson	4	1	0	0	13.7	12	8	6	5	7	1	0	1	0	1.000	3.95	5.27
Richardson, Henry Layton (Long Tom)	1	0	0	0	1.0	0	0	0	0	1	0	0	0	0	.000	0.00	0.00
Smith, Jake	1	0	0	0	2.0	4	4	4	1	1	0	0	0	0	.000	18.00	18.00
Streeter, Samuel (Sam)	23	17	15	3	158.0	127	67	45	39	97	2	1	13	6	.684	2.56	3.82
Wheeler, Joseph (Jodie)	25	17	11	2	146.0	135	74	59	33	102	2	0	7	8	.467	3.64	4.56
Williams, Andrew (Stringbean)	1	1	1	0	6.0	5	2	1	3	2	0	0	1	0	1.000	1.50	3.00
	80		**55**	**7**	**661.0**	**573**	**326**	**233**	**201**	**450**	**11**	**14**	**44**	**33**	**.571**	**3.17**	**4.44**

League-Level Opponents

	App.	GS	CG	SHO	IP	H	RS	ER	BB	K	WP	HB	WON	LOST	PCT.	ERA	RPG
Cramer	1	1	1	0	6.0	3	2	1	3	1	0	2	1	0	1.000	1.50	3.00
Harris	2	2	1	0	15.0	17	15	11	3	11	0	1	0	2	.000	6.60	9.00
Johnson, Nate (Speedboy)	5	5	5	0	43.0	34	23	15	20	33	2	5	3	2	.600	3.14	4.81
Lewis, Milton	2	2	1	0	12.3	15	6	4	1	6	0	0	0	2	.000	2.92	4.38
Lloyd	2	1	1	0	9.7	9	5	5	2	6	0	0	1	0	1.000	1.86	4.66
Mason, Charles (Corporal)	1	1	0	0	2.7	9	5	4	1	1	0	0	0	0	.000	13.50	16.87
McAttall	1	1	1	0	6.0	10	10	8	3	2	0	1	0	1	.000	12.00	15.00
Patterson	2	0	0	0	3.0	3	2	2	1	3	1	0	1	0	1.000	6.00	6.00
Streeter, Samuel (Sam)	5	5	3	0	36.3	31	22	12	15	23	0	3	3	2	.600	2.97	5.45
Wheeler, Joseph (Jodie)	1	1	1	0	8.0	6	2	2	5	7	1	0	0	1	.000	0.00	2.25
Williams, Andrew (Stringbean)	1	1	1	0	6.0	5	2	1	3	2	0	0	1	0	1.000	1.50	3.00
	19		**15**	**0**	**148.0**	**142**	**94**	**60**	**61**	**92**	**4**	**10**	**9**	**10**	**.474**	**3.65**	**5.72**

1922 (New York City Bacharach Giants)
All Games

	App.	GS	CG	SHO	IP	H	RS	ER	BB	K	WP	HB	WON	LOST	PCT.	ERA	RPG
Blane	1	0	0	0	2.0	1	0	0	0	0	0	0	0	0	.000	0.00	0.00
Johnson, Nate (Speedboy)	1	1	0	0	1.3	4	4	3	2	1	0	0	0	0	.000	20.25	27.00
McIntyre	1	1	1	0	9.0	11	5	4	0	6	0	0	1	0	1.000	4.00	5.00
Redding, Richard (Cannonball)	25	19	15	1	170.0	188	72	49	25	76	5	2	10	10	.500	2.59	3.81
Roberts, Leroy (Roy)	27	23	16	1	179.3	220	132	91	62	77	4	4	13	7	.650	4.57	6.62
Smith	2	2	0	0	13.3	13	12	8	6	6	0	0	1	1	.500	5.40	8.10

Appendix C: Batting and Pitching Statistics by Year

	App.	GS	CG	SHO	IP	H	RS	ER	BB	K	WP	HB	WON	LOST	PCT.	ERA	RPG
Treadwell, Harold E.	33	23	18	0	221.3	197	120	90	69	94	2	5	13	10	.565	3.66	4.88
Williams, Andrew (Stringbean)	11	8	3	0	55.7	60	35	29	13	34	0	1	2	5	.286	4.69	5.66
Winters, James Henry (Nip)	22	15	11	2	131.3	129	85	64	51	114	5	0	9	9	.500	4.39	5.82
	92	67	64	2	783.3	823	465	338	228	408	16	12	49	42	.538	3.88	5.34

League-Level Opponents

	App.	GS	CG	SHO	IP	H	RS	ER	BB	K	WP	HB	WON	LOST	PCT.	ERA	RPG
Blane	1	0	0	0	2.0	1	0	0	0	0	0	2	1	0	.000	0.00	0.00
Redding, Richard (Cannonball)	23	17	13	0	151.0	176	71	49	25	76	5	2	8	10	.444	2.92	4.23
Roberts, Leroy (Roy)	17	15	9	0	112.0	139	96	66	40	28	4	1	7	6	.538	5.30	7.71
Treadwell, Harold E.	25	18	13	0	168.3	156	102	76	62	62	2	5	7	10	.412	4.06	5.45
Williams, Andrew (Stringbean)	6	4	1	0	25.3	28	15	13	6	17	1	0	1	2	.000	4.62	5.33
Winters, James Henry (Nip67)	19	13	9	0	111.3	108	73	53	43	93	5	0	8	8	.500	4.28	5.90
		67	45	0	570.0	608	357	257	175	276	16	9	30	36	.455	4.06	5.64

1923

All Games

	App.	GS	CG	SHO	IP	H	RS	ER	BB	K	WP	HB	WON	LOST	PCT.	ERA	RPG
Carter, Clifford	1	1	1	0	6.0	2	4	0	3	4	1	1	1	0	1.000	0.00	6.00
Dennis	1	1	1	1	9.0	6	0	0	0	7	0	0	1	0	1.000	0.00	0.00
Downs, McKinley (Bunny)	1	0	0	0	3.0	4	6	4	2	2	0	0	0	0	.000	12.00	18.00
Gisentaner, William (Lefty)	1	1	0	0	6.3	8	4	3	4	1	1	0	0	1	.000	4.26	5.68
Hampton, Lewis	9	6	2	2	36.3	42	25	21	7	27	0	5	3	3	.500	5.20	6.19
Harper, John	27	21	16	2	184.3	166	86	61	47	104	1	7	11	11	.500	2.98	4.20
Henderson, Arthur Chauncey (Rats)	36	26	22	1	246.0	205	110	66	44	150	0	5	15	13	.536	2.41	4.02
Johnson, Nate (Speedboy)	19	15	8	0	124.0	156	96	74	36	62	0	7	6	5	.545	5.37	6.97
Lockhart, George Hubert (Prof)	21	16	15	3	150.3	131	69	48	32	77	0	2	8	5	.615	2.87	4.13
Marlin	1	1	0	0	1.0	6	5	5	2	0	0	0	0	0	.000	45.00	45.00
McLloyd	1	0	0	0	7.0	4	3	2	2	4	0	0	1	0	1.000	2.57	3.86
Reid, Ambrose Leevolia (Ambrose)	1	0	0	0	0.3	0	0	0	0	0	0	0	0	0	.000	0.00	0.00
Roberts, Leroy (Roy, Eveready)	8	7	3	1	50.3	47	31	23	9	23	0	1	2	4	.333	4.11	5.54
Robinson, George Washington (Sis)	1	0	0	0	1.0	7	4	3	0	1	0	2	0	0	.000	27.00	36.00
Smith, R. (Red)	1	0	0	0	3.7	5	2	2	0	2	0	0	0	0	.000	4.91	4.91
Treadwell, Harold E.	3	3	1	1	19.0	12	11	5	3	5	0	0	1	1	.500	2.37	5.21
White, Chaney Leonard (Reindeer)	1	1	1	0	9.0	8	4	3	3	6	0	1	1	0	1.000	3.00	4.00
	100		71	11	856.7	809	460	320	194	475	3	17	50	43	.538	3.36	4.83

League-Level Opponents

	App.	GS	CG	SHO	IP	H	RS	ER	BB	K	WP	HB	WON	LOST	PCT.	ERA	RPG
Carter, Clifford	1	1	1	0	6.0	2	4	0	3	4	1	1	1	0	1.000	0.00	6.00
Downs, McKinley (Bunny)	1	0	0	0	3.0	4	6	4	2	2	0	0	0	0	.000	12.00	18.00
Gisentaner, William (Lefty)	1	1	0	0	6.3	8	4	3	4	1	1	0	0	1	.000	4.26	5.68
Hampton, Lewis	7	5	1	1	26.3	37	20	17	5	18	0	2	2	3	.400	5.81	6.84
Harper, John	17	13	9	0	114.7	97	58	41	25	46	1	3	7	8	.467	3.22	4.55
Henderson, Arthur Chauncey (Rats)	26	20	16	1	177.7	154	93	54	34	104	0	5	11	11	.500	2.74	4.71
Johnson, Nate (Speedboy)	9	7	3	0	57.0	76	50	40	19	31	0	0	3	2	.600	6.32	7.89
Lockhart, George Hubert (Prof)	15	11	11	2	110.3	94	47	30	22	50	0	1	7	3	.700	2.45	3.83

1924

League-Level Opponents

	App.	GS	CG	SHO	IP	H	RS	ER	BB	K	WP	HB	WON	LOST	PCT.	ERA	RPG
Reid, Ambrose Leevolia (Ambrose)	1	0	0	0	0.3	0	0	0	0	0	0	0	0	0	.000	0.00	0.00
Roberts, Leroy (Roy)	2	2	0	0	12.3	17	14	8	5	4	0	0	0	1	.000	5.84	10.22
Robinson, George Washington (Sis)	1	0	0	0	1.0	7	4	3	0	1	0	0	0	0	.000	27.00	36.00
Treadwell, Harold E.	2	2	0	0	10.0	9	11	5	3	0	1	0	0	1	.000	4.50	9.90
	62	41		4	525.0	505	311	205	122	262	3	10	31	30	.508	3.51	5.33

All Games

	App.	GS	CG	SHO	IP	H	RS	ER	BB	K	WP	HB	WON	LOST	PCT.	ERA	RPG
Carr, Wayne	10	8	4	0	57.7	67	40	34	18	18	0	1	2	3	.400	5.31	6.24
Carter, Clifford	4	1	1	0	24.3	21	16	11	2	3	0	0	2	1	.667	4.07	5.92
Estrada, Oscar	2	0	0	0	3.0	9	5	4	2	1	0	2	0	0	.000	12.00	15.00
Evans, W.P.	8	7	4	0	47.0	40	21	19	16	33	1	0	3	2	.600	3.64	4.02
Hampton, Lewis	1	1	1	1	9.0	4	0	0	0	4	0	1	1	0	1.000	0.00	0.00
Harper, John	18	14	9	1	122.0	109	54	42	35	65	1	1	12	3	.800	3.10	3.98
Henderson, Arthur Chauncey (Rats)	12	10	8	1	83.7	66	26	21	32	67	1	0	6	3	.667	2.26	2.80
Hobson, Charles Johnson (Johnny)	8	8	7	1	65.0	80	42	36	15	25	0	0	3	5	.375	4.98	5.82
Jones, William (Willie)	1	1	0	0	3.7	10	13	9	1	2	0	0	0	1	.000	22.09	31.91
Lockhart, George Hubert (Prof)	22	18	13	1	165.3	163	89	56	43	72	1	0	13	5	.722	3.05	4.84
Lowell	1	0	0	0	7.0	5	1	1	0	3	0	1	1	0	1.000	0.00	0.00
Lundy, Richard Benjamin (King Richard)	1	0	0	0	1.3	1	0	0	0	2	0	0	0	0	.000	6.75	6.75
Mitchell, Benjamin Arnett [Ernest] (Hooks)	8	6	4	0	45.0	47	30	23	23	17	1	0	3	3	.500	4.60	6.00
Nuttal, H. (Bill)	12	7	5	0	67.7	77	33	26	14	32	0	2	4	4	.500	3.46	4.39
Roberts, Leroy (Roy)	8	8	6	1	60.3	57	25	20	11	45	0	1	4	2	.667	2.98	3.73
Starks, Otis (Lefty)	17	12	12	0	123.0	139	67	55	22	54	0	0	6	7	.462	4.02	4.90
Thompson	1	1	1	0	9.0	7	3	0	3	11	0	2	1	0	1.000	0.00	3.00
Williams, Andrew (Stringbean)	16	15	14	4	132.3	121	46	29	26	79	1	2	10	4	.714	1.97	3.13
	118		89	10	1,026.3	1,023	511	386	263	533	6	10	71	43	.623	3.38	4.48

League-Level Opponents

	App.	GS	CG	SHO	IP	H	RS	ER	BB	K	WP	HB	WON	LOST	PCT.	ERA	RPG
Carr, Wayne	7	5	2	0	40.7	43	27	23	12	11	0	1	1	2	.333	5.09	5.98
Carter, Clifford	2	0	0	0	7.3	10	6	4	2	3	0	0	1	0	1.000	4.91	7.36
Evans, W.P.	3	2	1	0	16.0	16	11	11	10	6	0	1	1	1	.500	6.19	6.19
Harper, John	13	9	4	0	80.0	85	48	38	29	27	1	1	7	3	.700	4.28	5.40
Henderson, Arthur Chauncey (Rats)	10	9	7	1	69.7	56	21	18	27	50	1	1	5	2	.714	2.33	2.71
Hobson, Charles Johnson (Johnny)	6	6	5	0	50.0	59	33	28	13	21	0	0	2	4	.333	5.04	5.94
Lockhart, George Hubert (Prof)	19	16	11	1	135.3	140	80	51	36	54	0	0	10	5	.667	3.39	5.32
Lowell	1	0	0	0	7.0	5	0	0	0	3	0	1	1	0	1.000	0.00	0.00
Mitchell, Benjamin Arnett [Ernest] (Hooks)	5	3	3	1	19.0	25	23	18	16	7	1	0	1	2	.333	8.53	10.89
Nuttal, H. (Bill)	6	3	2	0	28.0	40	21	17	5	9	0	0	0	4	.000	5.46	6.75
Roberts, Leroy (Roy)	3	3	2	0	20.3	24	9	8	6	6	0	1	1	1	.500	3.54	3.98
Starks, Otis (Lefty)	9	5	5	0	62.0	75	40	36	17	22	0	0	1	5	.167	5.23	5.81
Williams, Andrew (Stringbean)	7	7	7	2	61.0	55	23	14	18	34	1	1	4	2	.667	2.07	3.39
	68	47		3	596.3	633	342	266	191	253	5	5	35	31	.530	4.01	5.16

1925

All Games

	App.	GS	CG	SHO	IP	H	RS	ER	BB	K	WP	HB	WON	LOST	PCT.	ERA	RPG
Clark, Maceo Richard	2	2	1	0	10.0	11	7	6	2	5	0	0	1	1	.500	5.40	6.30
Farrell, Luther Alaner (Red)	15	12	11	1	110.3	103	48	38	33	91	1	1	9	4	.692	3.10	3.92
Gatewood, Ernest E.	1	0	0	0	1.0	2	1	1	0	0	0	0	0	0	.000	9.00	9.00
Gillespie, Henry	11	9	5	0	63.7	73	46	37	33	26	0	2	4	4	.500	5.23	6.50
Grier, Claude Bonds (Red)	15	12	9	1	107.3	117	50	42	36	66	1	1	10	3	.769	3.52	4.19
Henderson, Arthur Chauncey (Rats)	42	31	26	2	297.3	277	146	119	85	160	3	10	20	13	.606	3.60	4.42
Lockhart, George Hubert (Prof)	19	16	12	1	133.7	150	71	56	29	44	0	2	6	7	.462	3.77	4.78
Lundy, Richard Benjamin (King Richard)	1	0	0	0	1.0	2	1	1	0	0	0	0	0	0	.000	9.00	9.00
Mitchell, Benjamin Arnett [Ernest] (Hooks)	27	22	16	1	180.0	204	110	92	35	90	0	3	10	11	.476	4.60	5.50
Nuttal, H. (Bill)	8	6	3	0	61.0	61	30	28	13	25	3	0	2	2	.500	4.13	4.43
Reid, Ambrose Leevolia (Ambrose)	2	1	0	0	9.7	12	7	5	2	2	0	1	1	0	1.000	4.66	6.52
Roberts, Leroy (Roy)	18	16	11	1	119.7	103	55	41	47	83	4	3	7	7	.500	3.08	4.14
		127	**94**	**7**	**1,094.7**	**1,115**	**572**	**466**	**315**	**592**	**13**	**22**	**70**	**52**	**.574**	**3.83**	**4.70**

League Opponents

	App.	GS	CG	SHO	IP	H	RS	ER	BB	K	WP	HB	WON	LOST	PCT.	ERA	RPG
Farrell, Luther Alaner (Lefty)	11	8	8	1	79.0	74	36	28	25	56	1	1	5	4	.556	3.19	4.10
Gillespie, Henry	8	6	3	0	42.3	50	29	25	23	23	0	2	2	3	.400	5.31	6.17
Grier, Claude Bonds (Red)	11	9	7	0	84.7	91	41	35	32	61	0	0	7	3	.700	3.72	4.36
Henderson, Arthur Chauncey (Rats)	33	26	21	2	237.3	231	123	97	73	125	2	7	16	11	.593	3.68	4.66
Lockhart, George Hubert (Prof)	9	7	5	0	52.3	67	36	27	17	17	0	0	2	4	.200	4.64	6.19
Mitchell, Benjamin Arnett [Ernest] (Hooks)	15	11	6	0	93.3	108	63	55	26	34	1	3	4	7	.364	5.30	6.08
Nuttal, H. (Bill)	3	3	2	0	25.3	31	17	15	10	7	3	0	1	1	.500	5.33	6.04
Roberts, Leroy (Roy)	4	4	2	0	26.7	28	13	9	15	14	0	0	0	3	.000	3.04	4.39
		74	**54**	**3**	**641.0**	**680**	**358**	**291**	**221**	**337**	**7**	**13**	**36**	**36**	**.500**	**4.09**	**5.03**

1926

All Games

	App.	GS	CG	SHO	IP	H	RS	ER	BB	K	WP	HB	WON	LOST	PCT.	ERA	RPG
Farrell, Luther Alaner (Buck)	17	13	9	1	113.0	110	52	41	28	99	0	1	7	5	.583	3.27	4.14
Grier, Claude Bonds (Red)	42	34	26	5	283.3	216	128	92	103	224	2	11	21	13	.618	2.92	4.07
Henderson, Arthur Chauncey (Rats)	37	28	22	2	258.0	217	105	77	73	138	0	5	15	11	.577	2.69	3.66
Johnson	1	1	0	0	1.7	5	5	4	2	2	0	1	0	1	.000	21.60	27.00
Lockhart, George Hubert (Prof)	18	15	8	0	128.7	116	51	40	38	37	0	0	7	6	.538	2.80	3.57
Mitchell, Alonzo (Fluke)	13	8	6	2	69.0	67	40	29	21	25	0	1	4	5	.444	3.78	5.22
Reid, Ambrose Leevolia (Ambrose)	1	1	1	1	5.0	3	0	0	0	2	0	0	1	0	1.000	0.00	0.00
Roberts, Leroy (Roy)	26	19	13	0	161.7	148	95	77	64	91	1	3	10	5	.667	4.29	5.29
White, Chaney Leonard (Reindeer)	2	1	1	0	11.3	9	5	4	3	2	0	0	1	0	1.000	3.18	3.97
		120	**86**	**11**	**1,031.7**	**891**	**481**	**364**	**332**	**620**	**3**	**23**	**66**	**46**	**.589**	**3.18**	**4.20**

League-Level Opponents

	App.	GS	CG	SHO	IP	H	RS	ER	BB	K	WP	HB	WON	LOST	PCT.	ERA	RPG
Farrell, Luther Alaner (Red)	8	4	3	0	42.7	48	23	21	15	33	0	1	1	4	.200	4.43	4.85
Grier, Claude Bonds (Red)	29	24	20	3	200.0	143	74	54	73	157	2	8	16	8	.667	2.43	3.33

Appendix C: Batting and Pitching Statistics by Year

1927

League-Level Opponents

	App.	GS	CG	SHO	IP	H	RS	ER	BB	K	WP	HB	WON	LOST	PCT.	ERA	RPG
Henderson, Arthur Chauncey (Rats)	23	20	16	1	185.7	161	77	58	54	100	0	4	13	7	.650	2.81	3.73
Lockhart, George Hubert (Prof)	5	4	1	0	36.3	27	15	12	19	10	0	0	1	2	.333	2.97	3.72
Mitchell, Alonzo (Fluke)	7	3	2	1	32.7	28	14	11	10	9	0	0	2	1	.667	3.03	3.86
Roberts, Leroy (Roy)	12	10	6	0	70.0	63	45	36	25	32	1	2	4	3	.571	4.63	5.79
White, Chaney Leonard (Reindeer)	1	0	0	0	3.3	3	3	2	2	0	0	0	0	0	.000	5.40	8.10
	65	37	48	5	570.7	473	251	194	198	341	3	15	37	25	.597	3.06	3.96

All Games

	App.	GS	CG	SHO	IP	H	RS	ER	BB	K	WP	HB	WON	LOST	PCT.	ERA	RPG
Cooper, Samuel (Sam)	1	0	0	0	2.0	1	0	0	1	1	0	0	1	0	1.000	0.00	0.00
Farrell, Luther Alaner (Red)	43	32	24	2	286.0	273	149	109	79	181	0	6	20	14	.588	3.43	4.69
Gillespie, Henry	15	11	6	0	93.3	95	55	43	30	32	0	3	4	6	.400	4.15	5.30
Grier, Claude Bonds (Red)	7	6	3	0	40.7	47	32	23	10	17	0	0	2	2	.500	5.09	7.08
Henderson, Arthur Chauncey (Rats)	24	17	14	1	153.3	151	66	52	36	77	0	1	12	6	.667	3.05	3.87
Hubbard, Jesse James (Mountain Man)	23	21	16	1	173.0	166	93	73	42	80	0	2	13	7	.650	3.80	4.84
Lewis, Milton	1	0	0	0	4.0	1	0	0	1	0	0	2	0	0	.000	0.00	0.00
Lockhart, George Hubert (Prof)	24	16	11	1	149.3	160	93	71	51	61	0	3	8	6	.571	4.28	5.60
Lundy, Richard Benjamin (King Richard)	2	0	0	0	2.0	4	3	3	0	0	0	0	0	0	.000	13.50	13.50
Reid, Ambrose Leevolia (Ambrose)	2	0	0	0	3.0	10	10	7	1	1	0	0	0	0	.000	21.00	30.00
Roberts, Leroy (Roy)	31	19	9	0	176.7	170	104	84	66	79	1	6	12	6	.667	4.28	5.30
White, Chaney Leonard (Reindeer)	1	1	0	0	2.0	6	5	4	1	0	0	0	0	1	.000	18.00	22.50
	123	83	5		1,085.3	1,084	610	469	318	529	1	23	72	48	.600	3.89	5.06

1928

League-Level Opponents

	App.	GS	CG	SHO	IP	H	RS	ER	BB	K	WP	HB	WON	LOST	PCT.	ERA	RPG
Cooper, Samuel (Sam)	1	0	0	0	2.0	1	0	0	1	1	0	0	1	0	1.000	0.00	0.00
Farrell, Luther Alaner (Red)	32	24	16	2	208.7	192	101	72	51	128	0	2	16	10	.615	3.11	4.36
Gillespie, Henry	9	7	3	0	57.0	55	30	23	23	14	0	0	2	4	.333	3.63	4.74
Grier, Claude Bonds (Red)	4	3	2	0	21.3	24	14	11	6	6	0	0	1	0	1.000	4.64	5.91
Henderson, Arthur Chauncey (Rats)	24	17	14	1	153.3	151	66	52	36	77	0	0	12	6	.667	3.05	3.87
Hubbard, Jesse James (Mountain Man)	18	16	14	1	142.3	121	60	47	34	64	0	2	11	4	.733	2.97	3.79
Lewis, Milton	1	0	0	0	4.0	1	0	0	1	0	0	2	0	0	.000	0.00	0.00
Lockhart, George Hubert (Prof)	16	10	6	0	91.7	115	76	57	38	35	0	3	4	5	.444	5.60	7.46
Lundy, Richard Benjamin (King Richard)	2	0	0	0	2.0	4	3	3	5	0	0	0	0	0	.000	13.50	13.50
Reid, Ambrose Leevolia (Ambrose)	1	0	0	0	1.0	6	7	5	1	0	0	0	0	0	.000	45.00	63.00
Roberts, Leroy (Roy)	25	15	5	0	136.7	128	82	69	60	55	1	5	8	6	.571	4.54	5.40
	92	60	4		820.0	798	439	339	251	380	1	15	55	35	.611	3.72	4.82

All Games

	App.	GS	CG	SHO	IP	H	RS	ER	BB	K	WP	HB	WON	LOST	PCT.	ERA	RPG
Daniels, Fred	1	0	0	0	1.0	1	3	3	0	0	0	0	0	0	.000	27.00	27.00
Farrell, Luther Alaner (Red)	28	21	18	0	183.0	174	78	67	65	142	2	1	16	8	.667	3.30	3.84

Appendix C: Batting and Pitching Statistics by Year

	App.	GS	CG	SHO	IP	H	RS	ER	BB	K	WP	HB	WON	LOST	PCT.	ERA	RPG
Gardner, Kenneth Fuller (Ping)	26	20	14	0	171.0	195	124	103	38	66	2	3	7	14	.333	5.42	6.53
Green, Curtis (Cornelius)	8	6	3	0	51.7	53	29	23	21	23	0	0	3	2	.600	4.01	5.05
Henderson, Arthur Chauncey (Rats)	21	16	11	2	135.7	151	73	61	33	82	1	0	10	4	.714	4.05	4.84
Lockhart, George Hubert (Prof)	13	8	6	0	85.0	85	45	38	28	41	0	6	4	3	.571	4.02	4.76
Lundy, Richard Benjamin (King Richard,	1	0	0	0	2.0	2	3	3	1	0	0	1	0	0	.000	13.50	13.50
Mitchell, Alonzo (Fluke)	13	7	3	0	54.7	71	40	35	22	27	1	0	4	2	.667	5.76	6.59
Shields, James D. (Jaydee)	10	9	9	2	82.7	78	32	24	27	33	0	0	6	3	.667	2.61	3.48
Stanley, John Wesley (Neck)	2	2	0	0	10.0	11	9	6	1	1	0	0	0	1	.000	5.40	8.10
	89		**64**	**4**	**776.7**	**821**	**436**	**363**	**236**	**415**	**7**	**11**	**50**	**37**	**.575**	**4.21**	**5.05**

League-Level Opponents	App.	GS	CG	SHO	IP	H	RS	ER	BB	K	WP	HB	WON	LOST	PCT.	ERA	RPG
Daniels, Fred	1	0	0	0	1.0	1	3	3	0	0	0	0	0	0	.000	27.00	27.00
Farrell, Luther Alaner (Red)	21	16	13	0	135.0	140	65	55	49	102	2	1	11	7	.611	3.67	4.33
Gardner, Kenneth Fuller (Ping)	22	18	12	0	144.3	171	114	95	36	52	2	3	3	14	.176	5.92	7.11
Green, Curtis (Cornelius)	4	2	1	0	19.7	25	16	14	3	3	0	0	1	1	.500	6.41	7.32
Henderson, Arthur Chauncey (Rats)	16	11	6	2	91.7	104	53	44	25	60	0	0	7	2	.778	4.32	5.20
Lockhart, George Hubert (Prof)	10	5	4	0	60.7	55	30	23	18	30	0	0	3	2	.600	3.41	4.45
Lundy, Richard Benjamin (King Richard,	1	0	0	0	2.0	2	3	3	1	0	0	0	0	0	.000	13.50	13.50
Mitchell, Alonzo (Fluke)	12	6	2	0	45.7	58	32	28	20	22	1	3	3	2	.600	5.52	6.31
Shields, James D. (Jaydee)	7	6	6	1	59.7	48	15	11	22	21	0	0	4	2	.667	1.66	2.26
Stanley, John Wesley (Neck)	1	1	0	0	3.0	6	4	2	2	1	0	0	0	1	.000	6.00	12.00
	65		**44**	**3**	**562.7**	**610**	**335**	**278**	**175**	**291**	**6**	**7**	**32**	**31**	**.508**	**4.45**	**5.36**

1929

All Games	App.	GS	CG	SHO	IP	H	RS	ER	BB	K	WP	HB	WON	LOST	PCT.	ERA	RPG
Albright, Thomas (Pistol Pete)	11	4	2	0	40.3	59	35	27	21	13	0	0	2	3	.400	6.02	7.81
Cade, Joe	16	10	2	0	64.3	90	52	45	25	28	0	1	2	5	.286	6.30	7.27
Cooper, Samuel (Sam)	12	5	0	0	52.7	70	54	44	28	23	0	0	1	4	.200	7.52	9.23
Eggleston, Macajah Marchand (Mack)	1	0	0	0	1.0	0	0	0	0	0	0	0	0	0	.000	0.00	0.00
Farrell, Luther Alaner (Red)	4	3	2	0	22.3	39	24	18	15	9	0	1	0	3	.000	7.25	9.67
Gardner, Kenneth Fuller (Ping)	16	12	6	0	82.7	120	92	68	37	31	2	2	4	9	.308	7.40	10.02
Henderson, Arthur Chauncey (Rats)	33	24	13	1	188.3	226	135	110	62	91	2	3	11	13	.458	5.26	6.45
Lindsay, William Hudson (Red)	3	0	0	0	9.0	15	6	6	3	2	0	1	1	0	1.000	6.00	6.00
McClure, Robert E. (Bob, Big Boy)	35	17	8	1	166.3	202	120	100	43	64	4	3	8	11	.421	5.41	6.49
Miller	1	1	0	0	2.0	4	6	6	2	1	0	0	0	1	.000	27.00	27.00
Mitchell, Alonzo (Fluke)	7	4	1	0	25.0	34	21	16	10	14	0	2	2	0	1.000	5.76	7.56
Reid, Ambrose Leevolia (Ambrose)	3	2	1	0	13.0	17	12	9	5	4	0	0	1	0	1.000	6.23	8.31
Roberts, Leroy (Roy)	3	1	0	0	9.3	26	24	21	5	5	0	1	0	1	.000	20.25	23.14
Shields, James D. (Jaydee)	28	14	3	1	123.7	123	97	80	58	47	2	0	7	6	.538	5.82	7.06
Stevens, Frank L. (Lefty)	1	0	0	0	2.3	5	6	4	0	0	0	0	0	0	.000	15.43	23.14
	97		**38**	**3**	**802.3**	**1,030**	**684**	**554**	**314**	**332**	**7**	**8**	**39**	**56**	**.411**	**6.21**	**7.67**

League-Level Opponents	App.	GS	CG	SHO	IP	H	RS	ER	BB	K	WP	HB	WON	LOST	PCT.	ERA	RPG
Albright, Thomas (Pistol Pete)	7	2	1	0	19.0	34	23	19	8	6	0	0	0	2	.000	9.00	10.89
Cade, Joe	10	6	0	0	36.0	50	33	31	12	9	0	0	1	4	.200	7.75	8.25

Appendix C: Batting and Pitching Statistics by Year

League-Level Opponents	App.	GS	CG	SHO	IP	H	RS	ER	BB	K	WP	HB	WON	LOST	PCT.	ERA	RPG
Cooper, Samuel (Sam)	9	3	0	0	46.3	60	46	37	24	21	0	0	0	3	.000	7.19	8.94
Farrell, Luther Alaner (Red)	4	3	2	0	22.3	39	24	18	15	9	0	0	0	3	.000	7.25	9.67
Gardner, Kenneth Fuller (Ping)	11	8	3	0	56.0	82	67	49	28	24	2	1	4	5	.444	7.87	10.77
Henderson, Arthur Chauncey (Rats)	25	18	8	1	141.0	156	100	80	49	58	2	2	8	10	.444	5.11	6.38
Lindsay, William Hudson (Red)	1	0	0	0	2.0	5	5	5	1	0	0	0	0	0	.000	22.50	22.50
McClure, Robert E. (Bob)	25	10	2	0	99.3	126	78	66	26	45	1	2	4	8	.333	5.98	7.07
Mitchell, Alonzo (Fluke)	5	3	0	0	14.7	17	13	9	9	9	0	0	1	0	1.000	5.52	7.98
Reid, Ambrose Leevolia (Ambrose)	1	0	0	0	5.3	3	1	1	2	2	0	0	0	0	.000	1.69	1.69
Roberts, Leroy (Roy)	1	0	0	0	3.3	8	7	7	1	4	0	0	0	0	.000	18.90	18.90
Shields, James D. (Jaydee)	17	7	0	0	50.7	71	66	53	36	24	1	0	1	4	.200	9.41	11.72
Stevens, Frank L. (Lefty)	1	0	0	0	2.3	5	6	4	0	0	0	0	0	0	.000	15.43	23.14
		60	16	1	498.3	656	469	379	211	211	6	5	19	39	.328	6.84	8.47

Chapter Notes

Chapter 1

1. James B. Crooks, "Changing Face of Jacksonville, Florida: 1900–1910," *The Florida Historical Quarterly*, 62 (1984), 439–442.
2. Crooks, 455–458.
3. Crooks, 461.
4. James Weldon Johnson, *Along This Way* (New York: Penguin, 1990), 45.
5. Emmett J. Scott, "Negro Migration During the War," in *Preliminary Economic Studies of the War*, ed. David Kinley for Carnegie Endowment for International Peace. (New York: Oxford University Press, 1920), 52; "Views and Reviews," *New York Age*, August 24, 1916.
6. Robert Cassanello, "Violence, Racial Etiquette, and African American Working-Class Infrapolitics in Jacksonville During World War I," *The Florida Historical Quarterly*, 82 (2003), 157–9.
7. Nelson Johnson, *Boardwalk Empire* (Medford, NJ: Medford Press, 2002), xv.
8. Johnson, *Boardwalk Empire*, 21.
9. Nelson Johnson, *The Northside: African-Americans and the Creation of Atlantic City* (Medford NJ: Plexus Publishing, 2010), 14.
10. Johnson, *Boardwalk Empire*, 72.
11. Johnson, *Boardwalk Empire*, 39; Johnson, *The Northside*, 31–32.
12. Martin Paulson, *The Social Anxieties of Progressive Reform: Atlantic City, 1854–1920* (New York: New York University Press, 1994), 172; "New Commission Kuehnle's, 3 to 2," *Trenton Evening Times, July 10, 1912*; "9,000 Registered in Atlantic City," *Philadelphia Inquirer*, November 3, 1912.
13. Johnson, *The Northside*, 40.
14. "Bacharach Appoints Two School Directors," *Philadelphia Tribune*, July 29, 1912; "Bacharach in Promises to Colored Race," *Atlantic City Daily Press*, April 17, 1924.
15. Advertisement, *Atlantic City Daily Press*, May 9, 1916.
16. "Bacharachs Beat Vandals in First A.C. League Game," *Atlantic City Daily Press*, May 9, 1916.
17. Robert Peterson, *Only the Ball Was White* (New York: McGraw-Hill, 1970), 68.
18. "Spotless Town Is Ambition of Bacharach," *Atlantic City Daily Press*, June 27, 1916; "Not a Plague, but a Panic," *Philadelphia Inquirer*, September 16, 1916.
19. World War I Draft Registration Cards, s.v. "Loraine Melcher," accessed through Ancestry.com.
20. "Ask for Arrest of Tom Jackson," *Atlantic City Daily Press*, July 14, 1916.
21. "Mayors Pummel Manhattans, 10-1: Play Regs Today," *Atlantic City Daily Press*, June 7, 1916; "Bacharachs Scalp Vandals, 8 to 2," *Atlantic City Daily Press*, June 13, 1916; "Bacharachs Win in Slugging Bee," *Atlantic City Daily Press*, June 24, 1916.
22. "Bacharachs Picked as Sunday Sinners," *Atlantic City Daily Press*, July 6, 1916.
23. "Brooklyn Royals Blank Bacharachs," *Atlantic City Daily Press*, July 19, 1916.
24. "Ask for Arrest of Tom Jackson," *Atlantic City Daily Press*, July 14, 1916; "Try to Trick Bacharach Nine," *Atlantic City Daily Press*, July 21, 1916.
25. http://www.baseball-reference.com/nlb/player.cgi?id=lundy-000dic; James A. Riley, *The Biographical Encyclopedia of the Negro Baseball Leagues* (New York: Carroll & Graf, 1994), 497.
26. 1910 United States Census, s.v. "Richard Lundy," Jacksonville, Duval County, Florida, accessed through Ancestry.com; Riley, *The Biographical Encyclopedia of the Negro Baseball Leagues*, 497; 1920 United States Census, s.v. "Richard Lundy," Jacksonville, Duval County, Florida, accessed through Ancestry.com.
27. Riley, *The Biographical Encyclopedia of the Negro Baseball Leagues*, 201; 1920 United States Census, s.v. "Willis Crump," Jacksonville, Duval County, Florida, accessed through Ancestry.com.
28. "Marcel and Roy Roberts in Big Baseball Trade," *New York Amsterdam News*, May 13, 1925.
29. John B. Holway, *Black Giants* (Springfield, VA: Lord Fairfax Press, 2010), 10.
30. Holway, *Black Giants*, 13; Napoleon Cum-

mings, interview with Robert Peterson, October 4, 1967, in Atlantic City, NJ (National Baseball Hall of Fame and Museum, Cooperstown, NY).
　31. "B-Giants Defeat Ocean City, 5–3," *Atlantic City Daily Press*, August 25, 1916.
　32. "Bacharach Giants Will Open Season," *Atlantic City Daily Press*, May 18, 1918. "Eastern Sporting World," *Chicago Defender*, June 14, 1919.
　33. "Seashore Grafters Held," *New York Times*, September 27, 1912.
　34. "Colored Show Off, but Plenty of Excitement," *Atlantic City Daily Press*, August 26, 1919.
　35. "Eckholm Gives the Lie to T. Jackson," *Atlantic City Daily Press*, May 11, 1920; "Jackson Is Asked to Manage Cuban Team," *Chicago Whip*, May 15, 1920.
　36. "Food for Fans," *Bridgeton Evening News*, August 25, 1916.
　37. "Giants Win Get-Away Game," *Philadelphia Inquirer*, October 9, 1916.
　38. *North American*, May 15, 1910, quoted in Neil Lanctot, *Fair Dealing and Clean Playing: The Hilldale Club and the Development of Black Professional Baseball, 1910–1932* (Jefferson, NC: McFarland, 1994), 6.
　39. Lanctot, *Fair Dealing and Clean Playing*, 7.
　40. Napoleon Cummings interview with Robert Peterson.
　41. Napoleon "Chance" Cummings interview with John Holway, collection of Michael Everett (Linwood, NJ).
　42. "Black Sox Defeated," *Indianapolis Freeman*, July 15, 1916.
　43. 1900 United States Census, s.v. "William Lai," Hanalei District, Island of Kauai, Hawaiian Islands, accessed through Ancestry.com.
　44. "Bacharach Giants Beat Chinese, 6–5," *Chicago Defender*, July 29, 1916.
　45. "Dilworth a Big Mystery," *Bridgeton Evening News*, August 6, 1916.
　46. "Mayors Wallop Listless Vandals," *Atlantic City Daily Press*, May 30, 1916.

Chapter 2

　1. "Bacharach Giants Open Baseball Season," *Atlantic City Daily Press*, May 19, 1917.
　2. "Bacharach Giants Open Baseball Season," *Atlantic City Daily Press*, May 19, 1917.
　3. Riley, *The Biographical Encyclopedia of the Negro Baseball Leagues*, 247; http://www.baseball-reference.com/nlb/player.cgi?id=downs-000bun4.
　4. http://www.seamheads.com/NegroLgs/player.php?ID=670; 1910 United States Census, s.v. "Elihu Roberts," Fitzgerald City, Malitia [sic] District 1537, Georgia, accessed through Ancestry.com; *Polk's Atlantic City Directory* (New Brunswick, NJ: R. L. Polk, 1927), 783.

　5. Riley, *The Biographical Encyclopedia of the Negro Baseball Leagues*, 833.
　6. *Sol White's History of Colored Base Ball*, compiled and introduced by Jerry Malloy (Lincoln, NE: University of Nebraska Press, 1995), 65.
　7. "Chester Evens Up Giants Series, 8–3," *Atlantic City Daily Press*, June 14, 1917; "Havana Red Sox Take Two from The Ryans," *Watertown Daily Times*, June 18, 1917.
　8. "Loses Players; Jackson Calls Off Two Games," *Atlantic City Daily Press*, June 18, 1917.
　9. Riley, *The Biographical Encyclopedia of the Negro Baseball Leagues*, 623.
　10. "'Pop' Watkins May Move On," *Watertown Daily Times*, July 24, 1917.
　11. "M'Donald, Twirler Leaves Havana Reds," *Watertown Daily Times*, July 25, 1917; "M'Donald Forced to Quit Red Sox," *Watertown Daily Times*, July 26, 1917; "Bacharachs Lose in Final Sessions," *Atlantic City Daily Press*, August 9, 1917.
　12. "Giants Sick Man Beats Logan Square," *Atlantic City Daily Press*, September 3, 1917.
　13. "Bacharach Giants Defeat Chester, 4–1," *Atlantic City Daily Press*, June 13, 1917.
　14. "Colored Teams for a League," *Atlantic City Daily Press*, June 28, 1917.
　15. "Red Caps Hammer New Giants Twirlers," *Atlantic City Daily Press*, July 6, 1917.
　16. "Plainfield Nine Leaves Field in Giant Game," *Atlantic City Daily Press*, June 6, 1917.
　17. Johnson, *The Northside*, 42.
　18. "Giants Cop First in City Series," *Atlantic City Daily Press*, September 24, 1917; "Melrose Pick-Ups Lose to Giants," *Atlantic City Daily Press*, September 26, 1917.
　19. Bill Nowlin, "Vince Molyneaux," Society for American Baseball Research BioProject, http://sabr.org/bioproj/person/6e306df2.
　20. "Logans Win Game of Lively Scraps," *Atlantic City Daily Press*, October 1, 1917.
　21. Lanctot, *Fair Dealing and Clean Playing*, 10–11.
　22. "Alexander Wants $15,000 Contract," *Trenton Evening Times*, February 16, 1917; "Baker Denies Charge of Sothoron," *New Orleans Daily States*, July 18, 1917.
　23. Lanctot, *Fair Dealing and Clean Playing*, 10–11.
　24. "N.E. Phillies Beat Bacharach Giants in Close Game; 5–4," *Atlantic City Daily Press*, June 7, 1917.
　25. Riley, *The Biographical Encyclopedia of the Negro Baseball Leagues*, 618.
　26. Lanctot, *Fair Dealing and Clean Playing*, 16–25.
　27. "Brooklyns Win in Listless Ball Game," *Atlantic City Daily Press*, August 25, 1917.

28. "Giants Lost After Eleven Inning Play," *Atlantic City Daily Press*, August 8, 1917.

29. "Foster's Champions Take First in Series for World Pennant," *Atlantic City Daily Press*, August 28, 1917.

30. Robert Obojski, *Bush League* (New York: Macmillan, 1975), 18.

31. Delco Baseball League History, http://www.leaguelineup.com/miscinfo.asp?menuid=30&url=delcoleague; "Camden County Ball League Disbanded," *Philadelphia Inquirer*, April 7, 1918; "Form Baseball League," *Philadelphia Inquirer*, March 28, 1918; *Final Report of the Provost Marshal General* (Washington, D.C.: Government Printing Office, 1920), 103–104.

32. Lanctot, *Fair Dealing and Clean Playing*, 50–51.

33. Riley, *The Biographical Encyclopedia of the Negro Baseball Leagues*, 352.

34. Riley, *The Biographical Encyclopedia of the Negro Baseball Leagues*, 118.

35. "Bacharach Giants Win Both Games of Double Header," *Atlantic City Daily Press*, August 12, 1918.

36. "The Bacharach Giants Lose Exciting Game," *Chicago Defender*, May 25, 1918.

37. "Cuban Stars Take Deciding Game," *Atlantic City Daily Press*, June 20, 1918; "Parkesburg Iron Workers Down Hilldale Nine," *Philadelphia Inquirer*, June 20, 1918.

38. "Royal Giants Win Second Game, 8–4," *Atlantic City Daily Press*, July 17, 1918.

39. "Bacharach Giants Beat Foster's Club," *Atlantic City Daily Press*, August 3, 1918.

40. Brian McKenna, "Bethlehem Steel League," Society for American Baseball Research BioProject, http://sabr.org/bioproj/topic/bethlehem-steel-league.

41. McKenna, "Bethlehem Steel League"; F. C. Lane, "A Rising Menace to the National Game," *Baseball Magazine*, August 1918, 345; Edward M. Reulbach, "Shipyard Baseball and the Future of the Big Leagues," *Baseball Magazine*, December 1918.

42. "Camp May Section Base Here Monday," *Bridgeton Evening News*, August 30, 1918.

Chapter 3

1. Obojski, *Bush League*, 18–19.

2. *Sol White's History of Colored Base Ball*, 151; "Sol White Recalls Baseball's Greatest Day," *Pittsburgh Courier*, March 12, 1927.

3. Michael Lomax, "The Great Independents," in *Shades of Glory*, Lawrence D. Hogan, ed. (Washington, D.C.: National Geographic, 2006), 99; World War I Draft Registration Cards, s.v. "John Wilson Connor," accessed through Ancestry.com.

4. 1900 United States Census, s.v. "John W. Connor," Borough of Brooklyn, City of New York, State of New York, accessed through Ancestry.com; "Over-The-River Jurist on Adams Street Bench," *Brooklyn Daily Eagle*, March 5, 1906.

5. Advertisement, *New York Age*, May 28, 1914.

6. "Johnson Is Now Undisputed Champion," *New York Age*, July 7, 1910; Konrad Bercovici, *Around the World in New York* (New York: Century, 1924), 235.

7. United States Passport Applications, s.v. "Barron D. Wilkins," County of New York, State of New York, November 26, 1919, accessed through Ancestry.com; "Stay for Negro Resort," *New York Times*, July 17, 1910; "Dying Woman in a Hack," *New York Sun*, April 2, 1904.

8. "Barron D. Wilkins Slain in Harlem," *New York Times*, May 25, 1924; "Stay for Barron Wilkins," *New York Sun*, July 17, 1910.

9. Mary Sullivan, *My Double Life: The Story of a New York Policewoman* (New York: Farrar & Rinehart, 1938), 54–59.

10. "Barron D. Wilkins Slain in Harlem," *New York Times*, May 25, 1924; "Barron Wilkins Murdered," *Chicago Defender*, May 31, 1924.

11. Jervis Anderson, *This Was Harlem: A Cultural Portrait, 1900–1950* (New York: Farrar, Straus, Giroux, 1982), 171; Bercovici, *Around the World in New York*, 235–237.

12. "Sporting News," *Cleveland Advocate*, April 26, 1919; "Bacharach Club Opens Season at Inlet May 29," *Atlantic City Daily Press*, May 21, 1919.

13. Certificate of Incorporation, Bacharach Giants Athletic Club, April 28, 1919, New Jersey Secretary of State, Trenton, NJ; "To Change Its Name," *Chicago Defender*, May 10, 1919; "Giants Cop Two Important Games," *Atlantic City Gazette-Review*, June 23, 1919.

14. "Saloonmen Become Baseball Promoters," *New York Age*, April 26, 1919; "John W. Connors to Reopen His Cabaret," *New York Age*, January 16, 1926.

15. "'King of the Bush Leaguers'—He Directs 5,000 Ball Players," *Salt Lake Telegram*, December 19, 1914.

16. "In the World of Sport," *New York Age*, May 2, 1912.

17. "EXTRA!! Lloyd with Bacharachs," *Chicago Defender*, June 7, 1919; "Eastern Sporting World," *Chicago Defender*, June 14, 1919.

18. "Slavery Still in Existence—Even in New York," *Chicago Defender*, May 10, 1919; "Strong's Early Morning Ride," *Chicago Defender*, May 24, 1919; "Strong's Request to Be Complied With," *Chicago Defender*, May 31, 1919.

19. Riley, *The Biographical Encyclopedia of the Negro Baseball Leagues*, 761.

20. Riley, *The Biographical Encyclopedia of the Negro Baseball Leagues*, 712.

21. "Bacharachs Swamp Hal Chase's Team," *Chicago Defender*, June 7, 1919.
22. "EXTRA!! Lloyd with Bacharachs," *Chicago Defender*, June 7, 1919; "Eastern Sporting World," *Chicago Defender*, June 14, 1919.
23. "Internationals Hit Ball All Over the Lot, 14–1," *Atlantic City Daily Press*, September 18, 1919.
24. "B-Giants Turn Tables on Dooin's Star Troop," *Atlantic City Gazette-Review*, September 16, 1919.
25. "Stars Win Twice from the Giants," *Brooklyn Daily Eagle*, October 20, 1919.
26. Lawrence D. Hogan, "Organized League Ball," *Shades of Glory*, 149.
27. "Hilldale Loses," *Philadelphia Inquirer*, August 27, 1919.
28. "Bacharachs Take First Two Games of Series," *Philadelphia Tribune*, June 14, 1919.
29. "Bacharachs Take First Two Games of Series," *Philadelphia Tribune*, June 14, 1919.
30. "Defeats Bacharach in 10-Inning Battle," *Chicago Defender*, August 30, 1919; "Eastern Sporting News," *Chicago Defender*, September 20, 1919.
31. "Negro Nines Play on Shibe Grounds," *Philadelphia Evening Ledger*, September 8, 1919; "Bacharachs Win the Championship," *Chicago Defender*, September 20, 1919.
32. Adrian Burgos, Jr., *Cuban Star* (New York: Hill & Wang, 2011), 34.
33. "B-Giants Claim Forfeited Game," *Atlantic City Gazette-Review*, June 27, 1919.
34. "B-Giants Make It Three Straight with Cubans, 7–4," *Atlantic City Daily Press*, July 25, 1919.
35. Riley, *The Biographical Encyclopedia of the Negro Baseball Leagues*, 229–230.
36. "Benefit for War Heroes," *New York Times*, May 10, 1919.
37. "Strong's Death Knell Sounded," *Chicago Defender*, August 9, 1919.
38. "Semi-Pro Baseball," *Variety*, March 31, 1920.
39. Riley, *Biographical Encyclopedia of the Negro Baseball Leagues*, 434–435.
40. "Bacharach Giants Wallop the Ball, Winning 6 to 2," *Atlantic City Daily Press*, August 29, 1919.
41. "Eastern Sport World," *Chicago Defender*, May 8, 1920.
42. Lanctot, *Fair Dealing and Clean Playing*, 85–86; "Hilldale's Answer to Rube Foster," *Philadelphia Tribune*, August 21, 1920.
43. Lanctot, *Fair Dealing and Clean Playing*, 255; "One Time Hilldale Wins," *Chicago Defender*, June 12, 1920; "Bacharach Giants Favored in Court Decision," *New York Evening Telegram*, June 2, 1920.
44. Riley, *Biographical Encyclopedia of the Negro Baseball Leagues*, 511.
45. Riley, *Biographical Encyclopedia of the Negro Baseball Leagues*, 687.
46. "Big Jeff Tesreau and Connie Savage in Control of Dyckman Oval," *Chicago Defender*, April 3, 1920.
47. "Connors and Savage Disagree," *Chicago Defender*, June 5, 1920; "Bacharach Giants on Their Way Home," *New York Age*, April 17, 1920.
48. "Bacharach Giants Beaten by American Giants' Team," *Atlantic City Gazette-Review*, August 10, 1920.
49. "Bacharachs Quit Field; Game Forfeited; Detroit Fans Sore," *Chicago Defender*, August 14, 1920.
50. "Giants Wallop Easterners Sunday," *Chicago Whip*, August 14, 1920; "Rough Stuff!" *Chicago Defender*, August 14, 1920.
51. "Bacharachs Beat Chicago Giants," *Atlantic City Gazette-Review*, August 20, 1920.
52. "Bacharach Giants Refuse to Play Hilldale Club," *Philadelphia Tribune*, September 18, 1920.
53. "Redding and Williams Are Idolized by Adoring Fans," *New York Age*, August 7, 1920.
54. "Bacharach Giants and Lincolns Break Even," *Brooklyn Daily Eagle*, July 12, 1920; "Bacharachs and Lincolns Clash at Ebbett's [sic] Field," *New York Age*, July 17, 1920; "Redding Trims Williams," *Chicago Defender*, July 17, 1920.
55. "Bacharachs and Lincolns Clash at Ebbett's [sic] Field," *New York Age*, July 17, 1920; "Redding and Williams Are Idolized by Adoring Fans," *New York Age*, August 7, 1920; "Redding Trims Williams," *Chicago Defender*, July 17, 1920.
56. "Redding Stages 'Iron Man' Stunt," *Brooklyn Daily Eagle*, August 30, 1920; "Rain and Car Strike Keep Many Away While Redding Wins Two," *New York Age*, September 4, 1920.
57. "Bacharach Giants Lose on Opening Day," *New York Age*, May 18, 1920.
58. "Giants and Tesreaus Divide," *Chicago Defender*, May 15, 1920.
59. "Bacharachs Bow Twice," *Chicago Defender*, June 5, 1920.
60. www.shipbuildinghistory.com/history/shipyards/2large/inactive/bethbaltimore.htm.
61. "Baltimore Beats B-Giants, Score 8–3," *Atlantic City Daily Press*, September 14, 1920.
62. "Babe Ruth's Nine Beaten by Bacharach Giants," *Philadelphia Inquirer*, October 5, 1920.
63. "B-Giants Trim Beards 3–1," *Atlantic City Daily Press*, July 29, 1920.
64. "Whiskerless Joe Makes No Hit with the House of David," *Brooklyn Daily Eagle*, August 29, 1920.
65. Roberto Gonzalez Echevarria, *The Pride of Havana: A History of Cuban Baseball* (New York: Oxford University, 1999), 169.
66. "Ball Players Becoming Restless in Cuba,"

Philadelphia Tribune, January 8, 1921; "Bacharachs Lose 11-Inning Fray," *Chicago Defender*, January 22, 1921.

Chapter 4

1. "National Association of Colored Base Ball Clubs, Second Annual Meeting a Great Success," *Kansas City Sun*, December 11, 1920.
2. "Pettus Signs with Bacharachs," *Chicago Defender*, March 19, 1921.
3. "Hilldale and Bacharach Split Big Doubleheader," *Atlantic City Daily Press*, July 4, 1921.
4. "Rain Halts Bacharach–A.B.C.'s Game in 10th," *Atlantic City Daily Press*, July 30, 1921.
5. "Bacharachs Revel in Hits and Runs," *Brooklyn Daily Eagle*, August 1, 1921.
6. "Colored Game Ends in Row Over Rule," *Richmond Times-Dispatch*, October 21, 1921.
7. Gary Ashwill, "1999: A Tale of Two Sluggers," *Outsider Baseball Bulletin*, June 8, 2010, 2.
8. "Redding Continues Good Work, Beating Buckeyes," *Atlantic City Daily Press*, August 15, 1921.
9. "Bacharachs Must Find New Home," *Chicago Whip*, September 24, 1921.
10. "Louis Greenberg's Sport Talk," *Atlantic City Daily Press*, April 3, 1922.
11. "Louis Greenberg's Sport Talk," *Atlantic City Daily Press*, April 28, 1922.
12. "Jones Error Paves Way for Giant Victory," *Chicago Defender*, May 27, 1922.
13. Mueller's Map of Absecon Island, A.H. Mueller, 1924, Vol. 1, Sheet 22, at http://www.historicmapworks.com/Map/US/10968/Plate+022.
14. Riley, *Biographical Encyclopedia of the Negro Baseball Leagues*, 452.
15. "Bacharach Giants Oppose Melrose in Twin Bill," *Atlantic City Gazette-Review*, June 21, 1922.
16. "Jap All-Stars Beaten by Bacharach Giants," *Baltimore Sun*, September 15, 1922.
17. "Bacharach's Rally and Tie Black Sox in Ninth–Win Out in the Tweleth [sic] Inning, 5–4," *Wilmington News*, July 21, 1922.
18. "St. Thomas Takes First One from Bacharachs," *Wilmington Sunday Morning Star*, July 9, 1922.
19. "Saints Win Loose Game Over Rival," *Wilmington News*, September 19, 1922.
20. "Bacharachs Must Find New Home," *Chicago Whip*, September 24, 1921.
21. "John Conners Is Absent, But His Cigars—Oh, Boy!" *Chicago Defender*, December 13, 1924.
22. "Barron D. Wilkins Slain in Harlem," *New York Times*, May 25, 1924; "First Degree Murder Is Jury Verdict in Trial of Barron Wilkins' Killer," *New York Age*, November 1, 1924; "'Yellow Charleston' Pays Death Penalty," *New York Times*, September 16, 1925; "Barron Wilkins Murdered," *Chicago Defender*, May 31, 1924; Certificate of Death for Barron D. Wilkins, Department of Health of the City of New York, Bureau of Records.
23. "J. Connors, Pioneer Cabaret Owner, Dies at Age Of 50," *New York Amsterdam News*, July 14, 1926.

Chapter 5

1. "Name This City for New League," *Atlantic City Daily Press*, April 28, 1922.
2. Lanctot, *Fair Dealing and Clean Playing*, 93.
3. "Fans Surprised at Actions of Eastern League," *Chicago Defender*, January 13, 1923.
4. "Will Eastern Baseball Men Consolidate Their Interests?" *New York Age*, December 2, 1922.
5. "Bacharach Giants Open Season with Twin Bill," *Atlantic City Daily Press*, May 30, 1923.
6. Boyd's Atlantic City Directory (Philadelphia: C.E. Howe, 1909–1929); "New York City News," *Chicago Defender*, January 17, 1920; "Along the Color Line," *The Crisis*, March 1930; "Seven Ways to Compute the Relative Value of a U.S. Dollar Amount," http://www.measuringworth.com/uscompare.
7. John B. Dykes: Polk's Atlantic City Directory (Philadelphia: R. L. Polk, 1923); 1920 United States Census, s.v. "John B. Dykes," Atlantic City, Atlantic County, New Jersey, accessed through Ancestry.com; 1930 United States Census, s.v. "John B. Dykes," Atlantic City, Atlantic County, New Jersey, accessed through Ancestry.com; "Gambling Kings Nabbed at Shore," *Trenton Evening Times*, September 27, 1912; Advertisement, "The Modern City" (Baltimore: Modern City Publishing), May-June 1925, 29; Charles B. Johnson: Boyd's Atlantic City Directory (Philadelphia: C. E. Howe, 1910, 1917, 1919); Polk's Atlantic City Directory (Philadelphia: R. L. Polk, 1926); 1920 United States Census, s.v. "Charles B. Johnson," Atlantic City, Atlantic County, New Jersey, accessed through Ancestry.com; 1930 United States Census, s.v. "Charles B. Johnson," Atlantic City, Atlantic County, New Jersey, accessed through Ancestry.com; "Northside News," *Atlantic City Gazette-Review*, September 20, 1919; "Elks Present Fob to C. B. Johnson," *Atlantic City Gazette-Review*, October 8, 1919; "Politics," *Atlantic City Daily Press*, September 8, 1924; Advertisement, "The Modern City," May-June 1925, 29.
8. Reginald Weekes: List or Manifest of Alien Passengers for the U.S. Immigration Service Officer At Port of Arrival," S.S. *Piemonte* at New York City, 1904, s.v. "Reginald Weeks," accessed

through Ancestry.com; World War I Draft Registration Cards, s.v. "Reginald Weekes," accessed through Ancestry.com; 1910 United States Census, s.v. "Reginald Wicks," Atlantic City, Atlantic County, New Jersey, accessed through Ancestry.com; 1930 United States Census, s.v. "Reginald Weekes," Atlantic City, Atlantic County, New Jersey, accessed through *Ancestry.com; Polk's Atlantic City Directory* (Philadelphia: R. L. Polk, 1926); E-mail exchange with Justice John E. Wallace, Esq., September 30, 2013; "Fifty Indictments Against Northside Dens Returned by Grand Jury; Take Pleas," *Atlantic City Daily Press*, August 8, 1923.

Duncan Weekes: 1905 New Jersey State Census, s.v. "Duncan Weekes," Atlantic City, Atlantic County, New Jersey, accessed through Familysearch.org; 1920 United States Census, s.v. "Duncan Weekes," Atlantic City, Atlantic County, New Jersey, accessed through Ancestry.com; 1930 United States Census, s.v. "Duncan Weekes," Atlantic City, Atlantic County, New Jersey, accessed through Ancestry.com; *Boyd's Atlantic City Directory* (Philadelphia: C. E. Howe, 1919); *Polk's Atlantic City Directory* (Philadelphia: R. L. Polk, 1926); "Fifty Indictments Against Northside Dens Returned by Grand Jury; Take Pleas," *Atlantic City Daily Press*, August 8, 1923.

William Weekes: "List or Manifest of Alien Passengers for the U.S. Immigration Service Officer At Port of Arrival," S.S. *Piemonte* at New York City, 1903, s.v. "William Weekes," accessed through Ancestry.com; 1930 United States Census, s.v. "William Weekes," Atlantic City, Atlantic County, New Jersey, accessed through Ancestry.com; "Fifty Indictments Against Northside Dens Returned by Grand Jury; Take Pleas," *Atlantic City Daily Press*, August 8, 1923.

9. Advertisement, "*The Modern City*," May-June 1925, 29.

10. "Corona Assured of Getting Game This Afternoon," *Brooklyn Daily Star*, May 28, 1924; "Sport Briefs by F. C. F," *Brooklyn Daily Star*, May 30, 1924; "Eastern Snapshots," *Pittsburgh Courier*, September 26, 1925.

11. Riley, *Biographical Encyclopedia of the Negro Baseball Leagues*, 833–834.

12. Riley, *Biographical Encyclopedia of the Negro Baseball Leagues*, 374.

13. "Morris Brown 'U' Drops Two Games to Talladega," *Chicago Defender*, April 29, 1922; "Lockhart Ends Great 4-Yr. College Career," *Chicago Defender*, June 12, 1926.

14. "Eastern Snapshots," *Pittsburgh Courier*, July 31, 1926.

15. "Lockhart, Bacharach Giants Pitching 'Ace,' an Unsung Hero," *Pittsburgh Courier*, September 10, 1927.

16. "B-Giants Play Lincoln Today," *Atlantic City Daily Press*, June 12, 1923.

17. "Black Sox Drop; Both Sunday Games," *Baltimore Afro-American*, July 20, 1923.

18. "South Phils Take Sensational Battle," *Philadelphia Inquirer*, June 23, 1923.

19. Brian McKenna, "The Henriquez Long Branch Cubans," June 25, 2011, http://baseballhistoryblog.com/date/2011/06.

20. "Bacharach Giants May Leave City," *Atlantic City Daily Press*, August 4, 1916; "B-Giants Quit Baseball Field Until Summer," *Atlantic City Daily Press*, October 2, 1923.

21. John B. Holway, *Blackball Stars* (Westport, CT: Meckler, 1988), 45; John B. Holway, *Black Diamonds* (Westport, CT: Meckler, 1989), 8–9; "Suspension of Lloyd Made Permanent by Darby Mogul," *Pittsburgh Courier*, October 6, 1923.

22. "B-Giants Win Two; Play Here Today," *Atlantic City Daily Press*, April 28, 1924.

23. Riley, *Biographical Encyclopedia of the Negro Baseball Leagues*, 713, 834.

24. "Rollo Wilson Picks All-Eastern Team," *Pittsburgh Courier*, September 27, 1924.

25. "Eastern Snapshots," *Pittsburgh Courier*, September 13, 1924.

26. "Brooklyn Royal Giants Fired Out of Eastern League," *Baltimore Afro-American*, May 30, 1924; "Brooklyn Royals Promise to Be Good in Eastern League," *Baltimore Afro-American*, June 6, 1924; "Eastern Snapshots," *Pittsburgh Courier*, June 7, 1924.

27. Terry Bohn, "Socks Seibold," Society for American Baseball Research BioProject, http://sabr.org/bioproj/person/0dae01bf.

28. "Trenton Proves Superior to Morgans Before Large Crowd," *Trenton Evening Times*, August 24, 1924; "Swigler Saves Tiger Hurlers," *Trenton Evening Times*, August 3, 1924.

29. Shawn Weldon, "The Day the Bronx Bomber Played in Kensington," June 23, 2010, Philadelphia Archdiocesan Historical Research Center, http://www.pahrc.net/index.php/the-day-the-bronx-bomber-played-in-kensington.

30. "B-Giants Lose to Mainlanders," *Atlantic City Daily Press*, July 30, 1924.

31. "Marcel and Roy Roberts in Big Baseball Trade," *New York Amsterdam-News*, May 13, 1925; "Sport–Pickups," *Pittsburgh Courier*, May 9, 1925; "Kill Man and Escape in Taxi," *New York Amsterdam-News*, April 29, 1925; "Police Unable to Find Ballplayers," *Baltimore Afro-American*, May 16, 1925; "Local Baseball Players Alleged to Be Mixed in Shooting of Benj. Adair," *New York Age*, May 2, 1925.

32. "Marcell Comes Back to Bees in Big Trade," *Atlantic City Daily Press*, May 9, 1925; "Oliver Marcel and Roberts Figure in Big Baseball Trade," *Baltimore Afro-American*, May 16, 1925; "Eastern Snapshots," *Pittsburgh Courier*, June 20, 1925.

33. "Marcell Voted Off B-Giants," *Atlantic City Daily Press*, June 16, 1925; "Giants Trade Star Players," *Atlantic City Sunday Press*, June 21, 1925; "Marcell Is Again Traded to the Bacharach Giants," *New York Amsterdam-News*, June 24, 1925.

34. "George W. Robinson Throws Light on the Policies of the Eastern League," *Pittsburgh Courier*, August 8, 1925.

35. Riley, *Biographical Encyclopedia of the Negro Baseball Leagues*, 340.

36. "Bees Although Outhit Conquer Ocean City, 3-1," *Atlantic City Daily Press*, July 23, 1925.

37. "Cyclone Joe Williams Due to Wear Uniform of Bees," *Atlantic City Daily Press*, April 11, 1925; "Bees Release Milton Lewis," *Atlantic City Daily Press*, April 24, 1925.

38. "Fans of Country Select Mythical All East Team," *Pittsburgh Courier*, October 3, 1925.

39. Lanctot, *Clean Playing and Fair Dealing*, 132; "Black Sox Lead at Bat; Hilldale Is Fastest," *Pittsburgh Courier*, August 29, 1925; "Beckwith Suspended for Beating Umpire Sewell Last Tuesday," *Baltimore Afro-American*, August 8, 1925.

40. "Leaders in Eastern Colored Baseball League Hold Meeting in Philadelphia," *New York Amsterdam-News*, January 28, 1925.

41. "B-Giants Lose at Harrisburg," *Atlantic City Daily Press*, May 19, 1925.

42. "B-Giants Pound Pritchard Hard to Defeat Harrisburg," *Atlantic City Daily Press*, September 11, 1925.

43. "Bees Capture Slugging Bee by Lone Run," *Atlantic City Daily Press*, August 20, 1925.

44. "Giants in Hitting Mood Turn Back Camden, 10-1," *Atlantic City Daily Press*, June 8, 1925.

45. "Dad Played Ball, Aunt Was a Bloomer Girl and Schoolboy Was Future Dodger," April 1, 2004, Timesnewsweekly.com, http://www.timesnewsweekly.com/sites/ www.timesnewsweekly.com/files/archives/Archives2004/Apr.-Jun.2004/040104/ NewFiles/OURNEIGH.html.

46. "Bacharach Giants Conquer Bloomer Girls in Comedy," *Atlantic City Daily Press*, September 4, 1925.

Chapter 6

1. "500,000 Here Over 'Fourth' Despite Rain," *Atlantic City Gazette-Review*, July 6, 1926; "Half Million Here for the Week-End," *Atlantic City Daily Press*, August 9, 1926; "Land First Settler Valued at Hundred Dollars, Now Worth Hundred Millions," *Atlantic City Daily Press*, April 3, 1926.

2. "Atlantic City Branded as Wettest City in Nation," *Atlantic City Daily Press*, September 9, 1924.

3. "Liquor Traffic Here Is Directed by a Syndicate," *Atlantic City Daily Press*, September 13, 1924.

4. "Mayor Announces Retirement from Commission Fight," *Atlantic City Daily Press*, March 15, 1920; "Bacharach in His Platform Announcement," *Atlantic City Daily Press*, April 16, 1924.

5. "Eastern Snapshots," *Pittsburgh Courier*, September 26, 1925.

6. "John H. Lloyd Speaks," *Baltimore Afro-American*, July 4, 1925; "John Henry Lloyd Cause of Fight in Eastern Baseball League," *New York Age*, January 2, 1926; "Lloyd to Leave Bees for Post with Lincolns," *Atlantic City Daily Press*, March 28, 1926.

7. "Bacharach Giant Roster Molding Together for 1926," *Atlantic City Daily Press*, April 20, 1926.

8. Riley, *Biographical Encyclopedia of the Negro Baseball Leagues*, 208–209; "Lundy Says," *Baltimore Afro-American*, August 21, 1926; "Monarchs Picked to Win World's Series," *Baltimore Afro-American*, October 2, 1926.

9. "Eastern Snapshots," *Pittsburgh Courier*, September 11, 1926.

10. "Locals' Brilliant Work Too Much for Harrisburg," *Atlantic City Daily Press*, July 20, 1926.

11. "Bacharachs Resent League Action," *Baltimore Afro-American*, September 18, 1926; "B-Giants Win by Big Margin," *Atlantic City Daily Press*, September 26, 1926.

12. "'We Won for Rube,' Says the Chicago Team," *Baltimore Afro-American*, October 2, 1926.

13. "Bacharach Giants Defeat Harrisburg," *Atlantic City Daily Press*, July 5, 1926.

14. "Pitcher Cockrell Strikes Ump," *Atlantic City Daily Press*, August 9, 1926.

15. Ed "Dutch" Doyle, "The Milkman: Sandlot Legend Rube Chambers Stumps the World Champs," *The National Pastime, A Review of Baseball History*, 13 (1993), 79.

16. Jonathon Dunkle, "Claude Hendrix," Society for American Baseball Research BioProject, http://sabr.org/bioproj/person/fca42ef7.

17. "Allentown Out of the League," *Chester Times*, June 15, 1926.

18. "Lincolns Buy Garcia and Cummings," *Baltimore Afro-American*, June 11, 1927.

19. John B. Holway, *Black Giants* (Springfield, VA: Lord Fairfax, 2010), 15–16.

20. "Lincolns Buy Garcia and Cummings," *Baltimore Afro-American*, June 11, 1927; "Lundy Holding Crippled Team in League Lead," *Atlantic City Daily Press*, September 2, 1927.

21. Riley, *Biographical Encyclopedia of the Negro Baseball Leagues*, 397–398.

22. "Lundy Holding Crippled Team in League Lead," *Atlantic City Daily Press*, September 2, 1927.

23. "Lawyer Nutter, 71, Looks Back on His Ups and Downs," *Atlantic City Daily Press*, October 2, 1949; "State to Open Department of Negro Welfare," *Trenton Evening Times*, September 20, 1917.

24. "Legal Battle with Carrier Involes [sic] Race War," *Indianapolis Freeman*, August 26, 1908; "Republicans Ungrateful Says Nutter," *Norfolk Journal and Guide*, June 25, 1921.

25. "Lawyer Nutter, 71, Looks Back on His Ups and Downs," *Atlantic City Daily Press*, October 2, 1949.

26. William E. Frank and Joseph W. Burns, "The Case of Enoch L. Johnson," 76–77, New Jersey State Library, Trenton, NJ.

27. "Keenan at the Bat," *New York Amsterdam-News*, June 29, 1927.

28. *The Black Worker: A Documentary History from Colonial Times to the Present*, Philip S. Foner and Ronald L. Lewis, eds. (Philadelphia: Temple University, 1981), vol. 6, 34; Aryness Joy, "Index of Production of Manufactures Derived from Census Data, 1927," *Journal of the American Statistical Association*, 25 December 1930, 453.

29. Vincent P. Franklin, *The Education of Black Philadelphia* (Philadelphia: University of Pennsylvania, 1979), 61; Kenneth Kushner, *A Ghetto Takes Shape: Black Cleveland, 1870–1930* (Urbana: University of Illinois, 1976), 204; Elizabeth Ames Martin, "Detroit and the Great Migration 1916–1929," Bentley Historical Library, University of Michigan, http://bentley.umich.edu/research/publications/migration/ch3.php.

30. Milton Palmer, "Earning a Living in Atlantic City, NJ," New Jersey Ethnic Survey, Federal Writers Project, Atlantic City Free Public Library, Atlantic City, NJ.

31. "Eastern League Elects Nutter Pres. to Succeed Bolden," *Pittsburgh Courier*, January 22, 1927; "Moguls Vote to Discontinue Schedule," *Norfolk Journal and Guide*, July 2, 1927.

32. "Athletic Club in Bankruptcy Case," *Trenton Evening Times*, April 13, 1927; "Atlantic City Base Ball Park Closed," *Baltimore Afro-American*, June 25, 1927.

33. "Atlantic City Base Ball Park Closed," *Baltimore Afro-American*, June 25, 1927; "Bacharach Baseball Club Renews Lease on Park," *Atlantic City Daily Press*, June 23, 1927.

34. "Bees Not to Play Series If Harrisburg Gets Flag," *Atlantic City Daily Press*, September 17, 1927; "World's Series Opens on Sat., Oct. 1," *Chicago Defender*, September 24, 1927.

35. "B-Giants Open Titular Series in Windy City," *Atlantic City Daily Press*, October 1, 1927.

36. "Chicago Lays Low B-Giants in First Tilt," *Atlantic City Daily Press*, October 2, 1927.

37. "Chicago Whitewashes Bacharach Giants," *Atlantic City Daily Press*, October 4, 1927.

38. "Fay Says," *Chicago Defender*, October 22, 1927.

39. "Sixth Colored Series Game Still Undecided," *Atlantic City Daily Press*, October 11, 1927.

40. "Westerners Win Deciding Game from B-Giants, 11–4," *Atlantic City Daily Press*, October 14, 1927.

41. "Harrisburg Nine Trips Home Club in Thriller," *Atlantic City Daily Press*, May 16, 1927.

42. "Dallard and Lundy Hit Tricky Circuit Drives," *Atlantic City Daily Press*, June 17, 1927.

43. "Dihigo Drives Out Two; Dollard-Oms Smack One," *Atlantic City Daily Press*, June 7, 1927; "'Rats' Henderson Baffles Islanders to Win, 9 to 1," *Atlantic City Daily Press*, June 9, 1927.

44. "Brooklyn Royal Giants Spank Bacharach Giants, 9–8," *Atlantic City Daily Press*, August 31, 1927.

Chapter 7

1. "Sports Shots: Press Box & Ringside," *Pittsburgh Courier*, December 17, 1927; "George H. Lockhart Says Baseball Players Are Slaves," *Baltimore Afro-American*, January 21, 1928.

2. "Eastern League Collapse Far-Reaching in Effects," *Baltimore Afro-American*, April 28, 1928.

3. "Sports Shots: Press Box & Ringside," *Pittsburgh Courier*, March 24, 1928; "Nutter and Associates Continue League," *Pittsburgh Courier*, March 24, 1928; "Hilldale Out of Colored Loop," *Chester Times*, March 19, 1928.

4. *Boyd's Atlantic City Directory* (Philadelphia: C. E. Howe, 1914); *Encyclopedia of African American Business*, Jessie Carney Smith, Millicent Lownes Jackson, Linda T. Wynn, eds. (Westport, CT: Greenwood Press, 2006), 819–821.

5. World War I Draft Registration Cards, s.v. "Isaac Washington," accessed through Ancestry.com; *Polk's Atlantic City Directory* (New Brunswick, NJ: R.L. Polk, 1924, 1926, 1927–1929, 1931).

6. "Baseball Magnate Taken as 'Numbers Banker,'" *New York Amsterdam-News*, March 6, 1929; "U.S. Indicts 5 in Jersey Policy," *Indianapolis Recorder*, March 25, 1939; William E. Frank and Joseph W. Burns, "The Case of Enoch L. Johnson," Appendix, New Jersey State Library, Trenton, NJ.

7. "Bees Change Diamond Plans," *Atlantic City Sunday Press*, April 29, 1928; "Bacharach Giants Open at New Ball Park, May 30," *Atlantic City Daily Press*, May 16, 1928.

8. "Sports Shots: Press Box & Ringside," *Pittsburgh Courier*, March 24, 1928.

9. "Lincoln Giants in Big Raid," *New York Amsterdam-News*, June 6, 1928.

10. "Charleston and Dalty Cooper Sign with Hilldale," *Pittsburgh Courier*, March 31, 1928.

11. "Star Players Released in Baseball Shakeup," *Pittsburgh Courier*, July 21, 1928.

12. "Sports Shots: Press Box & Ringside," *Pittsburgh Courier*, July 28, 1928.

13. "Bacharach Giants Take Measure of Hilldale," *Atlantic City Daily Press,* July 4, 1928.

14. "Brooklyn Royals Divide with Bacharach Giants," *Atlantic City Daily Press,* September 10, 1928.

15. "Bees Score Too Many Runs and Cancel Game," *Atlantic City Sunday Press,* June 17, 1928.

16. "Bees Complain of Attendance," *Atlantic City Daily Press,* July 14, 1928; "Bees Disband as Home Club, May Barnstorm," *Atlantic City Daily Press,* September 26, 1928.

17. "Need of Baseball League in the East Apparent to Lovers of National Game," *New York Amsterdam News,* August 15, 1928; "Baseball League in East Vital to Future Welfare of All Clubs," *Pittsburgh Courier,* August 18, 1928.

18. Lanctot, *Fair Dealing and Clean Playing,* 192–193.

19. "The Sportive Realm," *Pittsburgh Courier,* January 29, 1927.

20. "Sports Shots: Press Box & Ringside," *Pittsburgh Courier,* March 24, 1928; "Lundy with the Bees," *Baltimore Afro-American,* July 21, 1928.

21. "Black Sox Swap Taylor in First Trade of New League," *Pittsburgh Courier,* January 26, 1929; "Taylor May Not Take Post with 'Bee' Giants," *Baltimore Afro-American,* February 2, 1929; "Taylor Signed for One Year as 'Bee' Manager," *Baltimore Afro-American,* February 16, 1929.

22. "Prominent Eastern Stars Are Involved in Big A.N.L. Trade," *Pittsburgh Courier,* March 30, 1929; "Lundy with the Bees," *Baltimore Afro-American,* July 21, 1928.

23. "Farrell Leaves Bees to Twirl for A.C. Cops," *Atlantic City Daily Press,* May 17, 1929.

24. "Taylor Hunts Bees' 'Jinx,'" *Atlantic City Daily Press,* July 11, 1929; "Bees Lose Hard- Fought Tussle to Lincoln, 3-1," *Atlantic City Daily Press,* July 3, 1929.

25. Riley, *The Biographical Encyclopedia of the Negro Baseball Leagues,* 225.

26. Riley, *The Biographical Encyclopedia of the Negro Baseball Leagues,* 374.

27. "Baltimore Black Sox Pound Bacharach Giants," *Atlantic City Daily Press,* June 19, 1929; "B-Giants Drop Doubleheader to Black Sox," *Atlantic City Daily Press,* August 19, 1929.

28. "B-Giants Nose Out Cops; Aided by Errors, 3-2," *Atlantic City Daily Press,* September 7, 1929.

29. Lanctot, *Fair Dealing and Clean Playing,* 200–202.

30. "Ben Taylor, Out as Bee Boss, Says Atlantic City Is Doomed," *Baltimore Afro-American,* October 19, 1929.

31. "Sports Shots: Press Box & Ringside," *Pittsburgh Courier,* August 2, 1930.

32. "Bacharach Giants May Disband," *Pittsburgh Courier,* March 8, 1930; "Sports Shots: Press Box & Ringside," *Pittsburgh Courier,* October 26, 1929.

33. Neil Lanctot, *Campy: The Two Lives of Roy Campanella* (New York: Simon & Schuster, 2011), 20–32; Rick Swaine, "Roy Campanella," Society for American Baseball Research BioProject, http://sabr.org/bioproj/person/a52ccbb5.

34. "Bacharach Slated to Succeed Ruffo," *New York Times,* July 7, 1930; "Outside Police Aid Atlantic City Drive," *New York Times,* August 17, 1930; "Harry Bacharach Dies at Age of 73," *New York Times,* May 14, 1947.

35. "Atlantic City, Gay Resort Spot, Is Nation's Bagdad-by-the-Sea," *Washington Post,* March 24, 1935; "Harry Bacharach Dies at Age of 73," *New York Times,* May 14, 1947.

Epilogue

1. 1920 United States Census, s.v. "John H. Lloyd," Atlantic City, Atlantic County, New Jersey, accessed through Ancestry.com.

2. Wes Singletary, *The Right Time: John Henry "Pop" Lloyd and Black Baseball* (Jefferson, NC: McFarland, 2011), 192.

3. John B. Holway, *Black Diamonds: Life in the Negro Leagues from the Men Who Lived It* (Westport, CT: Meckler, 1989), 120.

4. Singletary, *The Right Time,* 195; Michael Everett, interview with author, October 9, 2013, Linwood, New Jersey.

5. "Press Box," *The Press of Atlantic City,* March 23, 1964.

6. "A.C.'s 'Pop' Lloyd Park, Keep the Promise," editorial, *The Press of Atlantic City,* April 10, 1991; "About New Jersey," *New York Times,* April 26, 1992.

7. Everett interview; "Redinia C. Gilliam-Mosee," obituary, *The Press of Atlantic City,* January 12, 2010.

8. Everett interview.

9. Dr. Lawrence D. Hogan, email interview with author, August 22, 2013.

10. Everett interview.

11. Everett interview.

Bibliography

Books

Anderson, Jervis. *This Was Harlem: A Cultural Portrait, 1900-1950*. New York: Farrar, Straus, Giroux, 1982.

Bercovici, Konrad. *Around the World in New York*. New York: Century, 1924.

Boyd's Atlantic City Directory. Philadelphia: C. E. Howe, 1909-1929 editions.

Burgos, Adrian Jr. *Cuban Star*. New York: Hill & Wang, 2011.

Echevarria, Roberto Gonzalez. *The Pride of Havana: A History of Cuban Baseball*. New York: Oxford University, 1999.

Final Report of the Provost Marshal General. Washington: Government Printing Office, 1920.

Foner, Philip S., and Ronald L. Lewis, eds. *The Black Worker: A Documentary History from Colonial Times to the Present*. Philadelphia: Temple University, 1981, vol. 6.

Franklin, Vincent P. *The Education of Black Philadelphia*. Philadelphia: University of Pennsylvania, 1979.

Holway, John B. *Black Diamonds*. Westport, CT: Meckler, 1989.

_____. *Black Giants*. Springfield, VA: Lord Fairfax, 2010.

_____. *Blackball Stars*. Westport, CT: Meckler, 1988.

Johnson, James Weldon. *Along This Way*. New York: Penguin, 1990.

Johnson, Nelson. *Boardwalk Empire*. Medford, NJ: Medford Press, 2002.

_____. *The Northside: African-Americans and the Creation of Atlantic City*. Medford NJ: Plexus, 2010.

Kushner, Kenneth. *A Ghetto Takes Shape: Black Cleveland, 1870-1930*. Urbana: University of Illinois, 1976.

Lanctot, Neil. *Campy: The Two Lives of Roy Campanella*. New York: Simon & Schuster, 2011.

_____. *Fair Dealing and Clean Playing: The Hilldale Club and the Development of Black Professional Baseball, 1910-1932*. Jefferson, NC: McFarland, 1994.

Obojski, Robert. *Bush League*. New York: Macmillan, 1975.

Paulson, Martin. *The Social Anxieties of Progressive Reform: Atlantic City, 1854-1920*. New York: New York University, 1994.

Peterson, Robert. *Only the Ball Was White*. New York: McGraw-Hill, 1970.

Polk's Atlantic City Directory. Philadelphia: R. L. Polk, 1923.

Riley, James A. *The Biographical Encyclopedia of the Negro Baseball Leagues*. New York: Carroll & Graf, 1994.

Scott, Emmett J. "Negro Migration During the War," in *Preliminary Economic Studies of the War*, ed. David Kinley for Carnegie Endowment for International Peace. New York: Oxford University, 1920.

Singletary, Wes. *The Right Time: John Henry "Pop" Lloyd and Black Baseball*. Jefferson, NC: McFarland, 2011.

Smith, Jessie Carney, Millicent Lownes Jackson, and Linda T. Wynn, eds. *Encyclopedia of African American Business*. Westport, CT: Greenwood, 2006.

Sullivan, Mary. *My Double Life: The Story of a New York Policewoman*. New York: Farrar & Rinehart, 1938.

White, Sol. *Sol White's History of Colored Base Ball, Compiled and Introduced by Jerry Malloy*. Lincoln: University of Nebraska Press, 1995.

Periodicals and Websites

Advertisement, "*The Modern City*." May-June 1925.

"Along the Color Line." *The Crisis*, (37) March 1930.

Ashwill, Gary. "1919: A Tale of Two Sluggers." *Outsider Baseball Bulletin*, June 8, 2010. Copyright 2010 by Scott Simkus and Gary Ashwill.

Bohn, Terry. "Socks Seibold," Society for American Baseball Research BioProject. http://sabr.org/bioproj.

Casanello, Robert. "Violence, Racial Etiquette, and African American Working-Class Infrapolitics in Jacksonville During World War I." *The Florida Historical Quarterly*, 82, (2003).

Crooks, James B. "Changing Face of Jacksonville, Florida: 1900–1910." *The Florida Historical Quarterly*, 62, (1984).

"Dad Played Ball, Aunt Was a Bloomer Girl and Schoolboy Was Future Dodger." April 1, 2004. http://www.timesnewsweekly.com/sites.

Delaware County Baseball League History. http://www.leaguelineup.com/miscinfo.asp?menuid=30&url=delcoleague.

Doyle, Ed "Dutch." "The Milkman: Sandlot Legend Rube Chambers Stumps the World Champs." *The National Pastime, A Review of Baseball History*, No. 13 (1993).

Dunkle, Jonathon. "Claude Hendrix." Society for American Baseball Research BioProject. http://sabr.org/bio.proj.

Hogan, Lawrence D. "Organized League Ball." in *Shades of Glory*, ed. Lawrence D. Hogan. Washington: National Geographic, 2006.

Joy, Aryness. "Index of Production of Manufactures Derived from Census Data, 1927." *Journal of the American Statistical Association*, Vol. 25 (December 1930).

Lane, F. C. "A Rising Menace to the National Game." *Baseball Magazine*, XXI, August 1918.

Lomax, Michael. "The Great Independents." in *Shades of Glory*, ed. Lawrence D. Hogan Washington: National Geographic, 2006.

McKenna, Brian. "Bethlehem Steel League." Society for American Baseball Research BioProject. http://sabr.org/bioproj.

McKenna, Brian, "The Henriquez Long Branch Cubans." June 25, 2011, BaseballHistoryBlog.com. http://www.baseballhistoryblog.com.

Martin, Elizabeth Ames. "Detroit and the Great Migration, 1916–1929." Bentley Historical Library, University of Michigan. http://bentley.umich.edu/research/publications/migration/ch3.php.

Nowlin, Bill. "Vince Molyneaux." Society for American Baseball Research BioProject. http://sabr.org/bioproj.

Reulbach, Edward M. "Shipyard Baseball and the Future of the Big Leagues." *Baseball Magazine*, XXI, December 1918.

"Seven Ways to Compute the Relative Value of a U.S. Dollar Amount," MeasuringWorth.com. http://www.measuringworth.com/uscompare.

Swaine, Rick. "Roy Campanella." Society for American Baseball Research BioProject. http://sabr.org/bioproj.

Weldon, Shawn. "The Day the Bronx Bomber Played in Kensington." June 23, 2010, Philadelphia Archdiocesan Historical Research Center. http://www.pahrc.net.

Archival Material

Atlantic City Free Public Library (Atlantic City, NJ)

Certificate of Death for Barron D. Wilkins

Certificate of Incorporation, Bacharach Giants Athletic Club, April 28, 1919

Department of Health of The City of New York, Bureau of Records

Elihu Roberts player page

Free Library of Philadelphia (Philadelphia, PA)

Hugh M. Morris Library, University of Delaware (Newark, DE)

Indiana University–Purdue University Indianapolis Center for Digital Scholarship (http://ulib.iupui.edu/digitalscholarship/collections/IRecorder).

List or Manifest of Alien Passengers for the U.S. Immigration Service Officer at Port of Arrival

Mueller's Map of Absecon Island, A.H. Mueller, 1924, Vol. 1, Sheet 22

New Jersey Secretary of State (Trenton, NJ)

New Jersey State Census, 1905

New Jersey State Library (Trenton, NJ)

New York State Library (Albany, NY)

Palmer, Milton. "Earning a Living in Atlantic City, NJ," New Jersey Ethnic Survey, Federal Writers Project.

Sterling Memorial Library, Yale University (New Haven, CT)

Trinity College Library (Hartford, CT)

United States Census, 1900, 1910, 1920

United States Passport Applications

W. E. B. DuBois Library, University of Massachusetts (Amherst, MA)
William E. Frank and Joseph W. Burns, "The Case of Enoch L. Johnson."
World War I Draft Registration Cards

Newspapers and Magazines

Atlantic City Daily Press
Atlantic City Gazette-Review
Atlantic City Sunday Press
Baltimore Afro-American
Baltimore Sun
Bridgeton Evening News
Brooklyn Daily Eagle
Brooklyn Daily Star
Chester Times
Chicago Defender
Chicago Whip
Cleveland Advocate
Indianapolis Freeman
Indianapolis Recorder
Kansas City Sun
New Orleans Daily States
New York Age
New York Amsterdam-News
New York Evening Telegram
New York Sun
New York Times
Norfolk Journal and Guide
North American
Philadelphia Evening Ledger
Philadelphia Inquirer
Philadelphia Inquirer
Philadelphia Tribune
Pittsburgh Courier
The Press of Atlantic City
Richmond Times-Dispatch
Salt Lake Telegram
Trenton Evening Times
Variety
Washington Post
Watertown Daily Times
Wilmington News
Wilmington Sunday Morning Star

Websites

Ancestry.com
Baseball-Reference.com (http://www.baseball-reference.com/nlb)
Chronicling America (http://www.chroniclingamerica.loc.gov)
Dick Lundy player page
FamilySearch.org (http://www.familysearch.org)
Fulton History (http://www.fultonhisory.com)
GenealogyBank.com (http://www.genealogybank.com)
Historic Mapworks (http://www.historicmapworks.com)
Library of Congress (http://www.memory.loc.gov)
McKinley "Bunny" Downs player page
Mid-Continent Public Library (http://www.mymcpl.org)
NewspaperArchive.com (http://www.newspaperarchive.com)
Paper of Record (http://www.paperofrecord.com)
Seamheads.com (http://www.seamheads.com/NegroLgs)
Shipbuilding History, Construction records of U.S. and Canadian shipbuilders and boatbuilders (http://www.shipbuildinghistory.com)

Interviews

Napoleon Cummings, interview with Robert Peterson October 4, 1967, in Atlantic City, NJ (National Baseball Hall of Fame and Museum, Cooperstown, NY).
Napoleon "Chance" Cummings, interview with John Holway, collection of Michael Everett (Linwood, NJ).
Justice John E. Wallace, Esq., email exchange with author, September 30, 2013.
Michael Everett, interview with author, October 9, 2013, Linwood, NJ.
Lawrence D. Hogan email interview with author, August 22, 2013.

Index

Page numbers in ***bold italics*** indicate pages with illustrations.

Adair, Benjamin 132
Adams, Wallace "Dump" 22
Agnew, Sid 45, 108
Albright, Tom 187
Alexander, Grover Cleveland 36
All-Americans baseball team 59
All-Cubans 85
All Nations baseball team 27
Allen, Touissaint 81, 84
Allentown (Pennsylvania) Dukes 153–154
Almendares 84
American Chain Company baseball team 94, 105
American League (white major league) 172
American Negro League 179, 181, 187
Anchor City Giants 25
Aragon, Angel 68
Asbury Methodist Church, Atlantic City, New Jersey 196
Ascension of Our Lord Parish baseball team 129–130
Ashe, Arthur 196
Atlantic City, New Jersey 9–13, 21, ***69***, ***96***, 160, ***142***; Depression's effects on black employment 160; during Prohibition 141–142; economic decline 194; growth of tourism 141; importance of railroads 9–10; "Northside" black community 12, ***96***
Atlantic City Cemetery 197–198
Atlantic City Colored League 15, 17
Atlantic City Daily Press 5
Atlantic City Free Public Library 5
Atlantic City Giants 13–14, 17, 25
Atlantic City Police Department baseball team 182, 187

Bacharach, Harry 1, 11–14, ***11***, 16, 68, 75, 112, 142, 158, 161, 190
Bacharach, Isaac 12, 112, 161

Bacharach Athletic Association 161
Bacharach Giants, statistics 2–5, 135
Bacharach Park: (I) New York and Adriatic Avenues 14; (II and IV) Tennessee and South Carolina Avenues 29, 112, 119, 161, 163, 165, 172; (III) Inlet Park 16–17, 95, 109; (V) Absecon Boulevard 172, 178, 185, 187
Bader, Edward L. 14, 142
Baker, Frank "Home Run" 36, 80
Baker Bowl 147
Baltimore, Prince 15–16, 20
Baltimore Black Sox 26, 77, 85, 106, 112, 117–118, 126–127, 137, 145, 152, 161, 167, 171, 174, 179–181, 183, 188
Baltimore Dry Dock and Shipping Company baseball team 67, 82
Banks, (first name unknown) 36
Barbour (Barber), Jesse 71, ***86***, 87, 97
Barrs Field, Jacksonville, Florida 73
Baumgartner, Stan 35, 106, 135, 177
Bay Ridge, Brooklyn, New York, baseball team 139
Baynard, Frank 31, 43
Becker, Smith & Page (Philadelphia) baseball team 45
Beckwith, John 135, 137
Bender, Albert "Chief" 36, 49
Benson, Gene 189
Benton, Rube 65
Bercovici, Konrad 53
Bethlehem Steel Company baseball teams 48
Betty Bacharach Home for Afflicted Children 12
Big Six Atlantic City baseball team 15–16
Birmingham Black Barons 162
Blackwell, Charlie 84

Bolden, Edward 38, 61, 70, 77, 85, 90, 106, 111, 114, 116, 123, 132–133, 135, 145, 158, 171, 173, 179–180, 189; *see also* Eastern Colored League; Hilldale
boll weevil 8
Bourne, James F. 13
Bressler, Rube 25
Briggs, Otto 188
Bronx Giants 81, 101
Bronx Oval 81, 95
Brooklyn Daily Eagle 3, 79
Brooklyn Dodgers (Robins) 73
Brooklyn Royal Giants ***26***, 51, 54–55, 61, 70–71, 106, 112, 117–118, 126–127, 129, 135, 138, 145, 152, 156, 167, 170, 175; *see also* Strong, Nathaniel C. "Nat"
Brown, Dave 99, 132, 138
Bryant, Elias "Country Brown" 44, 55, 57, 70, 79, ***86***, 87, 97, 117, ***120***, 133–134, 137, 144–145, 198
Buckner, Emory 54
Busby, Maurice ***86***, 88
Bushwicks (Brooklyn, NY) baseball team 2, 4, 106, 121, 138, 169, 186

Cade, Joe 183
Cadore, Leon 139
Calderin, Evilio 38–39
California Winter League 153, 181
Camden (New Jersey) Skeeters 121–122, 129, 139, 153–154, 168
Campanella, Roy 189
Capone, Al 191
Carr, George "Tank" 173, 182, 189
Carr, Wayne 125–126, 181
Casey, Rev. Willliam J. 129
Cason, Johnny 174, 181
Catholic Protectory Oval, Bronx, New York 78–79, 107, 119, 128, 138, 151, 160, 168, 176, 184, 185
Chambers, Rube 153
Chapman, Ray 65

Charleston, Oscar 75, 84, 126, 165, 169, 173
Chase, Hal 58, 65
Chester (Pennsylvania) baseball team 121, 129, 153–154
Chicago American Giants 40, 70, 74, 76, 79, 91, 98–99, 146, 155, 162, 165, 177; *see also* Foster, Andrew "Rube"
Chicago Defender 78
Chicago Giants 75
Chinese University of Hawaii baseball team 27
Christiansen, Jappy 34
Citrano, Tony 153
Clark, Dick 2, 3, 5
Clark, Morton 84
Cleveland Tate Stars 85, 94, 100
Clinton, Jimmy 64, 139
Clinton, William 31
Cockrell, Phil 84, 92, 151
Columbus (Ohio) Buckeyes 85, 93, 97
Combined Stars baseball team 106
Committee to Restore Pop Lloyd Stadium 195–196
Comstock, Ralph 68
Conahan, Eddie 122, 154
Condon, Ethel 140
Connor, John W. 51–52, 54–56, 58, 61, 64, 69–70, 73, 77, 81, 85, **86**, 95, 97, 109–110, 111; *see also* Strong, Nathaniel C. "Nat"; Wilkins, Barron D.
Cooper, Darltie 173
Cozart, Winfield F. 158
Cressona (Pennsylvania) baseball team 37, 105
Crockett, Frank 9, 14, 19, 28, 30, 103, 114, **117**
Cronin, Joe 40
Cross, Monte 36
Crump, Willis 9, 18
Cuban Giants 14, 96, 197
Cuban Stars (East) 38, 61–63, 77, 106, 112, 118, 126–127, 129, 137, 145–146, 150, 161, 165, 171, 175, 179–180, 183, 185; *see also* Pompez, Alejandro "Alex"
Cuban Stars (West, also Cuban Stars of Havana) 94, 160
Cuban Winter League 83–84
Cummings, Napoleon "Chance" 4, 9, 14, 19, **20**, 24, 28, 30, 43, 56, 103, 114–115, **117**, 124, 133, 143, 150, 156, 173, 191
Cyclones baseball team 15–16

Dallard, Maurice "Eggie" 144, 155–157, 173
Dallas, Bill 135
Daniels, Hammond 112, 114, 123, 132–133, 143, 156, 161
Davis, Jack 103
Day, Wilson "Connie" 182
Dayton Marcos 85
Deas, James "Yank" 19, 28, 30, 43, 57, 62, 70–71, **86**, 87, 97, 102–103, 106–107, 115, **117**, 121
Delaware County League 2, 23, 34, 36
Delaware River Shipyard League 49, 82, 102
Demarest, Helen 140
Depression, effects on black urban economies 160
Detroit Stars 61, 63, 73–74, 79, 92, 100, 177
Dexter Park, Brooklyn, New York 106, 185–186
Dihigo, Martin 138, 165
Dilworth, Arthur 9, 14, 18, 28, 32, 43, 58, 121, 165, 191
Dismukes, Dizzy 75
Donaldson, John 47
Dooin, Charlie "Red" 59–60, 104
Dougherty, Romeo L. 179
Downs, McKinley "Bunny" 30, 43–44, 56, 114, **117**
Duncan, Joe 156
Duncan, Warren 97
Durbin, Bill 153
Duval Giants 9, 24, 156
Dyckman Oval, Manhattan, New York 55, 64, 69, 73
Dykes, John B. 112–113, 161, 170

Earle, Frank 40
East-West League 187
Eastern Colored League 111–112, 118, 120, 126, 132, 135, 143–145, 152–153, 155, 159–161, 170–171, 174, 178–179; *see also* Bolden, Edward
Eastern Sports Writers Association 178
Ebbets, Charles F. 73, 138
Ebbets Field 1, 60, 73, 76, 78, 83, 90, 95, 109
Edge, Walter 158
Eggleston, Macajah "Mack" 181, 183, 189
Empey, Arthur Guy 63, 73
Enzman, Johnny 60, 186
Evans, Charley 125
Everett, Michael 5, 196–198
Exclusive Club 52–53, 110

Farley, Frank S. "Hap" 14, 193
Farley Stars (Atlantic City, New Jersey) baseball team 193
Farmers (Queens, New York) baseball team 106, 121, 177
Farmers Oval 121, 169
Farrell, Luther 133–134, 143–144, 151, 157, 172, 174, 182, 187, 189, 191; World Series no-hitter 163
Federal League (white major league) 172
Finley, Tom 107, 132
Fleischer Yarn Company (Philadelphia) baseball team 80
Flournoy, Willis 84
Forbes, Frank 33
Forbes, Joe 33
Foster, Andrew "Rube" 40, 47, 68–70, 77, 85, 111, 146, 180; *see also* Chicago American Giants; Negro National League (first)
Foster, Bill "Willie" 146–147
Foster, William (aka "Julie Jones") 53
Francis, Bill **41**, 90, 114, **117**, 124, 132, 198
Frock, Sam 82
Fuller, Jimmie **86**
Fuller, William "Chick" 20, 27

Garcia, Romando "Cheno" 143, 156
Gardner, Kenneth "Ping" 174, 181, 183
Gatewood, Ernest **26**, 55, 57, 87, 125–126, 134, 144–145, 156
George, Johnny 124
George, Tom "Lefty" 105
Gibson, Bill 171
Gillespie, Henry 134, 157, 165
Gilliam-Mosee, Regina 195–196
Gilmore, Quincy 85
Gordon, Herman 33
Gottlieb, Eddie 188–189
Graham, Dennis **86**, 87
Grant, Frank 198
Gray, Emerson 39, 104
Green, Curtis 174
Greenberg, Louis 6, 95–96
Grier, Claude "Red" 128–129, 133–134, 144, 146, 157, 174; World Series no-hitter 147
Gruhler, Henry "Whitey" 44, 194

Hal Chase's All-Nationals 58
Hampton, Lewis 117, **117**
Handy, Bill **26**, 43–44, 55–57, 70, 86, **86**, 87, 97, 156
Harlan Field, Wilmington, Delaware 102
Harlem Renaissance basketball team 173
Harper, John 107, 115, 125–126, 132
Harrisburg Giants 117, 126–127,

135–136, 145–146, 150, 153, 161–162, 165, 170, 173
Harrisburg Senators 140
Harry Davis All Stars 59
Harvey, John **86**, 88
Harvey, Richard "Lefty" ***26***
Havana Red Sox 31
Havana Reds 84
Hawkins, P.J. 12
Heckle, Walter 104
Helm, William P., Jr. 141
Henderson, Arthur "Rats" 4, 107, 115, **116**, **117**, 125–126, 134, 144, 156–157, 174, 183, ***190***, 191
Hendrix, Claude 153–154
Henriquez family 122
Hewitt, Joe 84
Hilldale 38, 46, 57, 61, 70, 77, 85, 89–90, 106, 111, 117–118, 123, 126–127, 133, 135–136, 145–146, 151, 155, 158, 165–166, 171, 173–175, 179–180, 183, 185, 188; *see also* Bolden, Edward
Hobson, Johnny **117**, 126
Hog Island (Philadelphia) baseball team 49
Hogan, Dr. Lawrence 5, 194–196
Homestead Grays 179–180, 183–184, 187–188; *see also* Posey, Cumberland Willis, Jr.
House of David baseball team 2, 27, 83
Howell, Henry 43, 45
Hubbard, Jesse "Mountain Man" 56–58, 67, 157, 174, 189
Hudspeth, Bob 76, 93, 97, 117
Huff, Eddie 115
Hummel, John "Silent John" 59
Hutchinson, Fred 56–57, 71

Indianapolis ABCs 56–57, 70, 75–76, 90, 99; *see also* Taylor, Charles Isham "C.I."
Inter-City Baseball Association 54
International League All Stars 59
International League Stars 60
Interstate Commerce Commission 158
Interstate League 153–154

J. & J. Dobson (Philadelphia) baseball team 80, 104
Jackson, Richard 87, 97
Jackson, Thomas H. 1, 13–14, 16, 20–21, 29, 31, 54, 70, 95–96, 107, 109, 112–114, **117**, 123, 161–162, 165, 171
Jacksonville, Florida 1, 7, 73
Jamison, Cesar 33, 36, 60, 79, 187

J. B. Stetson (Philadelphia) baseball team 37
Jefferson, Ralph 90
Jeffries, Jim (baseball player) 57
Jeffries, Jim (boxer) 52
Jeffries Athletic Club, Atlantic City, New Jersey 122
Jenkins, Clarence "Fats" 79, 173, 182
Jewell, Warner 56
J. G. Brill (Philadelphia) baseball team 36–37
John Henry Lloyd Stadium 194–195, ***195***
John Henry "Pop" Lloyd Foundation 5, 196–197
Johnson, Ban 36, 48
Johnson, Cecil "Sess" 56
Johnson, Charles B. 113, 161
Johnson, Dan "Shang" 9, 19, 28, 32, 35, 43, 55, 57–58, 72
Johnson, Enoch "Nucky" 10–11, 14, 142, 158–159, 163, 172, ***190***, 191, 193
Johnson, George "Chappie" 57, 125
Johnson, Grant "Home Run" 67, 81
Johnson, Jack 52
Johnson, James Weldon 8
Johnson, Judy 134
Johnson, Nate 103, 115, **117**
Johnson, Nelson, Esq. 5, 9
Johnson Stars (Atlantic City, New Jersey) baseball team 193
Jones, Willie 4, 103, 114, **117**, 125–126, 134, 144–145, 156, 174, 182–183

Kansas City Monarchs 100, 146
Kavanagh, Marty 64
Keenan, James H. 40, 61, 71, 77, 112, 126, 132, 143, 152, 159–160, 171–172, 175, 179, 184; *see also* Lincoln Giants
Kentucky Reds (Atlantic City, New Jersey) baseball team 104
Klein Chocolate Company (Harrisburg, Pennsylvania) baseball team 67
Krock, Dr. Jeremy 198
Ku Klux Klan 142
Kuehnle, Louis 10–12

Lai, William "Buck" 27, 121, 153, 186
Lamar, Edward B., Jr. 84, 96
Lambert, William "Doc" 178, 181
Lanctot, Neil 5, 36
Landgraf, Ernest "Duke" 153–154
Lane, F.C. 48
Lee, Holsey "Script" 88

Lennox, Eddie 36
Lennox, Sam 59
Leonard, Jim "Bobo" 134
Lester, Larry 2, 3, 5
Lewis, Joe 144
Lewis, Milton 103, 125–126, 133, 156, 173
Lincoln Giants 40, 61, 77–78, 106, 112, 117–118, 126–127, 132, 138, 143, 145, 151–152, 156, 159–160, 171–172, 175, 179–180, 183–184; *see also* Keenan, James F.
Lindsey, Bill 181–183
Lit Brother Department Store (Philadelphia) baseball team 129–130
Little Savoy nightclub 52–53
Lloyd, Anna 193
Lloyd, John Henry "Pops" 1, ***41***, 55, 56–57, 60, 67, 70, 93, 97, 113, 114, **114**, 116–117, 123–124, 126, 133, 134, 143, 189, ***190***, 191, 193–194, 196–198
Lloyd, Nan 193, 196
Lockhart, George Hubert 4, 115–117, 125–126, 134, 144, 157, 170, 174
Logan Squares (Philadelphia) baseball team 24, 29, 34–35, 45, 67, 89
Lohr, Howard 153, 186
Lomax, Michael 51
Long Branch (New Jersey) Cubans 123
Lord, Bris 36
Lundy, Dick 1, 9, 17–18, 28, 30, 31, 32, 43, 56, 70, 81, 84, **84**, 86–88, 97, 102–103, 114, 115, **117**, 123–124, 126, 133–134, 143, 156, 162, 172, 180–181

Mack, Connie 36
Mack, Earle 66, 169
Mack, Paul 19–20, 28, 30
Mack Stadium, Detroit 92
Mackey, Raleigh "Biz" 75, 189
Madison Stars (Philadelphia) baseball team 70, 79–80
Malarcher, Dave 99, 146
Malloy, Charley 104
Manhattans (Atlantic City, New Jersey) baseball team 15–16
Manning, Belinda 197
Manning, Max 193–197
Marcell, Oliver "Ghost" 4, 44, 71, ***71***, 72, 74–75, 86, **86**, 87, 97, 99, 117, 123, 132–134, 137, 143, 145, 152, 156, 173, 181
Marshall E. Smith (Philadelphia) baseball team 80
Martin, Lou 36
Mason, Charlie 115, **117**, 124, 126, 132–134

Index

Maxwell Motor Car Company (Detroit) baseball team 67–68
Mays, Carl 65–66, 83
McClure, Bob 137, 181, 183
McDonald, Gifford 31, 32, **86**
McDuffie, Terris 189
McGowan, Malcolm 189
McGraw, John 64–65
McNichol, Edward 24
McNichol, Daniel 24
McNichol, Frank 24
McNichol, James P. 24, 29, 45
Means, Lewis 72, 103, 156
Mederos, Frank 71
Melcher, Loraine 14, 21
Melrose Athletic Club (Atlantic City, New Jersey) baseball team 34, 104, 122
Merchant Ship (Bristol, Pennsylvania) baseball team 66, 82
Middletown (New York) Cubans (All Cubans of Havana) 122
Miller, Julius W. "Yellow Charleston" 110
Miller, Louis "Red" 30
Mirabel, Juan 150
Mitchell, Alonzo 144, 174, 183
Mitchell, Benjamin Arnett **86**, 88, 126, 134, 144
Molina, Augustin 160
Molyneaux, Vince 35
Montalvo, Alonzo 160
Mullin, George 36
Munch, Jake 108, 153

National League 172
National Stadium, Atlantic City, New Jersey 102
Nativity Catholic Club (Philadelphia) baseball team 80, 101, 105
Negro American League 187
Negro League Researchers and Authors Group (NLRAG) 3
Negro Leagues Baseball Grave Marker Project 198
Negro National League (first) 68–69, 85, 97, 111, 160–162, 177, 179, 187
Negro National League (second) 180, 187, 189
Negro Southern League 187
Negro World Series: 1926 146–148, **149**; 1927 162–163
Nelson, Raymond "Ike" 2, 34, 44, **45**, 104
New York Age 78
New York Bacharach Giants 95–96, 101–102, 111
New York Black Yankees 188
New York Bloomer Girls 140
New York Giants 64–65, 68

New York Oval, Bronx, New York 95, 109
New York Ship (Camden, New Jersey) baseball team 66
Newark Stars 144–145
Norfolk, Virginia 161
Nuttal, Bill 125, 134
Nutter, Atty. Isaac H. 62, 158–159, **159**, 162–163, 171–173, 179

Olympic Field, Manhattan, New York 40
Original Bacharach Giants 95–96, 101–102

Paige, Satchel 28, 40, 47
Parkesburg (Pennsylvania) Iron Works baseball team 46, 94
Parpetti, Augustin 84, 114–115
Pasquarella, Tony 121
Passon, Harry 153, 188
Passon, Herman "Chickie" 105, 140, 153
Paterson (Doherty) Silk Sox 2, 140
Penn-Jersey League 129, 139
Pennsylvania Red Caps 4, 27, 37, 67
Perez, Heather Halpin 5
Perry, Carl 107
Pettus, Bill 31, **41**, 43, 86, **86**, 97, 107
Petway, Bruce 30
Philadelphia Athletics 94, 130
Philadelphia baseball culture 23, 135
Philadelphia Tigers 171, 177
Pieka, Lou 151
Pierce, Bill 44, 71, 86
Pittsburgh Crawfords 188
Pittsburgh Keystones 85
Pittsburgh Stars 67
Pleasantville (New Jersey) baseball team 22, 29, 33, 45, 131
Poles, Spotswood **41**, 57, 61–62
"Poles-Yank Affair" 62
Pompez, Alejandro "Alex" 38, 62, 112, 171; *see also* Cuban Stars (East)
Posey, Cumberland Willis, Jr. 179–180, 187, 189; *see also* Homestead Grays
Pugh, Johnny **26**, 55, 57, 70, **86**, 87

Quinn, Jack 169

Ramirez, Ramiro 97, 124
Rampersad, Arnold 196
Redding, Dick "Cannonball" 2, **41**, 55, 57–58, 66, 70, 72–73, 78–79, **78**, 81, 83–84, **86**, 87–88, **87**, 97, 110, 117, 152

Reese, John 43
Reeves, Norman "Bees" 33
Reid, Ambrose 4, 103, 114–115, **117**, 124, 133–134, 143, 157, 173, 182
Republican Party 158
Reulbach, Ed 48–49
R. G. Dun (Philadelphia) baseball team 37
Richard Stockton College 197
Richardson, Henry "Long Tom" 88
Richmond Giants 4, 107, 121
Richter, Pam 5
Riley, James 31, 37, 71, 115
Ring, Jimmy 186
Risley, Sherwood 33
Roadside Hotel, Philadelphia 120
Roberts, Elihu 30
Roberts, Leroy "Roy" 4, 9, 18–19, 28, 30, 32, 43–45, 55, 57–58, 72, 93, 97, **117**, **117**, 125, 132, 144, 157, 174, 189
Robinson, George (baseball player) 43, 45
Robinson, George W. (team owner) 120, 132–133, 135
Robinson Land Company, Atlantic City, New Jersey 112, 161
Rodriguez, Victor 84
Rojo, Julio 63, 71, 84, **86**, 87, 97, 99, 117
Rommel, Eddie 59, 94, 106
Rosner, Max 106
Rossitter, George 179
Royal Café and Palm Garden 51–52
Rudolfs (Atlantic City, New Jersey) baseball team 15–16
Rudolph, Dick 60
Ruffo, Anthony M. Jr. 190
Ruth, Babe 77, 83, 130
Ryan, Merven "Red" 72–73, **72**, 87, 89

St. Louis Giants 177
St. Louis Stars 100, 146, 177
St. Thomas "Saints" (Wilmington, Delaware) baseball team 108–109
Santop, Louis 39, 81, 84, 177
Santop's Bronchos 177
Savage, Connie 64, 69, 73, 81
Schaub, Lou 153
Seibold, Harry "Socks" 105, 129–130, 139, 153
Sellars, J. Henry 25
Shibe Park 60, 62, 73
Shields, Jimmy 173–174, 183
Shively, George 56–57, 71, **86**, 87, 97, 125, 133
Singletary, Wes 194

Sisler, George 36
Smith, Charlie "Red" 33, 43, 45
Smith, Clarence "Scally" 157
Society for American Baseball Research, Negro Leagues Committee 198
South Philadelphia baseball team 129, 186
South Philadelphia Hebrew Association (SPHAs) baseball team 80, 104–105, 139
Starks, Otis "Lefty" 125
Steen, Herb 122, 153
Stenton Field Club (Philadelphia) baseball team 105
Stephens, Jake 123–124
Stivers, Wayne 3, 5
Stone, Ed 189
Streeter, Sam 103, 117, 184
Strong, Nathaniel C. "Nat" *26*, 54–56, 61–62, 70, 73, 77, 85, 106, 109, 111–112, 118, 126–127, 133, 158, 159, 170–171, 189; *see also* Brooklyn Royal Giants
Sullivan, Det. Mary 53
Summers, Art 59
Sunday baseball: in Atlantic City 16; in New York City 65; in Pennsylvania 23, 34
Swigler, Adam "Ad" 2, 24–25, 35, 130, 135, 186
Sykes, Frank "Doc" 38

Taylor, Ben 56–57, 70–71, 120, 152, 181–182, 187
Taylor, Charles Isham "C.I." 56, 70, 180–181; *see also* Indianapolis ABCs
Taylor, Jim 56, 181
Taylor, Johnny 56
Teran, Recurvon 84
Tesreau, Jeff 64–65, 73, 81
Tesreau's Bears (Manhattan, New York) baseball team 73, 80, 94
Thomas, Clint 93, 123, 173, 182
Thomas, Jules 79
Thompson, J.W. "Gunboat" 56
Thorbahn, Stewart R. 6, 145

Tomm, (first name unknown) 31
Torriente, Cristobal 74, 91
Trautwein Brothers 137
Treadwell, Harold 72, 83, 87–88, 97, 99, 117
"Treat 'Em Rough" (World War I fighting slogan) 64
Treat-Em-Roughs (Manhattan, New York) baseball team 64, 65, 73, 81
Trenton (New Jersey) baseball team 129–130
Tucker, Henry 1, 9, 13–14, 20, 29, 31, 39, 56, 58, 95–96, 107, 109, 112, 114, 161
Tucker, Michael 9, 19, 28

Upland (Pennsylvania) baseball team 80

Vandal Athletic Club (Atlantic City, New Jersey) baseball team 15–16

Wagner, Bill 156
Walker, Jesse 182–183
Wallace, Dick 20, 28, 30
Wallace, John E., Esq. 5
Wallace, McKinley "Jack" 144
Walsh, Marty 66
Warfield, Frank 123, 181
Warhop, Jack 59
Washington, Isaac W. "Ike" 171–172, 178, 180–181, 187–188
Washington, Sarah Spencer 171
Washington (Wilmington) Potomacs 117, 120, 124, 126–127, 132, 135
Watkins, John "Pop" 31, 32
Watson, John "Mule" 66–67
Weatherspoon, (first name unknown) 33
Webster, Bill *117*
Webster, Pearl *26*, 45
Weekes, Duncan 113, 161–162
Weekes, Reginald 5, 113, 161–162
Weekes, William 113, 161–162
Weiden, Ellen 6

Wheeler, Joe "Jodie" 103–104, 117
White, Burlin 30, 57
White, Chaney 4, 114–115, *117*, 124–125, 133–134, 143, 157, 172, 182
White, Charles D. 16
White, Sol 31, 51, 54, 198
White, William 55, 58, 64
Whitman, Billy 121
Whitmire, Kathy 196
Whitworth, Dick 89
Wickware, Frank 47, 57, 72, 132
Wilkins, Barron D. 51–56, 58, 61, 64, 70, 81, 85, 95, 97, 109, *109*, 110; *see also* Connor, John W.
Williams, Andrew "Stringbean" *26*, 72–73, *86*, 87–88, 97, 120, 125
Williams, Bobby 183
Williams, Clarence 197–198
Williams, Jim 198
Williams, Joe "Cyclone" "Smokey Joe" 40, 55, 59–60, 67, 78–79, *78*, 184
Williams, Leroy 158–159, 172
Williams, Tom 19
Wilmington, Delaware 102, 109
Wilson, Jud 106–107, 181
Wilson, W. Rollo 113–114, 116, 123, 126–127, 132–133, 143–144, 170–172, 179, 188
Wilson, Gov. Woodrow 11
Winters, James "Nip" 87–88, 97, 99–100, 117
Woods, Willie 134
World Series Stars 102
World War I: defense industry teams 47–49; effect on baseball 41–42; effect on black migration from South 43; effect on U.S. immigration 8
Wylie, Fred 33

York, Jim "Lefty" 139, 153
Young, Berdell 103, 117, 133–134

Zimmerman, Heinie 65, 81, 139

www.ingramcontent.com/pod-product-compliance
Lightning Source LLC
Chambersburg PA
CBHW081158230426
43666CB00016B/2851